CORPVS CHRISTIANORVM

CONCILIORUM OECUMENICORUM GENERALIUMQUE DECRETA

Istituto per le scienze religiose – Bologna – fscire.it

CORPVS CHRISTIANORVM

CONCILIORUM OECUMENICORUM GENERALIUMQUE DECRETA

Edidit
Istituto per le scienze religiose
BOLOGNA

General Editors
GIUSEPPE ALBERIGO †
ALBERTO MELLONI

TURNHOUT
BREPOLS
2023

CONCILIORUM OECUMENICORUM GENERALIUMQUE DECRETA

EDITIO CRITICA

VI/1/1

Synods of the Churches
of and after the Reformation

The Dawn of the Reformation
(16th-17th Centuries)

Part 1

Curantibus
G. Braghi, E. Campi, Z. Csepregi, D. Dainese,
I. Dingel, P. Hildebrand, G. Murdock,
C. Scheidegger, J. Schilling, K. I. Stjerna

Edidit
A. Melloni

Adlaborante
G. Braghi

TURNHOUT
BREPOLS
2023

CORPVS CHRISTIANORVM

CONCILIORUM OECUMENICORUM GENERALIUMQUE DECRETA

The research and publication of this volume were made possible by the support of Ministero dell'Università e della Ricerca (MUR), Ministero della Cultura (MIC), and Regione Emilia Romagna

D/2023/0095/167
ISBN 978-2-503-54506-6 (2 vols.)
Printed in the EU on acid-free paper

© 2023, Brepols Publishers n.v./s.a., Turnhout, Belgium

All rights reserved. No part of this publication may be reproduced, stored in a retrieval system, or transmitted, in any form or by any means, electronic, mechanical, photocopying, recording, or otherwise, without the prior permission of the publisher.

INTRODUCTION TO THE CHRISTIAN CONCILIARITIES OF THE CHURCHES OF AND AFTER THE REFORMATION

This volume on the councils 'of and after the Reformation'[1] concludes the thirteen-tome series of the six-volume *Conciliorum Oecumenicorum Generaliumque Decreta*.

More than twenty years have elapsed since this series took shape under the scientific impetus of Giuseppe Alberigo, initially as a patient work of critically updated re-edition of the 'yellow volume' of the *Conciliorum oecumenicorum decreta*, born in Bologna in via san Vitale 114, published by Herder on the eve of the Second Vatican Council and later re-edited downstream of the Council, in the intellectual and theological wake opened by Giuseppe Dossetti in 1953 with the birth of the *Centro di documentazione*, which has now become the Foundation for Religious Studies. The *Centro* and the Foundation took heed, and continue to take heed, to the wisdom of Silesian scholar Hubert Jedin, thanks to whom the Council of Trent – and thus, par excellence, the historiography on the Christian councils – was rendered to its history: and in turn this history was rendered to our present. A present capable of understanding that what is needed is not a historiography bent to whatever 'concrete objectives', but to a rigour capable of disrupting the ideological schemes of the past that encumber it.

On the other hand, less than twenty years have elapsed since an article appeared in *L'Osservatore Romano* of 3 June 2007, signed by an Anonymous with three asterisks, in which the *ignorantia crassissima* of an officially unknown author imputed to Alberigo the addition of that *Generaliumque* to the title of the *Conciliorum oecumenicorum decreta* which he suspected of questioning the list of 'ecumenical' councils that, according to his superficial

---

[1] The choice made for the title and the substance of the present volume is to use 'Reformation' as an 'uncountable' name: thus, we have refrained – not only out of a certain distrust of historiographical mannerism – from the widespread tendency to use plurals of what is numerable for the creation of plurals: for instance *cristianesimi*, as in A. Capone, 'Cristianesimi e polemiche nei primi secoli: approcci e prospettive', in B. Sère (éd.), *Les régimes de polémicité au Moyen Âge*, Rennes 2019, p. 15-29, with a pioneering appearance in A. D'Anna – C. Zamagni – E. Jurissevich (a cura di), *Cristianesimi nell'antichità: fonti, istituzioni, ideologie a confronto*, Hildesheim – Zürich – New York 2007. More specifically for the churches born after 1517, see for example U. Rublack (ed.), *The Oxford Handbook of the Protestant Reformations*, Oxford 2017.

VI INTRODUCTION

views, the Roman Catholic Church had 'adopted'. All learned people know that this was not true: the so-called 'list' was only a seventeenth-century sequence, drafted by Bellarmine and his entourage on the basis of existing handbooks, which seemed useful in the defence of the *Tridentinum* hinging on the pope's authority over the councils (although the pope began to preside over them only from the beginning of second millennium onwards).

This vile attack, which came out while Alberigo was in a coma and on the verge of death (he died on 15 June), convinced me and my fellow workers at the Institute of via san Vitale to break the hesitation: not only did we offer a proper and inflexible response to those baseless objections,(2) but we also started working on extending the edition of conciliar decisions to all Christian churches. In parallel with the *Mansi3* digital library – which collected in the fscire.it website the editions of the acts, documents, epistles, and diaries related to the *Historia Conciliorum* – it was decided to promote not just an update of an important and widely-acclaimed instrument such as *COD*, but to take up in full the working hypothesis that had guided it: *id est*, that the *decisions* of the councils, and the history of such decisions, constitute a hermeneutical whole with large-scale critical issues, against which the obsession of some Roman Catholic voices, adamant that the problem of conciliar history can be encapsulated in a 'continuity versus discontinuity' frame (albeit without saying what, how much, when, and why), appears in all its ideological infantilism. Brepols' gentlemanliness, the advice of prominent scholars, authorities and friends, as well as time have thus made it possible to design an architecture covering the traditions (*sic*: *traditions*, with the plural so dear to Jean-Marie Tillard and so detested by the adversaries of ARCIC1) of many Wests and many Easts, in a rich and divided Christian geography.

The *COGD* volumes on the Latin church of the first millennium and on the Roman Catholic tradition were meant to be: the famous Bellarminian list provided a familiar first series of conciliar meetings, to which it was necessary to return just those fourteenth-century councils that had been omitted by the anti-conciliarist phobia so widespread in early modern and post-Tridentine Rome.

Setting up volumes on the councils of the churches of Byzantine and post-Byzantine Orthodoxy in communion with Constantinople (of Greek, Paleo-Slavic, Georgian, and Russian tradition), as well as volumes on the councils of the churches of Eastern Orthodoxy (of Syriac, Armenian, Coptic,

---

(2) Cfr. A. Melloni, 'Concili, ecumenicità e storia. Note di discussione', *Cristianesimo nella storia* 28 (2007), p. 509-542; Id., 'Essence, Concept, or History: What Is at Stake in a Dispute on COGD', *Catholic Historical Review* 101/4 (2015), p. 578-587.

INTRODUCTION VII

and Ethiopian tradition) was immediately relatively easy. The materiality of manuscript sources, the availability of the collections of canons, the normative sylloges, the acts of transposition or rejection – all this allowed specialists to draw a vast, consolidated, persistent conciliar perimeter, stretching to the English translations of the twentieth century at the service of the diasporas: such translations have no value for the authority that promulgates them, but function as a sort of *textus receptus*, moulding the lives of those believers and communities which came many centuries later and in a *toto caelo* different cultural context.

Therefore, the reader can come into contact with a stream of decisions of different kinds, canonical scope, doctrinal density, and formular maturity: amidst thickenings and rarefactions, convergences and contrasts, such a stream shows how the Council acted in very different contexts without losing its own physiognomy. Indeed, what these contexts have in common is neither the distillation of a *Konzilsidee* nor the summation of a phenomenology of synodal experiences, but the historical-critical evidence of a changing but constant nexus between the church's self-understanding and its decisions, at the bottom of which lies the search for authentic worship.

Much more complex, on the other hand, was the design of the present volume, which had to grapple with three interlinked historical problems, namely: i) verifying the existence of a conciliar tradition comparable to other Christian traditions, in a dogmatic and institutional framework in which no superior authority descends from the Council, nor the authority of Christ is deemed as the authority with which the Council is invested in the Constantinian paradigm, but prefers the word 'Synod', considered more expressive of the obedience to *sola Scriptura*; then ii) verifying whether it was possible to offer a critical account of such a tradition without risking to adhere – implicitly and fatally – to the old controversialists' myth portraying the institutional antagonist of the churches born after Luther as a 'Roman' monolith opposed to a fragmented, doctrinally chaotic, punctiform reality. This caricatured representation did not undermine the doctrinal self-awareness of these churches, but it created a stereotype which the critical and scholarly work can, and perhaps must, dismantle, while making its own distinctions and identifying the nuances of what was born from a thirst for reform on which the whole of Christianity was nourished (by antagonism, by osmosis, by cohabitation); and finally iii) to show how to do so in a non-extrinsic and non-arbitrary manner, in the name of an 'ecumenism' in the early-twentieth-century intra-Protestant sense, and in a panorama of sources in which a collection such as the one offered here had never been gathered before: and this in spite of the dynamics between Communions, Unions, Alliances, Concords, which, along-

VIII INTRODUCTION

side all the other churches, have equally contributed to the exodus from the time of religious war to that of the ecumenical truce.

The alternatives that the sixth volume of *COGD* had before itself to account for these dynamics, therefore, were several. One could have divided volume 6 by confessions and denominations, following and representing more or less forcibly the ten-page list of churches born since the sixteenth century that the World Council of Churches includes in its membership. Otherwise, it could have grouped the councils using, and if necessary forcing, the dominant adjectives of the self-definitions of these churches (Evangelical, Reformed, Methodist, Presbyterian, Baptist, Pentecostal, Anglican, and so forth) and then find a way to bring what dwells there into the *World aggregations*. In the end, what seemed the most objective choice was adopted – which makes sense if, and only if, one accepts the working hypothesis that the thirst for Reform that has been thriving since the sixteenth century in Latin Christianity constitutes a sufficient common factor: namely, to gather all conciliar and synodal variants which manifested in the various families adjacent to that thirst for Reform, placing them in a chronological sequence that always distinguishes 'time by time', and time by time only, the denominational origin of the individual organ of communion taking synodal decisions.

Hence the decision to use the wording 'Churches of and after the Reformation' in the title, in the strong conviction that such a chronological sequence is able to restore a unity that is constituted not by the themes at hand time by time, but by the basic question that the churches of these traditions pose to the conciliar institution, and the question that the Council poses to them. Indeed, when we began discussing this volume, there was an instinctive response that denied the possibility of envisaging such a volume, since 'Protestantism does not have councils' – meaning, by 'Council', the body that the Orthodox and other Latin churches consider having constituted power in the ways discussed above: an unexceptionable, and at the same time eloquent, answer.

Luther's refusal to participate in a Council that was not free, Christian, and on German soil,(3) together with the symbolic break with the *Corpus iuris canonici* in 1517, gave rise to a dogmatic theology mistrusting anything that might have called into question the duty to question – in the light of the three *sola* – every instrument standing in the way of the experience of salva-

---

(3) Cfr. C. Spehr, *Luther und das Konzil. Zur Entwicklung eines zentralen Themas in der Reformationszeit*, Tübingen 2010.

INTRODUCTION IX

tion.(4) It was after the foundation of the World Council of Churches and in the wake of the Second Vatican Council and its singular 'ecumenicity' – which for the first time made room for non-Roman Catholic observers(5) and for the instance of visible unity posed by the ecumenical movement(6) – that theologians of the various denominations of the Reformation seized the opportunity for a new analysis of the conciliar instance, impossible otherwise.(7) These churches – corroborated by historical research that has delved into the events of the councils, although not abdicating their own dogmatics in any way – have experienced the vitality of a 'system'/'mechanism' adopted when needed,(8) the possibility of keeping such a system within limits that do not elude their own ecclesiologies,(9) and the force of separation and unity

(4) To my knowledge, the thesis by K. G. Steck, 'Der Locus "De Synodis" in der lutherischen Dogmatik', in *Theologische Aufsätze. K. Barth zum 50. Geburtstag*, München 1936, p. 338-352 has yet to be further developed.

(5) M. Velati, *Separati ma fratelli. Gli osservatori non cattolici al Vaticano II (1962-1965)*, Bologna 2014.

(6) Cfr. A. Melloni (dir.) – L. Ferracci (ed.), *A History of the Desire for Christian Unity*, 3 vols, Leiden – Boston 2021-2025.

(7) Among several studies by Mauro Velati, one thinks of the cases studied by D. W. Norwood, *Reforming Rome: Karl Barth and Vatican II*, Grand Rapids (MI) 2015; P. Ricca, 'Le concile œcuménique: expression de collégialité des évêques ou de la *communio ecclesiarum* ou même de la communauté entière des fidèles?', *Concilium* 187 (1983), p. 129-137.

(8) J.-L. Leuba, 'Das ökumenische Konzil in der reformierten Theologie', in H. J. Margull (hrsg.), *Die ökumenischen Konzile der Christenheit*, Stuttgart 1961, p. 373-392. The same year, still a long way from the opening of the Second Vatican Council but coinciding with the General Assembly of the World Council of Churches in New Delhi, P. Meinhold, *Der Evangelische Christ und das Konzil*, Freiburg 1961 was published. Following the Council and the 1968 Assembly of Uppsala, numerous works rediscuss conciliarity as a principle of unity, among which J. Neumann, *Synodales Prinzip. Der grössere Spielraum im Kirchenrecht*, Freiburg 1973; R. Mehl, 'L'unité conciliaire de l'Église' and H. M. Biedermann, 'Die Synodalität. Prinzip der Verfassung und Leitung der Orthodoxen Kirchen und Kirche', both in L. Hein (hrsg.), *Die Einheit der Kirche. Dimension ihrer Heiligkeit, Katholizität und Apostolizität. Festgabe Peter Meinhold zum 70. Geburtstag*, Wiesbaden 1977, p. 69-79 and 296-314 respectively. An overall perspective was introduced in the light of the subject of reception by W. Beinert, 'Konziliarität der Kirche. Ein Beitrag zur ökumenischen Epistemologie', *Catholica* 33/2 (1979), p. 81-108; a more recent synthesis in C. Böttigheimer – J. Hofmann (hrsg.), *Autorität und Synodalität. Eine interdisziplinäre und interkonfessionelle Umschau nach ökumenischen Chancen und ekklesiologischen Desideraten*, Frankfurt am Main 2008.

(9) A first synthesis by K. Blaser, 'Le Synode en régime protestant', *Revue de Théologie et de Philosophie* 122/1 (1990), p. 67-84.

INTRODUCTION

stemming from an inescapable albeit negotiable communion instance: (10) and this with what all the scholarship cited in the individual introductions to the various synods included in this volume entails. This sixth volume of *COGD* wishes to make its own contribution to such debates: a contribution – it seems to me – that can be condensed into three main points, all rooted in the history of the conciliar events chosen here to draw a parable from the origins to the present day, and more generally at the end of the long journey of the *Conciliorum Oecumenicorum Generaliumque Decreta*.

The first point concerns the fact that even the 'Churches of and after the Reformation' have a continuous, constant, changing, unbroken, specific conciliar/synodal tradition of their own. Such a tradition did not develop 'in spite of' an original distrust of everything that is deemed as standing in the way of the lordship of the Word: it developed *thanks to* that very conviction about faith, about grace, and about Scripture. Experience shows how con-decision – Synod, Council, assembly – can certainly be the place in which the lamp is put under the bushel, but it can also be the place where, thanks to the πιστοῖς ἀνθρώποις (2 Tim 2:2), is made extraordinarily clear that the Word of God οὐ δέδεται (2 Tim 2:9).

A second point touches the subject of the legal cultures and political philosophies underlying diachronically the synodality of the churches 'of and after the Reformation'. The issue of the relationship with the conception of power runs through all traditions, and the mythical vessels which convey them over time are well known: suffice it to mention the figure of Constantine and the Christian emperor, the Byzantine conception of universalism, the senatorial models and the theologies of *translatio imperii*, the papal monarchy, the function of princes, the myth of Moscow as а третий Рим, and so forth. In the churches born with the *caesura* of the sixteenth century, such a relationship is both fundamental to a 'Protestant' identity, and at the same time it is the premise of an adherence to forms of state and government marked by liberal-democratic principles in which the old *de maioritate* mechanisms of canon law and monastic praxis – from which parliamentary devices derive – return as the Justinian aspiration reinterpreted by Innocent III: *quod omnes tangit ab omnibus tractari et approbari debet*. This goes along with a fear of seeing the uncertainty of consensus, increasingly demythologised by use in modernity and in post-secular societies, entrusted to what instead must be *Ein feste Burg*, a solid rock unavailable to compromises.

---

(10) For a recent literature review on the 1618 synod, see W. Frijhoff, 'Le synode de Dordrecht (1618-1619): théologie et confessionalisation', *Revue d'histoire du protestantisme* 4/3 (2019), p. 389-422.

INTRODUCTION   XI

Each tradition has given various answers to this issue, which lies in the systems of *decision-making* (conventionally used as a synonym for decisional processes) and *decision-taking* (which is the synonym for the *decreta* in the title of this series): but what emerges from experiences that have found a chance to survive by fleeing Europe to America and bonding with its deepest constitutional culture is that their synodal traditions have not been all that different from those of other churches which have adopted other politological references (*id est*, articulating relationships by sacrament, authority, class, *ordines*, nations). Borrowing an apt expression from a title of a work on political theology from a few decades ago, this whole issue is presented as *the need for the unnecessary*.[11] It would be pathetic and suspicious to think that such processes and decisions took place in an 'ecclesiosphere' in which all that lives in history and in the flesh is angelically 'purified' and sublimated, thus confusing the mundane deceits to be rejected with the world to be inhabited also through rules and procedures. However, it would be no less dangerous to identify the substance of deliberations with the manner in which they are deliberated (*il rivestimento*, as John XXIII labelled it on 11 October 1962). The latter constitutes a procedural and cultural language that the very diachronic spectrum offered here should make it easier to identify: not to delude ourselves that such a language can be discarded, but to be certain that new political philosophies will find their own place, once again underlining the issue of a *usus pauper* of juridical-cultural frameworks with their own gifts and predicaments.[12]

The third and last point concerns conciliarity and the desire for the unity of the church as it appears in Protestant and Anglican theology two centuries after its first sprouts on German soil. The 2020s have proven themselves capable of recapitulating and replicating the horrors of the short and blood-soaked twentieth century: the 'rites' of capitalism (*ça va sans dire*, in Walter Benjamin's connotation) and the optimistic puns about 'never again' have led many to believe that our yesterday could be relegated to a sort of distant prehistory, detached from willpower, civic engagement, superficiality, or at best characterised by sub-optimal forms of regulating conflicts and clashes. At the beginning of a twentieth century already replete with horrors, the churches – thanks to the endeavours of the pioneers and prophets of the desire for Christian unity – embarked on a path that made them feel (and in some cases

---

(11) G. Ruggieri, *La necessità dell'inutile. Fede e politica*, Genova 1982.

(12) Cfr. for instance M. Battle, *Reconciliation: The Ubuntu Theology of Desmond Tutu*, Cleveland (OH) 1997.

XII INTRODUCTION

foretell) (13) a connection between the evil ravaging the world, the churches' division, and the call to heal the former and the latter wounds with a word of faith.

Nowadays, the churches are faced with no less radical and no less demanding options, in the midst of an extremely harsh and persistent ecumenical winter, such that the centenary of the Council of Nicaea will see the celebration of the Symbol of faith as a goal to be achieved rather than as self-speaking, demanding evidence. (14) The fraternal courtesy among religious leaders that never becomes liturgical communion, the warring schisms that stain Orthodoxy with blood, the silent schisms that see the coming together of different ideological positions across the denominational boundaries of the West, the rise of Pentecostal forms of Christian life promoting different categories of or against Christian unity – all this poses the same problem that the twentieth century did: *id est*, the weight of the churches' inertia in the face of the division into Evil, which they condemn in words more or less heartfelt, more or less profound, but without seeing its connection with their own separation. Yet the 'visible' unity to which those churches can return or can continue to aspire cannot be confined to dialogues between theologians, or public gestures between church leaders with which to fill nothingness. It needs to put conciliarity back into the future of the churches: not conciliarity in the abstract, but lived conciliarity, full of engagements and missteps, splinters of wisdom and catastrophic setbacks.

I would like to conclude with some lines from a 2003 essay by Giuseppe Alberigo. In a lecture very dear to me, he said that 'if the Christian experiences of the past undeniably shape the future with the weight of their achievements and errors, they also liberate it, since they testify to the partiality, and therefore the inadequacy, of every single experience with respect to the wholeness

---

(13) It is well known that Dietrich Bonhoeffer was disillusioned, and at the same time convinced, that an ecumenical Council – in the sense of 'voice of all the churches' – could condemn the war, thus giving adequate content to the petition of which he was a witness and an actor in the early 1930s, which saw the churches of and after the Reformation in a position of leadership that gave them greater responsibility at that time. See E. Bethge et al. (hrsg.), *Dietrich Bonhoeffer Werke*, 16 vols, Gütersloh 1986-2013, vol. 13 (1994), p. 304-309, and cfr. K. Clements, 'The Legacy of Dietrich Bonhoeffer for Ecumenism Today', *Nederduitse Gereformeerde Teologiese Tydskrif / Dutch Reformed Theological Journal* 55 (2014), Supplementum 1, p. 956-972, now also in Id., *Dietrich Bonhoeffer's Ecumenical Quest*, Geneva 2015.

(14) Forty years ago, on the anniversary of the First Constantinopolitan Council, Karl Lehmann, Wolfart Pannenberg, and Alexandre Ganoczy, editors of *Glaubensbekenntnis und Kirchengemeinschaft. Das Modell des Konzils von Konstantinopel (381)*, Freiburg 1982, discussed the binding value (in an active sense) of the Symbol.

INTRODUCTION   XIII

of the mystery of Revelation and the multifaceted richness of the Gospel'. According to the Bologna master's lesson, therefore, 'over two millennia, the Christian experience of synodality', with its 'alternation of systole and diastole, that is, of dilations and contractions [...] allows us to recover intact the trust in the generating force of the Christian faith within any human condition'.[15] Treasuring Gregory the Great's analogy between the four Gospels and the four councils, Alberigo found something in it that it would be wrong to consider 'only an authoritative appreciation of the councils from Nicaea to Chalcedon. In truth, at least the *sensus locutionis* of Pope Gregory's formulation transcends the individual contents of conciliar conclusions and highlights the value of the conciliar fact as relevant to the very core of the faith'.

Indeed, the traditions that are strictest and most careful to ensure that this 'relevance' does not become an anti-evangelical *passepartout* are the ones that, at the end of this journey of a few thousand pages, mark the closing of the circle that was opened with the critical re-edition of the *Conciliorum Oecumenicorum Generaliumque Decreta* and redeliver the problem of defining a relationship between the church and the Gospel open to the future – *id est*, what John XXIII's most important and least understood adjective called *pastoral*: not the packaging of 'doctrines' distilled who knows where, but the faith that the Gospel speaks and sows in time and in history.

The concluding consideration of this introduction can therefore be expressed with the words of Giuseppe Alberigo himself, leaving him the last word at the end of the six volumes of the *Conciliorum Oecumenicorum Generaliumque Decreta*, which are not simply a heritage, but also a gift bestowed upon me as general editor, upon the authors, editors and coordinators of these volumes, and the readers:

> To take up an ancient distinction, the *status ecclesiae* – Christ and faith in him – must always constitute the common and permanent element of the church, while the *statuta ecclesiae* – everything proper to the life of the community – must again be the place of pluriformity. As a result, the overcoming of any univocal ecclesiological stance and the possibility of an even deeper reintegration of the church, and reflection on its life, into the universe of faith can be achieved. This means that the relationship between the church – communion and community of the faithful – and the Council can also have a programmatic profile, aimed at the future.

---

(15) G. Alberigo, 'Conciliarità futuro delle chiese', in A. Melloni – S. Scatena (eds), *Synod and Synodality. Theology, History, Canon Law and Ecumenism in New Contact [International Colloquium Bruges, 2003]*, Münster 2005, now also in G. Alberigo, *Transizione epocale. Studi sul Concilio Vaticano II*, Bologna 2009, p. 867-868.

XIV INTRODUCTION

The consequences of this turning point are multiple and of great importance, because they remove the synodal dimension from the exclusive judicial or normative function, which in any case pertains to the ecclesiastical service of order. As it was in part in the early centuries (and, in some Christian traditions, still is), synodality relives a rich and complex meaning: a style with which every Christian community, church, and ultimately the Great Church read the 'signs of the times' for today and for the future, by comparing them with the eternal Gospel. So conceived, synodality directly involves every believer and every community, however small and 'peripheral' it may be. It is a Christian right and above all a duty, which can give a new impact and authenticity to the faith's testimony. The clerical and episcopal monopoly of conciliarity can be overcome, as a glorious season now come to an end. With respect for charisms and different services, the appreciation of fundamental baptismal equality can generate a new era of Christian presence, all the more so after the rediscovery of the sacramental significance of the common priesthood of the faithful. [16]

Alberto MELLONI

(16) *Ibid.*, p. 878-879.

EDITOR'S NOTE

The editorial criteria for this volume combine the specific requirements of the texts of the traditions of and after the Reformation with the standard criteria of the *COGD* series: indeed, unlike a substantial share of source-texts of Christian conciliar and synodal traditions, manuscript sources constitute a relatively small subgroup of the texts edited for this volume, while many amount to printed sources. This has entailed slight adaptations to the way in which the contents of the traditional three-tier standard annotations of *COGD* (biblical references, historical and bibliographical notes, and philological annotations) are presented to the reader: such adaptations can be appreciated throughout the volume. The multi-lingual and diachronic nature of the synodal traditions represented in this volume has also entailed editorial choices – in philological and orthographic matters – which could only be effectively implemented on a case-by-case basis and are elucidated at the end of every introduction in a short note.

Following the rules of the *Corpus Christianorum*, a bibliography is offered at the end of each introduction and its entries are abbreviated in the footnotes (when relevant). A general list of abbreviations lists many, although by no means all, of the most important and well-known texts, sources and repertoires of the Reformation's scholarly tradition: for the entries which have not been given a general abbreviation siglum, the bibliographies of individual editions should be consulted for such abbreviations.

English introductions and translations follow editorial norms as set out in the consolidated use of the *COGD* tradition.

Alongside the great honour of being entrusted with the responsibility of the editorial coordination of the present volume, I owe a great debt to many: the *capitulum* of the researchers of the Foundation for Religious Studies, and in particular the expertise of Prof. Davide Dainese and Dr Federico Alpi who have been working at the wider *COGD* project for many years; to the professionalism and patience of Dr Bart Janssens and Dr Tim Denecker; to the general editor of the series, Prof. Alberto Melloni, for granting me the opportunity to work at the most complex, enriching, and inspiring endeavour of my career so far.

Gianmarco BRAGHI

LIST OF ABBREVIATIONS

BSELK	*Bekenntnisschriften der Evangelisch-Lutherischen Kirche*, hrsg. K. Breuer, I. Dingel, *e.a.*, Göttingen 2014
BSLK	*Bekenntnisschriften der evangelisch-lutherischen Kirche*, hrsg. P. Althaus, H. Lietzmann, *e.a.*, Göttingen ¹³2010
Calv., *Instit.* (1559)	*Ioannis Calvini Institutio Christianae religionis*, 2 vols, hrsg. A. Tholuck, Berlin 1834; 1835
CC SL	*Corpus Christianorum. Series Latina*, Turnhout 1953-
COGD	*Corpus Christianorum. Conciliorum Oecumenicorum Generaliumque Decreta*, Turnhout 2006-
CR	*Corpus reformatorum*, Halle 1834-
CSEL	*Corpus Scriptorum Ecclesiasticorum Latinorum*, Wien 1866-
EKO	*Die Evangelische Kirchenordnungen des 16. Jahrhunderts*, Leipzig – Tübingen 1902-
MWA	*Melanchthons Werke in Auswahl*, Gütersloh 1951
PL	*Patrologiae cursus completus. Series Latina*, vol. 1- 221, ed. J. P. Migne, Paris 1844-1864
PG	*Patrologiae cursus completus. Series Graeca*, vol. 1-161, ed. J. P. Migne, Paris 1847-1886
PSB	*Polski słownik biograficzny*, Kraków 1935-
RefBK	*Reformierte Bekenntnisschriften*, 8 vols, Neukirchen-Vluyn 2002-2016
SC	*Sources Chrétiennes*, Paris 1941-

XVIII	LIST OF ABBREVIATIONS
VD 16	*Verzeichnis der im deutschen Sprachbereich erschienenen Drucke des 16. Jahrhunderts* (online: bsb-muenchen.de)
WA	*D. Martin Luthers Werke, Kritische Gesammt-ausgabe* (*Weimarer Ausgabe*), Weimar 1883-2009
	WA = Abteilung Schriften / Werke
	WA DB = Abteilung Deutsche Bibel

CONCILIUM HOMBERGENSE
1526

edidit
Johannes SCHILLING

THE SYNOD OF HOMBERG AND
THE *REFORMATIO ECCLESIARUM HASSIAE*
1526*

INTRODUCTION

The *Reformatio Ecclesiarum Hassiae* (*REH*) (2) is one of the earliest documents aimed at (re)organising the churches at the beginning of the Reformation. As the cities and territories leaning toward the protestant faith began to object to canon law, it became necessary to regulate ecclesiastical relationships according to new demands and contexts. In place of the Roman Church's jurisdiction and law, the right of sovereign authority and municipal law took centre stage. The general rules which applied to the Church and ecclesiastical life – along with the provisions that excluded the interventions of ecclesiastical or clerical authorities – were no longer dictated by the Church (in a universal sense) or locally by individual churches, but by political authorities.

These resolutions were preceded by a series of events that had been in the making for more than a century, dating back to the period of the Western Schism. These events were punctuated by attempts by the temporal powers of territories and cities to free themselves from ecclesiastical authorities, with the main aim of restricting clerical jurisdiction to its own purview. This came about in the landgraviate of Hesse, for example, starting from the fourteenth century, specifically during the disputes with the archdiocese of Mainz, which exercised control over most of the territory.

(*) I would like to thank Dr Lars Adler and Barbara Tuczek (Hessisches Staatsarchiv Darmstadt) for kindly offering information, as well as Brinja Bauer, M. Ed. and Johann Lehmhaus, Dipl. Theol. (Theologische Fakultät der Christian-Albrechts-Universität zu Kiel) for their assistance in the preparation of the critical edition of the *Reformatio Ecclesiarum Hassiae*. Fidel Rädle (Göttingen) proved himself again a *fidelis amicus* in supervising my edition, and Carolinne White an *amica* in supervising the English translation of my German introduction.

(2) See the edition in *EKO*, vol. 8/1 (1965), p. 10-15 and 43-65. The oldest bibliography is here reported in its entirety. Schilling, *Klöster und Mönche* remains a fundamental reference as it elaborates on the older bibliography and also includes literature published after *EKO*, vol. 8/1. The bibliography included therein is cited by way of exception.

Unlike other ordinances and regulations of the time, the legal validity of the *Reformatio Ecclesiarum Hassiae* was never recognised. The reasons for this can be traced back, on the one hand, to its contents – hard to implement, especially in the version that has survived – and on the other hand to the fact that Martin Luther adamantly rejected its first draft, which had been sent to him for approval. ([3]) On 7 January 1527, Luther conveyed his harsh judgment in a letter to Landgrave Philip I of Hesse and advised the latter not to 'allow this ordinance be printed in these times'. Luther held that times were not yet ripe to 'take possession of such a considerable collection of rules with such powerful words'. The landgrave should instead choose to take small steps on the road to the Reformation, providing individual communities with capable pastors and preachers in the first place. Once a certain amount of time had elapsed, the provisions that had been imparted to them could 'be put together in a booklet'. ([4])

The landgraviate of Hesse did not see a thorough ecclesiastical ordinance until many years later. Following the promulgation of several narrowly-focused ordinances, only in 1566 – the year before the death of Philip I – was a broader ordinance meant for the entire territory approved. ([5]) Meanwhile, between 1527 and 1566, specific provisions had been promulgated, for example on pastoral visits. ([6]) After several meetings with the Baptists residing in the landgraviate, these included the *Ziegenhainer Zuchtordnung*, ([7]) a series of disciplinary rules specifically relating to the sacrament of confirmation. For the first time, confirmation became an integral part of an ecclesiastical ordinance and was understood as the way to be responsible for one's own faith and live as a Christian according to the Gospel.

I

The landgraviate of Hesse was one of those territories where the ideas of the Reformers were well received at an early stage. Hessian scholars attended the University of Wittenberg in large numbers. Sources show that the early followers of Luther, the so-called 'Martinians', were present in the city of Kas-

---

(3) These sources have not survived.

(4) *WA, Briefwechsel*, vol. 4 (1927), p. 157-158, no. 1071.

(5) VD 16, H 2851 (online); edition in *EKO*, vol. 8/1 (1965), p. 24-36 and 178-337.

(6) *EKO*, vol. 8/1 (1965), p. 18-19 and 71-74; VD 16, H 2867, H 2878.

(7) *EKO*, vol. 8/1 (1965), p. 20-23 and 101-112. Facsimile edition: *Die Kirchenordnungen von Ziegenhain und Kassel 1539. In ursprünglicher Form dargeboten und erläutert von Alfred Uckeley*, Marburg 1939; VD 16, O 880 (Wien, Österreichische Nationalbibliothek, 77 Cc. 323, online) and O 881=H 2860.

sel as early as 1521. Also in 1521, and for the first time, they held a 'Teutsche Meße', i.e. a religious service in the vernacular. Preaching and sermons in other territories of the landgraviate and in the nearby abbey of Hersfeld began to open up to the Reformation in the fashion of Wittenberg. The circulation of leaflets promoting the new faith also played a significant role in its spread, even if print shops did not exist prior to the founding of the University of Marburg.

The key figure in the Reformation in the landgraviate of Hesse was Philip I, who later earned the moniker of 'Philip the Magnanimous'. Born in 1504, in 1518 he assumed the government of Hesse, replacing his energetic and devoted mother Anna of Mecklenburg (1485-1525). Following the illness (1504) and subsequent death of William II (1469-1509), Anna had governed the territories and safeguarded her son's succession. The administration of the territories was seamlessly conducted by chancellor Johann Feige (1482-1543) from 1514 to 1542. Feige was the most important court functionary of the landgraviate and later chancellor of the University of Marburg. Young Philip was fascinated by Luther's magnetism and by the ideas of the Reformation after he met him at the Diet of Worms in 1521. The landgrave's encounter with Philip Melanchthon (1497-1560) in May 1524 was another decisive step towards the former's shift to evangelical christianity / protestantism. Immediately after the meeting, Melanchthon set about drafting his *Epitome renovatae ecclesiasticae doctrinae ad illustrissimum principem Hessorum.* ([8]) This was translated into German the same year. ([9]) In this work, Melanchthon elaborated the fundamental concepts of the new interpretation of Christian religion. Also in 1524, the landgrave issued a 'mandate regarding Christian order' ([10]) which obliged parish priests to 'convey teachings to the people in the authentic, pure, faithful, and Christian spirit of the Gospel and of the doctrine of Christ, our Redeemer, outside of Whom there is no salvation'. Luther viewed this mandate as the deliverance of the Gospel. ([11]) Correspondence between

---

(8) VD 16, M 3228, M 3229, M 3231, M 3232. *Melanchthon-Bibliographie 1510-1560*, hrsg. H. Claus (*Quellen und Forschungen zur Reformationsgeschichte* 87/1-4), 4 vols, Gütersloh 2014, vol. 4, p. 2410: seven Latin editions, five in German, one in French (1525). Latin edition in *Melanchthons Werke in Auswahl.* 1. Band: *Reformatorische Schriften*, hrsg. R. Stupperich, Gütersloh 1951, p. 179-189.

(9) VD 16, M 3235 (online).

(10) VD 16, H 2855 (Nürnberg: Hans Hergot, 1524), online; VD 16, H 2891 (Leipzig: Nickel Schmidt, 1524); VD 16, H 2892 (Wittenberg: Hans Luft, 1524), online.

(11) *WA, Briefwechsel*, vol. 3 (1933), p. 337, 17-18, no. 772.

Philip I and his father-in-law George, duke of Saxony, provides an early confirmation of his orientation towards Luther.

By 1524, Reformation theology – both its basic guidelines and the essence of its message – was familiar not only to Philip I, but also to the majority of the landgraviate's elites. Monastic communities showed a certain degree of uncertainty and disorientation in the face of these developments. There were reports of sporadic abuses of power towards the convents as well as towards the monks. Following the example of brothers belonging to other orders, especially within the electorate of Saxony, several monks and nuns left their monasteries and, like the ex-Franciscan Johannes Schwan, ([12]) publicly justified their decision to exchange the religious life for a lay profession. Philip's intention to adopt the Reformation in his territory emerges in his correspondence with Nikolaus Ferber (*c.* 1480-1535), provincial father of the Franciscans of Marburg, and with Duke George of Saxony.

In February 1525, Philip entered into a dispute with churches and convents. This was the first step towards the dissolution of monasteries in the landgraviate and was pursued vigorously in the aftermath of the Synod of Homberg. The implementation of the Reformation was also sped up by the appointment of various pastors, including Adam Krafft (1493-1558), who became the chaplain of the landgraviate's court. The dissolution of monasteries soon followed. Correspondence with the electorate of Saxony suggests that the landgrave was preparing more serious actions. The Diet of Speyer (25 June – 27 August 1526) paved the way for the progressive imposition of the Reformation on individual communities, thus leading to the elaboration of the *Reformatio Ecclesiarum Hassiae.* A number of states of the Holy Roman Empire – including Hesse by way of Philip I – insisted that the issue of religion be discussed. In response to the question of whether individual states could opt for the old or the new faith, the Diet concluded that each state should take 'responsibility assumed before God and the Imperial majesty'. The choice to adhere to Luther's teachings was relegated to sovereign discretion, of which the landgrave of Hesse subsequently made use.

II

This was the context in which the *Reformatio Ecclesiarum Hassiae* was born as a result – at least in the version of the document that has survived – of

---

(12) J. Schilling, 'Johannes Schwan aus Marburg. Sein Leben und seine Schriften', in D. Korsch – J. Lohrengel (hrsg.), *Das Evangelium in der Geschichte der Frömmigkeit. Kirchengeschichtliche Aufsätze*, Leipzig 2016, p. 73-106.

the Synod of Homberg. The assembly, which was called by Philip I to be held in the city of Homberg (Efze) in Lower Hesse, was a decisive moment for the landgraviate on the road to the implementation of the Reformation. This event continued to resonate within the Hessian Church: for example, celebrations were held in 1926 (although no anniversary was held in 1976). Philip drafted and sent his own invitation to a 'friendly and Christian dialogue' to be held either on 19 or 20 October 1526 in Homberg. ([13]) In 1530, it was labelled retrospectively both as a 'Synod and provincial meeting concerning the Christian faith' and as a disputation. The juridical nature of the meeting was a matter of discussion. Latin sources refer to the assembly as a 'synodus'. Representatives of the clergy as well as lay attendees participated in it as if it were a territorial Diet. Inasmuch as it was organised by a sovereign and not by ecclesiastical authorities, the event was illegal in terms of canon law. Nikolaus Ferber also harboured doubts as to its legitimacy.

No original proceedings of the meeting seem to have survived. Its details and dynamics must thus be reconstructed from reports of the two antagonists involved in the disputation, Nikolaus Ferber and François Lambert from Avignon (1486/1487-1530). Following the first two disputations of Zwingli in Zurich – which took place on 29 January and 26-28 October 1523 – several other disputations concerning the issue of religion were held. Some took place prior to Homberg – such as in Altenburg, Strasbourg, Constance, Nuremberg, and Basel – and others afterwards until 1536, in particular in Hamburg, Lübeck, Soest, Esslingen, Geneva, and Lausanne. ([14]) Local political authorities were officially invited to these disputations as witnesses to the protestant faith as the authentic religion in order to impose it against those who resisted the Church in the territory. It is possible that François Lambert brought knowledge of the religious practices of Zurich to Hesse through Strasbourg.

III

The Disputation of Homberg took place on 21-23 October 1526 in the Liebfrauenkirche. Chancellor Johann Feige inaugurated the assembly. From the accounts of those involved, it is possible to reconstruct the atmosphere of

(13) Schilling, *Klöster und Mönche*, p. 181-204; Franz, *Quellen*, no. 29.
(14) For a summary and analysis of individual disputations, see Moeller, *Zwinglis Disputationen*; particularly on the Synod of Homberg, p. 113-118.

8 CONCILIUM HOMBERGENSE – 1526

the event. ([15]) The most important figure in attendance was the young ruler of Hesse, Philip I, who had already developed his opinions on Luther, his person, and his ideas during the Diet of Worms in 1521. After the initial mistrust and strong opposition to the changes sought by the Reformation camp, Philip began to promote protestant ideas within his territory from 1524 onwards. The ex-Franciscan François Lambert was also a key figure. ([16]) Born in 1486 or 1487 in Avignon, he entered a monastery and became such an acclaimed travelling preacher that in 1517 he received the title of *praedicator apostolicus*. After leaving his monastery, in 1522 he moved to Wittenberg for his studies, and later taught at the local University. After spending some time in Strasbourg, he arrived in Hesse and participated in the Diet of Speyer. In Homberg, he styled himself as a defender of a new image of the Church; after the Synod, however, his importance diminished considerably. Lambert was not an instrumental figure in the achievement of the Reformation in the landgraviate of Hesse, although he did become a professor of theology at the University of Marburg. He published a number of significant works such as a commentary on the Apocalypse and a *Somme chrétienne*, dedicated to Charles V. ([17]) He died on 18 April 1530 in Frankenberg, a small town near Marburg.

During the Synod, Nikolaus Ferber confronted Lambert on multiple theological issues. From the start Ferber disputed the legitimacy of the assembly but attempted to use the debate to gain respect for the position of the old Church and its faith. Neither the participants nor the landgrave shared his positions. Once it became clear that the landgraviate had moved on from the old Church and the survival of Hessian monasteries was in jeopardy, Ferber left the city and lived for a time in the Franciscan convent of Brühl, near Cologne. He later became the provincial father of the Franciscan order of Cologne and was unrelenting in his opposition to the Reformation, both in southern Europe as well as during a meeting with royal counsellors (*Her-*

---

(15) QVE | FRAN. LAMBER | tus Auenionensis / apud | sanctā Hessorū Synodū | Hombergi congregatā / | pro Ecclesiarum refor = | matione / Dei verbo dis = | putanda et deseruien = | da proposuit. | EIVSDEM EPI = | stola ad Colonienses De ipsa | venerabili Synodo: aduersum | Nicolaū Herborn Minoritam | assertorem et consarcinatorem | mendaciorum. | Erphordie per Johan = | | nem Loersfelt. | 1527. | Also VD 16, L 154 (online).

(16) On Lambert, see *Pour retrouver François Lambert. Bio-bibliographie et études,* P. Fraenkel (*Bibliotheca Bibliographica Aureliana* 108), Baden-Baden – Bouxwiller 1987.

(17) Sŏme | Chrestienne | a tresuictorieux Em = | pereur Charles / de ce | nom le Cinquiesme / | Composee par Fran. | Lamb. Dauignon. | A Marburg. 1529. | - Jmprime a | Marpurg / Lan de Gra | ce. M. D. XXIX. | le xvij. iour de | Mars. | – Marburg: Franz Rhode 1529. | Also VD 16, ZV 26878; held in Dresden, Sächsische Landes- und Universitätsbibliothek, Theol. ev. gen. 744.

rentag) held in Copenhagen in 1530. On this occasion, his participation did not go unnoticed, and he earned himself the nickname of 'Stagefyr' (firebrand). He died on 15 April 1535 in Toulouse.

Lambert used the Scripture to explain and interpret a series of 158 Latin paradoxes subdivided on the basis of 23 *tituli*. As not every single participant could understand Latin, Adam Krafft provided a summary in German. Ferber set about refuting Lambert's position, although he eventually left the Synod on the second day. A second antagonist is recorded, but he presumably did not contribute to the disputation with any illuminating reflections. At the end of the Synod, a committee was established to clarify – based on the Scriptures – what the Reformation in the Hessian community should look like. Given these circumstances, even if the *Reformatio Ecclesiarum Hassiae* did not have any juridical validity, the Synod of Homberg marked the end of the Roman Church in the landgraviate.

IV

After the end of the Synod, Philip I sent the *Reformatio Ecclesiarum Hassiae* to Luther. On 7 January 1527, Luther replied to the Landgrave:

> [y]our sovereign Grace should not allow the Ordinance to be printed in these times: so far I have never been, and I am not, so daring as to think of appropriating with such vigorous words such a substantial collection of rules. ([18])

According to Luther, it would have been expedient for the landgrave to take the necessary steps and only then to issue an ordinance, as 'prescribing and passing to action are very different things'. ([19]) Luther's advice was certainly a decisive factor in the ordinance not entering into force in the landgraviate. Unlike other Reformation ordinances of the following years, the *Reformatio Ecclesiarum Hassiae* was not published. However, again in 1530 the landgrave spoke of the event in Homberg as a 'provincial meeting and synod concerning the Christian faith' as well as of the 'disputation' held there. ([20]) As mentioned above, an *Ecclesiastical Ordinance* was issued in 1566, a year before the death of Philip I. ([21])

([18]) *WA, Briefwechsel*, vol. 4 (1933), p. 157-158, no. 1071.

([19]) *WA, Briefwechsel*, vol. 4 (1933), p. 158, 29.

([20]) *Quellen und Forschungen zur Geschichte des augsburgischen Glaubensbekenntnisses*, hrsg. W. Gussmann, 6 vols, Leipzig – Berlin 1911-1930, vol. 1/1 (1911), p. 328 and following.

([21]) VD 16, H 2851 (online); edition in *EKO*, vol. 8/1 (1965), p. 24-36 and 178-337.

CONCILIUM HOMBERGENSE – 1526

The title of the *Reformatio Ecclesiarum Hassiae* itself attests to it being an ordinance regulated according to the Word of God ('juxta certissimam sermonum Dei regulam ordinata'); as is befitting, the *intitulatio* is expressed in solemn wording in the style of papal communications. After a preamble, the *Reformatio Ecclesiarum Hassiae* is laid out in 34 chapters of various lengths followed by a *conclusio*. In its conclusion, it once again underlines 'ut omnia in eisdem [ecclesiis] iuxta Dei verbum fiant'.

As the preamble suggested, this ordinance was drafted with the awareness that, after a long period of darkness, the light of eternal truth had returned and human traditions had been abolished. It must apply to all Hessian congregations, as well as to those that might follow their example. Furthermore, the decisions of the Diet of Speyer were expressly referred to. All believers must hold to the divine precepts (*institutiones*) laid out at the beginning of the *Reformatio Ecclesiarum Hassiae*: the administration of the Church, the Eucharist, and ecclesiastical discipline. Central focus is given to the elimination of abuses, the dismissal of members of the clergy unsuited to their roles, and the selection of new preachers who proclaim the Word of God to be pure and authentic ('lauter und rein') as expressed in the related texts in the German language. The Mass must be celebrated in the vernacular, and the element of sacrifice is rejected. The celebration of the Eucharist is to be considered a 'memorial' (Chapter 3) where Christ is truly present. It includes references to the Holy Scriptures as the sole standard, and to the absolute need to keep the holy Word pure. As a whole, the *Reformatio Ecclesiarum Hassiae* contains a number of uncompromising elements. The idea that one could impose the new doctrine with targeted sanctions and with the removal of those who held certain roles or positions would have been illusory if the *Reformatio Ecclesiarum Hassiea* had actually come into force.

NOTE ON THE EDITION

The history of the text's transmission is as disappointing as its actual historical significance. There is no original document or transcription from the sixteenth century. In 1629, the chancellor of Hesse, Nicolaus Vigelius, had knowledge of the ancient 'copy n. 139 that was found in Kassel, in the convent church of Saint Martin'. (22) The first publication was undertaken by Friedrich

---

(22) J. Friedrich, *Die Entstehung der* Reformatio Ecclesiarum Hassiae *von 1526*, Gießen 1905, p. 128.

CONCILIUM HOMBERGENSE – 1526

Christoph Schmincke (1724-1795) in his *Monumenta Hassiaca*, (23) which drew from the recollections of his father, Johann Hermann Schmincke (1684-1743).

The only (undated) manuscript is found in the Hessisches Staatsarchiv Darmstadt under the shelfmark V A 1 Konv. 1 Fasc. 3 (the first abbreviation stands for 'Konvolut', *convolutum*, meaning 'rolled manuscript', and the second stands for 'fasciculus'). Hannelore Jahr used this manuscript for her edition (*EKO*) prior to 1958. The original disappeared from the archives in 2012 but was found again in 2018. A digitalised version from a microfilm of the manuscript can be consulted online. (24) The present edition is based on the microfilm of the Darmstadt manuscript and the edition by Schmincke. Later editions were used for comparison purposes. The orthography of the Darmstadt manuscript has not been changed although it is inconsistent. The numbering of paragraphs has been reproduced as found in Credner's 1852 translation and in *EKO*, although it is not in the manuscript.

BIBLIOGRAPHY

Sources (and Their Abbreviations)

K. A. Credner, *Philipp's des Großmüthigen Hessische Kirchenreformations-Ordnung...*, Gießen 1852.

EKO, vol. 8/1 (1965), p. 43-65.

(23) *Monumenta Hassiaca darinnen verschiedene zur Hessischen Geschichte und Rechtsgelahrsamkeit dienende Nachrichten und Abhandlungen an das Licht gestellet werden*, hrsg. F. C. Schmincke, 4 vols, Cassel 1747-1765, vol. 2 (1748), p. 588-656. In the preamble, the editor explains: 'Habe die erste Hessische Kirchen-Ordnung / welche auf dem Synodo zu Homberg in dem Jahr 1527 [*sic*] in lateinischen [!] Sprache verfasset worden / aus einer alten glaubwuerdigen Handschrifft hier an das Licht gestellet. Man erblicket darinnen den ausnehmenden Eiffer fuer die reine Wahrheit des Evangelii / vnd wie nachdruecklich die bißher eingeschlichenen Mißbraeuche in der Kirchen nach der Richtschnur der heiligen Schrifft angewiesen / vnd gluecklich gehoben [!] worden'.

(24) <https://arcinsys.hessen.de/arcinsys/digitalisatViewer.action?detailid=-v4478414>. The text was first edited (but this is an undocumented detail) by Karl August Credner (1797-1857) in his *Philipp's des Großmüthigen Hessische Kirchenreformations-Ordnung...*, Gießen 1852, then by Friedrich, *Entstehung*, p. (79) 81-124. The latest edition is *EKO*, vol. 8/1 (1965), p. 43-65.

J. Friedrich, *Die Entstehung der Reformatio ecclesiarum Hassiae von 1526*, Gießen 1905, p. (79) 81-124 [= Friedrich, *Entstehung*].

Hessisches Staatsarchiv Darmstadt, V A 1 Konv. 1 Fasc. 3.

LITERATURE (AND ITS ABBREVIATIONS)

Urkundliche Quellen zur hessischen Reformationsgeschichte. Zweiter Band, 1525-1547, hrsg. G. Franz et al. (*Veröffentlichungen der Historischen Kommission für Hessen und Waldeck* 11/12), Marburg 1954 [= Franz, *Quellen*].

B. Moeller, *Zwinglis Disputationen. Studien zur Kirchengründung in den Städten der frühen Reformation. Mit einem Vorwort von Thomas Kaufmann*, Göttingen [2]2011 [= Moeller, *Zwinglis Disputationen*].

J. Schilling, *Klöster und Mönche in der hessischen Reformation* (*Quellen und Forschungen zu Reformationsgeschichte* 67), Gütersloh 1997 [= Schilling, *Klöster und Mönche*].

W. Schmitt, *Die Synode zu Homberg und ihre Vorgeschichte 1526-1926*, Homberg 1926 [= Schmitt, *Die Synode zu Homberg*].

MONITUM

Hessisches Staatsarchiv Darmstadt, V A 1 Konv. 1 Fasc. 3.

CONCILIUM HOMBERGENSE
1526

| REFORMATIO ECCLESIARUM HASSIAE

IUXTA CERTISSIMAM SERMONUM DEI REGULAM, ORDINATA
IN VENERABILI SYNODO PER CLEMENTISSIMUM HESSORUM
PRINCIPEM PHILIPPUM, ANNO, MDXXVI. DIE XX OCTOBRIS
HOMBERGI CELEBRATA, CUI IPSEMET PRINCEPS ILLUSTRISSI-
MUS INTERFUIT.

| SYNODUS HESSIACA IN NOMINE DOMINI APUD HOMBERGUM CONGRE-
GATA UNIVERSIS ET SINGULIS CHRISTI NOMEN INVOCANTIBUS, AD QUOS
HAEC NOSTRA PERVENERINT, PAX ET GRATIA A DEO PATRE NOSTRO ET
DOMINO NOSTRO IESU CHRISTO.

1. Benedictus Deus Dominus noster, qui post tam diutinas tenebras nostri
misertus, aeternae veritatis suae lucem immisit, et Christum, quem Spiritus
impostores et doctrinae Daemoniorum subobscurarunt, nobis denuo palam
fecit. Hinc nobis laetitia vera et perpetua sui nominis benedictio, cuius fiducia
decernimus abiectis impiis hominum traditionibus vivere et regi verbo suo,
quod omnium fidelium est unica et ea quidem certa ad salutem Regula.

2. Erravimus et ut caeci olim a via veritatis et salutis declinavimus, ambu-
lavimus in via erroris et perditionis. Iam Dei misericordia illustrati in ipsam, a
qua apostataveramus, viam sic nos rediisse laetamur, ut cupiamus ad eam
universos pellicere et agere, ut sic eam amplectantur, ut nunquam ab ea deficiant.

3. Ea ratione pro universis nostrae Hassiae Ecclesiis, et si deinde nonnul-
lae aliae ad idem nostro exemplo provocarentur, conscripsimus hic, quae ipsis
Ecclesiis utilia fore vidimus, de quibus parati sumus Deo et Caesari ex Dei
verbo reddere rationem, prout in novissimis Imperialibus Comitiis Sphyrae
celebratis fuit definitum.

---

25 Sphyrae] i.e. Speyer

---

14 sui nominis] nominis sui *S*   **22** nostrae Hassiae] Hassiae nostrae *S*

16 CONCILIUM HOMBERGENSE – 1526

| 4. Ex his nonnulla cunctis fidelibus sunt necessaria, quippe quia in eis 2v
purum Dei eloquiorum sensum expressimus. Tantum admonere voluimus, ut
omnes ecclesiae sint memores institutionum Dei. Eiusmodi sunt, quae posui-
30 mus de cultu Dei vero, De Ecclesiarum regimine, de Eucharistia sub pane et
vino sumenda, De excommunicandis notorie criminosis, de absolutione resipi-
scentium, et ut omnia coram Ecclesia lingua vulgi dicantur, nisi interpres adsit,
visitandas Ecclesias a piis et in verbo Dei eruditis, earum Synodos niti oportere verbo Dei, Episcopos et Diaconos ex piis et spiritu Dei plenis eligendos,
35 Coniugium universis honorabile, etiam Episcopis et Diaconis, Sectas in Ecclesiis nullatenus ferendas, et id genus alia.

5. Caetera, ut Coenae Dominicae laudumque matutinarum et vespertina-
rum ritus, numerus electorum Synodi et similia cuncta non pro necessariis
legibus scripsimus, quod et nobis haud quaquam licet, sed tantum ut in nostris
40 Ecclesiis impleatur illud praeceptum, non dubium quin Domini, scriptum a
Paulo 1. Cor. 14. 40: Omnia decenter et secundum ordinem fiant.

6. Haec autem in nostris Ecclesiis ob uniformitatem observari volumus,
parati interim locum dare, si in generali aut nationali Synodo meliora fuerint
ex | Dei sermonibus ordinata. 3r

45 7. Fecimus autem haec paulo fusius, ne in eiusmodi amodo plura ordinen-
tur. Admonemus proinde et obsecramus per nomen Dei omnes, qui in futuris
Synodis congregabuntur, ne ordinationum multitudine et varietate Ecclesias
onerent, scientes, quod, ubi tam multa ordinantur, ibi cuncta semper sint inor-
dinatiora. Sint sola Dei Scriptura, et his nostris circa Ceremonias ordinatiun-
50 culis contenti, faciant ut haec serventur unanimiter, et vitent ne Ecclesiae,
quas Christus suo sanguine liberas fecit, denuo incidant in servitutem et
laqueos pernitiosissimos traditionum hominum, sitque novissimus error peior
priore.

8. Proinde si ab Ecclesiis dubia nonnulla mittantur, paucis ex Dei verbo
55 respondeant, tamen ut nihil eis tradant sub novarum conscientiarum titulo.
Quod si Ecclesiae necessitas eos aliquid iubere cogat, non tam ipsi quam Deus
in eis suo praecipiat verbo.

9. Nemo autem miretur, quod aliquoties contra eos, qui Domino contradicunt et scandalo fiunt Ecclesiae Dei, ab eaque apostatant, precamur, ut Ana-

---

50/51 ne – servitutem] cfr Gal. 5, 1 **51/53** et – priore] cfr Matth. 27, 64

35 Ecclesiis] ecclesia *S* **37** Caetera] Caeterum *S* **47** et] ac *S* **49** Dei Scriptura]
scriptura Dei *S* **55** tamen] tamen tantum *S* conscientiarum] constitutionum *S*

CONCILIUM HOMBERGENSE – 1526　　　17

60　thema sint, quod zelus gloriae Dei et ueritatis eius salutisque omnium nos ad
id Pauli exemplo admodum impulerit. Caeterum id genus impii et apostatae
non ob nostram precationem, sed propterea quod Dominum nostrum Iesum
Christum | ac veritatem eius calcant, etiam tacentibus nobis, anathemati subii-　3v
ciuntur, tametsi nihil omnino dubitamus eos iuxta carnem nonnihil passuros,
65　et nisi resipuerint, horrendius disperituros, quod sanctum Ecclesiae Dei zelum
fuerint aspernati. Omnium quippe verum bonum et gloriam Dei quaerimus:
Unde et sancte irascimur impietati et Apostasiae.

10. Praemonemus autem, ne quis putet nos per Episcopos alios intelligere
quam ministros verbi Dei, sic enim ab Apostolis, quorum doctrinam sequi-
70　mur, vocati sunt, ut in Paulo et Actis Apostolicis est videre.

11. Hortamur autem per sanctum Christi nomen, ne quis nobis in re tam
seria tamque pio ac necessario instituto sit de caetero molestus. Causam enim
Dei agimus, et sermo eius, imo ipsemet nobiscum est. Magis autem precamur,
ut una sententia unoque ore ambulemus in viis iustitiae ac veritatis, honorifice-
75　musque Deum et patrem Domini nostri Iesu Christi, quem toto corde obsecramus, ut nos in dies magis illustret ac corroboret spiritu et veritate sua,
donetque nobis, ut ab eo nunquam deficiamus, sed augeamur et perficiamur
usque in diem suum. Cui honor, gloria, decus et imperium in secula seculorum Amen.

80　　　　　　　　　　　| DE CULTU DEI VERO　　　　　　　　　　4r

Cap. I

12. Venit hora, qua Deus vult spiritu et veritate coli, Iohann. 4., quod tum
fit, dum iuxta verbum aeternae veritatis suae colitur. Proinde in omnibus
Ecclesiis nostris iuxta idem verbum purissime colatur, et omnis diversus cultus
85　ab eis propellatur. Tametsi enim cultus ipse Dei in fidei puritate sit, opera
tamen quaecunque externa, quae iuxta verbum fidei a nobis fiunt, et quibus
nos Dei cultores esse testamur, ad cultum Dei pertinent. Sic Deus in omnibus
Ecclesiis colendus est.

74　ut – iustitiae] cfr Ps. 118, 1　**82**　Venit – coli] cfr Ioh. 4, 23

61　admodum] a modo *S*　　**68**　nos] nos hic *S*　　**69**　verbi Dei] Dei uerbi *S*
70　Apostolicis] Apostolorum *S*　**73**　Dei] Domini *S*　**77**　augeamur] augeamus *D*

CONCILIUM HOMBERGENSE – 1526

De Ecclesiarum Regimine

Cap. II

13. Quia grex Christi solam audit vocem Pastoris sui et non exaudit voces alienorum, Io. 10., Non admittimus verbum aliud, quam ipsius Pastoris nostri, quin potius in Dei virtute interdicimus, ne aliud omnino verbum ab Episcopis in Ecclesiis doceatur, et secundum illud de caetero ipsae Ecclesiae regantur. Quod si quis aliud verbum quasi ad salutem necessarium docuerit, deponatur et communione privetur.

14. Porro quaecunque hic pro decenti agendorum in Ecclesiis ordine conscripsimus, et Dei verbo speciatim haudquaquam iubentur, nolumus alioqui quam pro sanis et a verbo Dei non dissenti|entibus consiliis a quopiam haberi, 4v quae tamen possint urgente Christi gloria immutari.

De Eucharistia vel Coena Dominica

Cap. III

15. Quotquot Coenae Dominicae participes esse volunt, simul et pani et poculo benedictionis communicent, sicut Dominus instituit, et qui aliud docuerit et admonitus Dei verbo non acquieverit, communione privetur, et praeterea, si Episcopus est, deponatur.

16. Non celebretur ipsa Coena, nisi adsint, qui communicent. Admoneant autem Ecclesiam Episcopi, ut ad hanc venerabilem Coenam singulis Dominicis conveniant, eidem participaturi. Verum se ipsos prius probent, ne in iudicium conveniant ad idque, si desolatae sunt eorum conscientiae, laudamus et consulimus, ut adeant Episcopum vel illius adiutorem aut aliquem ex piis doctisque fratribus confitentes peccatum suum, et audituri ab eis verbum sanctum, ut infra de Confessionibus.

17. Caeterum qui eam cupiunt, Episcopo aut ministro eius seipsos indicent, et ante Coenam ipsam segregentur in locum unum ab his qui tum participare nolunt, ut eorum numerus sciri valeat. Admonemus autem universos in

---

91/92 Quia – alienorum] cfr Ioh. 10, 4; 10, 16; 10, 27   **109/110** Verum – conveniant] cfr I Cor. 11, 34

---

92 alienorum] aliorum *S*   **94** Ecclesiis] Ecclesia *S*   **99** quopiam] quoquam *S*
110 eorum] ipsorum *S*

CONCILIUM HOMBERGENSE – 1526

Domino, qui tum aderunt, etiam eos, qui sanctae mensae non sunt externe participaturi, ut sint memores sacrificii nostri Christi semel pro nobis | oblati, 5r cuius haec coena memoriale est, quod et paucis ab Episcopo semper est decla-
120 randum.

18. Canon ille Missarius, et universae orationes, in quibus reperitur sacrificii aut hostiae vox, a nemine ultra in hac Coena dicatur. Nemo praeterea audeat hanc coenam sacrificare, ut loquuntur, pro vivis et mortuis, aut quacunque occasione, quod non sit nostrum sacrificium, sed Dei Coena, et pro
125 accepta per Christum beneficentia gratiarum actio, ac specialis commemoratio sacrificii, quo semel pro nobis semet ipsum obtulit, omniumque mirabilium eius. Est quoque signum communionis omnium, quae Christi quo ad invicem nos membra esse sub ipso et eodem quidem uno capite Christo profitemur. Sumus enim invicem membra Rom. 12, 1. Cor. 6 et 12. Et ipse Caput nostrum
130 Eph. 5, Col. 1.

19. Praeterea nullae in ea dicantur orationes, quibus aut sanctorum invocatio aut meritorum eorundem memoria sit. Solus enim Christus est advocatus noster 1. Ioh. 2 et unus mediator Dei et hominum 1. Timoth. 2. Denique ipse solus est, qui pro nobis omnibus meruit gratiam, gloriam et omne bonum.
135 Quodsi haec nobis mereri possemus, gratis Christus mortuus esset Gal. 2.

20. Confitemur in hac Coena Christum Deum et hominem praesentem esse, et id quidem non vocibus imprecatoriis, ut de nobis quidam obloquuntur, sed decreto Dei vivi, quod est ipsissimum verbum suum, cuius ipsae voces signa sunt.

140 21. Omniaque in hac Coena agantur vulgi lingua praeter has | consuetas 5v voculas Kyrie eleyson, Halleluiah, Hosiannah, Sabaoth, Amen, quas Episcopi aliquando interpretentur, ut plebs omnia capiens in Dei verbo consoletur et spiritu et mente psallat. Servetur in ea ritus, quem servus Dei Martinus Lutherus ultimo Germanice conscripsit, et ut iuxta Paulum cuncta decentius fiant,
145 laudamus si in eius ministerio ad minus induatur superpellicium, incendantur cerei et decens Calix habeatur.

---

129 Sumus – membra] cfr Rom. 12, 5; I Cor. 6, 15; 12, 12 seq.   Et – nostrum] cfr Eph. 5, 23; Col. 1, 18   **132/133** Solus – noster] cfr I Ioh. 2, 1   **133** et¹ – hominum] cfr I Tim. 2, 5   **135** gratis – esset] cfr Gal. 2, 21   **144** ut – fiant] cfr I Cor. 14, 40

143/144 Servetur – conscripsit] cfr M. Luther, 'Deutsche Messe' (1526), in *WA*, vol. 19 (1897), p. 72-113

117 eos] *om. S*   **126** mirabilium] memorabilium *S*   **127** quae Christi quo ad] qui Christi quod ad *S*

20 CONCILIUM HOMBERGENSE – 1526

22. Amodo nullae fiant impensae pro altarium paramentis, casulis, cappis seu chlamydibus et similibus, sed magis dispensentur egenis, quae in his frustra consumi consueverunt. Nimirum qui se putat in his colere Deum, sine causa id facit, quod sint purae et vanae hominum traditiones. Liberum autem sit habenti casulam eadem in Coenae Dominicae ministerio uti vel non, tamen de caetero haud quaquam emantur, quod non in haec, sed in pauperum usus, quae donare volumus, sint convertenda.

23. Praeterea infirmorum solummodo causa iam emptis uti permittimus, certi quod nihil horum a nobis et maxime quidem ut egenis misericordiam praestemus et illis nostra partiamur. Denique semper habentur pauperes, quibus bene facere opus sit. Idcirco universis Ecclesiis in verbo eruditis liberum sit omnia id genus paramenta divendere, quod si fecerint, eorum pretium Diaconorum ministerio pauperibus dispensetur.

24. Dalmaticas, hoc est Papisticorum Diaconorum vestes aut sub | diaco- ⁶ʳ norum nemo de caetero induat. Nolumus enim favere ordinibus illis sine Dei eloquiorum testimoniis introductis. Caeterum Scriptura alios nescit ministros praeterquam Episcopos seu Presbyteros et Pauperum Diaconos. De Missariis autem Diaconis nec iota quidem unum in utroque instrumento reperimus, tametsi episcoporum adiutores non incongrue Diaconi, id est ministri vocentur. Diaconus enim ministrum, et Diaconia ministerium significat.

25. Admonemus deinde in nomine Domini, ut Organa nunquam aut rarissime pulsentur, ne in priscos relabamur errores. Si enim praesente Ecclesia non est lingua peregrina utendum, nisi interpres adsit, ne homines non intelligant, quod dicitur, minus profecto organis, quod solis auribus sine animi fructu inserviant. Plebs enim sonum quidem audit, sed sensum rei, quae organo pulsatur, ignorat. Neque a lege sumendum est exemplum, quod tum iusserit Dominus Musicalia Instrumenta pulsari in Christi et Ecclesiae figuram: At figura, praesente veritate evanuit. Praeterea eadem pulsatio ad levitici sacerdotii ministeria pertinebat, quae adveniente Christo cum ipso sacerdotio evacuata sunt.

26. Campanae ad Dominicae Coenae celebrationem et ad omnium fidelium congregationes sic pulsentur, ut audire valeat populus et congregari. Hortamur autem in Domino, ut vanus ille ac pomposus pulsationum strepitus ab

---

147 altarium] altariorum *D*   **151** tamen] tantum *S*   **156** nostra] necessaria *S* habentur] habeantur *D*   **163** seu] *om. S*   **164** autem] aut *S*   **171** sonum quidem] quidem sonum *S*

CONCILIUM HOMBERGENSE – 1526

180 universis vitetur. Satis enim atque abunde foret Campanam unam mediocrem
pro signo pulsari.

| Non reservandam in armariis Eucharistiam nec per plateas etiam infirmorum occasione circumferendam

Cap. IV

185   27. Quia usus sanctae Eucharistiae est perceptio eius et communio fidelium in Christi commemorationem, nullibi a modo in armariis seu arcellis
reservetur nullaque ratione circumferatur. Haec namque figmenta hominum
sunt, ideoque vitanda. Quod si quis infirmorum ipsam Eucharistiam petit,
accedat minister quacunque hora fuerit, et in domo infirmi coenam hanc cele-
190 bret, ad quam, si fieri potest, fratres aliquot vocet, qui cum infirmo communicent orentque pro eo et consolentur eum verbo Domini et minister ille paucis
tantae Coenae mysteria declaret.

De oratione, lectione et Canticis tam matutinis quam vespertinis

195   *Cap. V*

    28. Quaecunque in praesentia Ecclesiae dicuntur, nisi adsit interpres iuxta
Paulum 1. Corinth. 14 lingua cunctis notiori tradantur, sive orationes sive
lectiones sive psalmi sive cantica sint, ut ex eis cuncti consolentur et ad benedictionem loquentium respondere possint: Amen. Proinde absente interprete
200 linguae peregrinae sileant, quod non Pauli solius, sed Domini praeceptum sit.
Nimirum praescripto loco de his aliisque nonnullis dicit: Si quis Propheta aut
spiritualis est, agnoscat, quae scribo vobis, quia Domini sunt praecepta. Si quis
autem ignorat, ignoret. Admonendi autem sunt universi fideles, ut ad publi-
cam orationem et lectionem, item ad | Coenam Dominicam diligentissime
205 conveniant. Caeterum haec amodo non fiant in choro, sed in medio Ecclesiae
decenter celebrentur, ut omnes utriusque sexus discant et concorditer et una-

---

196/197 Quaecunque – tradantur] cfr I Cor. 14, 5

186 seu] sive *S*   **190** fratres] tres *S*   **191** eum verbo] eum cum verbo *S*

22 CONCILIUM HOMBERGENSE – 1526

nimiter psallant, nomenque Dei simul glorificent. Omnes enim in Christo sacerdotes facti sunt.

29. Ordinamus denique ut in universis Ecclesiis laudes matutinae et vespertinae hoc ritu quotidie serventur, et primum matutinae sic: Cantetur psalmus: *Venite Exultemus*, et unus duo uel tres alii secundum iudicium episcopi, et id quidem sub tonis communibus, quibus psalmi hactenus latine cantati sunt. Psalmus quoque *Venite exultemus* eodem tono, quo alii cantetur. Servetur autem is ordo in psalmis cum tonis, ut una hora omnes in primo, alia in secundo, alia in tertio et sic de aliis cantentur. Posthac cantent in rythmo Psalmum: *Deus misereatur* pro dilatatione regni Christi vel Psalmum: *Saluum me fac Deus, quoniam defecit sanctus*, aut alium ex his, qui in rithmo positi sunt. Deinde episcopus aut eius adiutor legat unum caput ex veteri instrumento, cui liberum sit aliquid interpretari, modo id paucis agat, maxime infra hebdomadam nihilque dicat, nisi diligentissime praemeditatum et examinatum. Denique cantetur: *Benedictus Dominus, Deus Israel*, et hoc tonis consuetis, tono quotidie iuxta ordinem mutato. His absolutis dicat Episcopus: Dominus vobiscum. Respondeatur: Et cum spiritu tuo. Postea, Oremus: Pater noster, quod totum alte dicat, et in fine Ecclesia respondeat: Amen. Item dicat Episcopus: Infunde nobis, | quaeso, Domine Deus noster, Spiritum tuum, qui nos in cunctis dirigat, illustretque et dirigat aeternam veritatem tuam ac confirmet sic in ea, ut nunquam dividamur a te, et faciat, ut ex fide vivamus, ac omnia ex eadem agamus per Dominum nostrum Iesum Christum filium tuum, qui tecum etc. Respondeatur: Amen. Dominus vobiscum. Respondeatur: Et cum spiritu tuo. Benedicamus Domino. Respondeatur: Deo gratias.

30. Quod spectat ad vespertinas laudes, omnia fiant sicut in matutinis, excepto quod non dicunt Psalmum: *Venite exultemus*. Et cantent Psalmum rithmicum ab eo, quem mane cantarunt, et non ex veteri instrument, sed novo legant caput unum et pro *Benedictus* cantent *Magnificat* aut *Nunc dimittis*,

---

211 Ps. 94, 1   **216** Ps. 67, 1   **216/217** Ps. 11, 2   **221** Luc. 1, 68   **232** Ps. 94, 1
234 Luc. 1, 46   Luc. 2, 29

207/208 Omnes – sunt] cfr M. Luther, 'An den christlichen Adel deutscher Nation von des christlichen Standes Besserung', in *WA*, vol. 6 (1888), p. 407   **216** Deus misereatur] when the *Reformatio Ecclesiarum Hassiae* was written, Luther's song based on Psalm 67 was available in a single-sheet print, titled 'Es wolt vnß Gott uns genedig sein'. Headline: 'Der Lxvj. Deus Misereatur'

215 Posthac cantent] Posthaec *S*   **216** Psalmum¹] *om. S*   Deus] Christus Deus *S*   vel Psalmum] *D*in marg.   **217** quoniam] quem *D*   alium] alius *S*   **226** et] ac *S*   **227** ac] et *S*   **232** Psalmum¹] Psalmos *D*   **234** cantent] canent *S*

CONCILIUM HOMBERGENSE – 1526

235 tonis consuetis. Dominicis tamen diebus ac festis cantent utrumque: prius
Magnificat: postea *Nunc dimittis*.

31. In lectione is ordo servetur. Mane legant per ordinem librorum et capi-
tum ex veteri instrumento, et dum totum compleverunt, denuo incipiant. Sic
faciant vespere ex novo instrumento. In psalmis vero is sit ordo, quod psalmo-
240 rum ordinem sequantur ut si mane legerint 20, vespere legant 21. Et cum
totum Psalterium absolverint, a capite denuo incipiant. Dominicis praeterea
festisque diebus tam mane quam vespere in fine laudum, et si visum fuerit
episcopo post coenam Dominicam haec oratio post alias dicatur:

32. Deus a quo, per quem et in quo omnia sunt, ac cui soli gloria est
245 reddenda, miserere Caesaris nostri | ac omnium regum ac Principum ac Magi-   8r
stratuum orbis terrae, illustra eos lumine tuo et fac ut iuxta uerbum tuum
praesint populis tuis, ad idque eos pertrahe vinculis sanctitatis ac veritatis tuae
ut conterantur universae impietates, quae a multis fuere seculis, augeaturque
populus tuus, et tu solus regnes in omnibus gentibus. Caeterum Principem
250 nostrum et omnes, quos iam ad te attraxisti fecistique aeternae veritatis tuae
participes, in ea sic confirma, ut nunquam in ea deficiant, sed verus eorum
zelus augeatur de die in diem. Perfice in eis Domine, quae coepisti spiritu tuo,
et suscita in eis spiritum per omnipotentiam manus tuae, sicut suscitasti spiritum servorum tuorum Danielis, Iosaphat, Ezechiae et Iosiae, terrorem autem
255 et reverentiam eorum immitte super omnes hostes veritatis tuae, ut erubescant
et conturbentur valde velociter: Nosque in gloriam regni tui magnificemus
nomen sanctum tuum. Et tu o pater noster ne deseras nos, et ne sinas nos
libertate, qua nos ditasti, abuti in carnis occasionem nec a pietate deficere: ne
denuo pristinis erroribus ac tenebris involvamur, sed dona, ut videamus sem-
260 per victricem manum tuam super hostes tuos, ac nos et omnem terram tuo
Spiritu regi, teque solum ubique regnare per Dominum nostrum Iesum Christum etc.

257/258 Et – deficere] cfr Gal. 5, 13

235 cantent] cantetur *S*   240 sequantur] sequatur *S*   244 omnia] *om. S*   ac] et *S*
245 ac¹] et *S*   249 regnes] regne *D*   253 per] *om. S*   258 occasionem] occisionem
D S   262 etc.] *om. S*

DE CONFESSIONE

Cap. VI

265   33. Nemo quenquam ad Confessionem illam peccatorum sine Dei eloquiorum auctoritate introductam compellere, ut hactenus audeat. Nimirum hae solae sunt peccatorum | gratae Confessiones. Primum, si quis iuxta Ps. 8v 31 suam iniustitiam adversum se Domino confitetur. Item dum quis fidelis non se negat peccatorem, sed id vere et ex animo etiam coram tota Ecclesia confite-
270 tur. Proinde laudamus publicam Confessionem, quae in Coenae Dominicae initio fieri consuevit, modo lingua vulgi distincte et ab omnibus simul fiat. Item si quis in peccato deprehensus non declinat os suum in verba malitiae ad excusandas excusationes in peccatis, Ps. 140. Item, dum si aliqui fratrum se invicem offenderunt, iuxta Iacobum suae epistolae cap. 5, confitentur alter-
275 utrum ipsa sua peccata, quibus alter alterum offendit. Item dum quis venit ad episcopum aut aliquem pium fratrem, in genere confitens peccata sua, et petens ab eo consolari verbo Dei, verbumque bonum, quo testificetur a Deo sibi peccata dimitti, ut est illud Matth. 9: Confide fili, remittuntur tibi peccata tua.

280   34. In quo genere confessionis laudamus, si primum frater confitetur incredulitatem suam, neglectum verbi sancti ac veritatis inquirendae, et abusum Evangelicae veritatis ac libertatis, itemque generatim incredulitatis fructus. Porro si is, qui confitetur, verbi sancti directione indiget, hoc quaerat humiliter, et alius id praestet, quantum a Deo accepit, quo facto dicat: Confi-
285 de fili, remittuntur tibi peccata tua in nomine Patris et Filii et Spiritus sancti.

DE IEIUNIIS

Cap. VII

35. Quia necesse est, ut omnia fidelium opera sint ex fide, | quod quicquid 9r non est ex fide, peccatum sit Rom. 14, interdicimus universis Episcopis in
290 virtute Dei, ne quis eorum dies aliquos ad ieiunandum Ecclesiis praescribant,

---

267/268 Primum – confitetur] cfr Ps. 32, 5   **272/273** Item – peccatis] cfr Ps. 141, 4
273/275 Item – offendit] cfr Iac. 5, 16   **278/279** Matth. 9, 2   **284/285** Confide –
sancti] cfr Matth. 9, 2   **288/289** Quia – sit] cfr Rom. 14, 23

---

267 iuxta] in Christo *S*   **269** etiam] *D*^{sup.l.}; et *S*   **273** excusationes] excursiones *S*
275 ipsa] *D*^{sup.l.}   dum] dum si *D*   **277** verbumque] utrumque *S*   **278** sibi peccata]
peccata sibi *S*   **283** is] quis *eras. et is corr. sup. l. D*   **285** et¹] *om. S*

CONCILIUM HOMBERGENSE – 1526

sed sinant unumquemque in divini Spiritus libertate vivere, ut omnia secundum verbum Dei atque ex fide faciant. Admoneant illos ad temperantiam atque sobrietatem, et iubeant constanter ex verbo Domini, ut commessationes atque ebrietates devitent et in omnibus vitam Christo dignam vivant, servantes omnia praecepta Dei, et satis fuerit. Nolumus ut cuiquam prohibeant ieiunia, sed neque volumus, ut speciatim praecipiant, quod neutrum eorum eisdem liceat.

36. Verum si quae gravis causa seu necessitas urgeat, liberum est Principi cum aliquo Ecclesiarum consilio et assensu diem unum et alterum ad ieiunandum instituere, non tamen de hac re legem perpetuam facere. Consulimus tamen et gratius erit Deo, ut id potius rogando quam iubendo faciat, neque enim competit Christiano Magistratui, qui inter fratres alioquin habetur, ut aliquid durum imponat per imperium suis ex fide confratribus, nisi in rebus maxime urgentibus et ad bonum publicum necessariis. Veruntamen si iusserit, ab universis, qui possunt, est parendum.

37. Licebit itidem cuilibet Ecclesiae, cum aliquid arduum est aggressura, ut ieiunii diem constituat. Sic tamen ut neminem cogant, et ne hoc pro lege tradant. Hortamur autem fideles omnes in Domino, ut in his casibus ad ieiunandum difficiles haud quaquam sint.

| De Festis et Commemorationibus

Cap. VIII

38. Praeter Dominicam diem nullum festum celebretur, nisi pro mysteriis nostrae redemptionis. Ideo haec sola de caetero habeantur, Nativitatis Christi, Circumcisionis, Epiphaniae, Praesentationis Domini in templum, Incarnationis Verbi Dei sive Annunciationis, diei Parasceves, Paschae die primo, Ascensionis et Pentecostes die primo: Item dies Visitationis Beatae Mariae.

39. Interdicimus autem in virtute omnipotentis Dei, ne quis in ipsis festis quicquam agat eorum, quae hactenus contra puritatem sermonum Dei introducta fuerunt, ut sunt Benedictio candelarum in die praesentationis, et superstitiones, quae in diebus aliis praescriptis servabantur. Horum quippe celebratio non in factis superstitiosis, sed in verbi sancti frequentia et operibus misericordiae est sita.

---

293 atque] et *S*   Domini] Dei *S*   **294** atque] et *S*   **306** aggressura] aggressum *S*
312 Dominicam] Dominicum *S*

CONCILIUM HOMBERGENSE – 1526

40. Proinde in his primum fiat matutina oratio et lectio vice Missae matutinae. Deinde facto modico intervallo celebretur Dominica Coena, et in ea fiat sermo, postmodum hora secunda a prandio fiat vespertina oratio, in qua, post lectionem capitis novi Testamenti habeatur sermo, post quem mox cantetur *Magnificat* et ipsae laudes absolvantur.

41. Quod si tempore quo nihil horum fit, aliquis vult operari, quae spectant ad artem suam, nihil dubitans operetur in nomine Domini: Nimirum | hoc illi verbo Dei iubetur potius quam otiari, ipsum autem otium interdicitur. Otium non vocamus, si quis studet aut meditatur, sed si nihil utile facit aut impia desideria sectatur. Maxime enim ut Dei sermo a toto populo libere audiri possit, et dies Dominicus et alia festa dimittantur, quod alioqui veris fidelibus omnes dies liberi sunt.

42. Non licebit autem ipsis diebus opificum famulos cogere ad opera, nisi eo casu, quo ultra conciones coenamque dominicam vacarent contra verbum Dei comessationibus, ebrietatibus, ludis atque aliis id genus, sed magis ipsi dies eisdem liberi permittantur in Domino, ut non nisi ad ea quae sunt domui in horas necessaria impellantur, verum qui operatur, viderit, ut id sine scandalo ex fide faciat, laudabilius tamen et sanctius fuerit, si post auditum verbum Domini infirmis aut carceratis aut aliis desolatis visitandis ac consolandis intenderint. Item si studiis sacris aut sanctis de Dei verbo colloquiis aut id genus aliis seipsos occuparint, cum id diebus reliquis operariis minime liceat, his saltem, qui opificibus inserviunt, consulimus quod magis conducit. Verum si quis a Deo est, a fide et charitate plenius dirigetur atque erudietur. Haec de festis.

43. Fiant deinde in universis Ecclesiis nostris memoriae Divi Iohannis Baptistae, Sanctorum Apostolorum et Evangelistarum, et Beati Stephani protomartyris, non ut his diebus non operetur arte sua quisquam, sed ut confestim post laudes matutinas | habeatur publicus sermo, quo facto vadant ad labores suos in nomine Domini. Admonemus autem universos, ut ad ipsum sermonem conveniant audituri verbum sanctum, quo ad fidem sanctorum imitandam provocentur.

335/342 Non – intenderint] cfr Matth. 25, 34-46   **344/345** Verum – est] cfr Ioh. 8, 47

323 Missae matutinae] matutinae missae *S*

CONCILIUM HOMBERGENSE – 1526

44. Nolumus autem, ut alicuius sanctorum praedictorum fiat commemoratio plusquam die uno, excepto quod Divi Iohannis Baptistae tam nativitas
quam decollatio memorandae sunt, quod ipsis diebus propria sint Evangelia.

45. Fiat quoque memoria Conversionis Diui Pauli, ob insignem ex Actis
Apostolicis epistolam.

46. Episcopi eorumve Diaconi sive Adiutores singulis diebus Dominicis
pronuntient tam dies festos quam memorias, quae per hebdomadam sunt
futurae. Si quis Episcoporum aut adiutorum eorundem audet ipsis diebus post
sermonem supra dictum aliquos de caetero praepedire a labore, diebus inquam
commemorationum, quod velit eos pro festis haberi, et admonitus non
resipuerit, deponatur et communione privetur, si notum est, quod fecit.

47. Interdicimus universis Ecclesiis nostris in virtute Christi ne ultra dedi-
cationes celebrent, quod non conveniant verbo Domini, et nihil fiat in eis,
quod non sit a pietate diversum: denique post Christum nullum proprie lapideum templum est in Dei Ecclesia, sed soli fideles et ipsa Ecclesia sunt viva Dei
templa. Nam quae nunc a nonnullis templa vocantur, nihil minus sunt quam
quod esse dicuntur. Nullum enim externum a Deo | constitutum est praeter
Hierosolymitanum, quod cum suo sacerdotio suisque mysteriis finem in Christo et Ecclesia habet. Iam si nullum est templum, profecto illorum dedicatio
non est celebranda. Celebret quisque fidelium in corde suo Ecclesiae consecra-
tionem, qua sanctius potest, quod toties facit, quoties laetus in Domino de sua
et omnium fidelium vocatione gratias agit et quotquot potest ad sanctum
Ecclesiae gaudium coelestesque epulas verbo sancto invitat.

48. Interdicimus denique, ne quis Sanctos invocet, quod sit contra
verbum Domini, et nemo illis dedicet locum, et qui contrarium fecerit, communione privetur, et locus sic dicatus conteratur. Praeterea nulla Ecclesia nullo
alio Patrono glorietur quam Deo et Domino nostro Iesu Christo. Et ne prae-
cedentium errorum reliquiae novos pariant, universi episcopi doceant populum ex verbo Dei, vocare domus, quae hactenus templa vocata sunt, domos
Ecclesiarum, et nulla amodo vocetur templum huius vel illius Sancti, sed simpliciter domus Ecclesiae talis civitatis, oppidi vel pagi. Verum quaelibet Eccle-

---

365/369 Interdicimus – templa[1]] cfr I Cor. 3, 16

354 commemoratio] concio *S*   **355** Divi – nativitas] *intellege* 24 Iunii
356 decollatio] *intellege* 29 Augusti   sint] sunt *S*   **357** memoria – Pauli] *intellege* 25
Ianuarii   **363** quod] quasi *S*   **368/369** Dei templa] templa Dei *S*   **384** talis
civitatis] ciuitatis talis *S*

28 CONCILIUM HOMBERGENSE – 1526

385 sia definiat de domo sua, qua ratione vocanda sit, tantum ne superstitiosa sit
vocatio eius.

EXTERMINANDUM IMAGINUM ET IDOLORUM CULTUM

Cap. IX

49. Quia statuae et imagines in Ecclesiarum domibus ac platearum angu-
390 lis locisque eminentioribus positae contra | Dei verbum a multis coluntur, 11v
auferantur et amodo nullae ad id fiant, et qui diversum fecerit, communione
privetur. Exod. 20 Deut. 5 illis a Domino fuit interdictum. Denique adversus
primum Dei praeceptum ex Diametro repugnant. Auferantur autem a Magistratibus cum tota Ecclesia, posteaquam ab Episcopis ablationis earundem
395 necessitas fuerit in templis Dei verbo ostensa, et si, plebe Dei verbo edocta
visitatores easdem adhuc repererint, agant cum Magistratibus, ut mox auferantur et exterminentur. Sic Rex Sanctus Ezechias delevit Serpentem aeneum,
quem etiam Deus fieri iusserat: Delevit autem eum, propterea quod colebatur.

50. Altaria cuncta ab universis Ecclesiarum domibus auferantur, eo demp-
400 to, ex quo Coena Dominica administratur, quod etiam non altare, sed mensa
vocetur. Universa quoque pseudotempla, quae tam in civitatibus quam in agris
et silvis impia superstitio extruxit ac supra modum multiplicavit, diruantur a
Magistratibus, aut in alios usus communitati utiles convertantur et solae
domus parochiales seu Ecclesiarum maneant. Memores quippe esse oportet
405 universos Principes et Magistratus eos solos Reges in sacris historiis laudatos et
Deo fuisse acceptos, qui omnia huiusmodi exterminarunt:

51. Veruntamen antequam aliquid horum fiat, verbum sanctum in tempus
praedicari necesse est, ut eruditus populus sponte ipsa idola Altariaque
illorum ac quaecunque ad ipsorum impium cultum spectant, execretur.

389/392 Quia – interdictum] cfr Ex. 20, 4; Deut. 5, 8 **397/398** Sic – colebatur] cfr
II Reg. 18, 4

393 Dei] *D^{sup.l.}* **395** Dei verbo²] verbo Dei *S* **396** visitatores easdem adhuc]
uisitatores adhuc easdem *S* **398** etiam] *om. S* **404** quippe] quoque *S* **408** ipsa]
ista *S*

CONCILIUM HOMBERGENSE – 1526   29

| DE SUPERSTITIOSIS BENEDICTIONIBUS

Cap. X

52. Nec panis, nec vinum, nec aqua, nec sal, nec fructus, nec aliud quidquam ullo tempore superstitiose benedicatur, neque aliquid tale in fidelium domibus habeatur. Nimirum creaturae per verbum Dei benedictio, de qua 1. Tim. 4, non est aliquid tale, sed ut cum gratiarum actione et Dei laude omnia percipiamus. Idcirco et ante cibum et ab eo sumpto aliquid ex Dei verbo a fidelibus recitetur, et orent aut gratias agant, tametsi hoc non adiicimus, ut quemquam obligemus ad externum verbum laudis et gratiarum actionis, sed ut spiritu et mente id faciant. Nimirum haec creaturae benedictio, de qua Paulus, ubi supra ait, maxime capitur, ut spiritu ac fide quis ipsis creaturis utatur. Verbum namque Dei spiritus est, in cuius fide dum creaturis utimur, per ipsum, cui credimus, verbum sanctificamur.

DE BAPTISMO

Cap. XI

53. Baptismus vulgariter administretur, in quo posteaquam verbum aliquamdiu fuerit praedicatum nolumus unctionem Chrismatis pigmentarii: magis cupientes baptizatis Spiritus Christi unctionem. Interdicimus autem in nomine Domini, ne quis prohibeat fidelium parvulos baptizari. Si quis vero contra fecerit, communione privetur. Interdicimus praeterea, ne quis denuo baptizetur. | Quod si qui parvulorum ab obstetricibus aut aliis quibusvis 12v secundum Christi institutionem in partus periculo fuere baptizati, nullatenus rebaptizentur. Si vero propter ignorantiam baptismi dubitatur, an recte fuerint baptizati, tum sub conditione baptizentur sic: Si tu non es baptizatus, ego te baptizo in nomine patris etc.

---

414 Nimirum – benedictio] cfr I Tim. 4, 4 seq.   **421** Verbum – est] cfr Eph. 6, 17

416 Idcirco] Idcirca *D S*

De infirmorum visitatione

Cap. XII

54. Si quis fidelium infirmatur, mox ut notum est Episcopo aut eius adiutori, visitet infirmum cum aliquot senioribus et orent Deum pro eo, ut sanus fiat, si sit ad gloriam Christi consolenturque eum verbo Domini. Episcopi autem admoneant frequenter Ecclesias ad infirmorum visitationem eorumque auxilium, si pauperes sunt, et ut orent pro eis, atque alia id genus Charitatis opera, et super ipsis infirmis pauperibus Diaconi maxime advigilent.

De ritu sepeliendi

Cap. XIII

55. Nemo sepeliatur in claustris, ne praeteritae abominationes denuo statui videantur, alioqui sepeliatur unusquisque ubi voluerit exemplo Abrahami et Patrum. Verum quia multi non habent propria sepulchra, eligat Ecclesia quaelibet locum unum, in quo liberum sit cuivis fideli sepeliri, modo non sit excommunicatus. In sepulturis Psalmi aliqui legantur ad iudicium cuius|libet Episcopi, et orent pro vivis ut sancte vivant et moriantur. Omnia autem vulgi lingua fiant, tamen si omnes, qui sepulturae intersunt, latini sunt, possunt etiam latine omnia dici.

56. Dimittantur Pompae et impensae funerales superfluae, magis autem pauperibus dispensentur, quae in his frustra insumerentur. Laudandum autem si in funere habeatur aut sincera praedicatio verbi Dei, aut saltem iuxta ipsum brevis admonitio. Nemo de conficto illo Purgatorio amodo quicquam doceat, alioqui communione privetur, et, si Episcopus fuerit, deponatur: Non est enim aliud purgatorium, quam Dei Ecclesia, in qua fide purgamur et mundamur a peccatis.

---

441 ut] *om. S*   atque] + ad *S*   **442** advigilent] inuigilent *S*   **446** alioqui] alioquin *S*   **452** etiam] et *S*

De Sacro Coniugio

Cap. XIIII

57. Qui uruntur et non se continent iuxta Paulum 1. Cor. 7, matrimonium contrahant, etiam Episcopi, monachi et moniales. Connubium nimirum venerabile est universis, honorabilis thorusque impollutus, Heb. 13. Porro hi uruntur et se non continent, qui in alterius sexus concupiscentia vivunt. Videat ergo quisque, ne in adustione vivens dispereat, et ne aut animo aut facto scortetur. Ad id vitandum habeat quilibet vir uxorem suam, et quaelibet mulier virum suum 1. Cor 7.

58. Quotiens aliquis uxorem ducturus | est, primum tractatum habeant partes, qui antequam omnino concludatur, notum fiat Episcopo, qui in publico sermone admoneat, ut si quis putet iuxta Dei sermonem impedimentum esse, infra aliquot dies palam faciat Episcopo, quibus diebus elapsis, si nemo obstiterit, desponsentur in Domino.

59. Advigilent autem Episcopi, ne quid in nuptiis fiat, quod earum non deceat sanctitatem, maxime ut ebrietates et spurca verba vitentur. Qui aequalibus potationibus aut obscaenis et spurcis cantilenis aut impuris gestibus nuptiarum sanctitatem conspurcarit a Christo anathema sit, quod non expavit contumeliam facere sacro coniugio, quod in Domino Iesu Christo et Ecclesia sua praeclarissima et sublimia admodum mysteria habet. Unde et Paulus Eph. 5 ipsum coniugium in Christo et Ecclesia magnum mysterium habere dicit.

60. Si quis verbi Dei auctoritate non solutus a priori uxore illam deseverit et aliam duxerit, communione privetur, praeterea quod secunda non uxor, sed scortum est, ab ipsa dividatur, et priorem ad se revocet.

61. Si qui graves casus matrimoniales inciderint, solo Dei verbo definiantur. Quod si quis Episcoporum perplexus in his est, consulat visitatores aut alios, qui ex scripturis sanctis de eiusmodi casibus iudicare possint. Et qui in his nonnihil contra Dei | verbum definierit, et res innotuerit, communione privetur, quod novam et alienam doctrinam attulit, praeterea ipsa eius definitio irrita fiat.

462/463 Qui – moniales] cfr I Cor. 7, 1 seq.   **463/464** Connubium – Heb. 13] cfr Hebr. 13, 4   **467/468** habeat – 1 Cor 7] cfr I Cor. 7, 2   **479/480** Unde – dicit] cfr Eph. 5, 32

465 concupiscentia] concupiscentiam *D*   **486** sanctis] sacris *S*

32 CONCILIUM HOMBERGENSE – 1526

490 DE CONVENTIBUS HEBDOMADARIIS ET QUI IN EOS ADMITTENDI

Cap. XV

62. Quia iuxta praeceptum Domini Matth. 18 Si quis e fratribus peccans in confratres suos, eos admonentes audire contemserit, Ecclesiae est dicendum: Ecclesia autem Dei congregatio fidelium est, fideles sunt aliquando con-
495 gregandi, ut eis dicatur fratris impii rebellio et contemtus. Item si iuxta Pauli verbum 1. Cor. 5 ad correctionem publice criminosorum et ut separentur ab Ecclesia, tradanturque Sathanae in carnis interitum, ut spiritus eorum salvus fiat in die Domini, fideles sunt congregandi. Quod et fieri debet aliis causis, nempe ut de Pastoris sui voce iudicent, eligantque sibi Episcopos et Diaconos,
500 id est ministros sive adiutores eorum ac pauperum Diaconos, de quibus infra, utque illos deponant, si causa exigit, et si quae alia a tota Ecclesia sunt iuxta Dei verbum definienda.

63. Ordinamus idcirco, ut in quavis parochia, posteaquam verbum Domini fuerit in ea aliquamdiu praedicatum singulis diebus Dominicis aut mox a
505 Coena Dominica aut a prandio fiat conventus fidelium in congruo loco, ad quem, quotquot ex viris Christi negotio favent, et in sanctorum numero habentur, | conveniant, ut cum episcopo de universis, quae in Ecclesia trac- 14v tanda occurrerint, definiant ex verbo Domini. Porro si Episcopus legitime praepeditus fuerit, non proinde non fiat ipse conventus, modo adsit, qui vice
510 Episcopi Ecclesiam ex verbo Dei dirigere possit, ut, quaecunque in ea fient, digna sint fidelium congregatione. Non enim licet, ut in eiusmodi conventibus quicquam prophanum agatur, ut Dei Ecclesia contemnatur.

64. Huic fideles mulieres interesse quidem possunt, verum eis loqui in Ecclesiis non permittitur 1. Cor. 14 et 1. Tim. 2. Soli ergo viri definient.

515 65. Quia autem ad fidelium congregationem admittendi non sunt, qui contra fidei rationem vivunt, et ne quidquam immaturo consilio agatur, volumus, ut pro hoc principio fiat separatio verorum fratrum a falsis fratribus ordine hic posito.

492/495 Quia – contemtus] cfr Matth. 18, 15-17   **495/498** Item – congregandi] cfr I Cor. 5, 1 seq.   **513/514** Huic – Tim. 2] cfr I Cor. 14, 34; I Tim. 2, 12

497 tradanturque] tradantur *S*   **500** adiutores] adiutores et ministros *S*   **501** exigit] existit *S*   **506** Christi negotio] negotio Christi *S*   **508** occurrerint] occurrerunt *S* **510** verbo Dei] Dei uerbo *S*   **516** quidquam] quicquam *S*

CONCILIUM HOMBERGENSE – 1526

66. Primo die Dominico, quo post verbum in tempus annuntiatum conveniant, Episcopus notam faciat Dei voluntatem ex Paulo 1. Cor. 5 et ex 2. Iohan. epistola. Nempe quod fidelibus veris non sit communicandum et his, qui in fratrum numero habentur, si sunt scortatores, ebrii, adulteri, raptores, maledici, aut alias criminosi aut qui aliam doctrinam adferunt, quam purissimum Dei verbum, quam ob causam iuxta idem Dei verbum, nullus amodo in ipsum conventum recipiendus, sed ab eo ex|communicandus, cuiuscunque sit conditionis aut sexus, qui praescriptis aut similibus criminibus offendiculum praebebit Evangelio. Ideo si quis nolit extra ipsam Ecclesiam fieri et videt se id genus criminibus irretitum, ad cor redeat veteremque exuat hominem et vitam vivat Christo et Ecclesia dignam, quod si infra XV dies non mutaverint vivendi rationem, ut non ultra sint scandalo Ecclesiae Dei, die XV, id est tertia Dominica, ab ipsa Ecclesia excommunicabuntur, etiam nominatim universi, quorum scelera nota sunt, donec resipiscant. Per totos autem illos XV dies Episcopi haec saepius inculcent, ne se non praemonitos fuisse, queri possint. Quod si quis huic legi et praecepto Domini non vult subiici, nec in ipsum Conventum nec ad Coenam Domini recipiatur, nec pro fratre habeatur: Non potest enim nec debet divinae mensae ac communionis particeps fieri, qui Deo iubente non vult pro criminibus suis extra communionem fieri.

67. Idcirco ut praescripta sine tumultu fieri possint, verbum sanctum, sicut praediximus, aliquamdiu praedicetur, ut prius sit Ecclesia Dei, quae fide in ipsum verbum constituitur, quam congregetur. Demum ut nemo dicere possit iudicio praecipiti quicquam factum, antequam fiat alicubi conventus iste, mense uno singulis Dominicis ac festis pronuntietur futurus Dominica, quae hunc mensem sequetur, | et praemoneant omnes, ne in ipsum Conventum veniant, nisi velint et praescriptae et omnibus Dei legibus subiici, sicut opus est fidelibus cunctis.

68. Mox autem ut praescripta Dominica congregati fuerint, qui in Sanctorum numero haberi volunt, etsi pauci sunt, nihil expavescant, certi quod eorum numerus Deo propitio brevi augebitur verbi Dei efficacia, etsi a principio nonnisi viginti aut 30 essent. Deinde interrogentur singulatim ab Episcopo, si volunt praedictis legibus subditi esse et iuxta Dei verbum excommunicari,

---

519/521 Primo – epistola] cfr I Cor. 5, 11; II Ioh. 10-11   **528** ad – hominem] cfr Rom. 6, 6

---

521 fidelibus veris] ueris fidelibus *S*   et] etiam *S*   **523** adferunt] adserunt *S*
524 nullus] nullus sit *S*   **528** irretitum] irritetitum *D*   **536** divinae mensae]
doctrinae, mensae *S*   **541** alicubi] talicubi *S*   **543** praemoneant] praemoneantur *S*
549 singulatim] sigillatim *S*

34   CONCILIUM HOMBERGENSE – 1526

quando causa esset: tum quotquot acquieverint conscribantur. Quod si qui
virorum contradicant, uxores eorum et liberi ac servi conscribantur, si acquieverint pietati. In Ecclesia enim non est personarum delectus, quod in nullis
externis sita sit. Qui vero acquiescere noluerint, exeant et pro Ethnicis ac his
555 qui foris sunt habeantur, in fratrum vero numero minime supputentur. Veruntamen in omnibus Conventibus fratrum admoneat Episcopus, ut tam pro ipsis
quam pro aliis omnibus oratio fiat a singulis.

69. Obsecramus per nomen Domini, ne ipsi Conventus differantur in
dies multos, ne hac occasione et iniquitas et multitudo eorum, qui Evangelica
560 libertate abutuntur, adaugeatur. Caeterum in ipso primo Conventu posteaquam eiecti fuerint hi, qui pietati acquiescere noluerint, praemoneat omnes
Episcopus, ut, qui ex eis criminosi fuerint, vitam mutent, adhorteturque singu-
los seorsim, ut non oporteat eos tertia | proximiori Dominica ab Ecclesia pelli,   16r
in qua, nisi resipuerint, nominatim excommunicabuntur.

565 70. Obsecramus autem omnes per Charitatem Dei, ut si pro suis criminibus a fratribus separentur, non indigne ferant, sed resipiscant et agnoscant,
quod Dei verbum sit et quod nonnisi in eorum salutem fuerint abiecti, praeterea viderint Ecclesiam nunquam fuisse sine excommunicatione, etiam Apostolorum diebus. Et Paulum pro nulla re tam durum fuisse Corinthiis, quam quia
570 fornicarium non excommunicaverant, quem praecepit ab eis congregatis in
spiritu et virtute Dei Sathanae tradi 1. Cor. 5. Tum ut ex eo loco patet criminosi per totam Ecclesiam a communione arcebantur, quod demum larvis quibusdam solis contra fas commissum est, atque eo usque progressa est insania, ut
quod in salutem et resipiscentiae stimulum a Deo constitutum est, factum sit
575 instrumentum vindictae, rapinae ac malignitatis in proximos, quod in Papistarum regno nemo non videt. Non enim solius est Episcopi, sed totius Ecclesiae
excommunicare et absolvere quenquam. Ideo nulla ratione id solis Episcopis
permittimus, sed simul ipsis cum Ecclesia. Non est ergo dimittenda excommunicatio, sed quae in ea hactenus perperam facta sunt, Dei verbo reformari
580 necesse est, sicut et caetera ferme omnia.

71. In his Conventibus tractentur omnia cuiuslibet Ecclesiae negotia,
eligantur Episcopi, Diaconi, excommunicentur criminosi et, dum vere resipuerint, ad communionem denuo recipiantur. Interroget semper omnes
Episcopus, si quis aliquid | novit, in quo sit admonenda Ecclesia, aut in quo sit   16v

---

554/555 Qui – habeantur] cfr Matth. 18, 17   **569/571** Et – Cor. 5] cfr I Cor. 5, 4 seq.

560 adaugeatur] adaugeantur *S*   **561** noluerint] noluerunt *S*   **563** ab Ecclesia] ab
Ecclesia ab Ecclesia *D*   **571** Dei] *om. S*

CONCILIUM HOMBERGENSE – 1526

iactura negotiorum regni Dei et salutis proximorum, aut aliquid fieri contra
charitatem, et audiatur quisquam patienter, modo non loquatur indigna fideli.
Nemo enim in hoc sancto conventu audiendus est, nisi adferat verbum Dei aut
aperte videatur, quod nonnisi iuxta Dei verbum loquatur. Quod si quis sua
garrulitate aut profanis et impiis sermonibus sanctam congregationem turbare
aut profanare non expavescit, et admonitus resipiscere contemnit, carpatur
durius ab Episcopo et Senioribus. Quod si adhuc contemserit, differatur usque
ad proximum Conventum, in quo, si peccatum suum non agnoverit, communione privetur.

72. In his conventibus praesint Episcopi, ut Dei verbo omnia dirigant et
nihil admittant, quod Dei verbo non competat. Verum tempore Visitationis,
Visitatores praesint.

73. Quoties autem in ipso conventu de persona Episcopi agitur, egre-
diatur, donec revocetur, et aliquis ex Senioribus praesit. Idem fiat, quoties
speciatim loquuntur de Diaconis aut adiutoribus aut aliquibusuis aliis, ut scilicet hi egrediantur, de quibus fit sermo.

74. Hos Conventus sic lingua vulgi concludat Episcopus aut qui praeest
vice eius. Qui abnegat Dominum Iesum Christum et verbum eius, anathema
sit, pax autem, misericordia et veritas omnibus invocantibus eum: Et respondeat tota Ecclesia Amen. Benedictus, qui in his sacris Conventibus negotium
Domini non egerit fraudulenter, id est, qui nec timore, nec odio, nec amore
proximorum aut alias contra Verbum Dei in huiusmodi aliquid fecerit aut
dimiserit etiam. Amen.

| DE EXCOMMUNICATIONE

Cap. XVI

75. Quia fieri non potest, ut Ecclesiae sint ordinatae, nisi ab eis separentur
falsi fratres, per quos nomen Dei inter exteros male audit, et sicut paulo ante
diximus nemini fidelium liceat cum eis habere consuetudinem, multi autem
falsi fratres sunt, necesse est, ut in omnibus Ecclesiis sit criminosorum separatio et vere, si ipsa excommunicatio dimittitur, sermo Dei in hac parte abiicitur,
ac impiis ac falsis fratribus ansa praebetur, ut deteriores fiant. Propterea constituimus in virtute Dei, ut in omnibus Ecclesiis nostris iste articulus diligentissime observetur.

---

586 quisquam] quisque *S*   **604** his sacris Conventibus] his conuentibus sacris *S*

36 CONCILIUM HOMBERGENSE – 1526

76. Igitur post verbum sanctum in tempus annuntiatum et post dies XV a primo Conventu hebdomadario, sicuti capite praecedente dictum est, separen-
620 tur ab Ecclesiis omnes adulteri, scortatores, ebriosi, maledici, usurarii et alii id genus publice criminosi.

77. Amodo autem, si quis in haec crimina notorie inciderit, mox a communione privetur et nominatim, neque enim admonitione nova digni erunt, antequam excommunicentur, qui perpetuum Dei verbi tam gloriose revelati
625 admonitionem contemnent, et tam turpiter Sanctae Ecclesiae forent offendiculo. Criminosorum excommunicationes autem nominatim fiant, quod ex Paulo notum sit ita velle Dominum, ut fideles sciant, quos vitare oporteat.

78. Servetur deinde is ritus in excommunicationibus: Primum qui excommunicandi sunt, iubeantur egredi ex conventu hebdomadario, et mox Episco-
630 pus dicat eos ex Dei verbo excommunicandos ac cuiuslibet crimen explicet, ubi autem Ecclesia | responsum et consensum dederit, surgat Episcopus et 17v nomine totius Ecclesiae dicat: Hunc qui adulterio aut usura aut ebrietate etc. scandalo fuit Ecclesiae Dei, privamus communione et conventibus nostris et prohibemus, ne quis fidelium cum eo habeat consuetudinem, ut confusus ad
635 cor redeat: praeterea in virtute Domini nostri Iesu Christi tradimus eum Sathanae in carnis interitum, ut spiritus eius salvus fiat in die Domini. Respondeatur: Amen. Posthac dicatur: Potens Deus misereatur nostri, sine cantu, et tandem sic oret Episcopus: Oramus te, omnipotens et misericors Deus, ut hunc, quem te volente a nobis separavimus, perire non sinas, sed da
640 tandem ei, ut redeat in ovile tuum, a quo digne abiectus est, nos autem confirma in fide et veritate tua, ne unquam dividamur a te, per Christum Dominum etc. Respondeatur: Amen. Haec de notoriis criminibus.

79. Caeterum de privatis, quae vel uni vel paucis nota sunt, ut sunt proximorum iniuriae, usurae occultae et alia id genus, de quibus Matth. 18 et
645 Luc. 17: Si peccaverit in te frater tuus etc. sciat fidelium quisque, se hoc Christi verbo obnoxium, ut si quis ex fratribus aliquid tale aut contra aut noscente se admisit, eundem inter se et ipsum corripiat, cuius admonitionem si contempserit, adhibeat secum duos aut tres et admoneant eum, quorum etiam admonitionem si spreverit, in conventu hebdomadario prius admonito, tum
650 advocetur ab Ecclesia et admoneatur, Ecclesiae admonitionem Episcopo

---

626/627 Criminosorum – oporteat] cfr I Cor. 5, 13   **632/636** Hunc – Domini] cfr
I Cor. 5, 5   **643/645** Caeterum – etc.] cfr Matth. 18, 15; Luc. 17, 3

---

618 et] est *D*   **619** praecedente] praecedenti *D*   **620** et] vel *S*   **623** et] etiam *S*
626 excommunicationes autem] autem excommunicationes *S*   **646** contra] contra se
S   **649** admonito] Episcopo *add. S*

CONCILIUM HOMBERGENSE – 1526

proferente, aut mittat Ecclesia | duos aut tres, qui suo nomine eum admo- 18r
neant, tandem, si Ecclesiam audire noluerit, communione privetur, et donec
resipuerit, vitetur ab fidelibus, quod sit a Christi grege alienus, et quia praeceptum Christi et admonitionem Ecclesiae contemsit.

655   80. Nolumus autem, ut quispiam excommunicetur pro causis civilibus,
nisi simul crimina intervenerint. Tum enim excommunicandi essent pro criminibus ipsis. Si quid autem inter fratres gravis contentionis pro terrenis
exorietur, remittat eos Ecclesia ad Christianum magistratum, apud quem
eorum negotia definiantur; non enim convenit, ut haec in sancta congregatio-
660 ne tractentur.

81. Diximus paulo ante nemini fidelium licere ex verbo Dei, ut cum
excommunicatis habeat consuetudinem, quod sic intelligimus, ut nemo cum
eis manducet aut bibat aut cum eis veniat ad convivia aut nuptias aut aliquid
negotietur, nisi sit, quod maxime urgeat, ut audire verbum Dei. Item si quid
665 illis necessario venditur aut ab eis emitur, ut vita necessaria: at tum sic fiat, ut
colloquantur in tempus et nihil interveniat aliunde consuetudinis. Licebit eos
veruntamen commonefacere ad resipiscentiam.

82. Nullus excommunicatus in sua pertinacia moriens in fidelium sepulchris condatur. Sic aliquando legimus impios non fuisse positos in sepulchris
670 piorum. Prophetae enim, qui Dei iussione venerat in Bethel, cadaver non fuit
illatum in sepulchrum patrum suorum, quia non obedivit voci Domini
3. Reg. 13. Et impiissimi reges Iudae, Ioram, de quo 2. Paralip. 21 et Ioas apostata, de quo 2. Par. 24 propter iniquitates suas non fuere sepulti in sepulchris
regalibus.

675 | 83. Si quis fidelium cum excommunicatis et scortatoribus sive ebriis aut 18v
alias publice criminosis habet consuetudinem et admonitus non resipiscit,
communione privetur, et si Episcopi idem faciunt, et communione priventur
et deponantur.

670/672 Prophetae – Reg. 13] cfr I Reg. 13, 22   **672/674** Et – regalibus] cfr II Par.
21, 20; 24, 25

661 ex verbo Dei] *om. D*   **669** condatur] condiatur *S*

38 CONCILIUM HOMBERGENSE – 1526

De Absolutione Resipiscentium

680 *Cap. XVII*

84. Nemo excommunicatorum ad communionem denuo recipiatur, nisi coram tota Ecclesia cognoscat peccatum suum, et cunctis nota sit resipiscentia eius, adsit autem, qui absolvitur, et peccatum suum confiteatur coram tota Ecclesia, quod si prorsus interesse nequit, alium mittat, qui ex ore eius loqua-
685 tur, petens suo nomine Absolutionem. Deinde ab Ecclesia duo aut tres mittantur, qui admoneant eum, ne se sinat horrendis Sathanae laqueis denuo vinciri. Cum vero est absolvendus, et ad id consentit Ecclesia, eius nomine dicat Episcopus:

Hunc N. fratrem nostrum, quem Dei voluntate ob ebrietatem vel adulte-
690 rium etc. a nostra communione excluseramus, iam Dei dono resipiscentem in eam denuo recipimus, et in virtute Domini nostri Iesu Christi a Sathanae potestate absolvimus, ne ei quicquam nocere praevaleat. Respondeatur: Amen. Mox dicant psalmum: *Beatus uir, qui timet Dominum.* Deinde oratio haec dicatur ab Episcopo: Benedicimus et laudamus nomen tuum Domine
695 Deus noster, qui hunc fratrem nostrum N. reduxisti in ovile tuum, a quo te iubente eundem abieceramus, quique nobis donasti, ut denuo ipsum receperimus. Confirma hoc, Domine, quod per nos de ipso operatus es et corrobora eum, et nos, | ac universas Ecclesias tuas in veritate tua, ut nunquam deficia- 19r
mus a te per Christum etc. Respondeatur: Amen.

700 85. Interdicimus autem universis fidelibus per nomen Dei, ne ipsis resipiscentibus improperent, quod fuerint communione privati. Omnes enim peccatores sumus, et nemo non est a se ipso indignus inter Ecclesiae filios numerari, qui vero contrarium fecerit, et ob id fratri publice contumeliam intulerit, communione privetur; quod si privatim fecit et ordine pro privatis criminibus
705 supra posito admonitus non resipuerit, etiam communione privetur. Maledicus enim fuit, et maledici vitandi sunt. 1. Cor. 5.

---

693 Ps. 111, 1   **701/702** Omnes – sumus] cfr Rom. 3, 23   **705/706** Maledicus – Cor. 5] cfr I Cor. 5, 11

689 N.] N. N. *S*   **691** nostri] *om. S*   **693** dicant psalmum] dicat Episcopus *S*
695 N.] N. N. *S*

CONCILIUM HOMBERGENSE – 1526

De Anniversaria Synodo

Cap. XVIII

86. Quemadmodum, sicut in superioribus visum est, pro specialium Ecclesiarum ordine ac regimine peculiares earum Synodi necessariae sunt. Ita pro omnibus cuiuslibet Regionis Ecclesiis maiores et provinciales Synodus congregare opus est, in quibus de his, quae totam provinciam circa regimen et ordinem Ecclesiarum concernunt, ex Dei verbo definiatur.

87. Proinde constituimus, ut semel pro tota Hassia celebretur Synodus apud Marpurgum tertia Dominica post Pascha, cuius tamen principium Sabbatho ante eandem Dominicam sit, ipsum tamen Princeps Illustrissimus occasione legitima immutare poterit.

88. Ad eam conveniant universi Episcopi, nisi sint infirmi, aut alioqui legitime praepediti, quo casu rescribant excusationem suam, quam tradant Commisso Ecclesiae, cui praeest.

89. Volumus autem, ut appropinquante ipsa Synodo quaelibet Ecclesia congregetur, | et eligat ex se ipsa unum plenum fide et spiritu Dei, cui committat vices suas in omnibus, quae ad Synodum pertinent. Tum videant, si quid dignum habeant contra Visitatores aut Episcopos aut adiutores eorum, et quae digna fuerint, mittant ad Synodum, nihil autem mittant contra aliquem nisi diligenter et sufficienter probatum. Praeterea si deponunt Episcopum, alium eligant et mittant Synodo causas depositionis prioris. Item si quid dubii est, a quo velint per Synodum certiores fieri, mittant singula fideliter conscripta.

90. Precamur autem omnes in Domino, ut ad summum infra triduum omnia Synodi negotia absolvant, et ideo faciant, ut quinta hora matutina cuiuslibet diei incipiant. Haec autem faciant.

91. Primum ex tota congregatione eligant tredecim plenos fide et Spiritu Sancto, quorum ministerium erit perplexa quaecunque delata ad Synodum ac omnia eiusdem negotia definire: Sic tamen, ut quicquid arduum fuerit, prius toti Synodo palam fiat. Ipsi incipient sequentem Synodum, et dirigant eandem, donec novi electi sint. Item si quid gravis quaestionis infra sequentem Synodum exoriretur, ita ut sine gravi discrimine in ipsam Synodum differri nequeat, hi cum visitatoribus congregabuntur apud Marpurgum, nisi aliud iusserit Princeps, et eos voluerit alibi congregari. Eo casu obsecramus omnes

---

710 regimine] regmine *D*; regimne *S* **718** alioqui] alioquin *S* **725** mittant²] mittatur *S* **731** faciant] faciant. (I) *S*

40 CONCILIUM HOMBERGENSE – 1526

740 Ecclesias, per quas transierint, ut ipsis laborantibus in via praebeant alimentum: quia enim Ecclesiis deserviunt, ab eisdem alendi sunt. Porro si plures tredecim electi fuerint, tredecim illi pro electis | habebuntur, qui plures caete- 20r ris voces habuerint. Visitatores etiam eligi possunt ex absentibus, Electi vero Synodi non nisi ex praesentibus.

745   92. II. Vocem habebunt primum Clementissimus Princeps. Item Comites et Nobiles, si eligere voluerint et praesentes fuerint, cum universis Episcopis et Commissis Ecclesiarum.

93. Nemo autem vocem habeat nisi praesens sit, propter quod volumus, ut mox a Synodi principio nominentur omnes Episcopi, et quilibet, ut audit se 750 nominari, respondeat voce intelligibili: Adsum. Et qui pro absentibus literas habet, idem coram omnibus dicat.

94. III. Omnes Commissi Ecclesiarum reddant literas suae Commissionis tredecim electis.

95. IV. Electi xiii segregabunt in unum locum et diiudicabunt de universis, 755 quae ab Ecclesiis sunt missa. Mox autem ubi inter se definierint, quid sit ad omnia respondendum, mittent duos ex se ipsis ad totam multitudinem, quorum unus dicat: Fratres tale dubium a vobis quaeritur, cui nos iudicamus ita respondendum moti hoc et illo Scripturae textu: Si cui vestrum aliud ex Dei verbo videtur, aedificet Ecclesiam, nec putet sibi liberum tacere, quod commu- 760 nis Christi gloriam omnes quaerere debeamus. Tum si quis aliud dixerit et habuerit certius ac clarius Scripturae testimonium, habeat locum, etiamsi solus esset. Maior est enim Dei sermo omni hominum multitudine, et melius est adhaerere uni habenti verbum Dei quam multis proprium iudicium sequentibus. Quod si nemo ab Electorum iudiciis dissentit, secundum ea ipsis Ecclesiis 765 respondeatur.

96. Precamur autem per nomen Dei, ut eiusmodi iudicia nemo statutorum nomine publica | faciat, sed si quis ea desiderat, hoc titulo eadem conscri- 20v bat: Responsiones talis Synodi Hessiacae ad dubia eidem ab Ecclesiis missa. Nulla quoque responsio edatur, quae non sit solius Scripturae locis roborata, 770 ut universae Ecclesiae aedificentur.

97. V. Primus Electorum iubeat singulos Episcopos et Commissos Ecclesiarum paratos esse, dum vocabuntur ad consilium illorum XIII qui tum segre-

---

745 II] *om. D*; (II) *S*   **754** segregabunt] segregabuntur *S*   **757** Fratres] Frater *S* **761** Scripturae – etiamsi] Scripturae locum et testimonium etiam, si *D*; scripturae testimonium et locum, etiamsi *S*   **763** Dei] Domini *S*   **765** respondeatur] respondeat *D*   **769** solius] solidis *S*

CONCILIUM HOMBERGENSE – 1526

gabuntur in locum unum, ut definiant de his, quae sunt ad eos commissa, tam de Episcopis quam Visitatoribus. Vocent deinde singulatim eos, sicut necessum fuerit, admoneant admonendos, criminosos deponant, communione privent. Notum est autem, qui sint pro criminosis habendi, ut supra de Conventibus hebdomadariis visum est.

98. Si accusati excusare se voluerint, patienter audiantur, et si quis falsus testis deprehenditur fuisse, etiamsi absens fuerit, coram tota Synodo communione privetur, et si in aliquo Ecclesiae ministerio fuerit, deponatur.

99. Episcopi iuste depositi a propriis Ecclesiis eodem anno nulli Ecclesiae praeficiantur.

100. Caeterum qui electi sunt, nisi indigni essent, confirmentur. Quod si aliquis in variis locis electus est, praeficiatur illi Ecclesiae, cui putatur fore utilior in gloriam Dei, aliis autem Ecclesiis, a quibus etiam electus erat, mittatur, ut alios eligant per Visitatores confirmandos.

101. Tandem vocent ad se Visitatores anni praecedentis, et si quis eorum aliquod crimen perpetravit, aut contemsit verbum Dei aut aliquid pro suo ministerio accepit, et haec sunt nota aliquot Ecclesiis, coram tota Synodo communione privetur, declareturque inutilis ad idem Visitatoris ministerium, priveturque | Episcopi functione, si in ea est, et amodo non possit eligi in Visitatorem, in Episcopum autem sic, modo fuerit per totam Synodum restitutus, nec restituatur, nisi patienter hoc iudicium Ecclesiae pertulerit.

102. Omnes qui per Synodum communione privati sunt, si vere resipiscant, ad communionem denuo recipiantur per Ecclesias, in quibus habitant, et illorum Absolutio publica fiat in vicinioribus Ecclesiis et in Synodi urbe nempe Marpurgo.

103. Durante Synodo sit quotidie bis sermo ad populum, sicut primus Electorum consilio fratrum suorum ordinaverit. Priusquam autem novi XIII eligantur, veteres de his, qui primo die praedicaturi sunt, ordinent. Laudamus etiam, si a Synodi principio sermo latinus habeatur.

104. Consiliis XIII Electorum nemo nisi ab eis vocatus intersit. Liberum tamen sit Principi Illustrissimo et Comitibus nostrae regionis verbo faventibus, cum his quos ipse Princeps secum habere voluerit, eorum actis interesse.

---

773 de his] *om. D* **776** privent] priuentur *S* qui – habendi] qui pro criminosis habendi sint *S* **778** excusare se] se excusare *S* **796** Synodi] synodali *S* **802** intersit] interfuit *S* **804** cum] et *S*

42 CONCILIUM HOMBERGENSE – 1526

805 105. Igitur completis omnibus, quae ad ipsam Synodum spectant, pro conclusione eius unus electorum praedicet lingua vulgi, et in eius sermone omnes utriusque sexus interesse poterunt. Is paucis explicet dubia, quae ex Dei verbo Synodus definivit, nominet Falsos Prophetas ac errores specificet, sicut hos Synodus ipsa damnavit, nominetque eos, quos communione privavit, itidem
810 eos, quos absolvit, quorum aut excommunicationem aut absolutionem pronuntiet, et pro eis in communi orent, ut supra capitibus de Excommunicatione et Absolutione. Quibus absolutis haec dicat alta voce et ad singula respondeat tota Ecclesia: Amen.

| 106. Omnes qui Domini nostri Iesu Christi verbum amplexi sunt et ad 21v
815 Ecclesiam eius attinent, non sinat Deus aliquando sic anathema fieri, ut pro sua cupiditate propriisve commodis unquam apostatent. Respondeatur: Amen.

Benedictus sit a te, Domine Iesu, Princeps noster ac universi Magistratus, qui gloriam Regni tui ex animo quaerunt videantque filios filiorum suorum et
820 pacem super omnem Ecclesiam tuam. Respondeatur: Amen.

Benedicti sint a te, Domine Iesu, omnes, qui amplectuntur veritatem tuam et permanent in ea. Benedicat illis Dominus et custodiat eos, ostendat faciem suam illis, et misereatur eorum, convertat vultum suum ad eos, et det eis pacem. Respondeatur: Amen.

825 107. Tum paucis scribant literas, quibus paucis respondeant Ecclesiarum dubiis, et si quae Ecclesiae tepide agant in verbo Domini, literis corripiant.

De Electionibus et depositionibus tam Electorum Synodi, quam Visitatorum, quae infra tempus Synodi fiunt

Cap. XIX

830 108. Si quis Electorum Synodi aut Visitatorum infra sequentem Synodum animam Christo reddiderit, alius eius loco mox eligatur ab Ecclesia Synodalis Civitatis et in ea ordinetur.

818/820 Benedictus – tuam] cfr Ps. 127, 6   **822/824** Benedicat – pacem] cfr Num. 6, 26

---

821 sint] sunt *S*   amplectuntur] amplectantur *D*   **822** permanent] permaneant *D*
828 Visitatorum] Visitatorem *S*   fiunt] sunt *D*

CONCILIUM HOMBERGENSE – 1526

109. Si quis Visitatorum aut Electorum aliquod crimen perpetravit, nempe aut adulterium aut fornicationem aut ebrietatem aut munera accepit pro
835 ministerio suo, idque certum sit et per hoc offendit unam aut plures Ecclesias, | 22r
ipsae Ecclesiae offensae ad Synodalem Civitatem mittant negotium totum, ut
in eadem deponatur et alius eligatur, ac tum communione privetur, itidem
functione Episcopatus, si Episcopus est; qui, si resipuerit vere, denuo ad communionem admittatur, nunquam autem admittatur ad ministerium aut visita-
840 tionis aut electionis Synodi neque etiam ad functionem Episcopi, nisi a tota
Synodo restitutus.

Qua ratione procedendum in electionibus

Cap. XX

110. Universae Electiones tam in anniversaria Synodo, quam in universis
845 Ecclesiis nostris sic fiant. Tres ex omnibus eligentibus segregentur in locum
unum ad signandas omnium voces, nec opus fuerit scribere eligentium nomina, sed satis fuerit nomina scribere eorum, qui electi sunt, deinde parvis lineis
signare, quot quilibet voces habet. Unus horum trium scribet et signabit, alii
duo testes erunt fidelis conscriptionis et signationis.

850 111. In electione Episcopi tres Episcopi complebunt hoc ministerium. In
electione XIII Electorum Synodi tres Visitatores anni praeteriti. In electione
trium Visitatorum tres primi ex electis XIII. In Electione Diaconorum tam
Ecclesiarum quam Episcoporum, item in electione Commissorum ab Ecclesiis
ad Synodum, Episcopus et duo seniores.

855 ### De ordinatione ministrorum Ecclesiae
per orationem et manuum impositionem

Cap. XXI

112. Episcoporum, Electorum Synodi, Visitatorum et omnium | ministro- 22v
rum ordinatio Apostolorum exemplo per orationem et manuum impositio-
860 nem fiat, et id quidem hoc ordine.

---

836 Synodalem Civitatem] civitatem synodalem *S*   **838/839** ad communionem
admittatur] admittatur ad communionem *S*   **846** omnium voces] voces omnium *S*
850 complebunt] implebunt *S*   **858** omnium ministrorum] Omnium ecclesiae
ministrorum *S*

CONCILIUM HOMBERGENSE – 1526

113. Congregabitur Ecclesia, et omnes simul pro his, qui electi sunt, orabunt primo eorum reliquos coram ad id admonente, denique electi statuentur in medium, et super singulos eorum tres ad minus manus imponant.

114. Si plures sunt electi, ut, dum Electi XIII Synodi aut Visitatores ordinantur, tres manus imponent super primo Electo, quorum unus alta voce dicet: Accipe Spiritum Sanctum, quorum remiseris peccata etc. Vel sic: Accipe claves regni coelorum, quodcunque ligaueris super terram etc. Et sic fiat super singulis.

115. Super XIII Electis Synodi manus imponent tres ex electis veteribus aut tres Visitatores. Super Visitatoribus manus imponent tres primi Electi. Quodsi quis Visitatorum non interest Synodo, ordinetur apud Marpurgum, et tres Episcopi manus illi imponant. Super Episcopis manus imponant tres alii Episcopi, si Visitatores aut Electi Synodi non intersunt. Super Diaconis Ecclesiarum et Diaconis seu adiutoribus Episcoporum manus imponant duo ex senioribus, nisi alii Episcopi intersint.

116. Dum Episcopi aut Visitatores aut XIII Electi aut adiutores Episcoporum ordinantur, unus manus imponentium dicat: Accipite Spiritum Sanctum etc. Dum vero aliis manus imponuntur, unus eorum dicat: Impleat te Dominus spiritu suo et erudiat cor tuum illudque fide roboret, ut digne perficias ministerium, ad quod electus es. Respondeatur: Amen.

117. In omni manuum impositione | tandem dicatur haec oratio ab eo, qui ₂₃ᵣ praeest ordinationi, hoc praemittens: Dominus vobiscum. Respondeatur: Et cum spiritu tuo. Oremus: Deus qui tuo spiritu et verbo praecipis populos tuos regi, supplices te deprecamur, ut his famulis tuis, supra quos invocauimus nomen tuum sanctum et in ipso nomine tuo manus nostras imposuimus tui spiritus charismate infundas, et da illis, ut digne, sancte, et ad gloriam nominis tui Ecclesiae tuae utilitatem impleant ministerium, ad quod electi sunt per Dominum nostrum Iesum Christum, filium tuum, qui tecum regnat etc. Si vero solus est, qui ordinatur, oratio in singulari fiat.

---

867 Accipe[1] – etc.] cfr Ioh. 20, 22-23   **867/868** Accipe[2] – etc.] cfr Matth. 16, 19
878/879 Accipite – etc.] cfr Ioh. 20, 22

886/888 tui – ministerium] cfr Offertorium of the Missal: 'Suscipiat Dominus etc. ad laudem et gloriam nominis sui, ad utilitatem quoque nostram totiusque ecclesiae suae sanctae'

862 coram] eorum *S*   **871** imponent] imponant *S*   **879** imponuntur] imponunt *S*

CONCILIUM HOMBERGENSE – 1526

118. Omnibus ordinationibus universi utriusque sexus interesse poterunt, propter quod vulgi lingua omnia fiant.

De Visitatoribus eorumque ministerio

Cap. XXII

119. Sanctus Rex Iosaphat misit nonnullos per omnes terras regni sui, ut quae in Dei cultu deformata erant, iuxta legem reformarentur. 2. Paral. 17.Eius exemplo visum fuit Spiritui Sancto mittere in Principis Illustrissimi cor, et nos verbo suo ad idem commonefacere, ut amodo eligantur per anniversariam Synodum in Hassia tres pleni fide et Spiritu Sancto, qui semel in anno omnes Hessorum Ecclesias visitent. Verum pro hoc anno Ecclesiis nondum in Dei verbo institutis pro Visitatoribus habebuntur, quos Princeps cum Electis Synodi eligent.

120. Horum ministerium est primum ipsa anniversaria Visitatio: Deinde iudicare, si Electi ab Ecclesiis in Episcopos digni sunt, abiicere | praeterea indignos et dignos confirmare semperque iuvare Ecclesias et illarum Episcopos iuxta Verbum Sanctum ac modis omnibus agere, ut Dei verbum et nostrae ordinationes, quas iuxta idem verbum conscripsimus, observentur.

121. Quaelibet Ecclesia solvat impensas Visitatorum ac ministrorum eorundem, nec ciborum delicias exigant, sed iuxta Christi verbum manducent, quae eis apponuntur. Interdicimus autem eis in nomine Domini, ne vel munuscula pro suo ministerio accipiant. Scriptum est enim: Non accipias personam et munera, quae excaecant oculos prudentum et mutant viam iustorum. Item Gratis accepistis, gratis date. Et qui diversum fecerit et sua functione et communione privetur, si alicui Ecclesiae res nota fuerit, quo casu Ecclesia, cui nota est res, id significet Ecclesiae Civitatis Synodalis, a qua tum deponatur et alius eligatur. Sed de his paulo ante diximus. Et quum impensae hospitiorum pro muneribus haberi possint, in Episcoporum domibus Visitatores nullatenus hospitentur, nisi ipsis Episcopis pro impensis satisfiat.

895/896 Sanctus – Paral. 17] cfr II Par. 17, 7-9   **911/912** Non – iustorum] cfr Ex. 23, 8 **913** Matth. 10, 8

897 Spiritui Sancto] spiritus sanctus *S*   **903** Deinde] (II) *S*   **904** Episcopos] episcopis *S*   digni – abiicere] digni sunt, (III) abiicere *S*   **908** solvat] solvet *S*   **912** viam] uerba *S*   **914** cui] cuique *S*   **916/917** Et – possint] et quia impensae hospitiorum pro munere haberi possunt *S*

46 CONCILIUM HOMBERGENSE – 1526

122. Interdicimus quoque eisdem cum Paulo 1. Tim. 5 ne cuiquam facile et
920 sine gravi iudicio manus imponant, sed prius diligenter expendant, an tales
sint in Episcopos electi, quales Paulus vult esse 1. Tim. 3 et ad Tit. 1. Nihil
expavescant abiicere indignos et per id displicere hominibus, quod melius sit
eos incidere in odia et manus hominum quam Dei.

De Episcoporum electione, ordinatione, provisione et aliis
925 ## quae ad eos spectant

Cap. XXIII

123. Eligat quaevis Ecclesia aut deponat Episcopum suum, quod | ad eam 24r
spectet iudicare de vice pastorum.

124. Pro hoc veruntamen anno et donec verbo Dei instructae sunt Eccle-
930 siae, a Principe Clarissimo et Visitatorum consilio Episcopi vocentur, insti-
tuantur aut deponantur, et literae ad id petantur a Principe, ut eius praecepto
Episcopi recipiantur.

125. Cum autem Ecclesiae verbo doctae fuerint et elegerint Episcopos
suos, sat illis erit, ut a duobus Visitatoribus, si tres adiri nequeunt, ipsa electio
935 confirmetur, et si ipsi Visitatores personaliter convenire nequeunt, ut eisdem
manus imponant, rescribant paucis Ecclesiae Epistolam, qua ostendant se
confirmasse Episcopum ab eis Electum committantque illi, ut vocet tres ex vi-
inioribus Episcopis ad sui Episcopi ordinationem. Si Ecclesia inutilem et insin-
cerum Episcopum elegerit, deponatur a Visitatoribus, et alium mittant.

940 126. Alat quaevis Ecclesia Episcopum suum, quod non sit claudendum os
bovi trituranti. Sicque illi administret, ut cum sua familia vivere possit, et sicut
Paulus iubet, hospitalis esse. Praeter id autem nihil exigant Episcopi pro mini-
steriis privatis. Nullis Episcopis quidquam detur nisi praesentibus et actu suo
ministerio incumbentibus, sicut Paulus dicit: Qui non laborat, non manducet.
945 Praeterea quisquis eius modi est, nihil minus est quam Episcopus.

127. Episcoporum autem ordinatio fiat coram Ecclesia per manuum impositionem cum oratione.

919/921 Interdicimus – 1²] cfr I Tim. 5, 22; 3, 1 seq.; Tit. 1, 7 seq.   **940/941** Alat –
trituranti] cfr Deut. 25, 4   **941/942** Sicque – esse] cfr Rom. 12, 13   **944** II Tim. 3, 10

922 expavescant] expauescat *S*   **928** vice] voce *D S*

CONCILIUM HOMBERGENSE – 1526

128. Si quis ad Episcopatum muneribus pertingere nititur, abiiciatur, quod voluerit ministerium sanctum pecunia adipisci.

950   129. Qui ob pauperiem Episcopi | functionem ambiunt, nullatenus admittantur. Cibos nimirum non Dei gloriam aut animas quaerunt.   24v

130. Qui idem cupiunt favore amicorum aut cognatorum, repellantur, quod rem sanctam petant medio impio atque profano. Imo proprie non quaerunt rem sanctam, sed ex ipsa suam gloriam propriumque bonum.

955   131. Si quis pius in verbo sancto exercitatus docere petit verbum sanctum, non repellatur, a Deo enim interne mittitur, quod solam Dei gloriam et animarum salutem velit: Hi sunt, qui dum Episcopatum cupiunt, bonum opus desiderant. 1. Tim. 3.

132. Qui ex Episcopis, qui hactenus fuerunt, deponuntur et pauperes alan-
960   tur ab Ecclesiis et iubeant Diaconis, ut eorum maxime rationem habeant, praesertim si sunt senes aut alias infirmi et ad labores inepti.

133. Parochiae admodum parvae et omnino vicinae, quae non sufficiunt alere Episcopos suos et dare quo hospitales esse possint, uniantur, praesertim cum pro tam multis parochiis, sicut modo in Hassia sunt, satis Episcoporum
965   reperiri non possint. Specialis autem parochiarum unio Illustrissimi Principis voluntati ac dispositioni relinquitur.

134. Qui Episcopos electuri sunt, viderint, ut quantum fieri potest iuxta Paulum 1. Tim. 3 et ad Tit. 1 sint sine crimine, unius uxoris uiri, ornati, prudentes, pudici, hospitales, doctores et fideles dispensatores mysteriorum Dei,
970   non superbi, non commessatores, non vinolenti, non percussores, non avari, non litigiosi, sed suae domui bene praesidentes et filios habentes subditos cum omni castitate, non neophyti, sed probati et | habentes testimonium bonum ac   25r
potentes exhortari, et eos qui contradicunt arguere.

135. Qui ex Episcopis aut mollitie, aut pompa vestitus, aut suae conversa-
975   tionis levitate Ecclesiae cui praeest praebet offendiculum, et admonitus resi-
piscere contemnit, ab Ecclesia deponatur. Oportet enim, ut Episcopi sint aliis in exemplum vanitatis huius seculi contemnendae atque calcandae. Si vero adulteri aut scortatores aut ebriosi aut alias criminosi sint, et deponantur et communione priventur.

957/958 I Tim. 3, 1   **967/973** Qui – arguere] cfr I Tim. 3, 2 seq.; Tit. 1, 7 seq.

965 Principis] Principi *S*

CONCILIUM HOMBERGENSE – 1526

980 136. Nemo in Episcopatus functionem admittatur ac confirmetur, nisi velit permanere cum populo etiam pestis ac cuiusvis tribulationis tempore. Et si quis tempore pestis et angustiae Ecclesiam suam dimiserit, a sua functione deponatur et alius eligatur.

137. Cives pii et docti ac irreprehensibiles cuiuscunque artis sint, in
985 Episcopos eligi possunt.

138. Ministri sunt Episcopi, ideo principes, Domini ac Magistratus non fiant, quod Dominus dixerit Apostolis suis: Reges gentium dominantur eis, non ita erit inter vos.

139. Qui novis aut peregrinis dogmatibus Ecclesias sibi commissas pertur-
990 bant, deponantur et communione priventur.

140. Nullus Episcoporum aut Diaconorum eorundem admittatur aut confirmetur, nisi sub conditione, scilicet quandiu sincere, pure sanctum verbum docuerint, et vitam vixerint Christi et Ecclesiae ministris dignam.

DE EPISCOPORUM DIACONIS

Cap. XXIV
995

141. Eligat quaevis Ecclesia sui Episcopi adiutorem, quem cum oratione et manuum impositione coram tota Ecclesia confirmet, | quibus ab ipsis Ecclesiis 25v de omnibus ad vitam necessariis provideatur.

142. Viderint autem, qui eos eligunt, ne indignos vocent, sed irreprehensi-
1000 biles, sicut de Diaconis aperte iubet Paulus 1. Tim. 3. Qui tametsi sunt hi, de quibus sequenti capite agemus, tamen non inconvenienter pro adiutore seu ministro Episcopi capitur. 'Diaconus' enim Graeca vox est et ministrum signi-ficat, et indubie Diaconi, de quibus Paulus ait, sunt nedum hi, de quibus sequenti capite, sed etiam ipsi coadiutores Episcoporum.

987/988 Reges – vos] cfr Marc. 10, 41-42   **999/1000** Viderint – Tim. 3] cfr I Tim. 3, 8

---

980 functionem] functione *S*   **981** etiam] et *S*   **986** principes] princeps *S*
992 scilicet] *om. S*   **993** docuerint] docuerit *S*   vixerint] uixerit *S*   **997** confirmet]
confirment *D*   **998** vitam] unum *D*   **1000** sicut] Sicuti *S*   **1004** coadiutores]
adiutores *S*

CONCILIUM HOMBERGENSE – 1526   49

1005   143. Si Ecclesia tam parva est, ut cum Episcopo adiutorem seu Diaconum eius alere nequeat, desistat ab ipsius adiutoris Electione, attamen si minores parochiae uniantur, prout supra diximus, cessabit haec causa.

144. Hortamur autem omnes Ecclesias in Domino, ut singulae suis Episcopis de uno aut pluribus Diaconis aut adiutoribus provideant. Curent 1010   autem, ut sint tales, quales eos Paulus describit 1. Tim. 3.

De Diaconis Ecclesiarum et pauperum provisione

Cap. XXV

145. Liquet ex actis Apostolicis Cap. VI Septem ab Apostolis ad Diaconiam id est ministerium quotidianum electos, quorum primus Stephanus fuit. 1015   Exemplo igitur Apostolorum ordinamus, ut a singulis Ecclesiis tres ad minus pleni fide et Spiritu Sancto eligantur ad quotidianum ministerium pauperum, ut scilicet fidelium eleemosynas pauperibus dispensent.

146. Erigantur ad id in omnibus Ecclesiis aeraria, in quae mittat quisque quantum potest, ad quod Episcopi populum diligentissime commonefaciant. 1020   Praeterea unus | Diaconorum diebus Dominicis et festis mane tam ad sermo-   26r nem quam post egenorum causa per Ecclesiam postulet, et quaecunque receperit, in aerarium ponat. Ipsum autem aerarium tribus clavibus occludatur, e quibus unam habeat Episcopus, alias Diaconi Seniores.

147. Ex his, quae in aerario congregantur, provideatur egenis cuiuslibet 1025   parochiae primum, deinde peregrinis et exulibus, praesertim his, qui pro verbi sancti confessione exulant.

148. Si aliquot praebendae et bona in hunc usum dentur, Diaconorum ministerio in auxilium pauperum convertantur. Benedictus, qui in hoc ministerio non ambulaverit fraudulenter.

1030   149. Nihil magnum a Diaconis tribuatur sine Ecclesiae consensu. Magnum dicimus, quod est ultra communes necessitates, ut si quis peteret X aut XX aureos.

150. Praeterea quoties aperietur aerarium, intersit Episcopus et adnotet, quantum receptum fuerit, ut sciat, quam largiter contribuerit Ecclesia ad pau-

---

1009/1010 Curent – Tim. 3] cfr I Tim. 3, 8   **1013/1014** Liquet – fuit] cfr Act. 6, 1-6 **1028/1029** Benedictus – fraudulenter] cfr Prou. 11, 13

1010 eos] *om. S*   **1013** VI] VII *S*   **1022** ponat] ponatur *S*

50 CONCILIUM HOMBERGENSE – 1526

1035 perum fratrum indigentiam et avaros possit opportunius et efficacius increpare. Quod si Episcopus interesse non potest, vocetur ad id adiutorum unus.

151. Hortamur autem per Christum, ut, si commode fieri potest, in Ecclesiarum Diaconos hi soli eligantur, pro quibus alendis non sit opus onerare Ecclesias, et ne propria egestas eisdem praebeat stimulum suffurandi et mentiendi Spiritui Sancto, verum in eis ante omnia pietas et Domini Spiritus requiratur.

De non ambiendo primatu, et de ordine ministrorum Ecclesiae, et quod faciles omnes in Domino sint

Cap. XXVI

1045 152. Qui primatum cupit ad Christi Ecclesiam spectare non potest. | Ideo 26v si quis aut Electorum Synodi aut Visitatorum aut Episcoporum aut Diaconorum cum fratribus suis de primatu contendit, ab ipso ministerio deponatur.

153. Verum ut omnia decenter fiant, ordinamus, ut in Synodis primi sint electi, deinde Visitatores, deinde Episcopi, deinde Ecclesiarum Commissi. Sint autem cuiuslibet Ecclesiarum Commissi iuxta Episcopum suum.

154. Porro inter Electos Synodi Visitatores et Diaconos ille primus censeatur, qui plures voces habuit, et secundum hunc ordinem loquantur et sedeant. Verum non proinde alius sit suo Collega maior aut dignior, ordinem quaerimus, superbis et ambitiosis favere non possumus.

1055 155. Admonet autem venerabilis Synodus per humilitatem, mansuetudinem et charitatem Iesu Christi universos Electos, Visitatores, Episcopos et Diaconos secundum voluntatem Dei, aliis non sibi vivant, quaerentes non quae sua sunt, sed quae proximorum.

156. Idcirco sint fratribus in sua functione in Domino faciles, audiant eos cum iudicio et dirigant ac consolentur in verbo Domini et tales omnino se exhibeant, ne difficultate ac severitate nimia absterreant a se fratres suos suo ministerio indigentes, aut oves sibi concreditas, et per id contingat aliquando aut perire aut nimium desolari, et ipsi fiant rei sanguinis eorum. Severos

---

1055/1058 Admonet – proximorum] cfr Phil. 2, 4

1039 eisdem] *om. S* **1050** Episcopum suum] suum Episcopum *S* **1052** habuit] habebit *S* **1060** ac] atque *S* **1061** suos] *om. S* **1062** aliquando] aliquem *S*

CONCILIUM HOMBERGENSE – 1526

quidem et graves eos esse opus est, verum hoc non sit in difficili consuetudine,
sed in hoc, ne sint praecipites in iudiciis, et non convivant ebriis, commessato-
ribus, lusoribus, scurris et aliis criminosis ac leviculis hominibus, propter quos
male audit sermo Dei et Ecclesia Christi.

| 157. Item ne sint pueri sensibus, ne puellarum more vestium quaerant 27r
mollitiem, ne inconstantes et varii sint in doctrina, sed semper magis firmi et
solidi in verbo veritatis. Quod si impii severi et graves esse volunt, quid minus
facient superbis illis larvis, ad quorum ianuas sexcenties frustra venire oportuit? Quod si a nobis fit, nonne ad priores abominationes revertimur?

158. Ideo si quis eiusmodi esse vult, a sua functione deponatur, quod
omnino illi ineptus sit. Et si quis eiusmodi est, electus fuerit, aut decernat
mutare hanc vivendi rationem, aut nullatenus admittatur ad functionem, in
quam electus est, quod nimirum in perniciem sibi verteretur.

159. Hoc non constituit Synodus, ut Episcopi aut Visitatores aut alii in
arduis negotiis Ecclesiae praepediti omnes pro quavis levicula occasione
admittere debeant, sed ne quis ab eis sine causa gravissima emittatur: et si
aliquando admittitur, sic fiat, ut nemo desoletur.

DE OTIOSIS, DEQUE VAGIS ET FALSIS FRATRIBUS

Cap. XXVII

160. Otiosis ne cibus quidem tribuendus est, quod iuxta Paulum qui non
laborat, nec manducet. Ideo egenis sanis et fortibus ac laborare nolentibus
nihil detur, sed si ex Ecclesia fuerint, ad laborem cogantur: si vero alieni, emit-
tantur. Secus est, si non reperiant, quod laborent. Advigilent autem Diaconi,
ut, si fieri potest, habeant, quod laborent. Illis vero non reperientibus provideant si possunt, aut aliquid auxilii in tempus praebeant.

| 161. Caeterum quum multi et vagi et falsi fratres omnia ferme loca 27v
circumeunt, a simplicitate verbi plurimos abducentes et multis misere imponentes, ordinamus, ut huiusmodi impostores a nostris Ecclesiis pellantur, et ut
nemo habeat cum eis consuetudinem.

1083/1084 Otiosis – manducet] cfr II Thess. 3, 10

1064 non sit] non situm *D*; non est situm *S*   **1074** est] *om. S*   **1076** verteretur]
uerteret *S*   **1089** quum] quia *S*

CONCILIUM HOMBERGENSE – 1526

DE PEREGRINIS ET EXULIBUS FRATRIBUS

Cap. XXVIII

162. Quoniam verbi Dei perpetua comes est crux, fieri non potest, ut non sit peregrinorum et exulum multitudo, quae nisi Christum negare velit, in propriis terris habitare non potest. Nolumus, ut fratres sic peregrini et exules a nostris Ecclesiis ulla ratione pellantur, cum scriptum sit: Frange esurienti panem tuum et egenos vagosque induc in domum tuam.

163. Verum quum, sicut praediximus, multi falsi fratres circumeunt, nolumus ut ipsi peregrini admittantur in conventum hebdomadarium, nisi noti sint aut alias vere probati. Prius enim probandi sunt, denique admittendi. Caveat autem sibi quisque a falsis fratribus.

164. Demum quia Christianismus non est in natione, sexu, aut quavis re externa, interdicimus, ne quis aliquem peregrinum fratrem nationis causa contumelia adficiat. Fratres enim sumus. Qui autem diversum fecerit, communione privetur, si nota res est: Maledicus enim fuit. Et nullus peregrinorum quantumlibet pauper a nostris Ecclesiis pellatur, modo velit Christiane vivere et ociosus esse nolit iubente namque Deo peregrinorum habenda est ratio.

DE UNIVERSALI STUDIO MARPURGENSI

Cap. XXIX

165. Quia placuit Deo movere cor Principis nostri, ut nunc ful|gente Evangelii gloria universale studium apud Marpurgum erigere velit, idque maxime necessarium sit, ut in Ecclesiis nostris multiplicentur, qui in verbo et doctrina eisdem praesidere ac quae recta sunt, consulere possint: Interdicimus in virtute Dei, ut nihil in ea legatur, quod negotiis regni Dei obesse possit.

166. In ea sint primum, qui sacras literas profiteantur, et id quidem purissime, alioqui deponantur. Deinde sint, qui leges civiles praelegant, sic tamen ut cautelae impiae Dei verbo circumcidantur, et quae Dei verbo non conueniunt, per illud corrigantur. Idcirco vocentur Iureconsulti docti simul et pii, qui sciant Dei verbum omnium doctrinarum adhibere censorem, e quibus si quis

---

1098/1099 Is. 58, 7 **1103** Caveat – fratribus] cfr II Cor. 11, 26

1098 ulla] nulla *S* **1100** quum] quia *S* **1104** Demum] Denique *S* **1106** adficiat] aficiat *S* **1107** res est] est res *S*

CONCILIUM HOMBERGENSE – 1526

nonnulla contra Dei verbum adseruerit et suo ministerio et communione privetur. Tertio habeatur ad minus unus medicinae Professor, doctus simul et pius. Quarto praelegantur artes liberales et politiores literae, adhibito in omnibus, praesertim in Mathematicis, censore tutissimo, nempe sermone Dei. Quinto sint professores linguarum.

167. Porro Ius illud contra fas vocatum Canonicum, omnino legi prohibemus. Qui in hoc venerabili studio aliquid contra Dei sanctum verbum decernere ausus fuerit, anathema sit.

De Scholis Puerorum

Cap. XXX

168. In omnibus Civitatibus, oppidis et pagis sint puerorum scholae, ubi rudimenta et scribendi rationem doceantur, donec qui desideraverint apti sint Studio Marpurgensi et ad illud veniant maiora audituri.

169. Et si in nonnullis | pagis omnia rudimenta tradi nequeunt, Episcopi 28v saltem aut eorum adiutores pueros legere et scribere doceant. Viderint autem Ecclesiae, ut aptos huic ministerio eligant, qui et ad bonos mores et ad laudabilia studia pueros cum efficacia commonefacere possint: quibus de necessariis omnibus provideatur, ut liberius se huic negotio totos dedant, et super his Visitatores et Episcopi advigilent, quod non parum, imo maxime retulerit, si fidelium iuventus bene instituatur.

170. Volumus autem, ut amodo in ipsis scholis et mane et vespere cantent unum, duos aut tres Psalmos pro voluntate Paedagogi et id quidem latine. Sequantur autem omnium Psalmorum ordinem. Et mox unus legat unum caput ex Bibliis: Mane ex vetere, vespere ex novo instrumento. Nihilque dicatur praeter psalmos et caput unum. Hac ratione volumus pueros sensim in divinis Eloquiis exerceri. Hoc fiat mane, cum primum ad scholas venerint, et vespere, cum ab eis discedere volunt.

1128 Dei] *om. S*   **1133** donec qui] *om. S*; lacer hic, et in aliis nonnullis locis Codex MS. *S*   qui] *D^{sup.l.}*   sint] sunt *D, scriba corr.* sint; sunt *S*

De Scholis Puellarum

Cap. XXXI

171. Sint praeterea in Civitatibus et oppidis, si fieri potest etiam in pagis, puellarum scholae, quibus doctae, maturae et piae foeminae praesint, quae eas doceant fidei principia. Item legere, nere, operari acu, solicitas ac operosas esse, ut bonae tandem matres familias sint. Episcopi autem et Visitatores instent, ut haec fiant. Praeterea volumus, ut tam mane quam vespere ipsae puellae exerceantur in divinis literis, ut psalmum unum communiter legant, et una earum caput unum Bibliorum, ut supra de pueris diximus. Legant autem haec vulgariter.

| Pro Studiosis Pauperibus

Cap. XXXII

172. Ordinamus, ut si fundatis et institutis lectionibus praebendae nonullae superfuerint, constituatur et dotetur Marpurgi una domus studiis apta, in qua certus studiosorum numerus pauperum ad triennium ad minus ali possint, hoc est, singuli tribus annis.

173. Interdicimus autem, ne in ea quisquam recipiatur, si aliunde ali potest. Et qui contra hoc institutum in ea receptus fuerit, quasi raptor substantiae pauperum expellatur, et qui eum recepit, pro Rectorum Uniuersitatis iudicio puniatur.

De Beneficiatis

Cap. XXXIII

174. Beneficiati omnes intersint lectioni et orationi tam matutinae quam vespertinae, item et Coenae Dominicae. Caeterum, qui absunt, notentur ab Episcoporum adiutoribus, et pro absentiis eorum census diminuatur Ecclesiarum arbitrio in conventu hebdomadario.

1153 operari acu] *om. S*   **1154** matres familias] matronae domus *S*   **1159** Pro] De *S*
1163 numerus pauperum] pauperum numerus *S*

CONCILIUM HOMBERGENSE – 1526

175. Porro qui ex eis Marpurgi habitant, liberi quidem sint istis, sed lectiones sibi frequentent, ne frustra panem suum manducent, quod de sanis et ad studia dispositis intelligimus.

176. Caeterum, qui non sunt studio dediti et sani sunt, faciant ea, quae paulo ante diximus, alioqui sui census diminutione puniantur,

177. quod etiam intelligimus de his, qui e claustris erepti sunt, et donec vixerint aut in tempus annuum censum e claustris habent, nisi alioqui Christiano negotio aut discendo opificio occuparentur.

178. Proinde volumus nomina eorum scribi et interrogari, quas lectiones audire cupiant, quas si neglexerint in conventu hebdomadario, et pro absentiis ab Ecclesia eorum census diminuatur.

179. Nemini ultra ut hactenus beneficia tradantur, sed mortuis | possessoribus convertantur in usus, qui conveniunt sermonibus Dei.

180. Quod diximus de mortuis possessoribus, non intelligimus de Episcopatibus. Functio enim Episcoporum perpetua esse non debet, nisi veritatis possessio constans et perpetua sit. Dignitas nimirum aut beneficium non est, sed opus; quod si quis non sicut oportet exequitur, deponendus est.

DE CLAUSTRIS ET MONACHIS

Cap. XXXIV

181. Quia Monastice pugnat ex diametro contra illud Pauli 1. Cor. 7: Empti estis pretio magno, nolite fieri servi hominum, nemo sani iudicii non videt eam contra sermonem Dei esse introductam, quae non solum huic loco Pauli, sed aliis multis est contraria et vere multis modis impia.

182. Ideo in virtute Dei interdicimus, ut nullus ex universis Ecclesiis nostris de caetero Monachus fiat. Sed neque puellae fiant Moniales, sed maneat quisque in vocatione baptismi, cui Monastice est oppositissima.

1194/1196 Quia – introductam] cfr I Cor. 7, 23

1176 sibi] ibi *S* **1179** alioqui] *om. S* **1180** quod – his] quod etiam in reliquis *S* qui] *om. S* **1181** aut – annuum] *om. S* **1183** interrogari] interrogare *S* **1185** ab Ecclesia] *D*[sup.l.] **1191** quis] qui *D* sicut] ut *S* **1195** nemo] Nemo *D* **1196** non solum] nondum *D* **1197** modis impia] modis est impia *S*

183. Praeterea iubemus omnia utriusque sexus Monasteria libera esse, quod non sint servanda, quae contra Dei verbum voverunt. Caeterum egredientibus reddantur, quae tulerunt.

184. Iuvenes laborent manibus, qui vero nesciunt, discant, et qui apti sunt studiis, studeant in nomine Domini.

185. Puellis aliquid detur, quo matrimonium contrahere possint.

186. Senioribus et ad laborem prorsus ineptis vel infirmis provideatur, quantum opus est.

187. Summa: Universis e Claustris egredientibus pro ratione et indigentia personarum provideatur de Monasteriorum substantia, ut nemo iuste queri possit.

188. Mox autem ut ex aliquo Monasterio omnes egressi fuerint, fiant ex eo fidelium Scholae, praesertim Marpurgi, nisi campestria sint. Quod si alioqui satis est scholarum, in usus Ecclesiae aut reipublicae convertatur pro Ecclesiae cuiuslibet iudicio.

| 189. Tandem si in nonnullis tam potens est erroris species, ut contra Dei verbum in Claustris velint esse servi hominum, tolerentur in tempus, hac tamen lege, ut nullatenus missent aut boent, sicut hactenus, nec campanas proinde pulsent. Nolumus autem, ut alicui ministrent sacramenta nec Confessiones audiant, publice uel privatim, aut egrediantur de Monasteriis eorum cum crucibus aut mortuos sepeliant. Summa: Volumus ut servent angulum suum et de Ecclesiarum nostrarum regimine nullatenus se admisceant.

190. Hos admonemus per sanguinem Iesu Christi, ut sint memores salutis suae orentque, ut illuminentur. Audiant praeterea lectiones sacras et intersint Coenae Dominicae, si tandem Dei misericordia a caecitate, qua tenentur, liberi fieri possint.

191. Si quis autem ex eis non est professus loci, in quo nunc est, nolumus, ut in eo alatur, sed mittatur in locum suum.

192. In Claustris autem, ubi adhuc supererunt aliquot Monachi aut Moniales, constituatur unus, qui eis praedicet Verbum Dei, nisi ad publicas conciones accedere velint.

1202 Dei verbum] verbum Dei *S*   **1206** quo] ut *S*   **1207** infirmis] (inutilibus) *S*
1209 e Claustris egredientibus] *om. S*   **1210** de Monasteriorum substantia] *om. S*
1216 tam potens est] est tam potens *S*   species] spiritus *S*

CONCILIUM HOMBERGENSE – 1526

193. Exterminet Deus omnes sectas perditionis, et reducat omnes dispersos in unum ovile sub uno pastore et Capite Christo.

194. Si quis autem denuo sectam inter fideles introduxerit, Anathema sit.

CONCLUSIO

195. Paucis hic conscripsimus, quae ad Ecclesiarum nostrarum ordinem pertinere visa sunt, et ut omnia in eisdem iuxta Dei verbum fiant. Superest ut unanimiter eadem serventur ad gloriam Domini nostri Iesu Christi, cui cum Patre et Spiritu Sancto sit honor, gloria, decus et imperium in secula seculorum. Amen.

FINIS REFORMATIONUM ECCLESIARUM HASSIAE HOMBERGI.

1232/1233 et – Christo] cfr Ioh. 10, 16; Eph. 4, 15

1232 perditionis] perditionum *S*

CONCILIUM IULIOMAGENSE
1527

edidit
Christian SCHEIDEGGER

THE SYNOD AND *ARTICLES* OF SCHLEITHEIM
1527

On 24 February 1527 in Schleitheim some of the leading exponents of the Anabaptist movement took part in a Synod that was probably presided over by Michael Sattler. The assembly claimed doctrinal authority in the firm conviction that they had recognised God's will. They formulated seven articles and a cover letter, with the aim of addressing the communities and groups that had sprung up in various towns and villages in the wake of the rapid spread of the movement. In addition to regulating ecclesiastical practices, these seven articles also clarified certain tenets of Anabaptist doctrine and affirmed the need for separation from the world, from the papacy, and from the territorial evangelical churches that were forming at this time.

THE HISTORICAL CONTEXT

In 1525 in Zurich a number of adults were baptised after confessing their faith in Jesus Christ. Aside from baptisms of Jews or in missionary areas, these were the first adults to do so in early modern times. Anabaptists – as these Christians were soon to be known – were an original offshoot of the Reformation. [1] In theological terms, they were in broad agreement with Huldrych Zwingli, although opinions diverged widely with regard to how reform ought to be implemented in Church life. Whereas the opponents of infant baptism were demanding swift and unconditional change based on their Biblical studies, Zwingli left the implementation of these measures up to political authorities. Tensions rose in the wake of the controversial reform of baptism. After a disputation between mainstream theologians and radicals was held in the Zurich council hall on 17 January 1525, the city magistrates forbade opponents of infant baptism from organising their own meetings and ordered them to baptise any previously unbaptised infants, threatening anyone who refused to comply with exile. [2] When the radicals gathered again, probably on the evening of 21 January 1525, they were overcome by such awe in the presence of

---

(1) Köhler, 'Die Zürcher Täufer', p. 48. A good recent introduction to early Anabaptism is Strübind, 'The Swiss Anabaptists'.

(2) *QGTS*, vol. 1 (1952), p. 32-36, no. 21-26.

God that Jörg Cajakob – known as Blaurock – asked Konrad Grebel to baptise him. In turn, Blaurock baptised others who had long hoped to found a holy community. (3)

In January 1525, the magistrates in Zurich turned what was fundamentally a theological doctrine into binding law. In fact, upon Zwingli's sanction, political authorities had filled the power vacuum that came into being after Zurich had severed its ties with the Roman Catholic Church. Zwingli believed that there could be a lasting legitimate collaboration with the authorities with regard to Church leadership. Power struggles taking place in the city were coming under fire not only from the Anabaptists but also from congregationalist preachers and various rural communities demanding free use of ecclesiastical property in the wake of its secularisation. (4) Although peasant revolts had been peacefully resolved through recourse to the law until August 1525, the Zurich city council proved unable to put down Anabaptist protests either through legislative measures or through theological debate.

The Anabaptist movement spread throughout the Zurich area and the Swiss Confederation, and eventually crossed the border. Wherever the Anabaptists appeared, they demanded the right to gather as and to build the true Church. Penitent believers promised, by the act of baptism, to follow the rule of Christ (as in Matth. 18, 15-18). Both baptism and the Lord's Supper were constitutive elements of the Church. It was not least for this reason that their beliefs found such fertile ground. In 1525 – even in evangelical areas – the official Church tended to adhere to Roman Catholic practices, albeit to varying degrees. The future direction taken by Anabaptists was determined by the truth identified in the Bible and experienced in their lives, standing as testimony to their missionary zeal in public as well as to their desire to build congregations. As the latter only admitted individuals who made a profession of faith and adhered to Anabaptist orthopraxy, strong commitment to the community characterised these assemblies. Already in this early phase there were

---

(3) [Carel van Ghendt], 'Het beginsel en voortganck der geschillen, scheuringen, en verdeeltheden onder de gene die Doops-Gesinden genoemt worden', in S. Cramer, *Zestiende-eeuwsche schrijvers over de geschiedenis der oudste Doopsgezinden hier te lande* (*Bibliotheca reformatoria Neerlandica* 7),'s-Gravenhage 1910, p. 516. Although sources do not reveal much about this occasion, for those involved it must have been a truly momentous occasion. They believed that with the participation of willing men, God would create a purified Christian community of saints. As Grebel and his friends wrote in a letter to Thomas Müntzer on 24 September 1524, 'Züch mit dem wort und mach ein christenliche gmein mit hilf Christi und siner regel'. According to the Anabaptists, this meant that Christ himself would have been at work in their decisive actions. Cfr. in this regard *QGTS*, vol. 1 (1952), p. 17, no. 14.

(4) Kamber, *Reformation als bäuerliche Revolution*, p. 417-428.

signs of the emergence of an ecclesiology of free churches in several territories. In St Gallen, Wolfgang Ullmann refused to preach the Word of God in church as – he argued – the truth had never been uttered from the pulpit. Ullmann wished to announce God's revelation elsewhere. (5) This was motivated by a deliberate strategy: to gather a community of believers and found a separate Anabaptist Church. A contemporary witness mentioned that Ullmann and his followers met both in private homes and in the open air, claiming to be the Church of Christ and considering everyone else to be heathens. (6)

As it spread, Anabaptism became more stratified. Theologian Balthasar Hubmaier – who advocated an ecclesiology based on a territorial Church – made an attempt to introduce Anabaptism at town level, in Waldshut in 1525 and in Nikolsburg in 1526. Hans Hut, baptised in 1526 in Augsburg by Hans Denck, drew upon mystical and apocalyptic aspects of the teachings of Thomas Müntzer. Later leaders influenced the Anabaptist faith in their own individual ways: there was the apocalyptic visionary Melchior Hoffmann in East Frisia, Menno Simons who travelled throughout northern Germany and the Netherlands, and Jakob Hutter, a leading exponent of the Anabaptist movement in Moravia. Most scholars support the idea of the polygenesis of Anabaptism. (7)

Wherever they went, Anabaptists clashed with political authorities. Already in 1525, the first Anabaptists were condemned as heretics and burned at the stake in Roman Catholic lands. (8) The first edict making the believer's baptism (*Bekenntnistaufe*) punishable by death was promulgated in Zurich on 7 March 1526. (9) On 5 January 1527, the day he was drowned in the river Limmat, Felix Mantz became the first victim of the edict and the first Anabaptist condemned to death by Zwinglians. (10) The situation worsened drastically for the Anabaptists, not only in Zurich but also in other areas. For example, Anabaptists were expelled from Strasbourg and any form of dialogue with them was interrupted. (11) Persecutory measures grew harsher and harsher as the hostility of evangelical theologians created an unsettling climate, making it

---

(5) *QGTS*, vol. 2 (1972), p. 604 and following.

(6) *QGTS*, vol. 2 (1972), p. 605. There is a lack of scholarly consensus with regard to the early phases of Anabaptism. See by way of example Strübind, *Eifriger als Zwingli* and C. Arnold Snyder, 'The Birth and Evolution of Swiss Anabaptism'.

(7) See 'From Monogenesis to Polygenesis'.

(8) *HLS*, vol. 4 (2005), p. 49, and vol. 7 (2008), p. 468.

(9) *QGTS*, vol. 1 (1952), p. 180-181, no. 172. Cfr. also the Council decree of 19 November 1526 in *QGTS*, vol. 1 (1952), p. 210-211, no. 192.

(10) *QGTS*, vol. 1 (1952), p. 224-226, no. 204.

(11) Deppermann, 'Die Straßburger Reformatoren'.

64 CONCILIUM IULIOMAGENSE – 1527

vital to consolidate the community to prevent the impending return of its members to the official Church. The growing pressure of political authorities had long-lasting effects on the development of the Anabaptist movement, forcing its adherents who did not wish to abandon their beliefs to live their lives underground.

The exact circumstances of the *Concilium Iuliomagense* are unknown. The only primary sources available are the *Articles* that were formulated and written in the name of all the members present, along with a cover letter. Participants are not known. The meeting place can be identified as Schleitheim, over which the abbey of Reichenau, the counts of Lupfen, and the *Spital* of Schaffhausen all exercised seigneurial rights. ([12]) It is likely that the meeting was chaired by the former Benedictine prior Michael Sattler, ([13]) given that he is considered the author of the *Articles*. This attribution was confirmed after the publication of an undated letter that he wrote to the theologians of Strasbourg. ([14])

THE *SCHLEITHEIM ARTICLES*

The *Brüderliche Vereinigung* (*Schleitheim Articles* or *Schleitheim Confession*, also known as the *Brotherly Union*) examined various questions: baptism, excommunication, the Lord's Supper, separation from the world, pastorate in the Church, political authority, and the issue of oaths. Unlike the creeds of the so-called magisterial Reformation, its articles were not an attempt to systematise the tenets of Anabaptist faith. Although Sattler preached on the work of redemption of Jesus Christ and on the doctrine of justification, the *Articles* did not provide any further explanations about these tenets but postulated them tacitly. For a long time, there were no exhaustive professions of faith in Anabaptism in spite of the existence of binding dogmas. Binding formulations were not necessary as the Anabaptists did not deem the profession of faith a social obligation or even less a social constraint, which is why it never acquired the juridical aspect that it had for Reformed and Lutheran believers.

The *Articles'* cover letter clearly showed that the observant community of Anabaptists had been disrupted by the intrusion of false teachings. Indeed the community faced threats both from the outside – i.e. the repressive measures of political authorities – and from the false believers who had managed to

---

(12) *Geschichte von Schleitheim*, p. 278.

(13) On Sattler, see Arnold Snyder, *The Life and Thought of Michael Sattler*.

(14) Bucer, *Briefwechsel*, vol. 2 (1989), p. 193-195. See also Stricker, 'Michael Sattler als Verfasser', p. 16-17.

creep in. The latter reference presumably referred to individuals such as Balthasar Hubmaier – who supported the idea of a defensive, territorial Anabaptism – as well as to spiritualists such as Hans Denck and the apocalyptic visionary Hans Hut. ([15]) The *Schleitheim Confession* was intended to help rebuild a community under jeopardy and to preserve it in the recognised truth. Its articles contributed to clarifying who belonged to the community, who its leaders were, and how community life was to be regulated. It also defined the relationship between believers and the corrupt established churches, politics, and society. The first article concerned baptism and did not add anything new to early Anabaptist teachings on this matter. ([16]) Baptism must necessarily be preceded by catechesis. The ceremony symbolically expressed the washing away of sin and the entry into a new existence. This inner process – often referred to by other texts as inner baptism – involved an act of God in the person's heart which necessitated the blood of Christ at an objective level and personal faith at a subjective level. God's work in humans, their belief, and the symbol of baptism belonged together and were not to be fragmented such as in the teachings of Huldrych Zwingli or Martin Bucer. The *Articles* also emphasised the conscious decision made by those about to be baptised: baptism was an act of obedience that caused the baptised to be incorporated into the Body of Christ. The doctrine of baptism found in the *Schleitheim Articles* was in opposition to the theology of Hans Denck and of other spiritualists.

The second article – on excommunication – was also connected to baptism as baptised believers subjected themselves to the brethren's discipline (Matth. 18, 15-18), defined as rule of the ban or excommunication. This issue, examined in a letter by Konrad Grebel, is the key to understand Anabaptism. Anabaptists placed the visible community of believers at the centre of the stage and the congregation as a whole was entrusted with the preservation of doctrinal purity and of an impeccable lifestyle. Later on, Anabaptists accused Reformed believers of not being a true Church because they did not abide by the rule of Christ. ([17]) There was no proper ecclesiastical discipline in Zurich or in other Reformed cities, as it was left to the authority of civil magistrates to

(15) Meihuizen, 'Who Were the «False Brethren»'.

(16) See Grebel's dispatch, in *QGTS*, vol. 1 (1952), p. 17-18, no. 14; the protestation of Felix Mantz, in *QGTS*, vol. 1 (1952), p. 23-28, no. 16; the Anabaptist letter of 1526 – unknown until recently – in Scheidegger, 'Ein unbekannter Brief eines Täuferlehrers'; theses 1 to 4 in Sattler's letter to the theologians of Strasbourg, in Bucer, *Briefwechsel*, vol. 2 (1989), p. 193.

(17) *Täufer und Reformierte im Disput*, p. 207.

watch over morality and punish un-Christian behaviour with fines or imprisonment.

On a doctrinal level, Anabaptists and Reformed believers were in agreement on the Lord's Supper, the subject of the third article. Both groups rejected the doctrine of transubstantiation and underlined the Supper's significance as a memorial. The Anabaptists allowed only the baptised to partake in the Lord's Supper because this involved the holy community and the need to become a single body. God was not present in the eucharistic elements, but in the action of the Church as the Body of Christ.

The first three articles were relatively brief and concise in comparison to the more detailed articles which followed. The reason for their differing lengths and scopes probably lies in the fact that the vast majority of Anabaptists were largely in agreement on the first three articles, and made it possible to refute Reformed, Roman Catholic, and spiritualist beliefs by falling back on the usual arguments. The pastoral intent was more crucial. The aim was to ensure that Anabaptists remained faithful to the recognised truth and did not revert to the established churches. The fourth article – on separation – invoked an extreme dualism between good and evil, light and dark, Christ and Belial. God's admonishment to leave Babylon and Egypt was a clear reference to corrupt churches and sin-ridden world. The separatism that the *Articles* advocated concerned the ecclesiastical, cultural, and political spheres, and effectively meant withdrawing from society. Aware that both secular and religious authorities would employ all available means to quash the Anabaptist movement, the *Concilium Iuliomagense* chose the path of social isolation. This option represented a survival strategy allowing believers to hold onto their convictions: the believer's baptism, excommunication, separation between Church and state, and the refusal to perform military service. A movement that had been present in churches, guild houses, and other public places, challenging society at large, was now becoming an underground Church. The *Concilium Iuliomagense* was the watershed between these two moments.

The fifth article underlined the role of the pastoral office. Several pioneering Anabaptists were either deceased or had been banished by the political authorities, making it necessary to replace them. Unlike in the established churches – where theological training was the main criterion for selection – Anabaptists referred to the directives contained in Paul's letters with regard to the appointment of elders and overseers. Pastors were appointed by elders, without the intervention of authorities, and were subjected to the discipline of the community. Anabaptist congregations were brotherhoods, meaning that they were generally more relationship-oriented and less hierarchical than the official churches.

The sixth article concerned Church-state relations. The very first sentence – 'das Schwert ist eine Ordnung Gottes ausserhalb der Vollkommenheit Christi' ('The sword is an ordinance of God outside the perfection of Christ') – rejected the state Church of the magisterial Reformation as well as any recourse to the sword to bring about reform. There was no place in the Church (the 'perfection of Christ') for the exercise of temporal authority – referred to as the 'sword' in the language of the times – a position that was certainly not new. Konrad Grebel had insisted that 'man soll ouch daß evangelium und sine annemer nit schirmen mit dem schwert oder sy sich selbs' ('One should not defend the Gospel and its followers by means of the sword nor should one defend himself in this way'). [18] In fact, the separation between Church and state became a distinctive trait of the Anabaptists. An Anabaptist believer who attended the Disputation of Zofingen in 1532 criticised those who failed to distinguish between worldly administration and Christian Church: 'Wir wend ymmerdar, das underscheyd sye zwüschend dem gwalt des waeltlichen regiments und der christenlichen kilchen'. [19] In the mid seventeenth century, Anabaptists in Zurich referred to the sixth article of the *Schleitheim Confession* during a dispute. [20] According to this article, while Anabaptists did not recognise the authority of the state in religious matters, they did recognise political authority as being ordained by God and exercised outside the community. The sixth article also stated that Christians must abandon any military, juridical, and legal power. This apolitical and pacifist position was in contrast with the theology of Balthasar Hubmaier. It was supported by several examples taken from the life of Jesus and was part of the Anabaptist interpretation of Christian discipleship.

The seventh article also dealt with the relationship between believers and the state. Until 1527, Anabaptists had continued to swear oaths, with a few exceptions. It was not until the *Concilium Iuliomagense* that the refusal to swear oaths was elevated to dogma: thus, it became necessary to examine the question in detail. Their experience with the Zurich judicial system certainly played an important role in this as the Anabaptists could not and would not swear not to attend meetings or not to baptise adults because they were bound by their consciences to follow Jesus Christ. Abiding by Christ's rejection of oaths (Matth. 5, 33-37), they refused to give their unconditional obedience to secular authorities. They refused to swear promissory oaths such as oaths declaring truces (*Urfehde*) or oaths of citizenship (*Bürgereid*). Assertory oaths

(18) *QGTS*, vol. 1 (1952), p. 17, no. 14.
(19) *QGTS*, vol. 4 (2008), p. 173.
(20) *Täufer und Reformierte im Disput*, p. 197.

68 CONCILIUM IULIOMAGENSE – 1527

– for example, testimonies in court – continued to be permissible. Theological misgivings concerning solemn oaths sworn before secular authorities (*Eidschwur*) cropped up at regular intervals throughout the history of the Church, beginning with some of the Fathers of the Church and going right up to Erasmus. In the sixteenth century, oaths acquired considerable importance as they merged personal conscience with political allegiance. Anabaptists, however, believed that it was necessary to respond to Jesus Christ alone when it came to matters of conscience.

The *Schleitheim Articles* were quickly and broadly circulated, first by means of manuscript copies. The extraordinary relevance of this text is confirmed by several re-editions and translations into French, and Dutch. Huldrych Zwingli, Johannes Oecolampadius, and John Calvin also reacted to the *Confession*, considering it to be one of the founding documents of Anabaptism. (21)

Note on the Edition

The critical edition offered below reproduces the *editio princeps* – the unsigned edition of Peter Schöffer d.J., Worms (D²) – of the *Schleitheim Articles*. In addition to the *Articles* and their cover letter, the *editio princeps* also includes a letter by Michael Sattler to the congregation of Horb as well as an account of his martyrdom. The German print abbreviations are the same used in Walter Köhler's edition, although the chronological order is different to the one that he adopted (see D¹ below). Josef Benzing's dating of the first edition (1527) is confirmed by Helmut Claus ('1527 or shortly afterwards') (22). Further confirmation is provided by an early copy owned by Augsburg weaver Simprecht Kröll. (23) In our edition, every aspect of the original has been reproduced exactly, including capital and lower-case letters as well as punctuation. On the other hand, abbreviations have been tacitly resolved. *U/u* and *V/v* have undergone vocalic or consonantal transliteration. The numbering of paragraphs corresponds to the original, but we have not reproduced line breaks. Dots next to Roman numerals have been eliminated. Signature marks have been used as sheet counting in the margins. Evident errors have been corrected in the text and signalled in Apparatus 3.

(21) Leu – Scheidegger, *Das Schleitheimer Bekenntnis 1527*, p. 16-22.
(22) Benzing, 'Peter Schöffer', p. 116 and Laube, *Flugschriften*, vol. 1, p. 741.
(23) Universitätsbibliothek Heidelberg, Cod. Pal. germ. 793, fol. 92r-97r. See Meyer, *Literarische Hausbücher*, p. 590-592.

BIBLIOGRAPHY

Sources (and Their Abbreviations)

M. Bucer, *Briefwechsel / Correspondance* (Studies in Medieval and Reformation Traditions), hrsg. / éd. Jean Rott et al., 10 vols, Leiden 1979 – [= Bucer, *Briefwechsel*].

Das Schleitheimer Bekenntnis 1527: Einleitung, Faksimile, Übersetzung und Kommentar, hrsg. U. B. Leu – C. Scheidegger, Zug 2004 [= Leu – Scheidegger, *Das Schleitheimer Bekenntnis 1527*].

H. Fast, '[Michael Sattler], Brüderliche Vereinigung', in L. von Muralt et al. (hrsg.), *Quellen zur Geschichte der Täufer in der Schweiz*, 4 vols, Zürich 1952-2008, vol. 2, p. 26-36.

Flugschriften vom Bauernkrieg zum Täuferreich (1526-1535), hrsg. A. Laube, 2 vols, Berlin 1992 [= Laube, *Flugschriften*].

J. M. Stayer, 'Brüderliche Vereinigung (Schleitheim)', online at http://www.mennlex.de/doku.php?id=top:bruederliche-vereinigung (last accessed 20 October 2023).

Literature (and Its Abbreviations)

J. Benzing, 'Peter Schöffer d.J. zu Worms und seine Drucke (1518-1529)', *Der Wormsgau* 5 (1961-1962), p. 108-118 [= Benzing, 'Peter Schöffer'].

K. Deppermann, 'Die Straßburger Reformatoren und die Krise des oberdeutschen Täufertums im Jahre 1527', *Mennonitische Geschichtsblätter* 30 (1973), p. 24-33 [= Deppermann, 'Die Straßburger Reformatoren'].

K. Deppermann – J. H. Yoder, 'Ein Briefwechsel über die Bedeutung des Schleitheimer Bekenntnisses', *Mennonitische Geschichtsblätter* 30 (1973), p. 42-51.

M. Jorio (Chefredaktor), *Historisches Lexikon der Schweiz*, 13 vols, Basel 2002-2014 [= *HLS*].

P. Kamber, *Reformation als bäuerliche Revolution: Bildersturm, Klosterbesetzungen und Kampf gegen die Leibeigenschaft in Zürich zur Zeit der Reformation (1522-1525)*, Zürich 2010 [= Kamber, *Reformation als bäuerliche Revolution*].

W. Köhler, 'Die Zürcher Täufer', in C. Neff (hrsg.), *Gedenkschrift zum 400jährigen Jubiläum der Mennoniten oder Taufgesinnten, 1525-1925*, Ludwigshafen 1925, p. 48-64 [= Köhler, 'Die Zürcher Täufer'].

H. R. Lavater, 'Calvin und die Täufer - Zur Entstehung der *Briève Instruction 1544*', in M. Sallmann – M. Mayordomo – H. R. Lavater (hrsg.), *Johannes Calvin 1509-2009: Würdigung aus Berner Perspektive*, Zürich 2011, p. 69-100 [= Lavater, 'Calvin und die Täufer'].

U. B. Leu, 'Das Zürcher Exemplar des Schleitheimer Täuferbekenntnisses', *Mitteilungen der Antiquarischen Gesellschaft in Zürich* 86 (Querblicke: Zürcher Reformationsgeschichten), Zürich 2019, p. 71-77 [= Leu, 'Das Zürcher Exemplar des Schleitheimer Täuferbekenntnisses'].

H. W. Meihuizen, 'Who Were the «False Brethren» Mentioned in the Schleitheim Articles?', *Mennonite Quarterly Review* 41 (1967), p. 210-220 [= Meihuizen, 'Who Were the «False Brethren»'].

D. H. Meyer, *Literarische Hausbücher des 16. Jahrhunderts: die Sammlungen des Ulrich Mostl, des Valentin Holl und des Simprecht Kröll (Würzburger Beiträge zur deutschen Philologie 2)*, Würzburg 1989 [= Meyer, *Literarische Hausbücher*].

G. Möncke, 'Friedrich Huber, ein pseudonymer Verfasser zweier Straßburger Täuferdrucke', *Mennonitische Geschichtsblätter* 60 (2003), p. 80-88 [= Möncke, 'Friedrich Huber'].

Quellen zur Geschichte der Täufer in der Schweiz, hrsg. L. von Muralt et al., 4 vols, Zürich 1952-2008 [= *QGTS*].

C. Scheidegger, 'Ein unbekannter Brief eines Täuferlehrers (1526) und ein neuer Blick auf die frühe Täuferbewegung in der Schweiz', in C. Christ-von Wedel et al. (hrsg.), *Basel als Zentrum des geistigen Austauschs in der frühen Reformationszeit*, Tübingen 2014, p. 273-296 [= Scheidegger, 'Ein unbekannter Brief eines Täuferlehrers'].

C. Arnold Snyder, 'The Birth and Evolution of Swiss Anabaptism, 1520-1530', *Mennonite Quarterly Review* 80 (2006), p. 501-645 [= Arnold Snyder, 'The Birth and Evolution of Swiss Anabaptism'].

—, 'The Influence of the Schleitheim Articles on the Anabaptist Movement: An Historical Evaluation', *Mennonite Quarterly Review* 63 (1989), p. 323-344.

—, *The Life and Thought of Michael Sattler*, Scottdale (PA) 1984 [= Arnold Snyder, The Life and Thought of Michael Sattler].

James M. Stayer – Werner O. Packull – Klaus Deppermann, 'From Monogenesis to Polygenesis: The Historical Discussion of Anabaptist Origins', *Mennonite Quarterly Review* 49 (1975), p. 83-122 [= 'From Monogenesis to Polygenesis'].

H. Stricker, 'Michael Sattler als Verfasser der «Schleitheimer Artikel»', *Mennonitische Geschichtsblätter* 21 (1964), p. 15-18 [= Stricker, 'Michael Sattler als Verfasser'].

A. Strübind, *Eifriger als Zwingli: Die frühe Täuferbewegung in der Schweiz*, Berlin 2003 [= Strübind, *Eifriger als Zwingli*].

—, 'The Swiss Anabaptists', in A. N. Burnett – E. Campi (eds), *A Companion to the Swiss Reformation*, Leiden 2016, p. 389-443 [= Strübind, 'The Swiss Anabaptists'].

Täufer und Reformierte im Disput: Texte des 17. Jahrhunderts über Verfolgung und Toleranz aus Zürich und Amsterdam, hrsg. P. Wälchli et al., Zug 2010 [= *Täufer und Reformierte im Disput*].

C. Wanner – H. Wanner, *Geschichte von Schleitheim*, Schleitheim 1985 [= *Geschichte von Schleitheim*].

J. H. Yoder, 'Der Kristallisationspunkt des Täufertums', *Mennonitische Geschichtsblätter* 29 (1972), p. 35-47.

MONITUM

Brüderliche vereynigung etzlicher kinder Gottes / siben Artickel betreffend, [Worms: Peter Schöffer d.J., 1527], VD 16 S 1882: München, Bayerische Staatsbibliothek, 8° Mor. 135/132 (Res) and Res. Polem. 875, suppl. vol. 6.

CONCILIUM IULIOMAGENSE
1527

CONSPECTUS SIGLORUM

h^1 Anonymous transcription, lacking the cover letter, 1527: Bern, Staatsarchiv, A V 1453 (U.P. 80, n. 9)

d^1 Partial translation into Latin by Huldrych Zwingli, in *In catabaptistarum strophas elenchus Huldrichi Zvinglij*, Zürich: Froschauer, 1527 (VD16 Z 860), p. 73-118. – Edition: *Huldreich Zwinglis sämtliche Werke*, vol. VI/1, Zürich 1961 [= Z VI/1], p. 1-196 (editor: Fritz Blanke)

D^2 *Brüderliche vereynigung etzlicher kinder Gottes / siben Artickel betreffend*, [Worms: Peter Schöffer d.J., 1527], VD16 S 1882: München, Bayerische Staatsbibliothek, 8° Mor. 135/2 (Res) and Res. Polem. 875, suppl. vol. 6. – Facsimile: Urs B. Leu – C. Scheidegger (hrsg.), *Das Schleitheimer Bekenntnis 1527: Einleitung, Faksimile, Übersetzung und Kommentar*, Zug 2004. – Editions: H. Böhmer (hrsg.), *Urkunden zur Geschichte des Bauernkrieges und der Wiedertäufer*, Bonn 1921, p. 25-35; A. Laube et al. (hrsg.): *Flugschriften vom Bauernkrieg zum Täuferreich, (1526-1535)*, 2 vols, Berlin 1992, vol. 1, p. 728-735

h^3 Transcription by Simprecht Kröll based on D^2, 1527/1529: Heidelberg, Universitätsbibliothek, Cod. Pal. germ. 793, fol. 92r-97r

D^1 *Brüderlich vereynigung etzlicher kinder Gottes / sieben Articel betreffend*, [Strassburg: Jakob Cammerlander, 1533], VD16 S 1881: Wittenberg, Reformationsgeschichtliche Forschungsbibliothek, EKU 1199 – Edition: W. Köhler (hrsg.), *Brüderlich Vereinigung etzlicher Kinder Gottes sieben Artikel betreffend: item ein Sendbrief Michael Sattlers an eine Gemeine Gottes samt seinem Martyrium (1527)* (*Flugschriften aus den ersten Jahren der Reformation 2/3*), Leipzig 1908, p. 277-337

d^3 Partial translation into French in J. Calvin, *Brieve instruction pour armer tous bons fideles contre les erreurs des Anabaptistes*, Genève: Jean Girard, 1544 (GLN-61). – Edition: *Ioannis Calvini opera omnia*, s. IV, vol. 2 – ed. M. van Veen, Genève 2007

d^4 Partial translation into Latin from the French by Nicolas Des Gallars, based on d^3, in J. Calvin, *Brevis instructio muniendis fidelibus adversus errores sectae Anabaptistarum*, Argentorati: Wendelium Rehelium, 1546 (VD16 C 286)

d^5 Partial translation into English from the French based on d^3 in J. Calvin, *A short instruction for to arme all good Christian people agaynst the pestiferous errours of the common secte of Anabaptistes*, London: John Day and William Seres, 1549 (ESTC S110993)

d^6 *Broederlicke vereeninge van sommighe kinderen Gods, aengaende seven articulen* [Emden: Willem Gaillart] 1560 (Typographia Batava 820), Amsterdam, Universiteitsbibliotheek, Bibliotheek der Vereenigde Doopsgezinde Gemeente, OTM: OK 65-206 (2). – Edition: *Nederlandsche Anabaptistica* (*geschriften van Henrick Rol, Melchior Hoffman, Adam Pastor, De Broederlicke vereeninge*), uitg. S. Cramer (*Bibliotheca reformatoria Neerlandica 5*), 's-Gravenhage 1909, p. 585-613

d^7 *Broederlicke vereeninge van sommighe kinderen Godts aengaende seven articulen* [Steenwijk: Herman 't Zangers] 1565 (Typographia Batava 821), Amsterdam, Universiteitsbibliotheek, Bibliotheek der Vereenigde Doopsgezinde Gemeente, OTM: OK 65-201

D^3 *Brüderlich vereinigung etlicher Kinder Gottes / sieben artickel betreffend*, [Oberursel: Nikolaus Henricus, 1560?], VD16 ZV 30530: Schleitheim, Ortsmu-

76 CONSPECTUS SIGLORUM

seum (Permanent loan from Sturzenegger-Stiftung, Schaffhausen), and Goshen (Indiana), Mennonite Historical Library, 238.43 S253b

h^5 Anonymous transcription based on D¹ or D³. The first page of the accompanying text is missing (the text begins: 'Aber ihr nit also'), sixteenth century, Zürich, Staatsarchiv, E II 446, fol. 117r-120r

h^6 Transcription in Codex 'Braitmichel' (epistolary), Austerlitz 1566. Now in Montana (USA), owned by the Hutterite Brothers. Cfr R. Friedmann, *Die Schriften der Huterischen Täufergemeinschaften: Gesamtkatalog ihrer Manuskriptbücher, ihrer Schreiber und ihrer Literatur, 1529-1667 (Denkschriften der Österreichischen Akademie der Wissenschaften, Philosophisch-Historische Klasse 86)*, Wien 1965, p. 69-71

h^7 Anonymous transcription, minor text loss at beginning, no earlier than 1568, in Prag, Bibliothek des Nationalmuseums, XV G 10, fol. 55r-72v. Cfr M. H. Rauert – M. Rothkegel – G. Seebass (hrsg.): *Katalog der hutterischen Handschriften und der Drucke aus hutterischem Besitz in Europa (Quellen zur Geschichte der Täufer 18/1-2)*, Gütersloh 2011, p. 1095

h^8 Hutterite transcription by S. R. based on one of the printed works, after 28 August 1576, in Bratislava (Pressburg), Stadtarchiv, Hab 17, fol. 644r-651r. Cfr *Katalog der hutterischen Handschriften*, vol. 1, p. 341-342

h^9 Transcription in Codex E.W.3 (epistolary), 1592, now in USA, owned by the Hutterite Brothers. Cfr Friedmann, *Die Schriften der Huterischen Täufergemeinschaften*, p. 68-69

h^{10} Transcription by G. H. based on one of the printed works, 1618, in Bratislava (Pressburg), Stadtarchiv, Rkp. zv. 305, fol. 17rᵃ-21rᵇ, 1618. Cfr *Katalog der hutterischen Handschriften*, vol. 1, p. 425

h^{11} Transcription by Johann Jakob Spleiss based on one of the printed works, 1640, in Schaffhausen, Staatsarchiv: Schleitheim, CC 1

h^{12} Transcription by Melcher [Hipscher?] based on *D¹* or *D³*, mid seventeenth century, in Bratislava (Pressburg), Stadtarchiv, Hab 20, fol. 187v-200v. Cfr *Katalog der hutterischen Handschriften*, vol. 1, 373. – Edition (abridged): *Die Geschichts-Bücher der Wiedertäufer in Oesterreich-Ungarn, betreffend deren Schicksale in der Schweiz, Salzburg, Ober- und Nieder-Oesterreich, Mähren, Tirol, Böhmen, Süd-Deutschland, Ungarn, Siebenbürgen und Süd-Russland in der Zeit von 1526 bis 1785*, hrsg. J. Beck (*Fontes rerum austriacarum* 2/43), Wien 1883, p. 41-44

D^4 *Bürderlich vereynigung etlicher Kinder Gottes / sieben Artickel betreffendt*, s.l. [1686], in Basel, Universitätsbibliothek, fb 681:5

Lost texts

H Presumed autograph text by Michael Sattler

h^2 Basel transcription sent by Johannes Oecolampadius to Huldrych Zwingli on 24 April 1527. Cfr Z VI/1, 6. Zwingli had a total of four transcriptions at his disposal, cfr Z VI/1, 122, Marginalie

d^2/h^4 French translation (1544) that probably appeared in print. It is likely that Pierre Chambrier d.J. († 1571), notary and translator for the governor of Neuenburg, prepared a translation into French of the German text of the *Schleitheim Confession* and then had it printed. The documents refer to a print run of 1500 copies printed in a German-speaking area

| BRÜDERLICHE VEREYNIGUNG ETZLICHER KINDER GOTTES / SIBEN ARTICKEL BETREFFEND.

A1r

| Freud / fried und barmhertzigkeyt / von unserm Vatter / durch die vereynigung des blůts Christi Jesu / mit sampt den gaben des Geysts / der vom vatter gesendt wirt / allen glaubigen zů stercke / und trost / und bestendigkeyt / inn aller trübsal / biß an das ende / Amen / Sei mit allen liebhabern Gottes / und kinden des liechts / welche zerspreyt seind allenthalben / wo sie von Gott unserm Vatter verordnet seind / wo sie versamlet seind eynmůtigklich inn eynem Got unnd Vatter unser aller / Gnad und fried imm hertzen sei mit euch allen / Amen.

A1v

Lieben inn dem Herrn brůder und schwestren / uns ist allweg zů dem ersten unnd fürnembsten angelegen / euwer trost und versicherung euwerers gewissens / welches etwan verwirret was / darmit jr nit immer alß die außlendigen von uns gesündert wůrden / und schier vast außgeschlossen nach billigkeyt / sonder das jr euch widerumb wenden möchten / zů den waren ingepflantzten glidern Christi / die da gerůstet werden durch gedultigkeyt / und erkennung sein selbs / und also widerumb mit uns vereynbart wůrden / in der krafft eynes göttlichen christenlichen geysts / und eifers nach Gott.

Es ist auch offenbar / mit was tausentlistigkeyt / der teufel uns angewendt hab / damitt er jhnen das werck Gottes / welches inn uns zům teyl barmhertziglich und gnediglich angehebt ist worden / zerstör und zůboden richt / Aber der trew hirt unser selen Christus / der solches angehaben hat inn uns / der wirt dasselb biß an das end richten / und leren / zů seiner eer und unserem heyl / Amen.

3/4 die – Jesu] cfr I Cor. 10, 16   **7/8** wo¹ – eynmůtigklich] cfr Act. 1, 14   **9** inn – aller] cfr Eph. 4, 6   **22** Aber – selen] cfr I Petr. 2, 25   **22/23** Christus – richten] cfr Phil. 1, 6

---

4 vereynigung] *intellege* communion   **7** zerspreyt] *intellege* scattered   **14** schier vast] *intellege* almost completely   **19** angewendt] abgewent D^1

CONCILIUM IULIOMAGENSE – 1527

25 | Lieben brůder unnd schwestern: Wir / die da versamlet seind gewesen   A2r
im Herren / zů Schlaten am Randen miteynander in stůcken und artickeln /
Thůnd kůndt allen liebhabern Gotts / das wir vereynigt seind worden / so uns
betreffen in dem Herren zůhalten / als die gehorsamen Gottes kinder und sůn
und tôchtern / die da abgesündert seind / und sollen sein von der welt / inn
30 allweg thůn und lassen / und Got sei eynig preiß unnd lob / on aller brůder
widersprechen / gantz wol zůfriden / Inn solchem haben wir gespürt / die
eynigkeyt deß Vatters und unsers gemeynen Christi / mit jhrem Geyst / mit
uns gewesen sein / Dann der Herr ist der Herr des frides / und nit des
zangks / wie Paulus anzeygt / Das jhr aber verstanden in was artickeln solchs
35 gschehen sei / sollen jr mercken und verstan.

Es ist von ettlichen falschen brůdern under uns vast grosse ergernuß inge-
fůrt worden / das sich ettlich von dem glauben abgewendt haben / inn dem sie
vermeynt haben die freiheyt des geysts und Christi sich uben unnd brauchen /
Soliche aber haben gefelet der warheyt / und seind ergeben worden (zů jrem
40 urteyl) der geylheyt unnd freiheyt des fleyschs / unnd haben geachtet der
glaub und liebe můg es alles thůn und leiden / und jhnen nichts schaden noch
verdamlich sein / dieweil sie also glaubig seien.

Merckent jhr glider Gottes inn Christo Jesu / der Glaub an himmelischen
Vatter / durch Jesum Christum / ist nit also gestaltet / wircket unnd hanndelt
45 nitt solche ding / so dise falsche | brůder und schwestern handeln und leren /   A2v
hůten euch und seint gemanet vor sôlchen / dann sie dienen nitt unserm
Vatter / sonder jrem vatter dem Teuffel.

Aber ir nitt also / dann die da Christi sind / die haben ir fleysch gecreutziget mitsampt allen gelůsten und begirden / ir verstan mich wol und die
50 Brůder / welche wir meynen / Absunderet euch von jnen dann sie sind
verkert / Bittent den Herrn umb jre erkantnuß zůr bůß / und für uns umb
bestendigkeyt / den angrifnen weg fürzůwandlen nach der eer Gottes / und
seines Suns Christi / Amen.

---

29 die – welt] cfr II Cor. 6, 17   **33/34** Dann – anzeygt] cfr I Cor. 14, 33   **46/**
47 dann – Teuffel] cfr Ioh. 8, 41-44   **48/49** Aber – begirden] cfr Gal. 5, 24
50 Absunderet – jnen] cfr II Cor. 6, 17   **50/51** dann – verkert] cfr Tit. 3, 11

26 zů Schlaten am Randen] i.e. Schleitheim, situated between Randen and Wutach. The spelling in the original corresponds to the dialect expression of the toponym still in use today. Cfr E. Joos et al., *Die Orts- und Flurnamen des Kantons Schaffhausen: eingeschlossen die deutsche Enklave Büsingen*, 2 vols, Zürich 2018, vol. 2, p. 945

47 sonder] *a.c.* sonde   **50** welche] *a.c.* welhe   **51** für] *supplevi*

CONCILIUM IULIOMAGENSE – 1527

Die Artickel so wir gehandelt haben / und inn denen wir eyns worden
sind / sind dise

j. Tauff. ij. Bann. iij. Brechung des Brots. iiij. Absundrung von greweln. v.
Hirten inn der gemeyn. vj. Schwerdt. und der vij. Eyd.

Zum ersten / So merckent von dem Tauff. Der Tauff soll geben werden
allen denen so gelert sind die büß und endrung des lebens / unnd glauben in
der warheyt / dz ire sünd durch Christum hinweg genommen seien / und
allen denen / so wöllen wandlen in der uffersteeung Jesu Christi / und mit jm
begraben wöllen sein inn tod / uff das sie mit jm ufferstan mögen / und allen
denen so es in solcher meynung von uns begeren und fordern / durch sich
selbs / Mit dem werden außgeschlossen alle kinder tauff / des Bapsts höchsten
und ersten grewel. Solchs habt ir grundt | und zeugnus der schrifft und brauch   A3r
der Apostel Math. xxviij. Mar. xvj. Act. ij. viij. xvj. xix. Deß wölln wir uns eynfeltigklich / doch vestiglich halten und versichert sein.

Zum andern / Sind wir vereyniget worden von dem Bann / also: Der
Bann soll geprauucht werden mit allen denen / so sich dem Herrn ergeben
haben / nach zůwandeln in seinen gebotten und mit allen denen die in eynen
leib Christi getaufft sind worden / und sich lassen Brůder oder schwestern
nennen / und doch etwan entschlipffen und fallen in eynn fal und sünd / und
unwissenlich ubereilt werden / Die selben söllen vermant werden zů dem
andern mal heymlich / und zům dritten mal offenlich / vor aller gemeyn
gestrafft oder gebannt werden / nach dem bevelch unsers Christi. Mat. xviij.
Solchs aber sol gschehen nach ordnung des geysts Gottes vor dem brotbrechen / damit wir eynmütigklich und in eyner liebe von eynem brot brechen
und essen mügen / und von eynem kelch trincken.

Zům dritten / Inn dem brotbrechen sind wir eyns worden / und vereynbart: Alle die eyn brot brechen wöllen zů der gedechtnuß des brochnen leibs
Christi / Unnd alle die von eynem tranck trincken wöllen zů eyner gedechtnuß des vergoßnen blůts Christi / die sollen vorhin vereyniget sein / in eynen

---

66 Math. – xix] cfr Matth. 28, 19; Marc. 16, 16; Act. 2, 38; 8, 36-37; 16, 31-33; 19, 4-5
71/73 und – werden¹] cfr Gal. 6, 1   **75** Mat. xviij] cfr Matth. 18, 15-17   **81/**
83 Unnd – Christi] cfr I Cor. 10, 16-17

54/55 eyns – sind¹] vereingt sind worden, das *h¹*   **55** sind¹] *deest D¹*   **64/**
65 höchsten und ersten] höchste und erste *D¹*   **65** und² – und³] testimonium atque
robur scripturae *d¹*; zügnuß und grundt der gschrifft *h⁵*   **66** Deß] Deßelben *h¹*   **66/**
67 eynfeltigklich – halten] einfalticklich und doch festencklich behalten *h¹*
70 denen] *deest h¹*   **72** fal] *intellege* lapse, moral failure   **75** oder gebannt] *deest h¹*
unsers] *deest h¹ D¹*   **77** wir] wir all *h¹*   **79** und] und also *h¹*   **81** von eynem tranck]
de uno poculo *d¹*; von einem kelch tranck *h¹*. *Atramento erasus* kelch *in h¹*

80 CONCILIUM IULIOMAGENSE – 1527

leib Christi / das ist in die gemeyn Gottes / uff welchem Christus das haupt
ist / nemlich durch den Tauff / dan wie der Paulus anzeygt / so mügen wir nit
uff eynmal teylhafftig sein des Herrn tisch / und der teuffel tisch / wir mügen
auch nit uff eynmal teylhafftig sein und trincken von des Herrn kelch unnd
des teuffels | kelch / das ist / alle die gemeynschafft haben mit den todten A3v
wercken der finsternuß / die haben keyn teyl am liecht / also / alle die dem
teuffel volgen und der welt / die haben keyn teyl mit denen die zů Got auß der
welt berüffen seind / Alle die in dem argen ligen / die haben keyn teyl an dem
gůten.

Also auch sol und můß sein / Welcher nit hat die berüffung eynes Gots
zů eynem glauben / zů eynem tauff / zů eynem geyst / zů eynem leib / mit
allen kindern gottes gemeyn / der mag auch nitt mit jnen eyn brot gemacht
werden / wie dann sein můß / wa man das brot inn der warheyt / nach dem
bevelch Christi brechen wil.

Zům vierden / Seind wir vereynigt worden / von der absůnderung / Sol
geschehen von dem bösen und von dem argen / das der teuffel inn der welt
gepflantzt hat / also / alleyn das wir nit gemeynschafft mit jnen haben / und
mit jnen lauffen inn die gemenge jrer greweln / das ist also / Dieweil alle (die
nit getretten seind in die gehorsame des glaubens / und die sich nit vereyniget
haben mit Got / das sie seinen willen thůn wöllen) eyn grosser greuwel vor
Got seind / So kan und mag anders nit von jnen wachsen oder entspringen /
dann greuliche ding. Nun ist ie nichts anders in aller creatur / dann gůtz und
böses / glaubig und unglaubig / finsternuß und liecht / welt / und die auß der
welt seind / tempel gottes und die götzen / Christus und Belial / und keynes
mag mit dem andern teyl haben.

Nun ist uns auch das gebot deß Herren of|fenbar / inn welchem er uns A4r
heyßt abgesůndert sein und werden / von dem bösen / so wöll er unser Got
sein / und werden wir seine sůn und töchtern sein.

83/84 das[1] – anzeygt] cfr I Cor. 10, 21 **87/88** alle – finsternuß] cfr Eph. 5, 11 **92/93** Welcher – leib] cfr Eph. 4, 4-6 **95/96** wa – wil] cfr Matth. 26, 26-28 **100/101** die[2] – glaubens] cfr Rom. 1, 5 **104/107** Nun – haben] cfr II Cor. 6, 14-16 **108/110** Nun – sein[2]] cfr II Cor. 6, 17-18

83 welchem] an welcher *h[1]*; in qua *d[1]* **87** des teuffels] der tufflen *h[1]* die] die do *h[1]* **88/89** die[1] – welt] *deest d[1]* **90** die[2]] *deest h[1]* **94** gemeyn] *deest d[1]* **97** absůnderung] de defectione, separatione aut deviatione *d[1]* Sol] Die sol *h[1]* **100** inn die gemenge] in communicatione *d[1]* **101/102** die[2] – Got] quique nondum domino nomen dederunt *d[1]* **104** in aller creatur] in der welt und aller creatur *h[1]*

CONCILIUM IULIOMAGENSE – 1527

Weiter vermant er uns darumb von Babylon / und dem irdischen Egypto außzůgan / das wir nit auch teylhafftig werden jrer qual unnd leiden / so der Herr uber sie fůren wirt.

Auß dem allem sollen wir lernen / das alles was nit mit unserm Gott und Christo vereyniget ist / nichts anders sei dann die greuwel / welche wir meiden sollen und fliehen. Inn dem werden vermeynt alle Båpstliche und widerbåpstliche werck / unnd Gottes dienst / versamlung / kirchgang / weinheuser / bůrgerschafften / und verpflichtung des unglaubens / unnd andere mer der gleichen / die dan die welt für hoch halt / und doch stracks wider den bevelch Gottes gehandlet werden / nach der maß aller ungerechtigkeyt / die in der welt ist / Von disem allem sollen wir abgesůndert werden / und keyn teyl mit solchen haben / dann es seind eitel greuwel / die uns verhasset machen / vor unserem Christo Jesu / welcher uns entlediget hat / von der dienstbarkeyt des fleyschs / und uns geschickt gemacht dem dienst Gottes / durch den geyst / welchen er uns geben hat.

Also werden nun auch von uns ongezweifelt die unchristliche / auch teufelischen wafen des gewalts fallen / als da seind schwert / harnascht / | und dergleichen / und aller jrer prauch / für frůnde / oder wider die feind / in krafft des worts Christi / *Ir sollend dem ubel nit widerstan.*

Zům fünfften / Seind wir vereynigt worden von den Hirten in der gemeyn Gottes also: Der hirt in der gemeyn gottes sol eyner sein nach der ordenung Pauli / gantz unnd gar / der eyn gůt zeugnuß hab / von denen die ausser dem glauben seind / Solches ampt sol sein lesen / vermanen / und leren / manen / straffen / bannen / in der Gemeyn / unnd allen brůdern unnd schwesternn zůr besserung vorbetten / das brot anheben zůbrechen / und inn allen dingen des leibs Christi acht haben / das er gebawt und gebessert werd / und dem lesterer der mund werde verstopfft.

111/113 Weiter – wirt] cfr Apoc. 18, 4   **129** Matth. 5, 39   **131/132** Der – Pauli] cfr I Tim. 3, 7   **133/134** Solches – leren] cfr I Tim. 4, 13   **134** straffen – in] cfr I Tim. 5, 20

---

113 wirt] wil *h¹*   **116** und fliehen] *deest h¹*   **117** widerbåpstliche] *intellege* repopish (i.e. Protestant)   Gottes dienst] idolatriȩ *d¹*   **118** bůrgerschafften – verpflichtung] burgschaften und verpflichten *h¹*; civitas et foedera *d¹*   verpflichtung] civitatem hodie civilegium vocant *d¹ in marg.*   **120** Gottes] Christi *d¹*   **126/127** Also – fallen] In dem werden ouch fallen von uns die tufelischen waffen des gewaltzs *h¹*   **130** Seind – worden] statuimus *d¹*   **131** Der – sein] ut pastor sit de grege unus aliquis *d¹*   **133** lesen] lesen und *h¹*   **134** straffen] straffen oder *h¹*   **134/135** brůdern – vorbetten] schwestern und brůdern wol furstan im bett, im brottbrechen *h¹*   **136** werd] werd, darmitt der nam gottes durch uns geprisen und geeret werd *h¹*

82 CONCILIUM IULIOMAGENSE – 1527

Diser aber sol erhalten werden / wa er mangel haben wůrd / von der Gemeyn / welche jn erwelet hat / darmit welcher dem Evangelio dienet / auch
140 von dem selben lebe / wie der Herr geordnet hat.

So aber eyn Hirt etwas handlen wůrd / das zů straffen wer / sol mit jm nichts gehandelt werden on zwen oder drei zeugen / Und so sie sünden / sollen sie vor allen gestrafft werden / damit die andern forcht haben.

So aber diser Hirt vertriben / oder durch dz creutz dem Herren hingefůrt
145 wůrd / sol von stund an eyn anderer an die statt verordnet werden / damit das vólcklin und heufflin Gottes nit zerstórt werde.

Zům sechsten / Seind wir vereynigt worden von dem schwert / also / Das schwert ist eyn gottes ordenung ausserhalb der volkommenheyt Christi / welches den bósen strafft unnd tódtet / | und den gůten schützt und schirmt / A5r
150 In dem gesatz wirt das schwert geordnet / uber die bósen / zůr straff und zům tod / und dasselbig zůbrauchen seind geordnet die weltlichen oberkeyten.

Inn der volkommenheyt Christi aber wirt der Bann gebraucht / alleyn zů eyner manung und außschliessung des der gesündet hat / on tod deß fleyschs / alleyn durch die manung und den befelch nit mer zůsündigen.

155 Nun wirt gefraget von vilen / die nit erkennen den willen Christi gegen uns / Ob auch eyn christ móg oder solle das schwert brauchen gegen dem bósen umb deß gůten schutz und schirm willen / oder umb der liebe willen?

Antwurt ist geoffenbart eynmůtiglich also / Christus lert und bevilcht uns / das wir von jm lernen sollen / dann er sei milt / und von hertzen
160 demůtig / und so werden wir růw finden unser selen / Nun sagt Christus zům heydnischen weiblin / das im eebruch begriffen worden was / nit das man es versteynigen solt nach dem gesatzt seines vatters (und er doch sagt / *wie mir der vatter befolhen hat also thůn ich*) sonder der barmhertzigkeyt und verzei-

---

138/140 Diser – hat] cfr I Cor. 9, 14   **141/143** So – haben] cfr I Tim. 5, 19-20   **147/ 148** Das – ordenung] cfr Rom. 13, 2   **151** und – oberkeyten] cfr Rom. 13, 3-4   **158/ 160** Christus – selen] cfr Matth. 11, 29   **161/162** nit – vatters] cfr Leu. 20, 10   **162/ 163** Ioh. 5, 19

153 on tod deß fleyschs] meaning 'without killing the body'. However, 'ad interitum carnis' refers to I Cor. 5, 5, meaning 'for the destruction of the flesh'

139/140 auch – lebe] sol ouch darvon leben *h¹*   **140** geordnet] verordnet *D¹* **141** sol] so sol *h¹*   **142** zwen – zeugen] zweyer oder trier zugen mund *h¹*   Und] *deest h¹*   **144** durch – hingefůrt] aber dem herren durch das crutz heimgefůrt *h¹* **146** werde] werd, sunder durch die manung erhalten und getröst werd *h¹*   **152** Christi aber] aber Christi *h¹*   **153** on – fleyschs] ad interitum carnis *d¹*; sans mort corporelle *d³*   on] an *h¹*   **158** und bevilcht] *deest h¹*   **160** unser] unseren *h¹*   **161** heydnischen] *deest h¹ d¹*   worden] *deest h¹*   **163** also – ich] sic loquor *d¹*

CONCILIUM IULIOMAGENSE – 1527   83

hung / und manung nit mer zůsünden / und spricht / *gang hin und sünde nit*
165 *mer* / Sollichs sollen wir uns gentzlich auch halten / nach der regel des Banns.

Zům andern wirt gefragt des schwerts halben / Ob eyn Christ soll urteyl
sprechen in weltlichen zangk und spån / so die unglaubigen miteynnander
haben? Ist das die eynig antwurt: Christus hat nit wôllen entscheyden oder
urteylen zwischen brůder unnd brůder / des erbteyls halben / sonder hat sich
170 desselben gewidert / also | sollen wir jhm auch thůn.   A5v

Zům dritten / Wirt gefragt des schwerts halben / ob der christ solle eyn
oberkeyt sein / so eyner darzů erwelt wirt? Dem wirt also geantwurt: Christus
hat sollen gmacht werden zů eynem künig / und er ist geflohen / und hat nit
angesehen die ordenung seins vatters / also sollen wir jhm auch thůn / und jm
175 nachlauffen / so werden wir nit in der finsternuß wandlen / Dann er sagt
selbs / welcher nach mir komen wôl / der verleugne sich selbest / unnd nem
sein creutz uff sich und volg mir nach / Auch so verbeut er selbst den gewallt
des schwerts / und sagt: *Die weltlichen Fürsten herschen* etc. *Jr aber nitt also.*
Weiter sagt Paulus: *Welche Gott versehen hat / die hat er auch verordnet / das sy*
180 *gleichbertig sein sollen dem ebenbild seines suns* etc. Auch sagt Petrus: *Christus*
hat gelitten (nitt gherschet) *unnd hat uns eynn ebenbild gelassen / das jr solt*
nachvolgen seinen füßstapffen.

Zů letst wirt gemerckt / das es dem Christen nit mag zimen eyn oberkeyt
zů sein in den stůcken / Der oberkeyt regiment ist nach dem fleysch / so ist
185 der Christen nach dem geyst / Jr heuser unnd wonung ist bleiblich in diser
welt / so ist der Christen im himel / Jr bůrgerschafft ist in diser welt / So ist
der Christen bůrgerschafft im himel / Jres streits unnd kriegs waffen seind
fleyschlich / und alleyn wider das fleysch / Der Christen wafen aber seind
geystlich wider die bevestigung des teuffels / Die weltlichen werden gewapnet
190 mit stahel und eisen / Aber die Christen seind gewapnet mit dem harnascht

---

164/165 Ioh. 8, 11   **168/170** Christus – gewidert] cfr Luc. 12, 13-14   **172/**
173 Christus – geflohen] cfr Ioh. 6, 15   **174/175** also – wandlen] cfr Ioh. 8, 12   **175/**
177 Dann – nach] cfr Matth. 16, 24   **178** Matth. 20, 25-26   **179/180** Rom. 8, 29
180/182 I Petr. 2, 21   **186/187** Jr – himel] cfr Phil. 3, 20   **188/189** Der – teuffels]
cfr II Cor. 10, 4   **190/192** Aber – Gotts] cfr Eph. 6, 13-17

---

164 und³] *deest h¹*   **167** zangk] sachen, zang *h¹*   **168** eynig] *deest h¹*   **171** ob der
christ solle] *sicut in h¹ et d¹*; Sol das *D²*   **173** und er ist] do ist er *h¹*   **173/174** und² –
vatters] Forte mendum est, sed omnia exemplaria sic habebant *d¹* ⁱⁿ ᵐᵃʳᵍ·   **177** so] *deest*
h¹   **178** Jr aber nitt] aber ir nitt *h¹*   **179** versehen] zůvor versechen *h¹*   **181** ebenbild]
furbild *h¹*   **182** nachvolgen] sequamur *d¹*   **184** oberkeyt] obrer *D¹*   **184/185** so –
geyst] Christianus autem est secundum spiritum *d¹*   **185** bleiblich] corporalis *d¹*
186 Christen] Christianorum autem omnium *d¹*   **187** bůrgerschafft] *deest h¹* streits
unnd kriegs] *deest d¹*   **188** aber] *deest h¹*   **189** weltlichen] mundani magistratus *d¹*

84 CONCILIUM IULIOMAGENSE – 1527

Gottes / mit warheyt / gerechtigkeyt / fried / glauben / heyl / unnd | mit dem A6r
wort Gotts. Inn summa / Was Christus unser haupt uff uns gesinnet ist / das
alles sôllen die glider des leibs Christi durch jn gesinnet sein / damitt keyn
spaltung inn dem leib sei dardurch er zerstôret werde / dann eyn yegkliches
195 Reich das in jm selbs zertheylt ist / wirt zerstôrt werden. So nun Christus also
ist / wie von jm geschriben stehet / so mûssen die glider auch also sein / damit
sein leib gantz unnd eynig bleib / zû seiner selbs besserung und erbawung.

Zûm Sibenden / Sind wir vereyniget worden von dem Eyd / also. Der
Eyd ist eyn bevestigung under denen die da zancken / oder verheyssen / unnd
200 ist imm gesatz geheyssen wordenn / das er sôlle geschehenn bei dem namen
Gottes alleyn warhafftig und nit falsch. Christus der die volkommenheyt des
gesatz leret / der verbeut den seinen alles schweren / weder recht noch falsch
weder bei dem hymmel / noch bei dem erdtrich / noch bei Jerusalem / noch
bei unserm haupt / und das umb der ursach willen / wie er bald hernach
205 spricht: Dann ir mügen nitt eynn har weiß oder schwartz machen. Sehent zû /
darumb ist alles schweren verbotten / dann wir mûgen nit / das inn dem
schweren verheyssen wirt / erstattenn / dieweil wir das allermindst an unns /
nitt mügen endern.

Nun sind ettlich / die dem eynfeltigen gebott Gottes nitt glauben geben /
210 sunder sie sagen und fragen also: Ey nun hat Got dem Abraham geschwo-
renn / durch sichs selbs / dieweil er Gott was (da er jhm verhieß / das er jhm
wol wôlte / und wôlt sein Gott sein / so er seine gebott hielt) | / warumb solte A6v
ich dann nit auch schweren / so ich eynem etwas verhieß?

Antwurt / Hör was die schrifft sagt: Got da er wolt den erben der ver-
215 heyssung uberschwencklich beweisen / das sein rath nit wancket / hat er
eynen eyd darzwischen gelegt / auff dz wir durch zwey unwanckliche ding
(dardurch es unmûglich ist das Got liege) eynn starcken trost haben / Merck
den verstand diser geschrift / Gott hat gewalt zethûn / das er dir verbeut /
dann es ist jm alles mûglich / Got hat dem Abraham geschworen eynen eyd
220 (sagt die schrifft) darumb das er beweise / das sein radt nitt wanckt: das ist: Es

---

192/193 Inn – sein] cfr Phil. 2, 5   **193/194** damitt – sei] cfr I Cor. 12, 25   **194/**
195 dann – werden] cfr Matth. 12, 25   **198/201** Der – falsch] cfr Leu. 19, 12   **201/**
205 Christus – machen] cfr Matth. 5, 34-36   **210/212** Ey – hielt] cfr Gen. 26, 3
214/217 Got – haben] cfr Hebr. 6, 17-18   **218/219** Gott – mûglich] cfr Luc. 18, 27
219 Got – eyd] cfr Gen. 22, 16-18

---

191 gerechtigkeyt / fried] mit gerechtickeit, mit frid *h¹*   **194** dardurch] dar mit *h¹*
196 stehet] ist *h¹*   **200** ist] *deest h¹*   **202** der] *deest D¹*   **203/204** noch³ – haupt]
neque per nosipsos *d¹*   **204** bald] *deest h¹*   **206/207** nit – erstattenn] nut erstaten,
das in dem schweren verheissen wirt *h¹*   **210** sunder sie] die *h¹*   Ey] *deest h¹*
212 wôlt] *deest h¹*   **213** dann] *deest h¹*   **216/217** auff – haben] ut spem habeamus *d¹*

CONCILIUM IULIOMAGENSE – 1527

mocht jm niemant seinem willen widerstan und hinderen / und darumb
mocht er den eyd halten / Wir aber mûgen nichts wie droben von Christo
gesagt ist / dz wir den eyd halten oder leysten / Darumb sollen wir nichts
schweren.

Nun sagen ettlich weiter also / Es sei nitt bei Got verbotten zûschweren /
in dem neuwen Testament / unnd doch im alten gebottenn / sonder sei alleyn
bei dem himel / erdtrich / Jerusalem / und bei unserm haupt verbotten
zûschweren / Antwurt / Hôr die schrifft: *Wer da schweret bei dem himel / der
schweret bei dem stûl Gottes / unnd bei dem der drauff sitzt* / Merck / schweren
bei dem himel ist verbotten der nûr eyn stûl Gottes ist / wie vil mer ist verbotten bei Got selbs? Jr narren unnd blinden / was ist grôsser der stûl oder der
darauff sitzt?

Noch sagen etlich / wan nun das unrecht ist / wan man Got zû der warheyt praucht / so haben apostel / Petrus und Paulus auch gschworn. Ant-
wurt / Petrus und Paulus zeugen alleyn dz | welches von Got dem Abraham   A7r
durch den eyd verheyssen was / und sie selbs verheyssen nichts / als die exempel klar anzeygen / Zeugen aber und schweren ist zweyerley / Dann so man
schweret / so verheyßt man erst künfftige ding / wie dem Abrahe Christus
verheyssen ist worden / welchen wir lange zeyt hernach entpfangen haben /
So man aber Zeuget / so zeygt man an das gegenwertig / obs gût oder bôß sei /
wie der Simeon von Christo zû Maria sprach und zeuget: *Sihe diser wirt
gesetzt zû eynem fal und auffersteung viler in Israel / und zû eynem zeychen dem
widersprochen wirt.*

Dergleichen hat uns Christus auch geleret / da er sagt / *Euwer red sol sein
ja / ja / und neyn / neyn / dann was uber das ist / ist von argem.* Er sagt / euwer
red oder wort sol sein ja und neyn / Das man nit verstan wôlle / das er die

---

228/229 Matth. 23, 22   **231/232** Jr – sitzt] cfr Matth. 23, 17   **233/234** Noch –
gschworn] cfr Rom. 1, 9; II Cor. 1, 23; 11, 31; Phil. 1, 8   **237/239** Dann – worden] cfr
Gen. 22, 18   **241/243** Luc. 2, 34   **244/245** Matth. 5, 37   **246/247** Das – neyn] cfr
II Cor. 1, 19

---

221 und¹] *deest* h¹   **221/222** darumb – halten] ideo necesse fuit, ut iusiurandum
servaret d¹   **225** also] *deest* h¹   **225/226** Es – gebottenn] in novo testamento non esse
vetitum, ne per deum iuremus, sed in veteri d¹   **227** bei unserm haupt] *deest* d¹
228 himel] per templum aut coelum d¹   **233** etlich] etlich also h¹   **233/234** wan¹ –
gschworn] Si nephas est iurare, etiam cum dominicum nomen ad veritatem adsciscitur,
peccaverunt Petrus et Paulus apostoli: ipsi enim iurarunt d¹   **234** apostel] die apostel
h¹   **239** worden] *deest* h¹   lange zeyt] nach langer zit h¹   **240** obs – sei] ob es gût sig
oder bös h¹   **245** und] *deest* h¹   was] das h¹   **245/247** Er – habe] Sic monet
Christus 'sermo vester debet esse: non, non', ne sic velimus eum accipere, quasi
admiserit iurationem d¹   **246/247** die meynung] es h¹

86 CONCILIUM IULIOMAGENSE – 1527

meynung zůgelassen habe / Christus ist eynfeltig / ja und neyn / Und alle die
jhn eynfeltig sůchen / werden sein wort verstan / Amen.

250 Lieben brůder und schwestern in dem Herren / das seind die artickel /
die ettlich brůder bißher irrig und den waren verstand ungleich verstanden
haben / unnd damit vil schwacher gewissen verwirt / dardurch der nam Gottes gar größlich verlestert ist worden / Darumb dann not ist gewesen / das wir
vereyniget seind worden im Herren / Got sei lob und preiß / wie dann geschehen ist.

255 Nun / dieweil jr reichlich verstanden habent / den willen Gottes ietzmal
durch uns geoffenbart sein / wirt nodt sein / das jhr den erkanten | willen A7v
Gottes harrigklich / onabgeweltz volnbringen / Dann jhr wissent wol / Was
dem knecht zů lone hŏret / der da wissenlich sündet.

Alles was jhr unwissenlich gethan / unnd bekannt habent unrecht
260 gehandlet / das ist euch verzihen / durch das gelaubig gebett / welches inn uns
inn der versamlung verpracht ist / für unnser aller fǎl unnd schůldt / durch die
genedig verzeihung Gottes / und durch das blůt Jesu Christi / Amen.

Habent acht auff alle die nitt wandlen nach der eynfeltigkeyt Gŏttlicher
warheyt / die inn disem brieff begriffen ist / von uns inn der versamlung /
265 damitt iederman geregiret werd under uns durch die regel deß Banns / unnd
fürohin verhüt werde der falschen Brůder unnd schwestern zůgang under uns.

Sůndert ab von euch was bŏß ist / so wil der Herr ewer Gott sein / und
jhr werdent sein süne unnd tŏchter sein.

Lieben Brůder seind eingedenck was Paulus seinen Titum vermanet / Er
270 spricht also: *Die heylsam genad Gottes ist erschinen allen unnd zůchtiget uns /
das wir sollen verleugnen das ungŏtlich wesen / und die weltlichen lüste / und
zůchtig / gerecht / und gottselig leben inn diser welt / unnd warten auff die selbig
hoffnung und erscheinung der herlicheyt des grossen Gottes / unnd unsers heylan-
des Jesu Christi / der sich selb für uns geben hat / uff das er uns erlŏset / |* von aller A8r
275 *ungerechtigkeyt / und reyniget jm selb eyn volck zům eygenthum / daß da eiferig
were zů gůten wercken*: Das dencket / und sind des geůbet / so wirt der Herr
des frids mit euch sein.

257/258 Dann – sündet] cfr Matth. 24, 48-51   **265** regel – Banns] cfr Matth.
18, 15-17   **267/268** Sůndert – sein] cfr II Cor. 6, 17-18   **270/276** Tit. 2, 11-14   **276/
277** Das – sein] cfr Phil. 4, 9

248 werden – verstan] invenient eum d¹   **257** onabgeweltz] *intellege* unswervingly

Der nam Gottes sei ewig gebenedeit unnd hoch gelobet / Amen. Der
Herr geb euch seinen friden / Amen.

Acta Schlaten am Randen / auff Matthie / Anno MDXXvij.

---

280 auff Matthie] i.e. 24 February

DISPUTATIO ET DECEM THESES BERNENSES

1528

edidit
Pierrick HILDEBRAND

THE *TEN THESES* AND THE DISPUTATION OF BERN
1528

INTRODUCTION

The *Ten Theses* of Bern, or *Schlussreden*, were composed by Franz Kolb (1465-1535) and Berthold Haller (1492-1536), both ministers at the Bern Minister, to be discussed in the city in 1528. ([1]) Not meant to be original, the *Theses* reflected the Swiss and Upper-German Reformed theological consensus that had Zurich as its epicentre. Their dependence on Johann Commander's (1484-1557) *Ilanz Theses* ([2]) and Stephan Stör's († 1529) *Basel Theses*, ([3]) which can themselves be traced back to Zwingli's statements, is evident. ([4]) Even on a more formal level, such a non-academic and civic disputation on ecclesiastical issues was modelled upon Zwingli's invention of the Zurich disputations of 1523. ([5]) As Locher argued, 'the Bern Disputation became the most powerful demonstration of Protestantism before the Diet of Augsburg of 1530 and the climax of early Zwinglianism'. ([6]) The immediate impetus eventually leading to the Disputation was a chaplain's refusal to celebrate Mass and the petition of the canons to the city council for legitimisation. The guilds sympathetic to the evangelical cause ceased making their donations to the Church and requested that the theological conflict be clarified by means of a disputa-

---

(1) My thanks go to Silvianne Bürki for her preparatory work under the supervision of Professor Peter Opitz.

(2) For a modern edition of the *Ilanz Theses*, see J. F. Goeters, 'Ilanzer Schlussreden von 1526', in *RefBK*, vol. 1/1 (2002), p. 173-179.

(3) For the *Basel Theses*, see S. Stör, *Von der Priester Ee Disputation durch Stephanum Stör von Diessenhoffen* [...], Basel 1524. For a translation in modern German, see E. Stähelin, *Das Buch der Basler Reformation. Zu ihrem vierhundertjährigen Jubiläum im Ramen der evangelischen Kirchen von Stadt und Landschaft Basel*, Basel 1929, p. 82-83, no. 25.

(4) See Schuhmann, 'Die "große" Disputation zu Bern', p. 210-215; Locher, 'Die Stimme des Hirten', p. 113-115; Locher, 'Von der Standhaftigkeit', p. 38, note 8.

(5) Cfr. Moeller, *Zwinglis Disputationen*, p. 37. See further Flückiger, *Dire le vrai*, p. 84 ff.

(6) Locher, 'Die Berner Disputation', p. 140.

tion. (⁷) On 15 November 1527, the city council of Bern consented to a disputation to be held on 5 January 1528. Two days later, invitations were sent off to print along with the *Ten Theses*.

This circumstance in Bern, however, must be put in a wider context, as the character of the 1528 Disputation was not merely local. The city council, through its invitation, hoped that 'with God's help and grace the [Swiss] Confederation [...] could also be brought to the unity of true Christian faith and upright worship'. The town magistrates added that it should take place 'regardless of the disputation held in Baden in Aargau'. (⁸) Part of the purpose of the Bern Disputation of 1528, in fact, was to undo what had taken place in Baden two years earlier. (⁹) Called by the Swiss Diet (*Tagsatzung*), the Baden Disputation had been spearheaded by Jan Eck. The event had resulted in the condemnation of Zwingli in terms similar to those experienced by Luther at the Diet of Worms. Zurich was left politically isolated within the Confederation. Bern had sent Haller and Peter Kunz (*c.* 1480-1544), two prominent evangelicals, as delegates to represent what was still – at least officially – a Roman Catholic Confederate. By the *Tagsatzung* of 1526, (¹⁰) Bern had become suspect in the eyes of the party dominated by the other Roman Catholic Lands (*Orte*). The *Tagsatzung* did not allow Bern to consult the original proceedings of the disputation before they were printed. As a result, Bern did not acknowledge the outcome of the disputation. The Bernese, traditionally promoting cohesion among the Confederates, were also offended by their harshness against Zurich. The most powerful city-state of the Confederation could still be won over to the Reformation and become a significant ally of Zurich. Since the early 1520s, the city council of Bern had had to deal with increasing support toward Zwinglian doctrines. By Easter 1527, the evangelicals had won the majority in the Grand Council, which elected the Small Council a year later. The implementation of the Reformation in Bern was only a matter of time.

The author of the announcement must have been the city clerk Peter Cyro (1498-1564), who is considered the 'actual reformer of Bern' (¹¹) behind

---

(7) Berchtold Haller to Ulrich Zwingli, 4 November 1527, in *CR*, vol. 96 (1925), p. 291-292, no. 664; the same to the same, 19 November [1527], *ibid.*, p. 307, no. 667a.

(8) *Aktensammlung zur Geschichte der Berner-Reformation 1521-1532*, hrsg. R. Steck – G. Tobler, 2 vols, Bern 1918-1923, vol. 1 (1918), p. 519.

(9) Cfr. Hendricks, 'Some Observations'; Backus, *Neutralizing the Early Church*, p. 122.

(10) Locher argued for an 'ingeniously-set trap' for both ('Die Berner Disputation', p. 138).

(11) Locher, 'Die Berner Disputation', p. 139.

the scenes. With the help of the city guilds, Cyro managed to persuade a cautious Small Council to hold the disputation. The bishops of Constance, Basel, Sion and Lausanne were summoned under threat of being dispossessed of their rights to Bernese territory if they did not attend the disputation. All ministers serving in Bernese parishes, both in town and in the countryside, were likewise summoned under threat of losing their benefices if they did not appear. The latter came, whereas the former did not. The Swiss *Orte* and several cities of southern Germany were also warmly invited to participate in the disputation. Eight Lands, however, declined the invitation referring to Baden and denied any right of way on their territories. The most important delegation arrived under military escort from Zurich with Zwingli and over seventy ministers or councillors. (12) Many German cities accepted the invitation as well. Prominent figures on the evangelical side included Johannes Oecolampadius (1482-1531) from Basel, Joachim Vadian (1484-1551), and Benedict Burgauer (1494-1576) from St Gallen, Ambrosius Blaurer (1492-1564) from Constance, Wolfgang Capito (1478-1541) and Martin Bucer (1491-1551) from Strasbourg, and Andreas Althamer (1500-1539) from Nurnberg.

The Roman Catholic side was represented, among others, by the Dominican friar Alexius Grat from Bern, the Augustinian monk Conrad Träger (*c.* 1480-1543) from Freiburg im Breisgau, Johannes Buchstab (*c.* 1499-1528) from Zofingen, Gilg Murer from Rapperswil and Theobald Huter from Appenzell. Charles V's summoning letter, which was intended to cancel the disputation, arrived 'too late', according to Bern's official response. (13) Unlike in Baden, the announcement stated that 'no other writing than both New and Old Testament, which are called biblical and are God's word, is allowed and should prevail'. (14) The guiding hermeneutical principle was to be *Scriptura sui ipsius interpres*. The *Ten Theses* were attached to the invitation letters, so that every disputant could prepare for the meeting.

At Haller's request the council accepted the announcement and the *Ten Theses* were printed in Zurich by Christoph Froschauer. Haller sent Zwingli both documents on 19 November 1527 with the printing commission, and asked: 'I beg you, that you might faithfully leave, alter, improve, augment or remove from the theses including the title, that which seems best to you'. (15) Zwingli, however, did not make any changes to the text. In Zurich, both a

---

(12) Wuhrmann, 'Die Zürcher Teilnehmer', p. 451-455.

(13) Cfr. Steck – Tobler, *Aktensammlung*, vol. 1 (1918), p. 384, no. 1453. For Charles V's letter, see p. 558, no. 1427.

(14) Steck – Tobler, *Aktensammlung*, vol. 1 (1918), p. 519.

(15) Berchtold Haller to Ulrich Zwingli, 19 November [1527], in *CR*, vol. 96 (1925), p. 309, no. 667a.

94   DISPUTATIO ET DECEM THESES BERNENSES – 1528

booklet including the announcement and the *Ten Theses* and 100 separate copies of the *Theses* were printed. Zwingli, at Haller's request, translated the *Ten Theses* into Latin for the 'Welsch'. (16) Later, Guillaume Farel translated the *Theses* into French from the Latin. (17) The exact number of printed copies remains unclear. (18) Haller, who had received his copies on 2 December 1527, spotted a slight mistake in the German version. The Latin version, however, was 'rectissime' printed. (19)

The first thesis, which is a nearly verbatim quote from Zwingli's 1524 letter to the bishop of Constance, (20) basically stated that the *solus Christus* and *sola Scriptura* were two sides of the same coin (against the Roman Catholic implicit *sola Ecclesia*). This first thesis was the ground for the following ones, especially the second and the third. The second thesis stated that ordinances grounded in God's Word stood against human, i.e. ecclesiastical, ones. The third thesis affirmed the sufficiency of Christ's work of redemption apart from any human merit. The fourth and fifth theses concerned the Mass, while the following three theses referred to the cult of the saints, the purgatory and the cult of images respectively. The last two theses rejected clerical celibacy. Theses 4 to 8 formed polemical responses to Eck's *Baden Theses*. (21)

The Bern Disputation began on 6 January and ended on 26 January 1528. Herald Niklaus Manuel (1484-1530) – who campaigned for the Reformation

(16) For a different view, see W. H. Neuser, 'Berner Thesen von 1528', in *RefBK*, vol. 1/1 (2002), p. 198.

(17) See Steck – Tobler, *Aktensammlung*, vol. 1 (1918), p. 524-525, no. 1372.

(18) Fluri referred to an argument by Gottlieb Emanuel von Haller (1735-1786), which is no longer verifiable. Haller reported that 400 copies of the booklet and 100 separate copies of the *Ten Theses* were printed in Zurich, and his statement seemed to imply 100 copies in early modern German and 100 in Latin, thus totalling 200 copies. Cfr. G. E. von Haller, *Bibliothek der Schweizer-Geschichte und aller Theile, so dahin Bezug haben* [...], 7 vols, Bern 1785-1788, vol. 3 (1786), p. 115, no. 313; Fluri, *Die Beziehungen Berns*, p. 29-30.

(19) Berchtold Haller to Ulrich Zwingli, 2 December [1527], in *CR*, vol. 96 (1925), p. 319, no. 672. However, there is a second error which must have been noticed only later on: one word ('und' resp. 'et', see the edition below) is deleted with ink in both versions.

(20) Ulrich Zwingli, *Christliche Antwort Zürichs an Bischof Hugo*, in *CR*, vol. 90 (1914), p. 168, no. 37: 'Das ist die christenlich kilch, die gottes wort einigen loset, und sich das allein fueren und wysen laßt, als Christus Jo. 10. [1-16] eigenlich lert under der glychnuß des hirten und der schaffen: das die schaff den frömbden nit nachvolgend, ouch ir stimm nit erkennend, sunder allein dem rechten hirten'. See also Karl Barth's reception in the first thesis of the *Barmen Declaration* of 1934 (ed. Fulvio Ferrario, in *COGD* VI.2, forthcoming).

(21) Cfr. Hendricks, 'Some Observations', p. 574-575.

with Haller and later became a member of Bern council – took care that there was strict impartiality. The Disputation was presided by Vadian, Niklaus Briefer (1484-1548) from Basel, Abbot Konrad Schilling and Commander Conrad Schmid. The speakers were allowed to use written notes. There were numerous recorded votes at the sessions, although some could be deleted afterwards by common consent. Over 650 votes took place, with 330 coming from the Reformed, 236 from the Catholics, and 72 from the Lutherans. On the first thesis alone there were 210 votes, and it took twelve and a half days to debate the hotly-contested first four theses. The latter six were dealt with more briefly. The fourth thesis, concerning Christ's presence in the Lord's Supper, was the most fiercely debated, taking almost a week. In the debate, Zwingli played a prominent role and there was considerable division between the Reformed and the Lutherans. The Bern ministers were summoned before the city council on 13 January to give their view of the *Ten Theses*. Forty-six rejected them. During the disputation, several prominent evangelical ministers, including Zwingli, preached to the common people.

The Bern Disputation did not end with any formal decision of the city council. However, a public consultation took place, and on 2 February 1528 the town population took an oath of allegiance to the council's authority in secular and religious matters. On 7 February, the city council promulgated a *Reformationsmandat* stating that the *Ten Theses* were 'grounded in divine Scripture', (22) and that if any minister of the Church failed to implement them or preached against them, he would lose his benefices. The *Ten Theses* were granted the status of a Church Council decision. In the 1946 constitution of the Reformed Church of Bern, the *Ten Theses* are deemed the 'historical foundations' of the Bernese Church, along with the *Reformationsmandat* and the 1532 Synod.

Notes on the Critical Edition

Our edition of the *Ten Theses* is based upon one of the 100 separate copies in Latin printed in Zurich in 1527 by Froschauer. The text is located in the Staatsarchiv Bern with the following signature: A V 1444: 73. (23) It consists of one 23 × 16.15 cm page containing 35 lines. The Latin text is based on the same source used in the edition of the *Reformierte Bekenntnisschriften* (*RefBK*), where it is together with the original early modern German, which is

---

(22) Steck – Tobler, *Aktensammlung*, vol. 1 (1918), p. 630, no. 1513.
(23) The Latin copy is to be found, alongside the early modern German version, in Peter Cyro's handwritten proceedings of the Disputation.

also based on one of the 100 separate copies from 1527 ([24]). The early modern German copy printed together with the announcement for the booklet is also still available (either the announcement or the *Ten Theses*, not as a booklet anymore) at the Staatscharchiv and the Burgerblibliothek, both in Bern ([25]). The *Ten Theses of Bern* are also available in a modern German ([26]) and in an English ([27]) translation. The proceedings of the Bern Disputation have never been edited as a whole so far. Fragments can nonetheless be consulted in the critical editions of Zwingli's and Bucer's works ([28]). The four handwritten, original records and two early imprints in-quarto and in-octavo of March 1528 are held in the Staatsarchiv Bern ([29]).

Our edition applies the following editorial guidelines. The wording of the source (including capitalisation) is reproduced faithfully, with punctuation following modern usage. Numerals also follow the source. The letters *u/v* are normalized in accordance with phonetics, and *j* is always recorded as *i*. E-caudata is resolved as *ae*, & as *et*. Ligatures (e.g. æ/ae), contractions (e.g. q̄/*quam*) and tildes (e.g. m̄/*mm*) have been expanded and abbreviations resolved without any specific note. Other diacritical signs have been silently ignored.

[24] Neuser, 'Berner Thesen von 1528', p. 203-205. The Latin edition contains some errors of transcription.

[25] For detailed bibliographic information, see Neuser, 'Berner Thesen von 1528', p. 199-200.

[26] See 'Die zehn Thesen, 17. November 1527', übers. E. Saxer, in M. Sallmann – M. Zeindler (hrsg.), *Dokumente der Berner Reformation. Disputationsthesen. Reformationsmandat. Synodus*, Zürich 2013, p. 39-41.

[27] 'The Ten Conclusions of Berne (1528)', in P. A. Lillback – R. B. Gaffin Jr (eds), *Thy Word is still Truth. Essential Writings on the Doctrine of Scripture from the Reformation to Today*, Philadelphia 2013, p. 98-101.

[28] *Voten Zwinglis an der Berner Disputation. 6. bis 25. Januar 1528*, in *CR*, vol. 93/1 (1961), p. 243-568, no. 113; 'Die Berner Disputation (1528)', in R. Stupperich et al. (hrsg.), *Martin Bucers Deutsche Schriften*, 15 vols, Guterslöh – Paris 1960-2015, vol. 4 (1975), p. 37-154.

[29] For detailed bibliographic information, see Neuser, 'Die Berner Disputation 1528: Einleitung', p. 25-27.

BIBLIOGRAPHY

SOURCES

W. H. Neuser, 'Berner Thesen von 1528', in E. Busch, H. Faulenbach et al. (hrsg.), *RefBK*, vol. 1/1 (2002), p. 203-205.

Staatsarchiv Bern, A V 1444: 73.

LITERATURE (AND ITS ABBREVIATIONS)

I. Backus, *The Disputations of Baden, 1526 and Berne, 1528: Neutralizing the Early Church* (*Studies in Reformed Theology and History* 1/1), Princeton 1993 [= Backus, *Neutralizing the Early Church*].

F. Flückiger, *Dire le vrai. Une histoire de la dispute religieuse au début du XVIᵉ siècle*, Neuchâtel 2018 [= Flückiger, *Dire le vrai*].

A. Fluri, *Die Beziehungen Berns zu den Buchdruckern in Basel, Zürich und Genf 1476-1536*, Bern 1913 [= Fluri, *Die Beziehungen Berns*].

K. Guggisberg, *Bernische Kirchengeschichte*, Bern 1958, p. 101-115.

D. L. Hendricks, 'The Bern Disputation: Some Observations', *Zwingliana* 14/10 (1978), p. 565-575 [= Hendricks, 'Some Observations'].

E. Koch, 'Ein unbekanntes Autograph Zwinglis zur Berner Disputation', *Zwingliana* 14/10 (1978), p. 576-580.

I. Leuschner, 'Berchtold Haller an den Disputationen von Baden (1526) und Bern (1528)', in D. Hasler (hrsg.), *Berchtold Haller 1494-1536*, Bern 1994, p. 30-33.

K. Lindt, 'Der theologische Gehalt der Berner Disputation', in Evangelisch-reformierter Synodalrat des Kantons Bern (hrsg.), *Gedenkschrift zur Vierjahrhundertfeier der Bernischen Kirchenreformation*, 2 vols, Bern 1928, vol. 1, p. 303-344.

G. W. Locher, 'Die Berner Disputation 1528', in Historischer Verein des Kantons Bern (hrsg.), *450 Jahre Berner Reformation: Beiträge zur Geschichte der Berner Reformation und zu Niklaus Manuel*, Bern 1980, p. 138-153 [= Locher, 'Die Berner Disputation'].

—, 'Die Berner Disputation 1528: Charakter, Verlauf und theologischer Gehalt', *Zwingliana* 14/10 (1978), p. 542-564.

—, 'Die Stimme des Hirten', in O. Farner (hrsg.), *Erinnerungen*, Zürich 1954, p. 111-115 [= Locher, 'Die Stimme des Hirten'].

—, 'Von der Standhaftigkeit. Zwinglis Schlusspredigt an der Berner Disputation als Beitrag zu seiner Ethik', in U. Neuenschwander – R. Dellsperger (hrsg.), *Humanität und Glaube. Gedenkschrift für Kurt Guggisberg*, Bern 1973, p. 29-41 [= Locher, 'Von der Standhaftigkeit'].

B. Moeller, *Zwinglis Disputationen. Studien zur Kirchengründung in den Städten der frühen Reformation*, Göttingen ²2011 [= Moeller, *Zwinglis Disputationen*].

L. von Muralt, 'Zwinglis Mitwirkung an der Berner Disputation: Einführung', in *CR*, vol. 93 (1961), p. 203-225.

W. H. Neuser, 'Die Berner Disputation 1528: Einleitung', in R. Stupperich et al. (hrsg.), *Martin Bucers Deutsche Schriften*, 15 vols, Gutersslöh – Paris 1960-2015, vol. 4 (1975), p. 17-30 [= Neuser, 'Die Berner Disputation 1528: Einleitung'].

G. Schuhmann, 'Die "große" Disputation zu Bern', *Zeitschrift für schweizerische Kirchengeschichte / Revue d'histoire ecclésiastique suisse* 3 (1909), p. 81-101; 210-215; 241-274 [= Schuhmann, 'Die "große" Disputation zu Bern'].

W. Wuhrmann, 'Die Zürcher Teilnehmer an der Berner Disputation im Januar 1528', *Zwingliana* 2/15 (1912), p. 451-455 [= Wuhrmann, 'Die Zürcher Teilnehmer'].

MONITUM

Staatsarchiv Bern, A V 1444: 73.

DISPUTATIO ET DECEM THESES BERNENSES
1528

AD SEQUENTIA SIVE AXIOMATA SIVE CONCLUSIONES
RESPONDEBIMUS, BERTOLDUS HALLER ET FRANCISCUS
KOLB EVANGELII APUD BERNAM MINISTRI CUM ALIIS EVAN-
GELII PROFESSORIBUS, OMNIRATIONEM POSTULANTI EX
5 SCRIPTURA SACRA, HOC EST BIBLICA VETERIS AC NOVI TES-
TAMENTI, AD CONSTITUTUM BERNAM DIEM, DOMINICUM
SCILICET, QUI PROXIMUS ERIT A CIRCUMCISIONE ANNI
M.D.XXVIII.

I

10   Sancta ecclesia catholica, cuius unicum caput Christus est, ex verbo Dei
nata est, in quo et permanet, nec ullius alieni vocem audit.

II

Ecclesia Christi non condit leges aut statuta praeter verbum Dei. Quo fit,
ut omnes humanae constitutiones, quae a nobis ecclesiae praecepta vocantur,
15 conscientias nostras non aliter alligent, quam quatenus in verbo Dei fundatae
aut praeceptae sunt.

III

Christus solus est sapientia nostra, iusticia, redemptio et precium pro
totius mundi peccatis. Quo fit, ut qui vel aliud meritum, quo beatitudo paria-
20 tur, vel aliam satisfactionem pro peccatis agnoscant, Christum negent.

IIII

Quod corpus et sanguis Christi per essentiam corporalem in pane gratia-
rumactionis edatur, scriptura biblica probari nullo modo potest.

---

10 Sancta – est] cfr Eph. 4, 15   **10/11** ex – audit] cfr Ioh. 10, 5

V

25 Missa, quomodo hodie habet, quasi Christus in ea Deo patri pro peccatis vivorum ac mortuorum offeratur, pugnat cum sacra scriptura et in sanctissimam oblationem, puta passionem et mortem Christi, blasphemia est atque propter abusus huiusmodi abominatio coram Deo.

VI

30 Sicut Christus solus pro nobis mortuus est, ita solus mediator et advocatus inter Deum et patrem atque nos fideles invocari debet. Quo fit, ut omnes alii mediatores et advocati, qui extra hoc saeculum invocantur praeter scripturae biblicae fundamentum, abdicati sint.

VII

35 Extra hoc saeculum emendatorius vel purgatorius ignis nullus in scriptura biblica invenitur. Quo fit, ut omnia obsequia mortuorum, puta vigiliae, missae pro defunctis, remedia, septimi, tricesimi, anniversarii, lampades, faces atque id genus alia inania sint.

VIII

40 Imagines facere ut ad cultum prostent, pugnat contra verbum Dei veteris ac novi testamenti. Quo fit, ut ubicunque sic prostitutae sint, ut periculum sit ne adorentur, abolendae sint.

IX

A sacro connubio in divinis literis nulli sive ordini sive statui interdictum 45 est, sed a scortatione et meritricatu omni omnium ordini.

30/31 Sicut – debet] cfr I Tim. 2, 5   **40/41** Imagines – testamenti] cfr Ex. 20, 4; Deut. 4, 15-19; 5, 8-10; Rom. 1, 23-25; Apoc. 14, 9-10   **44/45** A – ordini] cfr Ex. 20, 14; Deut. 5, 18; I Cor. 6, 13 et 18; Eph. 5, 3; Col. 3, 5; I Thess. 4, 3-5

31 et] *atramento erasus*

X

Cum ergo publicus scortator vi scripturae in excommunicationem vere incidat, fit, quod scortatio et meritricatus nulli ordini sit detrimentosior quam sacerdotali. Id autem propter offensionem.

Cuncta in gloriam Dei et sacrosancti verbi eius.

47/48 Cum – incidat] cfr I Cor. 5, 1-5 et 9-13

CONCILIUM AUGUSTANUM

1530

edidit
Kirsi I. STJERNA

THE *AUGSBURG CONFESSION*
1530

The *Augsburg Confession* (1530) continues to hold together the Lutheran tradition, both historically and theologically. ([1]) With the *sola scriptura* principle, Lutheran theology upholds the priority and authority of the Holy Scriptures in matters of faith. For their interpretation, the *Augsburg Confession* stands as the primary guide and lens. This pertains both to theological discourse – inter-Lutheran and ecumenical as well as inter-faith – and to the organisation of the practicing faith communities which call themselves Lutheran. ([2]) The weight of the *Augsburg Confession* was debated and clarified already at the initial stages of the Lutheran tradition. Its pivotal position was articulated in the *Book of Concord* (1580), ([3]) the foundational collection of the confessional texts that have offered a broad grounding for that particular expression of the Christian faith which has come to be known and recognised as the Lutheran theology and ministry. ([4])

Composed at a time when different evangelical congregations needed to come together or face the possibility of becoming dispersed if not eradicated, in the vulnerable period when the fate of the Reformation was far from settled, the *Augsburg Confession* demonstrates the early Lutherans' struggle

---

([1]) Gritsch, *Fortress Introduction to Lutheranism*, especially chapters 1-6, is a helpful overview of the Lutheran movement from Martin Luther to global Lutheranism, with discussion of topics and sources in Lutheran confessional discourse. See also Lohrmann, *Living Stones* and Kolb – Nestingen, *Sources and Context of the Book of Concord*.

([2]) See *History and Theology of The Book of Concord*. For a theological assessment of the parameters of a particularly Lutheran orientation with confessions and contemporary issues, see Stjerna, *Lutheran Theology*.

([3]) The *Book of Concord* includes the ecumenical creeds, the *Augsburg Confession* and its *Apology* by Philip Melanchthon (1531), Martin Luther's *Small Catechism* and *Large Catechism* (1529), the *Schmalkalden Articles* (1538), Melanchthon's *Treatise on the Power and Primacy of the Papacy* (1537), and the *Formula of Concord* (1577) in its two parts, the *Epitome* and the *Solid Declaration*. Cfr *Concilium Saxonicum 1577*, ed. Dingel – Hund, in *COGD* VI.1.2, p. 793-893.

([4]) The most recent critical edition of the German and Latin texts is Dingel, 'Die Konkordienformel'. For a critical edition in English, see Kolb – Wengert, *The Book of Concord*. Moreover, *The Annotated Luther* includes the *Schmalkalden Articles* and both the *Small* and *Large Catechism*.

with, and commitment towards, if not unity at least an amicable agreement on the matters at stake. In political terms, a unified front among the debating evangelicals was a matter of survival; theologically, specificity regarding the parameters of Lutheran orientation and praxis allowed for a distinction from both the Roman Catholic Church and other emerging Protestant streams (such as the Swiss Reformation). It had become clear from the visitations which the Saxon reformers organised to evangelical parishes that uniformity and education in matters of faith were urgently needed. (5) Under the cloud of the Diet of Speyer (1529) and the Holy Roman Emperor's ambition to bring the Reformation to an end, the *Augsburg Confession* – along with Martin Luther's *Small* and *Large Catechism* – embodied the need for a clear definition of the evangelical theological positions. The words 'confession', 'catechism', and 'concord' expressed Luther's associates' boldness in standing for their convictions at their own peril, along with their vision of the vitality of the teaching of the Christian faith and their efforts to find unity amidst diversity: in this spirit, notably, the early Lutheran confessions were built upon the ancient ecumenical creeds. (6)

The text of the *Augsburg Confession* was originally prepared with a view to, and presented at, the Diet of Augsburg. After meeting with Pope Clement VII in Bologna, and committed to squashing the nascent Reformation once and for all, on 21 January 1530 Emperor Charles V summoned the Diet of Augsburg for June of the same year. Charles' motivations included recruiting support in his potential war against the Ottomans – who had managed to besiege Vienna in 1529 – and securing his position in the German-speaking lands. (7) While not at all in favour of Luther's suggestions, the Emperor was aware of the need for sweeping reform in the life of the Church. Evangelicals, on the other hand, harboured hopes of making a clear case before the ruling princes and the Emperor. Under the protection of Prince-Elector John of Saxony, a team of theologians, spearheaded by Martin Luther and Philip Melanchthon, had collaborated on documents identifying the areas where reform was most needed. As an outlaw, Luther could not attend the

---

(5) Under the rule of the Prince-Elector John of Saxony, visitations prompted Melanchthon to write his *Instructions by the Visitors* along with Luther and Johan Bugenhagen. See Kolb – Wengert, *The Book of Concord*, p. 27.

(6) On the history and significance of the Lutheran confessions, see among others Gaßmann – Hendrix, *Lutheran Confessions*; Lohrmann, *The Book of Harmony*; Braaten, *Principles of Lutheran Theology*. See also *History and Theology of the Book of Concord*; Grane, *The Augsburg Confession*; Hendrix, *Recultivating the Vineyard*.

(7) On the background, writing, presentation, and publication of the text, see Seebaß – Leppin, 'Die Confessio Augustana', p. 65-83.

CONCILIUM AUGUSTANUM – 1530

Diet and was forced to remain in the nearby castle of Coburg, while Melanchthon travelled to the Diet, ready to argue for reform with the *Torgau Articles*. (8) Composed during a meeting in the castle of Torgau, these articles addressed a variety of human ordinances, the sacraments – with a particular focus on the Lord's Supper and the Lutheran teaching of Christ's real presence – clerical marriage and celibacy, the vows, the ordination of the clergy, the practice of confession and penance, the communion of the saints, the language of liturgy, and issues of ecclesiastical authority and jurisdiction. (9)

However, the *Torgau Articles* alone proved insufficient to counter the anti-evangelical propaganda promulgated by one of Luther's most dogged opponents, Johann Eck from the University of Ingolstadt. His *Four Hundred Four Propositions*, among other things, cunningly misrepresented evangelical theologians as Antitrinitarians associated with the Anabaptist movement and as blasphemers of the Lord's Supper. (10) Other working documents served Melanchthon in his hurried task to build an explicitly confessional document. By offering a concise corrective to false and un-Scriptural teachings, Melanchthon hoped to avoid a permanent fragmentation and offered evidence of the reformers' catholic faith and benign aspirations. (11) The *Articles of Schwabach* (1529), written for the league of evangelical princes, (12) the

(8) Melanchthon and the Saxon theologians arrived in Augsburg on 2 May, followed by the delegation from Hesse on 12 May (Seebaß – Leppin, 'Die Confessio Augustana', p. 66).

(9) For the text of the *Torgau Articles*, see Förstemann, *Urkundenbuch*, vol. 1 (1833), p. 68-84. An English translation based on this edition can be found in Kolb – Nestingen, *Sources and Context of the Book of Concord*, p. 93-104.

(10) An English translation of Eck's *Four Hundred Four Articles* is in Kolb – Nestingen, *Sources and Context of the Book of Concord*, p. 31-82.

(11) With their intention to prove their catholic faith, evangelicals wanted to prove that they were teaching and believing in the orthodox tradition of the Church Fathers and the ecumenical creeds, not changing anything in the teachings and practices of the Church: they wanted to reform what was not working from their point of view and purge the Church from what they considered harmful, thus steering the Church back to the teachings of the early Church and the Holy Scriptures.

(12) The *Schwabach Articles* were written for the Lutheran alliance poised to answer with arms the Edict of Speyer (1529) which tried to force their return to the Roman Catholic fold. Luther and Melanchthon, along with John of Saxony, had insisted on a confessional agreement which was eventually reached with the seventeen articles. These later served as the foundation for the colloquy of Marburg in autumn. The *Schwabach Articles* clarify Luther's doctrinal positions and were instrumental for Melanchthon in the drafting of the *Augsburg Confession*. For an English translation, see Kolb – Nestingen, *Sources and Context of the Book of Concord*, p. 83-87.

Marburg Articles, ([13]) written in the same year after Luther's notorious encounter with Huldrych Zwingli, ([14]) and Luther's *Confession Concerning Christ's Supper* (1528) laid the foundation for the twenty-eight articles of the *Augsburg Confession.* The first twenty-one doctrinal articles were complemented with seven additional – and longer – articles which expounded the rationale for religious reform. This was, in many ways, pragmatic in nature: Melanchthon's and the Saxon theologians' experience of parish visitations, encapsulated in the document entitled *Instructions by the Visitors,* along with several lingering doctrinal and practical questions, steered the writing of a confession which could serve multiple purposes. The original text of the *Augsburg Confession,* drafted in German, bore the signatures of seven Lutheran princes and of two municipal governments and was read aloud by Chancellor Christian Beyer on 25 June 1530 before the Diet and Emperor, ([15]) who also received a Latin version of the document prepared by Melanchthon. ([16]) Luther had explicitly approved the document even though he considered it too soft in tone, particularly regarding the matter of the papacy (on which there was no separate article in the *Augsburg Confession*).

The Roman Catholic *Confutatio* of the *Confession,* which was read on 3 August 1530 after it was swiftly prepared, thwarted any hope to convince the Emperor, ([17]) who formally reaffirmed the Diet of Worms' condemnation of Luther and of his teachings at the close of the Diet of Augsburg. This also included an ultimatum to suppress any unsanctioned ecclesiastical reforms by 15 April 1531. The Lutherans' response to the Emperor's threat was the publication of the *editio princeps* of the *Augsburg Confession* in May 1531. In the following years, Melanchthon proceeded to revise the text further, which

(13) An English translation can be found in Kolb – Nestingen, *Sources and Context of the Book of Concord,* p. 88-92.

(14) Zwingli brought his *Ratio fidei* to the Diet for consideration.

(15) Charles V arrived on 15 June 1530 (Seebaß – Leppin, 'Die Confessio Augustana', p. 68).

(16) See Kolb – Wengert, *The Book of Concord,* p. 27-28; Kolb, *Confessing the Faith,* p. 14-15.

(17) Eck's *Confutatio* saw the involvement of Bishop Johannes Fabri, Johannes Cochlaeus, Konrad Wimpina, Johann Dietenberger, Julius Pflug, and Cardinal Lorenzo Campeggio. For an English translation of the *Confutatio,* see Kolb – Nestingen, *Sources and Context of the Book of Concord,* p. 106-139.

resulted in the dissemination of different versions of the *Confession*. (18) The *Confessio Augustana Variata* (1540/1542) featured the most significant changes, particularly in the revised Article 10 on the Lord's Supper and Christ's presence in the sacrament, a subject of controversy among Lutherans in the following years. Whereas John Calvin was pleased with the *Variata*, it was judged unacceptable by those committed to uphold Luther's specific theological position on the matter of the real presence of Christ in the Lord's Supper, the so-called Gnesio-Lutherans. This doctrinal tenet had already proven an obstacle for earlier hopes for a pan-Protestant alliance: it had been over this very issue that Luther and Zwingli had vehemently disagreed in their fateful 1529 meeting in Marburg. (19) Eventually, the *Book of Concord* explicitly rejected the *Variata*. Another work penned by Melanchthon, and entitled the *Apology of the Augsburg Confession* (1537), which he revised multiple times over his lifetime, was included among the Lutheran confessions. (20)

The *Augsburg Confession*, with its twenty-eight articles, was a relatively short document which embodied the Lutherans' theological foundations and expounded those practical reforms they sought and considered pivotal to the benefit of the whole Church. The first twenty-one articles addressed doctrinal questions whereas the last seven tackled practical reform matters in considerable detail and length. Combined, they demonstrated which issues were of theological interest, or matters of controversy, for the Lutherans, such as the nature of God, sin, justification by faith, Church and ministry, the new obedience, the sacraments of baptism and the Lord's Supper, penance, human order and regulations, free will, the Mass, the saints, matters pertaining to Christian

(18) The first edition of the *Augsburg Confession* was unauthorised: to Melanchthon's dismay, it was also altered or corrupted. A second edition of the German text was again published in 1533. The following editions of the Latin text – third edition in 1540 and fourth edition in 1542 – also featured several changes. See Kolb – Wengert, *The Book of Concord*, p. 29, n. 1.

(19) At a Catholic-Lutheran meeting in Weimar in 1577, Gnesio-Lutherans – in opposition to the so-called Philippists – protested the *Variata*'s muddying of Lutheran identity. Unlike other Lutheran princes, Elector Palatine Fredrick III, while in Naumburg in 1561, formally endorsed the legitimacy of the *Variata* in hopes of winning over John Calvin, who indeed approved the *Variata* at the colloquies of Worms (1540) and Regensburg (1541).

(20) As he was initially unable to secure a copy of the *Confutatio*, Melanchthon took fifteen months to complete his first version of the *Apology*. An in-quarto edition was published in April/May 1531, and an in-octavo edition in September. The Schmalkalden League signed the latter, which was also translated into German by Justus Jonas.

perfection, spirituality, vocation, sacramental practices, clerical marriage, monastic vows and celibacy, repentance, and the episcopal office. (²¹)

The catholic intent of the *Augsburg Confession* is clearly expressed in articles 1 and 3, which state the belief in the triune God in agreement with the ecumenical creeds and confirm the Chalcedonian Christological doctrine of Christ's two natures. The rationale for the ministry of the Word of God and the sacraments (Articles 5, 7-13) is deduced from the human condition, due to original sin and the consequent lack of freedom on the one hand (Articles 2, 18, 19), and with the Gospel's promise of unmerited grace on the other (Article 4). The issues of penance, episcopacy, clerical marriage and monastic vows, along with questions pertaining to different aspects of Christian life and worship were discussed at greater length than doctrinal tenets. Article 4 on grace and justification by faith was pivotal as it articulated the foundations for the restoration of the relationship between God and humankind. Indeed, it also set the tone for the reorganisation of Christian teaching and practices of faith, and it fuelled the promise of reform that Luther and his collaborators came to argue for in the *Augsburg Confession*.

Note on the Edition

Although the text of the document which was read aloud at Diet of Augsburg in 1530 no longer exists, the critical edition below aims at offering the reader the transcription of two manuscripts, one in German and one in Latin, which are considered among the most faithful to the version which was used in Augsburg, known in the *Augsburg Confession*'s *traditio textus* as *Mar* and *Mar2* respectively. The German version was most probably Philip of Hesse's personal copy. (²²)

---

(21) For an in-depth analysis of the contents of the *Confession*, see Grane, *The Augsburg Confession*; Lohrmann, *The Book of Harmony*, especially Chapter 4; Stjerna, *Lutheran Theology*, passim.

(22) Seebaß – Leppin, 'Die Confessio Augustana', p. 76-77 and p. 79.

BIBLIOGRAPHY

SOURCES (AND THEIR ABBREVIATIONS)

I. Dingel, 'Die Konkordienformel (1577)', in I. Dingel (hrsg.), *Die Bekenntnisschriften der evangelisch-lutherischen Kirche*, Göttingen 2014, p. 1163-1652 [= Dingel, 'Die Konkordienformel'].

K. E. Förstemann, *Urkundenbuch zu der Geschichte des Reichstages zu Augsburg im Jahre 1530*, 2 vols, Halle 1833-1835 [= Förstemann, *Urkundenbuch*].

H. J. Hillerbrand – K. Stjerna – T. J. Wengert (gen. eds), *The Annotated Luther*, 6 vols, Minneapolis (MN) 2015-2017 [= *The Annotated Luther*].

R. Kolb – J. A. Nestingen (eds), *Sources and Context of the Book of Concord*, Minneapolis (MN) 2001. [= Kolb – Nestingen, *Sources and Context of the Book of Concord*].

R. Kolb – T. J. Wengert (eds), *The Book of Concord*, Minneapolis (MN) 2000 [= Kolb – Wengert, *The Book of Concord*].

G. Seebaß – V. Leppin, 'Die Confessio Augustana', in I. Dingel (hrsg.), *Die Bekenntnisschriften der evangelisch-lutherischen Kirche*, Göttingen 2014, p. 63-225 [= Seebaß – Leppin, 'Die Confessio Augustana'].

LITERATURE (AND ITS ABBREVIATIONS)

C. P. Arand – R. Kolb – J. Nestingen (eds), *The Lutheran Confessions: History and Theology of The Book of Concord*, Minneapolis (MN) 2012 [= *History and Theology of the Book of Concord*].

C. E. Braaten, *Principles of Lutheran Theology*, Minneapolis (MN) ²2007 [= Braaten, *Principles of Lutheran Theology*].

G. Gaßmann – S. Hendrix, *The Fortress Introduction to the Lutheran Confessions*, Minneapolis (MN) 1999 [= Gaßmann – Hendrix, *Lutheran Confessions*].

L. Grane, *The Augsburg Confession; A Commentary*, Minneapolis (MN) 1987 [= Grane, *The Augsburg Confession*].

E. W. Gritsch, *Fortress Introduction to Lutheranism*, Minneapolis (MN) 1994 [= Gritsch, *Fortress Introduction to Lutheranism*].

S. Hendrix, *Recultivating the Vineyard: The Reformation Agendas of Christianization*, Louisville (KY) 2004 [= Hendrix, *Recultivating the Vineyard*].

R. Kolb, *Confessing the Faith: Reformers Define the Church, 1530-1580*, St Louis (MO) 1991 [= Kolb, *Confessing the Faith*].

M. J. Lohrmann, *Living Stones in Global Lutheranism: A Historical Introduction*, Minneapolis (MN) 2020 [= Lohrmann, *Living Stones*].

—, *The Book of Harmony: Spirit and Service in the Lutheran Confessions*, Minneapolis (MN) 2016 [= Lohrmann, *The Book of Harmony*].

K. Stjerna, *Lutheran Theology: A Grammar of Faith*, New York – London 2021 [= Stjerna, *Lutheran Theology*].

MONITUM

German = Hessisches Staatsarchiv Marburg, Best. 3, n. 258, fols 58r-108r.

Latin = Hessisches Staatsarchiv Marburg, Best. 3, n. 258, fols 2r-39r.

CONCILIUM AUGUSTANUM
1530

PRAEFATIO AD CAESAREM CAROLUM V.

Invictissime Imperator, Caesar Auguste, Domine clementissime. Cum indixerit conventum Imperii Augustae, ut deliberetur de auxiliis contra Turcam atrocissimum haereditarium atque veterem Christiani nominis ac religionis hostem, quomodo illius scilicet furori et conatibus durabili et perpetuo belli apparatu resisti possit, Deinde et de dissensionibus in causa nostrae sanctae religionis et Christianae fidei et ut in hac causa religionis partium opiniones ac sententiae inter sese in caritate, lenitate et mansuetudine mutua audiantur coram, intelligantur et ponderentur, ut illis, quae parum forsan probe utrinque in scripturis tractata aut intellecta sint, sepositis et correctis, res illae ad unam simplicem veritatem et Christianam concordiam componantur et reducantur, ut de caetero a nobis una, sincera et vera religio colatur et servetur, utque quemadmodum sub uno Christo sumus et militamus, Ita in una etiam Ecclesia Christiana unitate et concordia vivere possimus. Cumque nos infra scripti, Elector et Principes cum aliis, qui nobis coniuncti sunt, perinde ut alii Electores Principes et Status ad praefata Comitia evocati simus, ut Caesareo mandato oboedienter obsequeremur, mature venimus Augustam. Et quod citra iactantiam dictum volumus, inter primos affuimus.

Cum igitur V.C.M. Electoribus, Principibus et aliis Statibus Imperii etiam hic Augustae sub ipsa initia horum Comitiorum inter caetera proponi fecerit,

CONCILIUM AUGUSTANUM – 1530

Aller durchleuchtigster Grosmechtigster Unüberwintlichster Keyser, Allerg-
nedigster herr, Als euer Keyserliche Maiestet kurtz verschiener zeit einen
gemeinen Reichstag alhie gen Augspurg gnediglichen ausgeschrieben, mit
anzeig und ernstem beger von sachen unsern und des Christlichen namens
erbfeind, den Türcken, betreffend und wie demselben mit beharlicher hülff
statlichen widderstanden, Auch wie der zwiespalden halben inn dem heiligen
glauben und der Christlichen Religion gehandelt müge werden, zu rathschla-
gen und vleis anzukeren, alle, eins jglichen gutbeduncken, opinion und
meynung, zwischen uns selbst inn lieb und güttigkeit zuhören, zuersehen und
zuerwegen und dieselben zu einer einigen Christlichen warheit zu bringen
und zuvergleichen, alles, so zu beyden teilen nicht recht ausgeleget oder
gehandelt were, abzuthun und durch uns alle ein einiche und ware Religion
anzunemen und zuhalten, und wie wir alle under einem Christo sind und
streitten, Also auch alle inn einer gemeinschafft, kirchen und einigkeit zu
leben. Und wir, die unden benanten Chürfurst und Fürsten sampt unsern
verwanten, gleich andern Chürfursten, Fürsten und Stenden darzu erfordert,
so haben wir uns darauff dermassen erwogen, das wir sonder rhum mit den
ersten hieher komen.

Und als denn auch Euer Keyser. Maie. zu underthenigster volgtuung
berurts Euer Kei. Maie. ausschreibens und dem selbigen gemes dieser sachen
halben, den glauben berürend, an Chürfursten, Fürsten und Stende inn

---

1 Keyser] Emperor Charles V (1500-1558) arrived in Augsburg on 15 June 1530   2/
3 einen – Reichstag] the *Preface* sheds light onto the specific situation in which the
Confession was written, a political meeting at the Reichstag, to address 'the dispute as a
party conflict' on which the Emperor should not be the final judge. Grane, *Confession*,
p. 27   3 Augspurg] January 1530   5 den Türcken] that the Emperor needed alliances
in order to encounter the approaching Ottoman troops added to his motivations to
meet at the German Diet   14/15 Also – leben] the document's introduction
articulates a strong desire to maintain unity in the one Christian church with roots in
the ancient creeds of faith articulated at the first ecumenical councils, without
intending to propose anything essentially new   16 Stenden] *Die Ständen* refers to the
different groups, constituencies, and territories represented by delegated individuals
17/18 mit – komen] among the first to arrive in Augsburg in May 1530 were the
Elector John of Saxony and Philip of Hesse; stating their early arrival expresses their
positive disposition towards the occasion

quod singuli Status Imperii vigore Caesarei Edicti suam opinionem et sententiam in germanica et latina lingua proponere debeant atque offerre. Et habita deliberatione proxima feria quarta rursum responsum est V.C.M. nos proxima feria sexta Articulos nostrae confessionis pro nostra parte oblaturos esse. Ideo,

25 ut V.M. voluntati obsequamur, offerimus in hac religionis causa nostrorum Contionatorum et nostram confessionem, cuiusmodi doctrinam ex scripturis sanctis et puro verbo dei hactenus illi in nostris terris, ducatibus, ditionibus et urbibus tradiderint ac in Ecclesiis docuerint.

Si nunc et caeteri Electores, Principes ac Status Imperii similibus scriptis

30 Latinis scilicet et Germanicis iuxta predictam Caesaream propositionem suas opiniones in hac causa Religionis produxerint, hic nos coram V.C.M. tanquam domino nostro clementissimo paratos offerimus nos cum praefatis principibus et amicis nostris de tollerabilibus modis ac viis amice conferre, ut, quantum honeste fieri potest, conveniamus et re inter nos partes citra odiosam conten-

35 tionem pacifice agitata Deo dante dissensio dirimatur et ad unam veram concordem religionem reducatur, Sicut omnes sub uno Christo sumus et militamus et unum Christum confiteri debemus iuxta tenorem edicti V.C.M. et omnia ad veritatem dei perducantur, id quod ardentissimis votis a deo petimus.

CONCILIUM AUGUSTANUM – 1530

gemein gnediglichen, auch mit hochstem vleis und ernstlich begert, das ein
jglicher, vermüge vorgemelts E. Kei. Maie. ausschreibens, sein gut beduncken,
opinion und meinung der selbigen irrungen, zwispalden und misbreuch
25 halben etc. zu Deudsch und Latein inn schrifft stellen und uberantworten
solten. Darauff denn nach gemeinem bedacht und gehaltenem Rath E. Keis.
Maie. An vergangner Mitwochen ist furgetragen worden, als wolten wir auff
unserm teil das unser vermoge E. Kei. Maie. furtrags in Deudsch und latein
auff heut freitag ubergeben. Hierumb und E. Kei. Ma. zu underthenigstem
30 gehorsam uberreichen und ubergeben wir unser Pfarner, Prediger und ihrer
leren, auch unsers glaubens bekentnus, was und welcher gestalt sie aus grunde
Göttlicher heiliger schrifft in unsern Landen, Fürstenthumen, Herschafften,
Stetten und gebieten predigen, leren halten und underrichten thun.

Und sind gegen E. Kei. Maie. unserm aller gnedigsten herrn wir inn aller
35 underthenigkeit erbottig, so die andern Chürfursten, Fürsten und Stende
dergleichen gezwifachte schrifftliche ubergebung ihrer meinung odder opinion inn latein und deudsch itzt auch thun werden, das wir uns mit ihren lieb-
den und ihnen gern von bequemen gleichmessigen wegen underreden. Und
die selbigen, so viel der gleicheit nach immer müglich, vereinigen wollen,
40 damit unser beiderseitz als parten schrifftlich furbringen und gebrechen
zwischen uns selbst in lieb und gütigkeit gehandelt und die selben zwispalden
zu einer einigen waren Religion, wie wir alle unter einem Christo sind und
streitten und Christum bekennen sollen, alles nach laut offtgemelts E. Kei. Ma.
ausschreibens und nach Gottlicher warheit, gefurt mügen werden, Als wir
45 denn auch Gott den Almechtigen mit höchster demut anruffen und bitten
wollen, sein Gottlich gnad dazu zuverleihen. Amen.

---

28 in – latein] the document was prepared in two languages, as requested by the
Emperor, to reach all the attending parties. The delegates outside German-speaking
lands, especially the papal delegates, needed the Latin version, whereas the German
text allowed the attending German representatives to hear the case in their own
language   **29** auff – ubergeben] on Wednesday 22 June 1530, the presentation of the
document was scheduled for Friday 24 June, but ended up being postponed till
Saturday 25 June   **29/33** Hierumb – thun] the document underscores the Holy
Scriptures as the foundation for the evangelicals' teachings, preaching, and serves as
both a theological and a political statement pertaining to questions of truth and
authority   **38/41** Und – gehandelt] the expected process for the official and orderly
receipt of the Lutherans' document is explained in accordance with the stipulations
coming from the Emperor, with hopes for an amicable conclusion   **42/43** wie –
sollen] one Christ and belief in the same Christ offer the foundation for the one
religion all parties (still) adhere to   **43/44** alles – ausschreibens] the document
repeats the role of the Emperor as the one who had called the meeting and under
whose authority the procedures were to follow

CONCILIUM AUGUSTANUM – 1530

40   Si autem, quod ad caeteros Electores, Principes et Status, ut partem alteram, attinet, haec tractatio causae Religionis eo modo, quo V.C.M. agendam et tractandam sapienter duxit, scilicet cum tali mutua praesentatione scriptorum ac sedata collatione inter nos non processerit nec aliquo fructu facta fuerit, nos quidem testatum clare relinquimus, hic nihil nos, quod ad Christia-
45 nam concordiam (quae cum Deo et bona conscientia fieri possit) conciliandam conducere queat, ullo modo detrectare. Quemadmodum et V.C.M., deinde et caeteri Electores et Status Imperii et omnes, quicunque sincero religionis amore ac studio tenentur, quicunque hanc causam aequo animo audituri sunt, ex hac nostra et nostrorum confessione hoc clementer cognosce-
50 re et intelligere dignabuntur.

    Cum etiam V.C.M. Electoribus, Principibus et reliquis Statibus Imperii non una vice, sed saepe clementer significaverit et in Comitiis etiam Spirensibus, quae anno domini etc. XXVI. habita sunt, ex data et praescripta forma vestrae Caesareae instructionis et comissionis recitari et publice praelegi fece-
55 rit. Vestram M. in hoc negotio religionis ex causis certis, quae V.M. nomine allegatae sunt, non velle quicquam determinare nec concludere posse, sed apud pontificem Romanum pro officio V.C.M. diligenter daturam operam de congregando Concilio generali. Quemadmodum idem latius expositum est ante annum in publico proximo conventu, qui Spirae congregatus fuit, Ubi
60 V.C.M. per dominum Ferdinandum, Boemiae et Ungariae Regem, amicum et dominum clementem nostrum, Deinde per Oratorem et Comissarios Caesareos haec inter caetera proponi fecit, quod V.C.M. intellexisset et expendisset Locum tenentis, V.C.M. in imperio et praesidentis et Consiliariorum in Regimine et Legatorum ab aliis Statibus, qui Ratisponae convenerant, deliberatio-
65 nem de Concilio congregando. Et quod iudicaret etiam V.C.M. utile esse, ut congregaretur Concilium, Et quia causae, quae tum tractabantur inter V.C.M. et Ro. Pontificem, vicinae essent concordiae et Christianae reconciliationi, non dubitaret V.C.M., quin Roma. Pontifex adduci posset ad habendum generale Concilium. Ideo significabat se quod V.C.M. operam daturam, ut praefa-

CONCILIUM AUGUSTANUM – 1530

Wo aber bey unsern herrn, freunden und besondern den Chürfursten, Fürsten und Stenden des andern teils die handlung dermassen, wie E. Kei. Maie. ausschreiben vermag bequeme handellunge, unter uns selbs inn lieb und
50 gütigkeit nicht vorsahen noch ersprieslich sein wolt, als doch an uns inn keinem, das mit Gott und gewissen zu Christlicher einigkeit dienstlich sein kan odder mag, erwinden sol, wie E. K. Maie., auch gemelte unsere freund, die Chürfursten, Fürsten, Stende und ein jeder liebhaber Christlicher Religion, so diese sachen furkomen, aus nachfolgen unser und der unsern bekentnussen
55 gnediglich, freuntlich und gnugsam werden zuvernemen haben.

Nach dem denn E. Kei. Maie. vormals Chürfursten, Fürsten und Stenden des Reichs gnediglichen zuverstehen gegeben und sonderlich durch ein öffentliche verlesene Instruction auff dem Reichstag, so im jar der mindern zal xxvi. zu Speyr gehalten, das E. Kei. Maie. inn sachen unsern heiligen glauben belan-
60 gend zuschliessen lassen aus ursachen, so dabey angezeigt, nicht gemeinet, Sondern sich bey dem Babst umb ein Concilium vleissigen und anhaltung thun wolten Und fur einem jar auff dem letzten Reichstage zu Speyr, vormüge einer schrifftlichen instruction, Chürfursten, Fürsten und Stenden des Reichs durch E. Kei. Maie. Stadhalter im Reich, Königliche W. zu Hungern und
65 Behemen, sampt E. Kei. Maie. Oratorn und verordenten Commissarien, dis unter andern haben furtragen und anzeigen lassen, das E. Kei. Maie. der selbigen Stathalter, Ambts verwalter und Rethen des Keiserlichen Regiments, Auch der abwesenden Chürfursten, Fürsten und Stenden Botschafften, so auff dem ausgeschriben Reichstag zu Regenspurgk versamlet gewesen, gutbe-
70 duncken, das General Concilium belangend, nachgedacht und solchs anzusetzen auch fur fruchtbar erkand. Und weil sich aber die sachen zwischen E. K. Maie. und dem Bapst zu gutem Christlichen verstand schickten, das E. K. Maie. gewis were, das durch den Babst das general Concilium zu halten nicht gewegert, So were E. Kei. Maie. gnedigs erbietens zufordern und zuhandeln,

---

51 gewissen] in the model of Martin Luther at the Diet of Worms in 1521, evangelicals continue to refer to their conscience – as well as the Scriptures – as their stimulus for the confession of their beliefs   **52/54** wie – furkomen] the suggested audience of 'friends' for the document is the 'lover of the Christian religion', with the Emperor and those attending the Diet   **62** dem – Speyr] the Diets of Speyer, 1526 and 1529, had re-enforced the Edict of Worms of 1521 to extinguish Protestant reform   **67** Keiserlichen Regiments] written instructions from Ferdinand and Balthasar Merklin, imperial vice-chancellor; Margrave Philip of Baden the viceroy; Count Wolfgang of Montfort as the deputy. Kolb – Wengert, *The Book of Concord*, p. 34, notes 18-19   **69** Reichstag – Regenspurgk] the Diet of Regensburg, 1527

70 tus Ponti. Maximus una cum V.C.M. tale generale Concilium primo quoque
tempore emissis literis publicandum congregare consentiret.

In eventum ergo talem, quod in causa religionis dissensiones inter nos et
partes amice et in caritate non fuerint compositae, tunc coram V.C.M. hic in
omni oboedientia nos offerimus ex superabundanti comparituros et causam
75 dicturos in tali generali libero et Christiano Concilio, de quo congregando in
omnibus Comitiis Imperialibus, quae quidem annis Imperii V.C.M. habita
sunt per Electores, Principes et reliquos Status Imperii, semper concorditer
actum et congruentibus suffragiis conclusum est. Ad cuius etiam generalis
Concilii conventum, simul et ad V.C.M., in hac longe maxima et gravissima
80 causa iam ante etiam debito modo et in forma iuris provocavimus et appellavi-
mus. Cui appellationi ad V.C.M. simul et Concilium adhuc adheremus neque
eam per hunc vel alium tractatum (nisi causa inter nos et partes iuxta tenorem
Caesareae proximae Citationis amice in caritate composita, sedata et ad Christianam concordiam reducta fuerit) deserere intendimus aut possumus. De
85 quo hic etiam solenniter et publice protestamur.

CONCILIUM AUGUSTANUM – 1530

75 das der Babst solch general Concilium neben E. Kei. Ma. zum ersten auszu-
schreiben bewilligen und daran gar kein mangel erscheinen solt.

So erbieten gegen E. Kei. Maie. vor uns hiemit inn aller underthenigkeit
und zum uberflus inn berürtem fal ferner auff ein solch gemein frey Christlich
Concilium, darauff auff allen Reichstagen, so E. Kei. Ma. bey ihrer regierung
80 im Reich gehalten, durch Chürfursten, Fürsten und Stende aus hohen und
tapffern bewegungen geschlossen, An welchs auch zusambt E. Kei. Maie. wir
uns von wegen dieser groswichtigsten sachen inn Rechtlicher weis und form
verschiener zeit beruffen und appellirt haben, der wir hiemit nachmals anhengig bleiben und uns durch diese oder nachvolgende handlung (es werden denn
85 diese zwiespaldigen sachen entlich inn lieb und güttigkeit, laut E. Kei. Maie.
ausschreibens, gehort, erwogen, beygelegt und zu einer Christlichen einigkeit
vergleicht) nicht zubegeben wissen, davon wir hiemit offentlichen bezeugen
und protestiren. Und sind das unser und der unsern bekentnus, wie under-
schiedlichen von Artickeln zu Artickeln hernach volget.

---

75 der Babst] Pope Clement VII (1378-1534)   75/76 Babst – solt] the Lutheran
delegation being fully aware of the possible unwillingness from the Pope's part, the
Emperor is offered a reminder of his power in calling a free council that the Pope could
not refuse   78/79 ein – Concilium] the Lutheran delegation expresses their
understanding of the roles of the Emperor and the Pope in disputes pertaining to
religious matters: the Emperor's authority to call a free council does not extend to the
discernment about doctrine and content   81/88 An – protestiren] the Lutherans
admit their protesting actions but defend themselves for having acted in an orderly
fashion and within their legal rights   88 bekentnus] the word 'confessing' would
become one of the hallmarks of Lutherans' identity as a Christian tradition, indicating
both a written statement of faith and the act of joining those supporting the document.
Leif Grane, *The Augsburg Confession: A Commentary*, Minneapolis 1987 [transl. from
the Danish original of 1981], p. 18, writes: 'The AC does not intend to initiate
anything. It does not intend to create any new church doctrine. Rather, its purpose is
simply to reproduce what is taught in the Christian church. Its entire design is alien to
any sense of what we have come to understand as confessionalism'

Articuli fidei praecipui

I.

Ecclesiae magno consensu apud nos docent Decretum Nicenae Synodi de unitate essentiae divinae et de tribus personis verum et sine ulla dubitatione credendum esse. Videlicet quod sit una essentia divina, quae et appellatur et est Deus, aeternus, incorporeus, impartibilis, immensa potentia, sapientia, bonitate, creator et conservator omnium rerum, visibilium et invisibilium, et tamen tres sint personae eiusdem essentiae et potentiae et coaeternae, Pater, Filius et Spiritus sanctus. Et nomine personae utuntur ea significatione, qua usi sunt in hac causa Scriptores Ecclesiastici, ut significet non partem aut qualitatem in alio, sed quod proprie subsistit.

Damnant omnes haereses contra hunc articulum exortas ut Manicheos, qui duo principia ponebant, Bonum et Malum, item Valentinianos, Arianos, Eunomianos, Mahometistas et omnes horum similes. Damnant et Samosatenos, veteres et Neotericos, qui, cum tantum unam personam esse contendant, de verbo et de spiritu sancto astute et impie rhetoricantur, quod non sint personae distinctae, sed quod verbum significet verbum vocale et spiritus motum in rebus creatum.

CONCILIUM AUGUSTANUM – 1530

90 ## ARTIGKELL DES GLAWBENS UND DER LERE

Der Erste

Erstlich wirdt eintrechtigklich gelert und gehalten laut des Beschlus Concilii Niceni, das ein einig Göttlich wesen sey, welchs genent wird und warhafftiglich ist Gott, und sind doch drey personen inn dem selbigen einigen
95 Göttlichen wesen, gleich gewaltig, gleich ewig, Gott vater, Gott Son, Gott heiliger geist, Alle drey ein Göttlich wesen, ewig, one stück, unermessener macht, weisheit und güte, one ende, ein Schöpffer und erhalter dinge, der sichtbaren und unsichtbaren. Und wird durch das wort persona verstanden nicht ein stück, nicht ein eigenschafft in einem andern, sondern das selb beste-
100 het, wie denn die Veter in dieser sachen dis wort gebraucht haben.

Derhalb werden verworffen alle ketzereien, so diesem Artickel zuwidder sind, als Manichei, die zweene Götter gesetzt haben, ein bösen und ein guten. Item, Valentiniani, Arriani, Eunomiani, Mahometisten und alle dergleichen, auch Samosateni, alte und neue, so nür ein person setzen und von diesen zwei-
105 en, wort und heilig geist, Sophistrey machen, sagen, das es nicht müssen underschiedne personen sein, sondern wort bedeut leiblich wort odder stimme und der heilig geist sey geschaffne regung inn Creaturn.

92/93 des – Niceni] evoking the memory of the 325 Council of Nicaea summoned by the Emperor who was concerned about divisions among Christians **95/98** Gott¹ – unsichtbaren] the creedal teaching of the Trinity is important here to associate the *Confession* with the teachings considered orthodox and fundamental for the Christian church. The document – just as the ensuing Lutheran documents – does not offer further deliberations on the mysteries of the Divinity and the trinitarian language of the early church **101** alle ketzereien] deliberately mentioning several movements condemned as 'heresies' by the early church councils, the Confession aims to prove the evangelicals' orthodoxy and unity with the ancient teachings of the Creeds. Especially pertinent are statements about the equal divinity of the three persons of one God and adhering to the Chalcedonian decision on Christ's two natures. The article was accepted by the *Confutation* (*Confutatio Pontificia*). Grane, *Confession*, p. 33. As condemned heresies, these are mentioned: Arius (condemned in Nicaea 325) who taught Christ as a lesser deity than the first person of the Trinity; the Persian Mani († 276); the Gnostic teacher Valentinus (mid second century); Eunomios († 395), new Arian teacher; Muhammad associated with movements denying Christ's divinity; Paul of Samosata († 275), bishop of Antioch, who denied the distinction of Logos. Article 1 relates closely to Article 3 vis-à-vis the doctrine of God and Christological orientation

---

90 Artigkell – lere] *addidi*

II.

Item docent, quod post lapsum Adae omnes homines secundum naturam propagati nascantur cum peccato, hoc est sine metu Dei, sine fiducia erga Deum et cum concupiscentia, quodque hic morbus seu vitium originis vere sit peccatum damnans et afferens nunc quoque aeternam mortem his, qui non renascuntur per baptismum et spiritum sanctum.

Damnant Pelagianos et alios, qui vitium originis negant esse peccatum, et ut extenuent gloriam meriti et beneficiorum Christi, disputant hominem propriis viribus rationis coram Deo iustificari posse.

CONCILIUM AUGUSTANUM – 1530

Der Ander

Weiter wirt bei uns gelert, das nach dem falh Ade alle menschen, so
natürlich geporn werden, in sunden empfangen und geporn werden, das ist,
das sie alle von mutter leibe an voller böser lust und neigung sind und keine
ware Gottes forcht, kein waren glauben an Gott von natur haben können, Das
auch die selbige angeborne seuch und erbsund warhafftiglich sund sey und
verdamme alle die jhenigen unter ewigen Gottes zorn, so nicht durch die
Tauffe und heiligen geist wider neu geporn werden.

Hie werden verworffen die Pelagianer und andere, so die erbsund nicht
fur sunde halten, damit sie die natur from machen durch natürliche krefft, zu
schmach dem leiden und verdienst Christi.

---

108 Der Ander] that this article comes second in the document indicates the
importance of the shift in viewing the impact of sin vis-à-vis the whole person. This is
expressed more drastically in, e.g., Luther's later *Schmalkalden Articles*, calling sin 'the
corruption so deep and terrible that it is beyond human reason, only to be accepted in
faith'. Grane, *Confession*, p. 43 **109/112** Weiter – können] the *Confession* agrees with
the Catholic teachings of original sin received in birth and entailing a wrong desire, but
it offers a new definition in naming the lack of fear and trust in God as the root of sin
112/113 Das – erbsund] in contrast, medieval scholastic teaching on original sin
pointed to lost righteousness (Anselm of Canterbury), on the one hand, and as the
sinful desire called concupiscence (Peter Lombard), the impact of both being removed
in Baptism while the tinder of sin remaining in human nature. Luther's emphasis was
on the holistic devastation the original sin causes in orienting the person away from
God, a condition in which there are no different degrees to be discerned in terms of its
impact or guilt: the former remains in Baptism, while the latter is expunged. See
Grane, *Confession*, p. 41-42 **114/115** die Tauffe] Baptism is named as the beginning
and the sign of a new relationship with God, as the cleansing from the guilt sin brings
about while not removing it completely from human life **115** neu – werden] with the
expression 'neu geporn warden', the article expresses the invasiveness of sin and the
depth of the effect of justification, to be articulated in Article 2. Luther uses a similar
expression in his *Rückblick* (his *Preface* to the 1542 edition of his Latin writings) **116/
118** Hie – Christi] the Council of Trent would address the question of original sin and
baptism's impact vis-à-vis forgiveness and removal of sin, except concupiscence, that
would remain as a kindle for sin **116** die¹ – andere] condemning the teachings of
Pelagius meant affirming Augustine's position on the freedom of will and the reality of
original sin. The 'others' imply Zwingli and the scholastic medieval theologians
117 damit – krefft] relying on natural powers to conquer the impact of sin would be in
line with the teaching of Erasmus

III.

Idem docent, quod verbum, hoc est filius Dei, assumpserit humanam naturam in utero beatae Mariae virginis, ut sint duae naturae, divina et humana, in unitate personae inseparabiliter coniunctae, unus Christus, vere Deus et vere homo, natus ex virgine Maria, vere passus, crucifixus, mortuus et sepultus, ut reconciliaret nobis Patrem et hostia esset non tantum pro culpa originis, sed etiam pro omnibus actualibus hominum peccatis.

Idem descendit ad inferos et vere resurrexit tertia die, deinde ascendit ad coelos, ut sedeat ad dexteram patris et perpetuo regnet et dominetur omnibus creaturis, sanctificet credentes in ipsum misso in corda eorum spiritu sancto, qui regat, consoletur ac vivificet eos ac defendat adversus diabolum et vim peccati. Idem Christus palam est rediturus, ut iudicet vivos et mortuos etc. iuxta symbolum Apostolorum.

CONCILIUM AUGUSTANUM – 1530

Der Dritte

120   Item: Es wirt gelert, das Gott der Son sey mensch worden, und geporen aus Maria der reinen jungfrauen, Und das die zwo natur, Göttliche und menschliche, inn einer person also unzertrenlich vereinigt ein Christus sind, welcher warer Gott, und war mensch ist, warhafftig geporn, gelidden, gecreutziget, gestorben und begraben, das er ein opffer were nicht allein fur die Erbs-
125   und, sondern auch fur alle andere sunde, und Gottes zorn versünet.

Item: Das derselbig Christus abgestiegen zur helle, warhafftig am dritten tag von den toden aufferstanden, auffgefaren gen himel, sitzend zur rechten Gottes, das er ewig hersche uber alle creatur und regiere, das er alle, so an ihn gleuben, durch den heiligen geist heilige, reinige, stercke, und tröste, ihnen
130   auch leben und allerley gaben und güter austeile und widder den Teuffel und widder die sunde schütze und beschirme. Item: Das der selbige Herr Christus entlich wird öffentlich komen, zurichten die lebendigen und die todten etc. laut des Symboli Apostolorum.

---

121 Maria – jungfrauen] this only mention of Mary's virginity affirms the creedal teaching of Jesus' birth   **121/122** Und – unzertrenlich] a Chalcedonian conviction: inseparably united natures of Christ   **124** das – opffer] Christ as the only sacrifice refutes any consideration of the Mass as a new or renewed sacrifice, a view also criticised in the *Confutation* (Article 24). The Council of Trent, however, names the sacrifice of the Mass as an atonement for human beings' sins. See Grane, *Confession*, p. 52   **129** den – geist] with no separate article on the Holy Spirit in the document, Article 3 includes the pneumatological statement

IIII.

Idem docent, quod homines non possint iustificari coram Deo propriis viribus, meritis aut operibus, sed gratis iustificentur propter Christum per fidem, cum credunt se in gratiam recipi et peccata remitti propter Christum, qui sua morte pro nostris peccatis satis fecit. Hanc fidem imputat Deus pro iustitia coram ipso. Roma. iii. et iiii.

CONCILIUM AUGUSTANUM – 1530

4.

Weither wirtt geleret, das wir vergebung der sunth und gerechtigkeit vor Got nicht erlangen mugen durch unsere verdienste, wercke und gnug thun, sonder das wir vergebung der sunden bekommen und vor Got gerecht werhen aus gnaden umb Christus willen durch den glauben, so wir glauben, das Christus fur uns gelitten hab und das uns umb seiner willen di sunde vergeben, gerechtigkeit und ewigs leben geschenckt wirdet, dan dissen glauben will Got vor gerechttikeit vor ime halten und zurechnen, wie Paulus sagt zun Rom. am 3. 4.

141/142 Rom – 4] cfr Rom. 3, 21-26; 4, 5

134 4] the pivotal article on justification with the previous statement on Christ's two natures builds on the creedal teaching of belief in God and Christ, and on the reinstated Augustinian view on the depth of sin in all human beings, thereby offering a lens to address the necessary reconciliation between God and humankind, and the church's role in this. The *Confutation* agrees with the rejection of Pelagianism but defends the idea of meritorious works, without discussing justification per se. The Council of Trent later made a more explicit refutation of the Lutheran position and articulation of the different stages vis-à-vis grace and the function of law. Grane, *Confession*, p. 64-65 **135** gerechtigkeit] a key word in Lutheran teaching of holiness and salvation: the satisfaction that Christ effects is described as an act of justification and righteousness-making that entails different aspects: a declaration of forgiveness (forensic justification) and being made righteousness and one with Christ (effective justification). The Lutheran interpretation of this tenet has varied and emphasises the forensic aspect more than the effective dimension that Luther himself explicitly addressed, e.g. in his interpretation of Paul's letters to the Galatians. Finnish Luther scholarship with Tuomo Mannermaa has suggested a new lens on this root doctrine. See T. Mannermaa, *Christ Present in Faith: Luther's View of Justification*, Minneapolis (MN) 2005 **135/136** vor Got] justification as a restoration and readjustment explicitly in the realm of *coram Deo* **136** nicht – verdienste] not by one's own merit – the main point of Article 4, that grace is free and a matter of faith. Also a Lutheran emphasis: grace comes *extra nos*. As Grane compares 'For Thomas [Aquinas], grace is a power by which human capability is strengthened so that a person can raise him[one]self up to God. For Luther, grace is the fact that God in his mercy is present as the one who fights for sinners who have nothing to hold on to but the alien righteousness of Christ'. (Grane, *Confession*, p. 86) **138** gnaden] the article addresses the change that involves the entire person, when in justification one becomes righteous, right with God, and thereby also holy. The agent for this is the Word, and the cause is Christ, who is the favour and the gift. In the context of Articles 2 and 3, justification is explained as a free gift durch – glauben¹] these words underscore the passivity of the person in receiving salvation and justification, 'through faith' that has Christ as the focal point, foundation, and subject **138/139** so – vergeben] faith in forgiveness, and grace received in faith. Faith that holds onto the promise is the faith that saves, distinct from belief or believing as human actions

V.

Ut hanc fidem consequamur, institutum est ministerium docendi Evangelii et porrigendi sacramenta. Nam per verbum et sacramenta, tanquam per
135 instrumenta donatur spiritus sanctus, qui fidem efficit, ubi et quando visum
est Deo, in iis, qui audiunt Evangelium, scilicet quod Deus non propter nostra
merita, sed propter Christum iustificet hos, qui credunt se propter Christum
in gratiam recipi.

Damnant Anabaptistas et alios, qui sentiunt spiritum sanctum contingere
140 sine verbo externo hominibus per ipsorum preparationes et opera.

VI.

Idem docent, quod fides illa debeat bonos fructus parere et quod oporteat
bona opera mandata a Deo facere propter voluntatem Dei, non ut confidamus
per ea opera iustificationem coram Deo mereri. Nam remissio peccatorum et
145 iustificatio fide apprehenditur, sicut testatur et vox Christi: *Cum feceritis haec*

CONCILIUM AUGUSTANUM – 1530

Der Fünffte

Solchen glauben zuerlangen, hat Got das predig ampt eingesatzt, Evange-
145 lium und Sacramenta geben, dadurch ehr alls durch mittel den Heiligen Geist
gibt welicher den glauben wirgkt, wo und wenn er wil, inn denen, so das Evangelium hören, welches do leret, das wir durch Christus verdienst nicht durch
unser vordinst ein gnedigen Gott haben, so wir solchs gleuben.

Und werden verdammet die Widderteuffer und andere, so leren, das wir
150 one das leibliche wort des Evangelii den heiligen geist durch eigene bereittung
gedancken und werck erlangen.

Der Sechste

Auch wirt geleret, das solcher glaub gute frucht und gute werck bringen
soll und das man müsse gute werck thun allerley, so Gott geboten hat umb
155 Gottes willen, doch nicht auff solche werck zuvertrauen, dadurch gnad vor
Gott zuvordienen. Denn wir empfahen vergebung der sunden und gerechtig-
keitt durch den glauben an Christum, wie Christus selbst spricht: 'So ihr das

---

144 hat – eingesatzt] the office of ministry is explained vis-à-vis faith and its origins
through the proclamation of the Gospel and the administration of sacraments as
mediums for the Holy Spirit. Proclamation is the first and foremost duty of pastors and
a means of grace in itself. While everyone belongs to the ministry of the baptised or the
priesthood of all believers, the proclamation duty is secured with a specific office
instituted for the purpose. The Lutheran parameters for the priestly office have
remained through centuries and distinct from both Roman Catholic and other
Protestant traditions **148** so – gleuben] the Latin text includes a reference to Gal.
3, 14 on receiving the Holy Spirit through faith **149** Widderteuffer] Anabaptists,
originating from Zurich, were heavily persecuted for their practice of re-baptism, and
for their refusal to swear oaths or carry arms for the government. No distinction is
made between rebaptizers and spiritualists andere] the 'others' refer to those labelled
as 'spiritualists' or enthusiasts, or *die Schwärmer* – movements that upheld the
reception of the Holy Spirit apart the Word and Sacraments **150** leibliche] the word
'leiblich' underscores the concrete impact of the Gospel **153** gute' – werck] good
works and good fruit are explicitly mentioned as part of justification, to be returned to
in Article 22 **156** zuvordienen] the word 'zuvordienen' expresses the opposite of
justification by faith. The language refutes any suggestion of human beings able to
'earn' or 'merit' grace. The necessity of good works is explained from faith that is
bound to yield so-called good works or new obedience, the true agent being God's own
Spirit

---

146 er] *intellege* the Holy Spirit

omnia, dicite, servi inutiles sumus. Idem docent et veteres Scriptores Ecclesiastici. Ambrosius enim inquit: Hoc constitutum est a Deo, ut, qui credit in Christum, salvus sit Sine opere, sola fide, gratis accipiens remissionem peccatorum.

VII.

Item docent, quod una sancta Ecclesia perpetuo mansura sit. Est autem Ecclesia congregatio sanctorum, in qua Evangelium recte docetur et recte administrantur Sacramenta.

Et ad veram unitatem Ecclesiae satis est consentire de doctrina Evangelii et administratione Sacramentorum. Nec necesse est ubique esse similes traditiones humanas seu ritus aut ceremonias ab hominibus institutas. Sicut inquit Paulus: *Una fides, unum baptisma, unus Deus et pater omnium etc.*

CONCILIUM AUGUSTANUM – 1530

alles gethan habt, solt ihr sprechen: «Wir sind untüchtige knecht»'. Also
leren auch die Veter. Denn Ambrosius spricht: 'Also ists beschlossen bey Gott,
das, wer an Christum gleubt, selig sey und nicht durch werck, sondern allein
durch den glauben one verdienst vergebung der sunden habe'.

Der Siebent

Es wirt auch geleret, das alzeit müsse ein heilige Christlich kirche sein
und bleiben, welche ist die versamlung aller gleubigen, bey welchen das Evangelium rein gepredigt und die heiligen Sacrament laut des Evangelii gereicht
werden.

Denn dieses ist gnug zu warer einigkeit der Christlichen kirchen, das da
eintrechtiglich nach reinem verstand das Evangelium gepredigt und die Sacrament dem Göttlichen wort gemes gereicht werden. Und ist nicht not zu warer
einigkeit der Christlichen kirchen, das allenthalben gleichformig Ceremonien,
von menschen eingesatzt, gehalten werden, wie Paulus spricht Ephes. iiii.: 'Ein
leib, ein geist, wie ihr beruffen seid zu einerley hoffnung euers beruffs, Ein
Herr, ein glaub, ein Tauffe'.

---

158 Wir – knecht] Luc. 17, 10   **171/173** Eph. 4, 5-6

159 die Veter] referring to the authority of the Church Fathers of the early Church
159/161 Denn – habe] in the Catholic view, as expressed in the *Confutation*, a
distinction is made between *fides formata* that justifies as a gift and *fides charitate
formata* that manifests in loving deeds. Luther in his *On Christian Freedom* crystallises
a different starting point: a Christian is free in faith, but in love one is bound to serve
everyone. The latter does not cause or merit justification but it is part of the
fermentation to be logically and necessarily expected. See Grane, *Confession*, p. 84-85
159 Ambrosius] see Kolb – Wengert, *The Book of Concord*, p. 40, note 51   **160/
161** allein – glauben] the central statement in the *Confession*, and in Luther's theology,
about salvation coming from faith only. Luther, in his translation of Romans 3:28,
coined the word 'only' with 'faith'. Per John 1:12-13, he spoke of faith as the 'living,
daring confidence in God's grace' *WA DB* 7:9, 30-10, 23. See Grane, *Confession*, p. 87-88
163/164 Es – versamlung] the article underscores the evangelicals' conviction of the
continuity of the one Christian church, understood as a community of faith, desiring
to cause no disruption in the Church's mission   **164/166** bey – werden] the holiness
and the foundation of the church as the assembly of believers is in the Word and the
sacraments. 'No one can speak of faith apart from its bond to Christ's institution in
Word and sacrament, for only here is found the faith which does not look at itself but
to Christ alone. Conversely, it must never be forgotten that Christ's institution does
not in itself save, but only as it creates faith in the heart of the individual'. (Grane,
Confession, p. 98) This principle would continue to guide the future Lutherans on the
indispensable mission of the church. Unity is another important focus in this article

VIII.

Quanquam Ecclesia proprie sit congregatio sanctorum et vere credentium, tamen cum in hac vita multi hypocritae et mali admixti sint, licet uti
sacramentis, quae per malos administrantur, iuxta vocem Christi: *Sedent Scri-
bae et Pharisaei in Cathedra Mosi* etc. Et sacramenta et verbum propter ordinationem et mandatum Christi sunt efficacia, etiamsi per malos exhibeantur.

Damnant Donatistas et similes, qui negabant licere uti ministerio malorum in Ecclesia et sentiebant ministerium malorum inutile et inefficax esse.

IX.

De Baptismo docent, quod sit necessarius ad salutem quodque per Baptismum offeratur gratia Dei Et quod pueri sint Baptisandi, qui per Baptismum
oblati Deo recipiantur in gratiam Dei.

Der Achte

175 Item: Wiewol die Christliche kirche eigentlich nicht anders ist denn die versamlung aller gleubigen und heiligen, Jdoch dieweil inn diesem leben viel falscher Christen und heuchler, auch öffentliche sunder unter den fromen bleiben, so sind die Sacrament gleichwol krefftig, ob sie schon durch die Priester, dadurch sie gereicht werden, nicht from sind, wie dann Christus selbst 180 anzeigt: 'Auff dem stuel Moisi sitzen die Phariseer etc.'.

Derhalben werden die Donatisten und alle ander verdammet, so anders halten.

Der Neundte

Von der Tauff wirt gelert, das sie nötig sey und das dadurch gnad angebo-185 ten wirt, Das man auch die kinder teuffen sol, welche durch solche Tauff Gott uberantwort und gefellig werden.

---

180 Matth. 23, 2

178 so – krefftig] an issue discussed in 1529 at the colloquy of Marburg. *WA* 30/3:157, 1-15. See Kolb – Wengert, *The Book of Concord*, p. 42, note 57 **180** Auff – etc.] in other manuscripts, different words were used, e.g., about the effectiveness of the means of grace even in the hands of priests who had transgressed. The Word is the basis of the church's power and the sacraments' effectiveness **181** und – ander] referring to the spiritualist movements teaching about the 'pure' community of faith **183** Der Neundte] this short article, accepted by the *Confutation*, does not mention faith; Article 13 addresses faith in the context of proper use of sacraments. This article reacts to Johan Eck's *Articles* accusing Lutherans of tying faith and baptism. See Luther, *Sermon on the Holy and Blessed Sacrament of Baptism*, WA 2:727-737. 'While Luther maintains that Baptism is of no use without faith, he also emphasizes that Baptism stands secure independent of faith.' 'For my faith does not constitute Baptism but receives it' [Large Catechism]... There is very little about all this in the AC.' For Luther, 'Baptism is the sacrament of justification'. See Grane, *Confession*, p. 105, 107, 109-111 **184** nötig] the meaning of the word 'necessary' leaves room for interpretation **186** uberantwort – gefellig] the words 'trusted' and 'pleasing' point to the impact of justification on the person *coram Deo*

138 CONCILIUM AUGUSTANUM – 1530

170   Damnant Anabaptistas, qui improbant baptismum puerorum et affirmant pueros sine baptismo salvos fieri.

X.

De Coena Domini docent, quod corpus et sanguis Christi vere adsint et distribuantur in coena Domini et improbant secus docentes.

XI.

175

De confessione docent, quod absolutio privata in Ecclesiis retinenda sit, quanquam in confessione non sit necessaria omnium delictorum enumeratio. Est enim impossibilis iuxta Psalmum: *Delicta quis intelligit?*

XII.

180   De poenitentia docent, quod lapsis post Baptismum contingere possit remissio peccatorum quocunque tempore, cum convertuntur, Et quod Ecclesia talibus redeuntibus ad poenitentiam absolutionem impartiri debeat.

CONCILIUM AUGUSTANUM – 1530

Derhalben werden die Widderteuffer verworfen, welche da leren, das die kindertauff nicht recht sey.

Der Zehende

190 Von dem Abendmal des Herrn wirt also geleret, das warer leib und blut Christi warhafftiglich unter der gestalt des brods und weins im Abentmal gegenwertig sey und da ausgeteilt und genomen wirt. Derhalben wirt auch die gegenlahr verworffen.

Der Eilffte

195 Von der Beicht wirt also gelert, das man inn der kirchen privatam absolutionem erhalten und nicht fallen lassen sol, Wiewol inn der beicht nicht not ist, alle missethat und sunden zuerzelen, die weil doch solchs nicht müglich ist, Psal. xviii.: 'Wer kennet die missetat?'

Der Zwelfte

200 Von der Busse wirt also gelert, das die jhenigen, so nach der Tauffe gesundigt haben, zu aller zeit, so sie zur buß kommen, vergebung der sunden erlangen, Und das ihnen die Absolutio von der kirchen nicht soll gewegert werden.

---

198 Ps. 19, 13

187 Widderteuffer] the Anabaptists were widely condemned for their practice of rebaptism and foregoing infant Baptism, which was regulated in the imperial law. This article makes clear that Lutherans do not condone their teachings **188** kindertauff] for Luther, children need Baptism just as adults do, due to original sin, and they are able to believe as well. Baptism works for all on the same basis: God's initiative and action. 'That Baptism then requires faith in order to 'profit' a person is a presupposition of the doctrine of justification, even though it is not mentioned here'. (Grane, *Confession*, p. 112) **190** Von – Herrn] i.e. the Eucharistic meal **192/ 193** Derhalben – verworffen] those who consider the eucharist as a memorial (Karlstadt, Zwingli) or spiritual event (Schwenkfeld) instead of teaching the real presence each time the meal happens. See Kolb – Wengert, *The Book of Concord*, p. 44, note 62 **195** privatam absolutionem] part of sacramental teaching in the Roman Catholic church, priestly absolution **196/197** Wiewol – zuerzelen] breaking off the practice since the Fourth Lateran Council that required enumeration of one's sins in the sacrament of penance prior to receiving the mandatory eucharist **200** Busse] the word in the Roman catholic tradition, refers to the sacrament of penance

140 CONCILIUM AUGUSTANUM – 1530

Constat autem poenitentia proprie his duabus partibus: Altera est contritio seu terrores incussi conscientiae agnito peccato. Altera est fides, quae concipitur ex Evangelio seu absolutione et credit propter Christum remitti peccata et consolatur conscientiam et ex terroribus liberat. Deinde sequi debent bona opera, quae sunt fructus poenitentiae.

Damnant Anabaptistas, qui negant semel iustificatos posse amittere spiritum sanctum. Item qui contendunt quibusdam tantam perfectionem in hac vita contingere, ut peccare non possint. Damnantur et Novatiani, qui nolebant absolvere lapsos post Baptismum redeuntes ad poenitentiam. Reiiciuntur et isti, qui non docent remissionem peccatorum per fidem contingere, sed iubent nos mereri gratiam per satisfactiones nostras.

XIII.

De usu sacramentorum docent, quod sacramenta instituta sint, non modo ut sint notae professionis inter homines, sed magis ut sint signa et testimonia voluntatis Dei erga nos ad excitandam et confirmandam fidem in his, qui utuntur proposita. Itaque utendum est sacramentis ita, ut fides accedat, quae credat promissionibus, quae per sacramenta exhibentur et ostenduntur.

CONCILIUM AUGUSTANUM – 1530

Nu ist ware rechte busse eigentlich nicht anders, denn reu und leid odder schrecken haben uber die sund und doch darneben gleuben an das Evangeli-
205 um und Absolution, das die sunde vergeben und durch Christum gnad erworben sey, welcher glaub widderümb das hertz tröst und zu frieden macht. Darnach sol auch besserung volgen und das man von sunden lasse. Denn dis sollen die früchte der busse sein, wie Johannes spricht Matthei. iii.: 'Wircket rechtschaffene früchte der busse'.

210 Hie werden verworffen die, so leren, das die jhenigen, so einest sind from worden, nicht widder fallen mögen. Es werden auch verdammet die Novatiani, welche die Absolutio denen, so nach der Tauff gesundigt hatten, wegerten. Auch werden die verworffen, so nicht leren, das man durch glauben vergebung der sunden erlangen, sondern durch unser genugthuunge.

215 Der Dreizehend

Vom brauch der Sacrament wirt geleret, das die Sacrament eingesatzt sind nicht allein darümb, das sie zeichen sind, dabey man eusserlich die Christen kennen möge, sonder das es zeichen und zeugnus sind Göttlichs willens gegen uns, unsern glauben dadurch zuerwecken und zu stercken, derhalben sie auch
220 glauben foddern und denn recht gebraucht werden, so mans im glauben empfahet und den glauben dadurch sterckt.

208/209 Matth. 3, 8

203 nicht anders] the words 'nicht anders' were not reproduced in the 1580 text: Kolb – Wengert, *The Book of Concord*, p. 44, note 66   **203/204** denn – schrecken] criticism of the then current practice of generating sorrow and terror rather than comfort of the conscience   **211** die Novatiani] Novatius rejected the return of those who had surrendered during the persecutions, and started his own community of believers   **213/214** Auch – genugthuunge] medieval practice of the sacrament of penance included contrition, confession with a priest, and satisfaction with good works. Indulgences, criticised by Luther in his *Ninety-Five Theses* for their abusive uses, belonged to the realm of satisfaction. See Kolb – Wengert, *The Book of Concord*, p. 46, note 72   **216/219** Vom – zuerwecken] sacraments were considered the visible Word and active agents in effecting the faith, not mere rituals   **219/221** derhalben – sterckt] in distinction from, e.g., Zwingli or the medieval Catholic teaching on the role of faith, the article explains that the sacraments themselves awaken faith while their reception involves faith as well. The first published edition included explicit rejection of *ex opere operato*, a wording omitted in later versions and not used in the first manuscript. Grane, *Confession*, p. 148

XIIII.

De ordine Ecclesiastico docent, quod nemo debeat in Ecclesia publice docere aut sacramenta administrare nisi rite vocatus.

XV.

De ritibus Ecclesiasticis docent, quod ritus illi servandi sint, qui sine peccato servari possunt et prosunt ad tranquillitatem et bonum ordinem in Ecclesia, sicut certae feriae, festa et similia. De talibus rebus tamen admonentur homines, ne conscientiae onerentur, tanquam talis cultus ad salutem necessarius sit.

Admonentur etiam, quod traditiones humanae institutae ad placandum Deum, ad promerendam gratiam et satisfaciendum pro peccatis adversentur Evangelio et doctrinae fidei. Quare vota et traditiones de cibis et diebus etc. institutae ad promerendam gratiam et satisfaciendum pro peccatis inutiles sint et contra Evangelium.

Der Vierzehend

Vom kirchen regiment wirt gelert, das niemant inn der kirchen öffentlich leren odder predigen odder Sacrament reichen sol on ordenlichen beruff.

Das Fünffzehend

Von kirchen ordenung, von menschen gemacht, leret man die jhenige halten, so one sunde mögen gehalten werden und zu frieden und guter ordenung inn der kirchen dienen, Als gewisse feier, Fest und dergleichen, doch geschicht unterricht dabey, das man die gewissen damit nicht beschweren sol, als sey solch ding notigk zur seligkeitt.

Darüber wirt geleret, das alle satzungen und tradition, von menschen der meinung gemacht, das man dadurch Gott versune und gnade vordiehne, dem Evangelio und der lere vom glauben an Christum entgegen sind. Derhalben sind Closter gelübd und andere tradition von underscheid der speis, etc., dadurch man vermeint, genadt zuvordiehnen und fur die sundt gnugk zuthun, untüchtig und widder das Evangelium.

---

222 Der Vierzehend] the article relates to Article 28 on the power in the church, together expressing the Lutheran rationale for the function and parameters for the priestly and episcopal office   **223** Vom – regiment] order in the church, referring to the authority of and within church affairs   **223/224** niemant – beruff] probably a response to Eck's *Articles*, an important articulation on the regulation regarding the office for the proclamation and sacraments. The Latin *rite vocatus* expresses the intent for a necessary and lawful calling for this office that is not considered sacramental. For Luther, the calling was indispensable while ordination was not. See *Grane, Confession*, p. 151-153   **225** Das Fünffzehend] in comparison to Luther's advice on loving dealing with ceremonies and affairs that did not clash with the Word of God, the article names practices to be eliminated, such as monastic vows and fasting; Article 26 spells out the harm of any practice becoming a law, replacing grace, or burdening the human conscience. See Grane, *Confession*, p. 161   **226** Von – ordenung] in the singular form in the 1531 *editio princeps* and in the 1580 *Book of Concord*   **229** gewissen] conscience, an undercurrent concern for many of the reforms proposed in religious practices   **234** Closter gelübd] the cloister vows and celibacy vows were early on targeted as an unnecessary or harmful human regulation   von – speis] with 'distinguishing foods' a wide variety of practices were criticised

XVI.

De rebus civilibus docent, quod legitimae ordinationes civiles sint bona opera Dei, quod Christianis liceat gerere Magistratus, exercere iudicia, iudicare res ex Imperatoriis et aliis praesentibus legibus, supplicia iure constituere, iure bellare, militare, lege contrahere, tenere proprium, iurare postulantibus magistratibus, nubere.

Damnant Anabaptistas, qui interdicunt haec civilia iudicia Christianis. Damnant etiam illos, qui Evangelicam perfectionem non collocant in timore Dei et fide, sed in deserendis civilibus officiis, quia Evangelium tradit iustitiam aeternam cordis. Interim non dissipat Politiam aut Oeconomiam, sed maxime postulat conservare tanquam ordinationes Dei et in talibus ordinationibus exercere caritatem. Itaque necessario debent Christiani oboedire Magistratibus

CONCILIUM AUGUSTANUM – 1530

Der Sechzehend

Von Policey und weltlichem regiment wirt gelert, das alle Oberkeit inn der welt und geordente regiment und gesetze gute ordenung, von Gott geschaffen und eingesetzt, sind, Und das Christen mögen inn Oberkeit, Fürsten und Richterampt one sunde sein, Nach Keiserlichen und andern ublichen Rechten urteil und recht sprechen, Ubeltetter mit dem schwert straffen, Rechte kriege füren, streitten, keuffen und verkeuffen, auff gelegte Eyde thun, eigens haben, Ehelich sein etc.

Hie werden verdammet die widderteuffer, so leren, das der obangezeigten keins Christlich sey. Auch werden die jhenige verdampt, so leren, das Christliche volkomenheit sey, haus und hoff, weib und kind leiblich verlassen und sich der vorberürten stück eussern, so doch dis allein rechte volkomenheit ist, rechte forcht Gottes und rechter glaub an Gott. Denn das Evangelium leret nicht ein eusserlich zeitlich, sondern ein innerlich ewig wesen und gerechtigkeit des hertzen und stosst nicht umb weltlich Regiment, Policey und ehestand, sondern wil, das man solchs alles halte als warhafftige Gottes ordnung und inn solchen stenden Christliche liebe und rechte gute wercke, ein jder nach seinem beruff, beweise. Derhalben sind die Christen schuldig, der Oberkeit unterthan

---

237 Der Sechzehend] the article concerning secular government and temporary affairs. The German word *Polizei*, from the Greek *politeia*, translates in English with 'secular', the word used in Kolb – Wengert, *The Book of Concord*, p. 48, note 84   **238/240** Von – sind] emphasis on good order as the rationale for worldly government, the roots of which can be found in God's institution. The respect of the orderly use of civil government allows the distinction of authorities, civil and religious, protecting the latter from entanglement with the former   **238** weltlichem regiment] a distinction is made between the two realms of authority, spiritual and secular, the article delineating the parameters for the latter, of temporal nature   **240/241** Und – sein] different positions of civil authority and those overseeing magisterial matters   **242/244** Ubeltetter – etc.] rights to participate in wars, punitive actions, transactional activities, and choices pertaining to marriage   **245** die widderteuffer] Anabaptists are mentioned as Christians confusing external and internal, political and religious. Lutherans present themselves as obedient and dutiful citizens within the Empire   **246/247** Christliche volkomenheit] the idea of Christian perfection is viewed in juxtaposition to monastic life, radically broadening the concept of perfection pertaining to daily Christian life in different vocations, without elevating the monastic option   **250/251** gerechtigkeit – hertzen] the Gospel's teachings pertain to the righteousness of heart, not civil matters under the law. This article continues the distinction of the realms of authority, the undercurrent being a critical view of the confusion of the swords in the medieval church with particular reference to the bishop's office   **252/253** inn – stenden] referring to different standings in society, including positions in government, public affairs, and in marriage

suis et legibus. Nisi cum iubent peccare, tunc enim magis debent oboedire
Deo quam hominibus, Act. v.

XVII.

Item docent, quod Christus apparebit in consumatione mundi ad iudi-
230 candum et mortuos omnes resuscitabit, piis et electis dabit vitam aeternam et
perpetua gaudia, impios autem homines ac diabolos condemnabit, ut sine fine
crucientur.

Damnant Anabaptistas, qui sentiunt hominibus damnatis ac diabolis
finem poenarum futurum esse. Damnant et alios, qui nunc spargunt Iudaicas
235 opiniones, quod ante resurrectionem mortuorum pii regnum mundi occupa-
turi sint, ubique oppressis impiis.

XVIII.

De libero arbitrio docent, quod humana voluntas habeat aliquam libertatem ad efficiendam civilem iustitiam et deligendas res rationi subiectas. Sed
240 non habeat vim sine spiritu sancto efficiendae iustitiae Dei seu iustitiae spiri-

CONCILIUM AUGUSTANUM – 1530

255 und ihren geboten und gesetzen gehorsam zu sein inn allem, so one sunde geschehen mag. Denn so der oberkeit gebo one sund nicht geschehen mag, sol man Gott mehr gehorsam sein denn den menschen, Actuum iiii.

Der Siebenzehend

Auch wird gelert, das unser Herr Jhesus Christus am Jüngsten tag komen
260 wird, zu richten und alle todten aufferwecken, den glaubigen und ausserwelthen ewigs leben und ewige freude geben, Die Gottlosen menschen aber und die Teuffel inn die hell und ewig straff verdamnen.

Derhalben werden die widderteuffer verworffen, so leren, das die Teuffel und verdampte menschen nicht ewige pein und qual haben werden. Item: hie
265 werden auch verworffen etliche Jüdische lere, die sich auch itzund ereigen, das fur der aufferstehung der todten eitel heilige frome ein weltliche reich haben und alle Gottlosen vertilgen werden.

Der Achtzehend

Vom freien willen wird also geleret, das der mensch etlicher masse ein
270 freien willen hat, eusserlich erbar zu leben und zu welen unter denen dingen, so die vernunfft begreifft. Aber one gnad, hülff und wirckung des heiligen geists vermag der mensch nicht Gott gefellig zu werden, Gott hertzlich zufürchten, odder zu gleuben oder die angeporn böse lust aus dem hertzen

---

257 Actuum iiii] cfr Act. 5, 29

256 Denn – mag²] the important condition on obedience to the emperor and the laws of the land. What the alternative could mean is left ambiguous, whereas the expressed desire for order is clear   **261/262** Die – verdamnen] Article 17 is accepted by the *Confutation*   **263/264** Derhalben – werden] e.g., Anabaptists such as Hans Denck who taught universal salvation   **264/267** hie – werden] alternative views had been and would be presented by more radical groups, e.g. Thomas Müntzer in 1525 and the subsequent Dutch Kingdom of Münster. See Kolb – Wengert, *The Book of Concord*, p. 50, notes 92-93. This article rejects hopes of a millennial reign or earthly kingdoms (including those of Judaising orientation)   **270** eusserlich – leben] outwardly honorable life, civil righteousness   **271** so – begreifft] the most contested argument of Luther and his peers on the bondage of the will in spiritual and salvation matters beyond human understanding   **271/274** Aber – zuwerffen] in the light of Article 2, original sin prohibits human beings from the right orientation towards God; even faith has to be a gift. Article 18 rejects William Ockham's view on will

tualis, quia *animalis homo non percipit ea, quae sunt spiritus Dei*, sed haec fit in cordibus, cum per verbum spiritus sanctus concipitur.

Haec totidem verbis dicit Augustinus lib. iii. Hypognosticon: Esse fatemur liberum arbitrium omnibus hominibus habens quidem iuditium rationis, non per quod sit idoneum in iis, quae ad Deum pertinent, sine Deo aut inchoare aut certe peragere, sed tantum in operibus vitae praesentis tam bonis quam etiam malis. Bonis dico, quae de bono naturae oriuntur, id est velle laborare in agro, velle manducare et bibere, velle habere amicum, velle habere indumenta, velle fabricare domum, uxorem velle ducere, pecora nutrire, artem discere diversarum rerum bonarum, velle quicquid bonum ad praesentem pertinet vitam. Quae omnia non sine divino gubernaculo subsistunt, immo ex ipso et per ipsum sunt et esse coeperunt. Malis vero dico, ut est velle Idolum colere, velle homicidium etc.

CONCILIUM AUGUSTANUM – 1530

zuwerffen, sondern solchs geschicht durch den heiligen geist, welcher durch
275 Gottes wort geben wird, denn Paulus spricht i. Corin. ii.: 'Der natürlich
mensch vernimpt nichts vom geist Gottes'.

Und damit man erkennen möge, das hierin kein neuigkeit gelert wird, so
sind das die klaren wort Augustini vom freien willen, hiebey geschrieben aus
dem dritten buch Hypognosticon: 'Wir bekennen, das inn allen menschen ein
280 freier wille ist, denn sie haben ja alle natürlich angeborne verstand und
vernunfft, nicht das sie etwas vermügen mit Gott zuhandeln, als Gott von
hertzen zu lieben, zuförchten, sondern allein inn eusserlichen wercken dieses
lebens haben sie freiheit, gutes odder böses zuwelen. Gut mein ich, das die
natur vermag, als auff dem acker zu arbeiten odder nicht, zu essen, zu trincken,
285 zu einem freund zugehen odder nicht, ein kleid an odder aus zuthun, zu bau-
en, ein weib zu nemen, ein handwerck zu treiben und der gleichen etwas nütz-
lichs und guts zu thun, Welches alles doch one Gott nicht ist noch bestehet,
Sondern alles aus ihm und durch ihnen ist. Dagegen kan der mensch auch
böses aus eigener wal furnemen, als fur einem Abgott nidder zuknien, ein
290 todschlag zuthun etc.'

275/276 I Cor. 2, 14

274/275 durch² – wird] the role of the Holy Spirit is essential in effecting faith and
godly kind of righteousness **277/279** Und – Hypognosticon] associated with *Sancti
Prosperi Aquitani (Pseudo-Augustini) Hypomnesticon Augustini contra Pelagianos siue
Caelestianos haereticos*, in *The Pseudo-Augustinian Hypomnesticon against the Pelagians
and Celestians*, II, ed. J. E. Chisholm (*Paradosis* 21), Fribourg 1980, p. 100-208 (= *PL*
45, col. 1611-1664). Kolb – Wengert, *The Book of Concord*, p. 52, note 95 **279/
283** Wir – zuwelen] this article draws from the distinction between freedoms *coram
hominibus* (civil righteousness) and no freedom *coram Deo* (alien righteousness):
choices in daily life are different matters than the existential choice of choosing faith in
God. See Grane, *Confession*, p. 183-189 **287/288** Welches – ist] as expressed in
Article 4, the human beings' dependency on God is absolute. God is the agent of
salvation, the effect of which human beings can only receive. See Luther's *Heidelberg
Disputation* (1518), particularly thesis 28 on God's love creating what is pleasing to God
288/290 Dagegen – etc.] the 1531 *editio princeps* includes a paragraph rejecting all
who taught that human beings could uphold the commandments and love God
without God's grace and the work of the Spirit. Kolb – Wengert, *The Book of Concord*,
p. 52, note 8

XIX.

De causa peccati docent, quod tametsi Deus creat et conservat naturam, tamen causa peccati est voluntas malorum ut diaboli et impiorum, quae non adiuvante Deo avertit se a Deo, sicut Christus ait Ioan. viii: *Cum loquitur mendacium, ex seipso loquitur.*

XX. De fide et bonis operibus

Falso accusantur nostri, quod bona opera prohibeant. Nam scripta eorum, quae extant de decem praeceptis, et alia simili argumento testantur, quod utiliter docuerint de omnibus vitae generibus et officiis, quae genera vitae, quae opera in qualibet vocatione Deo placeant. De quibus rebus olim parum docebant Contionatores, tantum puerilia et non necessaria opera urgebant, ut certas ferias, certa ieiunia, fraternitates, peregrinationes, cultus Sanctorum, rosaria, monachatum et similia. Haec adversarii nostri admoniti nunc dediscunt nec perinde praedicant haec inutilia opera ut olim. Incipiunt etiam fidei mentionem facere, de qua olim mirum erat silentium. Docent nos non tantum operibus iustificari, sed coniungunt fidem et opera et dicunt nos fide et operibus iustificari. Quae doctrina tolerabilior est priore et plus afferre potest consolationis quam vetus ipsorum doctrina.

CONCILIUM AUGUSTANUM – 1530

Der Neunzehend

Von ursach der sunden wird bey uns geleret, das, wiewol Gott der allmechtig die gantze natur geschaffen hat und erhelt, so wirckt doch der verkerte wille die sund inn allen bösen und verechtern Gottes, wie denn des
295 Teuffels wille ist und aller Gottlosen, welcher als bald, so Gott die hand abgethan, sich von Gott zum argen gewand hat, wie Christus spricht, Joh. viii. 'Der Teuffel redet lügen aus seinem eigen'.

20. Vom glauben und wercken

Den unsern wirt mit unwarheit ufgelegt, das sie gute werck verpieten,
300 dan ire schrifften von zehen gepotten und andere beweisen, das sie von rechten christlichen stenth und werck guten nutzlichen bericht und ermanunge gethan haben. Davon man vor disser zeit wenig gelernt hatt, sonder allermeist in allen predigen auf kundische unnottige werck als rosenkrentz, heiligen dienst, munch werden, walfarten, gesatzten fasten, feyern, bruderschafften etc.
305 getrieben; soliche unnotige werck rhumet auch unser widderpart nhun nicht mher so hoch als vor zeiten. Darzu haben sie auch geleret, nu vom glauben zurethn, davon sie doch in vortzeiten gar nichts gepredigt haben, leren dennocht nhu, das wir nicht allein aus wercken vor Got gerecht werth, sonder sezen den glauben an Christum dartzu und sprechen, glaub und werck mach
310 uns gerecht vor Got, wilche rede etwas mher trosts pringen magk, dan so man allein leret, uff werck zuvertrauen.

296/297 Ioh. 8, 44

292/295 Von – bald] in the spirit of Augustine, the perverted will is identified as the cause for sin, the cycle of which can be broken only by the Holy Spirit. Without God's steering, men will choose sin, freely, because of original sin. God is thus not responsible for human sins. See Grane, *Confession*, p. 190-193   **295** so – abgethan] the idea of God withdrawing support raises the question of predestination, which is not addressed in the document   **296/297** sich – eigen] see Aurelius Augustinus, *De gratia et libero arbitrio* (*PL* 44), Paris 1865, col. 889-890. Kolb – Wengert, *The Book of Concord*, p. 52, note 97   **300** von¹ – gepotten] the Ten Commandments, typically referred to in Lutheran discourse when speaking of the law in Christian's daily life and of good works. Cfr *Von den guten Werken* (*Treatise on Good Works*), 1520, and the *Catechisms*. See Grane, *Confession*, p. 200   **303** unnottige werck] needless works refer mostly to works of satisfaction and monastic vows as well as other central practices of medieval piety. See Grane, *Confession*, p. 201   **303/305** als – getrieben] a list of familiar practices deemed unnecessary meritorious works, including praying with rosaries, fasting, and joining medieval associations committed to charitable acts and devotional practices

Cum igitur doctrina de fide, quam oportet in Ecclesia praecipuam esse, tam diu iacuerit ignota, quemadmodum fateri omnes necesse est de fidei iustitia altissimum silentium fuisse in contionibus, tantum doctrinam operum versatam esse in ecclesiis, nostri de fide sic admonuerunt Ecclesias.

Principio, quod opera nostra non possint reconciliare Deum aut mereri remissionem peccatorum et gratiam et iustificationem, sed hanc tantum fide consequimur credentes, quod propter Christum recipiamur in gratiam, qui solus positus est mediator et propitiatorium, per quem reconcilietur pater. Itaque, qui confidit operibus se mereri gratiam, is aspernatur Christi meritum et gratiam et querit sine Christo humanis viribus vitam ad Deum, cum Christus de se dixerit: *Ego sum via, veritas et vita.*

Haec doctrina de fide ubique in Paulo tractatur, Ephes. ii.: *Gratia salvi facti estis per fidem et hoc non ex vobis; Dei donum est, non ex operibus etc.* Et ne quis cavilletur a nobis novam Pauli interpretationem excogitari, tota haec causa habet testimonia Patrum. Nam Augustinus multis voluminibus defendit gratiam et iustitiam fidei contra merita operum. Et similia docet Ambrosius de vocatione Gentium et alibi. Sic enim inquit de vocatione Gentium: Vilesceret redemptio sanguinis Christi et misericordia Dei humanorum operum praerogativa succumberet, si iustificatio, quae fit per gratiam, meritis praecedentibus deberetur, ut non munus largientis, sed merces esset operantis.

Quanquam autem haec doctrina contemnitur ab imperitis, tamen experiuntur piae ac pavidae conscientiae plurimum eam consolationis afferre, quia conscientiae non possunt reddi tranquillae per ulla opera, sed tantum fide, cum certo statuunt, quod propter Christum habeant placatum Deum. Quemadmodum Paulus docet Rom. v.: *Iustificati per fidem pacem habemus apud Deum.* Tota haec doctrina ad illud certamen perterrefactae conscientiae referenda est nec sine illo certamine intelligi potest. Quare male iudicant de ea re homines imperiti et prophani, qui Christianam iustitiam nihil esse somniant nisi civilem et philosophicam iustitiam.

Olim vexabantur conscientiae doctrina operum, non audiebant ex Evangelio consolationem. Quosdam conscientiae expuliet in desertum, in Monasteria, sperantes ibi se gratiam merituros esse per vitam monasticam. Alii alia excogitaverunt opera ad promerendam gratiam et satisfaciendum pro peccatis.

CONCILIUM AUGUSTANUM – 1530

Dieweil nhu di lere vom glauben, di das heuptstuck ist in christlichem wesen, so lange zeit, wie man bekennen muß, nicht getrieben worden, sonder allein wergler an allen orten gepredigt, ist davon von den unsern solich under-
315 richt bescheen.

Erstlich, das unser werck uns nit mugen mit Got versonen und gnade erwerben, sonder solichs beschicht allein durch den glauben, so man glaubt, das uns umb Christus willen di sunde vergeben werth, wilcher allein der mitler ist, den vatter zuversunen. Were nun solichs vermeint durch werck außtzurich-
320 ten und gnade zuverdienen, der verachtet Christum und sucht ein eigen weg zu Got widder das evangelium.

Dise lere vom glauben ist offentlich und clar im Paulo an vilen orten gehandelt, sonderlich zun Ephesern am andern: 'Aus gnaden seit ir selig wor-den durch den glauben und dasselbig nicht aus euch, sonder es ist Gottes gab,
325 nicht aus wercken, damit sich niemants rhume etc'. Und das hierin kein neuer verstandt eingefurt sei, kann man aus sanct Augustin beweisen, der dise sach vleißlich handelt und auch also leret, das wir durch den glauben an Christum gnade erlangen und fur Got gerecht werthn, nicht durch werck, wie sein gantz buch de spiritu et litera außweiset.

330 Wiewol nu dise lere bei unversuchten leuthen seer veracht wirdet, so befint sich doch, das sie den bloden und erschrocknen gewissen seher trostlich und heilsam ist. Dan das gewissen kan nicht zu rhu und frieden khommen durch werck, sonder allein durch glauben, so es bei sich gewißlich schleust, das es umb Christus willen ein gnedigen Got habe, wie auch Paulus spricht zun
335 Romern am funfften: 'So wir durch glauben seint gerecht worden, haben wir rhue und frieden vor Got'.

Disen troste hat man vorzeiten nicht getrieben in predigten, sonder di armen gewissen auff eigene werck getriben, und seint mancherlei werck furge-nommen. Dan etlicher hat das gewissen in die closter gejagt, der hoffnung,
340 daselbst gnade zuerwerben durch closter leben. Ettliche haben andere werck erdacht, damit gnade zuverdienen und vor die sunde gnug zuthun. Derselbi-

---

323/325 Eph. 2, 8-9   **335/336** Rom. 5, 1

329 buch – litera] Augustine's *De spiritu et littera*. See Kolb – Wengert, *The Book of Concord*, p. 54, note 104   **335/336** So – Got] Some versions have a quote from Pseudo-Ambrose. Grane, *Confession*, p. 194, note 2   **340/341** Ettliche – zuthun] rejection of monastic vows and lifestyle and any deeds considered as part of satisfaction

154   CONCILIUM AUGUSTANUM – 1530

305 Ideo magnopere fuit opus hanc doctrinam de fide in Christum tradere et renovare, ne deesset consolatio pavidis conscientiis, sed scirent fide in Christum apprehendi gratiam et remissionem peccatorum.

Admonentur etiam homines, quod hic nomen fidei non significat tantum historiae notitiam, qualis est et in impiis et diabolo, sed significat fidem, quae
310 credit non tantum historiam, sed etiam effectum historiae, videlicet hunc articulum, Remissionem peccatorum, quod videlicet per Christum habeamus gratiam, iustitiam et remissionem peccatorum. Iam qui scit se per Christum habere propitium patrem, is vere novit Deum, scit se ei curae esse, invocat eum. Denique non est sine Deo sicut Gentes. Nam diaboli et impii non
315 possunt hunc articulum credere, Remissionem peccatorum. Ideo Deum tanquam hostem oderunt, non invocant eum, nihil boni ab eo expectant. Augustinus etiam de fidei nomine hoc modo admonet lectorem et docet in scripturis nomen fidei accipi, non pro notitia, qualis est in impiis, sed pro fiducia, quae consolatur et erigit perterrefactas mentes.

320   Praeterea docent nostri, quod necesse sit bona opera facere, non ut confidamus per ea gratiam mereri, sed propter voluntatem Dei. Tantum fide apprehenditur remissio peccatorum ac gratia. Et quia per fidem accipitur spiritus sanctus, iam corda renovantur et induunt novos affectus, ut parere bona opera possint. Sic enim ait Ambrosius: Fides bonae voluntatis et iustae actionis geni-
325 trix est. Nam humanae vires sine spiritu sancto plenae sunt impiis affectibus et sunt imbecilliores, quam ut bona opera possint efficere coram Deo. Ad haec sunt in potestate diaboli, qui impellit homines ad varia peccata, ad impias opiniones, ad manifesta scelera. Quemadmodum est videre in philosophis, qui et ipsi conati honeste vivere, tamen id non potuerunt efficere, sed contaminati
330 sunt multis manifestis sceleribus. Talis est imbecillitas hominis, cum est sine fide et sine spiritu sancto et tantum humanis viribus se gubernat.

CONCILIUM AUGUSTANUM – 1530

gen viel haben erfaren, das man dadurch nicht ist zufriethn khommen,
darumb ist not gewesen, dise lere vom glauben an Christum zupredigen und
vleissig zudreiben, das den glauben, an verdienst, Gottes gnade ergreifft.

345 Es geschicht auch underricht, das man hie nicht von solichem glauben
rett, den auch die teuffel oder gotlosen haben, die auch die historien glauben,
das Christus geliden habe und aufferstanden sei von dodten, sonder man redet
von warem glauben, der do glaubt, das wir durch Christum gnade und vergebung der sunde erlangen und der nu weis, das er ein gnedigen Got durch
350 Christum hat, kennet also Got, rufft ine an und ist nicht on Got, wie di
heyden; dan teuffel und gotlosen gleuben dissen artickel, vergebung der sunden, nicht. Darumb sein sie Got vheindt, konnen ine nicht anruffen, nichts
guts von ime hoffen. Und also, wie itzo angetzeigt ist, redet die schrifft vom
glauben, und heist nicht glauben ein solichs wissen, das teufel und gotlosen
355 menschen haben, dan also wirtt vom glauben geleret zun Hebreern am eilfften,
das glauben sei nicht allein di historien wissn, sonder zuversicht haben zu
Gott, seine zusage zuentpfaen. Und Augustinus erinnert uns auch, das wir das
wortt glauben in der schrifft verstehen sollen, das es heiß, zuversicht zu Gott,
das er uns gnedig sei, und heiß nicht allein, solich historien wissen, wie auch di
360 teuffel wissen.

Ferner wirt geleret, das gute werck sollen und mussen gescheen, nicht das
man drauf vertraue, gnade damit zuverdienen, sonder umb Gots willen und
Got zu lobe. Der glaub ergreifft allezeit allein gnade und vergebung der sunde.
Und dieweil durch den glauben der Heilig Geist geben wirt, so wirt auch das
365 hertz geschickt, gute werck zuthun. Dan zuvor, dieweil es an den Heiligen
Geist ist, so ist es zuschwach, dartzu ists ins teufels gewalt, der die armen
menschliche natuer zu vilen sunth treibt, wie wir sehen in den philosophen,
wilche sich understanden, eherlich und unstrefflich zuleben, haben aber dannocht solichs nicht außgericht, sonder seint in vile grosse offetliche sunde
370 gefallen. Also gehet es mit dem menschen, so er ausser dem rechten glauben
und dem Heiligen Geist ist und sich allein durch eigene menschliche crafft
regiret.

357/358 Und – Gott] Augustinus, *In Iohannis epistulam ad Parthos tractatus X* 10, 2,
éd. W. J. Mountain (*Œuvres de Saint Augustin* 76), Paris 2008, p. 402 (= *PL* 35,
col. 2055), and Augustinus [= Honorius Augustodunensis], *Liber de cognitione uerae
uitae* (*PL* 40), Paris 1887, col. 1025. Kolb – Wengert, *The Book of Concord*, p. 56, note
108   **364/365** Und – zuthun] the meaning of works commanded by God is explained
as deeds springing from freedom effected by God in justification, with deeds
commanded by God   **370/372** Also – regiret] human powers addressed in
opposition to, e.g., Erasmus' more optimistic view

156 CONCILIUM AUGUSTANUM – 1530

Hinc facile apparet hanc doctrinam non esse accusandam, quod bona opera prohibeat, sed multo magis laudandam, quod ostendit quomodo bona opera facere possimus. Nam sine fide nullo modo potest humana natura primi aut secundi praecepti opera facere. Sine fide non invocat Deum, a Deo nihil expectat, non tollerat crucem, sed querit humana praesidia, confidit humanis praesidiis. Ita regnant in corde omnes cupiditates et humana consilia, cum abest fides et fiducia erga Deum. Quare et Christus dixit: *Sine me nihil potestis facere*, Ioan. xv. Et Ecclesia canit: Sine tuo numine nihil est in homine, nihil est innoxium.

XXI.

De cultu Sanctorum docent, quod memoria Sanctorum proponi potest, ut imitemur fidem eorum et bona opera iuxta vocationem, Ut Caesar imitari potest exemplum Davidis in bello gerendo ad depellendos Turcas a patria. Nam uterque rex est. Sed scriptura non docet invocare Sanctos seu petere auxilium a Sanctis, Quia unum Christum nobis proponit mediatorem, propitiatorium, Pontificem et intercessorem. Hic invocandus est et promisit se exauditurum esse preces nostras et hunc cultum maxime probat videlicet, ut

CONCILIUM AUGUSTANUM – 1530

Derhalben ist dise leer vom glauben nit zuschelthn, das sie gute werck verbiete, sonder viel mher zurhomen, das sie gute werck zuthun lere und hilff
375 anbiete, wie man zu guten wercken kommen moge. Dan ausser dem glauben und ausserhalb Christo ist menschlich natuer und vermugen viel zu schwach, gute werck zuthun, Got anzuruffen, gedult zuhaben im leithn, den nhesten liben, befolene aempter vleissig außtzurichten, gehorsam zusein, bosen lust zumeiden etc. Soliche hohe und rechte werck mogen nicht gescheen on di
380 hilff Christi, wie er selbst spricht, Joannes am funfftzehenth: 'An mich kont ir nichts thun'.

Der Ein und zwentzigst.

Vom heiligen dienst wirt von den unsern also geleret, das man der heiligen gedencken sol, auff dar wir unsern glauben stercken, so wir sehen, wie
385 ihnen gnad widderfaren, auch wie ihnen durch glauben geholffen ist, dazu, das man Exempel neme von ihren guten wercken, ein jeder nach seinem beruff, gleich wie Kei. Mai. Seliglich und Göttlich dem exempel David folgen mag, kriege widder den Türken zu füren, denn sie beide sind inn Königlichem ampt, welchs schutz und schirm ihrer unterthan foddert. Durch schrifft aber
390 mag man nicht beweisen, das man die heiligen anruffen odder hülff bey ihnen suchen sol. Denn es ist allein ein einiger versüner und mitler gesetzt zwischen Gott und menschen: Jhesus Christus, i. Thimo. ii., welcher ist der einige heiland, der einige öberste Priester, gnadenstuel und vorsprech fur Gott, Roma. viii. Und der hat allein zugesagt, das er unser gebeth erhoren wolle. Das
395 ist auch der höchste Gottes dienst nach der schrifft, das man den selbigen Jhesum Christ inn allen nöten und anligen von hertzen suche und anruffe, i. Joh.

380/381 Ioh. 15, 5   **392** Thimo ii] cfr I Tim. 2, 5; not in the Latin text   **394** Roma viii] cfr Rom. 8, 34

373/374 Derhalben – verbiete] this article reacts to Eck's *Articles* accusing Lutherans of omitting good works   **379/381** Soliche – thun] the paradoxical teaching of both necessity and freedom to do good deeds for the sake of one's neighbour is explicated in Luther's *On Christian Freedom* (1520). Works, for Luther, never work for satisfaction of sin or for the performance of holiness but are a logical consequence of being saved and freed to love one's neighbour   **383/386** Vom – wercken] the saints' good deeds can present a motivation and inspiration for good deeds. 'The lives of the saints are no longer of benefit to us by virtue of their acquired merits, but as a testimony to God's mercy toward weak human beings. Thus contemplation of the saints becomes a proclamation of the gospel' (Grane, *Confession*, p. 208). Luther on the proper relating to the saints, *Schmalkalden Articles*, part 2, article 3   **387** gleich – Göttlich] not in the Latin text   **388** kriege – füren] a unified military front was essential for the Emperor facing the challenge of the Ottoman army

invocetur in omnibus afflictionibus. 1. Ioan. ii.: *Si quis peccat, habemus advoca-*
350 *tum apud Deum etc.*

Haec fere summa est doctrinae apud nos, in qua cerni potest nihil inesse, quod discrepet a scripturis vel ab ecclesia catholica vel ab Ecclesia Romana, quatenus ex scriptoribus nobis nota est, quod, cum ita sit, inclementer iudicant isti, qui nostros pro haereticis haberi postulant. Tota dissensio est de pau-
355 cis quibusdam abusibus, qui sine certa autoritate in Ecclesias irrepserunt, in quibus etiam, si qua esset dissimilitudo, tamen decebat haec lenitas Episcopos, ut propter confessionem, quam modo recensuimus, tolerarent nostros, quia ne Canones quidem tam duri sunt, ut eosdem ritus ubique esse postulent, neque similes unquam omnium Ecclesiarum ritus fuerunt. Quanquam apud nos
360 magna ex parte veteres ritus diligenter servantur. Falsa enim calumnia est, quod omnes ceremoniae, omnia vetera instituta in Ecclesiis nostris aboleantur. Verum publica querela fuit abusus quosdam in vulgaribus ritibus herere. Hi quia non poterant bona conscientia probari, aliqua ex parte correcti sunt.

Articuli, in quibus recensentur abusus mutati

365 Cum Ecclesiae apud nos de nullo articulo fidei dissentiant ab Ecclesia catholica, tantum paucos quosdam abusus omittant, qui novi sunt et contra voluntatem Canonum vitio temporum recepti, rogamus, ut Caesarea Maiestas clementer audiat, et quid sit mutatum et quae fuerint causae, quo minus coactus sit populus illos abusus contra conscientiam observare. Nec habeat fidem
370 Caesarea Maiestas istis, qui, ut inflamment odia hominum adversus nostros, miras calumnias spargunt in populos. Hoc modo irritatis animis bonorum virorum initio praebuerunt occasionem huic dissidio et eadem arte conantur nunc augere discordias. Nam Caesarea Maiestas haud dubie comperiet tolerabiliorem esse formam et doctrinae et ceremoniarum apud nos, quam qualem
375 homines iniqui et malevoli describunt. Neque veritas ex vulgi rumoribus aut maledictis inimicorum colligi potest. Facile autem hoc iudicari potest nihil magis prodesse ad dignitatem ceremoniarum conservandam et alendam reverentiam ac pietatem in populo, quam si ceremoniae rite fiant in Ecclesiis.

CONCILIUM AUGUSTANUM – 1530

ii.: 'So jemands sundiget, haben wir einen fursprecher bey Got, der gerecht ist, Jhesum' etc.

Dis ist fast die Summa der lere, welche inn unsern kirchen zu rechtem Christlichem unterricht und trost der gewissen, auch zu besserung der gleubigen, gepredigt und geleret ist, wie wir denn unser eigen seele und gewissen ja nicht gern wolten fur Gott mit misbrauch Göttlichs namens odder worts inn die höchste gröste fahr setzen odder auff unsere kinder und nachkomen ein andere lere denn so dem reinen Göttlichen wort und Christlicher warheit gemes fellen odder erben. So denn die selbigen inn heiliger schrifft klar gegründ und dazu gemeiner Christlicher, ja auch Römischer kirchen, soviel aus der Veter schrifft zuvermercken, nicht zu widder noch entgegen ist, So achten wir, auch unser widdersacher können inn obangezeigten Artikeln nicht uneinig mit uns sein. Derhalben handeln die jhenigen gantz unfreundlich, geschwind widder alle Christliche einigkeit und liebe, so die unsern derhalben als ketzer abzusondern, zuverwerffen und zu meiden ihnen selbst one einigen bestendigen grund Göttlicher gebot odder schrifft furnemen. Dann die irrung und zanck ist fürnemlich uber etzlichen tradition und mißbreuchen. So dann nu an den heupt Artikeln kein befindlicher ungrund odder mangel und dis unser bekentnus Göttlich und Christlich ist, solten sich billich die Bischoven, wenn schon bey uns der tradition halb ein mangel were, gelinder erzeigen, Wiewol wir verhoffen, bestendigen grund und ursach darzu thun, warümb bey uns etliche tradition und misbreuch geendert sind.

Artickel, von welchen zwispalt ist, do erzelet werden die mißbreuch, so geendert seindt. So nu von den Artikeln des glaubens inn unsern kirchen nicht gelert wird zu widder der heiligen schrifft odder gemeiner Christlichen kirchen, sondern allein etzliche misbreuch geendert sind, welche zum teil mit der zeit selbst eingerissen, zum theil mit gewalt auffgericht, foddert unser notturfft, dieselbigen zuerzelen und ursach anzuzeigen, warümb hierinne enderung geduldet ist, damit Keiserliche Maiestet erkennen möge, das nicht hierinne unchristlich oder frevelich gehandelt, sondern das wir durch Gottes gepot, welches billich höher zuachten denn alle gewonheit, gedrungen sein, solch enderung zugestatten.

397/398 I Ioh. 2, 1

406 gemeiner] Latin equivalent of 'catholic' **412/413** Dann – mißbreuchen] not in the 1531 *editio princeps*; Kolb – Wengert, *The Book of Concord*, p. 60, note 122

[22] De utraque specie

Laicis datur utraque species Sacramenti in Coena Domini, quia hic mos habet mandatum Domini Matth. xxvi.: *Bibite ex hoc omnes*. Ubi manifeste praecepit Christus de poculo, ut omnes bibant, et ne quis possit cavillari, quod hoc ad Sacerdotes tantum pertineat, Paulus ad Corinth. Exemplum recitat, in quo apparet totam Ecclesiam utraque specie usam esse. Et diu mansit hic mos in Ecclesia nec constat, quando aut quo autore primum mutatus sit, tametsi Cardinalis Cusanus recitet, quando sit approbatus. Cyprianus aliquot locis testatur populo sanguinem datum esse. Idem testatur Hieronymus, qui ait, Sacerdotes Eucharistiae ministrant et sanguinem Christi populis dividunt. Immo Gelasius Papa mandat, ne dividatur Sacramentum, Distinctio ii. de Consecratione, Caput Comperimus. Tantum consuetudo non ita vetus aliud habet. Constat autem, quod consuetudo contra mandata Dei introducta non sit probanda ut testantur Canones, Distinctio viii., Caput Veritate cum sequentibus. Haec vero consuetudo non solum contra scripturam, sed etiam contra veteres Canones et exemplum Ecclesiae recepta est. Quare si qui maluerunt utraque specie sacramenti uti, non fuerunt cogendi, ut aliter facerent cum offensione conscientiae.

Et quia divisio sacramenti non convenit cum institutione Christi, solet apud nos omitti processio, quae hactenus fieri solita est.

CONCILIUM AUGUSTANUM – 1530

22. Von beider gestalt des Sacraments

430   Den Leien wirt bey uns beide gestalt des Sacraments gereicht aus dieser ursach, denn dis ist ein clarer bevhel und geboth Christi, Matthei am xxvi.: 'Trincket alle daraus'. Da spricht Christus mit klaren worten von dem kilch, das sie alle daraus trincken sollen. Und damit niemand diese wort anfechten und glosieren könne, als gehöre es den Priestern allein zu, so zeiget Paulus i.

435 Corin. xi. an, das die gantze versamlung der Chorinther kirchen beide gestalt gebraucht hat, und dieser brauch ist langezeit inn der kirchen blieben, wie man durch die historien und Veter schrifften beweisen kan: Cyprianus gedenckt an viel orten, das den Leien der kilch die zeit gereicht sey. So spricht S. Hieronymus, das die Priester, so das Sacrament reichen, dem volck das blut

440 Christi austeilen. So gebeut Gelasius, der Bapst, selbs, das man das Sacrament nicht teilen sol, Distinct. ii. de Consecra. c. Comperimus. Man findet auch nindert kein Canon, der da gebiete, allein ein gestalt zunemen. Es kan auch nimand wissen, wenn odder durch welche diese gewonheit ein gestalt zunemen, eingefurt ist. Wiewol der cardinal Cusanüs gedenckt, wenn diesse weise

445 approbirt sei. Nu ists offentlich, das solche gewonheit wider Gottes geboth, auch widder die alten Canones eingefurt, unrecht ist. Derhalben hat sich nicht gebürt, der jhenigen gewissen, so das heilig Sacrament nach Christus einsetzung zugebrauchen begert haben, zu beschweren und zwingen, wider unsers Herrn Christi ordnung zuhandeln.

450   Und die weil die teilung des Sacraments der einsetzung Christi zuentgegen ist, wirt auch bey uns die gewonliche Procession mit dem Sacrament unterlassen.

---

432 Matth. 26, 27   **435** Corin xi] cfr I Cor. 11, 23-24

429 Von – Sacraments] an article returning to the sacrament of the Eucharist, addressed in Article 10, and its practical offering: the focus being in lay participation. See Article 13 on the use of sacraments   **430** Den Leien] laymen and laywomen **431** bevhel – Christi] Christ's commands   **436** und – blieben] evidence of a long-term practice supports the argument made   **437** Veter] Nicholas of Cusa (1401-1464) Cyprianus] cfr Cyprianus, *Epistularium* 57, 2, 2, ed. G. F. Diercks (*CC SL* 3B), Turnhout 1994, p. 303. Kolb – Wengert, *The Book of Concord*, p. 60, note 126 **438** das – sey] the practice of excluding the laity from receiving both the Eucharist in both kinds was officialised at the Fourth Lateran Council of 1215   **450/452** Und – unterlassen] Lutherans dismissing the *Corpus Christi* feast associated with the transubstantiation doctrine

[23] De coniugio sacerdotum

Publica querela fuit de malis exemplis Sacerdotum, qui non sese continebant. Quam ob causam et Pius Papa dixisse fertur fuisse aliquas causas, cur ademptum sit sacerdotibus coniugium, sed multo maiores esse causas, cur reddi debeat. Sic enim scribit Platina. Cum igitur Sacerdotes apud nos publica illa scandala vitare vellent, duxerunt uxores ac docuerunt, quod liceat ipsis contrahere matrimonium. Primum, quia Paulus dicit: *Unusquisque habeat uxorem suam propter fornicationem.* Item: *Melius est nubere quam uri.* Secundo, Christus inquit: *Non omnes capiunt verbum hoc,* ubi docet non omnes homines ad coelibatum idoneos esse, quia Deus creavit hominem ad procreationem, Gene. 1. Nec est humanae potestatis sine singulari dono et opere Dei creationem mutare. Igitur qui non sunt idonei ad coelibatum, debent contrahere matrimonium. Nam mandatum Dei et ordinationem Dei nulla lex humana, nullum votum tollere potest. Ex his causis docent Sacerdotes sibi licuisse uxores ducere.

Constat etiam in Ecclesia veteri Sacerdotes fuisse maritos. Nam et Paulus ait Episcopum eligendum esse, qui sit maritus. Et in Germania primum ante

CONCILIUM AUGUSTANUM – 1530

23. Vom Ehestand der Priester

Es ist bey jederman hohes und niders standes ein grosmechtige klag inn
der welt gewesen von grosser unzucht und wilden wesen und leben der Priester, so nicht vermochten, keuscheit zuhalten, und war auch jhe mit solchen
greulichen lastern auffs höchste komen. So viel heslichs gros ergernus,
ehebruch und ander unzucht zuvermeiden, haben sich etliche Priester bey uns
in ehelichen stand geben, die selben zeigen diese ursachen an, das sie dahin
gedrungen und bewegt sind aus hoher not ihrer gewissen. Nach dem die
schrifft klar meldet, das der ehelich standt von Goth dem Hern eingesetzet sey,
unzucht zuvermeiden, wie Paulus saget in der ersten zu den Cor. am 7.: 'hure-
rey zuvermeiden, hab ein jglicher sein eigen eheweib'. Item: 'Es ist besser
ehelich werden, denn brennen'. Und nach dem Christus selbst sagt Matt. xix.:
'Sie fassen nicht alle das wort', da zeiget Christus an (welcher wol gewust hat,
was am menschen sey), das wenig leute die gabe, keusch zu leben, haben.
'Denn Gott hat den menschen menlin und freulein geschaffen', Genesis am
ersten. Ob es nu inn menschlicher macht odder vermögen sey, one sonder
gabe und gnade Gottes, durch eigen furnemen odder gelübde, Gottes der
hohen Maiestet kopf besser zu machen odder zuendern, hat die erfarung alzu
klar geben. Denn was guts, was erbar, züchtiges leben, was Christlichs, ehrlichs
oder redlichs wandels an vielen daraus erfolget, wie greulich, schrecklich unru-
he und quall ihrer gewissen wie viel an ihrem letzten ende derhalb gehabt, ist
am tag, und ihr viel haben es selb bekennet. So denn Gottes wort und gepot
durch kein menschlich gelübd odder gesetz mag geendert werden, haben aus
dieser und anderen ursachen und gründen die Priester und ander geistliche
eheweiber genomen.

So ist es auch aus den historien und der Veter schrifften zubeweisen, das
inn der Christlichen kirchen vor alters der gebrauch gewest, das die Priester
und Diacon Eheweiber gehabt. Darümb sagt Paulus i. Timo. am iii.: 'Es sollen
bischoffe unstrefflich sein, eins weibs man'. Es sind auch in Deudsche land erst
vor vierhundert jaren die Priester zum gelübde der keuscheit vom Ehestand
mit gewalt abgedrungen, welche sich dagegen semptlich auch so gantz ernst-

---

462 Cor – 7] cfr I Cor. 7, 2; I Cor. 7, 9   **465** Matth. 19, 11   **467** Gen. 1, 27   **480/
481** I Tim. 3, 2

456 keuscheit] the question of chastity related particularly to clergy and monks.
Clerical celibacy did not draw from the early church   **457/459** So – geben] clerical
marriage was a custom with a renewed teaching on the rationale of marriage and
human sexuality

470 kopf] *scriba correxit, a.c.* geschepffe

annos quadringentos Sacerdotes vi coacti sunt ad coelibatum, qui quidem adeo adversati sunt, ut Archiepiscopus Moguntinus publicaturus edictum Rom. Pontificis de ea re pene ab iratis Sacerdotibus per tumultum oppressus sit. Et res gesta est tam inciviliter, ut non solum in posterum coniugia prohibe-
420 rentur, sed etiam praesentia contra omnia iura divina et humana, contra ipsos etiam Canones factos non solum a Pontificibus, sed a laudatissimis Synodis, distraherentur.

Et cum senescente mundo paulatim natura humana fiat imbecillior, convenit prospicere, ne plura vitia serpant in Germaniam. Porro Deus instituit
425 coniugium, ut esset remedium humanae infirmitatis. Ipsi Canones veterem rigorem interdum posterioribus temporibus propter imbecillitatem hominum laxandum esse dicunt, quod optandum est, ut fiat et in hoc negotio. Ac videntur Ecclesiis aliquando defuturi pastores, si diutius prohibeatur coniugium.

CONCILIUM AUGUSTANUM – 1530

lich und hart gesetzt haben, das ein Ertzbischoff zu Mentz, welcher das Bepst-
liche erstlich neu Edict derhalb verkündigt, gar nahe inn einer empörung der
gantzen Priesterschafft inn einem gedrenge wer umbbracht. Und das selbige
verbot ist bald im anfang so geschwind und unschicklich furgenomen, das der
Babst die zeit nicht allein die künfftige Ehe den Priestern verboten, sondern
auch der jhenigen Ehe, so schon inn dem stand lang gewesen, zurissen, Welches doch nicht allein widder alle Göttliche, natürliche und weltliche Recht,
sondern auch den Canonibus, so die Bepst selb gemacht, und den berümpsten
Conciliis gantz entgegen und widder ist. Auch ist bey viel hohen Gottfurchti-
gen, verstendigen leuten der gleichen rede und bedencken offt gehort, das
solcher gedrungener Celibat und beraubung des Ehestandes, welchen Gott
selbst eingesetzt und frey gelassen, nie kein gutes, sonder viel grosser böser
laster und viel arges eingefurt habe. Es hat auch einer von Bapsten, Pius der ii.
selbst, wie sein historien anzeigt, diese wort offt geredt und von sich schreiben
lassen: Es möge wol etliche ursach haben, warumb den geistlichen die Ehe
verboten sey. Es habe aber viel hoher, grosser und wichtiger ursachen, warumb
man ihnen die ehe sol widder frey lassen. Ungezweivelt, es hat Bapst Pius als
ein verstendiger weiser man dis wort aus grossem bedencken geredt.

Derhalben wöllen wir uns inn unterthenigkeit zu Kei. Maie. vertrosten,
das ihr Maie. als ein Christlicher hochloblicher Keiser gnediglichen behertzi-
gen werde, das itzund inn letzten zeiten und tagen, von welchen die schrifft
meldet, die welt immer erger und die menschen gebrechlicher und schwecher
werden, Derhalben wol hochnotig, nützlich und Christlich ist, diese vleissige
einsehung zuthun, damit, wo der ehestand verboten, nicht erger und schentli-
cher unzucht und laster inn Deudschen landen mochten einreissen. Denn es
wirt ja diese sachen niemands weislicher odder besser endern odder machen
künnen denn Gott selbs, welcher den ehestand, menschlicher gebrechlickeit
zu helfen und unzucht zu weren, eingesatzt hat. So sagen die alten Canones
auch, man müsse zu zeiten die scherffe und rigorem lindern und nachlassen,
umb menschlicher schwacheit willen und ergers zuverhüten und zu meiden.
Nu were das inn diesem fall auch wol Christlich und gantz hoch von noten.
Was kan auch der Priester und geistlichen ehestand gemeiner Christlichen
kirchen nachteilig sein, sonderlich der Pfarrher und anderer, die der kirchen
dienen sollen? Es wirt wol künfftig an Priestern und Pfarhern mangeln, so dis
hart verbot des ehestands lenger weren solt.

---

484 ein – Mentz] Kolb – Wengert, *The Book of Concord*, p. 64, note 135   **496/
501** Es – geredt] attributed to Pius II by Bartolomeo Platina   **511** die – Canones]
Gratianus, *Decretum* I, dist. 34, c. 7 (col. 127); II, causa 1, q. 7, c. 5 (col. 430). Kolb –
Wengert, *The Book of Concord*, p. 66, note 138

166 CONCILIUM AUGUSTANUM – 1530

Cum autem extet mandatum Dei, cum mos Ecclesiae notus sit, cum
430 impurus coelibatus plurima pariat scandala, adulteria et alia scelera digna
animadversione boni magistratus, Tamen mirum est nulla in re maiorem exerceri saevitiam quam adversus coniugium Sacerdotum. Deus praecepit honore
afficere coniugium. Leges in omnibus rebus publicis bene constitutis etiam
apud Ethnicos maximis honoribus ornaverunt. At nunc capitalibus poenis
435 excruciantur et quidem Sacerdotes contra Canonum voluntatem, nullam
aliam ob causam nisi propter coniugium. Paulus vocat doctrinam daemoniorum, quae prohibet coniugium, 1. Timoth. iiii. Id facile nunc intelligi potest
cum talibus suppliciis prohibitio coniugii defenditur.

Sicut autem nulla lex humana potest mandatum Dei tollere, ita nec
440 votum potest tollere mandatum Dei. Proinde etiam Cyprianus suadet, ut
mulieres nubant, quae non servant promissam castitatem. Verba eius sunt
haec, lib. 1 Epistola xi: Si autem perseverare nolunt aut non possunt, melius
est, ut nubant, quam ut in ignem deliciis suis cadant, certe nullum fratribus aut
sororibus scandalum faciant.

445 Et aequitate quadam utuntur Canones erga hos, qui ante iustam aetatem
voverunt, quomodo fere hactenus fieri consuevit.

CONCILIUM AUGUSTANUM – 1530

So nu dieses, nemlich das die priester und geistlichen mögen ehelich wer-
520 den, gegründet ist auff das Göttliche wort und gepot, dazu die Historien
beweisen, das die priester ehelich gewesen, So auch das gelübde der keuscheit
soviel hesliche unchristliche ergernus, soviel ehebruch, schrecklich ungehörte
unzucht und greuliche laster hat angericht, das auch etliche redlich unter
Thumherrn, auch etliche Curtisan zu Rom solchs offt selbst bekent und klegli-
525 chen angezogen, wie solch laster inn Clero zu greulich und ubermacht, in
Gottes zorn würde erregt werden, So ist es ja erbermlich, das man den Christlichen ehestand nicht allein verboten, sondern an etlichen orten auffs
geschwindest, wie ein gros ubelthat zustraffen, unterstanden hat, So doch
Gott inn der heiligen schrifft den ehestand inn allen ehren zuhaben geboten
530 hat. So ist auch der ehestand inn Keiserlichen rechten und inn allen Monar-
chien, wo jhe gesetz und recht gewesen, hochgelobet. Allein dieser zeit begin-
net man die leute unschuldig, allein umb der ehe willen, zu martern und dazu
priester, der man fur andern schonen solt, Und geschicht nicht allein widder
Göttliche recht, sondern auch widder die Canones. Paulus der Apostel i.
535 Timo. iiii. nennet die lere, so die ehe verbieten, Teuffels lere; so sagt Christus
selbst Johan. am viii., Der Teuffel sey ein mörder von anbegin, welchs denn
wol zusamen stimmet, das es freilich Teuffels lere sein müssen, die ehe verbieten und sich unterstehen, solche lere mit blut vergissen zuerhalten.

Wie aber kein menschlich gesetz Gottes gebot kan weg thun odder end-
540 ern, also kann auch kein gelübde Gottes gepot endern. Darümb gibt auch
Sanct Cyprianus den rath, das die weiber, so gelobte keuscheit nicht halten,
sollen ehelich werden, und sagt Epist. xi. also: 'So sie aber keuscheit nicht
halten wollen odder nicht vermügen, so ists besser, das sie ehelich werden,
denn das sie durch ihre lust ins feuer fallen, und sollen sich wol fur sehen, das
545 sie den brüdern und schwestern kein ergernus anrichten'.

Zu dem, so brauchen auch alle Canones grösser gelindigkeit und equitet
gegen die jhenigen, so inn der jugend gelübd gethan, wie denn priester und
Mönche des mehrerteils inn der jugent inn solchen stand aus unwissenheit
komen sind.

534/535 i – iiii] cfr I Tim. 4, 1

528/530 So – hat] the sentence is not reproduced in the 1580 edition. Kolb –
Wengert, *The Book of Concord*, p. 66, note 139 **542** Epist xi] Cyprianus, *Epistularium*
4, 2, 3, ed. G. F. Diercks (*CC SL* 3B), Turnhout 1994, p. 20, 44-47. Kolb – Wengert,
The Book of Concord, p. 66, note 140

[24] De missa

Falso accusantur Ecclesiae nostrae, quod Missam aboleant; retinetur enim Missa apud nos et summa reverentia celebratur. Servantur et usitatae ceremoniae fere omnes, praeterquam quod Latinis cantionibus admiscentur alicubi Germanicae, quae additae sunt ad docendum populum. Nam ad hoc praecipue opus est ceremoniis, ut doceant imperitos. Et non modo Paulus praecepit uti lingua intellecta populo in Ecclesia, sed etiam ita constitutum est humano iure. Assuefit populus, ut una utantur sacramento, si qui sunt idonei, id quoque auget reverentiam ac religionem publicarum ceremoniarum. Nulli enim admittuntur nisi antea explorati atque auditi. Admonentur etiam homines de dignitate et usu sacramenti, quantam consolationem afferat pavidis conscientiis, ut discant Deo credere et omnia bona a Deo expectare et petere. Hic cultus delectat Deum, talis usus sacramenti alit pietatem erga Deum. Itaque non videntur apud adversarios Missae maiore religione fieri quam apud nos.

Constat autem hanc quoque publicam et longe maximam querelam omnium bonorum virorum diu fuisse, quod Missae turpiter prophanarentur collatae ad quaestum. Neque enim obscurum est, quam late pateat hic abusus in omnibus templis, a qualibus celebrentur Missae tantum propter mercedem aut stipendium, quam multi contra interdictum Canonum celebrent. Paulus autem graviter minatur iis, qui indigne tractant Eucharistiam, cum ait: *Qui ederit panem hunc aut biberit calicem Domini indigne, reus erit corporis et sanguinis Domini.* Itaque cum apud nos admonerentur Sacerdotes de hoc peccato, desierunt apud nos privatae Missae, cum fere nullae privatae Missae nisi quaestus causa fierent. Neque ignoraverunt hos abusus Episcopi, qui si correxissent eos in tempore, minus nunc esset dissensionum. Antea sua dissimulatione multa vitia passi sunt in Ecclesiam serpere. Nunc sero incipiunt queri de calamitatibus Ecclesiae, cum hic tumultus non aliunde sumpserit occasionem quam ex illis abusibus, qui tam manifesti erant, ut tolerari amplius non possent. Magnae dissensiones de Missa, de Sacramento extiterunt. Fortasse dat poenas orbis tam diuturnae prophanationis Missarum, quam in Ecclesiis tot seculis toleraverunt isti, qui emendare et poterant et debebant. Nam in Decalogo scriptum est: *Qui Dei nomine abutitur, non erit impunitus.* At ab initio mundi nulla res divina ita videtur unquam ad quaestum collata fuisse ut Missa.

24. Von der Mess

Man leget den unsern mit unrecht auff, das sie die Mess sollen abgethan haben. Denn das ist öffentlich, das die Mess, one rhum zureden, bey uns mit grösser andacht und ernst gehalten wird denn bey den widdersachern. So werden auch die leute mit höchstem vleis zum offtermal unterricht vom heiligen Sacrament, wo zu es eingesetzt und wie es zugebrauchen sey, Als nemlich die erschrocken gewissen zu trösten, dadurch das volck zur Communion und Messe gezogen wird. Dabey geschicht auch underricht wieder ander unrechte lehre vom sacrament. So ist auch inn den öffentlichen Ceremonien der Messe kein mercklich enderung geschehen, denn das an etlichen orten deudsch geseng, das volck damit zuleren und zu uben, neben Latinischem gesang gesungen wird, sintemal alle Ceremonien furnemlich dazu dienen sollen, das das volck daran lerne, was ihm zuwissen von Christo not ist.

Nach dem aber die Messe auff mancherley weisse fur dieser zeit misbraucht, wie am tag ist, das ein jarmarckt daraus gemacht, das man sie kaufft und verkaufft hat und das mehrerteil inn allen kirchen umb geltes willen gehalten ist. Solcher misbrauch ist zu mehrmaln auch fur dieser zeit von gelerten und fromen leuten gestrafft worden. Als nu die prediger bey uns davon gepredigt und die priester erinnert sind der schrecklichen bedrangnus, so denn billich ein jden Christen bewegen sol, das, wer das Sacrament unwirdiglich braucht, der sey schuldig am leib und blut Christi, Darauff sind solche kauffmesse und winckel Mess, welche bisanher aus zwang umb geldes und der prebenden willen gehalten worden, inn unsern kirchen gefallen.

---

562 von – ist] I Cor. 14, 9-11   **568/569** so – sol] I Cor. 11, 27

551/552 Man – haben] correcting misleading comments about Luther rejecting the practice of Mass per se. See also Luther, *Deutsche Messe und Ordnung des Gottesdiensts, 1526, WA* 19:72-113. See Kolb – Wengert, *The Book of Concord*, p. 68, note 142   **553/555** So – Sacrament] e.g., Luther in *Large Catechism* on the sacraments. Also *Schmalkalden Articles*, part 2, article 2; part 3, article 6   **556/557** Communion – Messe] from the 1520s onwards, the practice of penance before participation in the Mass continued in Wittenberg   **559/560** denn – geseng] a visible reform was represented by hymns and singing in the vernacular in Lutheran churches   **566/567** Solcher – worden] critique expressed by Nicholas of Cusa, Johann Tauler, Gabriel Biel, and others. Kolb – Wengert, *The Book of Concord*, p. 68, note 144   **571** kauffmesse – Mess] *Winckle Mess* and *Kaufmess* are words for private Masses

Accessit opinio, quae auxit privatas Missas in infinitum, videlicet quod Christus sua passione satisfecerit pro peccato originis et instituerit Missam, in qua fieret oblatio pro quotidianis delictis, mortalibus et venialibus. Hinc manavit publica opinio, quod Missa sit opus delens peccata vivorum et mortuorum ex opere operato. Hic coeptum est disputari, utrum una Missa dicta pro pluribus tantundem valeat quantum singulae pro singulis. Haec disputatio peperit istam infinitam multitudinem Missarum.

De his opinionibus nostri admonuerunt, quod dissentiant a scripturis sanctis et ledant gloriam passionis Christi. Nam passio Christi fuit oblatio et satisfactio non solum pro culpa originis, sed etiam pro omnibus reliquis peccatis, ut ad Hebraeos scriptum est: *Sanctificati sumus per oblationem Iesu Christi semel*. Item: *Una oblatione consumavit in perpetuum sanctificatos.*

Item scriptura docet Nos coram Deo iustificari per fidem in Christum, cum credimus nobis remitti peccata propter Christum. Iam si Missa delet peccata vivorum et mortuorum ex opere operato, contingit iustificatio ex opere Missarum, non ex fide, quod scriptura non patitur.

Sed Christus iubet facere in sui memoriam, quare Missa instituta est, ut fides in iis, qui utuntur sacramento, recordetur, quae beneficia accipiat per Christum, et erigat et consoletur pavidam conscientiam. Nam id est meminisse Christi, beneficia meminisse ac sentire, quod vere exhibeantur nobis. Nec satis est historiam recordari, quia hanc etiam Iudaei et impii recordari possunt. Est igitur ad hoc facienda Missa, ut ibi porrigatur sacramentum his, quibus opus est consolatione, sicut Ambrosius ait: Quia semper pecco, semper debeo accipere medicinam.

CONCILIUM AUGUSTANUM – 1530

Dabey ist auch der greulich irthumb gestrafft, das man geleret hat, unser Herr Christus habe durch sein tod allein fur die erbsunde gnug gethan und die
575 Mess eingesatzt zu einem opffer fur die andern sunde und also die Mess zu einem opffer gemacht fur die lebendigen und todten, dadurch sunde weg zun-hemen und Goth zuversonen. Daraus ist weiter gefolgt, das man disputirt hat, Ob eine Mess fur viel gehalten so viel verdiene, als so man fur ein itzliche ein sonderliche hielte. Daher ist die gros unzeliche menige der Messe komen, das
580 man mit diesem werck hat wollen bey Gott alles erlangen, das man bedürfft hat, Und ist daneben des glaubens an Christum und rechten Gottes dienst vergessen worden.

Darümb ist davon unterricht geschehen, wie one zweivel die not gefoddert, das man wist, wie das Sacrament recht zugebrauchen were. Und erstlich,
585 Das kein opffer fur erbsund und ander sunde sey denn der einige tod Christi, zeiget die schrifft an viel orten an. Denn also stehet geschrieben zun Ebreern, das sich Christus ein mal geopffert hat und dadurch fur alle sunde gnug gethan. Es ist gar ein unerhorte neuigkeit in der kirchen leren, das Christus todt solt allein vor die erbsunde und sunst nicht auch vor andere sünde genug
590 gethan haben, derhalben zuhoffen, das menniglich vorstehe, das solcher irthumb nicht unbillich gestrafft sey.

Zum andern, so leret Sanct Paulus, das wir fur Gott gnade erlangen durch glauben und nicht durch werck. Dawidder ist öffentlich dieser misbrauch der Mess, so man vermeint, gnade durch dis wergk zuerlangen, Wie man denn
595 weis, das man die Mess dazu gebraucht, dadurch di sunde abtzulegen, und gnade und alle güter bey Gott zu erlangen, Nicht allein der priester fur sich, sondern auch fur die gantze welt und fur andere lebendige und todte.

Zum dritten, So ist das heilig Sacrament eingesatzt nicht, damit fur die sunde ein opffer anzurichten (denn das opffer ist zuvor geschehen), Sondern
600 das unser glaub dadurch erwecket und die gewissen getröst werden, welche durchs Sacrament vernemen, das ihn gnad und vergebung der sund von Christo zugesagt ist. Derhalben foddert dis Sacrament glauben und wird one glauben vergeblich gebraucht.

---

586 Denn – Ebreern] cfr Hebr. 9, 28; 10, 14

583/586 Darümb – an²] this article's main concern about the erroneous teaching that the Mass – or anything – would serve as a work or that the Mass would function as a sacrifice. The Scriptures are evoked as a correction and a reminder of the once and complete sacrifice of Christ. The Mass is an occasion for remembering Christ and receiving the benefits of the sacrament, and this always in a community. Private masses are abolished. See also Grane, *Confession*, p. 225

Cum autem Missa sit talis comunicatio sacramenti, servatur apud nos una comunis Missa singulis feriis atque aliis etiam diebus, si qui sacramento velint uti, ubi porrigitur sacramentum his, qui petunt. Neque hic mos in Ecclesia novus est. Nam veteres ante Gregorium non faciunt mentionem privatae Missae. De comuni Missa plurimum loquuntur. Chrysostomus ait Sacerdotem quotidie stare ad altare et alios ad comunionem accersere, alios arcere. Et ex Canonibus veteribus apparet unum aliquem celebrasse Missam, a quo reliqui presbyteri et Diaconi sumpserunt corpus Domini. Sic enim sonant verba Canonis Niceni: Accipiant Diaconi secundum ordinem post presbyteros ab Episcopo vel a presbytero sacram comunionem. Et Paulus de comunione iubet, ut alii alios expectent, ut fiat comunis participatio.

Postquam igitur Missa apud nos habet exemplum Ecclesiae ex scriptura et patribus, confidimus improbari eam non posse, maxime cum publicae ceremoniae magna ex parte similes usitatis serventur, tantum numerus Missarum est dissimilis, quem propter maximos et manifestos abusus certe moderari prodesset. Nam olim etiam in Ecclesiis frequentissimis non fiebat quotidie Missa, ut testatur historia Tripartita liber ix. Capitulum xxxviii: Rursus autem in Alexandria quarta et sexta feria scripturae leguntur easque doctores interpretantur et omnia fiunt praeter solennem oblationis morem.

[25] De confessione

Confessio in Ecclesiis apud nos non est abolita. Non enim solet porrigi corpus Domini nisi antea exploratis et absolutis. Et docetur populus diligen-

CONCILIUM AUGUSTANUM – 1530 173

Dieweil nu die Mess nicht ein opffer ist fur ander lebendige odder todte,
ihre sunde weg zunemen, sondern sol ein Communio sey, das der priester und
andere das Sacrament entpfahen fur sich, So wirdet diese weise bey uns gehalten, das man an feiertagen, auch sonst, so Communicanten da sind, Mess helt
Und etliche, so das begeren, Communicirt. Also bleibt bey uns die Mess inn
ihrem rechten brauch, wie sie vor zeiten inn der kirchen gehalten, wie man
beweisen mag aus Sanct Paulo, i. Corin. xi., Dazu auch aus vieler Veter schrifften, denn Chrysostomus spricht: 'wie der priester teglich stehe und fodder
etliche zur Communio, etlichen verbitte er hinzu zutretten'. Auch zeigen die
alten Canones an, das einer das ampt gehalten hat und die ander priester und
Diacon Communiciret. Denn also lauten die wort in Canone Niceno: 'Die
Diacon sollen nach den priestern ordenlich das Sacrament entpfahen vom
Bischoff odder priester'.

So man nu kein neuigkeit hierin, die in der kirchen fur alters nicht gewesen, furgenomen hat auch inn den öffentlichen Ceremonien der Messen kein
mercklich enderung geschehen ist, allein das die andern unnötige Mess, etwa
durch ein misbrauch gehalten neben der Pfarmesse, gefallen sind, Sol billich
diese weise, Mess zuhalten, nicht fur ketzerisch und unchristlich verdamnet
werden. Denn man hat vorzeiten auch inn den grossen kirchen, da viel volcks
gewesen, auch auff die tag, so das volck zusammen kam, nicht teglich Mess
gehalten, wie Tripartita Historia lib. ix. anzeigt, das man zu Alexandria an
Mitwoch und Freitag die schrifft gelesen und ausgelegt habe und sonst alle
Gottes dienst gehalten one die Messe.

25. Von der Beicht

Die Beicht ist durch die prediger dis teils nicht abgethan. Denn diese
gewonheit wird bey uns gehalten, das Sacrament nicht zureichen denen, so
nicht zuvor verhört und absolvirt sind. Dabey wird das volck vleissig unter-

---

610 i Corin] cfr I Cor. 11, 23-33

611 Chrysostomus] Ioh. Chrysost., *In Epist. ad Ephesios* hom. III (*PG* 62), Paris 1862,
col. 29. Kolb – Wengert, *The Book of Concord*, p. 70, note 148   **614** in – Niceno]
Nicene canon 18 (*COGD* I, p. 29). Kolb – Wengert, *The Book of Concord*, p. 70, note
149   **624** Tripartita Historia] Cassiodorus, *Historia ecclesiastica tripartita* 9, 38, 24,
hrsg. W. Jacob – R. Hanslik (*CSEL* 71), Wien 1952, p. 562, 126-128   **624/626** das –
Messe] in his 1537 *Schmalkalden Articles* Luther expressed a more critical assessment of
the medieval practice of the Mass and, as he saw it, its abuses and 'idolatries', in an
effort to defend the 'chief acticle' about salvation by Christ's unrepeatable and
complete redeeming sacrifice. See *Schmalkalden Articles*, part 2, article 2

174 CONCILIUM AUGUSTANUM – 1530

tissime de fide absolutionis, de qua ante haec tempora magnum erat silentium. Docentur homines, ut absolutionem plurimi faciant, quia sit vox Dei et mandato Dei pronuntietur. Ornatur potestas clavium et comemoratur, quantam consolationem afferat perterrefactis conscientiis, et quod requirat Deus fidem, ut illi absolutioni tanquam voci de coelo sonanti credamus, et quod illa fides vere consequatur et accipiat remissionem peccatorum. Antea immodice extollebantur satisfactiones; fidei et meriti Christi ac iustitiae fidei nulla fiebat mentio, quare in hac parte minime sunt culpandae Ecclesiae nostrae. Nam hoc etiam adversarii tribuere nobis coguntur, quod doctrina de poenitentia diligentissime a nostris tractata ac patefacta sit.

Sed de confessione docent, quod enumeratio delictorum non sit necessaria nec sint onerandae conscientiae cura enumerandi omnia delicta, quia impossibile est omnia delicta recitare, Ut testatur Psalmus: *Delicta quis intelligit?* Item Ieremias: *Pravum est cor hominis et inscrutabile.* Quod si nulla peccata nisi recitata remitterentur, nunquam adquiescere conscientiae possent, quia plurima peccata neque vident neque meminisse possunt. Testantur et veteres scriptores enumerationem illam non esse necessariam. Nam in Decretis citatur Chrysostomus, qui sic ait: Non tibi dico, ut te prodas in publicum neque apud alios te accuses, sed oboedire te volo prophetae dicenti, Revela ante Deum viam tuam. Ergo tua confitere peccata apud Deum, verum iudicem, cum oratione. Delicta tua pronuntia non lingua, sed conscientiae tuae memoria etc.

CONCILIUM AUGUSTANUM – 1530

richt, wie tröstlich das wort der Absolution sey, wie hoch und teuer die Absolution zuachten, denn es sey nicht des gegenwertigen menschen stimme odder wort, sondern Gottes wort, der die sunde vergibt. Denn sie wird an Gottes stad und aus Gottes befehl gesprochen. Von diesem befehl und gewalt der
635 schlüssel, wie tröstlich, wie nötig sie sey den erschrocken gewissen, wird mit grossem vleis geleret, Dazu, wie Gott fodder, dieser Absolution zugleuben nicht weniger, denn so Gottes stimme vom himel erschulle, und uns der Absolution frolich trösten und wissen, das wir durch solchen glauben vergebung der sund erlangen. Von diesen nötigen stücken haben vor zeiten die prediger,
640 so von der beicht viel lereten, nicht ein wörtlein gerüret, sondern allein die gewissen mit langer erzelung der sunden, mit gnugthun, mit ablas, walfarten und der gleichen gemartert. Und viel unser widdersacher bekennen selbst, das dieses teils von rechter Christlicher Bus schicklicher denn zuvor inn langer zeit geschrieben und gehandelt sey.
645 Und wird von der beicht also geleret, das man niemand dringen sol, die sund namhafftig zuerzelen, denn solchs ist unmüglich, wie der Psalm spricht: 'Wer kennet die missethat?'. Und Jeremias sagt: 'Des menschen hertz ist so arg, das man es nicht auslernen kan'. Die elende menschliche natur stickt also tieff inn sunden, das sie dieselben nicht alle sehen odder kennen kan, und
650 solten wir allein von denen absolvirt werden, die wir zelen können, wer uns wenig geholffen. Derhalben ist nicht not, die leute zudringen, die sunde namhafftig zuerzelen. Also haben auch die Veter gehalten, wie man findet distinct. i. de poenitentia, do die wort Chrysostomi angezogen werden: 'Ich sag nicht, das du dich selbst solt öffentlich dargeben, oder bey einem andern selbst
655 verklagen odder schuldig geben, sondern gehorche dem Propheten, welcher spricht: «Offenbar dem Herrn deine wege», derhalben beichte Gott dem Herrn, dem warhafftigen richter, neben deinem gebet, nicht sage deine sunde mit der zungen, sondern inn deinem gewissen'. Hie sihet man klar, das Chrysostomus nicht zwinget, die sunde namhafftig zuerzelen. So leret auch die glosa
660 in Decretis de poenitentia Distin. v., das die beicht nicht durch die schrifft

---

647 Wer – missethat] Ps. 19, 12

631 der Absolution] as with the Mass, Lutherans defend their position on retaining the practice of confession. The focus is on absolution being free and removing any suggestions of meritorious performing   **646** unmüglich] enumeration considered impossible and unhelpful in the light of how sin and the dynamics of forgiveness are understood   **658** Chrysostomus] Ioh. Chrysost., *In Epist. ad Hebraeos* hom. XXXI (*PG* 63), Paris 1862, col. 216. Kolb – Wengert, *The Book of Concord*, p. 74, note 160 **659/660** die² – poenitentia] Gratianus, *Decretum* II, causa 33, q. 33, q. 3 (de poenitentia), dist. 5, c. 1 (col. 1238-1240). Kolb – Wengert, *The Book of Concord*, p. 74, note 161

176 CONCILIUM AUGUSTANUM – 1530

Et glosa de poenitentia, Distinctio v., Caput Consideret, fatetur humani iuris
550 esse confessionem. Verum confessio cum propter maximum absolutionis beneficium, tum propter alias conscientiarum utilitates apud nos retinetur.

[26] De discrimine ciborum

Publica persuasio fuit non tantum vulgi, sed etiam docentium in Ecclesiis,
quod discrimina ciborum et similes traditiones humanae sint opera utilia ad
555 promerendam gratiam et satisfactoria pro peccatis. Et quod sic senserit mundus, apparet ex eo, quia quotidie instituebantur novae ceremoniae, novi ordines, novae feriae, nova ieiunia, et doctores in templis exigebant haec opera
tanquam necessarium cultum ad promerendam gratiam et vehementer terre-
bant conscientias, si quid omitterent. Ex hac persuasione de traditionibus mul-
560 ta incommoda in ecclesiis secuta sunt.
Primo: obscurata est doctrina de gratia et iustitia fidei, quae est praecipua
pars Evangelii et quam maxime oportet existere et eminere in Ecclesia, ut
meritum Christi bene cognoscatur et fides, quae credit remitti peccata propter
Christum, longe supra opera collocetur. Quare et Paulus in hunc locum maxi-
565 me incumbit, legem et traditiones humanas removet, ut ostendat iustitiam
Christianam aliud quiddam esse quam huiusmodi opera, videlicet fidem, quae
credit peccata gratis remitti propter Christum. At haec doctrina Pauli, pene
tota oppressa est per traditiones, quae pepererunt opinionem, quod per discrimina ciborum et similes cultus oporteat mereri gratiam et iustitiam. In poeni-
570 tentia nulla mentio fiebat de fide; tantum haec opera satisfactoria propone-
bantur. In his videbatur poenitentia tota consistere.
Secundo: hae traditiones obscuraverunt praecepta Dei, quia traditiones
longae praeferebantur praeceptis Dei. Christianismus totus putabatur esse
observatio certarum feriarum, rituum, ieiuniorum, vestitus. Hae observationes
575 erant in possessione honestissimi tituli, quod essent vita spiritualis et vita
perfecta. Interim mandata Dei iuxta vocationem nullam laudem habebant,
quod paterfamilias educabat sobolem, quod mater pariebat, quod Princeps
regebat rem publicam; haec putabantur esse opera mundana et imperfecta et
longe deteriora illis splendidis observationibus. Et hic error valde cruciavit
580 pias conscientias, quae dolebant se teneri imperfecto vitae genere in coniugio,

CONCILIUM AUGUSTANUM – 1530

geboten, sondern durch die kirchen eingesatzt sey. Doch wirt durch die Prediger dieses teils vleissig gelert, das die beicht von wegen der absolution, welche das heuptstucke und fürnembste darinnen ist, zu trost der erschrocknen gewissen, dartzu auch umb etzlicher ander ursach willen, zuerhalten sey.

665 26. Von unterschiede der speise

Vor zeiten hat man also gelert, gepredigt und geschrieben, das unterscheid der speise und der gleichen tradition, von menschen eingesatzt, und dazu dienen, das man dadurch gnade verdiene und fur die sund gnug thue. Aus diesem grund hat man teglich neue fasten, neue Ceremonien, neue orden
670 und der gleichen erdacht und auff solchs hefftig und hart getrieben, als sind solche ding nötige Gottes dienst dadurch man gnade vordiene, so mans halte und geschehe grosse sund, so mans nicht halte; daraus sind viel schedlicher irthumb inn der kirchen gevolget.

Erstlich ist dadurch die gnad Christi und die lere vom glauben
675 vertunckelt, welche uns das Evangelium mit grossem ernst furhelt und treibet hart darauff, das man den verdienst Christi hoch und theuer achte und wisse, das gleuben an Christum hoch und weit uber alle werck zu setzen sey. Derhalben hat S. Paulus hefftig widder das gesetz Mosi und menschliche traditiones gefochten, das wir lernen sollen, das wir vor Gott nicht from werden aus
680 unsern wercken, sondern allein durch den glauben an Christum, das wir um Christus willen durch Christus gnad erlangen. Solche lere ist schier gantz verloschen dadurch, das man hat gelert, mit gesetzen, fasten undersiecht der speiß, kleider etc. gnad zuverdienen.

Zum andern haben auch solche traditiones Gottes gebot vertunckelt,
685 denn man setzt diese traditiones weit uber Gottes gebot. Dis hielt man allein fur Christlich leben: wer die feier also hielt, also betet, also fastet, also gekleidet war, das nennet man geistlich Christlich leben. Daneben hielt man andere nötige gute werck fur ein weltlich ungeistlich wesen, nemlich diese, so jeder nach seinem beruff zuthun schuldig ist, Als das der hausvater arbeit, weib und
690 kind zu neren und zu Gottes forcht auffzuziehen, die hausmutter kinder gebieret und wart ihr, Ein fürst und Oberkeit land und leut regiert etc. Solche werck, von Gott geboten, musten ein weltlich und unvolkomen wesen sein.

677/679 Derhalben – gefochten] Paul's letters are read in contrast with the word of the law in the Old Testament. In Lutheran discourse, the tension between the law and the Gospel is intentionally employed in the proclamation of grace **684/685** Zum – gebot] another central criticism of the religious teachings of the time: confusing Christian with human orders make the latter appear as superior to God's commands

in magistratibus aut aliis functionibus civilibus, mirabantur Monachos et similes et falso putabant illorum observationes Deo gratiores esse.

Tertio: traditiones attulerunt magna pericula conscientiis, quia impossibile erat omnes traditiones servare et tamen homines arbitrabantur has observationes necessarios esse cultus. Gerson scribit multos incidisse in desperationem, quosdam etiam sibi mortem conscivisse, qui senserant se non posse satis facere traditionibus et interim consolationem nullam de iustitia fidei et de gratia audierant. Videmus Summistas et Theologos colligere traditiones et quaerere ἐπιεικείας, ut levent conscientias, non satis tamen expediunt, sed interdum magis iniiciunt laqueos conscientiis. Et in colligendis traditionibus ita fuerunt occupatae Scholae et contiones, ut non vacaverit attingere scripturam et quaerere utiliorem doctrinam de fide, de cruce, de spe, de dignitate civilium rerum, de consolatione conscientiarum in arduis tentationibus. Itaque Gerson et alii quidam Theologi graviter questi sunt se his rixis traditionum impediri, quo minus versari possent in meliore genere doctrinae. Et Augustinus vetat onerare conscientias huiusmodi observationibus et prudenter admonet Ianuarium, ut sciat eas indifferenter observandas esse, sic enim loquitur.

Quare nostri non debent videri hanc causam temere attigisse aut odio Episcoporum, ut quidam falso suspicantur. Magna necessitas fuit de illis erroribus, qui nati erant ex traditionibus male intellectis, admonere Ecclesias. Nam Evangelium cogit urgere doctrinam in Ecclesiis de gratia et iustitia fidei, quae tamen intelligi non potest, si putent homines se mereri gratiam per observa-

CONCILIUM AUGUSTANUM – 1530

Aber die traditiones musten dennprechtigen namen haben, das sie allein heilige volkomene werck hiessen. Derhalben war kein mas noch ende, solche traditiones zumachen.

Zum dritten: Solche traditiones sind zu hoher beschwerung der gewissen
geraten. Denn es war nicht möglich, alle traditiones zu halten. Und waren
doch die leut inn der meinung, als were solchs ein nötiger Gottes dienst, und
schreibt Gerson, das viel hiemit inn verzweiffelung gefallen. Haben sich auch
selbs umbracht Derhalben, das sie kein trost von der gnade Christi gehort
haben. Denn man sihet bey den Summisten und Theologen, wie die gewissen
verwirret, welche sich unterstanden haben, die traditiones zu samen zu ziehen,
und equitet gesucht, das sie den gewissen hülffen, haben soviel damit zuthun
gehabt, das die weil alle heilsame Christliche lere von nötigern sachen, als vom
glauben, von trost inn hohen anfechtungen und der gleichen, darnidder gelegen ist. Darüber haben auch viel fromer gelerter leut vor dieser zeit seer geklaget, das solche traditiones viel zancks inn der kirchen anrichten und das frome
leut, darmit verhindert, zu rechtem erkentnus Christi nicht komen mochten.
Gerson und etliche mehr haben hefftig darüber geklaget. Ja, es hat auch
Augustino misfallen, das man die gewissen mit soviel traditionibus beschwe-
ret, Derhalben er dabey underricht gibt, das mans nicht fur nötige ding halten
sol.

Darümb haben die unsern nicht aus frevel odder verachtung geistlichs
gewalts von diesen sachen gelert, Sondern es hat die hohe not gefoddert,
unterricht zuthun von ob angezeigten irthumen, welche aus misverstand der
tradition gewachsen sind, denn das Evangelium zwinget, das man die lere vom
glauben sol und müsse inn der kirchen treiben, welche doch nicht mag
verstanden werden, so man vermeint, durch eigene erwelte werck gnad zuverdienen.

693/694 heilige – werck] criticism of setting a goal of *status perfectionis* through
particular religious practices while creating a hierarchy between callings considered
holy and normal statuses and vocations in life, such as parenthood   **696/697** Zum –
geraten] repeating criticism of practices and teachings that add to the burdens of the
human soul, already devastating, rather than offering the means of grace towards
freeing the suffering consciences   **699** Gerson] Iohannes Gerson, *Opera magistralia*
opus 97 (*De vita spirituali animae*), lectio 2, éd. P. Glorieux (*Jean Gerson, Œuvres
complètes*, III), Paris – Tournai, 1962; Kolb – Wengert, *The Book of Concord*, p. 76, note
166   **705** anfechtungen] a word characterising Luther's teaching and experience of a
spiritual trial and *Angst*   **710** Augustino] Augustinus, *Epist.* 54 (*ad Ianuarium*), 2, ed.
K. D. Daur (*CC SL* 31), Turnhout 2004, p. 227. Kolb – Wengert, *The Book of Concord*,
p. 76, note 170   **713/718** Darümb – zuverdienen] this argument defends Lutherans
against accusations about their disorderly motivations and reminds of their insistence
that faith only saves, and this must be properly taught

tiones ab ipsis electas. Sic igitur docuerunt, quod per observationem traditionum humanarum non possimus gratiam mereri aut satisfacere pro peccatis, quare non est sentiendum, quod huiusmodi observationes sint necessarius cultus.

Addunt testimonia ex scriptura: Christus Matth. xv. excusat Apostolos, qui non servaverant usitatam traditionem, quae tamen videbatur de re media esse et habere cognationem cum baptismatibus legis, et dicit: *Frustra colunt me mandatis hominum.* Igitur non exigit cultum inutilem. Et paulo post addit: *Omne, quod intrat in os, non inquinat hominem.* Item Roma. xiiii.: *Regnum Dei non est esca aut potus.* Coloss. ii.: *Nemo iudicet vos in cibo, potu, sabbato aut die festo.* Act. xv. ait Petrus: *Quare tentatis Deum imponentes iugum super cervices discipulorum, quod neque nos neque patres nostri portare potuimus, sed per gratiam Domini nostri Iesu Christi credimus salvari, quemadmodum et illi.* Hic vetat Petrus onerare conscientias pluribus ritibus sive Mosi sive aliis. Et i. Thimoth. iiii. vocat prohibitionem ciborum doctrinas daemoniorum, quia pugnat cum Evangelio talia opera instituere aut facere, ut per ea mereamur gratiam, aut quod non possit existere christiana iustitia sine tali cultu.

Hic obiiciunt adversarii, quod nostri prohibeant disciplinam et mortificationem carnis, sicut Iovinianus. Verum aliud deprehendetur ex scriptis nostrorum. Semper enim docuerunt de cruce, quod Christianos oporteat tollerare afflictiones. Haec est vera, seria et non simulata mortificatio: variis afflictionibus exerceri et crucifigi cum Christo.

Insuper docent, quod quilibet Christianus debeat se corporali disciplina aut corporalibus exercitiis et laboribus sic exercere et coercere, ne saturitas aut desidia extimulet ad peccandum, non ut per illa exercitia mereamur gratiam aut satis faciamus pro peccatis. Et hanc corporalem disciplinam oporteat sem-

CONCILIUM AUGUSTANUM – 1530

720 Und ist davon also gelert, das man durch haltung gedachter menschlicher tradition nicht kan Gott versünen odder fur die sunde gnugthun odder gnadt verdienen, Und sol derhalben kein nötiger Gottes dienst daraus gemacht werden.

Dazu wirt ursach aus der schrifft angezogen: Christus Matthei xv.
725 entschuldiget die Apostel, das sie die gewonliche traditiones nicht gehalten haben, Und spricht dabey: 'Sie ehren mich vergeblich mit menschen gepoten'. So er nu dis ein vorgeblichen dienst nennet, mus er nicht nötig sein. Und bald hernach: 'Was zum mund eingehet, verunreiniget den menschen nicht'. Item Paulus spricht Roma. xiiii.: 'Das himelreich stehet nicht inn speis und tranck'.
730 Colos. ii.: 'Niemand sol euch richten inn speise, tranck, Sabbat etc'. Actuum xv. Spricht Petrus: 'Was versuchet ihr dann nu Gott mit aufflegung des jochs auff der jünger hels, welchs widder unser Veter noch wir haben mögen tragen, sonder wir gleuben durch die gnad des Herrn Jhesu Christi selig zu werden, gleicher weise wie auch sie'. Da verbeut Petrus, das man die gewissen nicht
735 beschweren sol mit mehr eusserlichen Ceremonien. Und i. Timo. iiii. werden solche gebot Teuffels lere genennet. Denn also lauten S. Paulus wort: 'Der geist aber sagt deutlich, das inn den letzten zeiten werden etliche vom glauben abtretten und anhangen den irrigen geistern und leren der Teuffel durch die, so in gleisnerey luegen reder sind und brandmal inn ihren gewissen haben und
740 verbieten, Ehelich zuwerden und zu meiden die speise, die Gott geschaffen hat, mit dancksagung zunemen, den gleubigen und denen, die die warheit erkennet haben'. Denn dis ist stracks dem Evangelio entgegen, solche werck einsetzen odder thun, das man damit vergebung der sunde verdiene odder als möge niemands Christen sein one solche dienste.

745 Das man aber den unsern hie schuld gibt, als verbieten sie Casteiung und zucht, wie Jovinianus, wirt sich viel anders aus ihren schrifften befinden. Denn sie haben allezeit gelert vom heiligen Creutz, das Christen zuleiden schuldig sind. Und dieses ist rechte, ernstliche und nicht ertichte Casteiung.

Daneben wirt auch gelert, das ein itzlicher schuldig ist, sich mit leiblicher
750 ubung, als fasten und ander arbeit, also zuhalten, das er nicht ursach zu sunden gebe, nicht, das er durch solche werck gnad verdiene. Diese leibliche ubung solle nicht allein etlich bestimpte tage, sonder stetigs getrieben werden.

---

724 Matthei xv] Matth. 15, 9   **729** Rom. 14, 17   **730** Col. 2, 16   **731/734** Act. 15, 10-11   **736/739** Der – haben] I Tim. 4, 1-3

720/722 Und – werden] the fundamental criticism of medieval theology and religious practice is condensed in the rejection of humankind's ability to earn salvation by any human actions

182 — CONCILIUM AUGUSTANUM – 1530

per urgere, non solum paucis et constitutis diebus. Sicut Christus praecipit:
630 *Cavete, ne corpora e vestra graventur crapula.* Item: *Hoc genus daemoniorum non eiicitur nisi ieiunio et oratione.* Et Paulus ait: *Castigo corpus meum et redigo in servitutem.* Ubi clare ostendit se ideo castigare corpus, non ut per eam disciplinam mereatur remissionem peccatorum, sed ut corpus habeat obnoxium et idoneum ad res spirituales et ad faciendum officium iuxta vocationem suam.
635 Itaque non damnantur ipsa ieiunia, sed traditiones, quae certos dies, certos cibos praescribunt cum periculo conscientiae, tanquam istiusmodi opera sint necessarius cultus.

Servantur tamen apud nos pleraeque traditiones, ut ordo lectionum in Missa, feriae, quae conducunt ad hoc, ut res ordine geratur in Ecclesia. Sed
640 interim homines admonentur, quod talis cultus non iustificet coram Deo et quod non sit ponendum peccatum in talibus rebus, sii omittantur sine scandalo. Haec libertas in ritibus humanis non fuit ignota patribus. Nam in Oriente alio tempore servaverunt Pascha quam Romae, et cum Romani propter hanc dissimilitudinem accusarent Orientem schismatis, admoniti sunt ab aliis tales
645 mores non oportere ubique similes esse. Et Irenaeus inquit: dissonantia ieiunii fidei consonantiam non solvit, sicut et Dist. xii, Gregorius Papa significat talem dissimilitudinem non ledere unitatem Ecclesiae. Et in historia Tripartita lib. nono multa colliguntur exempla dissimilium rituum et recitantur haec verba: Mens Apostolorum fuit non de diebus festis sancire, sed praedicare
650 bonam conversationem et pietatem.

CONCILIUM AUGUSTANUM – 1530

Davon redet Christus Luce am xxi: 'Hüttet euch, das eure hertzen nicht beschwert werden mit fressen und sauffen'. Item: 'die Teuffel werden nicht ausgeworffen denn durch fasten und gebet'. Paulus spricht, Er casteye seinen leib und bringe ihn zu gehorsam, Damit er anzeiget, das Casteyung dienen sol nicht, damit gnad zuverdienen, sonder den leib geschickt zuhalten, das er nicht verhindere, was eim jglichen nach seinem beruffe zuschaffen befolhen ist. Und wirt also nicht das fasten verworffen, sondern das man ein nötigen dinst darauff auff bestimpte tag und speis zuverwirrung der gewissen gemacht hat.

Auch werden dieses teils die Ceremonien und tradition gehalten, als ordenung der Messe geseng Fest etc., welche dazu dienen, sie inn der kirchen ordenung gehalten werde. Daneben aber wirt das volck unterricht, das solch eusserlich gots dinst nicht from mache vor, und das man one beschwerung des gewissens halten sol, Also das, so man es nach lest one ergernus, nicht daran gesundiget wirt. Diese freiheit inn eusserlichen Ceremonien haben auch die alten Veter gehalten. Denn inn Orient hat man das Osterfest auff andere zeit denn zu Rom gehalten. Und da etlich diese ungleicheit fur ein trennung inn der kirchen halten wolten, sind sie vermanet von andern, das nicht not, inn solchen gewonheiten gleicheit zu halten. Und spricht Ireneus also: 'Ungleicheit im fasten trennet nicht die einigkeit des glaubens'. Wie Distinc. xii. von solcher ungleicheit inn menschlichen ordenungen geschrieben, das sie der einigkeit der Christenheit nicht zu widder sey. Und Tripartita historia li. ix. zeucht zusamen viel ungleicher kirchen gewonheit Und setzt ein nützlichen Christlichen spruch: 'Der Apostel meinung ist nicht gewesen, Feiertag ein zu setzen, sondern glauben und lieb zu leren'.

753/754 Hüttet – sauffen] Luc. 21, 34; cfr Marc. 9, 29   **755/756** Paulus – gehorsam] I Cor. 9, 27

767/768 Diese – gehalten] an important affirmation of the Lutherans' intent to maintain many forms in the practice of faith, as long as they are not required or treated as paths to salvation and forgiveness. The ancient Fathers and the reactions of human conscience serve as a compass in navigating unforeseeable situations   **772** Distinc xii] Gratianus, *Decretum* I, dist. 12, c. 10 (col. 29). Kolb – Wengert, *The Book of Concord*, p. 80, note 180   **774/777** Tripartita – leren] cfr Cassiodorus, *Historia ecclesiastica tripartita* 9, 38, 7, hrsg. W. Jacob – R. Hanslik (*CSEL* 71), Wien 1952, p. 559, 33-35. Kolb – Wengert, *The Book of Concord*, p. 80, note 181

[27] De votis monachorum

Quid de votis Monachorum apud nos doceatur, melius intelliget, si quis meminerit, qualis status fuerit Monasteriorum, quam multa contra Canones in ipsis Monasteriis quotidie fiebant. Augustini tempore erant libera collegia, postea corrupta disciplina ubique addita sunt vota, ut tanquam excogitato carcere disciplina restitueretur. Additae sunt paulatim supra vota aliae multae observationes. Et haec vincula multis ante iustam aetatem contra Canones iniecta sunt.

Multi inciderunt errore in hoc vitae genus, quibus, etiam si non deessent anni, tamen iuditium de suis viribus defuit. Qui sic irretiti erant, cogebantur manere, etiam si quidam beneficio Canonum liberari possent. Et hoc accidit magis etiam in Monasteriis Virginum quam Monachorum, cum sexui imbecilliori magis parcendum esset. Hic rigor displicuit multis bonis viris ante haec tempora, qui videbant puellas et adolescentes in Monasteria detrudi propter victum, videbant, quam infoeliciter succederet hoc consilium, quae scandala pareret, quos laqueos conscientiis iniiceret. Dolebant autoritatem Canonum in re periculosissima omnino negligi et contemni.

Ad haec mala accedebat talis persuasio de votis, quam constat etiam olim displicuisse ipsis Monachis, si qui paulo cordatiores fuerunt, docebant vota paria esse baptismo, docebant se hoc vitae genere mereri remissionem peccatorum et iustificationem coram Deo. Imo addebant vitam Monasticam non

27. Vom closter gelubden

Vom closter gelubden zureden, ist noth erstlich zugedencken, wie es
bissalher damit gehalten, wilch wesen in clostern gewesen und das seer viel
dorin teglich nit allein widder Gottes wortt, sonder auch bebstlichen rechten
zuentgegen gehandelt ist. Dan zu sanct Augustins zeiten seindt closter stende
frei gewesen; folgend, do die rechte zucht und lere zureut, do hat man closter
gelubd erdacht und domit eben als mit einem erdachten gefengnus di zucht
widderumb auffrichten wollen. Uber das hat man neben den closter gelubthen
viel andere stuck mehr uffpracht und mit solichen banden und beschwerthn
ire viel auch fur geburenthen jaern belathen.

So seint auch vil personen aus unwissenheit zu solichem closter wesen
kommen, wilche, wiewol sie sonst nicht zu jung gewesen, haben doch ir
vermugen nicht gnugsam ermessen noch verstanden. Dieselben alle, also
verstrickt und verwickelt, seint gedrungen und gezwungen gewesen, in solichen banden zupleiben, ungeachtet des, das auch di bebstlich recht ir viel frei
gibt. Und das ist beschwerlicher gewesen in jungfrauen clostern dan in
monich clostern, so sich doch getzimbt hett, der weibspild als der schwachen
personen zuverschonen. Dieselb strengheit und herttigkeit hat auch vil frommen leuth in vorzeiten mißverfallen, dan sie haben wol gesehen, das beide,
knaben und maegdlin, umb underhaltung willen des leibs in di closter
versteckt seint worden. Sie haben auch wol gesehen, wie ubel das selb furnemen geraten ist, wass ergernus und wasser beschwerung es gepracht, und
haben vil leuthe geclagt, das man in solichen ferlichen sachen di canones so
gar nicht achtet.

Zu dem, so hat man ein soliche meynung von den closter gelubth, die
unverborgen auch vilen monchen ubel gefallen hat, di wenig ein verstandt
gehabt, dan sie gaben fur, das closter gelubden der tauf gleich were und das
man mit dem closter leben vergebung der sonde und rechtfertigung vor Got
verdinet. Ja, sie sezten noch mher darzu, das man mit dem closter leben
verdient nicht allein gerechtigkeit vor Got und fromkeit, sonder auch das man

---

778 Vom – gelubden] an article on cloister vows and celibacy, amounting to a total
rejection of monastic life, while acknowledging the special gift from God for celibacy
applicable for few. The *Confutation* rejects the article. See Grane, *Confession*, p. 230
785/787 Uber – belathen] monastic orders multiplied in time the *Rule* of Benedict
setting the model   **797** knaben – maegdlin] a concern on the young age of some of
the individuals entering monastic life, forcibly or voluntarily   **802/806** Zu –
verdinet] the distinction or parallels between Baptism and monastic orders was a topic
of tension with Protestants rejecting such a comparison, and most definitely any
conception of monastic life as a path towards righteousness or status of perfection

186 CONCILIUM AUGUSTANUM – 1530

tantum iustitiam mereri coram Deo, sed amplius etiam, quia servaret non
modo praecepta, sed etiam consilia Evangelica. Ita persuadebant Monasticam
professionem longe meliorem esse baptismo, vitam Monasticam plus mereri
675 quam vitam Magistratuum, vitam pastorum et similium, qui in mandatis Dei
sine facticiis religionibus suae vocationi serviunt. Nihil horum negari potest,
extant enim in libris eorum.

Quid fiebat postea in Monasteriis? Olim erant scholae sacrarum literarum et aliarum disciplinarum, quae sunt utiles Ecclesiae et sumebantur inde
680 pastores et Episcopi. Nunc alia res est, nihil enim opus est recitare nota. Olim
ad discendum conveniebant, nunc fingunt institutum esse vitae genus ad
promerendam gratiam et iustitiam, immo praedicant esse statum perfectionis
et longe praeferunt omnibus aliis vitae generibus a Deo ordinatis. Haec ideo
recitavimus nihil odiose exaggerantes, ut melius intelligi posset de hac re doc-
685 trina nostrorum.

Primum de his, qui matrimonia contrahunt, sic docent apud nos, quod
liceat omnibus, qui non sunt idonei ad coelibatum, contrahere matrimonium,
quia vota non possunt ordinationem ac mandatum Dei tollere. Est autem hoc
mandatum Dei: *Propter fornicationem habeat unusquisque uxorem suam.*
690 Neque mandatum solum, sed etiam creatio et ordinatio Dei que cogit hos ad
coniugium, qui sine singulari Dei opere non sunt excepti, iuxta illud: *Non est
bonum homini esse solum.* Igitur non peccant, qui obtemperant huic mandato
et ordinationi Dei.

Quid potest contra haec opponi? Exaggeret aliquis obligationem voti,
695 quantum volet, tamen non poterit efficere, ut votum tollat mandatum Dei.

CONCILIUM AUGUSTANUM – 1530

domit hielte di gepott und rethe, im evangelio verfast, und wurth also di closter gelubdt hoher gepreiset dan die tauff; item, das man mer verdient mit dem
810 closter leben dan mit allen andern stenth, so von Got geordent sein, als pfarrer, prediger stant, oberkeit, fursten, hern standt und dergleichen, die alle nach
Gots gepott, wortt und befelch iren beruff on erdichte geistlichkeit dienen,
wie dan dieser stuck keins mag verneint werth, dan man findts in iren eigen
buchern.

815 Uber das, wer also gefangen und ins closter kommen, lernet wenig von
Christo. Etwan hett man schulen der heiligen schrifft und anderer konsten, so
der christlichen kirchen dienstlich seint, in den clostern vor alter, das man aus
den clostern pfarrer und bischoffen genommet hat. Itzo aber hats viel ein
andere gestalt mit den clostern; dan vor zeiten komen sie der meynung zusa-
820 men in closter leben, das man di schrifft lernet. Itzt geben sie fur, das closter
leben sei ein solichs wesen, das man Gots gnade und fromkeit for Got domit
verdiene, ya es sei ein standt der volkommenheit, und sezens den andern
stenth, so von Got eingesetzt, weitt fur. Das alles wirt dorumb angezogen on
alle verunglimpfung, domit man ye desterbaß vernemen und verstehen moge,
825 was und wie di unsern leren und predigen.

Erstlich leren sie bei uns von denen, di zur ehe greiffen, also, das alle di, so
zum ledigen standt nit geschickt seindt, macht, fug und recht haben, sich
zuverehelichen, dan die gelubd vermugen nicht Gottes ordnung und gepot
ufftzuhebenn. Nu laut Gots gepot also, 1. Corinth. 7.: 'Umb der hurerei willen
830 hab ein iglicher sein eigen wei und ein igliche habe iren eigen man'. Dartzu
dringt, zwinget und dreibt nicht allein Gottes gepott, sonder auch Gottes
geschopf und ordenung alle di zum ehestant, di on sonderlich Gots werck mit
der gabe der jungkfrauschafft nit begnadet seint, lauts dises spruchs Gots selbt,
Genesis am 2.: 'Es ist nicht gut, das der mensch allein sei. Wir wollen ime ein
835 geholffen machen, der umb in sei'.

Was mag man nu dawider auffsprengen? Man rhume das gelubd und di
pflicht wie hoch man welle, man mutz auf als hoch als man kand, so mag man
dennocht nit erzwingen, das Gottes gepott dadurch auffgehoben werde. Die

---

829/830 I Cor. 7, 2 **834/835** Gen. 2, 18

809/814 item – buchern] in medieval religious teaching, different sets of orders were
designated to different people with different levels of perfection to be expected **826/
829** Erstlich – ufftzuhebenn] while monastic vows are still respected as an option for
those with the gift of chastity (celibacy), the right to marry is drawn from God's
command. Luther wrote on this already in his 1520 *On the Babylonian Captivity of the
Church*, and even earlier in his critique of the celibate and monastic life marriage was
considered as instituted by God

Canones docent in omni voto ius superioris excipi, quare multo minus haec vota contra mandata Dei valent.

Quod si obligatio votorum nullas haberet causas, ut mutari possit, nec Romani Pontifices dispensassent. Neque tamen licet homini obligationem, quae simpliciter est iuris divini, rescindere. Sed prudenter iudicaverunt Romani Pontifices aequitatem in hac obligatione adhibendam esse. Ideo saepe de votis dispensasse leguntur. Nota est historia de Rege Arragonum revocato ex Monasterio et extant exempla nostri temporis.

Deinde cur obligationem exaggerant adversarii seu effectum voti, cum interim de ipsa voti natura sileant, quod debet esset in re possibili, quod debet esse voluntarium, sponte et consulto conceptum. At quomodo sit in potestate hominis perpetua castitas, non est ignotum. Et quotusquisque sponte et consulto vovit? Puellae et adolescentes, priusquam iudicare possunt, persuadentur ad vovendum, interdum etiam coguntur. Quare non est aequum tam rigide de obligatione disputare, cum omnes fateantur contra voti naturam esse, quod non sponte, quod inconsulto admittitur. Plerique Canones rescindunt vota ante annum xv. contracta, quia ante illam aetatem non videtur tantum esse iuditii, ut de perpetua vita constitui possit.

Alius Canon plus concedens hominum imbecillitati addit annos aliquot, vetat enim ante annum xviii. votum fieri. Sed utrum sequemur, maxima pars habet excusationem, cur Monasteria deserant, quia plurimi ante hanc aetatem voverunt. Postremo etiam si voti violatio reprehendi posset, tamen non videtur statim sequi, quod coniugia talium personarum dissolvenda sint. Nam

CONCILIUM AUGUSTANUM – 1530

doctores sagen, das di gelubd auch wider der babsts recht unbunding sein,
840 wieviel weniger sollen sie dan binden, stat und crafft haben wider Gottes
gebot!

Und wo di plicht der gelubd kein ander ursach hett, das sie mucht auffge-
haben werden, so hetten die bebst auch nit dowider dispensirt und erlaupt.
Dan es gepurt keinem menschen, di pflicht, so aus gotlichen rechten
845 herwechst, zu zureissen. Darumb haben die bebst wol bedacht, das in dise
plicht ein equitet soll gepraucht werthen, und haben zum offtermal dispensirt,
als mit einem konig von Arragon und viler ander. So man nu zuerhaltung zeit-
licher dinge dispensirt hat, sol viel pillicher dispensirt werden umb notturfft
willen der selen.

850 Volgend, warumb treibt der jegentheil so hart, das man di gelubd halten
muß und sicht nit an zuvornt, ab das gelubd sein art habe? Dan das gelubd sol
in muglichen sachen und willig, ungezwungen sein. Wie aber di ewig keuscheit in des menschen gewalt und vermugen stehe, weis man wol. Auch
seindt wenig beide mans und weibs personen, die von inen selbst willig und
855 wolbedacht das closter gelubnus gethan haben. Eher sie zu rechten verstandt
khommen, so uberredt man sie zum closter gelubd, zuweilen werthen sie auch
dortzu getzwungen und gedrungen.

Darumb ist es ye nit pillich, das man so schwind und hart von der gelubden pflicht disputirt, angesehen, das sie alle bekennen, das solichs wider di
860 natuer und art des gelubnus ist, das es nit williglich und mit guten rath und
bedacht gelobt wirdt. Ettliche canones und bebstliche recht zerreissen di
gelubd, die under funffzehen jaren geschen sein. Dan sie haltens dafur, das
man fur derselben zeit soviel verstants nicht hat, das man di ordnung des gan-
zen lebens, wie dasselb anzustellen, beschliessen konne.

865 Ein ander canon gibt der menschlichen schwacheit noch mher jar zu, dan
er verbeut das clostergelubd unther achzehen jaren zuthun. Daraus hat der
meiste theil entschuldigung und ursach, aus den clostern zugehen, das sie des
merentheils in der kindthait, vor disen jaern, in closter kommen seint. Entlich,
wan gleich die verprechung des closters gelubds mucht gedadelt werden, so
870 kont aber dannocht darus nit erfolgen, das man derselbigen ehe zerreissen solt.

---

847 einem – Arragon] Ramiro II Jiménez, king of Aragon (1086-1157), was a monk,
but the Aragonese nobility made him king after his brother Alfonso the Battler died
childless   **861/862** Ettliche – sein] Gratianus, *Decretum* II, causa 20, q. 1, c. 10
(col. 845). Kolb – Wengert, *The Book of Concord*, p. 86, note 193   **862/864** Dan –
konne] the reformers discussed on the reasonable age when a person could take a vow

Augustinus negat debere dissolvi, xxvii. quaest. 1 Cap. Nuptiarum, cuius non
est levis autoritas, etiamsi alii postea aliter senserunt.

Quanquam autem mandatum Dei de coniugio videatur plerosque liberare
a votis, tamen afferunt nostri et aliam rationem de votis, quod sint irrita, quia
omnis cultus Dei ab hominibus sine mandato Dei institutus et electus ad
promerendam iustificationem et gratiam impius est, sicut Christus ait: *Frustra
colunt me mandatis hominum*. Et Paulus ubique docet iustitiam non esse quaerendam ex nostris observationibus et cultibus, qui sint excogitati ab hominibus, sed contingere eam per fidem credentibus se recipi in gratiam a Deo propter Christum.

Constat autem Monachos docuisse, quod facticiae religiones satisfaciant
pro peccatis, mereantur gratiam et iustificationem. Quid hoc est aliud quam
de gloria Christi detrahere et obscurare ac negare iustitiam fidei? Sequitur
igitur ista vota usitata impios cultus fuisse, quare sunt irrita. Nam votum
impium et factum contra mandata Dei non valet neque enim debet votum
vinculum esse iniquitatis, ut Canon dicit.

Paulus dicit: *Evacuati estis a Christo, qui in lege iustificamini, a gratia exci-
distis*. Ergo etiam qui votis iustificari volunt, evacuantur a Christo et a gratia
excidunt. Nam et hi, qui votis tribuunt iustificationem, tribuunt propriis operibus hoc, quod proprie ad gloriam Christi pertinet. Neque enim negari
potest, quin Monachi docuerint se per vota et observationes suas iustificari et
mereri remissionem peccatorum, imo affinxerunt absurdiora, dixerunt se aliis

CONCILIUM AUGUSTANUM – 1530

Dan sanct Augustin sagt 27. quaestione distinct. 1, cap. nuptiarum, das man soliche ehe nit zerreissen soll. Nu ist ye sanct Augustin nicht in geringem ansehen in der christlichen kirchen, ob gleich ettliche hernach anders gehalten.

Wiewol nu Gottes gepott von dem ehestandt ire seer viel vom closter gelubd frei und ledig macht, so wenden doch di unsern noch mher ursach fur, das closter glubd nichtig und unbundig sei. Dan aller gots dienst, von den mentschen on Gottes gepott und befelch eingesetzt und erwelt, gerechtigkeit und Gots gnade zuerlangen, sei wider Got und dem heiligen evangelio und Gottes befelch entgegen, wie dan Christus selbst sagt Mathei 15.: 'Sie dienen mir vergeblich mit menschen gepothen'. So lerets auch sanct Paulus uberal, das man gerechtigkeit nit sol suchen aus unsern gepothen und gots diensten, so von menschen erdicht sein, sonder das gerechtigkeit und fromkeit vor Got kombt aus dem glauben und vertrauen, das wir glauben, das uns Got umb seines einigen sons Christus willen zu gnath nimbt.

Nu ist es ye am tage, das die monch gelert und gepredigt haben, das di erdachten geistlichkeit gnug thun vor di sunde und Gottes gnade und gerechtigkeit erlangen. Was ist nu das anderst, dan di herlichkeit und preiß der gnath Christi vermindern und di gerechtigkeit des glaubens verleucken? Darumb volgt aus dem, das soliche gewonliche gelubd unrechte, falsche gots dienst gewesen. Derhalben seint sie auch unbundig, dan ein gotloß gelubd und das wider Gots gepot bescheen, ist unbundig und nichtig, weil auch di canones leren, das der eydt nicht soll ein bandt zur sunden sein.

Sanct Paulus sagt zun Gal. am 5.: 'Ir seit abe von Christo, wie ir durch das gesetz gerechtfertigt werth wolt und habt der gnaden gefelet'. Derhalben auch di, so durch gelubdt wollen rechtfertig werden, seint von Christo ab und felen der gnaden Gots, dan dieselben rauben Christo sein eher, der allein gerecht macht, und geben soliche eher iren gelubthn und closter leben. Man kan auch nit leucken, das di munch geleret und gepredigt haben, das sie durch ire gelubde und closter wesen und weise gerecht werden und vergebung der sunden verdienen, ya sie haben noch wol ungeschikter und ungereumbter ding erdicht und gesagt, das sie ire gute werck den andern mittailten. Wan nu einer dis alles

---

879/880 Matth. 15, 9   **893/894** Gal. 5, 4

871/872 Dan – soll] a statement from Augustine received in canon law. Gratianus, *Decretum* II, causa 27, q. 1, c. 41 (col. 1060). Kolb – Wengert, *The Book of Concord*, p. 86, note 195   **880/884** So – nimbt] this article argues for a shift in considering which is more in line with God's commands, marriage or monastic life, dismantling the latter and deeming it a difficult, human choice, whereas marriage as God's institution stands higher as a calling. Monastic vows are considered as human promises and can be nullified with no ill consequences   **891** di canones] Gratianus, *Decretum* II, causa 22, q. 4, c. 2 (col. 881). Kolb – Wengert, *The Book of Concord*, p. 88, note 197

192 CONCILIUM AUGUSTANUM – 1530

mutuari sua opera. Haec si quis velit odiose exaggerare, quam multa possit colligere, quorum iam ipsos Monachos pudet. Ad haec persuaserunt hominibus factitias religiones esse statum Christianae perfectionis. An non est hoc iustificationem tribuere operibus? Non est leve scandalum in Ecclesia populo

745 proponere certum cultum ab hominibus excogitatum sine mandato Dei et docere, quod talis cultus iustificet homines. Quia iustitia fidei, quam maxime oportet tradii in Ecclesia, obscuratur, cum illae mirificae religiones Angelorum, simulatio paupertatis et humilitatis et coelibatus, offenduntur oculis hominum.

750 Praeterea obscurantur praecepta Dei et verus cultus Dei, cum audiunt homines solos Monachos esse in statu perfectionis, quia perfectio Christiana est serio timere Deum et rursus concipere magnam fidem et confidere propter Christum, quod habeamus Deum placatum, petere a Deo et certo expectare auxilium in omnibus rebus gerendis iuxta vocationem, Interim foris diligenter

755 facere bona opera et servire vocationi. In his rebus est vera perfectio et verus cultus Dei, non est in coelibatu aut mendicitate aut veste sordida. Verum populus concipit multas perniciosas opiniones ex illis falsis preconiis vitae Monasticae. Audit sine modo laudari coelibatum, ideo cum offensione conscientiae versatur in coniugio. Audit solos mendicos esse perfectos, ideo cum

760 offensione conscientiae retinet possessiones, negotiatur. Audit consilium Evangelicum esse de non vindicando, ideo alii in privata vita non verentur ulcisci, audiunt enim consilium esse non praeceptum. Alii omnes magistratus et civilia officia iudicant indigna esse Christianis. Leguntur exempla hominum, qui deserto coniugio, deserta reipublicae administratione abdiderunt se

765 in Monasteria. Id vocabant fugere ex mundo et quaerere vitae genus, quod

---

748 offenduntur] *correxi*, ostenduntur *Mar2*

CONCILIUM AUGUSTANUM – 1530

unglimpflich wolt dreiben und ufmutzen, wie viel stuck kont er zusamen pringen, dero sich di monche auch itzt selbst schemen und nicht wollen gethan
haben. Uber das alles haben sie auch di leuth des uberredt, das di erdichten
905 geistlichen orden stende seint christlich volkomenheit. Dis ist ja die werck
rhumung, das man dadurch gerecht werde. Nu ist es nicht ein geringe ergernus
in der christlichen kirch, das man dem volck ein solich gots dienst vortregt,
den di menschen on Gots gebot erdicht haben und leren, das ein solicher gots
dienst di menschen vor Got fromme und gerecht mache. Dan gerechtigkeit
910 des glaubens, di man am menisten in der christlichen kirchen treiben sol, wirt
vertunckelt, wan den leuthen di augen mit disser seltzamen engelgeistlichkeit
aufgespert werden und falsch vorgeben des armuts.

Uber das werth auch di gebot Gots und recht ware gots dienst dardurch
verdunckelt, wan di leuthe horen, das allein di monich im stande der volko-
915 menheit sein sollen. Dan di christlich volkomenheit ist, das man Got von
hertzen und mit ernst forchtet und doch auch ein herzlich zuversicht, glauben
und vertrauen fast, das wir umb Christus willen ein gnedigen, barmherzigen
Got haben, das wir mugen und sollen von Got bitten und begeren, was uns
not ist und hilff von ime in allen trubsalen gewisslich nach eins yder beruff
920 und gestandt gewarten, das wir auch in des sollen mit vleis eußerlich gute
werck thun und unsers beruffs warten. Darumb steht di rechte volkomenheit
und der rechte gots dienst nicht in betlen oder in einer schwarzen oder graen
kapfen etc. Aber das gemein volck fast viel schedlicher meynung aus falschem
lob des closter lebens, so es hort, das man den ledigen standt on alle maß lobt.
925 Dan daraus folgt, das es mit beschwertem gewissen im ehestandt ist. So der
gemein man hort, das di betler allein sollten volkommen sein, kan er nit
wissen, das er on sunde guter haben und hanttiren muge. So das volck horet,
es sei nur ein rath, nicht rach ubel, folgt, das etlich vormeinen, es sei nit sunde,
ausserhalb des ampts rach zuuben. Etliche meinen, rach gezime denn christli-
930 chen gar nit, auch nicht der oberkeit.

Man liset auch der exempel viel, das etlich weib und kindt, auch ire regiment verlassen und sich in closter gesteckt haben, das selbig, haben sie gesagt,
heis aus der wellt fliehen und ein solich leben suchen, das Got baß gefiele dan
der andern leben. Sie haben auch nicht konnen wisßen, das man Got dienen
935 sol in den geboten, di er gegeben hat, und nicht in den geboten, di von men-

---

911 engelgeistlichkeit] angelic spirituality of those living the monastic life   **915/
921** Dan – warten] this is the Lutheran view of Christian perfection, utterly rejecting
a hierarchy between those with and without monastic orders; an affirmation of
different aspects of life as part of the holy vocation each Christian bears, in the broader
framework of a vocational theology of ordinary life   **929/930** Etliche – oberkeit]
unlike the Anabaptists who, for instance, refused to bear arms

Deo magis placeret, nec videbant Deo serviendum esse in illis mandatis, quae ipse tradidit, non in mandatis, quae sunt excogitata ab hominibus. Bonum et perfectum vitae genus est, quod habet mandatum Dei. De his rebus necesse est admonere homines. Et ante haec tempora reprehendit Gerson errorem Mona-
770 chorum de perfectione et testatur suis temporibus novam vocem fuisse, quod vita Monastica sit status perfectionis. Tam multae impiae opiniones haerent in votis, quod iustificent, quod sint perfectio Christiana, quod servent consilia et praecepta, quod habeant opera supererogationis. Haec omnia, cum sint falsa et inania, faciunt vota irrita.

775   [28] De potestate ecclesiastica

Magnae disputationes fuerunt de potestate Episcoporum, in quibus non-nulli incommode commiscuerunt potestatem Ecclesiasticam et potestatem gladii. Et ex hac confusione maxima bella, maximi motus extiterunt, dum Pon-tifices freti potestate clavium non solum novos cultus instituerunt, reservatio-
780 ne casuum, violentis excomunicationibus conscientias oneraverunt, sed etiam

CONCILIUM AUGUSTANUM – 1530

schen erdicht sein. Nu ist ye das ein guter und volkomener stant des lebens, wilcher Gots gebot vor sich hat. Das aber ist ein ferlicher stant des lebens, der Gots gebot nicht fur sich hat. Von solichen sachen ist von nothen gewesen, den leuthen guten bericht zuthun. Es hat Gerson in vorzeiten den irthumb
940 von der monchen, von der volkomenheit, gestrafft und zeigt an, das bei seinen zeiten disses ein neuer rede gewest sei, das des closter leben ein standt der volkomenheit sein soll. Soviel gotloser meynung und irthumb leben in den closter gelubth: das sie sollen rechtfertigen und fromme vor Got machen, das sie di christliche volkomenheit sein sollen, das man domit beide, des evangeli-
945 ums rethe und gebot, halte, das sie haben di ubermas werck, di man Got nit schuldig sei. Dieweil dan solichs alles falsch, eitel und erdicht ist, so machets auch di closter gelubde nichtig und unbundig.

28. Von der bischoffen gewalt

Von der bischoffen gewalt ist vorzeiten vil und mancherlei geschrieben,
950 und haben etlich unschicklich den gewalt der bischoffen und das weltlich schwert under einander gemenget, und seint aus disem anordenlichen gemen-ge seher grosse kriege, uffrhuren und emporungen erfolget, aus dem, das di bischoffen im schein ires gewalts, der inen von Christo gegeben, nicht allein neue gots dienst angericht haben und mit vorbehaltung ettlicher felle und mit
955 gewaltsamem banne di gewissen beschwert, sonder auch sich underwunden,

---

939 Gerson] Iohannes Gerson, *Opera magistralia* opus 88 (*De consiliis evangelicis et statu perfectionis*), éd. P. Glorieux (*Jean Gerson, Œuvres complètes*, III), Paris – Tournai 1962, p. 10-26. Kolb – Wengert, *The Book of Concord*, p. 90, note 201 **946/ 947** Dieweil – unbundig] in spite of the criticism of monastic life and vows in particular as if binding and elevating the person, the monastic institutions in Lutheran regions were not abolished immediately. The process was slow and difficult, especially with women's convents, some of which continue to operate under different auspices. With the closing of the convents, Protestant women lost an important voca-tional option. The force with which women defended their convents speaks of this reality. See M. Wiesner-Hanks (ed.), *Convents Confront the Reformation: Catholic and Protestant Nuns in Germany*, Marquette (MI) 1996 **948** Von – gewalt] the article on the power of the keys. A specific article on papacy is missing, as is an explicit rejection of the papal office, for which workable parameters can (still at this point) be imagined. Melanchthon's *Treatise on the Power and Primacy of the Papacy* (1537) offers a more detailed treatment. See Grane, *Confession*, p. 76 **951** under – gemenget] two regimens; mixing spiritual and secular authority **954** mit[1] – felle] referring to the practice of penance and absolution and the designations in authority to absolve

---

954 gots dienst] *intellege Gottesdienst*, worship

196 CONCILIUM AUGUSTANUM – 1530

regna mundi transferre et imperatoribus adimere imperium conati sunt. Haec vitia multo ante reprehenderunt in Ecclesia homines pii et eruditi. Itaque nostri ad consolandas conscientias coacti sunt ostendere discrimen Ecclesiasticae potestatis et potestatis gladii et docuerunt utramque propter mandatum
785 Dei religiose venerandam et honore efficiendam esse tanquam summa Dei beneficia in terris.

Sic autem sentiunt potestatem clavium seu potestatem Episcoporum iuxta Evangelium potestatem esse seu mandatum Dei praedicandi Evangelii, remittendi et retinendi peccata et administrandi sacramenta. Nam cum hoc
790 mandato Christus mittit Apostolos: *Sicut misit me pater, ita et ego mitto vos. Accipite spiritum sanctum; quorum remiseritis peccata, remittuntur eis, et quorum retinueritis peccata, retenta sunt.* Marci xvi.: *Ite, praedicate Evangelium omni creaturae etc.*

Haec potestas tantum exercetur docendo seu praedicando verbum et por-
795 rigendo sacramenta vel multis vel singulis iuxta vocationem, quia conceduntur non res corporales, sed res aeternae: iustitia aeterna, spiritus sanctus, vita aeterna.

Haec non possunt contingere nisi per ministerium verbi et sacramentorum, sicut Paulus dicit: *Evangelium est potentia Dei ad salutem omni credenti.*
800 Itaque, cum potestas Ecclesiastica concedat res aeternas et tantum exerceatur per ministerium verbi, non impedit politicam administrationem, sicut ars canendi nihil impedit politicam administrationem. Nam politica administratio versatur circa alias res quam Evangelium. Magistratus defendit non mentes, sed corpora et res corporales adversus manifestas iniurias et coercet homines
805 gladio et corporalibus poenis, ut iustitiam civilem et pacem retineat. Non igitur commiscendae sunt potestates, Ecclesiastica et civilis. Ecclesiastica suum mandatum habet Evangelii docendi et administrandi sacramenta. Non irrumpat in alienum officium, non transferat regna mundi, non abroget leges Magistratuum, non tollat legitimam oboedientiam, non impediat iudicia de ullis

---

806 igitur] *correxi*, legitur *Mar2*

CONCILIUM AUGUSTANUM – 1530

keyser und konige zusezen und zuentsezen ihres gefallens; wilchen frefel auch
lange zeit hievor gelerte und gotforchtige leut in der christenheit gestrafft
haben. Derhalben di unsern zu trost der gewissen getzwungen seint worden,
di underschiede des geistlichen und weltlichen gewalts, schwerts und regi-
960 ments anzuzeigen, und haben gelert, das man beide regiment und gewalt umb
Gots gebots willen mit aller andacht als zwo hochste Gottes gaben auff erden
ehren und wol halten soll.

Nu leren di unsern also, das der gewalt der schlussel oder der bischoffen
sei laut des evangeliums ein gewalt und befelh, das evangelium zupredigen, di
965 sunde zuvergeben und zubehalten und di sacrament zureichen und handeln.
Dan Christus hat di aposteln mit disem befelch ausgesent, Joannis am 20.:
'Gleich wie mich mein vatter gesent hat, also sende ich euch auch. Nemet hien
den Heiligen Geist. Welchen ir ire sunde erlassen werdet, denselben sollen sie
erlassen sein, und denen ir sie furbehalten werdet, den sollen sie furbehalten
970 sein'.

Denselben gewalt der schlussel oder der bischoff ubt und treibt man
allein mit der lere und predig Gots worts und mit handtreichung der sacrament gegen vilen oder einzeln personen, darnach der beruff ist, dan damit
werth geben nicht leipliche, sonder ewige dinge und guther, als nemlich ewige
975 gerechtigkeit, der Heilig Geist und das ewig leben.

Dise guther kan man anderst nit erlangen dan durch das ampt der predig
und durch di handtreichung der heiligen sacrament, dan sanct Pauel spricht:
'Das evangelium ist ein crafft Gots, selig zumachen alle, di dran glauben'. Dieweil nu der gewalt der kirchen oder bischoffen ewige guter gibt und allein
980 durch das predig ampt geubt und getrieben wirt, so hindert er di pollicei und
das weltlich regiment nichts uberal, dan weltlich regiment gehet mit viel
andern sachen umb dan das evangelium. Weltliche gewalt schuzt nit die seel,
sonder leip und gut widder eusserliche gewalt mit dem schwert und leiplich
peenen. Darumb soll man di zwei regiment, das geistlich und weltlich, nicht
985 in einander mengen und werffen. Dan der geistlich gewalt hat seinen befelch,
das evangelium zupredigen und di sacrament zureichen, soll auch nicht in ein
frembdt ampt fallen, soll nicht konige sezen und entsezen, soll weltliche gese-
ze und gehorsam der oberkeit nicht auffheben oder zurüten, soll weltliche
gewalt nit gesez machen und stellen von weltlichen handeln, wie dan auch

---

967/970 Ioh. 20, 21-23 **978** Rom. 1, 16 **982** dan – evangelium] Ps. 119, 50

963 der¹ – schlussel] the bishop's office, to absolve sins

984 peenen] *intellege* power; violence

CONCILIUM AUGUSTANUM – 1530

810 civilibus ordinationibus aut contractibus, non praescribat leges magistratibus de forma rei publicae, sicut dicit Christus: *Regnum meum non est de hoc mundo.* Item: *Quis constituit me iudicem aut divisorem super vos?* Et Paulus ait Philip. iii.: *Nostra politia in coelis est.* ii. Corinth. x.: *Arma militiae nostrae non sunt carnalia, sed potentia Deo ad destruendas cogitationes etc.*

815 Ad hunc modum discernunt nostri utriusque potestatis officia et iubent utramque honore afficere et agnoscere, utramque Dei donum et beneficium esse.

Si quam habent Episcopi potestatem gladii, hanc non habent ut Episcopi ex mandato Evangelii, sed iure humano donatam a regibus et imperatoribus ad 820 administrationem civilem suorum bonorum. Haec interim alia functio est quam ministerium Evangelii.

Cum igitur de iuris dictione Episcoporum quaeritur, discerni debet imperium ab Ecclesiastica iuris dictione. Porro secundum Evangelium, seu ut loquuntur de iure divino, nulla iuris dictio competit Episcopis ut Episcopis, 825 hoc est, quibus est commissum ministerium verbi et sacramentorum nisi remittere peccata. Item, cognoscere doctrinam et doctrinam ab Evangelio dissentientem reiicere et impios, quorum nota est impietas, excludere a comunione Ecclesiae sine vi humana, sed verbo. Hic necessario et de iure divino debent eis Ecclesiae praestare oboedientiam iuxta illud: *Qui vos audit, me* 830 *audit.*

Verum cum aliquid contra Evangelium docent aut statuunt, tunc habent Ecclesiae mandatum Dei, quod oboedientiam prohibet: Matth. vii.: *Cavete a Pseudoprophetis.* Gal. i.: *Si Angelus de coelo aliud Evangelium evangelizaverit, anathema sit.* ii. Corinth. xiii.: *Non possumus aliquid contra veritatem, sed pro* 835 *veritate.* Item: *Data est nobis potestas ad aedificationem, non ad destructionem.* Sic et Canones praecipiunt, ii. q. vii. Cap. Sacerdotes et Cap. Oves. Et Augustinus contra Petiliani Epistolam inquit: Nec catholicis Episcopis consentien-

CONCILIUM AUGUSTANUM – 1530

Christus selbst gesagt hat: 'Mein reich ist nicht von disser welt'. Item: 'Wer hat mich zu einem richter zwisschen euch gesezt?' Und sanct Pauel zun Phil. am 3.: 'Unser burgerschafft ist in himel'. Und in der andern zun Corinthern am zehenden: 'Di waffen unserer ritterschafft sein nit vleischlich, sonder mechtig vor Got, zuverstoren die anschlege und alle hohe, di sich erhebt wider di erkantnus Gots'.

Disser gestalt underscheithen di unsern beider regiment und gewalt ampt und heisth sie beide als di hochsten gaben Gottes auff erden in eheren halten. Wo aber di bischoffen weltlich regiment und schwert haben, so haben sie dieselben nicht als bischoffen aus gotlichen rechten, sonder aus menschlichen, keyserlichen rechten, geschenkt van romischen keysern und konigen, zu weltlicher verwaltung irer guter, und gehet das ampt des evangeliums gar nicht an.

Derhalben ist das bischofflich ampt nach gotlichen rechten das evangelium predigen, sunde vergeben, lere urtheilen und di lere, dem evangelio entgegen, verwerffen und di gotlosen, der gotlos wesen uffenbar ist, aus christlicher gemein ausschlissen, on menschlichen gewalt, sonder allein durch Gots wortt. Und des fals seindt di pfar leuthe und kirchen schuldig, den bischoffen gehorsam zusein, lauts disses spruchs Christi, Luce am 10.: 'Were euch horet, der horet mich'.

Wo sie aber etwas dem evangelio zuentgegen leren, sezen oder auffrichten, haben wir Gotes befelch im solichen fall, das wir nicht sollen gehorsam sein. Mathei am 7. sagt Christus: 'Sehet euch fur den falßen prophethen'. Und sanct Pauel zun Gal. am 1.: 'So auch wir oder ein engel vom himel euch ein ander evangelium predig wurde, dan das das wir euch gepredigt haben, das sei verflucht'. Und in der 2. episteln zun Corinth. am 13.: 'Wir haben kein macht wider di worheit, sonder vor di worheit'. Item: 'Nach der macht, wilche mir der her zubessern und nicht zu verderben geben hat'. Also gebeut auch das geistlich recht, 2. q. 7 cap. sacerdotes und c. oves, und sanct Augustin schreibt in der episteln wider Petilianum, man soll auch den bischoffen, so ordentlich

---

990 Mein – welt] Ioh. 18, 36   **992** Phil. 3, 20   **993/995** II Cor. 10, 4   **1007/1008** Luc. 12, 14   **1011** Matth. 7, 15   **1012/1014** Gal. 1, 8   **1014/1016** Wir – hat] II Cor. 13, 8; II Cor. 10, 8

1017 sacerdotes – oves] *sacerdotes* and *oves*. Gratianus, *Decretum* II, causa 2, q. 7, c. 8 et 13 (col. 484 et 485). Kolb – Wengert, *The Book of Concord*, p. 96, note 209   **1017/1018** sanct – Petilianum] Aurelius Augustinus, *Ad catholicos epistola contra Donatistas* (*PL* 43), Paris, 1865, col. 410-411; Kolb – Wengert, *The Book of Concord*, p. 96, note 210

200 CONCILIUM AUGUSTANUM – 1530

dum est, sicubi forte falluntur aut contra Canonicas Dei scripturas aliquid sentiunt.

840 Si quam habent aliam vel potestatem vel iuris dictionem in cognoscendis certis causis videlicet matrimonii aut decimarum etc., hanc habent humano iure, Ubi cessantibus ordinariis coguntur Principes vel inviti suis subditis ius dicere, ut pax retineatur.

Praeter haec disputatur, utrum Episcopi habeant ius instituendi ceremo-
845 nias in Ecclesia et leges de cibis, feriis, gradibus ministrorum seu ordinibus etc. condendi. Hoc ius qui tribuunt Episcopis, allegant testimonium: *Adhuc multa habeo vobis dicere, sed non potestis portare modo. Cum autem venerit ille spiritus veritatis, docebit vos omnem veritatem.* Allegant etiam exemplum Apostolorum, qui prohibuerunt abstinere a sanguine et suffocato. Allegant sabbatum muta-
850 tum in diem Dominicum contra Decalogum ut videtur. Nec ullum exemplum magis iactatur quam mutatio sabbati. Magnam contendunt Ecclesiae potesta-tem esse, quod dispensaverit de praecepto Decalogi.

Sed de hac quaestione nostri sic docent, quod Episcopi non habeant pote-statem statuendi aliquid contra Evangelium, ut supra ostensum est. Docent
855 idem Canones ix. Distin. per totum. Porro contra scripturam est traditiones condere aut exigere, ut per earum observationem satis faciamus pro peccatis aut mereamur gratiam.

Leditur enim gloria meriti Christi, cum talibus observationibus conamur mereri iustificationem. Constat autem propter hanc persuasionem in Ecclesia
860 pene in infinitum crevisse traditiones, oppressa interim doctrina de fide et iustitia fidei, quia subinde plures feriae factae sunt, ieiunia indicta, ceremoniae novae, novi honores sanctorum instituti sunt, quia arbitrabantur se autores talium rerum his operibus mereri gratiam. Sic olim creverunt Canones poeni-tentiales, quorum adhuc in satisfactionibus vestigia quaedam videmus.

CONCILIUM AUGUSTANUM – 1530

gewelet, nit folgen, wo sie irren oder etwas widder die heilige gotliche schrifft leren oder ordnen. Das aber di bischoff sonst gewalt und gerichts zwenge haben in etlichen sachen, als nemlich ehesachen, wucher oder zehenden, diselben haben sie aus crafft menschlicher recht. Wo aber di ordinarien in solichem ampt nachlessig seint, so seindt di fursten schuldig, sie thuens gleich gern oder ungern, hierin iren untherdanen umb fridts willen recht zusprechen, zuverhortung unfridden und grosser unrhu in lendern.

Weither disputirt man auch, ob bischoffen macht haben, ceremonien in der kirchen auffzurichten, desgleichen satzungen von speis, feiertagen, von unterschiedlichen orden der kirchen diener, dan di den bischoff disen gewalt geben, ziehen dissen spruch Christi an, Joannis am 16.: 'Ich habe euch noch viel zusagen, ir aber konts itzo nicht tragen. Wenn aber der geist der warheit kommen wirt, der wirt euch in alle worheit fhuren'. Darzu fhuren sie auch das exempel Actuum am 15., do sie blut und erstickts gepothen haben. So zeugt man auch das an, das der sabath in sontag verwandelt ist worden widder di zehen gepot, darfur sie es achten, und wirt kein exempel so harth getrieben und angezogen als di verwandlung des sabaths, und wollen domit erhalten, das der kirchen gewalt groß sei, dieweil sie mit den zehen gepotten dispensirt und etwas dran verendert hat.

Aber di unsern leren in disser frage also, das di bischoffen nicht macht haben, etwas wider das evangelium zusezen und auffzurichten, wie dan obangezeigt ist, und di geistlichen recht durch di ganze neunte distinction leren. Nu ist dis offetlich wider gots befelch und wort, der meynung gesetz zumachen oder zugebieten, das man dadurch vor die sunde gnug thu und gnade erlange. Dan es wirt di ehr des verdiensts Christi verlestert, wan wir uns mit solichen sazungen gnade zuverdienen underwinnen.

Es ist auch am tage, das umb disser meynung willen in der christenheit menschliche aufsazung unzelich uberhandt genommen haben und in des di lere vom glauben und di gerechttigkeit des glaubens gar underdrukt ist gewesen. Man hat teglich neue feier tage, neue fasten gepoten, neue ceremonien und neue eher erbietung der heiligen eingesezt, mit solichen wercken gnade und alles gut bei Got zu verdienen.

1029/1031 Ioh. 16, 12

1040 di² – distinction] Gratianus, *Decretum* I, dist. 9, c. 8-11 (col. 17-18). Kolb – Wengert, *The Book of Concord*, p. 96, note 214

1021 zehenden] *intellege* tithes

CONCILIUM AUGUSTANUM – 1530

865 Item autores traditionum faciunt contra mandatum Dei, cum collocant peccatum in cibis, in diebus et similibus rebus et onerant Ecclesiam servitute legis, quasi oporteat apud Christianos ad promerendam iustificationem cultum esse similem Levitico, cuius ordinationem commiserit Deus Apostolis et Episcopis, sic enim scribunt quidam. Et videntur Pontifices aliqua ex parte
870 exemplo legis Mosaicae decepti esse. Hinc sunt illa onera, quod peccatum mortale sit etiam sine offensione aliorum in feriis laborare manibus, quod sit peccatum mortale omittere horas Canonicas, quod certi cibi polluant conscientiam, quod ieiunia non nature sed afflictiva sint opera placantia Deum, quod peccatum in casu reservato non possit remitti, nisi accesserit autoritas
875 reservantis, cum ipsi Canones non de reservatione culpae, sed de reservatione poenae Ecclesiasticae loquantur.

Unde habent ius Episcopi has traditiones imponendi Ecclesiis ad illaqueandas conscientias? Cum Petrus vetet imponere iugum discipulis, cum Paulus dicat potestatem ipsis datam esse ad aedificationem, non ad destructio-
880 nem. Cur igitur augent peccata per has traditiones? Verum extant clara testimonia, quae prohibent condere tales traditiones ad promerendam gratiam aut tanquam necessarias ad salutem. Paulus Colos. ii.: *Nemo vos iudicet in cibo, potu, parte diei festi, novilunio aut sabbatis.* Item: *Si mortui estis cum Christo ab elementis mundi, quare tanquam viventes in mundo decreta facitis? Non attin-*
885 *gas, non gustes, non contrectes, quae omnia pereunt usu et sunt mandata et doctrinae hominum, quae habent speciem sapientiae.* Item ad Titum aperte prohibet traditiones: *Non attendentes Iudaicis fabulis et mandatis hominum aversantium veritatem.* Et Christus Matthei xv. inquit de his, qui exigunt tradi-

CONCILIUM AUGUSTANUM – 1530

Item, di mentschliche sazung uffrichten, thun auch domit wider Gots gebot, das sie sunde sezen in der speise, in tagen und dergleichen dingen und beschweren also die christenheit mit der knechtschafft des gesezs, eben als muste bei den christen ein solicher gots dienst sein, Gottes gnade zuverdienen,
1055 der gleichen were dem levitischen gots dienst, wilchen Got solt den aposteln und bischoffen befolen aufftzurichten, wie dan etliche davon schreiben. Steht auch wol zuglauben, das etliche bischoff mit dem exempel des gesez Moisi seint bedrogen worth, daher so unzeliche satzung kommen sein, das ein dodt sunde sein soll, wan man an feiertagen ein handt arbeit thut, auch on ergernus
1060 der andern; das ein todtsunde sei, wan man di sieben zeide nachlest; das etlich speise das gewissen vorunreinigen; das fasten ein solich werck sei, domit man Got versune; das die sunde in einem furbehalten falh werde nicht vergeben, man ersuche dan zuvor den furbehalter des fals, unangesehen, das di geistlichen recht nicht von der vorbehalttung der schult, sonder von vorbehalttung
1065 der kirchen ban redden.

Woher haben dan di bischoffe recht und macht, soliche auffsetz der christenheit auffzulegen, di gewissen zuverstricken? Dan sanct Peter verbeut in geschichten der aposteln am 15., das joch uff der junger hels zulegen. Und sanct Pauel sagt zu den Corinthern, das inen der gewalt zu bessern und nicht
1070 zuverderben geben sei. Warumb mheren sie dan di sunde mit solichen auffsezen? Doch hat man helle spruch der gotlichen schrifft, di do verbieten, solich aufsetz aufftzurichten, Gotes gnade domit zuverdienen, oder als sollte sie von noten zur seligkeit sein. So sagt sanct Paulus zun Colossern am andern: 'So last nun niemant euch gewissen machen uber speise oder uber dranck oder
1075 uber bestimpte tagen, nemlich den feiertagen oder neu monden oder sabath'. Item: 'So ir dan nu gestorben seit mit Christo von den weltlichen satzungen, was last ir euch dan fahen mit sazungen, als weret ir noch lebendig in der welt, di do sagen, du solt das nicht anruren, du solt das nicht essen noch trincken, du solt das nicht anlegen, welchs sich doch alles under handen verzert und
1080 seint menschen gebot und lere und haben der weisheit ein schein'. Item sanct Pauel zu Tito am ersten verpeut offettlich, man sol nicht achten auff judische fabeln und menschen gebot, wilche di warheit abwenthen. So redet auch Christus selbst Mathei am 15. von denen, so di leuth uf menschen gepot dreiben: 'Last sie fharen, sie seint der plinden plinden leider', und verwirfft soliche

---

1068 aposteln – 15] cfr Act. 15, 10   **1073/1075** Col. 2, 16   **1076/1080** Col. 2, 20-23
1080/1082 Item – abwenthen] cfr Tit. 1, 14   **1084/1086** Last – außereuth] Matth.
15, 14, 15, 13

1060 di – nachlest] canonical hours regulating prayer times

204 CONCILIUM AUGUSTANUM – 1530

tiones: *Sinite illos, caeci sunt et duces caecorum.* Et improbat tales cultus: *Omnis*
890 *plantatio, quam non plantavit pater meus coelestis, eradicabitur.*

Si ius habent Episcopi onerandi Ecclesias infinitis traditionibus et
illaqueandi conscientias, cur toties prohibet scriptura condere et audire traditiones; cur vocat eas doctrinas daemoniorum? Num frustra praemonuit spiritus sanctus?

895 Relinquitur igitur, cum ordinationes institutae tanquam necessariae aut
cum opinione promerendae gratiae pugnent cum Evangelio, quod non liceat
ullis Episcopis tales cultus instituere aut exigere. Necesse est enim in Ecclesiis
retineri doctrinam de libertate Christiana, quod non sit necessaria servitus
legis ad iustificationem, sicut in Galatis scriptum est: *Nolite iterum iugo servi-*
900 *tutis subiici.* Necesse est retineri praecipuum Evangelii locum, quod gratiam
per fidem in Christum gratis consequamur, non propter certas observationes
aut propter cultus ab hominibus institutos.

Quid igitur sentiendum est de die Dominico et similibus ritibus templorum? Ad haec respondent, quod liceat Episcopis seu pastoribus facere ordina-
905 tiones, ut res ordine gerantur in Ecclesia, non ut per illas mereamur gratiam
aut satis faciamus pro peccatis aut obligentur conscientiae, ut iudicent esse
necessarios cultus ac sentiant se peccare, cum sine offensione aliorum violant.
Sic Paulus ordinat, ut in congregatione mulieres velent capita, ut ordine
audiantur in Ecclesia interpretes etc.

910 Tales ordinationes convenit Ecclesias propter caritatem et tranquillitatem
servare eatenus, ne alius alium offendat, ut ordine et sine tumultu omnia fiant
in Ecclesiis. Verum ita, ne conscientiae onerentur, ut ducant res esse necessarias ad salutem ac iudicent se peccare, cum violant eas sine aliorum offensione,
sicut nemo dixerit peccare mulierem, quae in publicum non velato capite
915 procedit, sine offensione hominum. Talis est observatio diei Dominici,
Paschatis, Pentecostes et similium feriarum et rituum. Nam qui iudicant

CONCILIUM AUGUSTANUM – 1530

1085 gots dienst und sagt: 'Alle pflantzen, di mein himelischer vatter nicht gepflantzt hat, werden außereuth'.

So nun di bischoffen macht haben, die kirchen mit unzelichen aufsezen zubeschweren und di gewissen zubestricken, warumb verbeut dan di gotliche schrifft so offt, di menschliche auffsetz zumachen und zuhoren? Warumb nen-
1090 ten sie dieselbe teuffels lere? Solt dan der Heilig Geist solichs alles vergeblich verwarnet haben?

Derhalben dieweil soliche ordenung als notig auffgericht, damit Got zuversunen und gnade zuverdienen, dem evangelio entgegen seint, so zimbt sich keins wegen den bischoffen, soliche gots dienst zuertzwingen; dan man
1095 mus in der christenheit die lere von der christlichen freiheit behalten, als nem-
lich, das di knechschafft des gesez nit notig ist zu rechtfertigung, wie dan sanct Pauel zun Gal. Schreibt am 5.: 'So bestehet nu in der freiheit, damit uns Christus befreiet hat, und last euch nit widderumb in das knechtische joch verk-
nupfen'. Dan es muß je der furnemst articel des evangeliums erhalten werth,
1100 das wir die gnade Gottes durch den glauben an Christum on unser verdienst erlangen und nicht durch gotes dienst, von menschen eingesetzt, verdienen.

Was sol man dan halten von sontag und dergleichen andern kirchen ordnungen und ceremonien? Darzu geben di unsern diese antwort, das di bischoffen oder pfarher mogen ordnung machen, domit es ordentlich in der
1105 kirchen zugehet, nicht domit Gots gnade zuerlangen, auch nicht domit fur di sund gnug zu thun oder di gewissen domit zuverplinthn, solichs vor notige gots dienst zuhalten und es dafur zuachten, das sie sunde theten, wan sie dieselben on ergernus prechen. Also hat sanct Paululs zun Corinthern veror-
denet, das di weiber in der versamblunge ire heupter sollen decken, item das di
1110 prediger in der versamlung nicht zu gleich alle reden, sonder ordentlich einer nach dem andern.

Soliche ordenung gepurt der christlichen versamblung umb der libe und fridens willen zuhalten und den bischoffen und pfarhern in dissen gefellen gehorsam zusein und dieselben sofer zuhalten, das einer den andern nit erger,
1115 domit in der kirchen kain unordenung oder wustes wesen sei, doch also, das di gewissen nit beschwert werden, das mans vor soliche dinge halte, di zur selig-
keit notig sein solten und es dafur achten, das sie sunde theten, wan sie diesel-
ben an der andern ergernus brechen, wie dan niemants sagt, das das weip sunde thue, di mit blossem haupt on ergernus der leuthe außehet. Also ist di orde-
1120 nung vom sontag, von der oster feier, von der pfingsten und dergleichen feier

---

1097/1098 So – verknupfen] Gal. 5, 1 **1108/1111** Also – andern] cfr I Cor. 11, 5 et 6

1102/1103 Was – antwort] necessary because of Eck's attack in his *Articles*. Kolb – Wengert, *The Book of Concord*, p. 98, note 218

206 CONCILIUM AUGUSTANUM – 1530

Ecclesiae autoritate pro sabbato institutam esse diei Dominici observationem tanquam necessariam, longe errant. Scriptura abrogavit sabbatum, quae docet omnes ceremonias Mosaicas post revelatum Evangelium omitti posse. Et
920 tamen, quia opus erat constituere certam diem, ut sciret populus, quando convenire deberet, apparet Ecclesiam ei rei destinasse diem Dominicum, qui ob hanc quoque causam videtur magis placuisse, ut haberent homines exemplum Christianae libertatis et scirent nec sabbati nec alterius diei observationem necessariam esse.

925 Extant prodigiosae disputationes de mutatione legis, de ceremoniis novae legis, de mutatione sabbati, quae omnes ortae sunt ex falsa persuasione, quod oporteat in Ecclesia cultum esse similem Levitico Et quod Christus comiserit Apostolis et Episcopis excogitare novas ceremonias, quae sint ad salutem necessariae. Hi errores serpserunt in Ecclesiam, cum iustitia fidei non satis
930 clare doceretur. Aliqui disputant diei Dominici observationem non quidem iuris divini esse, sed quasi iuris divini praescribunt de feriis, quatenus liceat operari. Huiusmodi disputationes quid sunt aliud nisi laquei conscientiarum? Quanquam enim conentur epikeizare traditiones, tamen nunquam potest aequitas deprehendi, donec manet opinio necessitatis, quam manere necesse
935 est, ubi ignorantur iustitia fidei et libertas Christiana.

Apostoli iusserunt abstinere a sanguine, quis nunc observat? neque tamen peccant, qui non observant, quia ne ipsi quidem Apostoli voluerunt onerare conscientias tali servitute, sed ad tempus prohibuerunt propter scandalum. Est enim perpetua voluntas Evangelii consideranda in decreto. Vix ulli
940 Canones servantur accurate et multi quotidie exolescunt apud illos etiam, qui diligentissime defendunt traditiones. Nec potest conscientiis consuli, nisi haec aequitas servetur, ut sciamus eas sine opinione necessitatis servari nec ledi conscientias, etiamsi traditiones exolescant.

CONCILIUM AUGUSTANUM – 1530

und weise; dan di es dafur achten, das di ordenung vom sontagk vor den sabath als notig auffgericht sei, di irren seher, dan di heilig schrifft hat den sabath abgethan und leret, das alle ceremonien des alten gesezs nach eroffenung des evangeliums mogen nachgelassen werden; und dennoch, weil von noethen gewest ist, ein gewissen tag zuverordnen, uff das das volck wuste, wen es zusamen kommen soll, hat di christlich kirch den sontag darzu verordnet und zu disser verenderung destomehr gefallens und willens gehapt, domit di leuthe ein exempel hetten der christlichen freiheit, das man wuste, das wider di haltung des sabaths noch eins andern tags von nothen sei.

Es seint vil unrichtige disputation von der verwandlung des gesezs, van den ceremonien des neuen testaments, von der veranderung des sabaths, wilche alle entsprungen sein aus falschen und irrigen meynung, als must man in der christenheit ein solichen gots dienst haben, der den levitischen oder juddischen gots dienst gemeß were, und als solt Christus den aposteln und bischoffen befolen haben, neue ceremonien zuerdenken, die zur seligkeit notig weren. Dieselben irthumb haben sich in di christenheit eingeflochten, do man di gerechtigkeit des glaubens nicht lauter und rhein gelert und gepredigt hat. Etliche disputiren also vom sontage, das man halten muße, wiewol nicht aus gotlichen rechten, dennoch schier als viel als aus gotlichem rechten, stellen form und maß, wie ferne man am feiertage erbeiten muge. Was seint aber soliche disputation anderst dan falh strick der gewissen? Dan wiewol sie sich understehen, menschliche auf setz zulindern und epiceyesern, so kan man doch kein epiceya oder linderung treffen, solange di meynung steht und pleibt, als solten sie vonnoten sein. Nun muß dieselbige meynunge pleiben, wan man nichts weiß von der gerechtigkeit des glaubens und von der christlichen freiheit.

Die aposteln haben geheisth, man soll sich enthalten des bluts und erstickten. Were helts aber izt? Aber dennocht thun di kein sunde, di es nit halten. Dan di aposteln haben auch selbst di gewissen nicht wollen beschweren mit solichen knechtschaft, sonder habens umb ergernuß willen ein tzeitlangk verpotten. Dan man muß achtung haben in disser sazung auf das heuptstuck christlicher lere, das durch dis decret nicht aufgehoben wirtt. Man helt schier kein alten canones, wie sie lauten. Es fallen auch derselben sazung deglich viel wegk, auch bei denen, die soliche aufsez auffs aller vleissigst halten. Do kan man den gewissen nicht rathen noch helffen, wo disse linderung nicht gehalten wirtt, das wir wissen, soliche aufsez also zuhalten, das mans nicht dafur achte, das sie notig sein, das auch den gewissen unschedlich sei, wo gleich soliche auffsez fallen.

1141/1144 Dan – sein] Kolb – Wengert, *The Book of Concord*, p. 104, note 225

Facile autem possent Episcopi legitimam oboedientiam retinere, si non
945 urgerent servare traditiones, quae bona conscientia servari non possunt. Nunc
imperant coelibatum, nullos recipiunt, nisi iurent se puram Evangelii doctrinam nolle docere. Non petunt Ecclesiae, ut Episcopi honoris sui iactura
sarciant concordiam, quod tamen decebat bonos pastores facere. Tantum
petunt, ut iniusta onera remittant, quae nova sunt et praeter consuetudinem
950 Ecclesiae catholicae recepta. Fortassis initio quaedam constitutiones habuerunt probabiles causas, quae tamen posterioribus temporibus non congruunt.
Apparet etiam quasdam errore receptas esse, quare Pontificiae clementiae esset
illas nunc mitigare, quia talis mutatio non labefacit Ecclesiae unitatem. Multae
enim traditiones humanae tempore mutatae sunt, ut ostendunt ipsi Canones.
955 Quod si non potest impetrari, ut relaxentur observationes, quae sine peccato
non possunt praestari, oportet nos regulam Apostolicam sequi, quae praecipit
Deo magis oboedire quam hominibus.

Petrus vetat Episcopos dominari et ecclesias cogere. Nunc non agitur, ut
dominatio eripiatur Episcopis, sed hoc unum petitur, ut patiantur Evangelium
960 pure doceri et relaxent paucas quasdam observationes, quae sine peccato servari non possunt. Quod si nihil remiserint, ipsi viderint, quo modo Deo rationem reddituri sint, quod pertinacia sua causam schismati praebent.

CONCILIUM AUGUSTANUM – 1530

Es wurden aber di bischoff leichtlich den gehorsam erhalten, wo sie nicht drauff trungen, di jenigen satzungen zuhalten, so doch on sunde nicht mugen gehalten werden. Itzt aber thun sie ein dinck und verbiten beide gestalt des heiligen sacraments, item den geistlichen den ehestandt, nehmen niemants uf, er thue dan zuvor ein eydt, er welle disse lere, so doch on zweiffel dem heiligen evangelio gemeß ist, nicht predigen. Unsere kirchen begeren nicht, das di bischoffen mit nachteil irer eher und wirden widderumb frieden und einigkeit machen, wiewol solichs den bischoffen in der noth auch zuthun gepuret. Allein bitten sie darumb, das die bischoffen ettliche unpilliche beschwerung nachlassen, die doch vortzeiten auch in der kirchen nicht gewesen und angenomen sein widder den brauch der christlichen gemeinen kirchen, wilche villeicht im anheben ettlich ursachen gehabt, aber sie reimen sich nicht zu unsern zeiten. So ists auch unleuckbar, das ettliche sazung aus unverstandt angenomen sein. Darumb sollten di bischoffen der gutigkeit sein, dieselbige satzung zumildern, seitenmal ein soliche enderung nichts schadt, di einigkeit der christlichen kirchen zuerhalten. Dan viel satzungen, von menschen auffkomen, seint mit der zeit selbst gefallen und nit notig zuhalten, wie di bebstliche recht selbst zeugen.

Kans aber ye nicht sein, es auch bei inen nicht zuerhalten, das man soliche menschliche satzung messige und abthue, wilche man on sunde nicht kan halten, so mussen wir der aposteln regel fulgen, di uns gepeut, wir sollen Gott mher gehorsam sein dan den menschen.

Sanct Peter verbeut den bischoffen di herschafft, als hetten sie gewalt, die kirchen, wortzu sie wolten, zutzwingen. Ytzt ghet man nicht domit umb, wie man den bischoffen iren gewalt neme, sondern man bit und begert, sie wolten di gewissen nicht zu sunden zwingen. Wan sie aber solichs nit thun wurden und disse bit verachten, so mugen sie gedencken, wie sie derhalben vor Got werden antwort geben mussen, dieweil sie mit solicher irer harttigkeit ursach geben zuspalttung und das scisma, das sie doch pillich sollten verhueten helffen.

1181/1182 Sanct – zutzwingen] not a rejection of the episcopal office but a condemnation of power abuses, drawing attention to the most important power of the keys, i.e. absolution   **1184/1187** Wan – helffen] for variants in the 1531 *editio princeps*, see Kolb – Wengert, *The Book of Concord*, p. 102, note 224

Epilogus

Hi sunt praecipui articuli, qui videntur habere controversiam, quanquam
965 enim de pluribus abusibus dici poterat, tamen, ut fugeremus prolixitatem,
praecipua complexi sumus, ex quibus caetera facile iudicari possunt. Magnae
querelae fuerunt de indulgentiis, de peregrinationibus, de abusu excomunica-
tionis Parochiae multipliciter vexabantur per stationarios. Infinitae contentio-
nes erant pastoribus cum Monachis de iure parochiali, de confessionibus, de
970 sepulturis, de extra ordinariis contionibus et de aliis innumerabilibus rebus.
Huiusmodi negotia praetermisimus, ut illa, quae sunt in hac causa praecipua,
breviter proposita facilius cognosci possent. Neque hic quicquam ad ullius
contumeliam dictum aut collectum est. Tantum ea recitata sunt, quae vide-
bantur necessario dicenda esse, ut intelligi posset in doctrina ac ceremoniis
975 apud nos nihil esse receptum contra scripturam aut Ecclesiam catholicam,
quia mani festum est nos diligentissime cavisse, ne qua nova et impia dogmata
in Ecclesias nostras serperent.

Hos articulos supra scriptos voluimus exhibere iuxta edictum C. M., in
quibus confessio nostra extaret, et eorum, qui apud nos docent, doctrinae
980 summa cerneretur. Si quid in hac confessione desiderabitur, parati sumus latio-
rem informationem Deo volente iuxta scripturas exhibere.

Caesareae Maiest. V.
Fideles et subditi.

Ioannes dux Saxoniae Elector.
985 Georgius Marchio Brandenburgensis.
Ernestus a Luneburg.
Philippus Landgravius Hessorum.
Ioannes Fridericus dux Saxoniae.
Franciscus dux Luneburgensis.
990 Volfgangus Princeps ab Anhalt.

CONCILIUM AUGUSTANUM – 1530

Beschluß

1190 Dis seindt die vornembsten artickel, di itzt fur streitig geacht werthn, dan wiewol man vielmeher mispreuch und unrechtigkeit hett anziehen konnen, so haben wir doch, di weitleuffigkeit und lenge zuverhueten, allein di vornembsten vermeldet, daraus di andern leichtlich zuermessen. Dan man hat in vortzeiten seer geclagt uber den aplaß, uber walfarten, uber mißprauch des bannes.

1195 Es hetten auch di pfarrer unentliche gezenck mit den munchen von wegen des beichthorens, des begribniß, der leichpredigten und unzelicher anderer stuck mher. Solichs alles haben wir im besten und umb glimpfs willen ubergangen, domit man die vornemste stuck in diser sach desterbaß vermircken mocht. Dafur sols auch nicht gehalten werden, das in dem ymants ichts zu haß und

1200 ungelimpf geredt oder angezogen sei, sonder wir haben allein di stuck erzelt, di wir fur notig antzutziehen und zuvermelden geacht haben, damit man daraus desterbaß zuvernemen habe, das bei uns nichts, weder mit der lere noch ceremonien, angenommen ist, das entweder der heiligen schrifft oder gemeiner christlichen kirchen zuentgegen were. Dan es ist ye am tage und offentlich,

1205 das wir mit allem vleis mit Gots willen on rhum zuredden verhut haben, damit je kein neu und gotlose lere sich in unsern kirchen heimlich einfluchte, einrissen und uberhant nemen.

Dise obgemelten artickel haben wir dem ausschreiben nach ubergeben wollen zu einer anzeigung unsers bekentnus und der unsern leren. Und ob

1210 ymants befunth wurde, der doran mangel hett, dem ist man fernern bericht mit grundt gotlicher heiliger gschrifft zuthun erputtig.

Euer Keiserlichen Maiestet
Undertheinigste churfursten, fursten und stedte

Johanns Hertzog zu Sachssen Churfurst.
1215 Georg Marggrave zu Brandenburg.
Ernst Hertzog zu Braunschweig und Lünenburg.
Philipps Landgrave zu Hessen.
Johan Friedrich Hertzog zu Sachssen.
Franciscus Hertzog zu Lünenburg.
1220 Wolffgang Fürst zu Anhalt.

1189 Beschluß] from an earlier draft by Melanchthon; different in the *editio princeps*. Kolb – Wengert, *The Book of Concord*, p. 104, note 225 **1203/1204** angenommen – were] repeating the premise that nothing un-scriptural is presented in the document

---

1213 Undertheinigste] *intellege* the emperor's subjects

Senatus Magistratusque Nurnbergensis.
Senatus Reutlingensis.

CONCILIUM AUGUSTANUM – 1530

Die Stad Norimberg.
Die Stad Reutlingen.

1221 Die – Reutlingen] the free cities of Windsheim, Heilbronn, Kempten, and Weissenburg also signed the document in July 1530

CONCILIUM BERNENSE
1532

edidit
Pierrick HILDEBRAND

THE SYNOD OF BERN
1532

INTRODUCTION

The resolutions adopted at the Synod of Bern, which took place in Bern from 9 to 14 January 1532, go back essentially to Wolfgang Capito. At a time when the achievements of the Swiss Reformation were under threat, the Synod was perceived as a further sanctioning of the Reformation implemented four years before by the Bern magistrates. It had a consolidating and appeasing effect on the newly-established Reformed Church. (1) Some scholars have argued that the decisions taken at the Synod of Bern have the character of a confession of faith. (2) The announcement of 14 December 1531 did not state precisely why the clergy were being summoned to a Synod. It is significant that the initiative was taken by the secular authorities. (3)

The preface to this document, which was probably authored by the city clerk Peter Cyro (1498-1564), (4) reveals the Synod's political and ecclesial background and indirectly refers to the crisis that the Synod was intended to resolve. We will address three interrelated aspects of this political and religious crisis. The first and foremost issue concerns the Bernese ministers' serious inadequacies 'in leer und leben', (5) i.e. discrepancies between the doctrine they were supposed to preach and their manner of life. (6) The document's title itself includes a clear reference to this issue: it is in fact a *Constitutio, vitae doctrinaeque formulam, quam verbi ministri urbis ac ditionis Bernatium sequantur, complectens...* The terms 'vita' and 'doctrina' were used several times

---

(1) See the *Ten Theses* of Bern in the present volume, p. 89-103.

(2) Cfr. G. W. Locher, 'Der Berner Synodus als Bekenntnisschrift', in Locher, *Berner Synodus*, vol. 2 (1988), p. 16-34.

(3) *Aktensammlung zur Geschichte der Berner-Reformation, 1521-1532*, hrsg. R. Steck – G. Tobler, 2 vols, Bern 1918-1923, vol. 2 (1923), p. 1484, no. 3258.

(4) Locher, 'Der Berner Synodus als Bekenntnisschrift', p. 17-18.

(5) F. Krüger, 'Lehrartikel des Berner Synodus 1532', in *RefBK*, vol. 1/1 (2002), p. 514, no. 16.

(6) It is interesting to note that Sulzer's translation only mentions the ministers' 'mor[es]', not their doctrine. This somewhat free translation is an indication of how the conflict was perceived, i.e. more as an ethical than a theological issue (see the edition below).

218 CONCILIUM BERNENSE – 1532

throughout the synodal proceedings, which was a sign of the fact that the Synod sought to tackle the issue of clerical morals. In his preface, Cyro argued on the one hand that the lack of clerical morals jeopardised the sanctification of the common folk, which risked incurring in the wrath of God. On the other hand, the 'people outside' (i.e. Roman Catholics but above all Anabaptists) could defame the purity of the Gospel that the Reformation had brought to Bern. (7)

The second and third aspects are not explicitly mentioned in the text of the preface. However, they can be reasonably deduced by two brief allusions, 'recentes nostros tumultos' and 'alia quoque ingruentia mala ac vitia', which a contemporary reader would have easily identified. The reference to recent turmoil was connected to the defeat of Zurich, Bern's ally in the *christliches Burgrecht*, in the Second War of Kappel in October/November 1531. Bern, strikingly absent from the crucial battle, was forced to sign along Zurich a humiliating capitulation to the Roman Catholic Confederates (*Orte*) on 24 November 1531. As happened in Zurich, the war debt prompted a stiff reaction by the territories subject to Bern's jurisdiction holding the magisterial Reformation accountable for this difficult situation. This reference to tumults refers to emerging tensions between the city of Bern and its subject territories.

When Cyro wrote about the 'other acute mischiefs or deficits', (8) he undoubtedly referred to the quarrels emerging around the person of Caspar Megander (1495-1545). After the 1528 disputation, This Zurich-born theologian had been appointed minister and professor in Bern. Ardently championing Zurich's cause, he distinguished himself for his policies toward the five Roman Catholic *Orte*, which eventually led to the Second War of Kappel. After the defeat, he harshly criticised Bernese authorities in his public sermons and accused them of having betrayed the Gospel and the city of Zurich. His sermons were so controversial that on 2 December 1531 he was forbidden to preach. Megander's removal, though, was perceived as being a limitation of the freedom to proclaim the Gospel imposed by secular authorities at a time when the clerical need to obtain more independence from the state, especially in terms of ecclesiastical discipline, was growing stronger.

(7) Krüger, 'Lehrartikel des Berner Synodus 1532', p. 515, no. 16: 'da durch dann das heylig Evangelium [...] von denen die usswenig syn *verlestret wird*' (emphasis added). Sulzer's translation has a softened reading: 'cur nostro vitio male apud exteros Evangelium audiat'.

(8) The early modern German original reads 'andren unlust'. See Krüger, 'Lehrartikel des Berner Synodus 1532', p. 515, no. 16.

CONCILIUM BERNENSE – 1532

Initially planned for May 1532, the second Synod of Bern (9) was first re-scheduled for October 1531 and later for January 1532 because of the Kappel war. Wolfgang Capito arrived unexpectedly in Bern on 29 December 1531 and was welcomed 'domino mittente'. (10) He was then officially invited to help oversee the synod, although he was distrusted by many for his tolerant ideas towards Anabaptists and so-called spiritualists. On 8 January 1532, Capito presented to the city council of Bern the articles he wanted the Synod to discuss; the council approved them. Some scholars have suggested that sixteen fundamental articles – strikingly formulated with the neutral article *das* in the original early modern German – had already been partly discussed at this 'pro-to-Synod'. (11) Presumably Capito also authored the remaining articles, but the final version was a result of several modifications and amendments brought forth during the synodal debates. The remaining articles have more the character of a record of the synodal proceedings. (12) The structure of the articles of Bern follow the sequence of the synodal proceedings: Doctrine (Chapters 1-23), Exhortation (Chapters 24-30), Improvement (Chapters 31-35), Ministry (Chapters 36-43), and Life (Chapter 44). (13)

Theologically speaking, the articles discussed at the Synod of Bern show how the *devotio moderna* influenced Humanist reformers of Upper Germany and their epigones, of whom Capito himself was a perfect example. This late-medieval reform was characterised by an ethical orientation of spirituality, firmly set in an individualistic and inwardly conception of the communion with the Christ 'intra nos'.

---

(9) The first Synod of Bern was held in September 1530. The regular meeting of the clergy in synods in the Reformed tradition goes back to Huldrych Zwingli's initiative in Zurich. Unlike occasional disputations, which mainly discussed doctrinal issues, the Synod was more concerned with the 'life' of the Church and with the consolidation and development of the Reformation.

(10) Berchtold Haller to Martin Bucer, 16 January 1532, in *Berner Synodus*, vol. 2 (1988), p. 357.

(11) H. R. Lavater, 'Verbesserung der Reformation', in *Berner Synodus*, vol. 2 (1988), p. 76. These are the following capita: 1-5, 7, 11, 17-18, 23, 27, 32a–b, 38, 41-42 (numbering of early modern original).

(12) Lavater, 'Verbesserung der Reformation', p. 78-82.

(13) Lavater, 'Verbesserung der Reformation', p. 83-85 (numbering of early modern original).

220   CONCILIUM BERNENSE – 1532

The 'cursus' or run of grace, embedded in an actualising Trinitarian economy, was foundational for the Synod of Bern. (14) God's grace ran from the Father to the Son through the Spirit. Emphasis was laid on Christ's spiritual indwelling in the believer, and less on his work in the flesh (Chapter III). (15)

To date, scholarship has not investigated how the Latin translation subtly tended to correct Capito's inclination to spiritualise Christ, which was inspired by Caspar Schwenckfeld's Christology. (16) For example, in the third article the Father speaks through Christ's Spirit, which establishes the presence of Christ in the believer's heart ('perque Spiritum eius, cuius interventu nostra corda inhabitat, etiamnum quotidie appellet'). In the German original the Father speaks through the Son, whose presence in the heart lies in the Spirit ('Der vatter redet zuo unns durch synen sun noch hüt by tag, welicher im heyligen Geyst unser hertzen jnwonet'). In the sixth article of the German original, Christ perfected his work in the flesh ('im fleysch') before ascending to heaven to reveal himself to the believers in the Holy Spirit ('im h[eiligen] geyst'). In Sulzer's Latin translation, Christ's 'cursus' in the flesh seems to include the ascension 'in coelis', from where he illuminates the believer 'per Spiritum Sanctum' (emphasis added). It is therefore not accidental that the programmatic Biblical quotation of 2 Corinthians 5:16 on the frontispiece of the original imprint in German does not feature in the Latin edition.

Capito, in comparison to Zwingli and later Reformed confessions, placed a clear emphasis on Christ's dwelling within the individual as the very goal of the graceful 'cursus' (Chapter XIIII). This led him to a strong inward spirituality holding a low view of the law (see especially Chapters IX-XIII) and of the Old Testament, which was hardly mentioned! (17) In contrast, most Reformed confessions stressed a redemptive direction of history epitomised in the crucified and risen Christ who sits at the right hand of the Father and will return in glory.

The Synod was held from 9 to 13 January 1532. The Synod's decisions were then ratified by the delegates. The original preface, authored by Capito, was

---

(14) It is a recurring expression in the first twenty-three articles (see chapters VI, VII, XIIII, XIX, and XXIII) and reiterated in the two prefaces. The 'gratiae cursus' appears prominently in the title of Chapter XIIII, but Capito spoke synonymously also of the 'Spiritus Sancti cursus' or 'Christi cursus'.

(15) The Latin translation preserved the explicit Trinitarian terminology of the early modern German original. Sulzer translated Father and Son as 'Maiestas' and 'Christus', respectively.

(16) Cfr. E. Saxer, 'Capito und der Berner Synodus', in *Berner Synodus*, vol. 2 (1988), p. 158-164.

(17) S. Lutz, 'Bibelstellenregister', in *Berner Synodus*, vol. 2 (1988), p. 395-399.

CONCILIUM BERNENSE – 1532

written in the name of the participants in the Synod. It addressed the Bernese civil magistrates with gratitude by acknowledging the need for an outward order of the Church, which the civil authorities were bound to preserve. Conversely, no clerical intervention in secular affairs was permitted. In the later preface written by Cyro, the magistrates of Bern acknowledged the decisions of the Synod but contradicted Capito's views on this precise argument, claiming that the Church held a prophetic ministry even in political matters.

The proceedings of the Synod were sanctioned by the city council on 14 January 1532 and passed into law. They were first printed in Basel by Hieronymus Froben and publicly posted across the Bernese territories on 4 April. Berthold Haller entrusted Simon Sulzer with a Latin translation to be circulated in the Francophone territories under Bernese jurisdiction. The translation was printed in the workshop of Andreas Cratander in mid-March 1532. ([18]) The Synod of Basel managed to pacify the conflicting parties and ultimately consolidated the Reformation in Bern. However, its decisions were supplanted shortly afterwards by Bullinger's Second Helvetic Confession (1566). The Synod of Bern was revived in the seventeenth and eighteenth centuries by Pietists such as Nikolaus von Zinzendorf (1700-1760), who elevated its proceedings to the status of an official confession of the Moravian Church. ([19]) In the Reformed Church of Bern's 1946 constitution, the Synod of 1532 is said to belong to the 'historical foundations' of the Church, along with the *Ten Theses* and the *Reformationsmandat* of 1528.

NOTES ON THE EDITION

We offer below the first critical edition of Sulzer's Latin translation of the decrees of the Synod of Bern. It is based on an in-quarto printed copy of the 1532 Latin edition, held in the Zentralbibliothek Zürich among the *Alte Drucke* collection (shelfmark: 18.563), consisting of 37 pages. This Latin translation does not follow the same numbering of articles as the one found in the original German:

German	Latin
Chapters 1-24	Chapters I-XXIIIIa
Chapter 25	Chapter XXIIIIb
Chapters 26-28	Chapters XXV-XXVIIIa

(18) See further A. Fluri, *Die Beziehungen Berns zu den Buckdruckern in Basel, Zürich und Genf 1476-1536*, Bern 1913, p. 42-44.

(19) See further Dellsperger, 'Einheitskonzeption und Bekenntnisrezeption', p. 206-225; Saxer, 'Zinzendorf und der Berner Synodus'.

Chapter 30	Chapter XXVIIIb
Chapter 31	Chapter XXVIIII
Chapters 32a + b	Chapters XXX-XXXII
Chapters 33-40a	Chapters XXXIII-XL
Chapters 40b-44	Chapters XLI-XLV

Other copies of this document are held, for example, in the Bibliothèque Cantonale et Universitaire (Fribourg) and in the British Library (London). The former was reproduced with the early modern German original and the first French translation as facsimiles in the first volume of *Der Berner Synodus 1532*. ([20]) This volume also includes a translation into modern German and a bibliographical study of various editions and translations up to 1978. ([21]) The first 24 articles of Capito's draft request have been edited in the *Reformierte Bekenntnisschriften* (*RefBK*). ([22]) A manuscript version of the proceedings of the Synod is held in the Staatsarchiv Bern (shelfmark A II 110 Band 232).

Our critical edition applies the following editorial guidelines. The wording of the source (including capitalisation except when punctuation requires otherwise) is reproduced faithfully, whereas punctuation follows modern usage. Numerals are reproduced as in the original source. The letters *u/v* are normalised in accordance with phonetics, and *j* is always recorded as *i*. E-caudata is resolved as *ae*, & as *et*. Ligatures (e.g. æ/ae), contractions (e.g. q̄/*quam*) and tildes (e.g. m̄/*mm*) have been expanded and abbreviations resolved without any specific note except for Biblical references and, etc.

BIBLIOGRAPHY([23])

Sources (and Their Abbreviations)

Der Berner Synodus von 1532, hrsg. G. W. Locher, 2 vols, Neukirchen-Vluyn 1984-1988 [= Locher, *Berner Synodus*].

([20]) *Berner Synodus*, vol. 1 (1984).

([21]) Lavater, 'Beschreibendes chronologisches Verzeichnis der Editionen', in *Berner Synodus*, vol. 1 (1984), p. 383-392. Lavater was not aware that a Latin copy is held in Zurich: see Lavater, 'Der "Synodus" in der Berner Kirche bis zum Anfang des 18. Jahrhunderts', in *Berner Synodus*, vol. 2 (1988), p. 304-329; Locher, 'Die Editionen vom 18. Jahrhundert bis zur Gegenwart', in *Berner Synodus*, vol. 2 (1988), p. 330-353.

([22]) Krüger, 'Lehrartikel des Berner Synodus 1532', p. 508-548, no. 16.

([23]) For a detailed bibliography, see Lavater, 'Annotierte Bibliographie zum Berner Synodus', in *Berner Synodus*, vol. 2 (1988), p. 388-414.

CONCILIUM BERNENSE – 1532

Staatsarchiv Bern, A II 110, Band 232.

LITERATURE (AND ITS ABBREVIATIONS)

R. Dellsperger, 'Der Berner Synodus. "...fleissig verlesen, erläutert, ausgelegt und erneuert...'", in R. Dellsperger – D. Lavater (hrsg.), *Die Wahrheit ist untödlich. Berner Täufer in Geschichte und Gegenwart*, Bern 2007, p. 213-242.

—, 'Einheitskonzeption und Bekenntnisrezeption. Die Bedeutung des Berner Synodus für Zinzendorfs Einheitsbestrebungen in Pennsylvanien', in E. M. Laine (hrsg.), *Der Pietismus in seiner europäischen und außereuropäischen Ausstrahlung*, Helsinki 1992, p. 206-225 [= Dellsperger, 'Einheitskonzeption und Bekenntnisrezeption'].

U. J. Gerber, 'Berner Synodus – Berner Täufertum. Gemeinsames und Trennendes', in J.-G. Rott – S. L. Verheus (hrsg.), *Täufertum und radikale Reformation im 16. Jahrhundert. Akten des internationalen Kolloquiums für Täufergeschichte des 16. Jahrhunders*, Baden-Baden – Bouxwiller 1987, p. 185-296.

F. Krüger, 'Huldrych Zwingli und der Berner Synodus', in A. Schindler – H. Stickelberger (hrsg.), *Die Zürcher Reformation: Ausstrahlungen und Rückwirkungen. Wissenschaftliche Tagung zum hundertjährigen Bestehen des Zwinglivereins (Zürcher Beitrage zur Reformationsgeschichte 18)*, Bern 2001, p. 77-85.

E. Saxer, 'Zinzendorf und der Berner Synodus', *Unitas Fratrum* 29/30 (1991), p. 157-174 [= Saxer, 'Zinzendorf und der Berner Synodus'].

CONCILIUM BERNENSE
1532

|ACTA SYNODI BERNENSIS.

A1r

CONSTITUTIO VITAE DOCTRINAEQUE FORMULAM, QUAM VERBI MI-
NISTRI URBIS AC DITIONIS BERNATIUM SEQUANTUR, COMPLECTENS
ADDITA UBERIORE QUADAM CHRISTI ET SACRAMENTORUM INTERPRETA-
TIONE, IN SYNODO HABITA ISTIC IX. IANUARII CONCORDITER FACTA ET
RECEPTA.

SIMONE SULTZAERO INTERPRETE. [...]
|SENATUS DECRETUM.

A3v

Nos, Consul et senatus uterque urbis Bernensis, omnibus nostrae ditionis
Parrochis ac divini verbi ministris oblata benevolentia notum facimus.

Postquam Papismo una cum omnibus vanis persuasionibus et superstitione abrogato reiectoque, sacrum Evangelium in urbe ac ditione nostra tota,
mox a disputatione ante quadriennium habita, ita sumus amplexi, ut parem
cum reipublicae nostrae legibus vim et autoritatem deinceps habiturum opitu-
lante deo et ad quod doctrina ecclesiarum et mores nostri emendentur,
omnium votis consentientibus, solenni insuper iureiurando professi sumus.
Quod institutum tamen nec recte geri nec propagari potest, nisi a vobis, qui
ecclesiarum sustinetis ministerium, sana doctrina vitaeque vestrae innocentia
tanquam e salubri fonte promanans plaebi veram sitienti iusticiam exhibeatur.
Ad eam rem consequendam quum totis animis propenderemus, omnis generis
decreta ad vos gregis domini pastores pertinentia et nostrae iam pridem refor-
mationi, quam vocant, institae insevimus et vestris quoque proposuimus Syno-
dis. Nec minus tamenmulta cum in institutione tum moribus etiam vestris | A4r
desiderari comperimus, quamobrem dei gloria pietasque omnis ac vitae integritas apud subditos non sine gravi morum corruptela deficit vehementer ac
impeditur, quo nomine cumulatim super nos ac plaebem universam irati dei
indignationem accendi et augeri constat. Quae causa etiam est, cur nostro vitio
male apud exteros audiat Evangelium, quando nulla plane vel modestia Christiana vel pietas solida, quod unicum veritatis sigillum est ac vivum testimonium, in nostris subditis verbi divini auditoribus elucescit. Cuius mali
atrocitatem non immerito diligenter summaque animi agitatione perpendendam esse duximus, praesertim quando plus, tam in ministrorum verbi, quam

---

18/19 sana – exhibeatur] cfr Matth. 5, 6

228 CONCILIUM BERNENSE – 1532

plaebis vita, timoris dei, emendatioris vitae, virtutum ac sanctimoniae extare nobis polliceremur, quam hactenus eluxerit. Quantum enim malorum ac
35 improbitatis invexerit illa factionum discordia quamque parum etiamnum Christianae disciplinae eniteat, post recentes nostros tumultos, etiamsi ignoratum fuisset hactenus, abunde perspeximus. Siquidem posthabita spretaque nostrarum legum autoritate plurimi nostrae ditionis Germani et Galli in pessima omnis generis flagitia impudenter eruperunt. Quamobrem primum nos
40 ipsos accurato exactoque examine ac indagatione perquisivimus, quemnam quisque ex nobis erga deum sacrumque eius Evangelium affectum animumque gerat, hoc est, num fluxas opes honoresque momentaneos et corpus denique ipsum magis quam coelestem illam et aeternam vitam, quam Christus nobis recuperavit, Apostoli praedicarunt atque per spiritum sanctum credentibus
45 aliquo modo communicata est, tueri et conservare paratus sit. Quibus ultro citroque perpensis nequaquam divina benignitas, quam ubertim per Christum in suos diffundit, eo prolabi amentiae nos permisit, ut, tametsi hoc tempore perpetuus fere calamitatum tenor pusillanimes multorum conscientias graviter | offensas deiiciat prosternatque, ut ullum ob afflictionis praesentis moles- A4v
50 tiam in sanctissimo suo nomine ac veracissimis promissionibus amplectendis et protegendis fastidium ac satietas nos ceperit. Quin potius de integro re studiosius pensiculata convenimus concordique suffragio Evangelium, quam late se nostrae ditionis extendunt pomeria, apud nos nostraeque commissos fidei propagare ac eius vim doctrina et vita exprimere, dignitatem vero eius pro
55 virili et gratia divina sartamtectam, quod dicitur, conservare decrevimus. Id quod uno ore omnium subditorum nuper ad nos missi legati petierunt eoque a nobis promulgata iam olim causa verae instaurandae religionis decreta ultro nunc rursus rata in posterum habenda receperunt. Quare cum non praeter causam, ad alia quoque ingruentia mala ac vitia removenda compelleremur,
60 Synodum omnium vestrum, qui docendi in ecclesiis munere fungimini, conscripsimus. Ad quam ubi die IX. Ianuarii hoc XXXII. anno in urbe nostra Bernensi convenissetis, supra nostram simul ac vestrum omnium spem et expectationem pie studiosissimeque eo, qui mox subsequet ordine, de forma doctrinae Christianae ac vitae tractantes vos ipsos commonefecistis, nec ex
65 vobis erat quisquam, qui tam synceram sanctamque monitionem non prompte animoque ardentissimo exciperet. Qua in re deus clementissimus vestras, ut speramus, mentes accendit atque negocium ab externo per sedulum quendam eius ac fidum ministrum suum et legatum tanquam idoneum instrumentum promovit. Qui suum porro opus tam in nostris quam in vestris etiam animis
70 absolvere dignetur. Amen.

---

36 tumultos] *a.c.* tumultus

CONCILIUM BERNENSE – 1532

Porro cum acta illa vestrae Synodi nobis Consuli et senatui offerretis, unice simul efflagitastis, ut si perlecta probarentur, nostra ea autoritate confirmaremus, ad nos quantum attinet exequeremur vobisque demanderemus exe|quenda. Ne gratia donumque dei, hoc est, tam piae consultationes irritae A5r
75 interciderent, id quod fit, dum in communi conventu etiam utiliter instituta, a pio magistratu non corroborantur. Ea itaque vestra scripta, ut intellecta a nobis sunt, singulari favore excepimus frugiferaque per omnia ac instituto Christi consentanea esse iudicavimus censemusque plane non aliter quam ad eiusmodi omnino praescriptum parrochorum doctrinam ac vitam esse
80 formandam, quo coeleste illud aeternumque aedificium spe uberiore accrescat carnisque reprimatur licentia, spiritus vero sancti internaeque gratiae cursui liber relinquatur progressus, ut cui nullam imperare creaturam conveniat, veluti hoc ipso libello disertae copioseque estis testati. Quamobrem acta haec Synodi communi adprobavimus consensu ac tanquam ad gloriam dei incre-
85 mentumque Evangelii promoventum, vel maxime pertinentia firma rataque esse volumus adque nos quatenus pertingunt moribus exprimere nostrisque subditis per universam ditionem studiose observationem eorum imperare statuimus. Atque vestris Parrochis et concionatoribus in verbi divini praedicatione plenam facimus potestatem ac in eo etiam tuebimur, ut unum Christum
90 Iesum annuntiare, errores refellere, flagitia quoque et scelera quum magistratuum tum subditorum iuxta fidei charitatisque analogiam ac praesentium auditorum profectum libere citraque tremorem carpere et obiurgare possitis. Verum quemadmodum etiam vos ipsi aequum esse piumque affirmastis, si quis e vobis non ad dei gloriam iuxta formam ac modulum spiritus doceat aedi-
95 ficationem, sed ex animi impotentia et libidine malitiosa convicia egerat, in cuiuscunque id sexus aut conditionis homines fiat, nequaquam impune ferre patiemur, qua tamen in re non rigide nimium omnia persequemur. Sed quoniam eorum quae pie instituistis maior pars ad vos vestrumque munus per|ti- A5v net, volumus, ut ea quum inter vos ipsos, tum apud plaebem in omni doctrina
100 moribus studiose praestetis. Decani vero ac alii, qui eruditione synceraque pietate antecellunt, ad ea praestanda se mutuo caeterosque hortentur, promoveant et impellant. Verum si quem huic tam salubri instituto oblatrare atque ex eius contemptu et praevaricatione munus iniunctum male tueri ac vitae improbitate malo esse exemplo aliis comperimus, eiusmodi illum poena afficie-
105 mus, ut intelligant omnes quanta nos gloriae dei verbique divini neglectus cura tangat. Proinde quanta possumus autoritate serio imperamus, ut haec acta subsequentibus Synodis, quae Calendis Maiis ex more fere celebrantur,

---

80 coeleste – aedificium] cfr II Cor. 5, 1

106 possumus autoritate] *a.c.* possums auroritate

230   CONCILIUM BERNENSE – 1532

diligenter relecta ac explicata in memoriam revocentur, nec usquam ab hoc
discedatur praescripto. Quod si autem a nostris Parrochis aut exteris profera-
110 tur deinceps, quod propius nos ad Christum perducere atque ex fide scripturae
sacrae Christianis moribus conducibilius esse queat, quam quae haec proposita
nobis formula complectitur, obviis, quod dicitur, ulnis excipiemus, suum spiritui sancto cursum, qui neglecta carnalium rerum concupiscentia ad absolutum
Christi exemplar contendit, nequaquam remoraturi. Cuius nobis gratia omni-
115 bus perpetuo adesse velit. Datum Bernae XIIII. Ianuarii.

|ACTA SYNODI IX. IANUARII CAEPTAE, XIIII. VERO EIUSDEM   Bir
MENSIS FINITAE, HOC XXXII. ANNO.
IN QUA CCXXX. PARROCHI URBIS AC DITIONIS BERNENSIUM
CONVENERUNT.

120   DE OFFICIO AC POSTESTATE MAGISTRATUS CIVILIS IN REBUS FIDEI,
     UNA CUM ADHORTATIONE AD INCLYTUM SENATUM BERNENSEM.

Quoniam ita comparatum est, viri celeberrimi, ut in his quae ad externarum rerum administrationem attinent, citra civilis potestatis adminiculum et
autoritatem nihil a verbi dei ministris vel institui vel confirmari queat, ob
125 corruptos adeo ac pertinaces cum doctorum ipsorum tum plebis animos, eo
quod spiritu dei ac virtute iam dum caremus omnes. Addecet sane eum magistratum, qui Christi nomine gaudet et gloriatur, studio vigilantissimo incumbere, ut potestas ea non terrenarum modo rerum, sed domini etiam ministra
efficiatur evangelicamque doctrinam et vitam, quatenus ea in externis est sita,
130 promoveat ac tueatur apud suae praesertim commissos fidei, pro quibus in
extremo illo iudicio, quo per Christum deus iudicabit damnabitque mundum,
ut reddant rationem, sistendi sunt omnes. Verum quod ad eum gratiae cursum
profectumque attinet, qui in ipso humanae mentis sinu atque recessu versatur,
excitandum aut propagandum non id facultatis est humanae, nec quisquam
135 vel magistratuum vel creaturae penitus ullius id negocium esse credat. Etenim
cum coelestium rerum perpetuitas atque constan|tia omne consilium huma-   Biv
num omnemque terrenam potestatem excedat, nemo tantum sibi sumere
debet, ut hominum conscientias conetur ullo praecepto edictove astringere, ne
adgravasse eas terminumque spiritui, cuius progressus liber est, praedefiniisse
140 videatur. Christus enim Iesus, qui omnem a patre coelesti autoritatem spiritus-

---

128/129 ut – vitam] cfr Rom. 13, 4   **140/141** Christus – accepit] cfr Matth. 28, 18

CONCILIUM BERNENSE – 1532

que sancti promissionem accepit, unus dominus et imperator mentium est humanarum. Unde satis liquet Papam, episcopos, sacerdotes et reliquos eius factionis homines Christo velut ex composito repugnare doctrinamque docere daemoniorum. Quoniam conscientias hominum regere noxamque, ubi nulla est, confingere nituntur atque ea quibus contra deum delinquitur gravissime crimina abolendi potestatem esse sibi concessam perque vana et efficta opera gratiam domini et favorem quum sibi tum aliis demereri se posse confidentissime asserunt. Cui impietati non solum se non ingerere magistratus debet, sed quantum potest fugere eamque ne ingruat praecavere. Interim tamen synceram atque solidam in iis praesertim, quae in crassis illis et conspicuis hominum actionibus consistunt, administrationem nunquam vel deseret vel intermittet a deo missa potestas. Quin ubi pietatis profectus et fructus promoveri posse speratur, tanquam dei sociam ac auxiliatricem sese adiunget, id quod ita fiet, si sanam doctrinam diligenter foveat, errores et imposturas excludat, offendicula avertat atque aeternam illam et inconcussam veritatem fortiter totoque pectore tueatur.

Quandoquidem igitur, viri ornatissimi, evangelium domini a vobis tanta alacritate et susceptum est et ad subditos propagatum, qui ex aequo se vobiscum omnes in hoc tanquam municipale ius, quo antiquius nihil habetis, iuramento obstrinxerunt, merito id etiam instar senatusdecreti aestimari et haberi a vestra amplitudine debet, eoque, etiamsi | mundum spectetis, citra ignominiam deseri a vobis recepta semel veritas nullo modo potest. Nec tamen inficiamur gladium illum terrenum vestrumque ministerium aliud nihil (nisi negocium ipse promoveat Christus) quam hypocritas efficere posse iamque pridem etiam effecisse nonnullos. Vitant enim missam tanquam rem abominandam non parum multi, quibus cum illa pulchre conveniret nihilque ab ea abhorrerent penitus, nisi per edictum vestrum publicum ea esset abrogata. Verum id neminem commoveat, ad Moysi respiciatur exemplum, cuius quum ministerium in domini lege (quae vitae tamen lex erat) amplius promovere nihil posset, non tamen ullo pacto cessandum sibi est ratus, sed magis strenue delegatum munus obeundum et exequendum, quo vivificam eam legem carni, quae potissimum illi nitebatur, in literam mortuam atque adeo in iram mortemque ipsam transmutaret. Nam in omni Moysi administratione nunquam plaebi dominus vel mentem sanam vel oculos apertos vel aures ad divina percipienda idoneos concessit, quadraginta licet annis cum ipsis tum convixisset Moyses, id quod in postremo suo quem ante mortem habuit sermone breviter conqueritur. Adeo parum in Christiana instituenda republica etiam seduli

---

154 sanam doctrinam] I Tim. 1, 10; II Tim. 4, 3; Tit. 1, 9; 2, 1   **172** in¹ – mortuam] cfr II Cor. 3, 6   in iram] cfr Rom. 4, 15

232 CONCILIUM BERNENSE – 1532

ministri opera et industria proficit. Interim vero utut suscipiatur Evangelium, non in magistratu, sed in his quibus id offertur, culpa residebit. Siquidem hoc
180 unum est vestrum et ardens votum, qui quantum in vobis est, plurimi ab errore ad verum numinis cultum alliciantur offendiculaque, et si quae extant publice scelera, coerceantur. Quae tamen omnia non ad emendationem vitae sed ad hypocrisim potius accipit mundus. Non aliter ac Moysi quoque accidit inter suos, id unum operam danti, qui ad dominum perquamplurimos adduceret,
185 labentique et inclinanti subinde verae pietati opem ferret.

| Et quanquam a nullo magistratu, ut vel animi puri vel conscientia tran- B2v quilla reddatur, praestari queat, adiuvatis tamen in hoc vestra potentia et autoritate, ut apud vos vestrosque verbum domini strenue exerceatur, gratia vera aperiatur atque ad fontem illum ducantur omnes, ex quo uno salutis et immor-
190 talitatis aquae hauriuntur, hoc est, Christum Iesum, unicum inter deum et homines mediatorem. Cui tam salubri doctrinae quicunque tandem pareant, imo si incassum (quod minime videtur consentaneum) vester exeat conatus, iniuncto tamen munere rite perfuncti animas vobis e noxa eripueritis, nec minus reipublicae Christianae adiumenti attuleritis quam Moyses et pii illi
195 Iuda reges, qui legem domini in plebe sua diligenter exercebant. Cuius cum praelectio assidua divini verbi praedicationi, quam unice fovebant reges, coniungeretur, ira iudiciumque dei adversus sceleratos est declaratum peccandique hoc pacto profligata licentia, pietas porro vera detegi et veris iam affectibus coli coepta, est cuius rei causa sanctissimi reges, praeclarum in scripturis enco-
200 mium a spiritu sancto sunt consecuti.

Hoc ergo tam pium vestrum et sanctum institutum neutiquam vel interturbare vel remorari debet, quod nonnulli parum prudentes homines obiiciunt afferentes Christianismum, cum in interiore homine sit positus, non a vestrae potentiae, sed verbi dei gladio regi debere et administrari adeoque de
205 integro novum exoriri papismum, si in fidei negocium autoritatem vestram sitis interposituri. Quibus ita responderi potest. Non negari posse ea, quemadmodum illi affirmant contingere, si magistratus in conscientias aut libertatem Christianam, qua una mens pia fovetur, imperium sibi assumat, cuiusmodi tamen suscipio in vos minime cadit, ut quibus id unum in Evangelii negocio
210 studio fuerit hactenus, qui pastores domini gregem synceriter et studiose | B3r docerent, ad leges pincipis sui Christi servandas admonerent, ad veritatem cohortarentur, flagitia praeterea cum magistratuum, tum subditorum carperent et obiurgarent, interim tamen externa illa religionis valere eatenus volentes, ne spiritus sancti cursus vel interclusus vel interruptus iudicari posset. Sed

---

188/190 gratia – hauriuntur] cfr Ioh. 4, 14   190/191 Christum – mediatorem] cfr I Tim. 2, 5   196 quam – reges] cfr IV Reg. 23, 2   214 ne – posset] cfr I Thess. 5, 19

CONCILIUM BERNENSE – 1532

215 earum rerum fidem tum facietis luculentam, si quae in praesenti Synodo, nos qui Evangelium domini apud vos vestrosque docendi in professo habemus, post diligentem consultationem ad gloriam dei promovendam instituimus, ea vestra autoritate confirmaveritis nobisque tanquam celsitudini vestrae obnoxiis et obstrictis observanda rataque in perpetuum habenda demandaveritis, 220 quod ut fiat etiam atque etiam petimus suppliciterque obsecramus. Habent autem ea se in hunc modum.

Quod nostrae professioni solerter nos vacare conveniat.
Caput I.

Principio cum parrochos et verbi divini praecones praeter caeteros ad 225 aedificandam ecclesiam missos ministros spiritus deique mysteriorum dispensatores et esse nos et dici par sit (nam et alii qui cum in hac, tum in caeteris urbibus publicis praesunt consiliis, ministri dei sunt et appellantur) aequum vel praecipue et necessarium etiam fuerit iuxta nuper promulgatum pro Evangelii successu a magistratu decretum, ut munus, quod a domino delegatum 230 sustinemus, sanctum et coeleste id omni cura rite atque ordine obeamus et tueamur. Quod ut praestetur sana et incorrupta doctrina vitaeque sanctimonia, non quod ad nos solum, sed quod ad universos etiam fidei nostrae consortes domesticosque attinet, requiritur.

Christum unice esse docendum.
235 *Caput II.*

Certum est autem doctrinam veram et salubrem aliud | esse nihil nisi B₃v aeternum illud verbum patrisque coelestis benignitatem et benevolentiam, quam in Christo generi humano exhibuit, hoc est, ille ipse Christus Iesus, qui nostri causa crucis subivit supplicium propterque nostri iustificationem a mor- 240 tuis est excitatus. Quicquid igitur huic dogmati repugnat, tanquam saluti nostrae contrarium habeatur, imo quicquid in se non ea, quae dicta sunt universa, complectitur, non pro Christiana, sed vana et inani doctrina censeri debet. Nam in hoc omnes vocati sunt veri Evangelistae, ut tanquam salutis per Christum consequendae annunciatores passionis eius sint testes velutque in 245 hoc unum amandati voluntatem eius et commissa obeant et exequantur. In

---

225 ministros spiritus] II Cor. 3, 6   deique – dispensatores] I Cor. 4, 1   **227** ministri dei] Rom. 13, 4   **231** sana ... doctrina] I Tim. 1, 10; II Tim. 4, 3; Tit. 1, 9; 2, 1 vitaeque sanctimonia] cfr Hebr. 12, 14   **232/233** fidei ... domesticosque] Gal. 6, 10 **238/240** Christus – excitatus] cfr Rom. 4, 25   **244** passionis – testes] cfr I Petr. 5, 1 **245/246** In – mundum] cfr Ioh. 5, 36

234 CONCILIUM BERNENSE – 1532

eum quoque modum et Christus a patre est demissus in mundum, quo paternum illius nomen et gloriam miseris nobis mortalibus aperiret et explicaret, id quod in omni vita studiosissime praestitit, ut qui perpetuo in patris sui negotio occupatus ea solum, quae ab ipso acceperat, docuerit et praedicarit.

250 *Deum plaebi tantummodo in Christo esse demonstrandum.*
Caput III.

Ridiculum autem fuerit Christi apostolum et ministrum domini sui voluntatem minus explorate cognitam perceptamque habere, aut rebus occupari aliis, quae a gloriae dei salutisque nostrae profectu, in quam promoven-
255 dam totus debebat incumbere, sint aliena. In Christo nanque paternam erga nos benignitatem operaque coelestia vel manifestissime deprehendimus, eo quod per hunc nos maiestas illa aeterna voluerit reconciliatos, perque Spiritum eius, cuius interventu nostra corda inhabitat, etiamnum quotidie appellet. Atque ea Christi cognitio accedente sedula ac perpetua admonitione fidem
260 solidam maiori indies incremento adauget. Verum si more Ethnicorum de deo disseratur | a verbi ministris, eo neglecto Christo, in cuius fulgore et imagine   B4r aeterna illa sapientia veritasque elucet, adeo non vel in emendatione vitae vel dei cognitione quicquam proficietur, ut et plaebs commissa sibi reddatur seipsa deterior et eo tandem provehamur impietatis, ut veritate desperata absque
265 omni dei cultu vitam transigamus, perinde ac Ethnicis accidit, qui cum de naturali numine multa acute et subtiliter disputarent, nunquam tamen vel deum legitime venerari vel clementiae illius paternae et bonitatis sensum firmiter ullum percipere potuerunt, tantisper donec in Christum annunciatum crederent, id quod ad Ephesios Paulus hisce verbis testatur: *Eratis* (inquit) *in*   Ephes.
270 *tempore illo sine Christo etc. Spem non habentes deoque carentes in Mundo.*

Christum esse verum fundamentum.
Caput IIII.

Iesus Christus, servator omnium, unicum est sacri illius aedificii fundamentum, sine quo, ut nulla speranda salus, ita huic constanter innitenti nulla

---

246/247 quo – nomen] cfr Ioh. 17, 6   **247** et gloriam] cfr Ioh. 1, 14   **248/
249** perpetuo – occupatus] cfr Luc. 2, 49   **249** ea – praedicarit] cfr Ioh. 8, 26 et 28;
15, 15   **257/258** Spiritum – inhabitat] cfr Eph. 3, 17   **261/262** in – elucet] cfr Col.
1, 15   **264/265** ut – transigamus] cfr Eph. 2, 12   **266/267** nunquam – venerari] cfr
Rom. 1, 21   **269/270** Eph. 2, 12   **273** Iesus Christus … fundamentum] I Cor. 3, 11
sacri – aedificii] cfr I Petr. 2, 5   **274** sine – salus] cfr Act. 4, 12

CONCILIUM BERNENSE – 1532

275 maledictio est formidanda, hic etenim lapis est ille angularis, introitus, via, veritas et vita, quam solam Apostoli ipsorumque discipuli, quorum vestigiis nos Parrochi insistimus, docuerunt, eoque Paulus eam, quae ex lege petitur, iustificationem reiecit simulque cum caeteris Apostolis pro fundamento solido Phil. 3 Christum collocavit. Quae omnia exemplis mox sequentibus clarius patebunt,

280 quanquam idipsum nulla non scriptura confirmet. *Ego* (inquit) *iuxta gratiam,* I Cor. 3 *quae data est mihi, ut sapiens architectus fundamentum posui etc. Nam fundamentum aliud nemo potest ponere, praeter hoc, quod positum est, quod est Iesus Christus. Siquidem gustastis, quod benignus est dominus, ad illum accedentes,* I Petri. 2 *qui lapis est vivus.* Hic Iesus Christus electus est lapis ille angularis et preciosus,

285 de quo Esaias 28 et Psalmus 118.

| *Per Christum absque omni medio benignum deum agnosci.* B4v
Caput V.

Sed quid longiore hic sermone est opus, cum *omnes scientiae sapientiaeque thesauri in hoc sint reconditi?* Colos. 2. Quae igitur sit causa quamobrem divini
290 verbi minister sapientiam veram ex aliis potius historiis librisque peregrinis, quam ex hoc domini nostri poenu, quod unum abunde complectitur omnia, petat aut depromat? Saepe equidem de deo praeter Christum loqui multa multi conantur, sed id absque fructu eo quod in operibus seipsum declararit, perque quarundam rerum effigies et indicia mortalium generi innotuerit: ut in Gen. 2
295 paradiso per arborem vitae, post casum Adae per mulieris semen, Abrahamo Gen. 3 | Gen. per id quod eum eduxit ex Ur Chaldaeorum. Servo suo et successori, cum 11 et 12 diceret e rubo: *Ego sum deus patris tui, deus Abraham, deus Isaac et deus Iacob.* Exo. 3 Similiter apud populum: *dominus deus patrum vestrorum, Deus Abraham etc.* In eremo ac in terra promissionis: *deus, qui nos eduxit ex Aegypto et de domo* Exo. 20
300 *servitutis.* Praeterea foederis illius causa, archa testimonii, templum atque ipsa etiam urbs Hyerosolimitana deus appellabatur, quibus rebus tanquam imaginibus creatorem omnium intelligebant, qui per certas eiusmodi notas et gratiae suae opera, obscuritate tamen quadam involuta, seipsum representare voluit, cum contra hodie sese vere piis in Christo lucide exeruerit. Quamobrem

---

275 lapis – angularis] cfr Ps. 117 (118), 22; Act. 4, 11; Eph. 2, 20; I Petr. 2, 7   **275/**
276 via – vita] Ioh. 14, 6   **276/277** quam – docuerunt] cfr I Cor. 1, 23; Col. 1, 28
278 iustificationem reiecit] Phil. 3, 9   **280/283** Ego – Christus] I Cor. 3, 10-11   **283/**
284 Siquidem – vivus] I Petr. 2, 3-4   **284** lapis² – preciosus] Is. 28, 16   **288/**
289 Col. 2, 3   **291** quod – omnia] cfr Eph. 1, 10   **293** sed – declararit] cfr Rom. 1, 20
294/295 ut – vitae] cfr Gen. 2, 9   **295** post – semen] cfr Gen. 3, 15   **295/**
296 Abrahamo – Chaldaeorum] cfr Gen. 11, 31; 12, 1-5   **297** Ex. 3, 6   **298** Ex. 3, 15
299/300 Ex. 20, 2; Deut. 5, 6   **304/306** Quamobrem – debet] cfr II Cor. 4, 6

236 CONCILIUM BERNENSE – 1532

305 lumen illud, quo claritas illucesscit divina non aliunde, quam in Christi facie excitari debet. 2. Cor. 4. Cognitio siquidem dei omnis, quam sine Christo consequimur, umbratilis est velutque e manibus nostris effluit. Cuius rei exemplum est apud Ciceronem Simonides, qui interrogatus, quid nam esset deus, post diutinam meditationem inquisitionemque magis ac magis, quid de deo

310 vel sentiret vel responderet ignorabat. Atque hic Iudaeos etiam hodie | hallucinari constat, quod plus nimio literae mortuae ac Arcae foederis, quae tamen obsolevit, inhaereant. Novum nunc est respiciendum symbolum, in quo deus ipse existit. Is enim cum nos aeternae irae ac maledictioni obnoxios non aliter quam in Christo placatos voluerit, merito non iam Arcae operculum, quod

315 propiciatorium priscis appellatur, sed eius loco Christum omnis gratiae certissimam sedem colemus et amplectemur, ut in quo et coelestes illae placidaeque benignitatis divinae voces percipiantur, et certum per hunc ad patrem consequamur accessum, de quibus Hieremias in hunc modum disserit: *Non dicent* ultra arca testamenti domini, neque ascendet super cor, neque recordabuntur

320 *illius. In tempore illo vocabunt Hierusalem solium domini.* Eo in loco de coelesti illo Hierusalem deque Christi regno, quod est liberum quodque Christus in cordibus hominum electorum inhabitat, Propheta loquitur, atque ex eo consequitur per caput et membra, hoc est, Christum hominesque fideles, Deum patrem tantummodo intelligi oportere, unde etiam in gentes diffusa est

325 gratia, quae illa absque lege per Christi sanguinem spiritusque sancti effectum cum Iudaeis ex aequo participarunt.

*Cir

1Hier.*

Concionem Christianam de Christo et ex Christo totam esse oportere. Caput VI.

Cum autem universam sapientiae aeternae cognitionem per manifestas
330 quasdam actiones ac figuras percipi a nobis voluerit dominus easdemque in Christo denotarit, qui perfecto in carne suo cursu, in coelis bonitate sua per spiritum sanctum illucescit cunque conforme adeo sit per omnia cum patre mysterium, ut ne cognosci quidem ille nisi per filium possit, in primis fuerit necessarium, ut, quibus verbi ministerium deique regnum annunciandi incum-

---

311 quod – mortuae] cfr Rom. 7, 6; II Cor. 3, 6   **314/315** quod – appellatur] cfr Ex. 25, 17-22   **315/316** Christum – sedem] cfr Rom. 3, 25; Hebr. 4, 16   **317/318** certum – accessum] cfr Rom. 5, 2; Eph. 2, 18 et 3, 12   **318/320** Ier. 3, 16-17   **320/321** coelesti – Hierusalem] cfr Hebr. 12, 22   **321/322** Christi – inhabitat] cfr Eph. 3, 17   **323** consequitur – fideles] cfr Eph. 5, 30; Col. 1, 18   **324/325** Deum – gratia] cfr Eph. 3, 8   **325** per – effectum] cfr Eph. 2, 13   **333** ut – possit] cfr Matth. 11, 27

308/310 qui – ignorabat] cfr Cicero, *De natura deorum* 1, 60

CONCILIUM BERNENSE – 1532

335 bit provincia, Ie|sum Christum, in quo aeternum illud dei est absolutum con-   Civ
silium, depraedicent et inculcent, ut cuius cognitio rebus omnibus sit praefe-
renda, ne vel tanquam legis doctores depraehendantur aut prophanorum
oratorum instar, rationis suae momenta obtrudentes, reiiciantur.

Doctrinam Christianam et vitam in morte resurrectioneque Christi et inchoan-
340   *dam et finiendam.*
                                   Caput VII.

Nec satis fuerit, si concionatores verba haec 'Christus Iesus servator
noster' identidem ingeminent aut inculcent, non enim in nudo vocum verbo-
rumque strepitu, sed in vi et potentia dei Evangelium regni consistit, quae
345 fidelium animos mutat innovatque et ex peccatoribus impuris iuxtaque
carnem et sanguinem affectis filios dei et coelestes homines efficit. At hoc
munus tam divinum eamque gratiam ut adipiscamur, in docendo a morte et
resurrectione Christi est sumendum initium moxque poenitentia et peccatorum remissio annuncianda, quae doctrinae Christianae summa est et colo-
350 phon. Hunc instituendi modum tradidit Christus, hunc observarunt Apostoli,
susceperunt ab illis electi spiritusque sanctus confirmavit nemoque est mortalium, qui illum, quin certus sit et indubitatus, inficiari queat. Huc pertinet
Lucae testimonium ita scribentis: *Tunc aperuit illorum mentem, ut intelli-*   Lucae. 24
gerent scripturas et dixit eis. Sic scriptum est et sic oportebat Christum pati et
355 *resurgere tertio die a mortuis et praedicari in nomine eius poenitentiam et remis-*
sionem peccatorum in omnes gentes. Hinc liquet poenitentiae remissionisque
peccatorum post resurrectionem domini prima subnasci semina, utpote quae
in illus, qui morti traditus denuo resurrexit, nomine est annuncianda, cui rei et
Apostolorum missio post resurrectionem primum facta astipulatur. Proinde
360 hisce omni|bus rite perpensis Christianarum concionum eo dirigatur institu-   C2r
tum, qui abiectis sublatisque erroribus mores emendentur pietasque vera
promoveatur. Interim vero haudquaquam ignorandum per Christi resurrectionem totum eius vitae cursum, hoc est ascensionem ad coelos spiritusque sancti
communicationem, una cum reliquis, quas credentium mentes percipiunt,
365 actionibus, intelligi oportere. Sunt autem et Petri accurate observandae
perscrutandaeque conciones, quae eandem salutis per Christum annunciandae
praeferunt seriem. Act. 2. 4. 11. 17. 20. Ubique enim per Christi mortem et resurrectionem poenitentiam urgent noxaeque contractae (quae summa nostri

---

335 Christum – consilium] cfr Eph. 1, 11   **344** sed – consistit] cfr I Cor. 4, 20   **345/**
346 ex – affectis] cfr Rom. 8, 5   **346** filios dei] cfr Eph. 4, 13; Phil. 2, 15   **348/**
349 poenitentia – annuncianda] Luc. 24, 47   **353/356** Luc. 24, 45-47

238 CONCILIUM BERNENSE – 1532

est Evangelii) indicant abolitionem. Cuiusmodi doctrinae forma et a nobis quoque expendi debet studiosissime, qui eodem, quo ipsi utamur initio, aequalique progressu et incremento in Christo proficiamus. Occlamant autem hic nonnulli, in hunc modum.

Si a morte Domini et resurrectione ordiendum est finiendumque negocium, quid prodest nativitatis illa totiusque vitae Christi apud Evangelistas descriptio? Responsio.

Nativitas vitaque Christi universa ad mortem eius est quaedam praeparatio, ita ut dispensatio vitaque eius praesens et corporalis ad salutem nostram perpetuo tendat. In hoc enim cum a patre sit in mundum demissus filius, omnia procul dubio, quum dicta tum facta eo instituit et direxit, quo legatione commissa rectissime fungerent, atque ea nisi praestitisset, patri suo (quod vel cogitare vel suspicari fuerit impiissimum) immorigerus videri posset. Spiritus ergo, qui in nobis est, in omni doctrina solum gloriae Christi crucisque verbum requirit. Opera autem et miracula ita respicit et observat, ut in iis omnibus internum gratiae profectum arcanamque quandam in cordibus nostris actionem intelligat. Siquidem eos, qui ob criminum suorum multitudinem caeci et surdi fue|rant, ad vivam iam dei vocem oculis auribusque perci- C2v piendam idoneos reddit, claudos autem ita agiles et expeditos heroas efficit, ut viam domini omnibus superatis difficultatibus currant inoffense, lepram flagitiorum per gratiam salutarem tollit mortuumque resurrectionis spiritu suscitat vitaeque restituit non periturae. Ita fides signa prodigiaque Christi sensibus quidem percipit, sed multo magis et suspicit et admiratur, eas quae in spiritu sancto peraguntur actiones rationemque omnem humanam longissimo superant intervallo. Caeterum facta illa in spiritu sancto nativitas nihil denotat aliud, quam nos in filios dei creari, si praeter eam, quae ex carne et sanguine provenit nativitatem, per eundem a Christo nobis concessum spiritum novi coelestesque homines efficiamur. Quamobrem et nativitatem et reliquam Christi vitam haudquaquam praeter rem Evangelistae describunt, quando ea ad liberationem nostri deservit mortificatioque carnis ac ea, quae iuxta spiritum fit, resurrectio in illa manifestissime declaratur.

386/387 ad – reddit] cfr Is. 35, 5   **387** claudos – efficit] cfr Is. 35, 6   **387/388** ut – inoffense] cfr Is. 40, 3   **388/389** lepram – suscitat] cfr Eph. 2, 5-6   **393** Caeterum – sancto] cfr Matth. 1, 18; Luc. 1, 35   **393/394** nativitas – creari] cfr Ioh. 1, 17-18   **397/ 399** quando – resurrectio] cfr Rom. 6, 8

CONCILIUM BERNENSE – 1532   239

400 *Quo pacto ex Christo peccata nostra sint intelligenda.*
     Caput VIII.

Divus Paulus in hoc Deum suam erga nos charitatem potissimum comen-
dare testatur, quod cum peccatores hostesque eius essemus *Christus pro nobis*
mortuus fuerit. Ro. 5. Unde sequitur abominabile odiosumque nobis fieri
405 peccatum, cogitantibus scilicet dei filium mortis afficiendum supplicio inque
cruce immolandum crudeliter quo et delicta nostra toleret et amissam parentis
nostri culpa salutem nobis inveniret et repararet, quod ipsum satis indicat
quantum noxae quantumque maledictionis in natura resideat humana, quod
ea nisi per sacri sanguinis effusionem hostiamque | tam preciosam nec munda-   C3r
410 ri nec a sceleribus expiari poturit, nullo alio praesidio vel spe ulla reliqua. Ergo
cum Deum et creatorem et servatorem nostri esse agnoscamus omnes, merito
nos illi dedere et consecrare totus conveniebat, in quo tamen nostra, qua duce
vehimur, natura repugnat, utpote quae creaturas potius, quam earum condito-
rem respiciat seque ipsam ita tenere amet, ita colat et admiretur, ut idolum
415 plane se, cui honores etiam divinos attribuere non dubitet, constituat. Hinc
est cur nostri neglectum contemptumque tam aegre et inique feramus omnes.

In Christo absque lege cognitionem peccati esse quaerendam.
Caput IX.

Quemadmodum Iudaei vix tandem maximaque cum difficultate peccata
420 sua ex lege potuerunt cognoscere, ita per mortem Christi inquinatam nostram
et deploratam naturam nullo negocio Apostoli depraehenderunt. Quare gentibus simpliciter delicta sua primum mox reconciliationem per Christum com-
monstrarunt, nullo ex iis ad Moysem remisso. Nam si ex lege peccati doceant
cognitio, frigida ea res est vique omni carens. Apostolis igitur cum tantum sit
425 desudatum, qui a Moyse abductis Iudaeis, Christo eos adiungerent, quae sit
insania nostram plebem a Christo avulsam ad legis adstringere servitutem?

402/404 charitatem – fuerit] cfr Rom. 5, 8-9   **403/404** Rom. 5, 9   **409** nisi –
effusionem] cfr Hebr. 9, 14; I Ioh. 1, 7   hostiamque] cfr Eph. 5, 2; Hebr. 10, 12   **410/**
415 Ergo – constituat] cfr Rom. 1, 25   **420/421** ita – depraehenderunt] cfr Rom.
3, 20   **421/423** Quare – remisso] cfr Rom. 10, 4

240 CONCILIUM BERNENSE – 1532

Quamobrem Paulus tam multa de lege inter gentes egerit.
Caput X.

Caeterum ubi Pseudoapostoli apud nonnullos propius sese ingessissent
430 praeterque Christum legem, tanquam necessariam docerent, quas nam ad res
prodesset cum suo ministerio Moyses quatenusque religioni Christianae sub-
serviret, ve|ro Apostolo explicandum fuit, quae sane cura apud Gentes fuisset C3v
supervacua, ut qui simpliciter credentes, peccatorum remissionem sperabant
in Christo, cui per omnia adhaerebant et obtemperabant. Quicunque enim in
435 Christum *credit, habet vitam aeternam*. Adeo ut fidelis homo paedagogo legitimo non habeat opus, eo quod filiorum libertatem iam sit consecutus.

Iudaeos sub lege quemadmodum Gentes absque lege ad fidem pervenisse.
Caput XI.

Ecclesia vero Iudaeorum ex libertate Christiana una cum Christo legem
440 observavit maximo zelo, nihil interim tamen decrescente in servatorem fiducia, atque eo etiam Malachias ubi Christi regnum describit, confirmantibus
idipsum caeteris quoque Prophaetis, dei illos persona hortatur. *Mementote*
(inquit) *legis Moysi servi mei quam praecepi in monte Horeb, mandatorum et*
iudicii. Sedenim quamobrem aut quam diu legis illos per os Prophetae me-
445 mores esse iubet? Eam ob causam et tam diu nimirum, dum legis vim et
potentiam cognoscerent, hoc est, ut maiore desiderio ardoreque erga domini
adventum accenderentur, tantisper dum Helias, poenitentiae doctor, Domini
viam apud desperabundum peccatorem dirigeret atque pararet. Tum enim
finem sortitur Moysi illa lex, nec minus tamen, non velut ex imperio, sed libere
450 et exprompta animi hilaritate observatur, quum quod per eius usum pie quendam vivendi habitum plerique sunt consecuti, tum quod operum legis externorum dum imaginationem oculis animoque versant, interni illi coelestesque
verae pietatis thesauri magis magisque in ipsis concitantur. Quamobrem
Paulus nec contemptum nec transgressionem legis ullam docet, sed et ipse
455 purificationem Hyerosolimis iuxta praescriptum Moysi suscipit, idque alios
respiciens Apostolos, quo non con|temnere legem, sed et ipse utilem esse et C4r
salutarem agnoscere videretur. E diverso autem et Hierosolymis in ea, quae
erat Apostolorum ex Iudaeis conflata ecclesia, nec subdere legi quenquam nec

---

429 Pseudoapostoli] II Cor. 11, 13   **429/430** apud – docerent] cfr Gal. 1, 7
435 Ioh. 6, 47   **435/436** Adeo – opus] cfr Gal. 3, 24-25   **436** eo – libertatem] cfr
Rom. 8, 21; Gal. 5, 13   **442/444** Mal. 4, 4   **445/447** dum – accenderentur] cfr
Mal. 3, 2   **447** tantisper – doctor] cfr Mal. 4, 5   **447/448** Domini – pararet] cfr Is.
40, 3   **456/457** quo – videretur] cfr Rom. 7, 12

CONCILIUM BERNENSE – 1532

obstringere volebat, quamvis mordicus eam illi tuerentur. Act. ca. 21. Nam
460 Iudaeis quidem credentibus, qui recte ea legitimeque utuntur, confert obvete-
rem consuetudinem non parum, quum ad Christi erga se clementiam intelli-
gendam, tum ad peccatorum molem exactius perpendendam. Verum imperitis
Ethnicis ante vel post Christum inculcata falsam quandam in opera sua,
tanquam in dei filio non omnia sita essent, fiduciam peperit. Atque eadem
465 tamen illa legis opera Iudaei credentes vel ob mysticas adumbrationes non esse
infrugifera satis usu ipso compererant, nec timebant, dum ea quam firmiter
conceperant gratia, eos non destitueret, ut ad fluxa denuo moxque interitura
huius mundi elementa delaberentur.

Discrimen concionatoris, qui inter Ethnicos et eius, qui inter Iudaeos Christum
470 *annunciant.*
Caput XII.

Differt igitur munus Apostolicum inter gentes obeundum, quod Paulo est
demandatum, ab eo quod est inter Iudaeos exequendum, quo functus est
Petrus. Hoc enim praeter detrimentum legem acriter tuetur, act. 21. Illud nec
475 legem curat, nec Moysen respicit ullo pacto, nisi quatenus ad doctrinam vitaeque emendationem confert etc. Nos autem, qui ex gentibus provenimus, cum
illis etiam non cum Iudaeis de fidei agentes negocio absque lege pure et caste
annunciare Christi gratiam convenit, non autem iuxta morem ecclesiae Hiero-
solimitanae in lege occupari. Siquidem satisfactio nostra Christus, quid est
480 igitur, quod ultra requiramus?

Unde nam Pseudoapostoli.
Caput XIII.

Hinc est quod pseudoapostoli Petri ecclesiam, quae magno zelo legem
complectebatur, praetendentes ab ea se in mandatis habere iactabant, sed falso,
485 ut gentes a Christo | seductas ad Moysi observationem pertraherent, cuius-   C4v
modi tamen nihil ea, quae Hyerosolimis erat ecclesia, vel instituebat vel molie-
batur, nec Paulus etiam fieri ullo modo admittebat, ut qui in hoc esset totus,

---

459 Act. ca 21] cfr Act. 21, 20-26   **464/468** Atque – delaberentur] cfr Gal. 4, 9
474 act. 21] cfr Act. 21, 20   **474/476** Illud – etc.] cfr II Tim. 3, 16   **476/479** Nos –
occupari] cfr Gal. 2, 14-16   **479/480** Siquidem – requiramus] cfr II Cor. 12, 9
483 pseudoapostoli] cfr II Cor. 11, 13   **484/485** praetendentes – pertraherent] cfr
Act. 15, 1

---

465 adumbrationes] *a.c.* abumbrationes

242 CONCILIUM BERNENSE – 1532

qui ad constantiam eas fidei non simulatae cohortatione sua quam evidentissi-
me alliceret. Ad quod efficiendum, ut vires et usum legis Moysique mini-
490 sterium explicaret, res ipsa poscebat, non quidem ut per legem eos, qui fide
iam in Christo solida praediti essent, ad penitiorem scelerum suorum, a quibus
iam repurgati erant, cognitionem induceret (nam per Christum quicquid est
flagitiorum apertius intelligitur), sed eo illa pertinuit disputatio, ut de lege
conceptam persuasionem tanquam rem periculosissimam aboleret eosque in
495 Christum consolidaret integre, qui spiritum legis vitae absque scripta lege affa-
tim elargitur, id quod permanet duratque in perpetuum.

Quamobrem et eadem nobis quoque doctrinae forma, qua usi inter Gentes sunt Apostoli, erit capessenda, hi enim absque lege in Christo peccata com-
monstrarunt remissionemque eorundem et gratiam ex ipso et per ipsum
500 annunciarunt.

Caeterum si locus incidat scripturae, qui eiusmodi pseudoapostolos et
eos, qui legem inculcant, impugnet, sane eum dilucideque inter docendum
interpretari Christumque nihilominus absque lege ostendere et docere oporte-
bit, ita et verae in Christo aedificationi consuletur et praevenientur errores
505 imponentes simplicibus, qui perfacile scripturae falso intellectui se implicant
moxque eum praeter rationem propugnare nituntur.

De resipiscentia et remissione peccatorum et cursu gratiae.
Caput XIIII.

Quando igitur ex morte Christi receptuque eius in gloriam patris pecca-
510 tum nobis innotuit, oboritur indubitato quoque poenitentia, hoc est, verus
quidam et al|tissimus ob admissa dolor nostrique fastidium et displicentia, Dır
quae coniunctam tamen firmam de criminum remissione fiduciam habet,
quando ad ea condonanda solum filius dei ad crucis supplicium a patre est
demissus, quo per ipsius mortem nos vitae coelestiumque bonorum fruitioni
515 restitueret. Ubi in hunc modum filium clementissimus pater hominum conscientiis patefactum offert, inconcussa statim de tanta tamque stupenda dei
erga nos benignitate certitudo concipitur. Atque haec unica illa per quam
sumus iusitificandi fides est.

Per mortem ille in coelos penetravit, ubi nihil vel sordidum vel immun-
520 dum esse potest.

Hic est Christi cursus, hic est gratiae per spiritum sanctum in nos supervenientis effectus, ut per mortem, resurrectionem ascensumque Christi ad

---

495 spiritum – vitae] cfr Rom. 8, 2   absque – lege] cfr Rom. 7, 6; II Cor. 3, 6   **519**/
520 ubi – potest] cfr Eph. 5, 5

CONCILIUM BERNENSE – 1532

patrem ex delicto iam cognito damnataque natura, ad divinae benevolentiae munus in Christo percipiendum idoneos nos exhibere illique nos totos committere addiscamus. Ita per eiusmodi iam partam in Christo securitatem gratiam eam adipiscimur, qua contra deum commissa abolentur flagitia, ut nihil porro eorum in poenam nobis sit imputandum, atque eius rei testimonio deprehendimus noxam absconditam latentemque in pectoribus hominum maledictionem consumi quotidie velutque argentum igne a peccati spuma sordibusque repurgari. Duas enim res in nobis potissimum agit spiritus, alteram, ut nos innovet atque ad verae pietatis fructus adducat, alteram, ut nos iuxta spem efficiat haeredes vitae sempiternae, id quod tum fit, cum in fidei perdurantes certamine carnem mortificamus divinaque iam et coelestia sapimus.

De poenitentia et remissione peccatorum, hic atque eiusmodi complures scripturarum loci sunt considerandi. Quapropter omisso qui in Christo rudes inchoat sermone, *ad perfecionem feramur non rursum fundamentum iacien|tes poenitentiae et fidei in deum.*

Poenitentia in Christo reperta solidae pietatis fundamentum est.
Caput XV.

Verae pietatis fundamentum est poenitentia, quae, ut dictum, in Christo uno quaeri debet. Quare Christi praedicatio poenitentiam docet, quia instet regnum caelorum ac si doceret poenitentiae causam esse, oportere disiderium regni coelorum per Christum percipiendi. Cuius voti tum demum reddemur compotes, cum spiritus nos sanctus Christi sanguine aspersos abluit purosque et sanctos homines efficit. Ad poenitentiam hortatur Ioannes eos, qui iram dei imminentem effugere ac evitare cuperent. Quamobrem illius et nobis quoque vestigiis est insistendum, id quod et Apostoli fecerunt studiosissime, veluti sequentes loci declarant.

Posteaquam Petrus in sua concione Christum a deo esse a mortuis excitatum probasset, in hunc modum Iudaeis est locutus.

Dextera igitur dei exaltatus et promissione spiritus sancti accepta a patre effudit hoc, quod nunc videtis et auditis et caetera.

---

531 ut[1] – innovet] cfr Eph. 4, 23-24   ad – adducat] cfr Gal. 5, 22   **531/532** ut[2] – sempiternae] cfr Tit. 3, 7   **532/533** in – certamine] cfr I Tim. 6, 12   **533** carnem mortificamus] cfr Rom. 8, 13   **537/538** Hebr. 6, 1   **542/543** Quare – caelorum] cfr Matth. 4, 17   **546/547** Ad – cuperent] cfr Matth. 3, 7   **552/553** Act. 2, 33

244 CONCILIUM BERNENSE – 1532

Certo sciat ergo tota domus Israel, quod dominum et Christum fecerit deus
555 *hunc Iesum, quem vos crucifixistis.* Interrogantibus autem quid agendum ergo
foret. Respondit.

Delictorum poenitentiam agite et baptisetur unusquisque vestrum in nomi-
ne Iesu Christi in remissionem peccatorum et accipietis donum spiritus sancti.
Act. 2.

560 Rursus alio in loco idem adducens inquit.

Deus patrum nostrorum suscitavit Iesum, quem vos interemistis suspenden-
tes de ligno. Hunc principem et servatorem exaltavit dextera sua ad dandam
poenitentiam Israeli et remissionem peccatorum atque nos sumus ei testes | eorum, D2r
quae dicimus insuper autem, et spiritus sanctus et caetera. Act. 5.

565 Quae succincta est et perfecta concio totum dei negocium in Christo
absolutum complectens.

De mysterio quod iam olim a principio latuit. Christum esse gentibus absque lege
praedicandum et de eadem re loci scripturarum quidam.
Caput XVI.

570 *Dedit igitur deus et gentibus poenitentiam ad vitam.* Act. 11. Inquibus
mysterii, quod a retroactis temporibus latuit, magnificentia, hoc est, Christi
intra gentes est patefactum. Ergo si cui docendi inter gentes est iniunctum
munus isque per legem et peccata arguere et poenitentiam excitare nitatur,
praecipuum potentiae Christi obscurat mysterium, eo quod spiritus sanctus ut
575 Iudaeis sub lege ita gentibus absque lege tribuatur. Quod altissima cogitatione
est perpendendum.

Paulus apud Thessalonicam in Iudaeorum Synagoga disserebat e scripturis
per tria sabata et aperiens et allegans, *quod Christum oportuisset pati et resurge-* 1Acto
re a mortuis, et quod hic esset Christus Iesus, quem ego, inquit, *annuncio vobis.*
580 Rursus Athenis in hunc modum loquitur. *Et tempora quidem huius igno-*
rantiae quum hactenus dissimularit, nunc annunciat hominibus, ut omnes
ubique resipiscant, eo quod statuit diem in quo iudicaturus est orbem terrarum
cum iustitia per eum virum, per quem decreverat, fide praestita omnibus cum Hoc e
excitarit illum e mortuis. regnu
coelo
585 Docui vos et caetera *testificans Iudaeis simul et Graecis eam, quae erga* instat.
deum est poenitentiam ac fidem, quae est erga dominum nostrum Iesum. Act. 20.

554/555 Act. 2, 36   **557/558** Act. 2, 38   **561/564** Act. 5, 30-32   **570** Act. 11, 18
571/572 Christi – patefactum] cfr Eph. 3, 8-9; Col. 1, 26-27   **572/575** Ergo –
tribuatur] cfr Act. 15, 8-9   **578/579** Act. 17, 3   **580/584** Act. 17, 30-31   **585/**
586 Act. 20, 21

CONCILIUM BERNENSE – 1532   245

| *Christianam poenitentiam etiam ex Prophetis doceri posse.*   D₂ᵛ
         Caput XVII.

Itaque si loci de poenitentia in veteri testamento nobis occurrant, non
aliter hi, quam ex Christi sensu vel accipi vel tractari debent, ut in quem unum
omnia Prophetarum oracula tendant. Exemplum sit hic Hieremiae locus.

Si poenitentiam egerit gens illa a malo suo quod locutus sum adversus eam
etc.   Hier. 18

Haec atque eiusmodi puris Christianisque auribus sunt accipienda et consideranda, quo poenitentiam in uno Christo quaeri et inveniri posse intelliga-
mus, ne quis praeter spiritus divini afflatum, poenitentiae aliquem zelum ex
seipso nitatur confingere, eamque ob causam proxime se ad deum accessisse
falso persuadeat.

Crescere in Christi cognitione oportere et suam unicuique fidem exploratam esse.
         Caput. XVIII.

Doctrina porro haec inter ecclesias magis magisque progredi et accrescere
debet, qui ex diligenti fidei suae examine et incremento suam per Christum
factam vocationem certius quotidie explorent. In Christi enim sensu, qui non
proficit, aut deficere se aut viam domini nunquam recte ingressum esse sciat,
huc pertinent Pauli paraeneses, quae studiose Parrochis sunt exercendae.

Porro electio et gratia, in quibus omnia sita sunt, non quidem deficiunt
unquam, doceri tamen plebem oportet, ut altissima cura secum perpendat et
examinet, num electio haec et benigna dei voluntas in recte vivendi exemplum
apud unumquenque eruperit, hoc est, ut quisque quantum a deo muneris acce-
perit, quantum ve cognitionis adhuc divinae desit probe intelligat. Quae
omnia cordium quaedam | sunt innovatio inaetaernumque illum et coelestem   D₃ʳ
hominem ab omni peccato, quatenus ex deo est natus, immunem, nec iuxta
carnem et sanguinem amplius affectum constituit. Siquidem fides evidens est
animi certitudo atque hic, quod in prophanis negociis solet, probabilibus nihil
efficitur.

Hactenus de doctrina christiana, quae in Christi morte ac resurrectione
est auspicanda.

In morte Christi peccati cognitio veraque poenitentia discitur. Remissio
autem criminum in eiusdem exaltatione, quae per fidem Christique spiritum

---

592 Ier. 18, 8   **602/603** qui – explorent] cfr II Petr. 1, 10   **612** ab – immunem] cfr
I Ioh. 3, 9

---

602 diligenti] *a.c.* diligeti

246 CONCILIUM BERNENSE – 1532

620 divino semine animos electorum gravidos reddit coelestesque homines aeternitati progignit, hoc est, qui relectis peccatis ad iusticiam pietatemque exercendam toto pectore incumbant, amoris simul erga Deum, qui sint in se fomites excitati per fidem animadvertentes. Atque haec doctrina in omnibus concionibus studiosissime est observanda.

625 Tantum de vera et sana doctrina, nunc nonnulla etiam de sacramentis adhuc adducemus.

De sacramentis et baptismate in genere.
Caput XIX.

De sacramentis autem sic statuimus, ut nihil nec prius nec antiquius
630 charitate, quantum id per nos stat, habendum censeamus, neque cum quoque in certamen descendendum sacramentorum praesertim gratia, quantisper mysterium Christi nobis relinquitur intactum, etiamsi tam clarum lucidumque, quam oportebat, non relinquatur, ne per contentionem, ut fit, totum amittamus.

635 Ad perfectionem nanque sacramenta non ad sensuum carnalium argutiam excitandam pertinent. Verum si quis perceptam semel et quodammodo indutam persuasionem adversum nos omnino tueri pergat, cedendum esse arbitramur sermonemque ad certas actiones, quas in nobis perficit | spiritus, D₃ᵛ derivandum, pro uniuscuiusque gratia quolibet vel loco vel tempore concessa.
640 Puta de fide eiusque virtute aut de bona conscientia, in quo et quam diu ea consistat, quamobrem aut quo pacto excidat, praeterea de perpetuitate ex interiore gratiae cursu et incremento proveniente et alias eius generis disputationes inferre. Tantum ut odiosas illas conflictationes, quibus alter alterum irretire inque suam pertrahere sententiam nititur, caveamus, alioquin plurimum et
645 malorum et abominationum subnascetur et erroribus fenestra latissima aperietur. Videtur autem de sacramentis tutissimo in hunc modum dici posse.

Primum, ea non templorum esse ritus aut eas ceremonias, quas hukim hebraei appellant. Nam umbrae tantum et figurae fuerunt Christi mox adventuri, qui nunc et praesens apud nos est et in perpetuum permanet, sed mysteria
650 dei vel ecclesiarum esse, per quae velut externis quibusdam indiciis Christus offertur, qui spiritu sancto animos nostros ab internis implet ac communit. Dominum ergo orabimus, quo externam illam sacramentorum tractationem in

---

639 pro – concessa] cfr Eph. 4, 7   **647** hukim] cfr exempli gratia Deut. 4, 1
648 umbrae] Col. 2, 17; Hebr. 10, 1

---

642 incremento] *cod.* incremenro   **647** hukim] chuqqim, חֻקִּים (sg. חֹק = rule,
decree)

CONCILIUM BERNENSE – 1532

divinae contemplationis habitum transmutet, hoc est, ut magnum illud mysterium, quo deus in carne denotatur, in nobis ita vivat et adolescat, quemadmo-
655 dum per externa sacramenta insinuatur. Deinde vero de sacramentis iis est
verbis agendum, quae et cuique sint tempori accomoda et ad nostri deserviant
emendationem neque omnino quisquam contentionibus est exagitandus.
Atque hic consideretur quod Paulus ad Romanos scribens iam baptisatos,
m. 13 monet hoc pacto: *Tanquam in die composite ambulemus, non commessationibus*
660 *et ebrietatibus et caetera, sed induamini dominum Iesum Christum et carnis*
curam ne agatis ad concupiscentiam. Ediverso Galatis scribit in hunc modum:
Gal. 3 *At postquam venit fides, non amplius sub paedago|go sumus. Omnes enim filii dei* D4r
estis, eo quod credidistis Christo Iesu. Nam quicunque baptisati estis, Christum
induistis. Quid hic legitur? Num sui oblitus spiritus sanctus sibi ipsi repugnat?
665 Romanos enim veluti praecibus ad induendum Christum hortatur, apud Galatas autem immutato sermone baptisatos omnes Christum iam esse indutos
affirmat. Ex quibus manifeste discimus, non tam ad verba ipsa sermonisque
proprietatem, quam ad sensum esse respiciendum, pro cuius varietate dicendi
forma eadem vel immutari vel adservari potest. Quapropter λογομάκοι quos
670 vocat Paulus, tanto sunt fugiendi magis, quanto altioribus contentionem suam
mysteriis infarciunt, cum Paulo itaque dicemus:
es. 4| *Induite novum hominem. Induite arma dei. Induite arma lucis. Induite vos*
es. 6| *sicut electi dei.* Item, *induite virtutem ex alto.*
n. 13| Aliaque eiusmodi multa, quae accommodari eo possunt, ubi vel nostram
los. 3 plaebem labi potissimum animadvertimus, vel dum ad progrediendum eam in
676 pietatis studio cohortamur. Etenim si recte, quantum bonorum quantumque
faelicitatis adepti simus omnes, qui per baptisma Christi in spiritu sancto baptisati veri credimus, sedula mentis agitatione expendamus, sine dubitatione et
Christum nos iam esse indutos possumus affirmare et ad intimius induendum
680 dominum nos mutuo cohortari. Cito nanque ex divinae erga nos benevolentiae consideratione nostram deprehendemus imbecillitatem, ne forte nimio
carnis studio insolescamus.
Perdidit autem hoc unum et evertit ecclesiam semper, quod plerique
novis studuerint dogmatis, paucissimique fuerint, qui spiritum sanctum, qui
685 unus recte animos imbuit, audirent doctorem. Simplicitatem ergo nos Christi
veluti supra eam descripsimus, constanter amplectemur | et intercedente dei D4v
auxilio omnibus ad pietatem promovendam mediis, cuiusmodi baptisma est et
domini coena, citra curiositatem utemur. Siquidem in omnibus per fidem in

---

659/661 Rom. 13, 13-14   662/664 Gal. 3, 25-27   672 Induite[1] – hominem] Eph.
4, 24   Induite[2] – dei] Eph. 6, 11   Induite[3] – lucis] Rom. 13, 12   672/673 Induite[4] –
dei] Col. 3, 12   673 induite – alto] Luc. 24, 49

unum Iesum Christum respicimus, aut saltem respiciendum esse constat,
690 dominus suam largiatur nobis gratiam, quo rite voluntatem eius ubique
exequamur.

De baptismo seorsim.
Caput XX.

Ecclesia dei ea est, quam Christus inhabitat quamque iuxta hominem
695 internum fovet ac tuetur, cuius sacramenta signa quidem sunt, sed eiusmodi
quae latentem dei vim et potentiam complectantur. Quemadmodum in sacro
baptismate, ubi minister quidem aqua, sed una cum illo etiam Christus in
spiritu sancto ex aequo baptisat. Caeterum in eo quod nostros tingimus infantes, ecclesiae eos dei inscribimus, certo sperantes dominum suum quoque apud
700 illos effecturum opus inque spiritu sancto baptisaturum, atque hunc paedo-
baptismum pro vero sacramento agnoscimus. Fides enim nostra nullo vel loco
vel tempori vel externis omnino ullis alligatur, in hoc tamen baptismo credenti
homini, qui verae illi et spirituali ecclesiae accensetur, mysteriorum dei ref-
ricatur memoria. Quare nequaquam ille inter inanes ceremonias, sed inter
705 ecclesiae sacramenta magnaque dei mysteria est adnumerandus. Quum enim
Christi nomine gloriemur omnes, non illum per figuras aut umbras explicare
contendimus, sed per sacramenta fidem nostram testamur et renovamus,
cuiusmodi licet a puero nihil dum praestari queat, apud nos tamen, qui actioni
adstamus, momenti aliquid habet, ut qui divini negocii imaginem non qua-
710 tenus id coram deo perpetuitate sua consistat, sed in nobis quantum et apud
nos proficiat, exprimimus. Baptismus cum Christo nos sepelit | rursusque iam   E1r
mortuos exuscitat cum eodem. Hoc vero interim Christianae libertati conce-
ditur, ut eum nobis baptisare liceat, quem ad eiusmodi mortificationis
studium informandum speramus. Atque ea una et praecipua nostrum omnium
715 cura sit, ne praeter mysterium, quantum in nobis est, sacramenta administre-
mus. Siquidem mysterii reconditi indicia apud nos permanere nec instar caete-
rorum rituum exerceri debent.

699/700 certo – baptisaturum] cfr Matth. 3, 11   **711/712** Baptismus – eodem] cfr
Rom. 6, 4

---

715 mysterium] *a.c.* mysterum

CONCILIUM BERNENSE – 1532

De Baptismi tractatione.
Caput XXI.

720   Quamobrem hortamur, ut quisque ex ministris assuefaciat suos, ut infantes diebus dominicis praesente caetera etiam plaebe baptisandos in templum perferant. Nam cum id ecclesiae, quae ex populo Christiano coalescit, sacramentum sit, non etiam nisi ea praesente tractari debet, adeoque si absit illa, non iam ecclesiae est sacramentum, sed tanquam commune puerorum
725 balneum. Eodem pacto si infans a male religiosa obstetrice a partu statim in aedibus baptisetur, quibuscunque id fiat praesentibus, pro baptismo nequaquam haberi debet, nam et id citra ecclesiae iussum facit et vana simul coniuncta superstitio est, qua certo persuadetur, nisi ab externo tinctus esset puer, desperandam eius fuisse salutem. Quamobrem alibi suos infantes, qui imbecil-
730 les sunt et intra spacium unius mensis aut duorum morituri videntur, non tingunt homines Christiani. Baptismo enim egent pueri non tam sui quam ecclesiae causa, quae nihil dum nisi iuxta futurae pietatis salutisque spem cum illis agit.

    Atque ut aequalitatis ubique habeatur ratio, volumus non extra templum
735 vel medio templi, sed apud baptisterium locumque consuetum baptisari infantes, nec totos, sed capite tantum, reliqua corporis parte involuta manente, morbos enim parit, si tenera adhuc et rubicunda a partu caruncula | neque E iv dum aeris assueta vel frigida aqua perfundatur, vel vento asperiore affletur.

    Nec turbet hac in re quenquam quod a veteribus nonnullis dictum est,
740 propter mysterii significationem infantem totum sub aquam mergi deberi, humana enim ea est et inanis cogitatio. Nam si tanta superstitione signa illa et externa symbola tractanda essent, quadraginta aquae mensuris iisdemque non haustis, quae in libris Talmuticis saytha vel sayn appellantur, opus foret. Sed et propter dilucidiorem explicationem ex Propheta Esaia etiam vivas et fluentes
745 aquas exigi oporteret. Siquidem aquae internae vivae sunt, semperque scaturiunt in vitam aeternam. Sed quo tum evadet nostra libertas? Quantum negocii facesserent nobis externa? Imo quantum ab aeternarum rerum, quae in fide fiunt, contemplatione impediremur? Quare fratres et cooperiarii in evangelio dei charissimi, in verbi divini annunciationem, quod praecipuum nostrum
750 munus est, omni studio incumbamus, nihil hominum contentiosorum morati

---

745/746 Siquidem – aeternam] cfr Is. 58, 11

742/743 quadraginta – appellantur] Miqwa'ot 1, 7 et 5. 6 (*non haustis*, Miqwa'ot 2, 4)

727 coniuncta] *a.c.* coiuncta   **743** saytha vel sayn] סאים dual. סאתים (sg. סְאָה = Seah (unit), lat. *satum*, pl. *sata*)

250 CONCILIUM BERNENSE – 1532

naenias, qui pio quidem affectu opinionem suam tuentur, sed semplices tamen animos ob sacramentorum usum in fraudem illiciunt falsamque superstitionem inducunt.

Parem ergo ubique baptisandi rationem omni cura tenendam esse ducimus, nec ferendos qui dicunt: 'Liber sum, pro meo arbitrio meos tingam nihil curans caeteros'. Absint voces tam impiae, charissimi fratres. Quanquam enim Christianus homo liber sit, idem tamen omnibus sese accommodare neminemque offendere studet. Liberi sumus omnes, sed ministri iusticiae omnium per Christum nos servituti subiicientes. Cuius autem sit charitatis aequalem cum tanta urbis ac ditionis multitudine externarum rerum communionem aversari? Verum neminem tam praefractum aut pertinacem fore speramus, qui nullo aliorum habito respectu tam contumaciter privatam opinionem vel inducere, vel tueri nitatur.

| Quoniam autem baptismus Ecclesiae sanctum est sacramentum, volu- E2r
mus illum inter nos summo studio et gravitate tractari locumque ex scripturis ad id deservientem exponi, adiuncta eius baptismi explicatione, qui in spiritu sancto peragitur, cuius innovatione filios dei in vitam aeternam progignit. Posthaec preces ad deum fundantur addita rursus adhortatione pia, quo auditores suum in oculis gerant baptismum ac per mortificationem carnis eam, quae per spiritum fit resurrectionem, inseipsis magis magisque absolvant, id quod tum fiet, si baptismus non leviter aut negligenter velut olim in Papismo fiebat, sed studiose graviterque exerceatur. Nam, ut saepe dictum, non hic ritus externus, sed altissimum mysteriorum dei est sacramentum.

De caena Domini.
Caput XXII.

In caena domini eadem, quae de caeteris sacramentis et baptismo memoravimus in genere, sunt consideranda, eo quod totius in se Christianismi negocium complectatur. In fractione nanque panis non ritus modo externus, sed mysterii etiam inest sacramentum, quo Iesu Christi pro nobis mortui corpus et sanguis offertur et caetera. Atque hoc corpus hicque sanguis ita nos interiore cibo potuque in spiritu pascit et rigat, quemadmodum per os corpus pane vinoque satiatur. Ac in hunc modum fides sursum ad internarum rerum contemplationem convertitur duasque in se comprehendit actiones, scilicet panis

---

756/758 Quanquam – studet] cfr I Cor. 10, 23 et 32   758 Liberi – iusticiae] cfr Rom.
6, 18   758/759 omnium – subiicientes] cfr I Cor. 4, 5   769 ac – carnis] cfr Rom.
8, 13   770 quae – resurrectionem] cfr Rom. 8, 11   779 quo – mortui] cfr I Thess. 5, 10

772 graviterque] *a.c.* gravitesque   782 satiatur] *a.c.* saciatur

CONCILIUM BERNENSE – 1532

fractionem externam et animarum cibationem internam. Quare sanguis et corpus domini in caena quidem sunt, sed nec substantiale corpus in pane, nec corporalis sanguis in vino, veluti pristini confidenter asserebant errores, existit. Ex quo sequitur reconci|liationis communionisque hoc esse sacramentum, quando hoc nobis corpus offert, cuius membra nos sumus, ut qui ex carne et ossibus eius provenimus, iuxta hunc Pauli locum. E2v

Panis quem frangimus, nonne communicatio corporis Christi est? quoniam unus panis, unum corpus multi sumus. Hinc facile patet, quid diiudicare sit corpus domini, nempe hoc ipsum quo alimur et per quod communicationem habemus. Quisquis igitur non suam apud se imbecillitatem probarit praeque caeteris seipsum inflatus extollat, non hic Christi corpus diiudicat eoque participatione ea caret, quoniam et sui ipsius nititur viribus hancque manducationem instar cibi communis praeter mysterium et sine Christo usurpat eoque ad iudicium sibi manducat et bibit. Christus nanque cum carnem peccatorum in nobis concitatricem per spiritum suum corripiat, nullum dum eius rei sensum in animo suo percepit, id quod certum est indicium dominum cum illo tanquam infideli nondum cohabitare.

Quod vero ad usum caenae attinet, visum est, ut panibus non fermentatis (quas hostias vocant) utamur, qui si haberi parui non queant, maiores in particulas concisas distribuemus. Interim etiam plaebs doceatur, manibus quoque panem et calicem ab ipsis accipi citra piaculum posse idque videri commodius, quam si in os a verbi ministro illa sint inserenda. Sin autem quis ab horum tanquam rerum sacrarum contrectatione abhorreat, huic ipsi panem calicemque, donec rem sanius intelligat, porrigemus.

Solemus autem ter in anno caenam domini celebrare, nempe in Pascatis, Penthecostes et natalis Domini festis. Quo non ad tempus quicquam alligamus, velut in Papismo fiebat, ubi singulo pascatis festo communicare caenae domini indicta detrectantibus piaculi poena omnes adigebantur. Nullius enim in hisce conscientiam gravare statuimus. In|terim tamen quid pietatis charitatisque habeant ii, qui a communi seipsos ecclesiae usu reddunt alienos, non est difficile deprehendere. E3r

Caenam porro ut dictum graviter studioseque peragi volumus, praesertim cum totius in se Christianismi negocium contineat. Quare mysterium explicetur cum praelectione scripturae ad eam rem deservientis, praecipue tamen verborum caenae domini quamadmodum ea vel Paulus, vel Evangelistae

---

788/789 ut – provenimus] cfr Eph. 5, 30   **790/791** I Cor. 10, 16-17   **791/792** diiudicare ... corpus] I Cor. 11, 29   **793** Quisquis – probarit] cfr I Cor. 11, 28   **796/797** ad iudicium sibi manducat et bibit] I Cor. 11, 29   **818** vel Paulus] cfr I Cor. 11, 23-26   vel Evangelistae] cfr Marc. 14, 22-25

252 CONCILIUM BERNENSE – 1532

describunt, quae mox subsequatur pia ad Deum praessiusque cogitata praeca-
820 tio. Deinde panis calicisque distributio, quae cum gratiarum actione, prout
cuiuslibet loci aut temporis oportunitas tulerit, concludetur. Verum et hoc
quoque moneatur, quibus ab hoc cibo sit abstinendum, ut qui regni dei non
sint particeps, veluti a Paulo I. Corin. 6. et aliis item locis enumerantur.

Quoniam autem circa harum adhuc rerum primordia laboramus neque
825 dum plerique negocii profunditatem intelligunt, ad internam potissimum
aedificationem respiciemus. Quare ad externa quod attinet flagitia, foro matri-
moniali, ut vocant, contenti neminem facile excommunicandum esse statuimus, quando ii iudices prava exempla avertere et coercere malosque ad
emendationem aliqua ratione pertrahere possunt. Interea tamen fraterna illa
830 correptio nullo pacto nobis est omittenda. Praeterea suapte natura homines
scelerati seipsos a nobis separant, ut qui ex animo nunquam nobis adhaeserint.
Sin autem eo provehantur insaniae aliqui, ut verbis ac factis in eo quod impie
in Evangelium moliri coeperunt, tuendo insolenter se perseveraturos ostend-
dant, a communione tamen temperare nolint, facile ea in re pius minister,
835 remedia quibus huic malo occurrat, excogitabit, ne indiligentiae unquam
culpari queat.

| *De usu legis et Prophetarum.* E3v
Caput XXIII.

Ex praedictis abunde cognoscimus sacramenta Christianorum non ritus
840 tantum ceremoniacos, sed magna dei esse mysteria Moysemque cum suis ceremoniis ad nos nihil pertinere, eoque neminem ex Christianis retrorsum in
Moysen prophetasque, ut ad illorum se comparet praescriptum esse deducen-
dum, sed ut in fide cognitioneque Christi accrescat esse cohortandum. Sed in
his nonnulli obiiciunt: Si nullus sit Moysi prophetarumque habendus respec-
845 tus, nec Bibliorum esse opus lectione, nec vetus omnino praedicandum esse
testamentum, quibus Paulum obiectionibus opponemus ad Timotheum ita
scribentem: *At tu persistito in his quae didicisti et quae tibi concredita sunt,* 12 Tim
sciens a quo didiceris et quod a puero sacras literas noveris, quae te possunt eru- Cap. 3
ditum reddere ad salutem, quae est in Christo Iesu. Omnis scriptura divinitus
850 *inspirata est utilis ad doctrinam, ad redargutionem, ad correctionem, ad institu-*
tionem, quae est in iusticia, ut integer sit dei homo ad omne opus bonum adpara-

---

823 veluti – enumerantur] cfr I Cor. 6, 9-10; Gal. 5, 19-21; Eph. 5, 5 **830/**
831 Praeterea – adhaeserint] cfr I Ioh. 2, 19 **843** ut – accrescat] cfr II Petr. 3, 18
847/851 II Tim. 3, 14-17

834 temperare] *a.c.* temprare

CONCILIUM BERNENSE – 1532

tus. Haec Apostolus, qui Timotheum et in Christi fide permanere constanter et scripturae usum non negligere iubet. Atque hic quinque causae, cur scriptura conducat, referri possunt.

855 Primo, scriptura, hoc est, lex et prophetae, sapientes nos reddunt ad salutem, in eo quod Christi nos fidem tanquam unici servatoris vitaeque largitoris aeternae deducunt. Quid enim aliud apud nos proficit Moyses, dum vel vitae emendationis formam praescribit, vel aberrantibus ab ea mortem minatur, nisi quod eius in nobis excitat desiderium, qui iustos efficit sceleratos, gratiamque
860 pure et sancte vivendi iuxta hominem internum elargitur. Etenim sum|mam E4r quandam fuerit sapientiam consecutus, qui ex lege prophetisque se alienum ab omni carnis concupiscentia esse debere intelligat. Sed quis nam mortalium id per legem praestare potest? Nemo. Sapientes ergo nos ad salutem per Christum Iesum consequendam ea efficit. Is enim primo crucis verbum, quo carnis
865 mortificantur desideria, nobis offert, mox verbum vitae vimque resurrectionis, quae rerum coelestium divinitatisque in nobis sensum parit. Ita legem rite utentibus plurimum conferre emolumenti apparet. Huc autem etiam tabernaculi, testimonii, candelabri aurei, mensae, panum propositionis, arcae et sanctificationis mysteria pertinent, postremo omnia sacrificia, una cum universo
870 Moysi ministerio.

Porro et ex hoc quam undequaque depravata sit nostra natura discimus, quando ab inito statim suorum praeceptorum Moyses, ea quibus vel in pietate erga deum, vel charitate erga proximum aberremus, ostendit. Docet autem in universa plaebe etiam crucem et resurrectionem, quae tum demum in veram
875 extollitur gloriam, cum maxime depressa humiliatur. Inque extremis discriminibus tuto innixus domino consistit animus summa etiam in praesenti vita tranquillitate, quemadmodum etiam per veram poenitentiam, dum in Christum credimus, aeternam salutem adipiscimur.

Atque haec eadem, quae ex Moyse hactenus memoravimus, etiam prophe-
880 tarum libri complectuntur, qui aliud nihil sunt quam perpetuae quaedam in Moysem enarrationes adiunctis simul historiis, quae salutem per Christum adumbrant, ut in quem unum, quum in Moyse tum in prophetis Spiritus Sanctus spectavit, huiusque unius causa opera dei eodem ordine et modo sunt

---

859/860 gratiamque – internum] cfr Rom. 7, 22   **860/862** Etenim – intelligat] cfr Rom. 7, 7   **864** Is – verbum] cfr I Cor. 1, 18   **865** verbum vitae] cfr Phil. 2, 16; I Ioh. 1, 1   **866** quae – parit] cfr Rom. 8, 5   **866/867** Ita – apparet] cfr I Tim. 1, 8 **867** tabernaculi] cfr Ex. 33, 7   **868** testimonii] cfr Ex. 25, 21-22   candelabri aurei] cfr Ex. 25, 31-39   mensae – propositionis] cfr Ex. 25, 23-30   arcae] cfr Ex. 25, 10-22 **871** undequaque – discimus] cfr Rom. 7, 18

858 emendationis] *a.c.* emendatioris

254 CONCILIUM BERNENSE – 1532

peracta quondam, quo gratiae per Christi spiritum supervenientis cursus in
885 hominum animis est absolutus. | Hisque recte perpensis facile, quid Christus E4v
Io. 5 voluerit, intelliget: *Si Moysi* (inquit) *credidissetis, credidissetis utique mihi,*
de me enim ille scripsit. Rursus, *scrutamini scripturas, quia vos videmini in ipsis*
vitam aeternam habere, et illae sunt, quae testificantur de me, nec vultis venire
ad me, ut vitam habeatis. Ex quibus consequitur, nullum scripturae sensum
890 vere consecutum esse hunc, qui nullum dum de Christo luculentum testimonium aut accessum ad illum animo suo percepit. Veruntamen si per ignorantiam hoc pacto Christum non in omnibus scripturae locis queamus eruere,
non est ut deterreamur, verum enim profectum modo pro nostra et ipsi virili
annitamur, spiritus suppeditabit. Cum autem in omni doctrina unus sit Chris-
895 tus perpetuo praedicandus, necesse est, ut ea loca, quae Christum nobis expli-
cant, identidem inculcemus. Ex aliis vero, quibus minus aperte exprimitur
Christus, boni aliquid excerpemus, certi, nonnihil intelligentiae nos scripturarum adeptos, dum aliquid ex ea comperimus usus ac utilitatis. Siquidem
scriptura plurimum ad omne bonum emolumenti confert.
900 Secundo, ad doctrinam scriptura prodest, quae fructuum gratiaeque ex
cruce Christi manantis est cognitio, cuiusmodi bonorum coelestium intellectus facile nobis innotescet, si ea, qua debemus, sedulitate in rerum divinarum
consideratione versemur. Huc autem pertinent externorum promissiones, quas
ad animi et spiritus profectum primum referre et per Christum spiritualiter
905 concedi doceri oportet, ac tum demum ad externa cum spiritus Christi suum
in nobis munus obivit. Eaque nisi observentur, periculum est, ne saepe praeter
Christum splendide promittamus multa, quae secus tamen evenire experiamur, atque ita falsi arguamur Apostoli, dum in mendaciis deprehensi conuin-
cimur, id quod recens nuper agricolarum declaravit exemplum, quibus cum
910 nonnulli | tormentorum ictus se per fidem suam aversuros manicisque involu- F1r
turos confidentissime pollicerentur, accepta clades tam miseranda falsos esse
illos Prophetas nihilque promissionum eiusmodi praestitisse probabat. Quare
cum ministri simus spiritus, omnia etiam spiritualiter a nobis sunt designanda,
quemadmodum in Christo ad veritatem et spiritum omnia referuntur.
915 Tertio, ad correctionem errorum. Quanquam enim nonnihil cognitionis
ex fide simus adepti, in densa tamen etiamnum caligine multarumque rerum
ignorantia versamur. Est autem scriptura non iuxta nudam literam, quod
quidam solent, sed ex fidei ratione et analogia contra errores adducenda.
Quarto, ad vitae emendationem. Nam historiae et figurae ad nos relatae
920 validas frugiferasque in se admonitiones complectuntur.

886/887 Ioh. 5, 46 **887/889** Ioh. 5, 39-40

CONCILIUM BERNENSE – 1532

Quinto, ad scelerum correptionem, quo relicto abiectoque peccato verum in nobis pietatis studium accendatur.

In his vero omnibus est summa cura observandum, quae nam coram Deo vere sint flagitia quo certissime ea, quae ex Prophetis corripere statuimus, cognita iam ante perspectaque habeamus. Nam falsos alioquin Prophetas nos esse hoc pacto declarabimus, si vel docuisse vel exegisse a nobis deum asseramus, quibus contrariam aliquando voluntatem illius reipsa experiamur. *Nam si dixerit* (inquit dominus) *falsus propheta in nomine dei et non evenerit, id dominus non est loquutus et hoc erit signum etc.* Deut. 18. Eiusmodi Prophetis et paulo ante capite 13 etiam mortis est indicta poena.

Porro propheticas correptiones Christi spiritu condiri et mitigari oportet, quo inter acerbitatem amoris quaedam vehementia emineat, quae correptionis austeritatem edulcet. Ita fiet, ut etiam eius scripturae usum aliquem deprehendamus, quam nondum per omnia intelligimus, hoc est, in qua Christum | nondum satis expresse comperimus. Spiritus enim dei iustificationem vitae et omne bonum docet. Tantum, fratres charissimi, in hoc omni incubamus studio, quo praedicationis de Christo delegatum nobis munus rite exequamur.

De impugnando Papismo.
Caput XXIIII.

Porro locos quosdam communes Pontificiorum, hoc est, praecipuos quosdam Papisticae Ecclesiae ritus Parrochus probe cognitos habeat oportet, quo iuxta Christi praescriptum, veluti supra diximus, refutare illos et ab Ecclesia sua avertere queat, quod tamen non simul, sed singillatim et ordine quodam pro oblata occasione est faciendum. Etsi enim quicquid vel imperii Papistici vel inanium ceremoniarum erat, per totam ditionem Bernensem a magistratu sit abrogatum, operepraetium tamen est et necessarium, ut plaebs solide et constanter erudiatur, ne conscientiae adhuc imbecilles ab adversa parte implicentur inque pristinos abstrahantur errores. Quae ut magis dilucide adpareant, fingamus verbi ministrum eiusmodi scripturae locum tractasse. *Christus caput est Ecclesiae, suique corporis servator* atque huic mox subiecisse themati. Ecclesiam Christi populum esse internum et spiritualem, quem Christus praeter ullius omnino creaturae medium gubernet, servet, purum sanctumque efficiat, quibus verbis haec quoque subiici possent. Quapropter Christum certo abnegat, quisquis papam vicarium eius vel constituere vel asserere ausit, Christus

---

928/929 Deut. 18, 22   **929/930** Eiusmodi – poena] cfr Deut. 13, 6   **949/950** Eph. 5, 23   **954/955** Christus – perpetuo] cfr Matth. 28, 20

924 certissime] *a.c.* certiffime   **926** si – exegisse] *a.c.* fi vel docuiffe vel exegiffe

956 CONCILIUM BERNENSE – 1532

955 enim cum praesens apud suos sit perpetuo, non aliter Ecclesiae atque caput
membris cohaeret, quibus vitam Spiritumque iugiter de supernis infundit. Ex
his itaque manifeste patet, quicquid de Pontifice tanquam vicem Christi
gerente deque institutis eius legibus decretisque traditur ex Sathana proficisci
Chri|stoque servatori nostro velut ex diametro repugnare et caetera. Quae F2r
960 paucioribus vel pluribus verbis pro cuiuslibet vel loci vel temporis oportunita-
te indicari posunt mentione interdum de missa aut lustrica illa scelerum confessio ne adiuncta.

Quando igitur eos, qui verbo praesunt, non aliunde quam ex spiritu sancto salutem nostram, hoc est Christum Iesum, annunciare convenit, qui afflatu
965 suo ad deum pertrahit mortales et mundum arguit peccatorum, sedulo illius
exemplo danda est et nobis opera, quo in singulis concionibus ad Christum
fructusque iusticiae hortemur et scelera, si quae in nostra plebe extant, corri-
piamus. Neque tamen in publica ista et crassa, quae nunquam non fortiter
impugnari debent, solum est invehendum, sed latentes magis et reconditae
970 carnis versutiae sunt detegendae, cuiusmodi sunt amor sui, hypocrisis, falsa
sanctimoniae persuasio, charitatis neglectus, inhumanitas et, si quae sunt alia,
quae in animo aestuantia illum adversus deum suum exagitant aut impellunt.
Quo pro fidei suae modulo quisque in crepatus in veram emendationem
incumbat, populusque Christianus ipsum fontem originemque, hoc est, ipsos
975 cordium sinus et involutas arcanasque cogitationes observet, easque ad fruge
meliorem perducat. Quare adprime in hisce est necessarium, ut procul omni
relegato affectu ex constanti veritate tanquam coram deo in conspectu Iesu
Christi corripiant concionatores. Quod dum fit, nunquam nisi ex mera abun-
dantique charitate, qua per Christum ipsorum sunt tincta corda, obiurgatione
980 adversus suos utentur neque id tamen ulterius quam ad aedificationem eam
conferre putarint. Quandoquidem in Ecclesia domini ad emendationem vitae
comparata, quae fiunt, omnia esse debent, adeo ut nihil vel ex studio carnis vel
contentionis zelo proficiscatur. Qua tamen in parte non paucos, qui Evangelici
mu|neris titulo glorientur, labi gravissime animadvertimus, qui ex affectuum F2v
985 suorum impotentia privatum odium in adversarios evomunt iracundiaque
ardentes in contumeliam feruntur praecipites, se ipsos potius quam Christum
praedicantes, ut munus plane ipsorum cathedra impudentiae condignius
quam ecclesiae appellari posset. Absit igitur omnis amarulentia, omnis acerbi-
tas ab his, qui Christum tam benignum et obvium servatore docendi in profes-
990 so habent. Quin potius charitate profusa eiusmodi esse pectora vel maxime

---

955/956 non – cohaeret] cfr Eph. 4, 15-16   **964/965** qui – peccatorum] cfr Ioh. 16, 8
967 fructusque iusticiae] cfr Phil. 1, 11   **974/975** ipsos – cogitationes] cfr Marc. 7, 21
988 Absit – amarulentia] cfr Eph. 4, 31   **990/991** Quin – illis] cfr Rom. 5, 5

CONCILIUM BERNENSE – 1532

convenit per spiritum, qui datus est illis. Idque si secus fiat, ut correptio non iuxta dei voluntatem ex Christi cognitione depromatur nulla item amoris permixta dulcedine, adeo ut non per omnia unica dei gloria salusque audito- rum quaeri intelligatur, malam esse eam et a Christi instituto alienam scelerum
995 carpendorum rationem, nemo est, qui negare queat. Atque haec veluti prae- scriptum hactenus sese habere in hunc modum aperte fatemur omnes, domi- numque obsecramus, ut ita pectora linguasque nostras moderetur, ut aequabili incedentes gradu medium ubique teneamus. Nam ad scelera vel connivere, vel leniori ea, quam oportebat, oratione coercere aeque fuerit pernitiosum.
1000 Verum, qui Domini mentem ac iustum iudicium respiciunt, facile in qualibet re, quid facto sit opus, ex praedictis cognoscent. Praeterea inter corripiendum sermo non levis aut scurrilis, sed gravis, solidus et constans esse debet, ne magnitudo Christi et potentia, quae libere poenas adversus hominum flagitia profert, ulla ex parte imminuatur. In ecclesia enim domini graviter omnia
1005 decenterque debent, cum contra nonnulli e nobis usqueadeo insulsos impudi- cosque sermones effundant, ut a castis auribus citra pudorem audiri plane nequeant. Id ne accidat, nos mutuo hortamur ac diligenter obsecramus, quo sermonibus sobriis purisque utamur omnes, qui ad aedificationem profectum- que | pietatis deserviant, non animos imbecilles conturbent.   F3r

1010
Qui sint corripiendi.
Caput XXV.

Praesentes igitur auditores flagitiorum suorum admoneri et corripi opor- tet. Quid enim adferat utilitatis, si in Bernatium urbe aut ditione in exteros principes, qui nec ad nos attinent nec nostram ecclesiam ulla ex parte agnos-
1015 cunt, acerbius insecteris? Paulus *ad emendationem omnia facienda esse* monet prima Corinthios 14. Sed quid emendemus, si magnis clamoribus in absentes detonantes nostrum gregem, qui plurima et doctrina et correptione eget, inani sermone suspendamus? Perinde sit, ac si mortuum in balnea perferas, relicto in sordibus suis furnario, hic enim, qui ablutione indigebat vel maxime, negli-
1020 gitur, in illo nihil balneum efficit aliud, quam ut cadaver citius ex calore foeteat et computrescat. Eodem pacto et nos quoque exteros, ubi linguae in- caluerunt, proscindimus, nulla gregis nostrae in carnis studio pereuntis habita ratione, cui tamen a nobis ad monitione commoda succurri et poterat et inpri- mis decebat. Atque ita dum minus nos ad Christi formulam comparamus, ex
1025 omni parte ecclesiae nostrae officimus. Nam eiusmodi tam acerbis in absentes

---

1004/1005 In – debent] cfr I Cor. 14, 40   **1015** I Cor. 14, 26; cfr II Cor. 12, 19

1016 14] *a.c.* 12

CONCILIUM BERNENSE – 1532

declamationibus plaebs nostra exacerbatur inque temeraria incidat iudicia, ita ut propriae oblita emendationis alienis examinandis criminibus tantum ingeniosa esse laboret. Quamobrem absentibus minime allatrandum esse censemus, nisi forte periculo vel reipublicae vel ecclesiae imminenti sit occurrendum, aut alioqui obiter ac veluti exemplo a sceleratis sumpto hominibus a paribus flagitiis auditores deterreamus. Sed Papam tamen silentio praeterire nullo modo possumus, eo quod imperio suo nostris cervicibus perpetuo incumbat simpliciumque hominum conscientias impediat et conturbet, alioqui facile traditiones illius | tam sordidas (utpote gravioribus occupati negotiis) corripere, omitteremus, nisi a sacri illius templi aedificio avertenda nobis impedimenta essent. Quare eatenus veluti praedictum de exteris est silendum. Nam si exoriri aliquos sentiat parrochus, a quibus incommodum Ecclesiae aut pernities ulla impendat, non eos negliget, sed ad plebem suam id negotium admonitione adiuncta referet, securus etiam si eos Evangelii hostes, quos arguit necessario, gravissime offendat et exagitet. Discrimen autem inter adversarios, qui pietatis aliquo studio tenentur et eos, qui seipsos tantum quaerunt, non difficile erit observare, quemadmodum et Paulus suos ab Alexandri et Hymenaei, licet absentium, imposturis monuit, quo, si Ephesi in illos inciderent, melius et praevidere et cavere eas possent. Alioqui solet non raro et accurate piorum hominum et alibi degentium pie facta velut testimonii loco adducere, nempe quo suos ad poenitentiam vitaeque integritatem alliciat, siquidem cum mala exempla passim citra investigationem occurrant, bonorum vero sit tanta ubique locorum paucitas, necesse est ut nihil, quod a bonis sit uspiam, taceatur. Ediverso autem quibusdam e nobis hoc unum est studio, qui omnium ignominiam detegant, nihil prorsus aput ullos comendatione dignum observantes. Id quod ipsum tamen e simplici et bono instituto provenire non negaverimus, quod vitandorum scelerum rationem magis inculcant plerique, quam ut in animis auditorum, id quod tamen huius muneris est praecipuum opus, ultroneam recte gerendi excitent propensionem.

Veritatem citra ullam humani favoris spem non ex magistratus iussu,
sed ex scripturae autoritate libere praedicandam.
Caput XXVI.

Gladium porro verbi dei ex aequo in omnes stringant Par|rochi, nec vir an mulier, dominus an servus, hostis an amicus, magistratus an subditus, gratum

---

1035/1036 nisi – essent] cfr I Cor. 3, 17 ; Eph. 2, 21 **1042/1043** quemadmodum – Hymenaei] I Tim. 1, 20 **1044/1046** Alioqui – adducere] cfr II Cor. 9, 2 ; I Thess. 1, 7-8 **1058** Gladium – dei] cfr Eph. 6, 17 ; Hebr. 4, 12

CONCILIUM BERNENSE – 1532

1060 item an ingratum fit verbum, penitus respiciant, sed libere proferant, quicquid ad vitae emendationem conducere ex scripturis compererint, sibi ipsis vero nec ad plausum venari, nec concitare factiones debent. Siquidem dei negotium simpliciter et constanter citraque ullum diei humanae respectum tractandum est.

1065 Neque ex nobis quenquam, veluti passim vulgi sermonibus iactatur, magistratus tantum praedicare autoritatem convenit, adeo ut pleraque quae docet eo, quod a magistratu praecepta et observanda et credenda esse dicat, ne, qui cognitionis sunt minus solidae, plus Senatus potentiae quam deo studii venerationisque deferant, is enim papistice tyrannidis vel praecipuus error est. 1070 Fides autem vera in unum deum spectat exque vivo eius verbo et cordis illumminatione promanat, non vel ex terrenae potestatis, vel hominis omnino ullius iudicio pendens. *Iustus enim ex fide sua vivit.* In hunc itaque modum negocium plaebi exponatur.

Quandoquidem magistratus Bernensis recepto nuper concordibus suffra-1075 giis dei Evangelio, missam et quicquid huic atque eiusmodi evidentibus scripturae locis fideique analogiae contrarium abrogavit, id quod ita clarum est, ut nullus inficiari queat obstante tam manifesta scripturae autoritate veraque Christi cognitione, cui utrunque testamentum certo astipulatur. Quare dei auxilium communibus votis est expetendum, quo veritatis istos sensus porro in 1080 animos vestros pro sua benignitate diffundat. Neque committendum nobis est, ut magistratum nostrum in Papae, qui conscientiarum sibi imperium vendicat, locum subrogemus, id quod nostris nos viribus nimium fidere externaeque potentiae plus aequo inniti argueret.

| *Favorem plebis Parrocho non esse captandum.* F4v
1085 *Caput XXVII.*

Sunt alii nimium acres et intemperantes in perstringendo magistratu presertim absente, quem tamen, si cora esset, ubi vel maxime erat profitenda veritas, turpi assentatione blandiciisque demulcere student, idque ob eam causam, quo plaebem sibi, quam potissimum eiusmodi conviciis et declamandi 1090 in magistratum licentia delectari sciunt, sibi concilient et adiungant. Ab utrisque vero ex aequo peccatur. Christi nanque minister non vel subditos vel magistratus subiicere sibi, aut ullo se pacto ambitiosus extollere debet, cum ex professione sua dei aedificationem promovere tantum citraque personarum

---

1062/1064 Siquidem – est] cfr I Cor. 4, 3   **1070** Fides – verbo] cfr I Petr. 1, 23 **1072** Rom. 1, 17   **1092/1093** ex – promovere] cfr Eph. 2, 21-22

1061 conducere] *cod.* coducere   **1077** manifesta] *a.c.* menifesta

CONCILIUM BERNENSE – 1532

respectum ad dominum suum credentes adducere et deceat et conveniat maxime. Atqui favorem nos hominum demereri invidiamque declinare nitimur, a qua ambitione fuisse Paulum alienissimum constat, qui parvi faciebat, quod a Corinthiis dieque humana iudicaretur. Quapropter omne in hoc est situm negotium, ut verbi minister aeternum dei observans consilium illius ex ore ea proferat potius, quae in extrema die verissimo iudicii adprobentur, quam quae mundo blandiantur presenti lascivasque et petulantes aures iucunde titillent.

Ubi dicentis fuerit erectus animus, rite etiam omnia fiunt et succedunt. Syncero sane et vero pastori prima haec est et praecipua cura, qui deus apud hominem internum fiat maximi pietasque solida et germana apud Ecclesiam suam eluceat. Quare mox ad virtutes hortatur, deinde corripit, nec tamen vehementius, quam ex divini spiritus impulsu, aut Christum ipsum corripuisse indicavit. Ergo ut recte ad|ministrentur omniaorandum sedulo, ut fidi in hanc Gir tam latam domini vineam operarii ab ipso immitantur.

> *Quando acriter sit increpandus, vel leniter admonendus peccator,*
> *exemplo Christi esse discendum.*
> *Caput XXVIII.*

Accidit autem, ut acriore nonnunquam correptione sit opus, interdum vero orationem vel maxime blandam res ipsa exposcit, iam parcitur, iam rursus asperior increpatio exercetur utrumque ad dei gloriam promovendam. Samuel abiectum a domino Saulem nec traducere nec infamare apud plaebem voluit. Elias vero Isabelem una cum caeteris Baal sacerdotibus acriter et publice insectatur, quorum uterque munus suum ex dei voluntate obibat, alter acerbius, alter vero lenius agens cum duobus aeque invisis domino peccatoribus.

Caeterum in his quae cuilibet vel loco vel tempori conveniant, nec canonibus ullis comprehendi, nec ratione humana reputari possunt, spirituali enim iudicio ea sunt examinanda, quod consequemur, si ad domini nos per omnia praescriptum comparare animo ardenti expetamus. Quod nostrum votum Ioan. haud gravate exaudiet dominus, sermonem qui singulis expediat temporibus suppeditans, etiamsi certa mox inde pericula subsequantur.

1095/1097 a – iudicaretur] cfr I Cor. 4, 3   **1099** quae¹ – adprobentur] cfr Matth. 12, 36   **1102/1103** qui – maximi] cfr Eph. 3, 16   **1105** ex – impulsu] cfr Rom. 8, 14 **1106/1107** ut² – immitantur] cfr Matth. 9, 38   **1113/1114** Samuel – voluit] cfr I Reg. 15, 30-31   **1115** Elias – insectatur] cfr III Reg. 21, 20-23   **1120/1121** si – expetamus] cfr Ioh. 7, 17

CONCILIUM BERNENSE – 1532

AD SENATUM BERNENSEM CLEMENTISSIMOS DOMINOS NOSTROS
ADHORTATIO

Quamobrem, viri celeberrimi, si vel adversum vos omnes vel singulos aut vestros etiam praefectos acerbius quidpiam insolentiusque dicatur, laudabile fuerit et praeclarum, si celsitudo id vestra non ferat iniquius, | sed cuius ea G1v nomine, ac iussu Parrochi proloquantur, consideraveritis. Nam velut legati et apostoli principis sui Christi verbum illi offerunt, a quibus, quae dicuntur, aequi bonique sunt consulenda. Sapientiam enim mundanam, cum pro sua voluntate variis modis infringat dominus, interdum per indoctum eiusmodi Parrochum paganum imbecillitatis nos nostrae commonet, in quo potissimum fidei praestabitis obedientiam, si eas increpationes tanquam ad emendationem vestri a domino profectas aequo animo tuleritis.

Nec vero commovere ac exagitare vos debet, si minus forte exacta in corripiendo vestrae existimationis ratio habeatur. Nam et a natura sic est comparatum, ut viciis nostris adplaudamus omnes correptionemque etiam aequissimam citra fastidium audire nequeamus. Culpam enim suam nemo est, qui sua sponte agnoscat, aut agnoscere etiam velit, ut non dicamus, quanto in periculo magistratus consistat, ut cui maior pars hominum ob excellentem potentiae autoritatem in os assentatur, et quae auditu iucunda sunt, ingerunt. Neque tamen interea, ut verba prae se ferunt, affecti, imo absentibus nonunquam calumniantes ac pessima quaeque imprecantes. Obiurgatio ergo publica potior vobis quam amicitia simulata esse debet, utpote quod vulnus amici, quod dici solet, utilitatem veram confert, osculum autem hostis certa pernicies comitatur, et ut uno rem fasce complectamur, omnino est in omnibus dicentis animus respiciendus. Praestat sane confictis vos onerari calumniis, quam gnatonicum illud, aio, 'assentabunde' passim ingeminari. Hoc enim falsam in vana opera fiduciam securitatemque parit, illud cautos perspicacesque oculos reddit, quo diligenter circumspicientes rectius omnia et geratis et administretis. Eximiae igitur et praeclarae cuiusdam virtutis laudem meretur magistratus, si quae in se dicuntur austerius, animo magno excelsoque | ferat nihil in G2r peiorem repuntans partem. Verum si communis exigat tranquillitas, ut effrenis illa calumniandi reprimatur libido, enitendum est, ut id modeste ac citra vio-

---

1131/1132 Sapientiam – dominus] cfr I Cor. 1, 19; Is. 29, 14 **1144/1145** Obiurgatio – debet] cfr Prou. 27, 5

1146/1147 osculum – comitatur] see *Deutsches Sprichwörter-Lexikon*, hrsg. K. F. W. Wander, 5 vols, Leipzig 1866-1880, vol. 5 (1880), p. 443, no. 21 **1148** gnatonicum] Gnatho is one of the main characters in Terence's *Eunuchus*, known for being a shameless flatterer

262 CONCILIUM BERNENSE – 1532

lentiam re non nisi probe comperta fiat, sic, ut magis obiurgatorem scelerum paulo vehementiorem, quam canem obmutescentem (sic enim a Propheta adpellatur), hoc est, ad omnia impie facta conniventem tolerare se posse declaret. Quae non eo dicimus, quod importunorum hominum insolentes nobis
1160 clamores probentur, sed quoniam veritas ipsa mordet suamque in se habet austeritatem et fere imminens incommodum, quod alii aut minus prospiciunt, aut non futurum credunt, sit parrocho a praevendiendum. Necessarium est longanimitate atque clementia in intempestivis etiam eiusmodi increpationibus excipiendis utamini, nisi fortassis pravitas malevola subsit correptioni, ubi
1165 aequa poena statui potest. Sed in his quid facto sit opus facile ipsi pro vestra prudentia decernetis. De nostrae nunc pietatis profectu potissimum agitur.

Quibus in rebus potissimum plaebs admonenda sit et corripienda.
Caput XXVIIII.

Enimvero Christus doceri nequit, nisi erroribus commonstratis in scelera
1170 invehamur ac ad solidam dei cognitionem veramque pietatem, quam ultro gignit animus, gnaviter cohortemur, id quod in docendo praecipuum esse debet. Sed quod ad communes illas ac prophanas rerum publicarum rationes attinet, sententia nostra mox ex sequentibus patebit.

Ad parendum magistratui cohortandam esse plebem et
1175 *de discrimine prophanae ac spiritualis potestatis.*
Caput XXX.

Principio cum plaebis adversus magistratus tenuiorisque fortunae hominum erga opulentiores animos, natura ipsa inobsequentes sediciosos et contumaces esse | videamus, cum tamen dissidium unum omnium maxime charitati G2v
1180 christianae, qui unicus hominum piorum est color, quo a pestilenti mundo separati discernuntur, repugnet, omni conatu est annitendum, quo debitum magistratui honorem tanquam a deo concessum apud imperitam multitudinem sedulo depingentes vindicemus, ut quem dei vices gerentem etiam propter conscientiae securitatem conveniat revereri. Quanquam enim homo vere
1185 Christianus subiectum se esse omni creaturae persuasus sit, in ecclesia tamen Apostolorum hic etiam perniciosae opinionis error irrepsit, ut homines pii,

---

1157/1158 sic – adpellatur] cfr Is. 56, 10   **1180** qui – color] cfr Ioh. 13, 35   **1183/**
1184 ut – revereri] cfr Rom. 13, 1

1180 pestilenti mundo] cfr Cassiodorus, *Expositio psalmorum* 53, 3, ed. M. Adriaen (*CC SL* 97), Turnhout 1958, p. 484, 44-45

CONCILIUM BERNENSE – 1532

quia coelestis illorum esset respective nec locum sedem ve in terris ullam constantem stabilemque haberent, sed expectarent futuram, magistratum terrenum ad se nihil attinere nec sua, quod institueret, interesse existimarent. Hinc domini confundebatur ordinatio, quae duos in terris constituit principatus, quorum sublimior et augustior est spiritualis et coelestis, quem administrat Christus, cui uni omnis gloria est assignanda, ad illum ab externo deserviunt ministri spiritus, hoc est, veri concionatores. Minor autem, cui magistratus Bernensis ac alii quoquo versus terrarum praesunt. Utrique autem homo obligatur Christianus, ad conscientiam enim quod attinet, spirituali, quam dominus solus citra ullius omnino creaturae interventum iudicat. Quod vero ad corpus bonaque attinet temporalia, gladio externo humanaeque administrationi subiicitur. Caelestes etenim, qui Christi nomen profitentur, omnes sunt, sed non per omnia, dum terrenam hanc habitationem corpusque periturum secum circumferunt, quamobrem nec se terreno subducere imperio debent, quanquam indies ex ea crescere et emergere ac magis magisque coelestes effici conveniat. Homo enim Christianus e mundo eiusque imperio per unctionem dei sese attollit, hoc est, minus minusque | concupiscentiis illius sordidisque G3r negociis adhaeret. Quae ut dilucidius pateant, ex biblicis historiis adduci exempla possunt, ex iis enim satis liquet, quanta severitate deus impiis etiam regibus inobsequentes puniverit. Cuiusmodi Davidis est contra Saulem exemplum, cui cum dominus omne renunciasset imperium, venerationem tamen Davidem etiam unctum iam regem detulisse et cum perdere illum posset, pepercisse constat, quod diligenter est considerandum.

De censu et decimis.
Caput XXXI.

Ex praedictis consequitur decimas iure esse persolvendas. Constitutio nanque externa est nec contraria charitati, id quod Iosephi testatur historia, qui ita Aegyptum universam tributariam reddidit, ut quintam bonorum suorum partem pendere Regi singuli adigerentur, quae fusius ex Pauli ad Romanos epistola explicari possunt. Neque enim aequior ullus est redditus quam decimae, in quibus tam qui accipit, quam qui dat, dei liberalem in nos benignitatem respicit et expectat, aequale uterque ex eo, quod provenit com-

---

1187 quia – esset] cfr Phil. 3, 20   **1188** sed – futuram] cfr Hebr. 13, 14   **1199/1200** dum – circumferunt] cfr II Cor. 5, 1   **1202/1203** Homo – attollit] cfr Col. 3, 2   **1207/1209** venerationem – constat] I Reg. 24   **1214/1215** ut – adigerentur] Gen. 41, 34   **1215/1216** quae – possunt] Rom. 13, 6-7

1214 bonorum] *a.c.* bonornm   **1217** accipit] *a.c.* accpit

264 CONCILIUM BERNENSE – 1532

modum incommodumque ferens. Verum quod ad censuum (quos vocant) attinet rationem, modum non raro excedi haudquaquam ignoramus, in quibus corrigendis magistratum advigilare, non Parrochum occupari decet, eo quod nec sui est muneris et fere publici status immutationem inducit, quae tamen non citra prudentum hominum consilia exactamque meditiationem est molienda, nisi fortassis nimia violentia apertaeque iniuriae, ut saepe in vini frumentique redditibus accidit, deprehendantur. Monebit autem suos Parrochus, si modo ad praesentes ea res auditores ullo pacto pertingit, non eum, qui etiam iniquos persolvit, redditus ulla esse in noxa, sed qui accipiunt, eos vero graviter in dominum delinquere. Atque | in his est unica charitatis praescri- G3v benda regula, ut omnes, quae sibi pari in re fieri cupiant, eadem quoque aliis diligenter et officiose praestent.

Verum et hoc observandum, emptionis venditionisque contractus maechanicaque artificia et manuarios omnis generis labores non evangelio simpliciter, quod ad conscientias tantum attinet, sed externis ordinationibus subiici eademque quodam modo ad charitatis formulam esse examinanda. Caeterum in vero christianismo, qui puris affectibus ad proximi utilitatem totus est comparatus, sibi mutuo student omnes mutuoque datur, nulla lucelli foenorisque spe proposita adeoque proprium nihil possidetur. Verum in his suum quisque observet spiritum, ne carnis quodam studio ea elargiatur, in quibus etiamnum tota mente acquiescat. Anna enim e pectore repurgato rationibus pecuniariis facilius rectiusque consuletur. Qua in re non parum lapsi et Catabaptistae sunt, qui externam potestatem, quantum in ipsis est, tollunt seque mutuo ad parentes, uxores, liberos aedesque deserendas urgent et impellunt. Id quod dei recte moderantis omnia voluntati repugnat, qui a nobis exigit, ut sua quisque sorte ac vocatione contentus nihil ex seipso instituat, quin potius charitate rebus omnibus praeposita Christum ultro amplectamur, qui ex interna animorum puritate in bona opera erumpit diversum a lege mosaica, quae exteriore illa ac simulata pietate hominum mentes coercuit.

1229/1230 ut – praestent] cfr Matth. 7, 12   **1234** ad – formulam] cfr I Cor. 16, 14
1236/1237 nulla – proposita] cfr Luc. 6, 34   **1237** adeoque – possidetur] cfr Act.
2, 44 **1239/1240** Anna – consuletur] Act. 5, 3 **1242** liberos – deserendas] cfr Marc.
10, 29

1221 magistratum] *a.c.* magistatum

CONCILIUM BERNENSE – 1532

Legum et decretorum senatus nostri autoritatem sedulo inculcandam, inque
scelera plaebi familiaria constanter invehendum.
Caput XXXII.

Posteaquam autem a magistratu nostro varia mandata et edicta ad Christianam modestiam moresque pertinen|tia prodierunt, diligenter ea nobis ac G4r
pro virili tuenda sunt et propaganda illorumque ostendenda aequitas, eo quod
flagitia eadem et scripturae iam olim prohibuerint et ne apud gentes quidem,
praesertim honestatis aliquo praeditas studio impune sint admissa. Cuiusmodi sunt scortatio, lusus, ebrietas, adulterium, lenocinium, blasphemiae in
deum et Carum instar belligerando sanguinem fundere Christianum eosque,
qui nunquam laeserunt perdere. Cuius rei turpitudinem ratio quoque humana
intelligit et quam honestiores etiam gentilium sunt aversati. Atque ea tam pia
decreta, ut rata habeat, fortiterque tueatur magistratus est cohortandus munerisque subinde sui commonendus.

Porro plaebis nostrae captus et ingenium studiosissime a nobis observari
debet, quo nostro illam ministerio per Christum ad timorem dei pelliceamus.
Neque enim apud omnes omnia flagitiorum genera comperiuntur saepeque
temporis mutatio etiam morum scelerumque variationem parit, cuiusmodi ex
conversatione diutina privataque subditorum interpellatione facile animadvertetur. Nunquam tamen non de matrimoniis et puerorum disciplina fraternaque correctione, quaeque communia omni carne adhaerent scelera, est
agendum, veluti sunt livor, odium, mendacium, perfidia et alia eiusmodi
humanarum tenebrarum opera. Quarum rerum tractationem quisque diligenter meditatam habere frequenterque usurpare debet.

De puerorum disciplina et cathechismo.
Caput XXXIII.

Quia non difficulter vereque discitur, quicquid discitur a primis statim
annis, contra autem aetate provectiores inepti ad omnia sunt, tum etiam quia
domini iugum a teneris statim subire conducit atque in hoc est incumbendum
Christia|nis praecipue, qui liberi Christo in mortem eius quamprimum conse- G4v
crentur, quos alioquin plus satis in humanis concupiscentiis et Sathanae imperio adolescere cernimus, opus est vel maxime ut Catechismus sive puerorum
docendorum ratio instituatur, in quo homines imperiti praesertim iam adulti
creatorem suum et amare et timere per Christum addiscant. Nec vero ea res
multis et variis scripturarum eget testimoniis, sed ex communi isto Apostolo-

---

1255/1257 Cuiusmodi – deum] cfr Gal. 5, 19-21

266 CONCILIUM BERNENSE – 1532

rum symbolo dominicaque oratione, omnibus nota multisque iam ante libellis explicata commode tradi possunt. In quo tamen prima ea sit ac praecipua cura,
1285 ut verus dei amor in nostris ipsorum pectoribus accensus ardeat, unde deinceps tenelli adhuc puerorum animi facile nostro exemplo ad pietatis studium incalescent. Nam quicquid alioquin vel alii docent, vel ratio ex libris compraehendit, actio quaedam est humana sicque permanet, donec verus praeceptor spiritus in opus progrediatur ipse, qui nos ad perennem illam et coelestem
1290 vitam creat, innovat et regenerat. Visum est autem necessarium nobis, ut totum Christum universumque fidei negocium ex symbolo investigemus simplicibusque commonstremus. Nam ut precatio dominica veram orationem omnem aperte copioseque complectitur, ita ut veterum praeces longe lataeque excedat, sic in hoc fides nostra fusissime est comprehensa.

1295 *De decem praeceptis.*
Caput XXXIIII.

Et quanquam in passionis mortisque Iesu Christi meditatione tantum peccatorum cognitio poenitentiaque comparetur, utile tamen est et operaepraetium, ut decem praeceptis statim pueri imbuantur ab externo atque ad
1300 animum ea a parrochis inter docendum explicatione dilucida referantur, ad | Hir eum modum, quem Christum in suis, quos in monte habuit, sermonibus tenuisse videmus, Matth. 5. 6. 7. Quo pueri dei notitiam fideique negocium in animis suis, quos dominus continue intuetur, percipiant tandem et recte intelligant. Sed utinam parentes eiusmodi catechismum et veram fidei doctrinam
1305 pueris suis inculcare minus puderet, quo sincera aliquando et germana pietas maiori cum studio coleretur, nec verbis tantum vanis sanctimoniam polliceremur.

De symbolo fidei, oratione dominica et decem praeceptis.
Caput XXXV.

1310 Fidei autem negocium tribus hisce partibus constat. Symbolo, oratione dominica et decem praeceptis. Symbolum docet deum et christum indicatque quo pacto gratia et vita nobis obveniat, accrescat et absolvatur. Oratio dominica perfecta est Christianorum hominum praecatio ac instar urnae, qua ex divinae benignitatis fonte gratia ea hauritur hominumque animis inseritur.

1285 ut – ardeat] cfr Luc. 24, 35   **1289/1290** qui – regenerat] cfr Tit. 3, 5; I Petr. 1, 3-4 **1313/1314** qua – inseritur] cfr Ioh. 4, 14

1308 dominica] *a.c.* domica

CONCILIUM BERNENSE – 1532

1315 Siquidem voto suo potitur, qui vero affectu petit adeoque citra petitionem frustranea est omnis gratiae oblatio. Ea enim mentem aperit atque ad dei benignitatem percipiendam idoneam reddit.

Porro decem praecepta exercitatio quaedam externa et usus sunt, quo caro depressa et flagitia sua agnoscere et agnita in memoria retinere potest, quae 1320 tamen cognitio nisi ex Christo petatur, nihil emolumenti habet. Praecepta igitur haec in animo suo reputantem, pari ratione cogitare convenit Christum innocentem ex dei praedestinatione pro peccatis suis mortuum esse. Atque ita rudium hominum et puerorum biblia sunt symbolum, oratio dominica et decem praecepta, ut quae totius in se christianismi rationem comprehendant. 1325 Sacramenta enim, velut baptismus et caena | domini sunt sacraeque conciones, H1v quoniam nihil agunt aliud, quam ut credentium animis mysterium filii dei offerant oblatique excitent considerationem, non est, quod pueros et simpliciores hisce gravemus, nisi quatenus ad Christum, qui his tribus veluti praedictum luculentissime exprimitur, intelligendum conducunt. Alioquin nimio 1330 verborum agmine negocium involuitur et oneratur, ut pii desperatione statim praesumpta sublimiora illa, quam quo suus pertingere captus queat, esse existiment. Sedenim et hoc quoque diligenter cogitandum, quod Christus *inperscrutabilem dei gratiam prudentibus huius seculi absconditam, parvulis tantum aperuisse se* tam disertis verbis testatur. Quare simplicium nos hominum intel- 1335 lectui, quantum fieri potest, accommodare nec ex cuiuslibet insani capitis commentatione novos fidei articulos confingere decet.

De vita ac innocentia Parrochorum et concionatorum in genere.
Caput XXXVI.

Non ab re est, quod Propheta testatur, perinde esse plaebem ac sacerdo- 1340 tem et sacerdotem iuxta ex plaebis moribus metiendum. Nam quos gratia sua benigne respicit dominus, pios Prophetas fidelesque ac prudentes *mysteriorum suorum dispensatores* illis immittit. Quocirca sibi ipsi imputet populus, quod nostro ei ministerio, ut par erat, non est consultum. E regione nos quoque culpandi, quod auditores tam insolentes et contumaces veritatique obluctantes 1345 experimur, nam idipsum et graviora etiam nostra merentur flagitia. Verum si assiduos nos in hac tam ampla et copiosa messe operarios praestiterimus, semper tractabiles reperientur animi, qui ad solidam dei iusticiam pertrahi queant. Quare danda unicuique opera, ut ad eorum nos praesidum formemus | exem- H2r

---

1315 Siquidem – petit] cfr Matth. 7, 8   **1320/1322** Praecepta – esse] cfr Rom. 4, 25; I Cor. 15, 3   **1332/1334** Matth. 11, 25   **1339/1340** perinde – metiendum] cfr Os. 4, 4 et 9   **1341/1342** I Cor. 4, 1   **1344** veritatique obluctantes] cfr Rom. 2, 8   **1345/ 1346** si – praestiterimus] cfr Luc. 10, 2

268 CONCILIUM BERNENSE – 1532

plar quales in Iudicum libro instituit Moyses, nempe ut sint sapientes, pruden-
1350 tes, stemmatum non imperiti, graves ac fortes viri, pii, veritatis amantes et
avaritiae osores, cuiusmodi donum et gratia in nobis quoque vel maxime eluce-
re debet. (Ut enim illi in temporali isto ac perituro regno, ita in coelesti nos
Ecclesiarum sumus ministri.) Ne minorem forte nostra veritas, quam illorum
umbra et imago, quae sub Moyse fuit, obtinere videatur. Porro ea maxime,
1355 quae ex cruce Christi profluit, sapientia intelligentiaque praeditos omnes
ecclesiarum ministros esse convenit atque hoc etiam hominum Christianorum
de se testimonium eumque favorem tenere, quae non ex carne et sanguine, sed
ex spiritus fructu opereque charitatis proficiscatur, iuxta Pauli exemplum, qui
iuxta carnem neminem agnoscebat, quem eundem affectum et ecclesias indue-
1360 re convenit, non quae carnis sunt porro sentientes. Neque hic vel dictorum, vel
operum etiam audacia, sed patientia constans charitasque officiosa, quae ex
fide provenit non fucata, respicitur. Atque haec tam solida fides veritatem per
se inducit omnemque non avaritiam modo, sed pravam etiam cupiditatem
excludit, quo etiam Petrus hortatus est. In hunc modum comparatus fuit Pau-
1365 lus, qui se tanquam exemplar et imaginem quatenus Christi mores exprimebat,
imitandum proposuit. Ad cuius formulam, si nostram quoque vitam forma-
verimus, hoc est, si cogitationes, os, manus omnesque actiones nostrae cum
doctrina paria faciant, possumus et nostram plaebem, ut nos ipsos tanquam
pietatis effigiem observet, cohortari. Sed ad huc id tuto nobis haudquaquam
1370 licet, quando ex divinis rebus nec ipsi dum satis nos explicare possumus, nec
dum opera pietatis ulla in nobis tanta eluxerunt. Verum tum ea gregi nostrae
erunt commendabiliora, si nostrum in ecclesia munus rite obeamus et cum
intra nos ipsos tum apud familiam | nostram modesti, graves, piique esse com- H2v
periamur. Sed primum de officio nostro in sequentibus tractabitur.

1375 *Quam in literarum sacrarum lectione ac caeteris studiis*
rationem Parrochi sequi debeant.
Caput. XXXVII.

Quoniam *divina scriptura per fidem, quae est in Christum Iesum, sapientes*
nos efficit ad salutem, omnis enim scriptura ad doctrinam, correptionem et emen-
1380 *dationem vitae in iusticia confert, ut vere homo dei ad pias actiones reddatur*
idoneus, necessarium est, ut in Bibliorum lectionem magno studio incumba-

---

1350/1351 veritatis – osores] cfr Ex. 18, 21; Deut. 1, 13   **1353/1354** Ne – videatur] cfr
Hebr. 8, 5   **1358** ex – fructu] cfr Gal. 5, 22   **1358/1359** qui – agnoscebat] cfr II Cor.
5, 16   **1360** non – sentientes] cfr Rom. 8, 5   **1361/1362** quae – respicitur] cfr I Tim.
1, 5   **1364** quo – est] cfr I Petr. 5, 1-3   **1365/1366** qui – proposuit] cfr I Cor. 11, 1
1373 modesti – comperiamur] cfr I Tim. 3, 4   **1378/1381** II Tim. 3, 15-17

CONCILIUM BERNENSE – 1532 269

mus, eo tamen ordine, ut prius, quam in manus sumatur liber, preces ad deum
fundantur, quae piae plane ac spirituales esse debent. Vera enim eiusmodi et ex
spiritu proveniens oratio ante omnia ad gratias ob acceptum a domino benefi-
1385 cium agendas impellit orantem, unde mox consolatio certa fidesque constans
enascitur, deinde ad eam urget precationem, qua inscitiam in praesentiarum
praementem ab sese tolli petit. Unde ardor quidam vehemens et cupiditas
exoritur, iusticiae fames ac sitis a domino appellata, quam semper saturitas
comitatur ac vera salus. Quamobrem constat per orationem mentes expurgari
1390 nostras ac velut praeparari, quo consilium ac dei sensum latentem in litera
compraehendere queat. Quod nisi fit, citra religionem in libris divinis
tanquam in prophanis historiis versari nostramque exercere rationem solemus,
ex quo nihil nisi sapientia quaedam carnalis ac insolentia exoritur, quae postea
ibi 1. tanquam dei oracula simplici plaebi obtruditur, quare non immerito monet
1395 Iacobus, ut *si cui desit sapientia postulet a deo qui dat simpliciter.*

Post orationem autem animi tam pii et divino amore flagrantis aperiri
liber, nec ut hominum, sed ut dei, quae revera | sunt, verba perlegi debent H₃r
manente eadem semper orationis ardore, tantisper dum intelligentiae alicuius
divinae de supernis infusae sensum percipiamus. In quo suscipiendo constan-
1400 ter sineque dubitatione lector sibi persuadeat ad correptionem vitaeque suae
emendationem omnia dici atque ita seclusis caeteris creaturis omnibus, totum
negocium inter se ac deum suum simplici synceroque animo expediat, non
solum quid populo sit dicturus, sed etiam quo pacto apertiorem ipse earum
rerum lucem et cognitionem consequi possit cogitans. Verum post nonnullam
1405 iam in fide concaeptam noticiam aliquos scripturae locos, qui cum suo nonnihil pugnare intellectu videntur, sibi ipsi lector opponat eosque ut rite inter
se possit conferre, domini imploret auxilium, donec ipsa nobis veritas certo
per omnia innotescat. Quae omnia gratiarum actio assiduaque muneris accepti
consideratio consequatur. Postremo vero his rite peractis, commentarii et libri,
1410 qui ea de re vel hac tempestate vel prioribus saeculis prodierunt, sunt evolven-
di atque cum nostro, quem hactenus adepti sumus, intellectu conferendi, ita
fiet, ut cum iudicio sano inoffense legi possint. Nec sane parum laetitiae attule-
rit, si quis eum se a domino intelligat percepisse rerum divinarum sensum, cui
vel aliorum dona consentiant, vel tantum reliqui nondum sint investigando
1415 assecuti. Qua tamen in re non seipsum insolentius efferet, utpote qui et praecibus a domino id impetrarit et probe, quantum pravam ambitionem malorum

---

1383/1384 ex – oratio] cfr Rom. 8, 26   **1388** iusticiae – appellata] cfr Matth. 5, 6
1393 sapientia ... carnalis] II Cor. 1, 12   **1395** Iac. 1, 5   **1397** dei – verba] cfr I Thess.
2, 13

1395 simpliciter] *a.c.* smpliciter

270 CONCILIUM BERNENSE – 1532

consequatur, prospiciat. Porro suas quilibet in scripturae studio meditationes assignet ac cum sequentibus, in quae mox incidit, studiose componat. In via enim domini ad sublimiorem semper profectum est enitendum. Quumque sit
1420 tam fallax et imbecillis saepe nostra memoria, utile est, ut veluti instructo poenu subsidium quoddam habeamus paratum, unde ad quamlibet oblatam occasionem quod de|promatur suppetat. Cuiusmodi exercitia mentes nostras H3v tanquam scientiae divinae armamentarium, ubi spiritualia adversus daemonis insidias arma reconduntur, efficiunt.

1425
Scripturam nobis inter nos mutuo amice esse conferendam.
Caput XXXVIII.

Ad hoc inprimis conduxerit, si cum scriptura nostrum intellectum idque sedulo ac diligenter conferre non pigeat, potissimum cum suo quenque vicino pio videlicet et divinae gratiae uberius consequendae cupido, quo ad maiorem
1430 domini nostri Iesu Christi cognitionem perveniatur atque adeo eiusmodi sermones nostros familiariaque esse colloquia erga omnes decet, ut pietatem Christique regnum ante omnia referant. Id quod et maioribus nostris solenne, et nobis repullulante nostris temporibus Evangelio non infrequens fuisse abunde constat, quos cum omnibus de nostro Evangelio adversus Papisticas
1435 fraudes disputare precipue iuvabat. Ubi tamen enixe cavendum, ne aut mordaces ac iritabiles nos exhibeamus aut durae cervicis et pertinaces, ut qui opinionem semel concaeptam propugnare ac obstinate tueri pergamus. Convenit enim, quicquid Christi donorumque eius apud unumquenque sentiscas, utut minutum fuerit, gratias deo agere eaque modeste administrare omnia, ut
1440 quicquid id sit divini muneris, prolicere potius quam spiritum extinguere studeas. Nam hinc vel maxime simplex et deo devotus animus ad magnam divinorum operum cognitonem provenire solet. Quinetiam id genus collationes eo conferunt, ut expeditiores et cum iis versemur, qui nostrae sunt curae commissi et adversariis nos minus praeter dignitatem obiiciamus. Quod
1445 quidem a filiis Dei longe alia fit ratione, quam in temporalibus illis adversarios suos opprimere ca|ro et sanguis consuevit. H4r

---

1422/1424 Cuiusmodi – efficiunt] cfr Eph. 6, 11   **1431/1432** ut – referant] cfr Matth. 6, 33   **1440/1441** prolicere – studeas] cfr I Thess. 5, 19   **1444/1445** Quod – ratione] cfr Phil. 2, 15

1432 Christique] *a.c.* Cristique   **1438** Christi] *a.c.* Chrsti

CONCILIUM BERNENSE – 1532

Quo pacto considerari sacra concio debeat.
Caput XXXVIIII.

Ubi concionandum est, scriptae aliorum homiliae sive commentaria legi a non paucis excipique tantisper solent, dum horae transigendae quod collegerunt, sufficiat, parum vero observatur, quid ad praesens tempus praesentis Ecclesiae aedificationi vel conferat, vel obsit. Unde fit, ut parum adeo quae dei sunt, solide tractentur. Nostrum ergo fuerit et adhortari nos invicem et promovere, ut scripturam ipsam ultro quisque meditari potius velit et expendere pro suo nempe commodo, ut dictum est, dein vero ad observatum sibi ecclesiae suae modulum intellectus sui acumen attemperare, ita ut vix decimam partem interdum eorum, quae sibi ad praesentem scripturae locum a deo tradita sunt, pro concione esse dicenda, existimet. Siquidem omnia cedere in ecclesiae bonum debent neque hic vel ingenii acumen, vel spiritus sublimitatem ostentare convenit, ubi toto pectore dei honor ad ecclesiae salutem per Christum posthabitis interim aliis omnibus quaerendus est.

Nihil ergo necesse fuerit, varias adeo canonum formas praescribere, quando veritas mentibus ipsa inest eamque charitas dei abunde distribuit. Atque hic nulli plane carni parceretur neque acerbe praeter rem irritaretur facile quisquam, ad populi vero aedificationem proficerent omnia, qui extra sunt, committerentur deo, nec tantum undique rixarum tumultuaretur, quemadmodum miseri non raro iam accidere experimur (qua de re satis iam antea dictum est), quae omnia in omnibus deum precamur, ut syncerius aliquando tractentur. Amen.

| Libros prophanos modeste legendos.
Caput XL.

H4v

Possunt vero prophanorum scriptorum libri, ut historiae, ab eo, qui verbo caeteris praeest, legi, sed diversa tamen a sacris existimatione et cum iudicio, nempe ut ad rationis exercitium ingeniumque carnis perdiscendum faciant. Neque est cur eos ad animi nostri profectum alioqui pertinere, vehementer arbitremur. Proinde ex spiritu Christi et sacris literis omnis instituendi, exhortandi, corrigendi proficiendique sumi ratio debet, quanquam accidit, ut interdum sed brevibus ethnica aliqua historia non incommode adduci pro concione possit, id quod usqueadeo non prohibemus, ut interim tamen unum-

---

1458/1459 Siquidem – debent] cfr I Cor. 14, 12

1448 XXXVIIII] *a.c.* XXXVII   **1459** spiritus] *a.c.* fpiritus

272 CONCILIUM BERNENSE – 1532

1480 quenque speremus, cogitaturum mysteriorum Christi se dispensatorem esse
eiusdemque spiritus ministrum proindeque spiritualibus literis quam carnali-
bus usurum potius. Et quamvis (quod dolendum profecto) qui per agrum
verbo praesunt, non perinde omnes studiosi sint, admonendum hoc tamen
non ab re iudicavimus.

1485 *Sacrae concionis habendae ratio.*
Caput XLI.

Haberi concio debet singulari cum animi ardentique charitate erga auditores ad emendationem et profectum in deo. Et quae talis fuerit concio, locum
apud pios invenit. Oves enim Christi vocem domini sui verique pastoris
1490 audiunt, ipsum agnoscunt, ipsum sequuntur, cum alioqui delicatae mentes
mordaciori correptionis aceto exacerbantur magis ac intereunt nostrisque e
concionibus invidiae tantum ac odii factionumque pestes contrahunt. Ubi
adeo non probatur quorundam remissior sermocinandi ratio, ut vehementer
etiam vitio dandam excludendamque censeamus, qua nonnulli e nobis ulcus,
1495 quod dici solet, tangere verentur | atque ita excomposito loquuntur ea tantum, I1r
quae esse iucunda auribus ducunt, potius quam quae aedificent, adversus quos
dictum illud Pauli quadrabit: *Si hominibus placere vellem, Christi servus non*
essem.

Servandas esse omnes dies concioni destinatos.
1500 *Caput XLII.*

Postquam in reformatione a dominis nostris constitutum est, ut quisque
Parrochus dominica, Lunae, Mercurii et Veneris diebus concionetur, nosque
interdum ob auditorum penuriam excusandi nobis ansam quaesivimus, ex
officio fore iam visum est, ut, quantum fieri potest, unusquisque nostrum det
1505 operam, quo dies illos concioni destinatos observet, etiam si praeter unum aut
duo auditores non adsint amplius. Quemadmodum et dominum non piguit
uni mulieri Samaritanae ac soli apud fontem colloqui, quanto igitur minus

---

1480 cogitaturum – esse] cfr I Cor. 4, 1   **1489/1490** Oves – sequuntur] cfr Ioh.
10, 4 et 27   **1497/1498** Gal. 1, 10   **1506/1507** Quemadmodum – colloqui] cfr Ioh.
4, 7-26

1501/1502 Postquam – concionetur] see 'Reformationsmandat für das Gebiet Bern',
in R. Steck – G. Tobler (hrsg.), *Aktensammlung zur Geschichte der Berner Reformation*
1521-1532, 2 vols, Bern 1918-1923, vol. 1 (1918), p. 634

1500 XLII] *a.c.* XXII   **1503** quaesivimus] *a.c.* quaesivimns

CONCILIUM BERNENSE – 1532

pigere debet ministrum Christi de domino suo in gloriam eius cum minimis etiam disserere? Quandoquidem apud deum nullus habetur personarum respectus uniusque fidelis hominis anima toto mundo in conspectu eius est praeciosior. Neque vero refert, si eiusmodi exhortatio profestis diebus non e suggestu, sed inter ipsa subsellia ad auditores atque id quam simplicissime fiat. Sed quia tam facile omittimus, abunde declarat, quam parum nobis curae sit dei honor, aut quanto plus ad multitudinem, quam pusillum Christi gregem ac pias mentes respiciamus, quibus tamen iuvandis identidem nos decebat esse ac iugiter intentos. Quanquam non desint interim fratres aliquot, quibus concionari quotidie placet, quorum certe diligentiam laudamus merito, siquidem boni zeli index est.

Sunt praeterea Parrochiae non paucae, quae complures ha|bent pagos et sua in hisce templa quoque. Ubi inprimis necessarium videtur piae plaebeculae in reliquis pagis per hebdomadam aliquoties concionari, die vero dominica nonunquam ab aliquo duas haberi conciones, quam rem tamen in Capitulis (quae vocant) tractandam porro censemus. Neque enim eadem omnium est oportunitas remorari, tamen in officio suo sedulum verbi preconem nemini fas esto, quando errantem reducere in viam, cum omnium Christianorum, tum maxime Parrochi interest. Neque nobis incertum est, quantum emolumenti adferat, ex animo se ac ultro pio alicui se ac simplici homini offerre et suam ei salutem per Christum declarare, qui alioqui forte in ignorantia sua misere periturus erat requirendusque eius sanguis de parrochi sui manibus, qui ut pastor minime verus gregem collapsam non sublevarit.

Privatim quoque docendos esse subditorum singulos.
Caput XLIII.

Quoniam autem officii nostri est, nihil eorum, quae ad adducendum deo populum omnino attinent, intermittere, non sufficiat in ipsa tantum parrochia docere publice aut reliquis quoque pagis, quemadmodum ex instituto nobis est commissum, verum etiam per singulas domos convenire subditos privatimque singulos, quantum fieri postest, viam salutis docere sedulo poenitentiamque annunciare, sicut ante nos fecerunt Apostoli quoque, conveniet.

1509/1510 Quandoquidem – respectus] cfr Act. 10, 34; Rom. 2, 11; Eph. 6, 9 **1510/1511** uniusque – praeciosior] cfr Matth. 16, 26 **1528/1529** qui – erat] cfr Eph. 4, 18 **1529** requirendusque – manibus] cfr Ez. 3, 18 **1529/1530** qui – sublevarit] cfr Ez. 34, 4 **1537** viam salutis] cfr Act. 16, 17

1511 eiusmodi] *a.c.* eusmodi **1525** omnium] *a.c.* omnum **1534** sufficiat] *a.c.* fufficiat

274 CONCILIUM BERNENSE – 1532

Siquidem privata illa institutio mentem occupare multo interdum solet magis,
1540 quam ea, quae ad multos etiam alios dici publice consueverunt.

De infirmorum visitatione.
Caput XLIIII.

Praecipuum est officium consolari afflictos, unde nos parrochi et animarum curatores, tam in urbe quam per agrum, dare operam debemus, ut ad
1545 infirmos venire nobis liceat, dum adhuc animo valent neque | operiri extrema. 12r
Debetque is admonitionis ordo apud infirmos observari, ut primo laborantem
gratiae divinae commoneamus per Christum, quomodo suis et adsit in afflictionibus et adesse omnino velit docebimusque veros Christianos adventum
domini sui liberationemque sive vocationem ex hoc seculo magno cum deside-
1550 rio expectare, quae ubi infirmi concepisse se sentiunt, consolari debent et ad
poenitentiam exhortari, unde sui amorem fideique suae infirmitatem agnoscere discant et pro augenda fide dominum orent, ne forte perversa aliqua fiducia
seducantur a nobis, quos divinae veritatis esse testes oportet. Deinde qui simul
adstant, exhortandi sunt, ut per infirmi huius dolorem ac discrimen suae quo-
1555 que reminisci miseriae velint deumque in veritate timere, quando omnis fiducia carnalis vana omnino sit ac incerta quantumque sit in id genus angustiis
solatium, misericordem habere deum Christumque filium eius pro se intercessorem et arbitrum agnoscere, quem per poenitentiam nostraeque vitae
emendationem ac veram in Christum fidem consequi liceat. Sed et praeveniri
1560 multos, qui cum fatuis virginibus venienti occurrere sponso negligant. Post
haec in genua procumbendum omnibus et infirmo pro gratia orandum inque
angustiis eius pro nostris etiam tam praesentibus, quam futuris malis divinae
gratiae praesentia magna cum devotione roganda. Neque inutile fuerit, quae
de passione et resurrectione Christi scripta sunt, ex Paulo et evangelistis aliis-
1565 que Apostolis legere vivaciterque interpretari etc. Atque haec actio interdum
melior est decem concionibus publicae praeter singularem auditorum atten-
tionem habitis, quoniam ea angustia similiter omnes percellit eiusdemque
solatii omnes disiderio tenentur, quod nusquam reperire est certius, quam in

---

1547 quomodo – afflictionibus] cfr Ps. 34, 19 **1548** et – velit] cfr Matth. 28, 20
1548/1549 docebimusque – sui] cfr II Petr. 3, 12 **1549** liberationemque – seculo] cfr
Phil. 1, 23 **1551/1552** unde – orent] cfr Luc. 17, 5 **1555/1556** quando – incerta] cfr
Phil. 3, 3 **1560** qui – negligant] cfr Matth. 25, 1-13 **1561** in – orandum] cfr Iac. 5, 14
1568/1569 quod – Christo] cfr II Thess. 2, 16

1540 consueverunt] *a.c.* confueverunt

CONCILIUM BERNENSE – 1532

domino Iesu Christo, postquam omni auxilio temporali diffisum est. Hactenus
1570 de officio parrochorum quomodo ipsi adesse eos deceat.

| *De vita Parrochi erga seipsum et familiam suam.*
Caput XLV.

I2v

Quisquis mandatum fecerit et docuerit, is magnus vocabitur in regno coelo-
rum, non enim auditores legis, sed qui legem factis adimplent iusti apud deum
1575 reputantur. Cuius diversum apparet in pharisaeis recte quidem de Mose
loquentibus graviaque onera hominum humeris imponentibus, quae minimo
tamen digito attingere ipsi non dignantur, id quod longe a nobis apostolorum
sectatoribus abesse debet. Sed quia crucem Christi praedicamus, circumferre
in mortali hac vita nostra Christi mortem aequum est perque vitam coelestem
1580 Christi resurrectioni efficaciter exhibere, quorum sane testes esse debemus,
non autem sumus, ubi fundamentum nostrum in hunc modum posuerimus, ut
alii, qui praeter carnem nihil sapiunt. Mansionem nostram habere nos in coelo
convenit veluti una cum Christo e mortuis experrectos, quo eos, qui nostrae
fidei traditi excitemus, ut de iis diligenter cogitent, quae vera, integra, iusta,
1585 casta, iucunda laudeque digna sunt, quae quidem discere a nobis accipereque
et audire ac in nobis ipsis denique videre ipsos consentaneum est. Tum securis
accedere tribunal Christumque nostrum iudicem ac dominum licebit et nostri
officii in die eius laudem mereri, id quod probe divus Paulus expendit discipu-
lo suo Timotheo praescribens, quales constituere episcopos, hoc est mysterio-
1590 rum Christi dispensatores, debeat. *Oportet,* inquit, *episcopum irreprehensibilem*
esse, unius uxoris maritum, vigilantem, sobrium, modestum, hospitalem, aptum
ad docendum, non vinolentum, non percussorem, non turpis lucri cupidum, sed
aequum, alienum a pugnis, alienum ab avaritia, qui suae domui bene praesit,
qui liberos habeat in subiectione cum omni reverentia. Quorum verborum
1595 expendere quedam decrevimus reliqua cuivis | porro inspicienda commitentes. I3r
Irreprehensibilem: Conversationem nostram esse honestam decet, sive stando,
sive incedendo, sive quicquid denique agendo, ut tam in dictis, quam in factis
nihil appareat, quod non integritas commendet. Unde consentaneum videtur,

---

1573 Matth. 5, 19   **1574/1575** non – reputantur] cfr Rom. 2, 13   **1576/1577** quae –
dignantur] Matth. 23, 2-4   **1578** Sed – praedicamus] cfr I Cor. 1, 23   **1578/**
1579 circumferre – est] cfr II Cor. 4, 10   **1579/1580** perque – debemus] cfr Act. 1, 22;
2, 32   **1582/1583** Mansionem – convenit] cfr II Cor. 4, 10   **1583** veluti – experrectos]
cfr Col. 3, 1   **1584/1585** ut – sunt] cfr Phil. 4, 8   **1586/1587** Tum – tribunal] cfr
II Cor. 5, 10   **1589/1590** episcopos – dispensatores] cfr I Cor. 4, 1   **1590/**
1594 I Tim. 3, 2-4

1582 sapiunt] *a.c.* sapiuut

ut (non contempta interim plaebe) honesto tamen amictu utamur, quo inter lixam et verbi ministrum, quod ad vestitum adtinet, nonnihil intersit. Eiusmodi enim neglectus, quod nihil differre quidam arbitrantur quacunque tamen veste utare, levis esse animi index plerunque solet. Domini nostri sectarum turpiter vestium luxum prohibent, et sacerdotem, qui esse aliis exemplo debet, levissimo quale esse usquam potest, amictus genere uti impune licebit? Neque tamen placere ideo nobis pharisaicam illam superstitionem existimare quenquam volumus. Verum ut in rebus omnibus ita hic quoque medium recte et synceriter amplectendum censemus. *Unius uxoris maritum*: Vult pro hoc Paulus castum ac mundum significare animum, sive in matrimonio, sive extra matrimonium, Iudeorum enim morem respicit, quo singulis habere plures uxores licebat, id quod impudici animi signum erat, praeter molestias quas secum ea uxorum varietas et turba afferebat innumeras. Nam qui in coniugio sunt, multas habent afflictiones per carnem, tametsi uxorem unam episcopo non prohibeat Paulus. Quia ad familiam curamque domesticam quod attinet, tum qui placeat uxori. Siquidem Christianam uxorem habet, quae una diem domini cum ipso identidem expectet, nihil est periculi. Sed unius tantum uxoris esse maritus debet, ut conversationem habeat castam. Neque vero aliter nobis liquet, quam quod attinet ad externa, ut nihil in nobis sit calumniae merito obnoxium, probe tamen interim expendendum nobis relinquitur, quam nos dedeceat faceciarum et turpium sermonum levitas vel adesse saltem | id genus colloquiis, quibus scortationis et adulterii incestuumque sordes improbi quidem pro libidine iactitant. Siquidem hoc ad nefanda scelera consensus quidam videtur, quod ipso facinore gravius omnino malum est. Cui ergo sacri verbi magna esse autoritas potest, ubi adeo levibus interdum ac immundis sermonibus vel ipsi indulgemus, vel arridemus aliis? *Sobrii* esse debemus: Qualem enim speciem praese ferat, si in oenopoliis cum abiectissimis hominibus praeter temporis rationem desideamus inter pocula, perinde quasi officium nostrum nihil aliud sit, quam epulis ac potationibus dies noctesque incumbere. Quanquam de his non agere amplius decrevimus, ubi crux Christi mentem occupaverit, reliquis omnibus facile consulet, id quod inprimis respiciendum erit. Atque interea ab omni turpitudine ac vicio vehementer cavendum donec ulterius ad sublimiora spiritus negocia penetrare nobis liceat, quae secum omnis generis bonas artes ac virtutes adferunt, quo tota haec Synodus potissimum est instituta. Deus gratiam suam nobis largiatur, qua iugiter ea consequi liceat. Amen.

I3v

1611/1612 Nam – carnem] I Cor. 7, 28   **1613/1614** Quia – uxori] I Cor. 7, 33
1619 quam – levitas] cfr Eph. 5, 4   **1626/1628** perinde – incumbere] cfr Rom. 14, 17

1625 abiectissimis] *a.c.* abiectiffimis

CONCILIUM BERNENSE – 1532

Ut autem Christianae huiuscemodi exercitationi diligentius incumbamus, quotannis celebrari talis Synodus ab omnibus parrochis et qui urbi praesunt, et qui agro, ipsis Calendis Maiis debet, qua semper memorata instituta renoventur. Adhaec duo Capitula cogantur annis singulis, quatenus hoc dominis nostris visum fuerit, in quibus similiter id agemus, quod pertinere cum ad nostri, tum ad gregis profectum videbitur, quemadmodum amplius cum dominis nostris deliberare ac decernere constituimus.

Postremo vero oramus, ut omnipotens deus nos tueatur ac dirigat idque augere pergat, quod sex hisce diebus misericorditer nobis largiri dignatus est, quo reliqua vita nostra omnino ad gloriam eius et plaebis profectum instituatur.

|Coepta est haec Synodus IX. Ianuarii eiusdemque XIIII. finita.

Basilaeae apud Andr. Cratand.

Anno MDXXXII.

1647 Andr Cratand] *intellege* Andream Cratandrum

CONCILIUM CAMPI FORANEI (IUXTA HENGRONIAM)
1532

edidit
Gianmarco BRAGHI

THE *CONCILIUM GENERALE* OF CHANFORAN (*)
1532

In his 1982 commemorative booklet – printed on occasion of the four-hundred-fiftieth anniversary of the Synod of Chanforan, held on 12 September 1532 – pastor Giuseppe Platone called this Synod a 'consilium generale' and a 'turning point' of Waldensianism. [1] In this publication, Platone recalled the installation of a monument in the fields of the valley of Angrogna in 1932: 'around 1,800 people were present, the majority of whom were young ... for the first time in [the twentieth] century, under the old chestnut trees of Chanforan (no longer extant), the image of the ancient assembly of 1532 ... had become reality'. [2] The statute of Chanforan as a watershed in the history of the Waldensian movement has been disputed, to the point that the *Concilium generale* has been labelled a 'myth'. It has been argued that scholarship is characterised by a 'farrago of misreading' in that it tends to imply a degree of 'coherence and organisation' which Waldensianism and indeed the Reformation 'did not possess at this period'. [3]

More recently, a call has been made for a much-needed inversion of 'the hierarchy between the synodal event and its institutionalisation' in the assessment of the significance of Chanforan in the history of Waldensianism. [4] Indeed, the 'identity crisis' the Piedmontese Waldensians experienced in the wake of the Reformation reached its climax in the events surrounding the *Concilium generale* itself. [5] Regardless of any implied degree of coordination and organisation of the Waldensian movement at this particular stage, Chanforan had the incontrovertible effect of prompting the latter's shift from its medieval heritage to different forms of Christian religiosity: in the end, it was after 1532 that many Waldensian *barbes* embraced the Reformation and slowly

---

(*) Dr Braghi is thankful to the staff of the Manuscript and Archives Research Library of Trinity College Dublin for their kind assistance in the consultation of the rare and important manuscript containing the source-text used for this critical edition.

(1) Platone, *1532, Chanforan*.

(2) Platone, *1532, Chanforan*, p. 5.

(3) Cameron, *The Reformation of the Heretics*, p. 139 and 267.

(4) Foresta, 'Da barba a pastori', p. 740, 'invertire la gerarchia tra il fatto sinodale e la sua istituzionalizzazione'.

(5) Audisio, *Preachers by Night*, p. 205.

282 CONCILIUM CAMPI FORANEI – 1532

turned into pastors – especially after 1555, as a result of Genevan interest in the valleys. (6) The question remains open as to whether this event might be regarded as the 'end of Waldensianism', (7) or at least as the swansong of the late-medieval parabolic development of the Poor of Lyon's multifaceted movement. What is indisputable, however, is that after 1532 the Waldensian Church became something that could not possibly have been foreseen before the *Concilium* of Chanforan. It has also been argued that the *Concilium* was one among several events of sixteenth-century Waldensianism which allowed the transformation of a 'heresy' into a fully-fledged 'Church'.[8] Recently, Giuseppe Platone himself has commented once again on the 'significant transition' of Chanforan, when 'old and new aspects interlocked in a most peculiar way' as the solidarity ties between the Waldensians and the newborn Reformation movement tightened. (9)

'Nudi Nudum Christum Sequentes' ([10])

In the Middle Ages, the Waldensian movement stemmed from widespread moral, social, and disciplinary concerns in the Western Church. Waldo, a wealthy merchant from Lyon (*c.* 1140–*c.* 1205) – the initiator of the movement – and his *fratres* and *sorores* adhered to a pauperistic understanding of Christian life and to a strong idea of the centrality of Scripture, under the lodestar principles of the Sermon of the Mount and the three vows of chastity, poverty, and obedience. Their activities were initially encouraged by Guichard de Pontigny, archbishop of Lyon: Roman authorities, however, soon took issue with the Poor of Lyon's particular way of imitating the Apostles, and especially with their unsanctioned, itinerant, public preaching of the Gospel, along with their demand for its availability in the vernacular. ([11]) Some of the members of the newborn movement travelled to Rome in 1179 to be heard by the Third Lateran Council, while Waldo tried to defend his brothers' and

---

(6) See for instance Tron, 'La creazione del corpo pastorale valdese'.

(7) 'La fin des vaudois (XVIe siècle)?', in Audisio, *Les vaudois des origines à leur fin*, p. 77-99, especially 95-96.

(8) Armand Hugon, 'Popolo e chiesa', p. 5.

(9) Platone, *Valdesi e Riforma*, p. 5-6.

(10) W. Map, *De nugis curialium (Courtiers' Trifles)*, ed. and transl. M. R. James, Oxford 1983, p. 126. 'Hii certa nusquam habent domicilia, bini et bini circueunt nudi pedes, laneis induti, nichil habentes, omnia sibi communia tanquam apostoli, nudi nudum Christum sequentes. Humillimo nunc incipient modo, quia pedem inferre nequeunt; quos si admiserimus, expellemur'.

(11) Based upon Merlo, *Valdo*, p. 21-27.

sisters' doctrinal stance in the presence of a papal legate in 1180 with a profession of faith. Nonetheless, the Poor of Lyon's perceived usurpation of the *genus clericorum*'s prerogatives led to a first injunction to abandon any preaching of the Gospel. Refusal to comply prompted an initial condemnation of Waldo and his followers at the Council of Verona (1184) with Lucius III's decretal *Ad abolendam*, and to the eventual excommunication issued by the Fourth Lateran Council under the watchful eye of Innocent III. ([12])

It was then that the Waldensian movement went into hiding. Clandestine groups of followers of Waldo's intuitions and way of life began to appear in Piedmont, Lombardy, southern Italy, Dauphiné, Languedoc, and elsewhere in Europe. However, not only did underground activities conflict in many ways with the Waldensians' original vocation (the public preaching of the Word of God): they also rapidly changed both the nature and the membership of the movement. While Waldo and his associates had chosen the city of Lyon as the stage for their preaching – and the social composition of the first generation of the Poor of Lyon reflected an urban and relatively wealthy membership – in the thirteenth century Waldensianism rapidly moved from towns to the countryside and came to be composed mainly of skilled labourers or ordinary peasants. Moreover, while the initial drive to announce the Word of God openly and freely, living in towns as beggars of alms – not unlike the *Ordo fratrum minorum* and the *Ordo fratrum praedicatorum* – faded, Waldensians began to develop a complex identity based on a different self-image, imbued with persecution and martyrdom characterising the true children of Israel. ([13]) The doggedness with which inquisitors persecuted Waldensians, especially after the eradication of Catharism, contributed to these changes in a significant way.

While the thirteenth century represented – despite mounting persecution – the height of the missionary expansion of the Waldensian movement, ([14]) the second half of the fourteenth century saw a general decline in proselytising. ([15]) This has created several problems for those scholars who

---

(12) 'Concilium Lateranense IV', ed. A. García y García – A. Melloni, in *COGD* II.1, p. 168. 'Quia vero nonnulli sub specie pietatis virtutem eius, iuxta quod ait apostolus, abnegantes, auctoritatem sibi vendicant predicandi, cum idem apostolus dicat Quomodo predicabunt nisi mittantur?, omnes qui prohibiti vel non missi, preter auctoritatem ab apostolica sede vel catholico episcopo loci susceptam, publice vel privatim predicationis officium usurpare presumpserint, excommunicationis vinculo innodentur, et nisi quantocius resipuerint, alia competenti pena plectantur'.

(13) Based upon Audisio, *The Waldensian Dissent*, p. 35-38.

(14) For a detailed analysis of the expansion of the movement until the end of the thirteenth century, see Papini, *Il primo secolo*.

(15) *Storia dei Valdesi*, vol. 2 (1974), p. 121.

have tried to flesh out the traditions and customs of late-medieval Walden-sianism, as the evidence stems mainly from inquisitorial trials, which are replete with heterogenous and sometimes even contradictory elements. Certainly, as we have seen, the particular form of Christian worship which characterised the Waldensian movement in the late Middle Ages was not perceived by its adherents as a wealth to offer others through proselytising, but as a legacy to be treasured and defended. (16) The *barbes*, entrusted with the preaching of the Word of God, were the keepers of this legacy: theirs are the hands behind the written culture of the Waldensian movement in these centuries. The *barbes* – by forsaking the *saeculum* to embrace their vocation – were itinerant preachers who were entrusted with the care of souls and followed rigorous ethical tenets, often in remote places where the need for a simple (albeit not naïve) Biblical exegesis modelled upon pastoral and practical concerns was prevalent. (17) They changed their names after the laying of hands, lived in poverty as beggars, and pronounced the three religious vows. (18)

The fifteenth century saw the emergence of what has been called the 'Waldensian-Hussite International', (19) which could count its members across most of continental Europe, including the Italian peninsula, southern France, Switzerland, Austria, the Holy Roman Empire – in particular the margraviate of Brandenburg – Pomerania, Bohemia, Moravia, Poland, and Hungary. At the beginning of the sixteenth century, however, the Waldensian movement was a mere shadow of its former self. The secrecy in which it had been silenced by repeated waves of persecution in the fifteenth century became one of its hallmarks and one of the core features of its identity. However, unexpected events, culminating in the Piedmontese and Dauphinois Waldensians' 'brief dialogue' with the first reformers, changed its destiny forever. (20)

THE TURN OF THE TIDE (*C.* 1526–*C.* 1535)

The path which led the alpine Waldensians of Piedmont and Dauphiné to the decisions of the *Concilium generale* of Chanforan was somewhat rugged: the lack of sources itself stands as testimony to these difficulties. Indeed, the late fifteenth and early sixteenth century saw a recrudescence of persecution in Dauphiné and in the valleys under the overlords of Savoy and

---

(16) Merlo, *Valdesi e valdismi*, vol. 2 (1991), p. 29-30.
(17) Merlo, *Valdesi e valdismi*, vol. 2 (1991), p. 31.
(18) See Audisio, *Preachers by Night*, Chapter 6.
(19) *Storia dei Valdesi*, vol. 2 (1974), p. 159.
(20) Vinay, 'Il breve dialogo'.

CONCILIUM CAMPI FORANEI – 1532

Saluzzo. ([21]) According to Reformed pastor Girolamo Miolo – author of one of the earliest histories of the alpine Waldensians, probably written in the 1580s ([22]) – persecution did not prevent the brave *barbes* from holding synods every year, in about September. ([23]) However, Miolo's marked (and confessional) retrospective illusion led him to affirm that in the time of the *barbes* – i.e. before Chanforan – ecclesiastical discipline in the Waldensian Church was not as pure and orderly as it became later, when the Reformation was implemented and consistories were founded. ([24]) On the other hand, Miolo was quick to blame this lack of discipline on persecution and on nicodemism, as well as on a 'pinch of papal wheat' which still remained 'in some points of [the Waldensians'] doctrine'. ([25]) In this sense, in the eyes of Miolo and other early commentators, the *Concilium generale* was providential as it cleansed Waldensianism from its residual flaws which it had inherited from the corrupt Roman Church of the late Middle Ages.

The *Concilium generale* was preceded by two synods, held in Laux in 1526 and in Mérindol in 1530. In Laux – where 140 *barbes* allegedly convened ([26]) – it was decided that two envoys, Giorgio of Calabria and Martin Gonin, be sent to Switzerland and Germany to gather knowledge about the Reformation. Apparently, they returned from their journey with great enthusiasm for the newborn religious movement, along with hoards of printed books. Discussions over what Giorgio of Calabria and Martin Gonin had brought back to their homeland culminated in the decision taken in Mérindol to dispatch other two *barbes*, Georges Morel and Pierre Masson, once again to Germany and Switzerland. This time, their mission was to seek the advice of a few 'out-

---

(21) Gonnet, 'Valdesi franco-italiani e riformatori d'Oltralpe', p. 9-11.

(22) For his biography, see Miolo, *Historia breve e vera*, p. 19-43. On Waldensian historiography in the sixteenth century, see J.-F. Gilmont, 'L'historiographie vaudoise du XVIe siècle: Jean Crespin, Étienne Noël et Scipione Lentolo', in Balmas, *I Valdesi e l'Europa*, p. 165-202.

(23) It is also what *barbe* Pierre Griot told the inquisitors (Audisio, *Le barbe et l'inquisiteur*, p. 103). Curiously, Chanforan is also known to have taken place in September.

(24) On this retrospective illusion, see for instance Gonnet, 'Chanforan e la storiografia valdese', especially p. 5-6, where the issue of the 'pregiudiziale filoriformata' is discussed – notwithstanding Gonnet's understanding of it being 'quasi del tutto assente nei primi storici del Cinquecento'.

(25) Miolo, *Historia breve e vera*, p. 99-100. 'Domanda 7. Se in queste valli vi erano de consistorii antiquamente del tempo di detti Barba. Risposta. Vi era bene qualche forma di disciplina, ma non già in tale libertà et ordine come hoggi dì nelle Chiese Riformate. Imperochè in quel tempo tutto si faceva secrettamente per causa delle persecutioni'.

(26) Miolo, *Historia breve e vera*, p. 99-100.

286   CONCILIUM CAMPI FORANEI – 1532

standing Doctors of whom God availed for the Reformation of the Church' in order to settle their doctrinal and ecclesiastical uncertainties. ([27]) Morel and Masson travelled to Neuchâtel, Morat, Bern, and later to Basel and Strasbourg.

Morel and Masson first addressed a long letter to Johannes Oecolampadius (1482-1531). They hoped that 'the [Holy] Spirit', through the reformer of the city, 'would clarify many things' to them. Due to their 'ignorance and sloth', these uncertainties prevailed, 'to the detriment of [themselves] and of the people to whom [they] taught in such an inadequate way'. ([28]) They described to Oecolampadius the customs and traditions of the *barbes* and the Waldensians and succinctly affirmed their theological and sacramental beliefs. They also listed eleven queries on various matters of doctrine and discipline which they asked the Basel reformer to clarify. Among these issues, there were the degrees of hierarchy in the ministry (or lack thereof), the legitimacy of civil authorities, the validity of civil laws before God, usury, the extent of original sin, celibacy, and the relationship between free will and predestination. Oecolampadius' replies – two letters survive – to Morel and Masson's message were generous, detailed, and full of encouraging expressions, which stand as testimony to his consideration for the Waldensians' cause. ([29]) The very same doubts were submitted to the attention of Martin Bucer (1491-1551), the reformer of the imperial free city of Strasbourg, following Oecolampadius' recommendation to do so. Bucer replied in an equally magnanimous way, with a somewhat more systematic dispatch. While they returned to the valleys of Piedmont, Masson was arrested in Dijon and later executed. It was Morel's responsibility to translate Oecolampadius' and Bucer's replies into the vernacular and bring them to the attention of his fellow *barbes* who later met in Chanforan, including many who came from the Waldensian diaspora in Calabria, Apulia, and elsewhere. ([30]) These questions and answers constituted the key items on the agenda of the *Concilium generale*. A third journey – on which Martin Gonin and a certain *barbe* Guido embarked – was organised in summer 1532 in order to invite some Swiss reformers to the *Concilium*. Eventually, the *barbes* managed to invite Guillaume Farel (1489-1565) and his collaborator Antoine Saunier to participate in the debates of Chanforan. ([31])

The proceedings of the *Concilium generale* – which amount to a concise *propossicione* – are considered evidence of the obliteration of 'all the typical

(27) Gilles, *Histoire ecclésiastique*, vol. I, p. 47-48.

(28) *[1]Morel-Masson*, p. 36.

(29) See *[1]Oecolampadius* and *[2]Oecolampadius*, whose relevant passages are quoted in the critical edition offered below, along with *[1]Bucer*.

(30) Gonnet, 'Valdesi franco-italiani e riformatori d'Oltralpe', p. 14.

(31) Jalla, 'Farel', p. 291-293.

CONCILIUM CAMPI FORANEI – 1532

characters of medieval Waldensian piety'. While there is undoubtedly some truth to this argument, this nonetheless seems exaggerated in the light of the very decisions of the *Concilium generale*. While Waldensian worship, through Chanforan, did acquire a significant degree of – so to speak – spiritualisation, it did not follow blindly the advice offered by either Oecolampadius or Bucer. The result was an original mix of both theological stances, coupled with a quasi-Zwinglian understanding of the Lord's Supper (Chapter 23) and other matters, certainly owing to Farel's sway over many among the *Concilium*'s attendees. (32) Although Chanforan has been interpreted as the Waldensian Church's gateway to the Reformation, the absence of any explicit reference to justification by faith alone is an elephant in the room with which scholarship has refrained from engaging seriously. Other decisions, such as the possibility to swear oaths (Chapter 1), the un-Scriptural nature of auricular confession (Chapter 5), the adiaphoric statute of the imposition of hands (Chapter 9) and of fasting (Chapter 12), the recognition of secular authority (Chapter 11), and the legitimacy of congruous interest rates (Chapters 17 and 18) followed the lines of contemporary magisterial Reformation. So did strictly theological statements such as the denial of free will and the assertion of predestination (Chapters 19-21) as well as the disavowal of all sacraments except baptism and the Lord's Supper (Chapter 23).

The extent of the discussions over the changes to the Waldensians' traditions (both in theology and in ecclesiastical organisation) which Oecolampadius and Bucer required – as well as the difficulties which their implementation certainly underwent – is impossible to reconstruct. (33) Shedding some new light on those events, thus going beyond an unspecific statement of the *Concilium generale*'s decisions as having been 'not without internal contrasts', is a desideratum in this field of studies. (34) The two most contentious issues were free will and nicodemism: denial of the former was a keystone principle of the early Reformation, while extirpation of the latter in favour of the acceptance of martyrdom was needed to correct the alpine Waldensians' tendency to disguise themselves as Roman Catholics to avoid persecution – which often included participation in the Mass and other pollutions, as Oecolampadius and Bucer would have put it. According to the inquisitorial deposition of *barbe* Pierre Griot, disagreements arose between two (former) monks and two noblemen from Grenoble in the midst of an assembly of 'great

(32) Vinay, *Le confessioni*, p. 27-28.
(33) Not by chance the years between 1534 and 1549 have been labelled 'the years of silence' (Cameron, *The Reformation of the Heretics*, p. 144).
(34) Foresta, 'Da barba a pastori', p. 733.

clergymen and doctors', weeks before Chanforan. The ex-monks supported justification by faith alone, while apparently the noblemen held a more ambiguous theological position, according to which 'faith without works' was 'dead'. The monks retorted that works were mere testimonies of faith and did not have any place in salvation. Moreover, they accused the noblemen of being 'more occupied with, and encumbered by, ceremonies and external works than those of the Roman Church' were. This discussion caused much scandal among the Waldensian *barbes*, as did subsequent disagreements over marriage and clerical celibacy. (35) This anecdote – not found elsewhere – does not match Gilles' reconstruction of the disagreements which emerged during the *Concilium generale*, blaming those who had once served as monks and priests 'in the papacy' for trying to bring forth some 'relics of their old opinions' and force the Synod to approve them. (36)

It is clear that several *barbes* did not agree with some of the decisions of the *Concilium generale*, and this was mainly for three reasons: firstly, they did not deem some of the new regulations really necessary; secondly, they feared that the new order of the Waldensian Church as approved in Chanforan – which strongly disapproved of nicodemitic attitudes – might prompt Roman Catholic authorities to persecute it even more strongly; thirdly – and most crucially – they believed that by establishing these new regulations, the Church 'dishonoured the memory of those who had blessedly guided [it]

(35) Audisio, *Le barbe et l'inquisiteur*, p. 107-109, 'Aussi dict et confesse que ceste année présente se sont trouvéz de grands clercz et docteurs à leur congrégation. Entre les autres en y avoit ung en habit noir, l'autre blanc; et estoient religieux. Et deux autres, lesquelz estoient gentliz hommes du pays de Grenoble. Et ont tenu desputation entre eulx de la foy. Les deux religieux disoyent que la foy seule justifioit et les deux autres disoient que la foy sans les eouvres [*sic*] est morte. Et *contra* les religieux disoient que les eouvres ne servoient de rien à justification mais seulement estoient tesmoings de la foy et que les eouvres n'estoient que une superstition qu'on avoit trouvée et que Dieu ne demandoit point icelles eouvres extérieures mais seullement demandoit le cueur de l'homme. Aussi disoient les deux religieux: «Vous estez plus occupéz et empeschéz après vous cérémonies et eouvres extérieures que ne sont ceulx de l'esglise romaine»'.

(36) Gilles, *Histoire ecclésiastique*, vol. 1 p. 52, 'Outre que entre les Vaudois se trouvoyent plusieurs qui avoyent esté moines ou Prestres en la papauté, et qui depuis s'adjoignans aux Eglises Réformées y apportèrent des reliques de leurs anciennes opinions, qu'il cherchoyent de faire recevoir'.

CONCILIUM CAMPI FORANEI – 1532

until then'. (37) This disgruntled circle of *barbes* (of which very little is known) sent two of its spokesmen, called Daniel de Valence and Jean de Molines, to Bohemia to meet the Waldensian movement's old friends and supporters in the Bohemian Brethren. (38) As soon as they were informed of the decisions taken at Chanforan and of the contacts that the alpine Waldensians had with the Swiss and German reformers, the Bohemians were 'utterly upset in [their] souls'. They were shocked by the fact that the Waldensians, who had 'firmly persevered with [their] fathers' in the Christian faith in the previous centuries, had allowed some Swiss theologians, with their corrupt teachings, to 'intrude' in the Waldensian Church and provoke a schism which the *barbes* should have avoided at all costs, 'in the same way as sailors avoid Scylla and Charybdis'. (39) It has been claimed that the Bohemian Brethren's rebuke was discussed and rejected at a subsequent assembly, held in a small village called Prali, in 'Val S. Martin' – now known as the Germanasca valley – on 15 August 1533. (40)

The role of Guillaume Farel and his associate Antoine Saunier in the evolution of the Waldensian movement has not been overlooked by scholarship. In particular, Saunier's concern for the disagreements stirred by the malcontents who had resorted to the Bohemian Brethren prompted a new mission to Switzerland by Martin Gonin and *barbe* Guido, which ultimately resulted in the participation of Robert Olivétan in the Waldensians' activities in the valleys. (41) Olivétan's translation of the Bible (1535), one of the major achievements of the first years of the francophone Reformation, was financed by the Waldensians, who rapidly abandoned – in matters of worship – their vernacular languages in favour of French also as a result of the use of this translation. Other mid-term results of the *Concilium generale* of Chanforan were the relinquishment of nicodemism, the implementation of public worship, and the slow but real replacement of the *barbes* with Reformed pastors, educated in Reformed institutions across Europe. In the wake of the *Concilium*, this was greatly facilitated by the French occupation of Piedmont in 1536-1559.

(37) Gilles, *Histoire ecclésiastique*, vol. 1, p. 52, 'Il est vray que quelques-uns des Barbes ne consentirent pas à toutes les conclusions de cette Assemblée, estimans que ces règlemens nouveaux n'estoyent pas totalement nécessaires, et qu'en les establissant on deshonotoit la mémoire de ceux qui avoyent tant heureusement conduit ces Eglises jusqu'alors; et en outre, en se descouvrant plus que de coustume, il est vraisemblable que les adversaires s'en irritoyent, et en pourroyent prendre occasion de persécuter l'Eglise'.
(38) Vinay, *Le confessioni*, p. 28.
(39) *Bohemian Brethren*, p. 144, 146.
(40) Gilles, *Histoire ecclésiastique*, vol. 1, p. 56-57; Vinay, *Le confessioni*, p. 146, n. 9.
(41) Gonnet, 'Les relations des vaudois des Alpes', p. 50-52.

(42) From 1555, after the sending of pastor Jean Vernou to Piedmont, the Genevan guise of the Reformation came to characterise the Waldensian Church as it slowly became one of the numerous pieces of the composite mosaic of international Calvinism.

Notes on the Edition

The decisions (*propossicione*) of the *Concilium generale* of Chanforan survive in a unique manuscript held at Trinity College Dublin (MS 259), at fol. 118-125. The various documents bound in this manuscript are known, following Jean-Paul Perrin's seventeenth-century label, as *Mémoires de Georges Morel* (43) and have been thoroughly studied, commented, and edited by several scholars, and in particular by Valdo Vinay. (44) The manuscript is the result of *barbe* Morel's notes, written down to serve as a memorandum of the correspondence between the Waldensian Church and the reformers of Basel and Strasbourg, as well as the talks the envoys had with the latter. In his learned study of the Waldensian material held in Trinity College Dublin, James Henthorn Todd described this item as 'obviously an original, written soon after Morel and Masson were sent on their expedition'. (45)

How exactly this manuscript arrived in Dublin remains somewhat of a mystery. It is unlikely that MS 259 was included in a larger hoard of Waldensian manuscripts which were gathered *in loco* by Samuel Morland (1625-1695), a close collaborator of Oliver Cromwell who was sent to an embassy at the court of Savoy in 1655 to voice Cromwell's disapproval of the series of massacres collectively known as the *Pasque piemontesi*. (46) James Ussher (1581-1656), archbishop of Armagh and primate of All Ireland, had entrusted Morland with the collection of Waldensian manuscripts in the valleys of Piedmont. At some stage, this manuscript was certainly in the possession of Jean-Paul Perrin – who was entrusted with a bundle of documents by the Waldensian Synod in order to write his *Histoire des Vaudois* – as reported by Jean Léger. (47) Jean himself and his uncle Antoine were behind the transfer of the

(42) Vinay, 'Il breve dialogo', p. 113.
(43) Perrin, *Histoire des Vaudois*, t. 1, p. 106 and 157.
(44) See the detailed analyses provided in Vinay, '*Mémoires*', especially p. 35-41 and in the introduction to Vinay, *Le confessioni*.
(45) Todd, *The Books of the Vaudois*, p. 8 and 20.
(46) On the *Pasque*, see *Storia dei Valdesi*, vol. 2 (1974), p. 73-102. Morland, however, had probably seen the manuscript independently from Perrin's witness. Cfr. Morland, *History of the Evangelical Churches*, p. 224 and Léger, *Histoire générale*, t. 1, p. 21-25.
(47) Léger, *Histoire générale*, t. 1, p. 24.

CONCILIUM CAMPI FORANEI – 1532

collection of Waldensian sources to Morland now held in Cambridge. ([48]) Although the presence of an important collection of Waldensian manuscripts in Dublin is certainly connected to Archbishop Ussher's interest in such sources and to Morland's activities in Piedmont, the exact succession of owners of the material now held in Dublin has not yet been fully reconstructed.

MS 259 is 15 × 10.5 cm. An indistinct number of *peticions* (around 50) by the *barbes* to the reformers fills the pages of this manuscript, alongside the *propossicione* of Chanforan. Each *peticion* is followed by the answers received. Chapters 3 and 4 are not numbered ([49]) and two different handwritings are displayed (the second starts from Chapter 19). It has been argued that the numerous erasures in the original manuscripts may have been the result of Perrin's preparation of the Chanforan *propossicione* for printing in his *Histoire des Vaudois*. ([50])

The edition of the decisions of Chanforan offered below comes with the original spelling of the source-text, without any arbitrary modernising. Tildes and contractions have been silently expanded.

BIBLIOGRAPHY

Sources (and Their Abbreviations)

'I barba Georges Morel e Pierre Masson a Ecolampadio (primi di ottobre? 1530)', in V. Vinay (a cura di), *Le confessioni di fede dei valdesi riformati, con documenti del dialogo fra «prima» e «seconda» Riforma*, Torino 1975, p. 36-51 [= *¹Morel-Masson*].

'Prima risposta di Ecolampadio ai valdesi (Basilea, 13 ottobre 1530)', in V. Vinay (a cura di), *Le confessioni di fede dei valdesi riformati, con documenti del dialogo fra «prima» e «seconda» Riforma*, Torino 1975, p. 52-63 [= *¹Oecolampadius*].

---

(48) Léger, *Histoire générale*, t. 1, p. 21.

(49) Cfr. Vinay, '*Mémoires*', p. 38.

(50) Cameron, *Waldenses*, p. 246; cfr. the succinct edition in Perrin, *Histoire des Vaudois*, p. 158-160. Todd had 'no hesitation' in affirming that the 'intention' behind these erasures was 'dishonest', especially if they were 'made with a view to the publication of the document': the objective was to 'omit everything, properly speaking, Waldensian', thus 'concealing the original difference in doctrine and discipline between the Vaudois and the Reformed' (Todd, *The Books of the Vaudois*, p. 20); the same argument in Vinay, '*Mémoires*', p. 35.

'Seconda risposta di Ecolampadio ai valdesi (Basilea, ca. metà o fine ottobre 1530)', in V. Vinay (a cura di), *Le confessioni di fede dei valdesi riformati, con documenti del dialogo fra «prima» e «seconda» Riforma*, Torino 1975, p. 64-69 [= *2Oecolampadius*].

'Risposta di Martin Bucero (Strasburgo, fine ottobre 1530)', in V. Vinay (a cura di), *Le confessioni di fede dei valdesi riformati, con documenti del dialogo fra «prima» e «seconda» Riforma*, Torino 1975, p. 74-117 [= *1Bucer*].

'Barba Morel e Bucero sulla giustificazione per fede', in V. Vinay (a cura di), *Le confessioni di fede dei valdesi riformati, con documenti del dialogo fra «prima» e «seconda» Riforma*, Torino 1975, p. 118-137 [= *2Bucer*].

'I fratelli di Boemia e di Moravia ai Valdesi (Dalla Boemia, 25 giugno 1533)', in V. Vinay (a cura di), *Le confessioni di fede dei valdesi riformati, con documenti del dialogo fra «prima» e «seconda» Riforma*, Torino 1975, p. 144-151 [= *Bohemian Brethren*].

P. Gilles, *Histoire ecclésiastique des églises vaudoises de l'an 1160 au 1643*, éd. P. Lantaret, 2 vols, Pignerol 1881[= Gilles, *Histoire ecclésiastique*].

J. Léger, *Histoire générale des églises évangéliques des vallées de Piémont; ou Vaudoises...*, 2 vols, Leyde 1669 [= Léger, *Histoire générale*].

G. Miolo, *Historia breve e vera de gl'affari de i Valdesi delle Valli*, a cura di E. Balmas, Torino 1971 [= Miolo, *Historia breve e vera*].

S. Morland, *The History of The Evangelical Churches Of the Valleys of Piemont. Containing A most exact Geographical Description of the Place, and a faithfull Account of the Doctrine, Life, and Persecutions of the Ancient Inhabitants...*, London 1658 [= Morland, *History of the Evangelical Churches*].

J.-P. Perrin, *Histoire des Vaudois. Divisee en trois parties ...*, Genève 1619.

J.-P. Perrin, *Histoire des Vaudois. Divisee en trois parties ...*, Genève 1618 [= Perrin, *Histoire des Vaudois*].

LITERATURE (AND ITS ABBREVIATIONS)

A. Armand Hugon, 'Popolo e chiesa alle Valli dal 1532 al 1561', *Bollettino della Società di Studi Valdesi* 110 (1961), p. 5-34 [= Armand Hugon, 'Popolo e chiesa'].

G. Audisio, *Preachers by Night: The Waldensian Barbes (15th–16th Centuries)* (*Studies in Medieval and Reformation Traditions* 118), Leiden 2007 [= Audisio, *Preachers by Night*].

—, *The Waldensian Dissent: Persecution and Survival, c. 1170–c. 1570* (*Cambridge Medieval Textbooks*), Cambridge ²1999 [= Audisio, *The Waldensian Dissent*].

—, *Les vaudois. Histoire d'une dissidence, XIIᵉ-XVIᵉ siècles*, Paris 1998.

—, 'Chanforan 1532: quel changement?', *Bollettino della Società di Studi Valdesi* 154 (1984), p. 25-38.

—, 'Une mutation: les vaudois passent à la Réforme', *Bulletin de la Société de l'Histoire du Protestantisme Français* 126 (1980), p. 153-165 [= Audisio, 'Une mutation'].

—, *Le barbe et l'inquisiteur. Procès du barbe vaudois Pierre Griot par l'inquisiteur Jean de Roma (Apt, 1532)*, Aix-en-Provence 1979 [= Audisio, *Le barbe et l'inquisiteur*].

E. K. Cameron, *Waldenses: Rejections of Holy Church in Medieval Europe*, Oxford 2000 [= Cameron, *Waldenses*].

—, *The Reformation of the Heretics: The Waldenses of the Alps, 1480-1580*, Oxford 1984 [= Cameron, *The Reformation of the Heretics*].

R. Cegna, 'Appunti su Valdismo e Ussitismo', *Bollettino della Società di Studi Valdesi* 131 (1972), p. 3-42.

Le confessioni di fede dei valdesi riformati, con documenti del dialogo fra «prima» e «seconda» Riforma, a cura di V. Vinay, Torino 1975 [= Vinay, *Le confessioni*].

E. Comba, 'Relazione originale del sinodo valdese tenuto a Angrogna l'an. 1532 (secondo un manoscritto del Trinity College, Dublino)', *La rivista cristiana* 4 (1876), p. 265-269 [= Comba, 'Relazione originale'].

P. Foresta, 'Da barba a pastori. Il *concilium generale* di Chanforan (1532)', *Cristianesimo nella storia* 32 (2011), p. 733-753 [= Foresta, 'Da barba a pastori'].

J. Gonnet, *Il grano e le zizzanie. Tra eresia e riforma (secoli XII-XVI)*, 3 vols, Soveria Mannelli 1989.

—, 'Chanforan e la storiografia valdese (da Scipione Lentolo a Ernesto Comba, 1542-1932)', *Bollettino della Società di Studi Valdesi* 154 (1984), p. 3-23 [= Gonnet, 'Chanforan e la storiografia valdese'].

—, 'Le développement des doctrines vaudoises de Lyon à Chanforan', *Revue d'histoire et de philosophie religieuses* 4 (1972), p. 397-406 [= Gonnet, 'Le développement des doctrines'].

294 CONCILIUM CAMPI FORANEI – 1532

—, 'Les relations des vaudois des Alpes avec les réformateurs en 1532', *Bibliothèque d'humanisme et Renaissance* 23 (1961), p. 34-52 [= Gonnet, 'Les relations des vaudois des Alpes'].

—, 'I rapporti tra i valdesi franco-italiani e i riformatori d'Oltralpe prima di Calvino', in D. Cantimori et al. (a cura di), *Ginevra e l'Italia. Raccolta di studi promossa dalla Facoltà Valdese di Teologia di Roma*, Firenze 1959, p. 3-63 [= Gonnet, 'Valdesi franco-italiani e riformatori d'Oltralpe'].

J. J. Hemardinquer, 'Les Vaudois et la Réforme tchèque', *Bollettino della Società di Studi Valdesi* 103 (1958), p. 37-56.

J. J. Herzog, *Die romanischen Waldenser, ihre vorreformatorischen Zustände und Lehren, ihre Reformation im 16. Jahrhundert und die Rückwirkungen derselben, hauptsächlich nach ihren eigenen Schriften dargestellt*, Halle 1853.

J. Jalla, 'Farel et les Vaudois du Piémont', in Comité Farel (éd.), *Guillaume Farel 1489-1565. Biographie nouvelle, écrite d'après les documents originaux par un groupe d'historiens, professeurs et pasteurs de Suisse, de France et d'Italie*, Neuchâtel – Paris 1930, p. 285-297 [= Jalla, 'Farel'].

G. G. Merlo, *Valdo. L'eretico di Lione* (*Piccola collana moderna – Serie storica* 133), Torino 2010 [= Merlo, *Valdo*].

—, *Valdesi e valdismi medievali* (*Studi Storici*), 2 vols, Torino 1984-1991 [= Merlo, *Valdesi e valdismi*].

A. Molnár, *A Challenge to Constantinianism: The Waldensian Theology in the Middle Ages*, Geneva 1976.

A. Muston, *L'Israël des Alpes. Première histoire complète des Vaudois du Piémont et de leurs colonies...*, 4 vols, Paris 1851.

Olivétan, traducteur de la Bible, éd. G. Casalis – B. Roussel, Paris 1987.

C. Papini, *Valdo di Lione e i «poveri nello spirito». Il primo secolo del movimento valdese (1170-1270)*, Torino ²2001 [= Papini, *Il primo secolo*].

G. Platone, *Valdesi e Riforma nel passaggio di Chanforan (1532)*, Torino 2014 [= Platone, *Valdesi e Riforma*].

—, *1532, Chanforan: svolta del valdismo*, Torre Pellice 1982 [= Platone, *1532, Chanforan*].

G. Scuderi, 'Carisma e istituzione nelle chiese della Riforma, con particolare attenzione alla chiesa valdese in Italia', *Ecclesia Mater* 3 (1982), p. 181-189.

K.-V. Selge, *Die ersten Waldenser. Mit Edition des* Liber antiheresis *des Durandus von Osca*, 2 vols, Berlin 1967.

Storia dei Valdesi, a cura di A. Armand Hugon – A. Molnár – V. Vinay, 3 vols, Torino 1974-1980 [= *Storia dei Valdesi*].

V. Subilia, 'Chanforan 1532 o la presenza protestante in Italia', *Protestantesimo* 37/32 (1982), p. 65-94.

J. Henthorn Todd, *The Books of the Vaudois: The Waldensian Manuscripts Preserved in the Library of Trinity College Dublin*, London – Cambridge – Dublin 1865 [= Todd, *The Books of the Vaudois*].

D. Tron, 'La creazione del corpo pastorale valdese e la Ginevra di Calvino', *Bollettino della Società di Studi Valdesi* 207 (2010), p. 77-161 [= Tron, 'La creazione del corpo pastorale valdese'].

—, 'Un profondo mutamento. Da barba a pastori', in R. Genre (a cura di), *Valdismo e cattolicesimo prima della Riforma (1488-1555), dai conflitti alla convivenza*, Villareto-Roure 2010, p. 253-292.

I Valdesi e l'Europa, a cura di E. Balmas (*Collana della Società di Studi Valdesi* 9), Torre Pellice 1982 [= Balmas, *I Valdesi e l'Europa*].

Les vaudois des origines à leur fin, éd. G. Audisio, Torino 1990 [= Audisio, *Les vaudois des origines à leur fin*].

Vaudois languedociens et Pauvres Catholiques (*Cahiers de Fanjeaux* 2), Toulouse 1967 [= *Vaudois languedociens*].

V. Vinay, 'Il breve dialogo fra prima e seconda Riforma 1530-1533', *Bollettino della Società di Studi Valdesi* 136 (1974), p. 99-115 [= Vinay, 'Il breve dialogo'].

—, '*Mémoires de George Morel*. L'importanza del codice valdese c-5-18 (MS 259) del Trinity College di Dublino per la storia dell'adesione dei valdesi alla Riforma', *Bollettino della Società di Studi Valdesi* 132 (1972), p. 35-48 [= Vinay, '*Mémoires*'].

Waldenser. Geschichte und Gegenwart, hrsg. W. Erk, Frankfurt am Main 1971.

MONITUM

Trinity College Dublin, MS 259, fol. 118-125.

CONCILIUM CAMPI FORANEI (IUXTA HENGRONIAM)
1532

CONSPECTUS SIGLORUM

CODEX

T   Trinity College Dublin, Ms 259, fol. 118-125

EDITIONES

b   E. Comba, 'Relazione originale del sinodo valdese tenuto a Angrogna l'an. 1532 (secondo un manoscritto del Trinity College, Dublino)', *La rivista cristiana* 4 (1876), p. 265-269

h   J. J. Herzog (hrsg.), *Die romanischen Waldenser, ihre vorreformatorischen Zustände und Lehren, ihre Reformation im 16. Jahrhundert und die Rückwirkungen derselben, hauptsächlich nach ihren eigenen Schriften dargestellt*, Halle 1853, p. 382-388

n   W. H. Neuser (hrsg.), 'Die Erklärung von Chanforan 1532', in *RefBK*, vol. 1/1, p. 549-570

v   'La dichiarazione del sinodo di Chanforan 1532', in V. Vinay (a cura di), *Le confessioni di fede dei valdesi riformati, con documenti del dialogo fra «prima» e «seconda» Riforma*, Torino 1975, p. 139-143

| LE PROPOSSICIONE CHE SONO STATE DISPUTATE EN 118
ANGRONIA LANNO DEL SEGNOR 1532. ET ADI 12. DE SETEM-
BRO. ENPRESENCIA DE TUTI LI MINISTRI ET ECIAN DIO DEL
POPULO.

5   El primo di fu disputato se hera licito al christiano de jurar inalcun modo.

C. I.

El christiano po iurare licitament al nome de dio sencza fare contra le
parolle che sono script ensancto Mat. 5 c. la conclusione he stata don modo

---

5 se – modo] cfr Ex. 20, 7   **7/9** le – jurare] cfr Matth. 5, 33-37

5/14 El – etc.] cfr *Oecolampadius*, p. 56, 'Magistratum secularem audimus in his, quae
contra Deo non sunt, honoramus etiam, etiam esse christianum posse credimus.
Juramentum, si exigat, non negamus, non obstante eo, quod apud Matthaeum legimus.
Nihil enim ibi prohibuit Christus, quod per se non est peccatum, prohibuit malam
conscientiam, avaritiam, iram et vindictae cupiditatem, mendacium omne et
periurium'; cfr *Bucer*, p. 84, 'Quod plebem a juramentis et aliis saeculi hujus vitiis
abstrahitis, christiane factis, jusjurandi tamen religionem in loco exhibere nemo
damnet. Neque enim hanc Christus Matth., sed vulgaria et levia juramenta, quae in
cottidiano sermone accidunt, quem voluit dominus simplici affirmatione et negatione
constare, prohibuit', as well as *Bucer*, p. 102, 104, 'Summa est haec: deus in lege sua
praeceperit jusjurandum deferre et facere, ergo in se peccatum non est, non potuit
igitur ipsum Christus prohibere. Item de Christianis prophetae praedixerunt juraturos
in nomine domini, et psalter dicit, laudabuntur omnes qui jurant in eo, ergo per se
jusjurandum res sancta est, qua et Apostoli usi sunt, ut Rom. 9 et II Cor. 2 patet. Quid
enim mali, invocare nomen dei ad testimonium veritatis? Dilectio proximi legem
complet, ergo nihil contra legem et dei voluntatem quam quod proximo nocet'

---

1 propossicione] propossitione *b*   che] ch' *b*   **2** angronia] angrogna *n v*   lanno]
l'âno *b*   del] d'l *b*   **2/3** Et – Enpresencia] Et adi 12 d'Setembro en presencia *b*   **3/
4** ecian – populo] eciandio d'l populo *b*   **5** di] dì *b*   fu] fo *b n v*   de – modo] d'jurar
in alcun modo *b*   **7** iurare] jurare *h*   de dio] d'Dio *b*   sencza] senza *b*   **8** che] ch' *b*
ensancto] en sancto *b*   la] La *b h n*   **8/9** don modo che] dy modo ch' *b*

che colluy che jura non pilha el nome de dio in vano che el po jurare. Non pilha il nome de dio in vano quando el juramento suo redonda in maiore gloria de dio et salut del prossimo he dio si po jurare jniudicio per che colluy que exerce potesta, sie inffidelle overo fidelle, exerce la potesta de dio, eper questo in qualunque sorte visia dacto el juramento intendemo jurare al nome de dio etc.

C. 2.

Nulla opera he quiamata bona si non quella che dio ha comandato. Nulla opera he quamata cativa si non quella che dio ha prohibito. Inquanto ale opere

---

11/12 si – dio] cfr Rom. 13, 1   **12/14** eper – etc.] cfr Deut. 6, 13   **17/19** Inquanto – etc.] cfr Matth. 12, 5

16 Nulla[1] – comandato] cfr *¹Bucer*, p. 90, 'Alterum unde poteritis agnoscere haud bono illos spiritu agi, est, quod ea tantopere urgent, quae non per se ad pietatem attinent. Paulus cum supervacaneas legis quaestiones damnaret, posuit nobis scopum, ad quem necesse est dirigantur et spectent quaecunque rite ex lege observantur et tractantur. Finis inquit praecepti est dilectio ex corde puro et conscientia bona et fide non simulata, a quibus quod aberrarunt quidam, deflexerunt ad vaniloquium volentes esse legis doctores, non intelligentes quae loquuntur neque de quibus asseverant. Jam isti omissa charitate quae fit omnia omnibus et ibi majorem operam impendit lucrandi, ubi plus periculi est pereundi'   **17/18** Inquanto – dio] cfr *¹Bucer*, p. 86, 'Circa baptismum in nostris Ecclesiis primum coorta disputatio est, num sint pueri baptizandi. Mox satana cogente, secesserunt multi, et nostras Ecclesias satanae tradunt, propterea quod pueros baptizamus, quanquam simul in alios multos errores inciderint. Contemnunt enim dona dei cum linguarum, tum cognitionis scripturarum et jactant neminem ex doctis posse veritatem percipere, nam ipsi omnes fere praeter germanam nullam linguam habent et operis externis quibus victum conquirunt, adducti sunt.

---

9 colluy – jurare] colluy, que jura, non pilha el nome de dio en vano, que el po jurare *h*   che[2]] ch' *b*   de dio] d'Dio *b*   che el] ch'el *b*   **9/12** Non – dio] Non pilha el nome de dio in vano, quando el juramento suo redonda in majore gloria de dio e salut del prossimo. He Dio si po jurare in judicio, perque colluy, que exerce la potesta, sie inffidelle o vero fidelle, exerce la potesta de dio *h*   **11** de dio] d'dio *b*   salut] salute *b n v*   del] d'l *b*   prossimo he] prossimo. He *b*   jniudicio] in iudicio *b*, iniudicio *n v*   che] ch' *b*   **12** potesta[1]] potesta d' dio *b (err.)*   inffidelle] infid'lle *b*, infidelle *n v*   fidelle] fid'lle *b*   de dio] d'dio *b*   **12/14** eper – etc.] *non extat in h*   **12** eper] e per *b*   **13** dacto] datto *b*   juramento intendemo] juramento, intend'mo *b*, juramento. intendemo *n v*   **14** dio] Dio *b v*   etc.] *non extat in b*   **16** Nulla[1]] Nullo *h*   che dio] ch'dio *b*   comandato] comandata *b*   **16/17** Nulla[2] – prohibito] *sub cap. 3 in n*   **17** quamata] quiamata *h*   che dio] ch'dio *b*   prohibito] prohibita *h*   **17/19** Inquanto – etc.] *sub cap. 4 in n*   **17/19** Inquanto – peccato] *atramento erasus T*   **17** ale] a le *h*

CONCILIUM CAMPI FORANEI – 1532

externe lequalle non sono state prohibite de dio lomo lepo fare o non fare
secondo la conclussione dacta sencza peccato etc.

20 | Le due prime propossicione sono note per se afidelli deontiuone. Non [119]
faray tuto quello que te pare esser ben facto liochi toy ma faray quello che
tecomando, alfine del c. Tanto solamente quello che yo tecomando faray non
aiostare ne tolhere ala parolla mia fa tuto solamente quello che te comando.
Non declinaray adestra ne ala sinestra fa tanto solamente quello que te coman-
25 do et questa sea la toa reglea en tote le toe opere externe tu poy fare tute quante le opere externe de qual conque sorte siano. Don modo que non te jnduca-
no affare contra lo comandamente de dio que he delo amare. Ne ecian contra

---

20/22 Non – del c.] cfr Num. 15, 39-40   **22** Tanto – faray] cfr Ier. 50, 21   **22/
23** non – mia] cfr Deut. 4, 2   **24** Non – comando] cfr Deut. 5, 29   **26/27** Don –
amare] cfr Deut. 6, 5; Matth. 22, 37   **27/29** Ne – anoy] cfr Matth. 7, 12

Multos alioqui bonos seducunt vitae severitate et persecutionum tolerantia. Quid
namque sit, angelum Satanae transfigurari in angelum lucis et angelorum religionem
prae se ferre, ut Christi interim gratia obscuretur, miseri ignorant. Sed nec vident quod
apud deum nullum gravius peccatum sit quam placere sibi, damnare tam temere alios.
Aliquot crassioribus vitiis sese eximunt et incidunt in subtilia illa et spiritualia, quae
hoc nocentiora sunt quod pro virtutibus habentur'   **20** Le – deontiuone] cfr
²*Oecolampadius*, p. 64, 'Principio, de meritis unctio docet sanctos Dei ad exemplum
Christi nihil sublime de seipso sentire, et quum omnia fecerunt, quae servorum sunt,
dicere, se fecisse, quae debuerunt, et si recte discusserint opera sua, semper aliquid in
sanctis suis desiderant et inveniunt, quod vel plurius vel ardentius vel suavius fieri
debuerit. Itaque sibiipsis semper vilescunt et pro magno habent se sibi delicta sua, a
Deo in peccatum imputantia, tantum abest, ut aliquid suis operibus deberi cogitent, id
quod Pharisaei faciunt'

18/19 lequalle – etc.] lequelle non son prohibit de dio, l'omo le po fare o non fare –
sencza peccato *h*   **19** conclussione] conclusione *b n v*   dacta] datta *b*   sencza] senza *b*
20 Le – deontiuone] *non extat in h*   propossicione] propossitione *b*   afidelli] a fid'lli
b, a fidelli *n v*   deontiuone] *non extat in b*   **21** liochi toy ma] hochi toy, ma *h*   liochi]
li ochi *b*   **21/22** che tecomando] que te comando *b*   **22** alfine – faray] *non extat in h*
del c.] d'l *b*   che yo] ch'yo *b*   **23** ala – comando] a la parolla mia, fa tuto solament
quello ch' te comando *h*   che te] ch'te *b*   **24/29** Non – anoy] Non declinarey a
destra ne a la senestra, fa tanto solament quello que te comando. Aquesta sera la toa
regula en tote le toe opere externe. Tu poy fare tute quante le opere externe de
qualconque sorte siano, don modo que non te iudicairo affare contra lo comandamente
de dio, que he de lo amare; ne etiam contra quello que he proibito czo e non fare al
proximo nostro quello que non voressimo que fosse facto a noy *h*   **24** adestra] a destra
b   **25** sea] la *b*, sera *n v*   reglea] regl'a *b*   **26** de] d' *b*   qual conque] qualconque *b n v*
siano. Don] siano dy *b*   jnducano] inducano *b*   **27** de dio] d'dio *b*   delo] d'lo *b*
ecian] eciam *b*

302 CONCILIUM CAMPI FORANEI – 1532

quello que he proibito czo e non fare al proximo nostro quello quello que non
voressimo que fosse facto anoy.

30   C. 5.

La conffessione auriculare non he comandata da dio he stato concluso
secondo le sacre scripture che lavera confesion del christiano sie de confessare al solo dio el qualle apartiene honore e gloria. Et alui medessimo tanto solamente confessione etc. La 2ᵃ confessione si he reconciliare al proximo suo
35 como avemo en s. Mat. 5 c. he s. Jacobo ultimo confessamo etc. La 3ᵃ sie en
sancto Mat. 18 de colui que pecca alencontra de me. czo e yo savente che yo
debe adare alui e non luy ame. Esi non se vole coregire ne per me ne per testi-
moni ne ecian dio per tota moltitudine. | Et cosi como publicamente apeccato 120
publicamente habia a confessar el peccato suo. Altra confessione noy non
40 troviamo en la sancta scriptura etc.

31/34 La – etc.] cfr Ps. 32, 5   **35** como – Mat. 5 c.] cfr Matth. 5, 23-24   he – ultimo]
cfr Iac. 5, 16   **35/36** La – me] cfr Matth. 18, 15-17

30 5.] in *T*, 3 is replaced with 5. However, this should not be taken as proof that
chapters 3 and 4 were omitted. Throughout the other documents included in the
manuscript, sequence numbers are also quite disorderly: thus, it cannot be argued that
the absence of sequence numbers 3 and 4 stands as testimony to the omission of two
chapters   **31** La – dio] cfr *¹Bucer*, p. 84, 'Quod singulorum confessionem auditis,
probamus, sic enim potestis unius cujusque morbis melius adhibere remedium.
Tantum nolite exigere ut singula peccata fateantur, cum id deus non praeceperit'

---

28 proibito] prohibito *b*   czo e] czoe *b*   quello quello] *sic*   quello²] *non extat in b*
30 C. 5.] *del.* 3 *T*   **31/33** La – gloria] La confessione auriculare non he comandata da
dio; he stato concluso secondo le sacre scripture, ch' la vera confessione del christiano
sie de confessare al solo dio, el quello apartiene honor e gloria *h*   **31** conffessione]
confessione *b*   dio he] dio. He *b*   **32** che lavera] ch'la vera *b*   del] d'l *b*   de] d' *b*   **33/**
34 Et – etc.] *non extat in h*   **33** alui] al *b*   medessimo] med'ssimo *b*   **34/36** La –
me] La 2a confessione, si he reconciliare al proximo suo, coma avemo en sancto Mat. 5.
he S. Jacob: confessiamo etc. La 3a sie en sancto Mat. 18 de coluy que pecca etc. *h*
35 como] come *b*   Jacobo] Iacobo *b*   **36** colui] coluy *b*   **36/37** alencontra – ame]
non extat in b   **36/40** czo – etc.] *non extat in h*   **37** Esi] E si *b*   **38** ecian dio]
eciandio *b*   cosi] così *b*, ecsi *n*   como] come *b*   apeccato] a peccato *b*

CONCILIUM CAMPI FORANEI – 1532

C. 6.

La cessacione de opere nel jorno de la dominica non he proibita de dio al christiano. La conclussione he stata que per ben che hlomo possa operare el jorno de la dominica sencza peccato como havemo ne li evangeli. Et eciam en li gallacian al 4 c. et ali collocenczi al 2 c. nientedimeno per exercitare la carita ali nostri servitori. Et eciam per vacare alla parolla de dio dovemo cessare quel jorno como cellatore delo honor et gloria de dio.

C. 7.

La parolla non he necessaria nela oracion.

---

44 como – evangeli] cfr Marc. 2, 23-28   **44/46** Et – servitori] cfr Gal. 4, 10; Col. 2, 16

42/43 La – christiano] cfr ²*Oecolampadius*, p. 66, 'Tertio quaesivit, an die festo liceat operari. Scimus autem neminem iudicandum esse propter ferias; est enim christianis libertas per Christum parta, posse quovis die operari, ad Col. 2, Gal. 4 et Rom. 16. Atqui charitas docet, ut, cum infirmis fratribus illo die ociosi simus et quum propter infirmitatem etiam nostram cogimur alias dies in nostras necessitates insumere, vel hunc diem peculiariter in preces et ad audiendum et recogitandum verbum Dei insumamus. At si necessitas vel fratrum utilitas aliquid requirat, sciamus nos esse dominos sabbati, non sabbatum dominari nobis'; cfr ¹*Bucer*, p. 114, 'De die dominico item in Mattheo et Psalmis'

---

41 C. 6.] *atramento erasus* T; C 6 *ipsa manus add. in marg.* T   **42** cessacione] cessacion *h*   jorno] giorno *b*   dominica] domenica *b*   proibita] prohibita *h*   de dio] d'dio *b*   **43** christiano] cristiano *h*   **43/47** La – dio] La conclussione he stata, que per ben que hl'omo possa operare al jorno de la dominica sencza peccato, coma havemo ne li evangeli, e eciam en li gallacian al 4 e a li Collocenczi al 2 Cap., mentedimeno per exercitare la carita a li nostri servitori, e eciam per vacare alla parolla de dio, devemo cessare quel jorno como cellatore de lo honor et gloria de dio *h*   **43** conclussione] conclussione *b n*   che] ch' *b*   **44** de la] d'la *b*   dominica] domenica *b*   sencza] senza *b*   como] come *b*   **45** gallacian] gallaciani *b*   collocenczi] collocenzi *b*   carita] carità *b*   **46** servitori. Et] servitori et *b*   de dio] d'dio *b*   **47** delo] d'lo *b*   **48/52** C. 7. – oracion] *atramento erasus*   **49/52** La – oracion] La parolla non he necessaria ne la oracion engenolvament, ne hore determinate ne descopiment del capo ne altre cose externe non sono necessarie ne requeste en la oracion *h*

304   CONCILIUM CAMPI FORANEI – 1532

50   C. 8.

Engenochiamenti ne hore determinate ne descoprimenti del capo no altre cose externe non sono necessarie ne requeste jnla oracion. He stato concluso che el colto divino non sipo fare si non in sperito e en verita como havemo ensancto johane al 4 c. dio he sperito et qui vol parllar con luy besogna que
55 parlla con lo sperito. La parolla et altre cose externe non si fanno si non ha exprimere e demostrare grande affecione al proximo etc. | con que hlomo ha 121 versso el suo dio.

                                 C. 9.

La inposicione de le mane non he necessaria la conclusione he stata per
60 ben che li apostoli la habiano usata. Et li antiqui padri nientedimeno per que he cosa externa sia en liberta de uno chasqueduno.

52/55 He – sperito] cfr Ioh. 4, 24   **59/60** La – usata] cfr I Tim. 4, 14

59 La – necessaria] cfr *Oecolampadius*, p. 114, 'Sacramenta praeter baptismum et Eucharistiam nulla novimus quam forte manuum impositionem et unctionem, utraque celebris etiam apostolis videtur, sed non tamen, quantum priora duo. Sive autem in usu sint, sive non, certum est, quicquid exterum est, symbolum tantum esse internorum'

---

50 C. 8.] *deest b*   **51** Engenochiamenti] Engenochiament *b*   ne[1]] he *n*   del] d'l *b* no] ne *b*   **52** jnla] en la *b*, enla *n v*   **52/57** He – dio] *sub* C. 8 *in b (suppl.)*   **53** che el] ch'el *b*   che] ch' *h*   sipo] si po *b h*   sperito] spirito *b h*   verita como] verità come *b*, verita, coma *h*   **54/55** ensancto – sperito] en sanco Johanne al 4 c.: dio he spirito, e qui vol parlar cum luy, besogna que parlla cum lo spirito *h*   **54** johane] Johane *b* sperito] spirito *b*   parllar] parlar *b*   **55** parlla] parla *b*   sperito. La] spirito la *b*   et] e *b h*   **56** demostrare] demonstrare *h*   affecione] affecion *b*   etc.] *non extat in h*   **56/ 57** con – dio] cum que hl'omo ha conversato el suo dio *h*   **57** versso] verso *b*   **58/ 61** C. 9. – chasqueduno] *atramento erasus T*   **59/61** La – chasqueduno] La imposicione de le mane non he necessaria. La conclusione he stata per ben che li apostoli la habiano usata e li antiqui padri; mentedimeno per que he cosa externa, sera en liberta de uno chasqueduno *h*   **59** necessaria la] necessaria. La *b*   he[2]] è *b*   **60** che li] ch'li *b*   usata. Et] usata et *b*   **61** sia] sera *n v*   liberta] libertà *b*   de uno] d'uno *b*

CONCILIUM CAMPI FORANEI – 1532

C. 10.

Non he licito al christiano vindicarsi del suo jnimico jnsorte nulla que sia.
La presente propossicione et patente per se como habiamo en sancto matheo
65 al 5 c. Et s. paulo Rom. 12 e ensancto pietro en la prima etc.

C. 11.

El christiano po exercitare el magistrato sopra li christiani delinquenti. La
propossicione he clara como havemo en s. paulo Rom. 13. Corint. 6 c. e
ensancto pietro en la soa prima epistolla.

70 ## C. 12.

El christiano non ha tempo statuito dovere jeiunar questo he chiaro per
tuta la scriptura per que non si trova que dio lo habia comandato.

64/65 como – etc.] cfr Matth. 5, 38-47; Rom. 12, 19-21; I Petr. 3, 9   68/69 como –
epistolla] cfr Rom. 13, 1-4; I Cor. 6, 1-4; I Petr. 2, 15-17

63/65 Non – etc.] cfr *1Oecolampadius*, p. 58, '... qui seipsos gladio defendunt ultionis
aviditate inque propria causa, nequamquam iuxta evangelium agunt, quod iubet, ut in
patientia possideamus animas nostras et porrigamus dexteram percutienti sinistram' as
well as *1Bucer*, p. 104, 'Sic etiam, quae de propulsione injuriae Christus vetuit, de ea
intellexit, qua quis suam caussam ulciscitur'   67/69 El – epistolla] cfr
1Oecolampadius, p. 58, 'Item iudices et magistratus seculares animadvertere in flagitiosos
et defendere patriam viduasque ac pupillos gladio, non arbitramur legi divinae
contrarium. Hoc enim non agunt suo nomine, sed vicarii Dei sunt et ab illo gladium,
non a seipsis acceperunt'; cfr *1Bucer*, p. 104, 'Quae per magistratus fiunt, dei sunt
judicia, non hominum. Haec cum pater praeceperit ut bona et necessaria, filius
prohibere non potuit tamquam mala, unum enim sunt'

---

62 C. 10.] *T in marg.*   63 licito] lecito *b*   del] d'l *b*   jnimico jnsorte] inimico in sorte *b*
h, inimico insorte *n v*   64/65 La – etc.] *non extat in h*   64 propossicione]
propossitione *b*   et] he *b corr.*   en sancto] ensancto *n v*   matheo] Matheo *b*   65 Et –
paulo] et ... Paulo *b*   e ensancto] e en sancto *b*, eensancto *n v*   pietro] Pietro *b*
66 C. 11.] *T in marg.*   67 delinquenti] *atramento erasus*; deliquenti *h*, de li quenti *n v*
67/69 La – epistolla] *non extat in h*   68 propossicione] propossitione *b*   havemo]
havemc *n*   paulo] Paulo *b*   Corint.] 1 Corint. *suppl. b*   68/69 e ensancto pietro] e en
sancto Pietro *b*   70 C. 12.] *T in marg.*   71 El] Il *b*   statuito] statuto *h*   dovere] devere *b*
n v   jeiunar questo] jeiunar. Questo *b*, jeunar; questo *h*   72 tuta] tutta *h*   scriptura
per que] scriptura, perque *h*

C. 13.

El matremonio non he proibito ha alcuno de quallunque stato ho ordine
75 che sia.

C. 14.

Quicunque proibisse el matrimonio a quelli que el volleno ensegnano
doctrina diabolica.

| C. 15.

122

80　　Ordinare stato hovero ordine de verginita he doctrina diabolica.

73/78 C. 13. – diabolica] cfr *¹Oecolampadius*, p. 58, 60, 'Porro quod illis prohibentur
coniugia, non arbitramur esse ex spiritu Christi; neque enim donum illud summum et
angelica vita in carne plurimis concessum est. Unde fit, ut multorum conscientiae male
habeant, et gravissima oriantur offendicula. Ne tanti faciamus, fratres, aestimationem
sanctimoniae cum tanto periculo! Est et in coniugio continentia, quae multum Deo
placet. Fuerunt et prophetae et apostoli coniugati et nihilominus in ministerio verbi
diligentissimi. Coniugium non perdit sacerdotes, sed ignavia, amor ventris ac metus
crucis'; cfr *¹Bucer*, p. 76, 78, 'Permittitur igitur cuique liberum, vel connubium amplecti
vel caelibatum, ut quemque dominus impulerit, vivantque apud suos, qui caelibatum
sibi deligunt, quo inter suos serviant, nec otiosum caelibatum, quod papistarum est,
colant, tum etiam quo mutare illum minore offendiculo queant, dum ratio poscit. Hic
natus est error humani generis, admirari quae insolentia, non quae utilia sunt, et
innumera mala orbi invexit. Si quis honorabile connubium fastidit, si cibos quos deus
creavit ad sumendum, non sumit, si praeter hominum conditionem aliquid facit, quae
omnia et satan et satanae discipuli possunt, tantum non adoratur pro deo et plus quam
angelicam sanctimoniam adferre creditur'　**79** C. 15.] the erasures of chapters 15 and
17 have been described as made by a later hand in *b*. This argument is based on the
difference between the text's ink and the erasures' ink. See Comba, 'Relazione
originale', p. 266　　**80** Ordinare – diabolica] cfr *¹Oecolampadius*, p. 58, 60, 'Idipsum
etiam sentimus de virginibus coenobitis, quae nonnunquam, quia uruntur, in pessimas
tentationes, incidunt, quibus esset satius nubere, non obstante stulto et infideli voto,
quod nec ligat nec a Deo approbatur. Etenim ubi in illis irrepit tanta hypocrisis,
periclitatur simul tota ipsorum religio, amarescitque omne, quod antea dulce in
Christo, et durum fit, quod antea leve erat iugum. Nos sane virginitatem maximi

---

73 C. 13.] *T^{in marg.}*　　**74** matremonio] matrimonio *b*　proibito] prohibito *h*　de] d' *b*
75 che] ch' *b*, que *h*　**76** C. 14.] *T^{in marg.}*　　**77** proibisse] prohibisse *b h*　el¹] deest *h*
a quelli] aquilli *h*　volleno ensegnano] volleno, ensegnano *h*　ensegnano] ensegnanno
b　**79/80** C. – diabolica] *atramento erasus*　**79** C. 15.] *T^{in marg.}*　**80** stato – verginita]
stato honorato cum ordine de verginita *h*　de verginita] d'virginità *b*

C. 16.

Coluy che non ha el dono de continencia he obligato al matrimonio. Le conclussione asay sono manifeste jnquanto ala doctrina prima noy havemo nel gen. che non he bon ahlomo que el sia solo. La 2ª he chiara como havemo en sancto paulo I Timoteo 4 c. La 3ª encara emanifesta perque he sencza fondamento de lescriptura. La 4ª he verissima cosi como scrive paulo ali corinti al 7 dela prima.

C. 17.

Non tuta usura he proibita de dio. Questo è chiaro perche dio non proibisse sinon lusura che agrava el proximo como contiene la lege non fare ha altro quello che non voresti che fosse facto atte.

83/84 noy – solo] cfr Gen. 2, 18   84/85 como – Timoteo 4 c.] cfr I Tim. 4, 3   86/87 La – prima] cfr I Cor. 7, 1-6   90/91 non – atte] cfr Matth. 7, 12

facimus, sed fictam Deo abominabilem scimus. Absit autem, ut propter pauperes et continentes in matrimonio quam divites in foedo coelibatu esse'   89/91 Non – atte] cfr *Oecolampadius*, p. 56, 58, 'Similiter non ita austeri sumus, ut omnes mutuantes et aliquid inde recipientes usurarios dicamus; Christus enim avaritiam mentis damnat, quam nos non videmus. Alia praecepta omnia per legem charitatis interpretari nos vult'; cfr *Bucer*, p. 108, 'De usura in quinto Matthaei multa disserimus. Omnis usura, quae proximum premit, prohibita est, ubi autem quis ex alterius labore partis lucrum usum facit, hoc est, usuram percipit, debet utrique proximo suo, cujusque labore lucrum fecit, ex eo aliquid impertire. Sic fiet, ut pecuniam de pecunia accipere non sit semper usura prohibita.... Atqui ubi ad sustinendam vitam datur mutuum, quod proximus mox in alimenta convertit, non lucratur inde, id debet dari, etiamsi nulla spes sortis sit, aut ullius responsionis. Quaecunque dominus Matth. 5 et Luc. 6 de his praecepit, huc instituta sunt, ut gratuito doceret proximis benefacere, ab ipso Domino expectaturi mercedem'

---

81 C. 16.] *T in marg.*   82 che non] ch'non *b*   che] que *h*   continencia he] continentia he *b*, contenencia, he *h*   82/87 Le – prima] *non extat in h*   83 manifeste jnquanto] manifeste. Inquanto *b*   85 paulo] Paulo *b*   Timoteo 4 c.] 3 c. *b*   encara] è chiara *b* emanifesta] e manifesta *b n*   sencza] senza *b*   86 de lescriptura] d'la scriptura *b* verissima] certissima *b*   cosi] così *b*   paulo ali corinti] Paulo ali Corinti *b*   87 dela] d'la *b*   88/91 C. 17. – atte] *atramento erasus*   89 tuta] tota *h*   chiaro perche] chiaro, perche *h*   89/90 proibisse – agrava] prohibisse si non l'usura que agrava *h* 90 sinon] si non *b h*   che] ch' *b*   proximo como] proximo, coma *h*   lege non] lege: non *h*   91 che¹] ch' *b*, que *h*   voresti] voressi *h*   che²] que *h*   atte] a te *b*, a tu *h*, acte *n v*

C. 18.

Le parolle che sono en sancto luca dantes etc. non se jntende de usura. Le propossicione he chiara perque Cristo non voleva dire altro he ensegnare
95 sinon el modo que devemo tenere con el nostro proximo eprestare luno alautro en lo officio di carita che devemo exercitare luno alaltro czo e che dovemo non solamente prestar | ha poveri ma donare se la necessita el requere.   123

C. 19.

Tucti quelli que sono stati et siano salvati sono preelleti avanti la costitu-
100 tione del mondo.

C. 20.

Quelli que sono salvati non possono essere non salvati. La 1ª he chiara como havemo en sancto paulo ali hephitian c. 1. La 2ª encora ali Romanj ne 8, 9 etc. cap.

---

93 Leᶦ – usura] cfr Luc. 6, 34   99/100 Tucti – mondo] cfr Eph. 1, 4   103 como – c. 1.] cfr Eph. 1, 4-6   103/104 La – cap.] cfr Rom. 8, 29-30; 9, 14-18

102 Quelli – salvatiˢ] cfr ²*Bucer*, p. 136, 'Donca cum dio haya predestina li ben celestial tant solament a li bon, e aquilh bon non pon essere degita e car non pon esser entendent las cosas celestials'

---

93 Leᶦ – usura] Le parolle que son en sancto Luca danter. 2. (?) non se intende de usura *h*   che] ch' *b*   jntende] intende *b h n v*   93/94 Le proposicione] La proposicione *b*   94 perque] perche *h*   95 el modo] deest *h*   devemo] d'vemo *b*, d'veon *h*   eprestare luno alautro] e prestare l'uno alautro *b*, e prestare l'un a l'autro *h*
96 di carita che] di carità ch' *b*, de carita, que *h*   luno – cheˢ] l'uno al altro czoe ch' *b*, l'uno a l'altro, czo e, che *h*   czo e] czoe *b v*   97 prestar] prestare *h*   poveri – la] poveri, ma donare si la *h*   necessita] necessità *b*   98 C. 19.] Tⁱⁿ ᵐᵃʳᵍ·   99 Tucti] Tuti *b h n*   que] ch' *b*   et] e *h*   siano] serano *b h n*   salvati – constitutione] salvati, sono predestinati ananti la constitution *h*   101 C. 20.] Tⁱⁿ ᵐᵃʳᵍ·   102 que] ch' *b*   salvati non] salvati, non *h*   possono] posseno *b h n v*   essere] esser *h*   102/104 La – cap.] *non extat in h*   103 paulo] Paulo *b*   hephitian] hephesian *b*   encora] enculca *b*   Romanj] Romany *b*   104 cap.] *non extat in b*

CONCILIUM CAMPI FORANEI – 1532

105

C. 21.

Quicunque statuise elibero arbitrio dinegua jntuto la predestinatione et la gratia de dio. Questo epiu che chiaro como havete ali romani cosi pertuta la epistola ali galati per tuto ali ephesi encora.

C. 22.

110   Li menistri dela parolla de dio non si debeno mutare de loco jnloco sinon que sia agrande utilita dela chiesa.

106/107 Quicunque – dio] cfr [1]*Oecolampadius*, p. 62, 'Liberum arbitrium, quatenus gratiae repugnat, non approbamus, neque propterea necessitatem peccandi inducimus. Qui enim peccant, sponte et voluntarie peccant. Orignale peccatum suam rationem habet. Neque propterea, quia tot praecepta ponuntur, maior nostra virtus est, sed magna vis Spiritus, per quem operamur voluntatem Dei, et magna nostra ignavia, propter quam indigni censemur. Est quidem fati ratio apud Deum, quod immutabile, etiamsi omnia vobis mutabilia appareant. At non oportet vos ad arcana Dei attendere, sed ad verbum eius, cui fidem habere debemus, per quod et salvabimur. Praedestinationem negare non possumus; falli eam non posse certissimum est'; cfr [2]*Bucer*, p. 130, 132, 'Acer lo liberale arbitre es en aquisti: ilh amenon, non solament son amena. Ilh slegisson librament czo qu'es, mas emperczo totas aquestas cosas son dons e obras de christ, regenerant e amenant e formant enaysi per lo seo sperit. Mas dio dona la fe e quant ela es veraya, eneyra tota bona obra de si, las quals tant coma son plus resplandent enapres alcun, de tant declayron plus grant delition de dio en luy.... Las nostras obras non son bonas si non que sian faytas de fe. Si aquesta es cum nos, nos sen ja fayt salf. Ephesia 2: mas nos sen amena a la deleytacion plena de la salu per las bonas obras. Dont quant dio parlla cum nos enayma cum enfans, appella marczi que sec / / las bonas obras, ben que segua de gracia e non de nostre merit' **110/111** Li – chiesa] cfr [1]*Oecolampadius*, p. 58, 'Deinde neque hoc videtur ex mente apostolorum, ut singulis trienniis mutetis ministros verbi in alia loca. Discrimen enim est inter apostolos et pastores. Apostoli mittuntur, episcopi et pastores cum suis ovibus manere debent. Ita constituit apostolus presbyteros oppidatim, quamvis pro apostolis visitatores utilissime constituantur'; cfr [1]*Bucer*, p. 82, 'Commutari ministros pro utilitate Ecclesiarum placet, ubi id secus accidat, peccatur in libertatem christianam, quae poscit ut omnibus rebus libere ad aedificationem utamur, nec certis regulis, quae non semper utiles sunt, nos addicamus; hoc enim papistarum est, qui elementis mundi rursus servire volunt Christo neglecto. In omnibus rebus nostris hoc in primis exquirendum: an quid regnum Christi promoveat?'

---

105 C. 21.] *supplevi, suppl. b*   **106/107** Quicunque – dio] Quicunque statuit libero arbitrio, denega in tuto la predestination e la gracia de dio *b*   **106** Quicunque] Quicunqne *b*   statuise] statuisse *b*   dinegua jntuto] denegua intute *n*, denegua intuto *b v*   **107/108** Questo – encora] *non extat in h*   **107** epiu] e piu *b n v*   pertuta] per tuta *b*   **109** C. 22.] $T^{in \ marg.}$ **110** menistri] ministre *h*   dela] de la *b h*   debeno]

310 CONCILIUM CAMPI FORANEI – 1532

C. 23.

Havere li menistri per nutrire la sua familha qualque cosa jnparticulare non he contra la communione apostolica. Queste due conclusione sono chiare como havemo neli acti deli apostoli.

| Circa la materia de li sacramenti he stato concluso per la scriptura che noy non havemo sinon doy segni sacramentali che Christo ne ha lasati luno he il baptismo laltro sie la heucarestia laquale noy Usemo en demostramento la perseveracion nostra nela fede la quale havemo promesso nelo baptismo essendo filholi. Et ancora alamemora dequello grande beneficio che Jesu Cristo hà facto anoy morendo per la redentione nostra elavando noy del suo pretioso sangue. Pertanto fratelli da poy che estato el bon piasere de dio de congregare

---

115 como – apostoli] cfr Act. 2, 44; 4, 32; 6, 1-4   **116/119** Circa – fede] cfr Matth. 10, 22; 24, 13; Marc. 13, 13   **119/120** la – filholi.] cfr Gal. 3, 26-27   **120** alamemora – beneficio] cfr Luc. 22, 19; I Cor. 11, 25   **121/122** morendo – sangue] cfr Apoc. 1, 5

113/115 Havere – apostoli] cfr *1Oecolampadius*, p. 60, 'Poterint nihilominus bona ministrorum omnia esse communia, communiter ali liberi et uxores, et sui quibusque iniungi labores'; cfr *1Bucer*, p. 80, 82, 'Quod ministri habent inter se omnia communia, sic probamus, ut tamen velimus vos vobis non hoc nomine sed dilectionis, quae sola omnia rite communia facit, apostolorum imitatores videri. Optamus quoque abesse superstitionem. Apostoli enim, dum usus ferret, utebantur rebus in communi, ubi minus habebat quisque sua, et tamen non ut sua. Dum igitur, charitati hoc vestrum institutum conduxerit, probandum est, dum minus, non est capturanda christiana libertas.... Placet tamen ut ministris prospiciatur, ne victus cura a causa Evangelii avocentur'

---

debino *b*   mutare] mutar *h*, putare *n*   jnloco] in loco *b h*   sinon] se non *b* **111** agrande] a grande *b*, a granda *h*   utilita] utilità *b*   dela] de la *h*   **112** C. 23.] *T in marg.*   **113** Havere li menistri] Haver li ministri *h*   jnparticulare] in particulare *b*, in particulari, *h*   **114** communione] communion *h*   **114/115** Queste – apostoli] *non extat in h*   **114** conclusione] conclusioni *b*   **116** per – scriptura] *deest h*   **116/117** che noy] ch'noy *b*, que nos *h*   **117** sinon] si non *h*   segni – lasati] signi sacramentals, che Cristo noy ha lasat, *h*   che] ch' *b*   lasati] lassati *b*   **117/118** luno – laquale] l'uno he il baptismo laltro sie la heucarestia laquale *b*, l'uno he il baptismo, l'altro sie la heucaristia, laqual *h*   **118** Usemo] usemo *b h n v*   **119** perseveracion] perseverancia *h*   **119/120** nela – dequello] ne la fede la quale havemo promisso nelo baptesimo essendo filholi, et ancora a la memora de quello *b*, en la fen, de laqual havemo promisso in lo baptismo essendo filholi, e ancara a la memoria da quello *h* **120** filholi. Et] filholi, et *b*, filholi Et *v*   beneficio che] beneficio ch' *b*, beneficio, que *h* Jesu] Jesù *b*   hà] ha *b h n v*   **121** anoy morendo] a noy morendo *b*, a noy, morendo *h* elavando noy] e lavando noy *b*, e lavando nos *h*   **121/122** pretioso sangue] sprecioso sangui *h*   **122** sangue. Pertanto] sangue pertanto *b*, sangue, pertanto *v*   **122/123** Pertanto – scriptura] *non extat in h*   **122** che estato] ch'e stato *b*   el] il *b*   dio] Dio *b*

CONCILIUM CAMPI FORANEI – 1532

ne insieme per la soa sanctissima scriptura et que mediante il suo adiutorio siamo venuti aprender dichiaration dela presente conclusione et tuti siamo stati uniti et duno medessimo sperito. Et publicamente sono state exputate non comodate deli homini ma comendate del sperito sancto cosi como Veramente sono. Ve pergiuriamo | nele Viscere dela carita che da poy che noy saremo partiti de jnsieme que non ne siamo discordanti nelo jnsegnare tanto nele desuso dicte conclusione coma nela jnterpretatione dela scriptura et cosi como Uno medessimo sperito la composta faciamo che sia jnterpretata per questo medessimo sperito.

125/127 Et – sono] as in *b* this wording was transcribed partly in the masculine and partly in the feminine forms, it is unclear whether Benrath thought that this sentence referred to the delegates to the Synod or to the Synod's decisions

---

123 per] scriptura *inser. et eras. T*   **123/125** et – sperito] E que medianti el suo adjutorio siamo uniti *h*   **124** aprender] a prender *b*   dela] de la *b*   conclusione] conclusion *b*   et] en *b n v*   tuti] tuto *b*   **125** duno] in uno *b*   sperito. Et] spirito et *b*   Et – exputate] *deest h*   state] stati *b*   **126** non – sancto] non comodate de li homini ma comendati dello spirito sancto *b*, Non comendati de li homini ma comendati del spirito sancto *h*   **126/127** cosi – carita] *non extat in h*   **126** Veramente] veramente *b n v*   **127** sono. Ve] sono Ve *v*   nele] nelle *b*   Viscere] viscere *b n v*   dela carita] de la carità *b*   **127/128** che' – discordanti] ch'da poy ch'noy saremo partiti de insieme que non siamo discordante *b*, Que depoy que noy siamo partent, que non he siamo discordante *h*   **128/129** nelo – scriptura] *non extat in h*   **128** jnsegnare] insegnare *b*   tanto] tuto *b*   **129** desuso] de suso *b*   conclusione] conclusioni *b*   coma] come *b*   jnterpretatione] interpretatione *b*   dela] de la *b*   **129/131** et – sperito] et cosi como uno medesimo spirito la composta faciamo che sia interpretata per questo medesimo sperito *b*, E cosi como suo medissimo spirito la composta, faciamo che sia interpretata per aquesto medissimo spirito *h*   **130** Uno] uno *b n*   medessimo] medesimo *b n v*

SYNODUS TIGURINA

1532

edidit
Emidio CAMPI

THE *PREACHERS' AND SYNODAL ORDINANCE* OF THE REFORMED CHURCH OF ZURICH
1532

INTRODUCTION

Zurich, a free city of the Holy Roman Empire, joined the Swiss Confederation in 1351 and it became home to another pattern of Reformation which had little more than an indirect debt to Luther. The chief reformers of the city were Ulrich Zwingli (1484-1531) and Heinrich Bullinger (1504-1575). Following the so-called First Disputation of Zurich (29 January 1523), Zwingli obtained the city council's permission 'to continue to preach the holy Gospel as heretofore, and to proclaim the true, divine Scriptures until he was better informed'. (1) This helped pave the way to the birth of the Reformed Church of Zurich. Further steps taken in 1524 and 1525 combined ecclesiastical reform with measures of social welfare. Along with the removal of images, the dissolution of religious houses, the replacement of the Mass with a simple Communion service, and the reconstitution of the cathedral school as both a grammar school and a theological college (*Prophezei*) to train Reformed pastors, the city council introduced a marriage court (*Ehegericht*) to supervise the moral life of the town as well as one of the most effective bodies of poor relief (*Armenfürsorge*) of the sixteenth century. (2)

The Zurich reformers introduced in the Reformed tradition a new institution which they called the Synod, in the manner of the ancient provincial and diocesan synods. Although the association of synodal government with reform was well established in the Middle Ages – particularly in the diocese of Constance under whose ecclesiastical jurisdiction the *Ecclesia Tigurina* fell – the Synod, as it came to function in and for the Reformed Church of Zurich, was something different. A Synod is a formal assembly of the clergy meeting at regular but infrequent intervals; in Zurich, however, it was held

---

(1) *Die Erste Zürcher Disputation (1523)*, in *CR*, vol. 88 (1905), p. 442-471, especially p. 471, no. 1-3.

(2) Gordon, *Swiss Refomation*, p. 46-71; Gäbler, *Zwingli*, p. 61-84; F. E. Sciuto, *Ulrico Zwingli: la vita, il pensiero, il suo tempo (Geminae Ortae* 9), Naples 1980, p. 189-248 and 249-337; Campi, 'Reformation in Zurich', p. 76-80.

twice a year and attended by the clergy and the representatives of the town magistrates, including the *Bürgermeister* and the *Stadtschreiber*, the principal city clerk. (³) The purpose of this gathering was to exercise legislative authority and jurisdiction in all matters affecting the general interest of the Church and to regulate the life and preaching of pastors.

The first 'reformed' Synod of Zurich gathered on 21 April 1528; it then met regularly under Zwingli's supervision until his death in the Second War of Kappel (October 1531). (⁴) At this first meeting, Zwingli jotted down agenda items for discussion which included the following points:

1) That the resolutions made at Bern (⁵) should be made public and that the preachers in Zurich will preach in accordance with them.

2) The assembly will consider the life and morals of the pastors and where there are questions individuals will give account of themselves.

3) The pastors may then say whether their oaths have been in any way challenged.

4) The members of the congregation who are present may then bear witness.

5) Answer is made to the Anabaptists.

6) The lives of the deacons and helpers are examined.

7) Encouragement is given to all.

8) Suggestions are made about preaching against usury. (⁶)

The records of the synods held between 1528 and 1531 give the impression of meetings characterized by lively discussions among pastors on a wide variety of subjects concerning Church reform, e.g. festive days of the Church; the persistence of Roman Catholic forms of worship; problems posed by Anabaptists. But they also show the breadth and frankness of the debates between clergy and magistrates over Church polity as well as social issues, e.g. directives against gambling or alcohol consumption and the difficulties connected to

---

(3) See the mandate of the city council from 8 April 1528 in Egli, *Actensammlung*, p. 597, no. 1383.

(4) Egli, *Actensammlung*, p. 600-610, no. 1391.

(5) The Disputation of Bern took place in January 1528 and led to the immediate implementation of the Reformation in Bern (ed. P. Hildebrand, see p. 89-103).

(6) The text of the *Synodalordnung* of 21 April 1528 is in Egli, *Actensammlung*, p. 602-603, no. 1391 and in *CR*, vol. 93/1 (1961), p. 533-534. The English translation is found in Biel, *Doorkeepers*, p. 57. The list of the pastors who attended the Synod, along with its proceedings, are published in Egli, *Actensammlung*, p. 603-610, no. 1391.

their implementation, payment of tithes, and marriage requirements for young couples. (7)

Zwingli's death on the battlefield of Kappel engendered crisis in the newborn Reformed Church, and brought the internal political tensions that had developed immediately before and during the war to their apex. (8) A large portion of the population of both the town and the countryside, albeit amenable to the Reformation, was dissatisfied with the adventurous religious policies that had determined the course of events in the Republic over the previous two years. Preachers and lay supporters belonging to Zwingli's close circle, who had sponsored the war, represented ideal scapegoats. Thus, not only did their opponents demand the expulsion of Zwingli's radical supporters from both levels of the city council: they also called for stricter methods of supervision of the clergy's dealings as well as the formal exclusion of pastors from any political decision. In an effort to combine faithfulness to religion and *raison d'état*, on 10 February 1532 the city magistrates officially ratified these demands.

On 9 December 1531, just two months after Zwingli's death, a memorable joint session of the Grand and Small council of Zurich bestowed upon a 27-year-old religious refugee from Bremgarten the difficult responsibility to lead the newborn Reformed Church. His name was Heinrich Bullinger. (9) The delicate reorganisation of the Zurich Church began in October 1532, when Bullinger, assisted in this task by Leo Jud, drafted the *Prädikanten- und Synodalordnung* (*Preachers' and Synodal Ordinance*), which gave an institutional form to the religious arrangement accompanying his appointment as chief pastor (*antistes*) of the Zurich Church. The *Ordinance* was approved by the Synod held on 22 October 1532 and published by the city council on 6 November 1532 with a confirmation of the magistrates (*Bewilligung und confirmation eines Bürgermeisters und ersamen kleinen und grossen Rates der stadt Zürich*). It remained operational until the end of the *ancien régime*, before a new Church order was introduced in 1802, reflecting the fact that the substance and the purpose of the Synod's meetings had changed.

(7) Gordon, *Clerical Discipline*, p. 73-78.

(8) H. Meyer, *Der Zweite Kappeler Krieg: die Krise der Schweizerischen Reformation*, Zurich 1976; Id., 'Krisenmanagement in Zürich nach dem Zweiten Kappeler Krieg', *Zwingliana* 14 (1977), p. 349-369; Büsser, *Bullinger*, vol. 2 (2005), p. 10-19.

(9) The standard biography is Büsser, *Bullinger*, vol. 1 (2004), p. 93-107.

318 SYNODUS TIGURINA – 1532

The text of the *Ordinance* is divided into three parts. ([10]) A first section concerns the calling and training of pastors; the second part concerns the life, learning, and duties of pastors; the last section outlines the rules of order and procedure of the Synod. The fact that in 1532 – a year after he took the office of *antistes* – Bullinger felt compelled to draft the *Ordinance* stands as testimony to the need to codify the agenda and to broaden the scope of the Synod. Bullinger was convinced that a Synod was necessary to govern the Church, which partly explains the speed at which the Zurich Synod was reshaped in the process of institutionalisation of the Church, as well as why it ultimately became an essential body in the political structure of the state. The half-yearly meetings of the Synod retained their original structure. It was a gathering of roughly 150 ordained pastors and professors of theology who resided in Zurich's territory and was also attended by seven members of the city council (four from the Grand council and three from the Small council), the *Bürgermeister* and the *Stadtschreiber*. The composition of this body, over which Bullinger presided for 43 years as the head of the Reformed Church of Zurich, reveals the strategic goals of this early Reformed *Ordinance*. The Synod was the place where clergy and magistrates together exercised their shared responsibilities in the administration of the Church.

It may come as a surprise that synodal discussions were not focused either on theological matters or on issues over Church administration and funding. The schedule included the following items:

1) The *invocatio*, praying God to send His blessing upon the gathering.

2) The *catalogus*, or the drafting of a list of attendees.

3) The *sacramentum*, by which newly-ordained preachers swore their synodal oath.

4) Procedures dedicated to the *externi* determined whether any guests from other churches or whom among the laity were allowed to participate in the Synod.

5) Afterwards, the delegates of both levels of the city council (*senatus*) brought forward initiatives or admonitions from their commissions; at this moment, pastors were also allowed to address the magistrates.

6) The *censura* – the main business of the Synod – consisted of an evaluation of each pastor's conduct and performance in his office, including the *antistes*. The synodal proceedings of Bullinger's times show that order and discipline were poor. The Synod's punitive measures ranged from fraternal

---

(10) The text is found in Egli, *Actensammlung*, p. 825-837, no. 1899; a new critical edition is available in Campi – Wählchli, *Zürcher Kirchenordnungen*, vol. 1, p. 129-150, no. 59.

admonition to public rebuke to reassignment to another congregation. When there was no hope for improvement, a pastor was discharged from the ministry.

Unlike in Geneva, the Zurich Reformed Church was prevented from developing an independent ecclesiastical discipline. This power was exercised jointly by the civil and ecclesiastical authorities, and *de facto* by the city council and the Examiners' Committee (*Examinatorenkonvent*). The original function of this body was to examine candidates for the ministry and to ordain them; but the Committee was also the highest court in the Church of Zurich and was entrusted with the oversight of the whole institution. It was composed of four members of the city council (two from the Grand and two from the Small), three pastors serving in town parishes, two professors of theology, and two archdeacons from the *Grossmünster*. Thanks to his extraordinary longevity as *antistes*, Bullinger shaped the theory and practice of pastoral training and greatly influenced the recruitment policies of the Zurich Church.

Other ecclesiastical and political bodies collaborated with the Synod in its disciplinary effort. The marriage and morals court (*Ehe- und Sittengericht*) was responsible for the supervision and preservation of morals in town, while the countryside fell under the jurisdiction of another court, the so-called *Stillstände*. (11) This name was used until 1798 for lay Church wardens, as this group literally 'stood still' after the worship service in the Church, i.e. they remained standing while they discussed their monthly business before the pastor. In both cases, the reach of moral discipline extended far beyond ecclesiastical concerns to encompass practically every single area of life.

The membership of the Synod undoubtedly reflected the self-confidence of an urban citizenry composed of educated burghers and literate artisans proud of their own political traditions, and in particular the far-reaching power wielded by the city magistrates over the internal affairs of the Church. This, however, should not overshadow the fact that the *Ordinance*'s intentions were essentially theological. The principles of the priesthood of all believers and of Reformed ministry were the pillars lying beneath the configuration of the Synod. That the laity took upon itself to reform the Church was theologically suitable, and in turn this was perfectly compatible with a concern for the importance and dignity of the pastoral office. Yet, to fully appreciate the

---

(11) The multiple duties of this oversight authority were established in the *Stillstands-protokollen* written by individual pastors. This remains a largely underused source, not least because these notes were taken very quickly and can be very difficult to read. See http://www.staatsarchiv.zh.ch/internet/justiz_inneres/sta/de/ueber_uns/organisation/editionsprojekte/stillstand.html.

features of this new institution one must consider in particular Zwingli's and Bullinger's understanding of the relationship between the spiritual and temporal spheres, which entailed important consequences on the interactions between the Church and the civic community. ([12]) For the two reformers, Church and commonwealth were not different entities or entirely separate bodies based on fundamentally different principles; rather, they were two elements of the very same reality. Although they were entrusted with different tasks, they were inseparable and drawn upon the same paradigm of righteousness. Within this framework, it becomes crucial to secure the distinction between ministerial and magisterial functions. By virtue of the interrelatedness of the two spheres, civil magistrates must care for the well-being of the community and protect and cultivate true religion (*cura religionis*). ([13]) For the same reason, preachers are entrusted with the *Wächteramt*, the prophetic office of watching over the political community and the magistrates. Just as commonwealth and Church are inseparable (as body and soul), so a reciprocal obligation between the magisterial and ministerial office exists. Thus, the membership of the Zurich Synod made explicit what had remained implicit in the theology of Zwingli and Bullinger.

Neither the former nor the latter seem to have ever recognised the risk of political dominance over the Church. However, they made every possible effort to avoid any overlap of spiritual and secular powers, as clearly emerges in the synodal proceedings and in the texts of the orations delivered at the Synod. ([14]) Bullinger also inaugurated the unique practice of the *Fürträge* (formal addresses), which lasted well into the seventeenth century. The pastors addressed the city council in the manner of the Old-Testament prophets when they denounced abuses or could not abide by certain political decisions. The *Fürträge*, which Bullinger and his successors held at the behest of the clergy, show how difficult it was to achieve critical cooperation between the offices of minister and magistrate. ([15]) On the whole, pastors often succeeded in having

---

(12) Campi, *Shifting Patterns*, p. 60-69.

(13) T. Kirby, 'The Civil Magistrate'; Campi, 'Bullingers Rechts- und Staatsdenken'.

(14) These sources, immensely valuable for our understanding of the period, have not been thoroughly examined, let alone edited. See for example Staatsarchiv Zürich, *Synodalprotokolle*, E.ii, 1 and E.ii, 1a; Zentralbibliothek Zürich, *Sermones synodales*, MS D.220. The most important contributions on this subject are Biel, *Doorkeepers*; Gordon, *Clerical Discipline*; Büsser, *Bullinger*, vol. 1 (2004), p. 127-142; J. D. Wood, *Reforming Priesthood in Reformation Zurich*, Göttingen 2019.

(15) A large selection of these *Fürträge* is available in Bächtold, *Bullinger, Schriften zum Tage*. See Bächtold, *Bullinger vor dem Rat*.

SYNODUS TIGURINA – 1532

their voices heard, thus creating an efficient means of participating in civic debates.

The Synod so effectively developed by Zwingli and Bullinger in Zurich served as a model for Bern, St Gallen, Basel, Schaffhausen, the Three Leagues, and other Reformed churches far beyond the borders of the Swiss Confederation. This model clearly rejected the Anabaptist views that the Christian community should remain radically separate from the secular sphere, or that believers should refuse any secular or religious offices. Even more momentous for the Reformed churches was John Calvin's struggle for the independence of the Church in managing its own affairs.

EDITORIAL CRITERIA

The edition reproduces the text of the critical edition included in the *Zürcher Kirchenordnungen 1520-1675*. Biblical references found in the margins have been put in Apparatus 1, while titles of sections found in the margins have been put at the beginning of relevant sections in square brackets. For an English translation of the section of the *Ordinance* from 6 November 1532 pertaining to the Synod, see Biel, *Doorkeepers*, p. 207-212.

BIBLIOGRAPHY

SOURCES (AND THEIR ABBREVIATIONS)

Actensammlung zur Geschichte der Zürcher Reformation in den Jahren 1519-1533, hrsg. E. Egli, Zürich 1879 [= Egli, *Actensammlung*].

Heinrich Bullinger. Schriften, hrsg. E. Campi – D. Roth – P. Stotz, 7 vols, Zürich 2004-2007 [= *Bullinger Schriften*].

Heinrich Bullinger. Schriften zum Tage, hrsg. H. U. Bächtold et al., Zug 2006 [= Bächtold, *Bullinger. Schriften zum Tage*].

Heinrich Bullinger. De scripturae sanctae authoritate deque episcoporum institutione et functione (1538), hrsg. E. Campi – P. Wählchli (*Bullinger Werke*, Abt. 3: *Theologische Schriften*, 4), Zürich 2009.

Zürcher Kirchenordnungen 1520-1675, hrsg. E. Campi – P. Wählchli, 2 vols, Zürich 2011 [= Campi – Wählchli, *Zürcher Kirchenordnungen*].

LITERATURE (AND ITS ABBREVIATIONS)

W. Baltischweiler, *Die Institutionen der evangelisch-reformierten Landeskirche des Kantons Zürich in ihrer geschichtlichen Entwicklung*, Zürich 1904.

H. U. Bächtold, *Heinrich Bullinger vor dem Rat: zur Gestaltung und Verwaltung des Zürcher Staatswesens in den Jahren 1531 bis 1575*, Bern 1982 [= Bächtold, *Bullinger vor dem Rat*].

P. Biel, *Doorkeepers at the House of Righteousness: Heinrich Bullinger and the Zurich Clergy (Zürcher Beitrage zur Reformationsgeschichte* 15), Bern 1991 [= Biel, *Doorkeepers*].

F. Büsser, *Wurzeln der Reformation in Zürich*, Leiden 1985, p. 231-241.

—, *Heinrich Bullinger (1504-1575): Leben, Werk und Wirkung*, 2 vols, Zürich 2004-2005 [= Büsser, *Bullinger*].

E. Campi, 'Bullingers Rechts- und Staatsdenken', *Evangelische Theologie* 64 (2004), p. 116-126 [= Campi, 'Bullingers Rechts- und Staatsdenken'].

—, 'The Reformation in Zurich', in A. N. Burnett – E. Campi (eds), *A Companion to the Swiss Reformation*, Leiden 2016, p. 59-125 [= Campi, 'Reformation in Zurich'].

—, *Shifting Patterns of Reformed Tradition*, Göttingen 2014 [= Campi, *Shifting Patterns*].

U. Gäbler, *Huldrych Zwingli: eine Einführung in sein Leben und Werk*, Zürich ³2004 [= Gäbler, *Zwingli*].

B. Gordon, *Clerical Discipline and the Rural Reformation: The Synod in Zürich, 1532-1580*, Bern 1992 [= Gordon, *Clerical Discipline*].

—, *The Swiss Refomation*, Manchester 2002 [= Gordon, *Swiss Refomation*].

Heinrich Bullinger: Life – Thought – Influence. Zurich, Aug. 25-29,2004, International Congress Heinrich Bullinger (1504-1575), ed. E. Campi – P. Opitz, 2 vols, Zürich 2007 [= *Heinrich Bullinger: Life – Thought – Influence*].

A. Holenstein, 'Reformatorischer Auftrag und Tagespolitik bei Heinrich Bullinger', in E. Campi – P. Opitz (eds), *Heinrich Bullinger: Life – Thought – Influence. Zurich, Aug. 25-29,2004, International Congress Heinrich Bullinger (1504-1575)*, 2 vols, Zürich 2007, vol. 1, p. 177-232.

T. Kirby, 'The Civil Magistrate and the "cura religionis": Heinrich Bullinger's Prophetical Office and the English Reformation', in E. Campi – P. Opitz (eds), *Heinrich Bullinger: Life – Thought – Influence. Zurich, Aug. 25-29,2004, International Congress Heinrich Bullinger (1504-1575)*, 2 vols, Zürich 2007, vol. 2, p. 935-950 [= Kirby, 'The Civil Magistrate'].

H. Meyer, *Der Zweite Kappeler Krieg: die Krise der Schweizerischen Reformation*, Zürich 1976.

—, 'Krisenmanagement in Zürich nach dem Zweiten Kappeler Krieg', *Zwingliana* 14 (1977), p. 349-369.

B. Moeller, *Zwinglis Disputationen: Studien zur Kirchengründung in den Städten der frühen Reformation*, Göttingen ²2011.

H. A. Oberman, *Masters of the Reformation: The Emergence of a New Intellectual Climate in Europe*, Cambridge – New York 1981.

J. D. Wood, *Reforming Priesthood in Reformation Zurich*, Göttingen 2019.

MONITUM

Zürcher Kirchenordnungen 1520-1675, hrsg. E. Campi – P. Wählchli, 2 vols, Zürich 2011, vol. i, p. 129-150.

SYNODUS TIGURINA
1532

| Bewilligung und Confirmation eines Burgermeisters unnd Ersammen 129
kleinen und grossen Radts der Statt Zürich / über die Restitution und verbesserung ettlicher månglen und mißbrüchen / so sich by den Dienern des wort
Gottes zůgetragen: yetzt von dem ganntzen Synodo Zürich 22. Octobris imm
5 1532. jar gehalten / angesåhen und angenommen.

Wir Burgermeyster und Radt / unnd der groß Radt / so man nempt die
Zweyhundert der Statt Zürich. Embieten allen und yetlichen unsern Burgeren / Vôgten / Amptlüten / Landsåssen / Zůgehôrigen und verwandten / und
besunderlich den dienern / so den Gemeinden und kilchen Gottes / zů
10 verkündung sines heyligen wordts / und rechter waarer Christenlicher leer /
in unser Statt und Landschafft fürgestelt / was nammens / stands / wåsens
oder wirdigkeit die yemer sind / unsern grůß unnd geneygten willen / mit
erfordrung schuldiger und Christenlicher gehorsamigkeit. Und fůgend üch
darby zůvernemmen. Demnach der erbfygend unsers heyls / dasselb zehinde-
15 ren nie gerůwet / sunder allweg die warheit / und den rechten waaren Gottge-
felligen Gotsdienst / nit allein yetz by unseren zyten / sunder so dickest die
wålt ye bůß und besserung / und sich Gottes willen zenåhern angenommen /
mit etwas unmaassen unnd mißordnungen zeundergraben unnd zůver-
dungklen understanden. Deßhalb die gemelten diener der Christenen gemein-
20 den / diewyl etwas mångel und unordnungen yngerissen / uß schuldiger trüw
bevolhens ampts / inn bysin / ouch mit hilff und gunst unserer darzů verord-
neter Radtsfründen / sôllich / ouch künfftig mångel und gepresten damit
zůverbesseren und zůfürkommen / zů meererem ufwachs gůter Christenlicher
sitten und tugenden / ouch bekeerung unsers sündtlichen lebens und
25 versůnung Gôttlichs zornns / inn yetzgehaltnem gemeinem Synodo / diß
nachvolgend erbar gôttlich Artickel / Restitution und verbesserung uff wyter
unser gfallen uß gůtem yfer / mit bystand unnd | grund heyliger gôttlicher 130
gschrifft angesehen / geordnet / inn gschrifft verfaßt / und uns die zůverwilli-
gen und zůbeståten / hüt datum fürbracht. Und so dann all unser gemůt und
30 fürnemmen / syd bekannter warheit har (bezügen wir an Gott) allweg und
noch dahin gereicht / das wir vorab Gottes Eer / sin ewige warheit / und
damit ein fromms erbars Gott seligs leben by und under den unsern / gefür-
dern und züchten / und die Gottverletzlichen laster abstellen môchten. Und
wir in uns anders nit finden kônnen / dann das sollich nachvermerckt Chris-
35 tenlich ordnung und verbesserung Gôttlicher gschrifft und warheyt gemåß /
mit der selben begründt / ouch zů ufnung unnd pflantzung eines gôttlichen
Christenlichen låbens / hoch dienstlich syge.

328 SYNODUS TIGURINA – 1532

So haben wir sy uns gfallen lassen / mit gůtter vorbetrachtung und woler-
wegnem radt / gunst und willen daryn geben / unnd sy uß ordenlicher Oberg-
40 keits macht bekrefftigt / confirmiert / und bestǎtigt. Wellend und gebietend
ouch daruf zum ernstlichsten gemelten Dienern deß wordts / unnd sunst allen
denen / so inn unser Statt gerichten und gebietten wonhafft / und die dise
ding belangen sind: das sy sǒllich gůtt erbar Ansehungen / Ordnungen / und
Christenlich Artickel haltind / daby belybind / denen strax und styff gelǎbind
45 und nachkommind: ouch darwider nüt thůgind / redind / noch handlind / so
lieb jnen Gottes und unser huld syge / unnd sy unser schwǎre straaff vermyden
wellind. Dann sǒlte sich yemands frǎfler wiß hiewider setzen / und disem
frommen fürnǎmen nit gelǎben / der wurde empfinden / das wir darab schwǎr
mißfallen / unnd zur straaff billich ursach gehebt hettind. Deß wellend wir
50 mǎngklich hiemit gewarnet. Und damit die erhaltung diser und anderer
Christenlichen Ordnungen dem gwaltigen allergůtigsten Gott / und sinem
fürgeliebten Sun Jesu Christo/ dem es alles zů gefallen beschicht / darzů uns
und üch / inn sein gǒttlichen schütz und schirm demůtigklich bevolhen
haben. Erkennt und in Truck verfert[i]gget / des vj. tags im Wyntermonet.
55 Anno / etc. M.D.XXXII.

Und lutet die gemelt Restitution und verbesserung von wort zů wort als
hǎrnach volgt.

Ghein fryheyt wǎder geistliche noch wǎltliche mag noch kan nit durch
gǒttlich rechtmǎssig ordinantzen gefangen / verhindert oder undergetruckt
60 werden. Dann die fryheit eins frommen Christen menschen nit der aart ist /
das sy begǎre von dem gůten waaren und erberen gefryet sin. Diewyl sy von
dem bǒsen unordenlichen fry / und des gůten eygen sin / die rǎcht fryheit | 131
achtet. So dann ein gǒttlich erber ansǎhen / nützid dann zucht und alles gůts
pflantzt / mǒgend kein rechtmǎssig ordinantzen mit dem tittel der fryheit
65 abgeschupfft werden. Sunder es soll bevor bybracht werden / das das ansǎhen
an imm selbs ungǒttlich und unbillich sye. Da wir uns yetzdan bevor behal-
tend / wo es mit Gottes wort erfunden / das einer oder vil artickel unsers
volgenden ansǎhens / unbillich / und dem wort Gottes zewider wǎre / der
oder die nützid gǎlten / und nach der warheit sǒllind gebessert werden. Damit
70 die waar fryheit / gar mit gheinem menschlichen ansǎhen getrǎngt werde.

Von der waal / sendung / und hǎnduflegen der Predicanten.

Diewyl das pfarr oder predigampt das hǒchst unnd notwendigist inn der
kilchen Gottes ist / und aber bißhar groß mangel und prǎsten inn der
berůffung / waal / und sendung gewǎsen: habend wir für das erst von einer

---

54/55 des – M.D.XXXII] id est, 6 Novembris 1532

SYNODUS TIGURINA – 1532

75 verbesserung red gehalten / angesåhen / das uns Gott nit allein bevelch abze-
bråchen / sunder ouch ufbuwens gegåben hat. Darumb so mit Gottes wort die
Bischofflich wyhe / ölung und Character abgethon / ist das nåchst / das wir
das henduflegen / nach dem bevelch des Herren und Apostolischen bruch /
an des ußgerüteten Bischoflichen mißbruchs stat / ynpflantzind: welches mit
80 volgenden mittlen angesåhen.

Und so nun Paulus spricht / Niemands mißt jm selbs die eer oder verwaltung zů / sunder der von Gott berůfft wirt / wie Aaron: ouch inn den Epistlen
an Timotheum und Titum / vil hoher gaaben inn dem Pfarrer fordert: ist gar
nit göttlich noch billich / das / so ein Pfarr ledig worden / ein yeder louffe /
85 båttle / gyle / gaaben verheysse unnd gåbe / die underthonen anfåchte /
parthen an sich håncke / gantz schaaren fürbitter mit jm fůre: und da jm die
pfarr uß ansåhen gunsts / früntschafft / lyplicher diensten / oder gaaben /
verlihen werde. Dann damit åben als übel gesündet wirt wider Gott und die
waarheit / als do der Römisch hof sin Curt ůbt / und uff die | pfarren die   132
90 satzt / die jm gefielend / und die er vereeren wolt / die doch nit zun Pfarreren
geschickt: dardurch aber das gantz volck verderbt und gar verfůrt ist.

Sömliches fürohin abzestellen und ze verkummen / sind wir desse uß
Gottes wort einß worden: das wo sömlicher unbill und vorteil / wider Gottes
ordnung gebrucht / und yemands erfunden / der selbs gelüffen / sölle der selb
95 billich mit Simone dem zouberer zů sömlicher göttlicher verwaltung nit zůgelassen werden. Deßhalb das er das hoch geistlich ampt nit anders geschetzt /
dann das es jm umb gållt / gunst unnd fürschub werden sölte [Ezech. 13] / das
er sinen buch damit spyßte / und nit achtet ob er zů diser verwaltung berůfft /
begabet und geschickt sye / oder wie er die schåfly Gottes weyden wölle und
100 möge.

Wenn aber ein pfarr ledig wirt / soll dannethin der Decanus / inn deß
Capittel die pfarr gelågen / einer ersammen obergheit des pfarrers tod antragen: ouch erfaaren und bericht gåben / wer der Låhen herr sye: damit man

---

75 das – bevelch] cfr Ier. 1, 10   **76/77** Darumb – wyhe] cfr II Cor. 10, 8   **78** nach –
Herren] cfr Act. 13, 2 seq.   **79** an – ynpflantzind] cfr I Tim. 4, 14   **81** Und – spricht]
cfr Hebr. 5, 4   **83** Timotheum] cfr I Tim. 3, 1-13; 4, 6; 5, 25; II Tim. 1, 3; 4, 8   Titum]
cfr Tit. 1, 5 et 3, 11   **93/94** wider – gebrucht] cfr Ier. 23, 21   **94/95** sölle – zouberer]
cfr Act. 8, 9-25   **99** oder – Gottes] cfr Ioh. 10, 1-16

75 das – bevelch] Ier. 1, 10 was already used by Ulrich Zwingli in 'Der Hirt' in *CR*,
vol. 90 (1914), p. 23, art. 3-12 to denote the spiritual office, as well as by Heinrich
Bullinger in his *De prophaetae officio*, Zürich 1532, fol. 3r-3v, as well as in *De scripturae
sanctae authoritate deque episcoporum institutione et functione* 1538), Zürich 2009, lib. I.
See *Bullinger Schriften*, vol. 4 (2006), p. 107, art. 3-5

330 SYNODUS TIGURINA – 1532

fürderlich einen anderen pfarrer der kylchen fürstelle: ouch niemands mitt-
105 hinzů nützid an siner fryheit und geråchtigkeit abbrochen werde.

[Examen] Und so dann yemands von dem Låhenherren fürgestelt / oder
unseren gnedigen herren / da sy nit Låhenherren / fürzestellen vergünstiget /
soll der oder die so fürgestelt / jro leer und låbens halben flyssig ersůcht: und
das sômlichs fůgklich beschåhen môge / ein bestimpter tag examinis / hie inn
110 der Statt Zürych / angestelt werden: dahin die vilgenampten fürgestålten jre
manråcht oder kuntschafft jres harkummens und låbens bringind: Damit nit
etwan harverlouffen / ufrůrig / meyneyd und verlümbdet lüt / die anderstwo
jro übelthat halben vertriben / hie unbedacht und unerfaren / an sômliche
gôttliche åmpter gesetzt werdint: dero schand hernach zů schmaach deß heyli-
115 gen Evangelij reyche.

Und nach dem dann die kuntschafften von Examinatoribus erlåsen / soll
dannethin einer nach dem andern examiniert werden: es sye dann sach das
einer vor bekant / probiert / und examiniert sye / denocht soll er sich uff den
tag Examinis erzeigen. Und wie man denn einen yeden findt: also soll es in
120 einen brieff gestelt / verschlossen / und einem ersammen Radt überschickt | 133
werden / das er da nach gstalt der frommgheit und gschiktligheit eines yeden
handle und waal nåme.

Wenn aber die waal imm Radt soll fürtragen werden / sôllend die Examinati / so inn brieff gestellt / für den ersammen Radt keeren / dem ouch jre
125 mannråcht oder kuntschafft fürlegen / sich allein anzeigen / und nit bitten /
noch fürbitt mit jnen fůren: damit die waal fry / und nit nach gunst beschåhe:
also die kilch mit frommen / geleerten / und gotsfôrchtigen dienern versåhen
werde.

[Examinatores] Hie ist aber ouch das billich / das unser G[nedige] H[er-
130 ren] den Examinatoribus by jro eyden befelhind zum trülichsten on alle gfaar
allein Gottes eer und der kilchen nutz angesåhen ze examinieren. Jtem das dz
examen fürnåmlich also gehalten werde / das man für das erst Locos communes religionis anzühe. Demnach erfare wie belåsen und geůbt die fürgestelten
inn beyden Testamenten syend: was sy für ein iudicium in Scripturis habind /
135 wie sy die bruchind / låsind unnd dem volck erklårind. Und das darzů verordnet werdind zwen von den Predicanten / zwen von den Rådten / und zwen
von den Låseren der heyligen geschrifft.

[Fürstellen der Predicanten] Nach dem aber das Examen beschåhen / die
zügknuß für Radt gefertiget / die waal geoffnet / und yetzdann einer zum
140 Pfarrer verordnet / wil inn vil wåg nit gebüren / das er grad hinlouffe und
anstande: sunder jm soll einer von einem ersammen Radt / oder der Vogt deß

113/114 an – werdint] cfr I Tim. 3, 1-13

SYNODUS TIGURINA – 1532

331

selben orts zůggåben werden / unnd uff den nåchstvolgenden Sontag inn die
Pfarr keeren: dahin sóllend ouch der Decanus deß selben Capittels / und der
nåchst Pfarrer / kummen. Unnd so dann das volck versammlet / soll der so
145 von einem ersammen Radt verordnet die waal der kilchen offnen / und ermanen / ob yemands da sye / der etwas lündens unnd unredlichs uff den
erwólten wüsse / sólle das offnen.

Und so sich dann nützid erfindt / ouch kein klag ist / soll der Decanus
predgen / fürnemlich was des Pfarrers ampt / und wie sich die kilch mit und
150 gågen jm halten sólle / etc. Unnd nach der predge stelle er den Pfarrer der
kilchen für / und språche zů jm / Sich lieber brůder / dise biderbe gemeind
befålhend wir dir mit den worten Pauli / Hab gůt acht uff die gantze hård / | 134
über die dich der heilig geist zum wåchter und hirten gesetzt hat / zeweyden
sin volck / das er mit sinem eignen blůt an sich erkoufft hat. So biß jnen ein
155 vorbild imm wort / imm wandel / inn der liebe / imm geist / imm glouben
und luterkeit: unnd Gott verlyhe dir sinen heyligen geist / das du wie ein
getrüwer diener sines herren / handlist / inn dem namen Gottes. Und damit
lege er jm die hend uff. Demnach ermane das volck umm gnad anzerüffen.
Aber nach vollendetem gebått / bevelhe der Vogt oder Radtsbott den Pfarrer
160 der Gemeind inn namen der Christenlichen oberghcyt. Das sy jn bevolhen
habind / jm beholffen und beradten syend zů allem dem das sin ampt betrifft /
nit beleydigind. Ob er dann nit handlete das geschickt / nit von einem yeden
gepalget sunder der ordenlichen Oberghcit angezeigt / die jn nach gebür
straaffen: glich wie sy ouch gheinen unbeschulter sach / sines ampts entsetzen
165 wólle: ouch nach luth und sag der letsten verkumnuß zwüschen Statt und
land.

Uff sómlichs wo er noch den Eyd jm Synodo nit gethon / soll jm denocht
uff trüw unnd glouben; zepredgen vertruwt werden: doch das er in dem
nechstkünfftigen Synodo schweere.

170 Von der Leer und låben der Predicanten.

[Die Leer] So dann ouch unmaß / und allerley unordnung in dem predgen und leeren von etlichen gebrucht: daruß aber vil ergernuß / unwillens und
unradts volgt: ouch die an den anstóssen mee von dem predgen verwildet /
dann herzů gebracht werdint / habend wir uns eigentlich erinneret deß
175 bevelch Gottes und eyds den wir thůnd / allein nüw und alt Testament
zepredgen / und was darinn grund hat. / Deßhalb wir ouch abgeredt / das

---

150/151 Unnd – für] cfr Act. 13, 1-3 **152** mit – Pauli] cfr Act. 20, 28 **154/155** So –
wort] cfr I Tim. 4, 12 **159** Aber] cfr II Par. 17, 9 **162/163** nit[3] – gepalget] cfr I Tim.
5, 19 **167/168** denocht – glouben] cfr Gal. 2, 7-10 **168** zepredgen – werden] cfr
II Tim. 4, 1-5

332 SYNODUS TIGURINA – 1532

niemands jm selbs ettwas erst erdachts / mit stuckwerch unordenlicher und unnôtiger matery fürnåme: sunder das jm ein yeder uß Biblischer geschrifft das siner kilchen gmåß und notwendig ist erwôlle / das fürtrage / interpretie-
180 re / daruß leere / ermane / trôste und straaffe: und das alles mit geist / ernst und trüw / ye das hierinn unnser fleischliche anfåchtung nit gespürt: oder das wir sôliches / mit so ungebürlichen / lychten / unzüchtigen / schalckhafften schmütz oder spitzworten thûgind / das einfallte biderbe lüt abgeschreckt / unwillig / und die warheit selbs verdacht / lycht / oder verhaßt gemacht.

185 | [Straaffen]Nit das darumb die mißbrüch / aberglouben / sünd und 135 laster nit sôllind dapfferlich ye nach gestalt der sach und gelågenheit der lastern oder lasterhafften / mit ruhen / doch gschrifftmåssigen worten / angetaast und bescholten werden. Dann wôlcher wôlte den für ein predger der waarheit halten / der aller valscher religion / allen lasteren und lasterhafften
190 verschonte / klüßlete unnd zentzlete? Sunder wir wellend hiemit ein maaß bestimpt haben / und das alle ding mit dapfferem ernst / nit mit låcherlichem gspey / schmützen / schimpffen und spåtzlen beschåhind: ja das die warheyt selbs / die lütere unnd klåre der håndlen / mee tringe / zühe und überwinde / dann das unbegrünt / gschrifftloß håderig balgen: Dann nützid sterckers /
195 dann die warheit ist. So ist ghein ander ding das mee berede und überwinde / dann hålle gûtte ordnung / unnd so man ein ding mit trüw / liebe und ernst darthût. Jn summa: es soll sich ein yeder also inn handel schicken / das all unser leer und straaff zû ufbuwnuß und eren Gottes beschåhe damit wir vil menschen Gott und der gerechtigkeit gewünnind.

200 [Die Mandata] Deßglych ist abgeredt / das die Mandaten so von unsern herren wider unmaß und laster ußgangen / vil an den Cantzlen angezogen werdind / wie es sich dann ye mit dem Text zûtreyt / damit das volck zû zucht / friden / und gehorsamme ermanet / der lastern nit nun der vorcht halben / sonder ouch von liebe Gottes wågen abstande. Deßhalb soll ouch nit
205 vergåssen werden / das ein yeder jårlich / nach unser herren bevelch / die ordnung wider kupplen / hûren / eebrechen / und derley laster fürlåse. Jtem kriegen / spilen / Gotslestern / und zûtrincken / ouch unmaaß in kleyden / und andern stucken / mit dem wort Gottes / und ußgangnen Mandaten weere. Deßglych das ein yeder die sinen ernstlich zû dem kilchengang erma-
210 ne / das doch der Sabbath gehalten / und Gottes wort nit so gar verachtet wer- de. Jtem das man sich vor allem valsch / liegen und vertragen goume / inn

---

188 Dann] cfr Matth. 5, 13   **197/198** das – beschåhe] cfr II Tim. 2, 1-13 et 4, 1-5
210 das – gehalten] cfr Ex. 20, 8-11; Ier. 17, 19 seq.; Act. 13, 13-47

188 Dann] *in marg.* Matth. 5, 13: Jr sind das salz der erden

SYNODUS TIGURINA – 1532

richten / lyhen / und kouffen nit verrůcht sye was man schuldig ist / bezaale /
niemands nützid veruntrüwe / recht gwicht und maaß habe und gåbe. Dann
gemelte stuck nit minder / dann das Bapsthůmb zůbeschålten und zeverwerf-
215 fen sind: und so vil ernstlicher / sovil schådlicher sy ynbråchind.

| [Die Armen] Und so uns die Armen von Gott in sonders bevolhen /   136
habend wir wyter einandren ermanet / das ein yeder uß mitlyden / die / siner
kilchen ernstlich mit Gottes wort fürstelle: in sonders deß kilchengůts vil
gedencke / wie man es bruchen sôlle. Daby von einet ermanen / das man
220 getrülich damit umbgange: wie ouch inn unser herren mandat jårliche råch-
nung bestimpt ist: damit wir uns nit übel ann den Armen wider Gott versünd-
int / und die kilchengůter größlicher dann der Bapst / München und Pfaffen
mißbruchind.

Jn summa / das sich ein yeder fürohin mit der leer flysse / nit nun die
225 abgethonen mißbrüch zebeschålten oder da uß zebehalten / das sy nit widerumb kummind: sunder ouch Gôttlichers und das besser ist / an des hingetho-
nen mißbruchs stat / zestellen. Also das wie wir vorhin die Gôtzen / stein und
holtz bekleydt / geziert / und mit opffern und anderen kostlichen gaaben
vereeret: das wir uns yetzund über die låbenden bilder Gottes / über die
230 Armen erbarmind / die bekleydind / spysind und haltind / wie Christus
Matth[åj] am xxv. bevolhen. Wie wir vor der Måß nachgelouffen / das wir
yetzund das wort Gottes liebhabind / dem nach haltind / und uß dem selben
die frucht des lydens råcht leerind verston: damit man ouch das Nachtmal
Christi mit waarem glouben / råchter dancksagung begange. Jtem wie wir vor
235 unser heil und fromgheit uff die Ceremonien und usseren schyn gegrünt: das
wir yetzund uff Gott allein gründint / unnd den mit glouben / liebe unnd
unschuld vereerind.

Jtem wie wir vor inn der unordnung gehorsam gsin: also yetzund der
warheit und erberen gůtten gsatzten nit widerstråbind / etc.
240 [Straaff der Laastern] Und das hie das volck gebåtten / und mit Gottes
wort genôtiget werde jr unråcht unnd ungehorsamme zeerkennen: fürnemm-
lich aber in Stetten die Rådt / und uff dem Land die Ober und Undervôgt /
ouch die Elteren in den Kilchhôrinen gar trüwlich und ernstlich ermanet
ufzesåhen: damit doch die laster nit so gar überhand nåmmind / sunder nach

---

212 und – sye] cfr Col. 3, 5-11   **213** niemands – veruntrüwe] cfr Rom. 13, 7   **230/
231** wie – xxv] cfr Matth. 25, 35-40; 25, 42 seq.   **244/245** sunder – xviij] cfr Matth.
18, 15-20

220 inn – mandat] this is a reference to the ordinance of 19 May 1528 concerning the
report on ecclesiastical goods, in Campi – Wählchli, *Zürcher Kirchenordnungen*, vol. 1,
p. 60-61, no. 33

245 der leer Christi Matt[håj] am xviij. mit warnen / oder so das nit hulffe / mit
straaffen abgethon / und damit zucht und gehorsamme gepflantzt werde.

| Hierumb bitten wir ouch unsere gnedige herren zum hôchsten und umb 137
Gottes willen / das sy hie in jro Statt mit den verordneten / und uff dem Land
mit jro Ober und Undervôgten / mit ermanen oder bevelch verschaffind / das
250 die gemelten Mandaten zů der eer Gottes trüwlich und redlich gehandthabt.
Und welche dann dapffer und rechtmåssig nach der warheit und ußgangnen
Mandaten handletind / das sy die schützind / schirmind / ouch jnen fůß haltind. Dann sol das trincken / zeeren / spilen / suffen / unmaaß in essen und
kleidern fürgon / zůnåmen / unnd nit abgestelt werden / ist zesorgen / das uß
255 uns nützid werde / dann ein verhergt volck / das all sin hab liederlich
verthon / yetzt umb gålt feyl / ouch wir einandern vor armůt nützid werdint
halten / ja gar nit bezaalen / betriegen / und mit tåglichem zanggen / råchten / und ufrůren zenüty machen.

Das nun alles one zwyfel wol damit mag vermitten werden / wenn man
260 zů allen jaren / oder so man sust uff dem Land zeschweeren pflågt / die Mandaten (wie ouch vornaher gebrucht) måldete und ernüwerte: ouch den fürgesetzten und verordneten eltern in den Gemeinden by jro eyden ynbunde /
sorg zetragen / die übertretter mit trüwen zewarnen / und so ghein früntliches
nützid beschusse / anzezeygen / damit das überfaren unnd ungehorsamme
265 nach verdienst gestraafft.

[Ordnung des predgens und båttens] Jnn der ordnung aber des predgens /
habend wir ouch das ein můtigklich angesåhen / das alle und yede Pfarrer alle
Sonntag jnn jro pfarren einist am morgen vor mittag predgind: und uff die
predge die allgemein form deß gebåtts / so uns Christus Jesus Mat[thåj] am vj.
270 geleert / vormeldint: daruff ouch den Decalogum / die gebott Gottes uß dem
ij. bůch Mosis xx. cap[itel] unnd zeletst die Artickel unsers waaren Christlichen gloubens vorspråchind. Damit dise drü stuck / das Gebått / die Gebott /
und der Gloub / dem gemeinen menschen wol ynbildint.

[Kinderzucht] Jtem das die uff dem Land ouch all Sonntag umb die drü /
275 wie man vornaher die vesper gehebt / yetzdan gemein gbått und predge halt-
ind / und | die für die dienst unnd das volck das morgens vor gschåfften zur 138
predig nit kummen mag: in sunders aber für die jugend / die in sonders Gott
geeignet und zů zucht und frommkeit sol uferzogen werden. Dorumb ist
abgeredt / das diser stund meerteils sôll Catechismus gehandlet / unnd
280 einfaalt was der gloub / welchs die Artickel des gloubens / was gebåttet / unnd

---

269/270 so – geleert] cfr Matth. 6, 9-13 **270/271** uß – xx] cfr Ex. 20, 1-17
277 in¹ – jugend] cfr Luc. 18, 15-17; Deut. 6, 20-25

271/272 die – gloubens] i.e. the *Apostles' Creed*

SYNODUS TIGURINA – 1532   335

wie man båtten sôlle: Jtem welchs die gebott Gottes / und was jr innhalt und
verstand sye / erkleert werden. Das nit ettwann verrůchte mennschen funden / die wåder des gloubens noch gebåtts / unnd wie sy joch låben sôltend /
bericht syend: also ouch unwüssend zů dem Tisch des Herren gangind: sun-
285 der das ein yeder vorhin denocht bericht / wüsse was er handle / und fürohin
thůn sôlle.

Doch in disem allem ist yeder kilchen heimgesetzt / welche stunden hierzů am allerfůglichsten erwôlt: so ferr das der Catechismus uff die Sonntag
geůbt werde. So ist allen denen vergünstiget die Filialen und deßhalb ferr
290 unwåg habend / das sy den Catechismum ze Monaten einist mit flyß haltind /
und das nit übersåhind.

[Fürbitt] Das ouch nüt disterweniger in der wochen zemol einist ein
predig und gemein gebått für alles anligen der kilchen Gottes: wie es yetzund
ouch hie in der Statt am sibenden Octobris tåglich zevolfůren angesåhen /
295 gehalten werde. Deßglych die tag der heyligen Apostlen unnd andere wie sy
von unsern herren bestimpt / mit predgen wie von alter har versåhen.

[Heimsůchen der krancken] Und sydmal der vynd unsers heils den menschen nimmer grusammer anfiht / dann inn der kranckheit und stund des
todts: deßhalb der mensch nimmermee trosts underricht und sterckung /
300 dann imm todtbett bedarff: habend wir unns erinnert der leer Jacobi am v. das
füro hin ein yeder Pfarrer die sinen (wo man anders sin begårte) besůchen /
die krancken trôsten und berichten sôlle / båtten / und von verzyhung / von
dem erlôsen Christi / von der urstendy und eewigem låben reden / das sich die
krancken dultigklich inn willen Gottes ergåbind / und fürohin der zytlichen
305 dingen vergessind / etc.

| [Die todten] Deßglych das ein yeder sin kilchen ermaane / das man die   139
krancken besůche / die werck der barmhertzigkeit erzeige / sy trôste / jnen
beholffen und beraten sye. Und so sy abgestorben / mit zucht und Christenlicher demůt / als mitgnossen der urstendy Christi / eerlich bestatte: und die
310 demnach (wie bruch ist) der kilchen verkünde / etc.

[Diaconi] Hierzů sôllend fürohin alle Diaconi / so sy vonn den Pfarreren
gefordert / beholffen sin / es sye dann mit predgen / zůdienen der Sacramenten / mit heimsůchen der krancken. Es ist ouch luter abgeret / das niemands
fürohin yemands ungeordneten und unbekannten / dem volck an die Kant-
315 zlen fürstellen sôlle: damit das ouch hie dem Evangelio ghein nachteyl
entstande.

---

300 Jacobi am v] cfr Iac. 5, 13-18   **309** als mitgnossen] cfr Act. 8, 2 seq.   **313**/
314 das – ungeordneten] I Tim. 3, 1-13

336 SYNODUS TIGURINA – 1532

[Kilchendienst / und zůdienen der Sacramenten] Wyter. habend wir ermåssen / das tråffenlich nottwendig sin wil / das alle diener des worts unnd der kilchen / grossen ernst inn den diensten der kilchen gebruchind. Dann so
320 die Diener one ernst jro ampt verwaltend / ist ghein wunnder ob schon ouch das volck nit nun die Diener / sunnder ouch die heiligen ding selbs verachtet. Dorumb wenn die kilch zesamen kumpt / die predig zehören / unnd zebåtten: so flysse sich mengklich des ernsts: das / wie das wort der warheyt ein ernst ist / also ouch des Dieners wanndel ernsthafft sye. Ouch das das volck vom
325 schwåtzen zum gebått gehalten werde. Ouch imm zůdienen der heyligen Sacramenten / die leer und das zůdienen gemåß sye hoher heiliger geheimnuß. Nit das man von den Sacramenten rede / wie von gemeinem zeichnen: und demnach den Touff gåbe / samm man one geheimnuß die kind mit gemeinem wasser begiesse. Oder also das Nachtmol Christi zůdiene / samm man sunst
330 gmein brot und wyn åsse und trincke: sunder es ist billich das man mit der leer / in sonders / wenn man dz Nachtmol begon wil / ouch sust wenn es sich von Sacramenten zereden begibt / eigentlich erklåre / das mengklich die hohen geheimnuß unnd heiligen pflicht der Sacramenten verstande / unnd dannethin mit glouben / ernst / und råchter andacht sy gebruche / in sunders
335 Gott umb gnad bitte / und umb syne gůtthåten dancksage. Dann die Corinther mit tod und kranckheyten gestraafft wurdint / das sy das Nachtmol Christi nit inn der wirde hieltend / inn dero sy es billich gehalten håttind. Und so der Bapst zevil daran gethon / und gestraafft worden / wirt ouch Gott uns | nit verschonen / wenn wir die Sacrament zevil verkleinern / und nit 140
340 recht bruchen wurdint. Darumb gedenck ein yeder das er nach abgethonem mißbruch / ghein annderen mißbruch / sunder den råchten bruch / nach vermög der gschrifft / råcht und wol ynpflantze. [Die Ee bestått en] Deß glych ouch mit dem ynfüren und beståten der Ee ernst bruche / damit die heilig ordnung Gottes unsers lychtfertigen diensts / by den einfallten / nit in argkw-
345 hon kumme: sunder wie die formen zebåtten / die Ee zebeståten: ouch die Sacrament den Touf und Nachtmol Christi zů zedienen / uß der gschrifft gestelt / den ernst und geist der gschrifft herfür tragend: also wir ouch gedenckend / das wir der gschrifft und geist Gottes diener sind. Hie ist ouch eigentlich beschlossen / das / irrung unnd spån / ouch valsch zevermyden /
350 gheiner unerloubt dem anderen die sinen ynfüren sölle.
[Låben und wandel der Predicanten] Also können d wir ouch wol erkennen / das nützid grössere verachtung der Predicanten gebirt: dann so sy sich selbs mit unordenlichem wandel befleckend und ze nüty machend. So aber die

---

323 das¹ – warheyt] sicut in Ps. 119, 43; II Cor. 6, 7; Eph. 1, 13; Col. 1, 5; II Tim. 2, 15; Iac. 1, 18 **335** die Corinther] cfr I Cor. 11, 30

SYNODUS TIGURINA – 1532

verachtung der Predicanten zů verkleinerung der predigy reichen wil / ouch
355 gantzer kilchen Gottes ergerlich unnd schådlich ist / wenn die Pfarrer inn
unmaaß / trunckenheit / üppigheit / unzucht in worten / wysen und geber-
den verschreyt / oder dero mittgsellen / die inn obernempten unrådten
verargwhont sind: ouch mit kleidung / weery / unnd anderem usserlichem
wandel sich der maassen gstaltind / das man ein lycht üppig gmůt ann usseren
360 zeichen spüren mag: habend wir uns hie uß hochanligender not entschlossen /
wóllend ouch die / so hierinn villycht verhafft und verargwhont / zum thüris-
ten ermant haben / das sy sich fürohin der stucken måßgind / der offnen
ober nempten verergerenden lastern abthůgind / die Wirtzhüser und gesell-
schafften (welche nit in sonders ze eeren dienend) gantz und gar vermydint: in
365 summa / das sy sich also mit reden / wandel / kleydung / und weery gestalt-
ind / das es unserm berůff und ampt gemåß / und yedem unverwyßlich sye /
ouch schynbarliche verbesserung in nåchst künfftigem Synodo spüre. Dann
treffenlich groß ist das wort des Herren / Jr sind das saltz und liecht der menschen. Also soll üwer liecht lüchten / das die menschen üwere gůte werck
370 såhind / und Gott prysind. Und das der heilig Paulus geredt / der Pfarrer sólle
heilig sin / ein züchtig fromm hußgesind haben / unnd eins unstråfflichen
wandels sin.

| [Studium und übung der Predicanten] Das ouch kein mangel und 141
gebråst ann Christenlicher leer uß unberichte ungeleerte oder unwissenheit
375 gefunden / sunder das ein yeder geschicklich / gewüß / klar / ordenlich und
mit vernunfft das wort Gottes der kilchen fürtrage / habend wir eigentlich
abgeredt / das sich mengklich / so ferr und jm lybs nodt müglich / der usseren
handarbeit entschlahe / aller usseren gwårben sich entzühe / und sich einig
uff das anrůffen zů Gott / für sin volck / und demnach uff das låsen und emp-
380 sig studieren begåbe: angesåhen das wir sómlichs in dem byspil der heiligen
Propheten un[d] Apostlen erleernt: und das Paulus von dem Pfarrer forderet /
das er also bericht unnd beredt sye / das er mit gsunder leer / leeren und ermanen / deßglych die widerfåchter überwinden / und jro valsch ans liecht herfür
zühen móge. Welches alles nit one besonderbare gnad Gottes / tråffenlichen
385 ernst / und grosse übung erlangt wirt. Dorumb dann grosser flyß notwendig
ist: in sunders / so wir fürnemlich mit der lybs narung dorumb erhalten
werdind / das wir der leer unnd aller kilchen håndlen dister baaß gewarten
mógind.

Von dem Synodo und wie der gehalten.
390 [Wenn die versammlung gehalten] Damit aber diß oberzelt ansåhen
dister baaß erhalten / ouch zucht / einigkeit / råchtmåssige ermanung und

---

367/368 Dann – Jr] cfr Matth. 5, 13-14 et 16   **370/371** der² – sin] cfr I Tim. 3, 2-4

338 SYNODUS TIGURINA – 1532

straaff under den Dienern des worts blybe: alle simulation und ambition vermitten und ußgeschlossen werde / solljårlich ein allgemeiner Synodus zweymalen hie inn unser herren Statt Zürich besammlet werden. Des ersten
395 uff nåchsten Montag nach dem Meytag: unnd zum anderen uff den nåchsten Montag nach Galli: und ob dann die zwen tag uff den Montag selbs vielend / so ist der volgend Montag bestimpt / das mengklich hie zů abind sye: damit man morndes zů gůter zyt anhebe. Hie soll ouch niemands ußblyben / one merckliche ursachen / die er sinen nåchsten mitpfarreren anzeigen. Unnd by
400 disen bestimpten tagen soll es fürohin one wyters beschryben und berüffen blyben. So môchtend ouch die zyten so rûwig werden / man wurde sich ze jar mit einem Synodo vernůgen lassen.

| [Presidenten] Jn disem Synodo sôllend zwen Presidenten verordnet wer- 142 den: einer von den Predicanten / und einer von den Rådten: welche die anfrag
405 habind / berüffind / ußstellind / anbringind und handlind. Wir bitten ouch unsere herren / das sy uns noch siben man uß jro Rådten verordnind / die by allen hånden sitzind / uns beradten und beholffen syend.

[Ordnung des Synodi] Der Synodus aber ist fürohin also angesåhen. Erstlich [1] soll man Gott umb gnad anrüffen / damit man da von siner eer / unnd
410 der kilchen heil mit ernst handlen / niemands beschwåren noch verforteylen / die warheit finden / und die yrrigen widerumb an den råchten wåg bringen môge. Das die warheit erhalten / zucht unnd alle gottseligkeit råcht gepflantzt werde / etc.

[2] Demnach låse man aller Pfarren naamen / damit man vinde welche
415 gehorsamm / und welche ungehorsamm erschynen.

Und sind die Pfarren also ußgeteylt unnd zů Capitlen verordnet volgender gstalt.

Zürich.
Das groß Münster
420 Die Lectores
S. Peter / sin Diacon
Frowenmünster / sin Diacon
Spital
Die siechen
425 Zollicken
Schwamedingen
Ryeden

---

395 Meytag] id est, Calendae Maii   **396** Galli] id est, dies sancti Galli (16 Octobris)
423 Spital] *intellege* S. Jacob   **424** Die siechen] leprosarium in Spanweid iuxta Tigurum   **425** Zollicken] *intellege* Zollikon

SYNODUS TIGURINA – 1532   339

Wytticken
Alltstetten
430 | Der See.   143
Ståfen
Humbråchtingen
Månendorff
Meylen
435 Küßnach { Herliberg // Erlibach
Richtischwyl
Wådischwyl
Horgen. Hirtzel
Dallwyl
440 Kilchberg
Das Fryampt.
Cappel
Husen
Knonow
445 Maschwanden
Rifferschwyl
Måttmenstetten
Ottenbach
Affhollteren
450 Hedingen
Bonstetten
Stallickon
Birmensdorff
Steiner cap[itel].
455 Stein
Stammheym
Ossingen
Trüllickon
Martelen
460 Louffen
| Winterthurer cap[itel].   144
Winterthur.

---

428 Wytticken] *intellege* Wiedikon   **435** Erlibach] *intellege* Erlenbach
436 Richtischwyl] *intellege* Richterswil   **437** Wådischwyl] *intellege* Wädenswil
439 Dallwyl] *intellege* Thalwil   **442** Cappel] *intellege* Kappel am Albis
444 Knonow] *intellege* Knonau   **446** Rifferschwyl] *intellege* Rifferswil

340   SYNODUS TIGURINA – 1532

Oberwinterthur
Dôß
465   Rickenbach
Dynhart
Alltickon
Dorlickon
Sôützach
470   Nåfftenbach
Hettlingen
Andelfingen
Tågerlan
Hengkhart
475   Berg
Flaach
Embrach
Lufingen
Rorbiß
480   Dåttlickon
Pfungen
Brütten
Velthen
Wülfflingen
485   Bůch
Elgôwer cap[itel].
Ellgôw
Aelsow
Wysedangen
490   Schlatt
Tzell
Durbentaal
Wyla
| Wetzikommer cap[itel].   145
495   Grůningen
Gryfensee
Pfåfficon. Diac[on]

---

464 Dôß] *intellege* Töss   **468** Dorlickon] *intellege* Torlikon   **469** Sôützach]
intellege Selzach   **473** Tågerlan] *intellege* Dägerlen   **475** Berg] *intellege* Berg am
Irchel   **479** Rorbiß] *intellege* Rorbas   **487** Ellgôw] *intellege* Elgg   **488** Aelsow]
intellege Elsau

SYNODUS TIGURINA – 1532

Kyburg
Alltorff
500 Yllnow. Diac[on]
Rußickon. Diac[on]
Wyßling
Lindow
Wangen
505 Schwertzenbach
Důbendorff
Vållanden
Muur
Uster. Diac[on]
510 Folckenschwyl
Seegråben
Wetzickon
Oetwyl
Hinnwyl
515 Wald
Bårotschwyl
Dürten
Vischental
Rüty
520 Goßow
Egg
Bůbickon.
Reginsperger cap[itel].
Hóngg
525 Wyningen
Rågenstorff
| Dellickon
Otelfingen
Buchs
530 Dielstorff
Wåningen. Diac[on]
Steinmur
Stadel

---

500 Yllnow] *intellege* Illnau   **503** Lindow] *intellege* Lindau   **510** Folckenschwyl]
intellege Volketswil   **513** Oetwyl] *intellege* Oetwil an der Limmat   **520** Goßow]
intellege Gossau

342 SYNODUS TIGURINA – 1532

Bülach
535 Niderhaßlach
Oberglatt
Rümmlang
Kloten
Basserstorff
540 Eglisow
Glattfelden
Wyl
Rafftz.

[3] Dannethin berůffe man die noch nit geschworen habend / das sy
545 unsern herren den gemeinen Eyd Synodi schweerind. Aber die form des Eyds
ist dise.

Das ich das heilig Evangelium und wort Gotts / darzů ich berůfft bin /
trüwlich und nach råchtem Christenlichen verstand / ouch nach vermóg Allts
und Nüws Evangelischen Testaments / lut miner herren von Zürich voruß-
550 gangnen Mandats / leeren und predgen / und darunder kein dogma und leer /
die zwyflig und noch nit uff der ban und erhalten sye / nit ynmischen / sy sye
dann zevor gemeiner ordenlicher versamlung / so jårlich zwey mol gehalten /
anzeigt / und vor der selbigen erhalten. Darzů soll und wil ich einem Burger-
meister unnd Radt / ouch den Burgeren / als miner ordenlichen Oberghheit
555 trüw unnd hold sin: gemeiner Statt unnd Lands Zürich nutz und frommen
fürdern / jro schaden warnen und wenden / so ferr ich vermag: ouch jren
unnd jren nachgesetzten Vógten und amptlüten gebotten und verbotten / inn
zimlichen billichen sachen gehorsamm unnd gewårtig sin: Jtem die heimlig-
heiten des Synodi verschwygen und nit offen-|baren / daruß schad und verwy-
560 sen móchte erwachsen / alles getrüwlich und on alle gfård / etc. 147

Danåben melde man / das / die nit in Synodum gehórend oder berůfft
sind / ußstandint: oder so ettliche / doch ersamme vertruwte personen /
begårtind zůzehóren / und es jnen vom Synodo nachgelassen / uff glübt der
trüw und gloubens getuldet werdint.

565 [4] Nach disem frage man die verordneten von einem ersammen Radt /
ob sy neiswas von wågen unser G[nedigen] H[erren] an den gantzen Synodum anzebringen habind.

[5] Ze letst soll einer uß den Predicanten ein kurtze ermanung thůn / das
sich inn der Censura yederman der warheit flysse / one anfåchtung nyds und
570 hasses handle / rede und radte / etc. Jtem kurtz erzellen / wie nutzlich die
straaff sye / so sy gůtlich ufgenommen wirt / etc.

[Censura] Hierufstelle man zum ersten uß die Predicanten / unnd Lectores Theologie / von der Statt / einen nach dem andern. Und Censiere man die

SYNODUS TIGURINA – 1532

mit ernst / glych wie die andern. Fürnemlich das hiemit allerley ambition
575 ouch argwhon der beherrschung abgethon / und sy sich als brüder und mitar-
beiter im Evangelio Christi erkennind.

Die nachfrag aber in der censura soll erstlich von der Leer / demnach von
dem Studio liebe und flyß der gschrifft: item von dem wandel / låben und
sitten / unnd ze letst von wågen des hußhabens und hußvolcks gehalten wer-
580 den. Und wer der stucken angezogen / soll mit warheit was jm zewüssen bezügen / es sye gůts oder bôß.

[Decani] Der gstalt soll ouch eines yeden Capittels Decanus ußgestelt
werden / damit jm keiner eignen gwalt schôpffe / und den wider sine brüder
gebruche: sunder / wie mencklich / dem Synodo underworffen sye. Wenn
585 aber der Decanus widerumb heryn berůfft / unnd sinen bescheid empfangen /
soll er | die naamen der Pfarreren / so ettlich strâfflich gehandlet / gschrifftlich 148
ynlegen. Die sôllend dannethin einer nach dem anderen ußgestelt / jro mißhandlung erkonnet / und censiert werden. Hat aber der Decanus ghein klag
und mangel an sinen brüdern / soll er das selb ouch mit kurtzen worten dar
590 thůn.

Nütdisterweniger / das mit der zeit ghein fürhaltens erwachse / sôllend
zwo fragen von den Presidenten gehalten werden. Die ein. Ob yemands inn
diesem Capitel sye / der unordnung / mangel / oder unzucht von dem andern
wüsse? Die ander. Ob sust yemands da imm gantzen Synodo zegågen mangel
595 und unrâcht über yemands dises Capitels wüsse. Und so dann ouch also nützid erfunden / mag man ein ander Capitel and hand nemmen.

[Des Dåchens ampt] Sôlichs aber ist dem Decano sines ampts halben
bestimpt / das er ein flyssig ufsåhen uff die pfarren habe / so jm befolhen / das
er die zun zyten heimsůche / erfaare was yedes studium sye / was er predgy /
600 und wie es in der kilchen stande. Und so er dann etwas mangels funde / dannethin einen oder zwen der nåchsten Pfarreren zů jm nåme / und den miß-
handleden warne / und straaffe / Christenlich und brüderlich / das man da
trüw und liebe / nit stôltze und ufsatz spüre. Wo aber sômliches nützid
hulffe / soll demnach die selb mißhandlung und verachtung / dem gantzen
605 Synodo antragen werden.

[Caplonyen] Dasouch ghein unordnung / uß mangel der straaff / under
den Caplonen und anderen / so der kilchengůtern gelåbend / erwachse / soll
ein yetlicher Decanus die Caplonen / so under jm unordenlich låbtend / uff
den nåchstvolgenden Synodum betagen / und da dem Synodo die unordnung
610 anzeigen / damit er sines unråchten abgewisen und widerumb zerâcht
gebracht werde.

[Consilia] Nach dem aber die censura / wie gebürlich / volbracht / soll
der Presidenten einer anfragen / Ob yemands uß den pfarreren ettwas der

leer / irrungen / mißverstands / oder sust kilchenhåndlen halb / nutzes oder
615 schades / habe anzebringen? denen soll ouch nach vermügen / von dem Synodo geholffen und geradten werden. Und was dann einem ersammen Radt
zůstat / ufzeichnen / unnd innet Monatsfrist / gůtlich fürgetragen / radts und
hilff zebegåren. Hierumb bitten wir ouch unser G[nedige] H[erren] sy wöll-
ind sömlich | anbringen Synodi gůtlich verhören: nit unserthalb allein / sun- 149
620 der vil mee der gemeinen kilchen halben: ouch angesåhen das sömlichs nit
mee dann zwey mol imm jar zeverfertigen kumpt / und aber vil nutzes und
gůts gebåren mag.

[Welche håndel imm Synodo ze handlen] Das ouch jr ersamm wyßheit /
unser censur und håndlen imm Synodo fürtragen / sovil minder bemůygt und
625 beunrůwiget: und aber nütdistweniger alle sachen so der kilchen notwendig
nit verhinderet: bittend wir hie abermols unser G[nedige] H[erren] das sy uns
doch nit wöllind versperren Ecclesiasticam authoritatem / die verwaltung inn
håndlen der kilchen / die uns unnser herr Jesus Christus bevolhen / nit zebe-
herrschen oder zůverderben / sunder zůdienen und uf buwen. Namlich das
630 der allgemein Synodus fürohin / mit sampt den acht Radtsfründen dem Synodo von einem ersammen Radt (wie obgemeldt) zůgesetzt / in allen denen
Articklen / so die leer unnd das låben der Predicanten beträffend / nach form
unnd gstalt / wie hierinn vergriffen / unnd wie es die warheyt Gottes vermag /
handlen möge / und was da ußgesprochen und verhandlet wirt / vest sye und
635 krafft habe. Was aber nit betrifft die leer unnd das låben der Predicanten /
oder daruß erwachsen / sunder usserlich und hierinn nit vergriffen ist / wil
sich Synodus gnodt entschlahen unnd nützid beladen. Deßglych wo die
gemelten acht Radtsfründ ein handel wie der wåre / für unnsere herren
zühen / wöllend wir gůtlich lassen beschåhen. Dann wir sömlichs nit der mei-
640 nung begårend / das wir eignen gwalt uffrichten / und uns (wie imm Bapst-
humb beschåhen) der ordenlichen Obergheit wöllend entzühen: sunder das
ein ersammer Radt mit disen kilchen håndlen / nit überlåstiget / ouch so er
sust mit anderen håndlen überladen / deßhalb er dise unsere anligende nodt /
nit allwåg nach nodturfft verhören mag / doch der leer und kilchen håndlen
645 darzwüschend nützid verwarloset oder versumpt werde.

[Abred] Aber ze end des Synodi / soll einer uß den Predicanten ein ernstlich ermanung thůn / ye wie sich die zyten zůtragend: fürnemlich aber das ein
yeder | siner kilchen mit der leer der warheit unnd gůtem byspil sines låbens 150
vorstande / etc.
650 Und in allen disen Articklen / wo sich ein fügklichers / waarers und
bessers erfunde / wöllend wir alle zyt der waarheit underworffen sin / und das
besser mit danckbarkeit and hand nemmen.
U[nser] W[yßheit] underthånige

SYNODUS TIGURINA – 1532   345

Verordnete Pfarrer / diener des worts / Låser der heiligen gschrifft / und
655 Diaconi / all gemeinlich unnd sunderlich uß der Statt und ab der Landtschafft
Zürich.

Yetzdan aber so tragend wir üch U[nsern] G[nedigen] H[erren] dise
Artickel inn aller gstalt wie sy verlåsen / inn naamen des gantzen Synodi für:
und begårend umb Gottes und der warheyt willen / üwer als einer Christli-
660 chen Obergheit / verwilligung hierzů: und damit sy allen zeglych werden
mögind / dz jr uns vergünstigen wöllind / dise inn den Truck zeverfertigen /
und das sy sovil mee krafft und ansahens habind / sóliches mit zůgethoner
verschribner bewilligung bewaren / das wöllend wir zů grossem danck ufnem-
men / und uns so getrüwlich inn diensten Gottes worts und der kilchen
665 halten / das U[nser] W[yßheit] erkantnuß und danckbargheit erkennen soll.

U[nser] W[yßheit] willige
Heinrych Bullinger und Leo Jud.

---

667 Leo Jud] pastor at St Peter in Zurich

CONCILIUM ARGENTORATENSE

1533/1534

ediderunt
Gianmarco BRAGHI – Graeme MURDOCK

THE SYNOD AND *ECCLESIASTICAL ORDINANCES* OF STRASBOURG[*]
1533/1534

INTRODUCTION

The free imperial city of Strasbourg (Strassburg) had an assembly of 300 aldermen (*Schöffen*) made up of fifteen representatives from each of the twenty guilds in the city. Each guild sent a representative to serve on the city's Senate alongside ten representatives of two noble corporations. The representatives of guilds on the Senate annually elected an *Ammeister* as the effective head of the city's government with four noble senators appointed to the role of *Stettmeister*. The Senate met in regular joint session with two executive councils. One of these councils was charged with responsibility for internal affairs and the other with external matters. These joint meetings (called the 'Senate and XXI') between senators and members of the executive councils were the highest legislative authority in the city. Celebrations of Mass had been prohibited by the city authorities in February 1529. In June 1533 the Senate and XXI called for a Synod to be held to agree on doctrine to be taught in the seven urban and fourteen rural parishes under their authority. In November 1534 the Senate and XXI published new ordinances about the approved teaching, organisation and religious practices of the Church in Strasbourg. (1)

One significant context for Strasbourg's 1534 *Ecclesiastical Ordinances* is provided by the evolving political and religious state of the Empire. When Philip Melanchthon produced a confession to be presented to the Diet of Augsburg in 1530, Martin Bucer and his colleagues in Strasbourg were unable to accept its clauses on the contentious issue of communion. Bucer wrote his own confession known as the *Tetrapolitan Confession* (it was also adopted by Constance, Memmingen, and Lindau). Strasbourg's leading reformers attempted through this confession to navigate an increasingly difficult path between Wittenberg and Zurich. Some in the city favoured a closer partnership with Zurich, Bern, and Basel. However, Strasbourg's leading political figure, Jacob Sturm, worked to achieve an alliance with Lutheran states in the

---

(*) Introduction by Graeme Murdock; critical edition by Gianmarco Braghi.
(1) Brady, *Ruling Class*.

Empire. In 1531 the city was accepted as a member of the League of Schmalkalden on the basis of Bucer's *Tetrapolitan Confession*. In 1532, the truce of Nuremberg reached between Charles V and the League of Schmalkalden provided a temporary respite from the threat of any military or legal action by the Emperor against Strasbourg. Bucer continued his efforts to reach an agreement with Lutherans over how to understand the presence of Christ in the sacrament. This culminated in the 1536 *Wittenberg Concord* which suggested that through a sacramental union the bread of communion is the body of Christ and that the power of the sacrament does not rest on the worthiness or unworthiness of the minister or of those who receive the elements. (2)

Further context for Strasbourg's *Ecclesiastical Ordinances* is provided by the changing pattern of religious life within the city. (3) One of the chief concerns of Bucer, Wolfgang Capito, Caspar Hedio, and their supporters was the challenge posed by Anabaptists and others who they considered to be troublemaking sectarians. The city council had established a committee in 1530 to investigate suspected radicals but this body was normally satisfied if those who appeared before it took oaths of obedience to the city authorities. In November 1532 the pastors asked the Senate and XXI to expel radicals who – Bucer and his colleagues claimed – were disturbing the unity and peace of the city. The Senate and XXI did not act on these complaints but responded to concerns expressed by its Church assembly (*Kirchenconvent*). This assembly was attended by the city's ministers as well as by parish wardens (*Kirchenpfleger* or *Kirchspielpfleger*). These lay wardens had first been appointed by the Senate and XXI in October 1531 to serve each of the city's urban parishes. Three wardens were appointed for each parish; one was a senator, the second an alderman, and the third a member of the parish. Parish wardens and ministers in the Church assembly were charged to ensure that agreed doctrine was being preached by all pastors and to discuss any other matters of concern. If the assembly was uncertain over any problem that arose, they were instructed to refer the question back to the Senate and XXI. It was this process that led to the decision taken by the Senate and XXI to call for a Synod to be held in Strasbourg in June 1533. (4)

---

(2) 'The Wittenberg Concord, 1536', transl. A. N. Burnett, *Reformation and Renaissance Review* 18/1 (2016), p. 25-27.

(3) There are a number of excellent studies of the era of reform in Strasbourg. See, for example, Adam, *Kirchengeschichte*; Wendel, *L'église de Strasbourg*; Chrisman, *Strasbourg and the Reform*; Abray, *The People's Reformation*.

(4) J. Rott, 'The Strasbourg *Kirchenpfleger* and Parish Discipline: Theory and Practice', in Wright, *Martin Bucer*, p. 122-128.

The Synod was instructed to agree on true Christian doctrine that would be taught in Strasbourg and thereby provide the basis for unity and good order in the city. This 1533 Synod was led by four commissioners nominated by the city council. The most significant of these commissioners was Jacob Sturm. The Synod was made up of parish wardens, pastors, and teachers. Bucer presented a proposed statement of doctrine to the Synod in sixteen articles. The Synod also examined the beliefs of Anabaptist and radical preachers. In the wake of this meeting the Silesian noble Caspar Schwenckfeld quickly left the city while the Swabian lay preacher Melchior Hoffman was imprisoned. A second meeting of the Synod was convened in October 1533. However, the magistrates temporised when the pastors requested that its results be formally accepted. The authorities continued to proceed cautiously not least because of the diversity of religious opinions among the city's elite. The pastors, led by Bucer and Capito, appealed again to the Senate and XXI at the beginning of 1534 to adopt the results of the Synod and to accept a revised version of Church ordinances which had been drafted by Bucer. In a sermon given at a civic ceremony in January 1534 Caspar Hedio decried 'a shameful, poisonous opinion that Satan is presently putting forth... that the authorities should not concern themselves with religious matters'. (5) The Senate and XXI finally acted in March 1534 and in principle adopted the *Tetrapolitan Confession*, Bucer's sixteen articles, and the *Ecclesiastical Ordinances*. The *Ecclesiastical Ordinances* were formally published in November 1534. (6)

THE *ECCLESIASTICAL ORDINANCES*

Through the 1534 *Ordinances*, the Senate and XXI sought to establish their authority to uphold good order in the religious life of the city. The *Ordinances* placed confidence in the Word of God as the only basis upon which a Christian community could be built. It was the responsibility of the city's authorities to promote a true understanding of the Gospel and to prevent the spread of error. Church services in the city must be orderly and lead to the edification of congregations without any disruption. A key objective of the *Ordinances* is revealed through the use of Paul's warnings to the church at Corinth about the need for orderliness in services of public worship. Citing

(5) J. Kittelson, 'Martin Bucer and the Ministry of the Church', in Wright, *Martin Bucer*, p. 86.

(6) *Ordnung und Kirchengebreuch, für die Pfarrern und Kirchendienern, zu Straßburg, und der selbigen angehörigen, vff gehabtem Synodo fürgenommen* [Straßburg 1534].

I Cor. 14, 33 as support, the 1534 *Ordinances* suggested that 'God is a God of order' ('Got ist ein Got der ordnung') rather than quote the conventional translation of this passage, 'God is not a God of disorder, but of peace' ('Denn Gott ist nicht ein Gott der Unordnung, sondern des Friedens'). The *Ordinances* suggested that divisions over matters of religion had led to the weakening of the peace and civil order of the city. Therefore, good order was needed among the ranks of the city's preachers. No teaching contrary to agreed doctrine would be tolerated, and pastors could not introduce any innovations without the prior knowledge and agreement of the city's authorities.

Strasbourg's 1534 *Ordinances* also set out the process of examination and appointment of pastors as pious servants of God's Word. Existing ministers were to examine and propose any candidates for appointment. Parish wardens and other chosen parishioners were given the final decision to endorse all candidates. The *Ordinances* affirmed a wide range of other roles for parish wardens in the religious life of the city. These wardens were tasked to oversee the lives and work of pastors in their parishes. Wardens were to ensure that ministers preached doctrine consistent with the *Tetrapolitan Confession* and Bucer's sixteen articles. Wardens were also to collaborate with pastors to encourage good attendance at Church services, to maintain standards of Sabbath observance, and to warn backsliders and encourage them to change their ways. Those who did not wish to repent were to be warned of God's judgement but there was no provision in the *Ordinances* for excommunication from the Church. (7)

The 1534 *Ordinances* required that all children in Strasbourg must be baptised in the parish in which they lived within six weeks of their birth. This regulation was backed up by a threat of banishment against those who refused to comply. If the city council was made aware of a refusal by parents to baptise their child, then it could instruct ministers to conduct the baptism. Communion services were to be held every four weeks in each parish. The *Ordinances* set out the important work of ministers in the Christian education of the young with the suggestion of occasional sermons to instruct parents in how to bring up their children. The *Ordinances* also set out regulations for the conduct of marriages which were validated under civil law in Strasbourg. Although marriage was no longer a sacrament, there was strong encouragement in the *Ordinances* for marriages to be confirmed and celebrated in Church services to be blessed by God. (8) Finally, the *Ordinances* set out a regime of inspection of Strasbourg's rural parishes through regular visitations

(7) van 't Spijker, *Ecclesiastical Offices*.
(8) Selderhuis, *Marriage and Divorce*.

CONCILIUM ARGENTORATENSE – 1533-1534

to check on the state of the faith of rural parishioners. Visitations were also intended to check on the quality of preaching as well as the conduct of pastors. A list of books was provided that pastors were expected to use, including the Bible in Latin and German as well as sermons and commentaries by Luther, Konrad Pellikan, and Johannes Oecolampadius. (9) The *Ordinances*' closing remarks on rural visitations highlighted the need for vigilance to remove any remaining images in churches that might lead to idolatry. (10)

At the 1533 Synod and through the 1534 *Ecclesiastical Ordinances*, Bucer and his colleagues sought to work with magistrates in Strasbourg to bring unity and order to the practice of religion in the city and to provide a firm basis upon which to improve understanding of the Gospel and standards of moral conduct. Bucer and others soon became concerned at the lack of progress of efforts to advance moral reform. In January 1539 the *Ammeister* Mathis Pfarrer reported to the Senate that the regulations about parish wardens had proven ineffective and that the city's ministers had asked for their role to be strengthened. The Senate reminded the wardens of their duties and ordered any troublesome members of parishes to be identified to the magistrates for appropriate action. (11) John Calvin observed these debates about the powers of the clergy and lay elders from when he arrived in Strasbourg in 1538 until he returned to Geneva in 1541 with his own draft *Ecclesiastical Ordinances*.

Note on the Edition

The text of *Ordnung vnd Kirchengebreuch, für die Pfarrern vnnd Kirchendienern, zu Straßburg, vnd der selbigen angehörigen, vff gehabtem Synodo fürgenommen* is reproduced following the 1534 printed edition (see Bibliography and Monitum). Rings diacritic (such as in 'ů') as well as letters bearing apical letters (such as 'ǒ') have been preserved. Contractions and tildes have been silently expanded.

(9) Chrisman, *Lay Culture, Learned Culture*.
(10) Wandel, *Voracious Idols*.
(11) Rott, 'The Strasbourg *Kirchenpfleger*', p. 124; Burnett, *The Yoke of Christ*.

354 CONCILIUM ARGENTORATENSE – 1533-1534

BIBLIOGRAPHY

Sources

Primary Sources

Bayerische Staatsbibliothek, München, Res./Liturg. 1467.

Ordnung vnd Kirchengebreuch, für die Pfarrern vnd Kirchendienern, zu Straßburg, vnd der selbigen angehörigen, vff gehabtem Synodo fürgenommen [Straßburg 1534].

Critical Edition

R. Stupperich, 'Ordnung und Kirchengebreuch für die Pfarrern und Kirchendienern zů Straßburg und derselbigen angehoerigen uff gehabtem Synodo fürgenommen, 1534', in S. E. Buckwalter – A. Cornelis et al. (hrsg.), *Martin Bucers Deutsche Schriften*, 18 vols, Gütersloh 1960-2015, vol. 5 (1978), p. 15-41.

Literature (and Its Abbreviations)

L. J. Abray, 'Confession, Conscience, and Honour: The Limits of Magisterial Tolerance in Sixteenth-Century Strasbourg', in O. P. Grell – B. Scribner (eds), *Tolerance and Intolerance in the European Reformation*, Cambridge 1996, p. 94-107.

—, *The People's Reformation. Magistrates, Clergy, and Commons in Strasbourg, 1500-1598*, Oxford 1985 [= Abray, *The People's Reformation*].

J. Adam, *Evangelische Kirchengeschichte der Stadt Straßburg bis zur französischen Revolution*, Straßburg 1922 [= Adam, *Kirchengeschichte*].

R. Bornert, *La Réforme protestante du culte à Strasbourg au XVIe siècle (1523-1598). Approche sociologique et interprétation théologique* (Studies in Medieval and Reformation Traditions 28), Leiden 1981.

T. A. Brady Jr, *Protestant Politics: Jacob Sturm (1489-1553) and the German Reformation*, Atlantic Highlands (NJ) 1995.

—, *Ruling Class, Regime and Reformation at Strasbourg, 1520-1555* (Studies in Medieval and Reformation Thought 22), Leiden 1978 [= Brady, *Ruling Class*].

Bucer zwischen den Reichstagen von Augsburg (1530) und Regensburg (1532). Beiträge zu einer Geographie, Theologie und Prosopographie der Reformation, hrsg. W. Simon (*Spätmittelalter, Humanismus, Reformation / Studies in the Late Middle Ages, Humanism, and the Reformation* 55), Tübingen 2011.

A. N. Burnett, 'Confirmation and Christian Fellowship: Martin Bucer on Commitment to the Church', *Church History* 64 (1995), p. 202-217.

—, *The Yoke of Christ: Martin Bucer and Christian Discipline* (*Sixteenth Century Essays and Studies* 26), Kirksville (MO) 1994 [= Burnett, *The Yoke of Christ*].

—, 'Church Discipline and Moral Reformation in the Thought of Martin Bucer', *Sixteenth Century Journal* 22 (1991), p. 438-456.

M. U. Chrisman, *Lay Culture, Learned Culture: Books and Social Change in Strasbourg, 1480-1599*, New Haven (CT) 1982 [= Chrisman, *Lay Culture, Learned Culture*].

—, *Strasbourg and the Reform. A Study in the Process of Change*, New Haven (CT) 1967 [= Chrisman, *Strasbourg and the Reform*].

Die evangelischen Kirchenordnungen des sechszehnten Jahrhunderts: Urkunden und Regesten zur Geschichte des Rechts und der Verfassung der evangelischen Kirche in Deutschland, hrsg. A. L. Richter, 2 vols, Weimar 1846; repr. Nieuwkoop 1967.

R. Friedrich, *Martin Bucer – Fanatiker der Einheit? Seine Stellungnahme zu theologischen Fragen seiner Zeit (Abendmahls- und Kirchenverständnis) insbesondere nach seinem Briefwechsel der Jahre 1524-1541*, Bonn 2002.

M. Greschat, *Martin Bucer. Ein Reformator und seine Zeit*, München 1990.

G. Hammann, 'Les motifs ecclésiologiques sous-jacents à la création des *Christlichen Gemeinschaften* par Martin Bucer à Strasbourg en 1546-1548', *Bulletin de la Société de l'Histoire du Protestantisme Français* 139 (1993), p. 168-186.

—, *Martin Bucer (1491-1551) zwischen Volkskirche und Bekenntnis-Gemeinschaft* (*VIEG Abteilung für Abendländische Religionsgeschichte* 139), Stuttgart 1989.

D. Kaplan, *Beyond Expulsion: Jews, Christians and Reformation Strasbourg*, Stanford (CA) 2011.

J. M. Kittelson, *Toward an Established Church: Strasbourg's Reformation from 1500 to the Dawn of the Seventeenth Century*, Mainz 2000.

356 CONCILIUM ARGENTORATENSE – 1533-1534

—, *Wolfgang Capito. From Humanist to Reformer* (*Studies in Medieval and Reformation Thought* 17), Leiden 1975.

M. Lienhard – J. Willer, *Straßburg und die Reformation*, Kehl 1981.

Martin Bucer and Sixteenth Century Europe: Actes du colloque de Strasbourg, 28-31 août 1991, ed. C. Krieger – M. Lienhard, 2 vols, Leiden 1993.

Martin Bucer: Reforming Church and Community, ed. D. F. Wright, Cambridge 1994 [= Wright, *Martin Bucer*].

Martin Bucer zwischen Luther und Zwingli, hrsg. M. Arnold – B. Hamm, Tübingen 2003.

H. Selderhuis, *Marriage and Divorce in the Thought of Martin Bucer* (*Sixteenth Century Essays and Studies* 48), Kirksville (MO) 1999 [= Selderhuis, *Marriage and Divorce*].

Strasbourg au cœur religieux du XVIe siècle: hommage à Lucien Febvre. Actes du colloque international de Strasbourg, 25-29 mai 1975, éd. G. Livet – F. Rapp – J. Rott, Strasbourg 1977.

D. Trocmé-Latter, *The Singing of the Strasbourg Protestants, 1523-1541* (*St Andrews Studies in Reformation History*), Abingdon 2015.

W. van 't Spijker, *The Ecclesiastical Offices in the Thought of Martin Bucer* (*Studies in Medieval and Reformation Thought* 57), Leiden 1996 [= van 't Spijker, *Ecclesiastical Offices*].

L. P. Wandel, *Voracious Idols and Violent Hands: Iconoclasm in Reformation Zurich, Strasbourg, and Basel*, Cambridge 1994 [= Wandel, *Voracious Idols*].

F. Wendel, *L'église de Strasbourg, sa constitution et son organisation, 1532-1535* (*Études d'histoire et de philosophie religieuses* 38), Paris 1942 [= Wendel, *L'église de Strasbourg*].

MONITUM

Bayerische Staatsbibliothek, München, Res./Liturg. 1467.

Ordnung vnd Kirchengebreuch, für die Pfarrern vnnd Kirchendienern, zu Straßburg, vnd der selbigen angehörigen, vff gehabtem Synodo fürgenommen [Straßburg 1534].

CONCILIUM ARGENTORATENSE
1533-1534

| ORDNUNG VND KIRCHENGEBREUCH /   A1r
FÜR DIE PFARRERN VNND KIRCHENDIENERN /
ZU STRASSBURG / VND DERSELBIGEN ANGEHOERIGEN /
VFF GEHABTEM SYNODO FÜRGENOMMEN.

⁵ | Nach dem hieuor durch Unsere Herren / Meyster / Rhådt / vnnd die   A2r
Ein vnnd zwentzig / auch Schôffel vnnd Amman diser Stat Straßburg / erkennet vnnd fürgenommen worden / das heylsam wort Gottes / nach dem rechten vnnd waren verstand / zů leren vnnd predigen / vnd so vil Gott genad
geben wolt / demselbigen zůgeleben / vnd nach zůkommen / vnd sich aber
¹⁰ allerley secten / rottungen vnd sônderungen eingerissen / zů zerrittung
gemeyner kirchen / außlôschung brüderlicher liebe / vnd endlicher zerstôrung
burgerlicher policy vnnd friden / vnnd allem anderen vnraht dienet.

Demselben zů begegnen / haben Unsere Herren / Meyster / Råht / vnnd
die Ein vnd zwentzig / als von Gott die geordnet Oberkeyt / auß schuldigem
¹⁵ ampt / des verscheynenden drei vnnd dreisigisten jars / vff den eylfften tag
Junii / ein gemeyne versamlung anfahen zů haben / darinn von rechter einhel-
liger Christlicher lere / auch kirchen ordnungen / vnnd erforschung des lebens
der vorgesetzten diener des worts / zů handlenn /

Unnd damit das selbige desto statlicher geschehen môchte / haben Unn-
²⁰ sere Herren / Meyster / Råht / vnnd die Ein vnnd zwentzig / zů solicher
verhôr / von jnen selb vnnd dem Regiment / vier personen zů Presidenten
oder vorsitzern / vnnd dann die Ein vnnd zwentzig gemeyn kirspelpfleger
verordnet / Damit aber jmm selben / auß zůlauffung des gemeynen volcks /
kein vnordnung erwůchse / vnnd doch jemand von der gemeyn dabei were /
²⁵ haben sie beuelch gethan / das ein jede zunfft / durch jre Schôffel vnnd
gericht / vier von den Schôfflen ordnete / ob die wolten / vnd jrer gelegenheyt
nach / bey solcher verhôre auch zů sein / damit sie der warheyt / auch wie /
vnnd was inn solcher verhôre gehandlet würde / zeügnüs geben môchten.

5/12 Nach – dienet] the central concern of the Senate and XXI is established that all
manner of sects have divided the city's parishes and this has led to the destruction of
civil order and peace   **13/18** Demselben – handlenn] the Synod called by the Senate
and XXI opened on 11 June 1533   **19/23** Unnd – verordnet] the Synod's four
commissioners appointed by the Senate and XXI were led by Jacob Sturm. The twenty-
one appointed wardens (*Kirchspielpfleger*) served the city's seven urban parishes

360 CONCILIUM ARGENTORATENSE – 1533-1534

Nach dem dann inn solichem gesprech / die Summa Christlicher lere /
30 wie die alhie bekennet / geleret / vnd geprediget / nach rechtem vnnd warem
verstandt der heyligen Euangelien / Apostolischer vnnd Biblischer schrifften /
nach aller notdurfft inn etliche Artickul verfasset / fürgetragen / disputiret
vnd erkläret / Auch die jenigen / so etlichen Secten anhengig / vnnd die
vorgemeldten Articul zů widerfechten vnderstanden / genůgsam verhöret /
35 vnd nachmals aller Prediger / pfarrer vnnd helffer / sampt den Ein vnd zwent-
zig kirspel pflegeren / raht vnd gůt|beduncken vernomen / vnnd jr bedencken A2v
jnn schrifften verfasset / Haben vnsere Herren / den vier geordneten Presidenten oder vorsitzeren beuolhen / über soliche gehandlete puncten zů sitzen / jr
raht vnd gůtbeduncken / wes zů besserung Christlicher gemeyn / vffbawung
40 gemeyner kirchen / inn lere / leben / vnd Ceremonien fůrzunemen sein solte /
zů begreiffen vnd anzůzeygen / das dann / als ein hochwichtig werck / on zeit
vnd weil nit beschehen mögen / hat sich also diser handel / von wegen der
hochwichtigheyt sein selb / vnd dann auch vile derschefften so tåglich fürfal-
len / eben lang verzogen / jedoch haben zů letst vnsere Herren / Meyster /
45 Råht / vnnd Ein vnd zwentzig / nach gehabten vilbedachten / vnd fleissigen
erwegungen des gantzen handels / sich entschlossen / erkennet vnd geordnet /
wie volget.

WIE OB DER EINIGEN CHRISTLICHEN LERE ZŮ HALTEN / VNND DEN
GEGEN JRRIGEN LEREN ZŮ BEGEGNEN.

50 Als der Synodus / furnemlich dreier puncten halb gehalten ist / Erstlich /
vergleichung Christlicher lere betreffen / vnnd abtreibung der Secten vnnd
trennungen / so solicher lere zůwider. Zům anderen / eüsserliche vnnd besser-
liche ordnung vnnd gebreüch der kirchen vff zůrichten. Und zům dritten /
Inquisition vnd erforschung des lebens vnnd wandels der jhenen / so der
55 kirchen fürgesetzet seind / zůthůn.
So ist vff den ersten puncten / die lere vnnd Secten belangen / entschlossen vnd erkennet / bey der Confession / zů Augspurg Keys. May. vberantwor-
tet / vnnd den Articulen / jmm Synodo fürgetragen vnnd gehandlet / zů plei-
benn / dieselbigen / als die recht Christlich lere / alhie lassen predigen / vnnd
60 ob der selbigen ernstlich zů halten / Auch keyne leren vnnd Secten / so derselbigen lere zů wider seind / hie zů gedulden / Unangesehen der langen schriff-

---

47 wie volget] discussion of the sixteen articles proposed by Martin Bucer **57** der
Confession] i.e. Martin Bucer's *Confessio Tetrapolitana*

CONCILIUM ARGENTORATENSE – 1533-1534

ten / so durch Clement Ziegler / Melchior Hoffmann / vnnd andere / jnn vnnd nach dem Synodo übergeben. Unnd damit also gesunde lere Christi / bey meniglich alhie / desto baß erhalten vnnd fürbracht / vnnd alle jrthumb
65 vnnd verfürische lere abgetriben vnd verhúetet werden. Haben Unsere Herren / Meyster / Råth vnnd Ein vnnd zwentzig / über andere weg vnd mittel / die | sie hiezů dienstlich erkennet vnnd fürgenomen / auch diß bedacht vnd   A3r geordnet / das die kirspyl pfleger ein getrewes ufsehen haben sollen / das soliche bekante lere / wie die inn offtgemeldter Confession / vnd Articulen des
70 Synodi / verfasset ist / alhie getrewlich geleret vnnd gepredigt werde / Unnd das niemand vberal / solicher lere zů wider / inn winckeln / oder offenlich / etwas außgiesse oder verlestere / oder auch die leüt von derselben abziehe / sonder wa sie solichs erfüren / das selb einem Ersammen Raht / oder den hienachgesetzen Verhóreren anzeygen / damit darinn ein getrewlichs vnd not-
75 durfftiges einsehen geschehe.

Zum andern / damit aber niemand vrsach nemme zů sagen / mann wólle dem heyligen geyst rygel fürschieben / vnd nichts weiters lernen oder hóren / Seind durch einen Ersa. Raht geordnet / zwen des Rahts vnd regiments / vnd von den kirspylpfegeren drey / welche fünff zwen von den Predigern zů jnen
80 berúffen sollen / der gestalt / so jemand were / der da vermeynen wolte es were fehl an der lere / die man hie als die lere Christi treibet / der soll sich genanten fünff verordneten anzeygen / vnd jnen in beisein der zweien Prediger / die auch dagegen verhóret werden sollen / sein meynung / vnd der selbigen grund fürtragen / vnd also mit jnen inn Christlicher zůcht handlen /
85 zůvor vnd ee er solich sein meynung jemand anderem fürgibet. Unnd wa diße verordneten bei einem solchen befinden / das der rede wert ist / gůts oder bóses / sollen sie dasselbig ann einen Ersa. Raht bringen / vnnd one eins Ersamen Rahts zůlassung / soll niemand vberahl der lere Christi / so alhie dafür erkennet / vnd zů treiben geordnet ist / etwas entgegen zů leren gestattet wer-
90 den. Wo dann solche geordnete jemand zů lerenn abweisen / vnnd des selben sach nit für ein Ersa. Raht bringen wolten / So mage ein jeder für sich selb bei einem Ersa. Raht vmb zůlassung seiner lere ansůchen / vnd also eins Rahts bescheyd darunder erwarten.

Zum dritten / damit dann alle lere zůuor / wie der Almechtig das allet-
95 halb leret / vnd gebeutet / ordenlich von den gleubigen verhóret vnd beweret / ee die vnder den einfaltigen außgossen / vnd nit also an Christlicher

---

62 Clement Ziegler] cfr R. Peter, 'Le maraîcher Clément Ziegler, l'homme et son œuvre', *Revue d'histoire et de philosophie religieuses* 34 (1954), p. 255-282   Melchior Hoffmann] (1495-1543) was a lay preacher from Swabia who had travelled to Saxony, the Baltic region, East Friesland, and Amsterdam before arriving in Strasbourg. Hoffman advanced a prophecy of Christ's return in 1533

362 CONCILIUM ARGENTORATENSE – 1533-1534

lere / daran doch all vnser heyl staht / von einem jeden / seinem můtwillen
nach / gefreůlet / vnd die einfaltigen verwirret werden / wie leyder bißher
beschehen. Wo dann jemand sich vernemmen liesse / vnd anndere lere
100 einzůfůren vnderstünde / So solle keyn burger oder einwoner dieser Stat
Straßburg / fur sich selb einem solichen gehőr geben. | sonder den / oder die A3v
vermanen / das er sich / nach jetzgemelter eins Rahts ordnung vnd erkantnüß / zů den obgesetzten verhőreren der leer verfůgen soll / vnd sein meynung
zůuor mit den selbigen handlen. Wo dann ein solicher sich des widern / vnnd
105 nichts desto minder sein fürgesatzte meynung / wider die lere Christi / die
alhie offentlich gefůret wurdt / auß zůgiessen nit ablassen wolte / Als dann
solle ein jeder burger / der eins solichen verfůrers innen wurdt / dasselbige den
gedachten geordneten verhőrern anzeygen / damit sie nach einem solichen
schicken / vnd Christlicher gebůr nach / freuntlich vnd auß dem wort Got-
110 tes / mit jm handlen mőgen / Uff das / was gůts von jemand mőchte angezey-
get werden / angenommen vnd gefurderet / vnd was verfůrisch / abgewisen /
vnd die einfaltigen daruor bewaret werdenn. Unnd sol diser articul auch den
zunfften / durch den Herren Ammeyster vnnd die Alten herrenn bracht werden / damit ob jemand / der sich andere leer einzufůren / vndernemmen vnd
115 anzeygen wolt / das sie wissen wemm sie es fürbringen sollen.

Ursach der vorgesetzeten Articul.

Wer eins gůten geistes ist / vnnd gesunde lere fůret / würt seiner lere
nirgend lieber rechenschafft geben / dann vor denen / die ein Oberkeyt / vnd
also gantze gemeyn / die auch nach vnserem Herren Jesu Christo fragen /
120 darzů verordnet / Wie vnnser lieber Herr Jesus Christus vonn jhm selb saget /
das er offentlich zůr welt geredet / alweg inn der Synagog vnnd tempel / da
alle Juden hynkahmen / geleret / vnnd inn den winckelen nichs geleret habe.
Dergleichen auch Paulus allethalben gethan / wa er je hynkommen / hat er
sich zů erst in die Synagogen / da mann offentlich von Gott geleret /
125 verfůget / Also handlete er auch zů Jerusalem zůuor mit Jacobo / Petro /
Johanne vnnd den eltisten.
Got ist ein Got der ordnung. I. Cor. 14. Wa man der selbigen nach kommet / würt es alweg fürdernüs / vnnd keyn hindernüs der warheyt jemer pringen kőnden / Hat Got jemand / hie oder anderswo zů leren / gesandt / vnnd
130 seind hie oder anderswo / denen er will solich lere fürgebracht werden / ob
dann schon nit alleyn soliche verhőr Christlicher | lere / sonder auch die A4r
Oberkeyt vnd gemeyn / mit allem gewalt / solchem zůwider sein wolten /

---

127 Got¹ – ordnung] cfr I Cor. 14, 33

CONCILIUM ARGENTORATENSE – 1533-1534

würde es dannoch nit helffen / Dann je keyne creaturen / jrem schöpffer seinen willen zů schaffen / wehren mögen.

135 Das ist ein mal gewiß vnnd war / dieweil der h. geist jhm selber nit mage zůwider sein / würt sich gedachter ordnung der verhör niemand / der den geyst Christi hat / jmermehr wideren könden / dann der selbig h. geist selb geleret / das die Christen nit solten einen jeden lassen (auch das war Euangeli) predigen / wir geschweigen ein noch vnbekante / vnbewehrte lere. Den / die
140 bewehret seind / sagt er / vnnd andere zů leren tauglich / die ein gůte zeügnüs haben / denen solle man diß ampt beuelhen / vnnd niemand die hend bald vflegen / 2. Thimo. 2. I. Thimo. 3. 5. Bringet dann jemand ein'andere leer oder Euangelj / dann die gleubigen erkennen das Euangeli sein / das vnns die Apostel gepredigt haben / den sollen sie verbannet haben / vnd wans ein Engel
145 vom hymel were / Gala. I. Dermassen leret er anderswo / vnd ermanet gantz ernstlich / sich vor falscher lere selb zů verhütenn.

Es gibt auch anders nit / das der h. Paulus, I. Cor. 14. von dem leret / das alle mögen nach ordnung weissagen / vnnd wa einem vonn sitzenden etwas geoffenbaret würt / das die anderen schweigen / vnd disem losen sollen. Dann
150 der h. Paulus redet des orts von denen / die die gabe der prophecy hatten / inn der kirchen zů Corintho sich hielten / vnd da bekant waren / Und gar nit von denen / die daher lauffen / vnd sich selb des h. geystes rhümen / on eynige kundschafft oder zeugnüs der kirchen. Wa noch heütigs tags weren / die die gab der Prophecey hetten / vnnd das den gleübigen möchte kundt sein / solte
155 mann soliche wol hören / vnnd darnach was sie sagten / richtenn. Dann wa schon recht Propheten sein / die den geyst der prophecy warlich haben / seind sie dennoch auch noch menschen / vnnd haben dabei auch den geyst des fleysches. Das man aber gleich solte lassen / ein jeden allenthalb leren vnd außgiessen / was er wolte / der sich des geysts Gottes berhümte / man kennete jn
160 aber nit / das hat S. Paulus nie gewölt / sonder wie vor anzeyget / das wider spyl geleret / das man nemlich alles beweren / vnnd dem alleyn stat geben solle / das mann gůt erkennet / Diß beweren / wil er auch ordenlich beschehen. Derhalben er allethalben den kirchen Eltisten verordnet hat / vnnd zů

135/142 Das – vflegen] cfr II Tim. 2, 2; I Tim. 3, 7; 5, 22   **142/145** Bringet – were] cfr Gal. 1, 8   **147** Es – leret] cfr I Cor. 14, 30   **155/167** Dann – am 15.] cfr Tit. 1, 9-11; Act. 15

---

147 Es – leret] as discussed in the text, this passage refers to the importance of orderly worship and the need for prophecy to be carefully weighed by others   **155/167** Dann – am 15.] this passage from the letter to Titus concerns the role of elders to encourage sound doctrine and to oppose rebellious people. The related passage of Acts 15 concerns the Council of Jerusalem and right authority in the Church to decide on divisive questions

verordnen beuolhen / die ob gesunder lere halten / den widersprecheren die
165 meüler verstopffen. Tit. I. vnd was | spennigs fürfallet / die warheyt vleissig
auß der geschrifft ersůchen sollen / vnnd andere deren berichten / wie zů Jerusalem geschahe / Actorum am 15.

Diß ist Gottes ordnung vnd beuelch / der můß gůt sein vnd bleiben /
dem auch alle Christen nachkommen sollen / Unangesehen / das auß rechtem
170 vrtheyl Gottes / wann die leüt die erkante warheyt nit wóllen / offt geschicht /
ja bey dem mehrer teyl der welt also gesehen würt / das niemand der warheyt
Christi mehr widerstrebet / dann eben / die sich selbs außgeben / als die eltisten vnd fürgesetzten der kirchen / die alle lere furnemlich verhóren vnd
bewehren sollen.

175 Auß dem gesatz / das Gott gepotten die falschen propheten zů dódten /
seind so vil warer propheten / Christus selb / vnd die Apostolen getódtet wordenn / Darumb aber haben sie dises gesatz nirgend ye angetastet oder
verworffen / sonder den mißbrauch des gesatzes. Die gericht seind allenthalb,
das die frommen vnd vnschuldigen / vor gewalt der bósen geschützet werden /
180 wie vil gericht seind aber / ab denen man anders claget? noch můß man
gericht haben. Also das die genanten geystlichen in aller welt / vnder dem
namen Christlicher ordnung / jre tyranney eingefüret / vnd damit alle warheyt zů vndertrucken nichs vnderlassen / solle man aber darneben / die
ordnung / die der H. geyst selbs geben / weder verwerffen / noch nachlassen /
185 sonder jederman ermanen / vnnd Gott vmb sein genad pitten / das solicher
ordnung recht nachkommen werde.

Es ist aber auch / Gott dem herren sey lob / mit disem verhóren vnd
bewehren / dauon wir hie reden / auch denen die hiezů sollen verordnet werden / weit ein anders / dann mit dem / das sich die genanten geystlichen
190 hierinn halten / Bei vns will man hóren / jhene greiffen fluchs zum leib on
verhór / Hie will man alles / nach dem wort Gottes / verhóren vnd beweren / dort pleibts beidem / das dem Pabst gefellet / So soll das auch die frucht
des lebens beweisen / das man die ehr Gottes des orts sůchet / so man wol
sihet / das es dem Pábstlichen hauffen / vmb das leiblich zů thůn ist.

195 Und da Gott vor seie / dises zur Tyranney wider die warheyt Christi
geriete / noch würde dennocht ein jeder warer Christ / den Gott zů leren
gesandt / alweg zům fürdersten den verordneten darzů / seine ler für zů tragen
begeren / wie Christus vnd die Apostel gethon / vnd sich alle rechte prediger
des Euangelij heutigs tags zů thůn erbieten / vnd von | anfang erbotten
200 haben / Auch vor dem Pabst vnd Bischouen / irer lere gründ vnd vrsach dar zů
thůn / so man sie alleyn hóren wolte / vnnd nit on / vnd vor aller verhór hyn-

CONCILIUM ARGENTORATENSE – 1533-1534

thůn. Man hat alwegen den trost / die leut so die warheyt fürderen sollen / halten sich inn dem / wie sie wöllen / so kennet Gott die seinen. 2. Thimo. 2. die würt er endtlich nit lassen / vnd jnen sein warheyt / alweg zů rechter zeit
205 erôffnen / Darumb wurt der Christ der ordnung Gottes sich alweg begeben / vnd deren geleben / vnd wol wissen / so er Gott vmb die warheyt bittet / das er jn vor der lůgen wol behůten würt / Gott würt er alleyn glauben / vnd sich im gentzlich ergeben / Aber daher würt er der ordnung / die Gott bei den leüten will gehalten haben / zům aller trewlichsten nachkommen / vnd wurt
210 jm Gott auch verleihen alle vnordnung vnd mißbreuch / so sich für Christliche ordnung verkauffen wôllen / bei zeit zů erkennen / vnnd sich deren zů entziehen.

Uff den Anderen puncten des Synodi / eusserliche ordnung vnd gepreuch der kirchen belangenn / seind nachuolgende puncten für nutz vnd gůt angese-
215 hen worden.

Wie die Pfarrer vnd helffer dienst zů versehen / vnnd inn rechtem besserlichen thůn zů erhalten seien.

Zům ersten / Nach dem zwischen den hirten Christlicher weyde / vnnd schâfflin Christi / die hôchste liebe vnd freüntdtschafft sein / auch S. Paulus
220 wille das ein Bischoff solle ein gůte zeugnüs von meniglich haben / gebüret sich / mit annemung vnd einsatzung der kirchen diener / also zů handlen / das man soliche diener einsetze / die / so vil jnen môglich / der Christlichen gemeyn anmůetig seien / Darumb dann auch von altemhar / der gemeyn will / inn wahl vnd annemmung der kirchen diener / alweg erfordert worden. Der-
225 halben ist erkant / so ein pfarr ledig würt / sollen die gedachten verhôrer Gôtlicher lere / einen oder mehr / nach dem man die haben mage / vnd die sie zů solichem ampt der pfarren oder helffern tauglich erkennen / oder durch das Examen tauglich befunden hetten / zů vor etlich predig inn der | pfarren / da B ıv der pfarrer oder helffer manglet / lassen thůn / damit sie / die gemeyn der
230 selben pfarr hôre / Unnd demnach / Nemlich wo ein pfarrer anzůnemmen / die gemeyn der pfarr inn einer predig / durch einen frommen diener des worts berichten lassen / was eins pfarrers ampt / vnnd wie vil an dem / das soliches recht verwesen werde / gelegen seie / mit ermanung Got mit hôchstem ernst zů bitten / das er solich wahl / vnd annemung so vorhanden / regieren vnnd
235 fůren wôlle / Unnd vff das / sollen die kirchen pfleger deren pfarr ein pfarrer

---

202/203 Man – Thimo. 2.] cfr II Tim. 2, 17-19

219 freüntdtschafft] *sic*

366 CONCILIUM ARGENTORATENSE – 1533-1534

zů erwelen ist / zwelf gotsförchtiger menner / die bey der gemeyn / Christliches wandels gůte zeügnüs haben / zů jnen nemmen / vnnd dann sampt den Examinatoren zů gelegner zeit vnnd statt / von den Examinatoren zů ernennen / mit allem ernst die wahl / so zů thůn ist / halten / vnd das alles bei jnen

240 ordenlich erwegen vnd vnderreden / das zů solicher wahl von nôten / welches erwegen vnnd berichten / in einer grossen gemeyn / der massen / wie die notdurfft das erheyschet / nit beschehen mage. Welchen dan also die verordneten Examinatoren / sampt kirchspylpflegeren vnd zwelffen von der gemeyn / die eins pfarrers mangelt / erwehlen / den sollen sie einem Ersamen Raht an-

245 zeygen / Und so dan ein Ersamer Raht den selben erwehleten / taugenlich erkennen vnd bestetigen / so sollen dan die vilgedachten Examinatores vnd kirchspylpfleger / abermal verschaffen vnd ordnen ein frommen diener des worts / inn derselbigen pfarr / deren mann ein pfarrer gewehlet / ein predig zuthůn / vnnd darinn der gemeyn solichen erwehlten beuelhen / jhm sein

250 ampt gegen der gemeyn / deßgleichen der gemeyn gegen jhm erzelen / vnnd daruff vermanen / Got trewlich anzurůffen vnd zů betten / das er seinen heyligen geyst / beden pfarrern vnnd gemeyn / sich also / wie beder ampt eruorderet / gegen einander zůhalten verleihen / vnnd also geben wôlle / das der pfarrer fruchtbarlich dienen môge. So aber ein helffer anzůnemmen / den

255 sollen die Examinatores / kirchenpfleger / vnd der pfarrer inn dem kirchspyl da man eins helffers manglet / annemmen / vnnd das man die / so man zů solichem ampt tauglich achtet / lasse zů vor etliche predigen thůn / mit ermanung an die gemeyn / die der pfarrer thůn solle / ob jemand vileicht an solichen die mann gehôret / vermeynet mangel zů sein / darumb sie zů disem

260 ampt nit tauglich weren / das der / oder die selbigen solichs wolten den kirchspyls pflegeren anzeygen. Wa auch mehr dann einer gehôret / vnnd jemand achtete besonder vrsachen sein / einen vor dem | anderen zu erwehlen / das solle man auch den kirchspyl pflegeren anzeygen. Unnd solle dann der pfarrer derselben pfarr / den erwehleten helffer der gemeyn / inn der

265 predig beuelhen / jhm sein ampt erzelen / vnnd für jhn betten lassen. Es sollen auch die vilgedachten Examinatores vnnd kirchen pfleger / der gesatzten Pfarrer vnnd helffer lere vnnd leben gůt acht haben / so mangel an jhnen befunden / das selbige besseren / wa das will stat haben / wa nit / die helffer vrlauben / der pfarrer halb die sach für ein Ersamen Raht gelangen lassen.

B2r

270 *Ursach dises Articuls.*

Das ampt die herd Christi zů weyden / ist so groß vnnd wichtig / das man inn der wahl solicher diener Christi / vnnd hirten seiner schäfflin / niemar vleissig genůg vfsehen / vnd alles erforschen würt / So ist soliches ampt recht

CONCILIUM ARGENTORATENSE – 1533-1534   367

verwalten / auch so weit über alles menschlichs vermögen / das Got für
275 solichs warlich mit höchstem ernst / vnd grosser andacht gebetten vnd ange-
rûffet werde solle. Daher dann kommet / das mann inn jnsetzung oder wahl
der Bischouen / die nichs dann pfarrer gewesen / von der Apostel zeit her / so
vil ceremonien vnnd solennitet geûbet hat.

CONUOCATZ.

280   Zum anderen / damit aber nun soliche lere Christi von den Pfarrern /
Helffern / vnd Predigern / mit rechtem ernst vnnd Christlicher massen
einhellig getriben werde / sie sich auch in jrem leben vnnd thûn / solicher leer
gemäß halten / So hat ein Ersamer Raht geordnet / vnd achtet es nutzlich
sein / nach dem sie / die prediger / biß her gepfleget alle wochen ein mal zû
285 samen kommen / vnd da sich mit einander zû besprechen / wie die lere Christi
zû fûren / wes die kirch yeder zeit zû ermanen seie / vnd alles so ir ampt erforderet / besserlich außgerichtet werden môge / Das hinfür die Ein vnnd zwentzig Kirchspyl pfleger alle mal drey von jnen / zû solichen Conuocatzen der
Prediger verordnen / darinnen yeder zeit / mit sampt den Predigern / zû
290 berahtschlagen / vnd sich zû vergleichen / wes notdurfft der kirchen er|vorde- B2v
ren würt / Ob aber sach für fielen / die jnen / den Kirchspyl pflegeren / zû
schwer sein wolten / oder darinn sie sich mit den Predigern nit vergleichen
kônthen / sollen sie es für die anderen Ein vnnd zwentzig Kirchspyl pfleger die
sie zû jnen berûffen môgen / oder für einen Ersa. Raht bringen / vnd die
295 Prediger also in solicher sachen still stohn / vnd nit für faren / sonder / des
beschluß der anderen Kirchspyl pfleger / oder eins Ersa. Rahts darunder
erwarten / Und sollen die selben Conuocatzen von vierzehen tagen zû vier-
zerehen tagen / je vff einen donerstag ordinarie gehalten werden / vnd die
erste conuocatz / einer von den kirchspyl pflegeren abgohn / vnnd die anderen
300 pleiben sitzen / vnnd an des abgohnden stat ein anderer geordnet werden
solle / vnnd also für vnnd für / das alweg inn einer jeden conuocatz zwen alten
vnnd ein newer kirchspylpfleger seyen / damit der new angehnd kirspylpfleger
von den alten bericht môge werden / was dauor gehandelt sey / Doch so sich
sachen oder notdurfft der kirchen zûtrügen / die die ordenlich conuocatz vnd
305 versamlung der vierzehen tag / wie obstat / nit erwarten môchten / mag vnd
soll mann soliche versamlung je nach gelegenheyt kürtzen / wie sollichs die
verordneten kirchspylpfleger vnnd pfarrer für nutz vnnd not wendig ansicht.

290/291 der – würt] the *Kirchenconvent*, or Church assembly

301 conuocatz] *a.c.* couocatz

368 CONCILIUM ARGENTORATENSE – 1533-1534

Es sollen aber alle pfarrer vnd helffer in der Stat / desgleichen der zů
Rǔprechtsaw vnnd zů Schlicken zů solichen Conuocationen kommen / vnd
310 on redliche vrsach solle sich keyner absentiren. So es auch die notdurfft erforderet / mǒgen sie die ordinarios Lectores / Schůl vnd leermeyster / sampt vnd
sonders / wie sie das für nutz vnd gůt ansihet / zů jhnen berǔffen / doch sollen
sie nichs namhafftigs beschliessen / oder kein sonder newerung fürnemmen /
sonder eins Ers. Rahts / dahin sie es pringen sollen / vorwissen.

315   VON DEN H. SACRAMENTEN.

Demnach die heiligen Sacrament / die haupt vnd ernstlichen Gottes hendel inn der kirchen sind / so eüsserlichen geůbet werden / dan da / sampt dem
Euangeli vnd gebet / auch die gnaden zeychen gereychet vnnd empfangen
werden / gebüret sichs je das bey solichen der hǒchst ernst / vnd grǒst andacht
320 bewysen werde / Dernhalb als der tauff der anfang vnd jngang ist ins Christ-
lich we|sen / vnd aber auß mißbrauch leyder bey vilen inn liederlicher   B3r
achtung / vnnd mit geringer andacht gehalten würt / Ist geordnet vnnd
erkant / das alle kinder inn diser stat Straßburg inn den pfarren / inn die sie
gehǒren / getauffet werden / vnnd das selbig inn den nebenpfarren vff die
325 Sontag nach der predig / oder zům vespergebet / vnd jm Münster vff den
kinderbericht oder mittag predig / so die gemeyn Gottes bey einander ist / das
der handel des taufs desto bas außgelegt / gebettet / vnd alles mit ernst vnnd
andacht beschehe. Unnd demnach die Münster pfarr etwas groß / so soll
mann auch vff den Mitwoch zů end der morgenpredig / noch ein tauf stund
330 halten. Trůge sich aber zů / das jemand sein kind zů anderen zeyten zůtauffen
begerete / das solle nit abgeschlagen werden / Doch soll das selbig nit geschehen
/ dann inn beysein einer zimlichen versamlung / welche die so jre kind zů
tauffen begeren / mit bringen sollen / damit das h. Sacrament des tauffes /
dannoch mit seinem ernst vnnd herlichkeyt gehandlet werde.
335   Zum andern / dieweil die geuatterschafft so ein alter Christlicher
gebrauch / auch von anderen kirchen allen / bei welchen das reyn Euangelion
geprediget würt / on wider sprechen gehalten würt / wie er auch wol mag
gehalten werden / so solle man niemand dauon abziehen / sonder mehr
darzů / vnd aber auch ernstlich ermanen / das man recht gots forchtige
340 Christliche leüt / auß recht Christlicher meynung neme / nit vmb gebens /
oder sunst weltlicher vrsachen willen / dahyn man die leüt von den Cantzlen
offt vnd trewlich ermanen solle.

308/309 zů Rǔprechtsaw vnnd zů Schlicken] two villages under the authority of
Strasbourg

CONCILIUM ARGENTORATENSE – 1533-1534

Zum dritten / spaltungen vnd secten zů verhůten / vnd zů verkommen /
So hat ein Ersa. Raht geordnet / vnnd wôllen / das keyn burger oder hinder-
345 saß seine kind / nach außgang der sechs wuchen der kindbet / mehr vngetaufft
lasse / ehe mag ers wol lassen tauffen / vnd die selbigen kinder vnserem Herren Christo Jesu zu bringen / den selbigenn vmb sein erlôsung vnd segen mit
glauben zů bitten / vnnd soliches segens sich zů getrôsten / die kindlin vff den
namen Christi vnnd in seinen todt tauffe / wie die Kirch den brauch von den
350 Apostolen / als die vralten vnns bezeügen / empfangen / biß anher gehalten /
wie dann auch die Juden jre kinder beschnitten / vnd sunst mit opfferen ge-
heyliget / vnd sich Gottes genaden vber sie / erinneret vnd getrôstet haben /
Welcher burger oder hinersaß aber das verbreche / sein kindlin / gehôrter
massen / vngetauffet liesse / den soll vnd will ein Ersa. Raht darvmb straffen /
355 vnd seins | burgerrechten verweisen. Zů dem / so last ein Ersa. Raht bey soli-   B3v
cher straff gebieten / welche burger oder hindersaß noch vngetauffte kinder
haben / die vber die zeit der sechs wochen alt seind / das sie die auch tauffen
lassen / Welcher aber solichs nit thůn wolte / die selben kinder soll vnd will
ein Ersa. Raht / so jnen das fürkommet / ordnen zů tauffen / vnd tauffen
360 lassen. Welcher burger oder hindersaß das aber auch nit wolte gestatten / den
soll vnd will ein Ers. Raht auch darumb straffen / vnd seins burgerrechten
verweisen.

Das H. Abentmal belangen.

Zum vierden / das H. Abentmal / in dem vns die gemeynschafft vnd
365 erlôsung vnsers Herren Jesu Christi zům hertzlichsten gehandlet / fürtragen /
dargereychet / vnd vbergeben würt / solle auch mit hôchster andacht / vnd
von gantzer gemeyn gehalten werden / Dernhalb ist geordnet / damit desto
mehr hynzů gangen / vnd alles mit ernst vnnd dapfferkeyt gehandlet / auch
das volck durch vorgohnde predigen / hie zů ordenlich vermanet werde / das
370 man das h. Abentmal hinfür inn den neben pfarren / zů vier wochen ein mal
halten / vnd inn disen vieren / S. Thoman / Claus / jung vnd alt S. Peter /
nach vnd vff einander / das alle Sontag inn disen vier pfarren einer / das
h. Abentmal begangen werde. Zů den Wilhelmeren vnd Aurelien / môgen
deßhaben zů jrer gelegenheyt / doch das es auch bey jnen nit lenger / dan die
375 vier wochen / verzogen werde / vnnd wie inn gedachten vier Pfarren.
Und solle alweg vorgonds Sontags / das volck des handels vleissig vnder-
richt vnnd erinneret werden. Im Münster / von wegen der grossen menig die

---

343/362 Zum – verweisen] given the context of this *Kirchenordnung*, it is not
surprising that an area of strict compulsion is expressed over the issue of infant baptism

370 CONCILIUM ARGENTORATENSE – 1533-1534

dahyn kommet / solle das Abentmal Christi wie biß har / alle Sontag gehalten / vnnd je zů zeiten / das volck inn den predigen auch dises handels vnder-
380 richtet / vnd sich zů dem recht zůschicken vermanet werden.

Zum fünfften / Nach dem vnser herr Jesus Christus / sein h. Abentmal
mit seinen jüngeren inn gemeyn halten / vnd der h. Paulus vß den worten vnd
einsatzung Christi schleüsset, das die nit des Herren Abent|mal halten / die es B4r
besonder / vnd nit inn / vnnd mit der gemeyn der gleubigen halten / Ist
385 geordnet / das mann die gleübigen ermanen solle / inn der gemeyn / zum
tisch des herren zů gohn / da sampt den anderen Christen jren brůderen vnnd
glyderen / jren Herren Jesum / das ware hymelbrot zů empfahen / vnnd sich
ein leib vnnd brot mit den gleübigen zů sein / auch damit zů beweisen / das sie
sich mit jnen / eins brots des Herren / teylhafftig machen. Uß dem sie so vil
390 lernen werden / das / so sie kranck vnd von hinnen berůfft werden / wan sie
nur glauben / Christum schon genossen haben / vnd niessen / wie das auch zů
aller zeit / wann mann bey der gemeyn Gottes nit sein kan / gar nit von nôten
ist / mund oder bauch zů bereyten / sonder glaubet jemand / so hat er / wie
der hey. Augustinus recht sagt / die speiß schon genossen / Dahyn sie auch /
395 durch die diener des worts / vnnd die jren / sollen gewisen werden / damit
nit / wie hieuor gewesen / die leüt das h. Sacrament inn der gemeyn zů empfahen / verlassen / vnnd dann inn jren kranckheyten / da sie etwann disen
heyligen hohen handel zů betrachten / den Herren mit rechtem glauben zů
empfahen / vnd seine gedechtnus mit warer danckbarkeyt zů halten / weder
400 vermôglich noch geschicket seind / meynen wôllen / jnen solle das eusser
empfahen des Sacraments für sich selb / wie es joch bei jnen / des glaubens
halb / stande / zů trost vnnd hilff kommen / vnd ein sichere wegspeiß sein inn
jhene welt / oder ein erleüchterung der kranckheyt.

Aber dieweil etwan leüt seind / die die gemeynschafft vnsers Herren in
405 disem h. Sacrament / noch nit empfangen vnnd hierinn den dienst der
kirchen nit geprauchet / vnd sich also noch nit bewisen / ein brot vnd ein leib
sein mit den anderen gleubigen / Wo dann soliche vor jrem abscheyd mit
anzeygung recht Christlichs hertzens / begerten auch dises Sacraments theyl-
hafftig zů werden / Den selbigen sollen die Pfarrer / vnd helffer hierinn
410 dienen / doch das sie sehen / das etliche mit jnen vnd dem krancken / diß
Abentmal Christi halten. Gleicher massen sind zů halten / die so schon in der
gemeyn etwan das Abentmal Christi gehalten / weren aber durch kranckheyt

---

394 die speiß schon genossen] cfr Augustinus, *In Iohannis evangelium tractatus
CXXIV* 25, 10, ed. R. Willems (*CC SL* 36), Turnhout 1954, p. 252-253 (= *PL* 35,
col. 1600-1601)

407 abscheyd] *a.c.* absheyd

CONCILIUM ARGENTORATENSE – 1533-1534   371

dahin bracht / das sie zů der gemeyn nit mehr kommen kônden. Wo sich von
anderen zů trůge / das sie soliches auch begereten / vnnd keynen sonderen
415   aberglauben in dem anzeygten / dieweil mit krancken alles vff Christlichen
trost / on vil disputierens / zů handlen ist / Soll jr Pfarrer / doch mit raht
seiner kirchen pfleger vnd der prediger / auch eins die zů den Examinatoren
verord|net seind / solichen auch zů willen werden / Doch das man / so vil   B4v
jnen môglich / darauff handle / das die Sacrament / nach der ordnung Chris-
420   ti / von meniglichen jnn der gemeyn gehalten / vnnd keyn aberglaub durch
die sondere Communion eingefůret / oder gehalten werde.

    Man soll auch die leüt von der Cantzel trewlich ermanen / das sie jre
krancken / durch jre seelsorger zů trôsten / nit verachten / vnnd aber auch die
selben bei zeiten beschicken wôllen / damit was da zů fürderung der seelen
425   heyl zů handlen / mit rechtem ernst / verstand vnd frucht / gehandlet werden
môge / es seie gleich des worts alleyn / oder auch der Sacramenten halb.

Der Jugend halb.

    Uff das aber an Christlicher zucht der jugend / so imm tauff dem Herren
ergeben würt / da sich auch die gantz kirch / sampt den elteren vnd gauat-
430   tern / begibt / die selbigen dem Herren vff zů ziehen / weniger versaumet werde / Hat ein Ersam. Raht geordnet / das vber die gemeynen kinder bericht /
so alle Sontag gehalten / vier gemeyne kinder bericht imm jar gehalten werden / den einenn den ersten Sontag Martij / den anderen den ersten Sontag
Junij / den dritten den ersten Sontag Septembris / den vierden den ersten
435   Sontag Decembris. Und soll alweg den vorgohnden Sontag / ein besonder
predig / von der zůcht der kinder / an die elteren beschehen / mit ernstlicher
ermanung / das jedes seine kinder vnd gesind / fleissig zům kinder bericht
schicken wôlle. Imm kinderbericht aber / die Articul des glaubens / Vatter
vnser vnd Zehen gepot / vffs kurtzest vnd hellest / erklâret werden. Zů soli-
440   chen gemeynen kinderberichten / solle auch meniglich / wie inn der schrifft
an die zünfften gestellet / die burger ermanet werden / jre kinder vnnd gesind
zů pringen / Dann sie getauffet vnnd also Christo ergeben seind / vnnd aber
der verderbten natur halb / nur durch andere gezogen werden můssen. Dern
halben auch niemand / inn einer Christlichen Stat vnnd gemeyn zů zůlassen /
445   an seinen kinden vnd gesinden so farlessig zů sein / das sie die doch nit solten
zů den kinder berichten fůren.

    Zum anderen / sollen die pfarrer das volck fleissig ermanen / das je|der-   Cir
man seine kind / so man sierstlich will lassen zum tisch der Herrenn gohn /
wôlle zůuor zů dem diener des worts / auff die Sontag zů dem kinderbericht

372 CONCILIUM ARGENTORATENSE – 1533-1534

450 bringen / vnnd nach dem selbigen lassen Christlicher leer halben inn seinem
beisein / etwas verhôret vnd bericht werden.

Zum dritten / Das die Schůl vnnd leer heüßer zum fürnemisten darumb
verordnet seind / das da die kinder / sampt gůten Gotseligen künsten zů rechtem Christlichen leben geleret vnnd gezogen werden / So sollen die Schůl-
455 meyster / die jenigen so bey jnen zů hauß vnd kost seind / also jre elteren nit
haben / alle Sontag zur predig fůren / oder schaffen das die selbige zur predig
bracht werden / Die anderen / jre leer knaben / Soll ein jeder vatter sein kind
vnd gesind zur predig vnd kinderbericht ziehen / Vnnd solle doch inn beden
Lateinischen schůlen / durch die prediger vnd jre helffer / wie sie das ordnen
460 môgen / alle wochen vff ein genanten tag / inn der schůl ein ermanung vnd
predig / den jungen dienstlich beschehen.

FÜR DIE GANTZE GEMEYN.

Dieweil der glaub auß dem gehôre kommet / vnd das Gotswort mit
frucht nit kan gehôret werden / es begeben sich dan die gemůter / mit aller
465 begirden vnd gentzlich hie zů / Dernhalben es Got zů aller zeit gefallen / das
mann zum wenigsten einen tag inn der wochen hiezů heyligte / vnd an dem
selben aller anderen geschefft můssig stůnde / damit mann das wort Gottes /
mit recht Got ergebnem gemůt hôren / die Sacrament empfahen / gebet vnnd
andere Gôtliche werck ůben môchte. Sollichs solte nun bey niemand ernstli-
470 cher / dann bey vns / die wir vns der reynen erkantnüß des h. Euangelij
rhůmen wôllen / gehalten werden / Vnd mann aber findet / die vff die Sontag / auch vnder den morgen predigen / vff den pletzen / greben / vnd vor der
stat spacieren gohnd / inn würts vnd scherheüseren sitzen zů schwetzen /
zechen vnnd spilen. Desgleichen vnder der Mittag predig / alles wider eins
475 Ersamen Rahts hieuor außgangene Mandaten vnd gepotten / Vnnd auch
etliche zünffte seind / die alweg / so sie zů schaffen haben / zů der stund der
Mittag predig zůsamen gepieten / so mann doch darnach zeit genůg hette / da
solle mann die voraußgangne Mandaten wider erfrischen / vnd vff den
zünfften mit allem ernst verkünden / | auch darob halten / vnd die prediger C IV
480 mit trewem vleis das volck ermanen / das nemlich jederman / sich vnnd die
seinen / vff die Sontag zur predig schicken solle. Item das vnder den predigen

---

463/489 Dieweil – solle] treatment of the issue of Church attendance reflected
concerns to promote unity in parishes, to uphold moral standards of Sabbath
observance, and to prevent any disturbance of Sunday services, including anyone
conducting shooting practice

---

478 Mandaten] *a.c.* Manten

CONCILIUM ARGENTORATENSE – 1533-1534

niemand solle feyl haben / keyn würt / scherer / oder andere vnder der zeit
der morgen oder Mittags predigen / inn seinem hauß jemands zů zechen /
oder spylen / gestatten / das auch niemand vff die Sontag offentlich one notdurfft arbeyte / noch vff den Sontag bauche / noch bauch außwesche. Item das
niemand vnder den morgen vnd Mittags predigen vff die Sontag / offentlich
vergeblich spacieren / gehen / stehn / oder vff den pletzen / greben / vnd
sunst inn den würts vnd scherheüseren sitze. Item sich auch morgens vnder
den Predigen niemands beschiessen solle. Item das auch vff keiner zunfft
mehr / zů der zeit der predigen / zůsamen gebotten / oder etwas gehandelt
werde / die weil die feirtag abgangen / damit der Sontag nit also wider
Gŏtlich / Christlich / der alten Keyser / vnd eins Ersamen Rahts außgangen
gepot / so übel gehalten werde / vnd frembd vnd heymisch / darab vrsach
nemmen / das h. Euangeli vnd den gantzen handel zů lesteren.

Zum anderen / So ist auch ein geuahrlicher mißbrauch / so mann imm
Münster / auch inn etlichen anderen pfarren oder kirchen / prediget / das die
leüt in den kirchen spacieren vnd schwetzen / welchs / bede die prediger vnd
zůhŏrer / verstŏret / das bei dem volck Gottes je vnd je ein vntreglicher grewel
gewesen / vnd dann solichs jnn einem weltlichen raht vnd zunffthauß / da
mann etwas zů handlen hat / nit gestattet würde / Unnd vnser lieber herr
Jesus / als er zů Jerusalem den ernst imm Tempel erzeygte mit dem außtreiben
der kauffer vnd verkauffer / liesse er auch keyn geschirr durch den Tempel
tragen. Mar. 11. So haben auch etliche priester / die es weniger thŭn solten /
vnd andere / den mißbrauch / das sie zur zeit der predigen / an den bŭchleden
hart amm Münster ligen zůschwetzen. Dieweil dann wir Christen die versam-
lungen zum heylig seligmachenden Euangeli je also halten / vnnd zů halten /
mit hŏchstem ernst verschaffen sollen / das wir die krafft Gottes zur seligkeyt /
allen die daran glauben / erkennen / vnd die leüt auch gern dazů fürderen
sollen. So hat ein Ersamer Raht zur ehren Gottes / vor dem mann je mit
hŏchster zucht vnd andacht erscheinen soll / vnd auch zů verhütung erger-
nüß / heymischer vnnd frŏmbder / sampt verstŏrung der prediger vnnd
zůhŏrer / geordnet / vnd wellen das niemand zů der zeit / so man prediget
vnd singet / | jmm Münster oder anderen kirchen / gehen / oder darinnen C2r
spacieren solle. Auch das die priester oder andere / zur zeit der predigen / vff
den leden ann der Münster thŭr ligen / oder jre thenth da auß zůrichten sich
mŭssigen sollen. Damit dise stet / doch soliche kurtze zeit / gŏtliche lere vnd

---

495/503 Zum – tragen] cfr Marc. 11, 15 seq.

495/503 Zum – tragen] the Gospel of Mark is cited in defence of the purity of
churches as spaces for the worship of God

betheüser seien / vnd darfür gehalten werden. Alles bei peen 5 schilling pfennig die man jedem verbrecher abnemmen würt. Vnnd damit solichs gehalten / so solle es den sibnen vnd jren knechten zů růgen vnd straffen / beuolhen werden / Doch welcher das nit gewüst hete / vnd sich bei seinen trewen des mócht purgieren vnd entschuldigen / solle der straffe vberhaben seyn.

Zům dritten / ist ein mißbrauch / das man was verloren würt / kinder / vihe / kleyder / gelt vnnd anders / zů end der Predig / da man das volck zům gebet vnd gesang ermanet / vnd besonder andacht pflegen soll / verkündet / Dernhalb haben vnsere Herren / ein Ersa. Raht erkennet vnd wóllen / das wer etwas verloren / das selbig inn zedelen verzeychnet / dem Sigristen imm Münster bringe / der ein taffel ann predigstůl hencken solle / vnd soliche hendel an den selbigen hefften / wie man hie vor deren namen / welchen man geleüet / an ein taffel ankleybet hat / Dabei soll er auch solicher zedel abschrifft bei jm behalten / damit jeder der verloren oder funden hat / bei jhm bescheyd finden móge / vnnd man nit zůr zeit der fünemisten andacht / von sewen / oder anderem verlieren vnnd finden / handlen můsse / Doch der krancken halb / da man das bett begeret / solle man der massen wie herkommen / verkünden.

Zům vierden / Dieweil den Pfarrern vnnd Kirchspyl pflegern eygentlich gebůret / das sie deren / die zů der pfarr gehóren / sich Christlichs namens berhůmen / vnd getauffet seind / besonder sorg tragen / vnd an dem nichs vnderlassen / da durch zů verhoffen / das soliche Christum vnseren Herren in der warheit lerneten / sich zů seinem wort vnd Sacrament / als glider seiner gemeyn / mit aller andacht fůgten / vnd in allem jrem leben also beweisen / als die jren tauff / vnd die genad Gottes / das er sie zů seinem Sůn berůffet / auch etwar für halten / Da hat ein Ersa. Raht erkant / nach dem leyder durch die vil trennungen der Religion / so sich erhaben / eben vil leüt seind / die weder für sich / noch die jren / der Predigen vnd Sacramenten achten / Auch nit wenig / ob sie schon etwan predig hóren / vileicht auch zům tisch des Herren gohn / doch also leben / das durch sie nichs dann der namme Gottes / vnd das heilig Euan|geli gelesteret würt / das die kirchspyl pfleger gewalt vnnd beuelch haben sollen / vff die Sontag oder andere tag jegliche in jrer pfarr zůsamen kommen / vnd wa soliche leüt inn pfarren / alle mal der selbigen etliche beschicken / oder von jhnen verordnen / die solche besonders ansprechen / wie sie das für fruchtpar erkennen / Und so die selbigen von denen weren / die sich von der gemeyn Christi gar sónderen / sie mit aller sennft můt vrsach fordern / warumb sie sich also von der gemeynschafft der kirchen

---

517 bei peen] *intellege* punishment by fine   5 schilling pfennig] *supplevimus*; *a.c.* v. ß. pfen.

CONCILIUM ARGENTORATENSE – 1533-1534

abhalten / vnd ab der leer vnd Sacramenten scheuhen / die doch die Oberkeyt
vnd gantz gemeyne Statt / für Christlich erkennen vnnd halten / Und so sie
dessen etwas vrsachen fürwenden / das sie ihnen dann in aller freundtlicheyt /
christlichen bericht thůen / vnd sie zů gewinnen vnderstanden. Sehe mann
dann / das soliche keyn besundere vrsachen hetten / weren sunst so einer
kleynen forcht Gottes / sie ermanen Gottes mer zůachten / vnd vor augen
zůhaben. Wo dann seind / die sich wol dahyn vermögen lassen / das sie selb
predig hören / vnd die ihren auch darzů halten wolten / vnd sich aber noch
nit dahyn begeben / das sie auch zům tisch des Herren gehn wolten / die
sollen sie also dem Herren lassen stohn / vermanen das sie dem wort vnd gebet
dapffer anhangen / vnd Gott zů bitten / das er jhnen verleihe sich an ihn
volkummen zůbegeben / vnd sie halten / wie vorzeyten die Catechumenj
gehalten worden seind / das ist / die sich der Christlichen leer begeben / vnnd
doch noch nit gemeynschafft der kirchen / durch die Sacrament angenommen
hatten.

Befinden sie aber dann / die sich soliche grosse offenbare veråchter Gôtli-
ches worts / oder widersprecher bewysen / das mann jnen das heyligthumb
vnd berlin Gôtlichs worts / nit kônde fürwerffen / die lassen sie faren / vnd
beuelhen sie Gôtlichem gericht / doch das mann jnen dennoch burgerliche
freündtschafft vnd dienst / mit aller senftmůt vnd gůtem willen leyste / vnnd
zů leysten vermane. Dann die Christen / wie jr himlischer vatter / gůts thůn /
vnd allen menschen / auch Juden vnnd Heyden / on anstoß leben sollen. Dergleichen sollen sie auch handlen mit denen die sich wol mit predig hôren vnd
gemeynschafft der h. Sacramenten / etwan Christen beweisen / aber also
leben / das sie offentliche ergernüs geben / vnd Christo vnserem Herren vnd
seiner kirchen / zů schand vnd schmach seind / vnd sich dauon durch leren /
vermanen / noch Christlichem anhalten nit wôllen abwenden lassen / Soliche
sorg vnd vleis für die zů haben / so getauffet vnd den namen Christi tragen / | C3r
sie also zů jrem heyl zů fürderen / hat vns der Herr gebotten / vnd môgen keyn
Christi genant werden / wa wir nit der massen vns vnserselb durch einander
annemmen / So werden dise auch nit Christen sein / welche sich solichen
ermanen vnd anfůren zů Christlichem leben entziehen wôllen / wie wir dann
das so auß getrucket haben / Mat. 18. Roma. 12. I. Corin. 12. vnnd zwar jnn
allen Epistolen Pauli / wie dann ein jeder wol erkennen kan / das da gar keyn
leib Christi sein můß / wo man solichen dienst vnd fürderung zur seligkeyt /

569/571 Befinden – fürwerffen] cfr Matth. 7, 6-8   **584/590** So – hat] cfr I Cor. 12;
Matth. 18, 15-17; Rom. 12, 2

569/571 Befinden – fürwerffen] regarding those who openly despise the pearls of
God's Word

376   CONCILIUM ARGENTORATENSE – 1533-1534

den menschen nit beweiset / oder den selbigen / wo jemand der bewysen
590 würt / nit zů gůt hat. So vil zwar will der Herr / das der kirchen leer / verma-
nung / vnd gemeynschafft gelte / das er gesagt hat / Wen die kirch vff erden
binde oder lôße / der sol imm hymel bunden oder loß sein / vnd welchen sie
die sünden behalte / oder nachlasse / denen sollen sie behalten oder nachgelassen sein. Unnd so jenen / den kirchspylpflegeren / hierin schweres zů fiele /
595 jnn dem môgen sie der Pfarrerraht pflegen vnd haben.

DER EHE HALBEN.

Zum ersten / Nach dem die Ehe bezeügung vnd einsegnung ein Christlich gotselig werck ist / da mann die eheleüt jres stands jmm Herren berichtet / vnd vmb genade inn dem selbigen Christlich zů leben bittet / Ists ja
600 vnfůglich / das man sie entweders verstohlner weis frů vor tag / oder jmm
tag / mit so üppigem bracht / pfeiffen vnd trummen außrichtet / vnd darzů
zeüchet. Man soll je vor Got frey vnnd offentlich / aber mit demůtigem
erschlagnen hertzenerscheinen. Da ist geordnet vnd erkant / das keyn helffer
oder pfarrer niemand / es seye wer der wôlle / vor dem morgen gepet jnfůren
605 solle / sonder wa ein ehe jnzůsegnen / vnd man das frů will haben / das sich
sollich Ehe vnd brautleüt zům morgen gepet verfůgen / daselben das worts
Gottes hôren / jr gebet mit anderen glaubigen thůn / vnnd als dann eingesegnet werden sollen. Welche aber zur tagzeyt wôllen kommen / so sie inn das
Münster pfarren / sollen zur tag predig da selbst mit allen züchten erschei-
610 nen / die predig mit andacht hôren / vnnd daruff eingesegnet werden / vnd
inn den andren pfarren / solle es beschehen vff die tag / so mann die tagpredi-
gen darinn haltet. Wo es aber jemand vff andere tag thůn wolte / so sollen die
brautleüt mit jren lieben freünden vnd gesten / inn al|ler zůcht zur kirchen   C3v
kommen / zů der zeit / wie jnen darzů gelegen sein mage / vnd die versamlung
615 am grôsten ist. Den selben soll dann der diener des worts / desto ein dapffere
ermanung / auß dem wort Gottes thůn / Und solle jn alweg hiemit verbotten
sein / zů solichen kirchgang / paucken / seytenspyl / oder etwas weltlicher
üpigkeyt zů gebrauchen oder ůben / Dan so diser stand so heylig / vnd so vil
allem menschlichen geschlecht daran / das er wol vnd Christlich angefangen
620 vnd gehalten werde / gelegen / vnd der kirchgang vnd das einsegnen je
darumb angesehen ist / das man solichen stand / inn vnd mit Got anzutret-

---

590/594 So – sein] cfr Matth. 18, 18; 16, 19

594/595 Unnd – haben] facing difficult cases, parish wardens are encouraged to seek
the help of ministers

CONCILIUM ARGENTORATENSE – 1533-1534

ten / vnd darinn zů leben geleret werde / vnnd darzů genad vnnd segen von
Got erlange / so solle je das mit besonder ernstlicher Gotsforcht vnd andacht
bewysen werden / so man doch zůuor / wa etwas erberkeyt vnd Gotsforcht
was / gebeichtet / vnd zum einsegnen / alweg Meß gehóret / vor vnd ehe
gebettet hat. Was nun Gotselig ist / solle bey vns so vil ernstlicher geůbet werden / so vil wir vns mehr Gótlichs wissens berhůmen.

Zum anderen / Es ist auch ein brauch von altem her / das sie landleüt / so
inn der nehe sein / jre Ehen inn der stat lassen einsegnen / fürnemlich imm
Münster / als sie sagen costen zů vermeiden / den sie dussen halten můsten /
inn dem sie vil leüt darzů zůladen / nit vmbgehn kónden / So tregt sich aber
dabei zů / das sie ehen haben / die nit richtig seind / die man jnen dussen nit
einsegnen würde / wischen also hie hindurch / da mann sie nit kennet / vnd
bringet also ergernüs. Dem zů begegnen / so sollen die diener des worts /
allemal von den selben eruordern, das sie etliche burger zů gegen bringen zů
zeügen. Ob nun gleich wol die selben den dieneren der worts nit so bekant /
etwan auch selb nit grüntlich wissen von sachen / mage mann dieselben vff ir
gefahr infůren / vnd jnen damit darzů dienen / das sie des ehstandts ein mal
gründtlich berichtet werden / vnd vff Got gewisen / Doch so man also
jemand vff ein vngewisses wil einsegnen / solle souil jmmer móglich / mit
ernst daruff gesehen werden / das niemand jhm seines vnrechten behilff sůche.

| FÜR DIE KIRCHEN VFF DEM LAND.   C4r

Zum ersten / So haben die pfarrer vff dem land vil mengel / die kirchen
ordnung betreffen / fürbracht / denen nit anders / oder satt geholffen werden
mage / dann durch ein Visitation. Der halben hat ein Ersamer Raht erkant /
jårlich zwen von kirchspylpflegeren / vnd einen von den Predigern erwehlet /
vnd hinauß geschickt sollen werden / ein trewe / leyische lere vnd ermanung
zů thůn zů rechtem Christlichem leben / welches der prediger zům ernstlichsten erzelen / vnd daruff trewlich ermanen / wa man fehl vnd mangel an leer
vnd leben des Pfarrers / oder anderer hette / das man soliches wólle den genanten Visitatoren getrewlich anzeygen. Zů solichem predigen solle auch
jederman / alt vnnd jung / gebotten werden / Unnd daruff sollen dann die
Kirchen pfleger / den Schuldheyß / das gericht / vnd pfarrer besonder befra-
gen / vnd so jemand etwas mangel an zů zeygen hette / verhóren. Auch etwan
so sich die vrsach zü trůge / fragen / vnd dann zur besserung / vnnd nach dem
das hie als Christlich verordnet / alles anrichten / so vil jnen das móglich. Was
jnen aber zů schwer sein wolte / das sollen sie heryn für die gemeynen kirch-

---

655 besserung] *a.c.* besseruug

378 CONCILIUM ARGENTORATENSE – 1533-1534

spyl pfleger / vnd als dann so es die notdurfft erforderet / für einen Ersamen
Raht bringen.

660   Zům anderen / So sollen die zwen kirchspyl pfleger / so also zů Visitieren
hinauß gesandt / die rechnug der kirchen geschworen besehen / wie solich gůt
gebrauchet würt / vnd auch verschaffen / das es Christlich / das ist vff die
armen gewendet werde. Und so man zů vor auß solichem gůt / so vil kosten
hat můssen haben / mit Meß vnnd gesang bůcheren / darnach kirchen
665 gezierd / kertzen vnd dergleichen / So sollen darauß zů allen pfarren vff dem
land / etliche notwendige bůcher gekauffet werden / die weil die pfarrer der
mehrer teyl schmal versehen sein / vnd solichs selb nit vermögen. Und vor
allem soll ein jede pfarr haben ein latinische vnd teütsche Bibel / Historiam
Ecclesiasticam / Commentaria in vetus testamentum Pellicani / Postillam
670 Lutheri / In Epistolam ad Galatas / Petri / in Deuteronomium / vnd etliche
Propheten. Item was von D. Oecolampadio / vnd hie vber die H. schrifft außgangen / Als vber den Esaiam / Jeremiam / die drey letsten kleinen Propheten / vber Ezechielem / Danielem / Job / Hoseam / Abacuc / Zephaniam /
den Psalter / die vier Euangelia / vber die Epistel zůn Rőmerern / Ephesern /
675 vnd was | sunst mag nutzlich vnd jeder pfarr zů kauffen treglich sein. Und die   C4v
bůcher so also kauffet / sollen auch jnventiret vnd vffgeschriben / vnnd nit
von der pfarr genommen werden. Soliche Visitation vnd heymsůchen / haben
die alen / eh der abfall so grob eingerissen / mit grossem ernst gehalten /
Dauon noch in etlichen Stifften das vber bliben / das man heysset den send
680 bereiten / vnd derhalben haben auch alle Euangelische stend / die etwas Land-
schafften haben / soliche Visitation wider an die hand genommen / vnd schaffen damit nit geringe frucht.

    Zům dritten / Ist aller Pfarrer vff dem land einhellig clag / das inn allen
flecken ein grosse verlassung seie / das wort Gottes zů hőren / welche verlas-
685 sung am mehrteyl orten durch die eingefüret / erhalten vnnd gemehret
würdt / die soliches billich vor anderen solten verhůten. Dann vff die Sontag
pflegen eben vil / die zeit so man prediget / vff den kirchhőffen / vnder den
lauben / an anderen pletzen / in würtsheüseren / vnnd sunst zů stehn vnd
sitzen / da selbet schwetzen / etwan auch spylen / zechen / vnd ander vnor-
690 denlich wesen füren. Es seind auch die / so man prediget / vnder den kirchen
stohnd zů gleyen vnd můtwill zůtreiben / das sie die so predigen vnd hőren /
jrr machen / An etlichen orten / die Schultheyß zůr zeit der predig / gericht

---

669 Pellicani] Konrad Pellikan (Kürsner or Kürschner) was born in Alsace, taught at
Basel, and then in 1526 moved to teach Greek and Hebrew in Zurich
671 Oecolampadio] Johannes Oecolampadius (Heussgen, Hussgen or Hausschein)
was the Palatinate-born leading supporter of reform in Basel from the early 1520s to his
death in 1531

CONCILIUM ARGENTORATENSE – 1533-1534

vnd gemeyn halten. Dieweil dann nůn alle feyertag ab sein / vnd das gantz menschlich heyl daran staht / das man Gottes wort hôre vnd glaube / auch das arm arbeytsam Landvolck amm verstand so schwach vnd vnerůbet / das jm gar vil mehr / dann anderenn / von nôten ist / das es durch die Oberkeyt gezogen / vnd zů seinem nutz gefůret werde / So solle jnen von der Oberkeyt wegen / gebotten werden / vff die Sontag sich vnd jre knecht vnd gesind zur predig zů schicken / vnd bey pen 3 schilling pfennig verbieten / das zur zeit der predig niemand sich ann der gassen / vff den kirchhôuen / vnder den lauben / inn würtsheüseren / oder anderswo / finden lassen. Noch vil weniger bey peen 10 schilling pfennig zeche / spyle / dantze / oder andere leichtigheyten treibe. Gleicher straff der zehen schilling / solle auch daruff gesetzet sein / wa mann zů solcher zeyt der predig / gericht oder gemeyn hielte.

Zum vierden / demnach vff dem land ein grosser / vnnd den armen leüten ein beschwerlicher mißbrauch ist / mit den kirchweihenen vnnd meßtagen / vff welche die Armen leüt / das jr mit hauffen verschwenden / geübet werden / das es bei den Heyden nit erlitten were / dadurch das jung vnd frembd volck hôchlich verergeret würt. Soliche Heyd|nische / ja vihische miß- Dir breuch sollen abgestellet / vnd in allen flecken mit namen verpotten werden / das niemand vberal / weder fremd noch heymisch gestattet werde / vnder den zeiten / so man vff soliche tag predigt / zů thantzen / zechen / oder ander üppikeyt zů treiben. Und so man mitler zeit freüntlich zeren / oder auch jungem volck ein thantz erlauben würde / so sollen alweg etliche besonder dapffere menner verordnet werden / die alwegen darbey seien / vnd ein ernstlich einsehen haben / das in dem zechen eins Ersamen Rahts Constitution vnd ordnung / nit vber tretten / vnd imm thantzen keyn unzůcht / wie dann das jung landuolck etwann gar zů vil vnuerschammet ist / begangen / vnd zů rechter zeit auch vff gehôret werde / damit sie nit biß in die mitnacht vnd lenger dantzen / vnd dabey alle vnzůcht treiben / vnnd dann erst bei nacht heym ziehen. Ob auch Schuldheyß vnd gericht darinn fahrlessig sein würden / die selbigen solle man darumb straffen.

Zům fünfften / der H. Sacramenten halben / ist bedacht das / so vil môglich / der tauff wie alhie in der Stat / vff die Sontag / vnd das H. Abentmal zů vier wochen eynist gehalten würde / oder vffs lengist zů acht wochen / nach einer jeden kirchen gelegenheyt.

Zům sechsten / So sollen die Visitatoren beuelch habenn / wa sie noch ergerliche bilder / die zů offenlicher abgôtterey vnd aberglauben gebrauchet werden / inn kirchen vff dem land funden / dieselbigen ab zů schaffen.

---

699 3 schilling pfennig] *supplevimus*; *a.c.* iij. ß. pfen. **702** 10 schilling pfennig] *supplevimus*; *a.c.* x. ß. pfenig.

CONCILIUM GENEVENSE

1541

ediderunt
Gianmarco BRAGHI – Graeme MURDOCK

THE *ECCLESIASTICAL ORDINANCES* OF GENEVA*
1541

INTRODUCTION

In 1541 the civil authorities in Geneva approved ordinances to regulate religious life in the communities under their jurisdiction. These *Ecclesiastical Ordinances* were of immediate and lasting importance for the structure of the Reformed Church both in the city and in surrounding villages and hamlets under Genevan authority. The *Ordinances* also marked a significant moment in the relationship between the Genevan magistrates and their French employee, John Calvin. Geneva's 1541 *Ordinances* reflected many of Calvin's views about the model of ecclesiastical government set out in the Bible. The application of Calvin's ideas in Geneva also proved to have a broad and long-lasting legacy across Europe's Reformed churches.

The Genevan republic was ruled by magistrates in different councils. Four syndics headed the Small Council (*Petit Conseil*) which was the key executive body within the state. A Council of Sixty included members of the Small Council and thirty-five representatives from the Council of Two Hundred. The Council of Two Hundred (established in 1527) elected most of the members of the Small Council and voted on measures presented to it by the Small Council. A General Council of all citizens met irregularly and elected the city's syndics. In October 1534 the Small Council declared that the office of prince-bishop was vacant (candidates for this office were nominated by the dukes of Savoy). In pursuit of independence from Savoyard domination, Geneva turned to Bern for support. However, this alliance was far from unproblematic given Bern's expansionist designs and promotion of its own brand of religious reform. In August 1535 Guillaume Farel and his supporters seized control of the cathedral of Saint Pierre. Following a subsequent wave of iconoclasm, the Council of Two Hundred voted to suspend celebrations of the Mass. As the tide turned in favour of reform, most Roman Catholic clergy and members of religious orders left Geneva in the autumn of 1535. A Savoyard siege of the city was relieved by Bernese forces in February 1536. Bern occupied the lands around Geneva from the Pays de Vaud to the Chablais. In May 1536

(*) Introduction by Graeme Murdock; critical edition by Gianmarco Braghi.

a meeting of the General Council proclaimed that Geneva had embraced reform and the Mass was banned. The authorities had already laid claim to Roman Catholic churches, property, lands, and the rights previously exercised by the prince-bishop, cathedral chapter, and by the priory of Saint Victor (the prior was later offered a pension as compensation). The republic asserted that it had gained rights to appoint clergy and to collect tithe payments in the parishes under its jurisdiction. Geneva and its new neighbour Bern contested the precise extent and character of their overlapping rights, particularly with respect to the rural parishes in the city's hinterland. The revenue gained from Roman Catholic property, lands, and rights was significant for the new republic and used in part to pay the salaries of appointed ministers and to support a new hospital on the site of a former convent. ([1])

In January 1537 Guillaume Farel (on behalf of the city's ministers) presented the Small Council with proposed ecclesiastical articles. These proposals included plans for monthly services of communion, required an oath of allegiance to the 1536 Genevan *Confession*, and included protection of the purity of communion through the right to excommunicate persistent rebels and moral offenders. However, the Council baulked at holding more than four communion services each year and at the suggested powers of exclusion from the sacraments. Tensions between ministers and magistrates escalated over the consequences of the need to maintain good relations with Bern. In 1538 the dominant faction on the Small Council favoured bringing Genevan religious practices into alignment with those of Bern. Calvin and Farel objected to being asked to use unleavened bread in communion and to the civil authorities holding the power to excommunicate members of the Church. After Calvin and Farel refused to administer communion using unleavened bread at Easter in 1538, the Small Council demanded that they leave the city within three days. ([2])

Calvin moved to Strasbourg where he led a small congregation of French refugees. Calvin oversaw the appointment of elders and deacons to assist in the governance and discipline of this community. Calvin also completed the 1539 revision of the *Institutes of the Christian Religion* setting out his views on ecclesiastical government. Turbulence in the Genevan Church did not abate following Calvin's departure. In October 1540 a majority on the Small Council voted to seek to bring Calvin back to the city. Calvin protested his reluc-

---

(1) On the structures of governance in Geneva see Monter, *Studies in Genevan Government*. For an overview of the religious history of Geneva in this period see Balserak, *The Reformation in Geneva*.

(2) Significant biographies of Calvin include Doumergue, *Jean Calvin*; Bouwsma, *John Calvin*; Gordon, *Calvin*.

CONCILIUM GENEVENSE – 1541

tance to return to Geneva, despite encouragement to do so from Farel, Pierre Viret, and the leaders of the churches in Basel and Zurich. Calvin finally agreed to leave Strasbourg and first appeared before the Small Council on 13 September 1541. The Small Council agreed to set up a committee to draft proposed regulations for the Genevan Church. Calvin drafted a text for review by this committee (councillors on this committee had supported Calvin's return and some would soon be appointed as elders). The committee was able quickly to agree a draft text that was presented to the Small Council on 27 September. The Small Council then debated this text at length over the following weeks. Amendments were introduced to clarify the rights and prerogatives of magistrates and other changes were made including about the frequency of services of communion. An amended text was then presented to the Small Council on 25 October. Once agreed, it was then approved by the Council of Two Hundred on 9 November, and subsequently by a General Council held on 20 November 1541.

FINDING A NEW BALANCE BETWEEN STATE AND CHURCH

The 1541 *Ecclesiastical Ordinances* were a product of this process of discussion and amendment but remained clearly influenced by Calvin's understanding of the model of ecclesiastical government found in Paul's letters to early churches. However, as Bruce Gordon comments, Calvin was 'largely indifferent to precise forms of organization and practice as long as they were grounded in scripture'. (3) Thus, while Calvin included the term bishop ('*evesque*') as another word used in Scripture to describe a pastor in a draft of the *Ordinances*, he was not concerned that Genevan sensitivities about their recent history with bishops meant that the term was removed from the final text. (4)

The 1541 *Ordinances* set out a vision of how civil magistrates, pastors, and lay officials should work together to lead the Church, and established four orders of ministry: pastors, doctors, elders, and deacons. The *Ordinances* set out the functions and processes of appointment for these offices, as well as disciplinary procedures against those who failed to uphold expected standards in the performance of their duties. Pastors were responsible for preaching, for administering the sacraments of baptism and communion, and for reprimanding those who held false beliefs or who exhibited poor standards of personal morality. The *Ordinances* required that pastors attend weekly meetings – known as *congrégations* – to discuss passages of Scripture with the aim of

(3) Gordon, *Calvin*, p. 126.
(4) See the critical edition below.

ensuring unity in doctrine. In the event of intractable disputes or problems about divisions over doctrine among the pastors, they were to turn to the civil magistrates for assistance (a significant concession to magisterial authority). From 1546 ministers also met as a Company of Pastors with Calvin as moderator to discuss all sorts of practical matters. Candidates for the role of pastor were examined on their knowledge of the Bible, on their ability to preach, and on their moral conduct. While existing pastors could nominate candidates, it was the Small Council that decided on appointments: successful candidates were then presented to congregations without any ceremonial ordination. The Council had the power to move pastors from urban posts to serve in rural parishes – which meant a drop in salary – or to remove pastors from office altogether following serious misconduct. (5)

Pastors alone could conduct sacraments. The *Ordinances* included a requirement for pastors to keep baptismal registers and to list the names given to children as well as the names of parents. This was no abstract enthusiasm for record-keeping: the *Ordinances* made clear that pastors should inform the civil authorities about children born outside of marriage. This written record of children's names proved of further use in 1546 following state regulations listing names that could not be used in baptisms. This was implemented by pastors in the face of some popular resistance. (6) The *Ordinances* approved the frequent holding of communion services. However – in a further concession by Calvin to the views of the magistrates – it was advised that only four services of communion would be held at Christmas, Easter, Pentecost, and on the first Sunday in September. Anyone wishing to participate in communion had to receive instruction in their faith. The *Ordinances* stressed the dangers for anyone who partook in communion without a clear understanding of the meaning of the ritual. Church members also had to be in good moral standing with the Church to gain access to communion. (7)

Elders shared with pastors the responsibility for moral oversight of the Church. Elders were appointed from among the four syndics and other members of the Small Council, from the Council of Sixty, and from the Council of Two Hundred. Each elder was responsible for a particular district of the city and charged to oversee the conduct of those in their area, arranging for fraternal correction of individuals when necessary. The elders and pastors met as a consistory on Thursdays – a syndic normally presided at meetings – to con-

---

(5) Manetsch, *Calvin's Company of Pastors*; de Boer, *The Genevan School of the Prophets*.

(6) Spierling, *Infant Baptism*; Naphy, 'Baptisms, Church Riots and Social Unrest'.

(7) Grosse, *Les rituels de la Cène*. From 1550 Communion services were held on the nearest Sunday to Christmas day. See Kingdon, *Reforming Geneva*, p. 111.

duct formal interviews of those called to answer for their opinions or behaviour. While the consistory could concern itself with disputes over engagements and marriages, the *Ordinances* made clear that the civil authorities had ultimate jurisdiction over marriages. The *Ordinances* outlined the disciplinary procedures that the elders and pastors were to follow. The consistory could admonish people about their conduct and warn offenders about the consequences of persistent disobedience. People were commonly reprimanded for poor attendance at services and instructed to attend more sermons. The consistory's aim was that offenders should repent of their sins. When the consistory did not see any evidence that people had accepted their errors or that they were attempting to mend their ways, it could instruct people to abstain from communion. This punishment of suspension from communion was intended to prompt offenders to repentance and was a very different matter from excommunication. (8) On the excommunication of members of the Church, the *Ordinances* suggested that very serious offenders and criminal matters were to be reported by the consistory to the civil authorities. The Council's intent that rare cases that might merit excommunication were matters for the magistrates was made clear by amendments made to the draft text that stressed that the consistory only held spiritual powers and its existence did not diminish in any way the authority of the city's magistrates.

The *Ordinances* also outlined the role of doctors in the Church to maintain sound doctrine and to ensure that there was no infection of false ideas among pastors. The *Ordinances* proposed that a college should be established capable not only of instructing children – a school had already been set up in the city – but also able to prepare students for the ministry. Long delayed through a lack of resources, a higher-level college with instruction in theology was only begun within a new academy opened in 1559 under its first rector, Theodore Beza. Until 1559 the practical role of doctors in the Genevan Church had therefore remained unclear. (9) The *Ordinances* suggested that deacons should be appointed to provide for the needs of the poor and the sick. The role of deacon was taken to be fulfilled by existing officers appointed within the system of poor relief that had already been established in Geneva through a hospital (or poor house). Officials with financial, administrative, and practical responsibilities (*procureurs* and *hospitalliers*) were charged with managing funds provided for the poor and with distributing support and medical care to those unable to work because of illness or old age whether

(8) Watt, *The Consistory and Social Discipline*.
(9) Maag, *Seminary or University?*

resident in the hospital or living elsewhere in the city. The *Ordinances* also included a provision against begging as contrary to good order. ([10])

The *Ordinances* set out further practical rules intended to structure religious life in the city, including details about the timing and frequency of services. The regulations suggested the number of pastors required to serve the three churches within the city's walls (Saint Pierre, the Madeleine, and Saint Gervais on the right bank of the river Rhône). These churches did not operate strictly as parishes, although the *Ordinances* encouraged people to receive communion, have their children baptised, and send their children to catechism class in their parish. Some details were provided about the conduct of funerals with a concern to avoid 'all superstitions contrary to the word of God'. The *Ordinances* encouraged people to seek spiritual support from pastors during periods of ill-health and to call on their pastors to visit and to pray with them. ([11]) In 1547 separate ordinances were approved with further regulations for Geneva's rural parishes. Rural pastors were given responsibility for two or three village churches each and wardens were appointed by the Small Council to assist rural pastors in their work of moral discipline. ([12])

The Significance of the *Ordinances*

Some aspects of the 1541 *Ordinances* were not implemented immediately and other points remained open to interpretation. Divisions remained over where authority should lie to excommunicate members of the state Church. Calvin and his supporters pressed from the early 1550s for the consistory to hold the exclusive right to excommunicate. This was conceded in 1555 following a failed effort by some members of leading Genevan families to reverse their diminishing political and social influence. Amid growing numbers of migrants arriving from France, resentment among a faction known as Perrinists focussed on the claims of authority by the French-born pastorate and the issue of excommunication. However, this dispute should not obscure a well-established pattern of collaboration between elders and pastors in the consistory and between the consistory and the Small Council. Opposition to the consistory holding the exclusive power to excommunicate was not driven by a desire to overturn the exercise of moral discipline in Geneva (although that was how Calvin portrayed matters). Concern about relations with Bern,

---

(10) McKee, *John Calvin on the Diaconate.*
(11) McKee, *The Pastoral Ministry.*
(12) *Registres de la Compagnie des Pasteurs*, p. 14-19. Revised ordinances were issued in Geneva in 1561 and 1576.

CONCILIUM GENEVENSE – 1541

opposition to the impact of French migration, and personal animosities were also all significant in determining different perspectives on where the balance of jurisdiction should lie between the civil authorities and the consistory. ([13])

The broader influence of Calvin's ideas about ecclesiastical government as set out in the *Institutes* and Geneva's *Ordinances* can be traced in later regulations in Reformed churches across the continent. However, just as we cannot read these 1541 *Ordinances* as somehow marking the beginning of a new era of 'Calvin's Geneva', likewise different Reformed churches adapted or ignored different aspects of Calvin's ideas and Genevan practices. Some aspects of the *Ordinances* proved to be exceptional among Reformed churches. While in Geneva a single consistory had oversight over all the residents of the state, in other Reformed churches consistories – if they were established at all – were normally set up in each congregation. This diversity among Reformed churches was hardly surprising or particularly problematic from Calvin's perspective since he had only intended to apply principles and models of ecclesiastical government identified in Scripture to the context of Geneva and since aspects of the *Ordinances* were the product of a delicate compromise reached between Calvin and his employers.

NOTE ON THE EDITION

The critical edition of the 1541 *Ecclesiastical Ordinances* of Geneva offered below stems from a collation between two manuscripts. The body of the text reproduces the only extant handwritten copy of the *Ordinances*, placed at the beginning of the first volume of the records of the Venerable Company of Pastors of Geneva. ([14]) The critical apparatus reflects the variants and proposals included in the so-called *Projet d'ordonnances ecclésiastiques* (siglum *P*), an earlier draft of the *Ordinances* featuring different hands – including Calvin's – which was used during discussions between state and Church delegates to agree upon a final, and official, version of the text. ([15]) *P* appears to be an original minute of the draft *Ordinances* with alterations effected as the draft proceeded through the Genevan councils. ([16]) Most of the annotations in *P* – or at least most of the substance of such annotations – made it through the

(13) Naphy, *Calvin and the Genevan Reformation*, p. 166-235.
(14) Archives d'État de Genève, Cp. Past. R1, fol. 1-15. The text is reproduced in *Registres de la Compagnie des Pasteurs*, p. 1-13.
(15) Archives d'État de Genève, Pièces historiques, 1384. The text is reproduced in *CR*, vol. 38 (1871), col. 15-30, although this transcription is unreliable in some instances.
(16) See *CR*, vol. 38 (1871), col. 10, n. 1.

final version of the *Ordinances*: however, if compared to the body of the text of the *Projet*, the overall tone of the official version of the *Ordinances* clearly reflects an increase of the weight of the state in ecclesiastical matters vis-à-vis the city's religious authorities.

Any arbitrary modernising in spelling and punctuation has been kept to a bare minimum; tildes and contractions have been silently resolved.

BIBLIOGRAPHY

Sources (and Their Abbreviations)

'Draft Ecclesiastical Ordinances', in J. K. S. Reid (ed.), *Calvin: Theological Treatises*, Philadelphia 1954, p. 56-72.

Ordonnances ecclésiastiques, Archives d'État de Genève, C p. Past. R1, fol. 1-15.

Les ordonnances ecclésiastiques de l'église de Genève, Genève 1561.

Ordonnances ecclésiastiques de l'église de Genève, Genève 1576.

'Ordonnances ecclésiastiques, Genf 1541/1561', hrsg. P. Opitz, in *RefBK*, vol. 1/2 (2006), 229-278.

Projet d'ordonnances ecclésiastiques, Archives d'État de Genève, Pièces historiques, 1384.

Registres de la Compagnie des Pasteurs de Genève au temps de Calvin, éd. J.-F. Bergier – R. M. Kingdon, vol. 1, Genève 1964 [= *Registres de la Compagnie des Pasteurs*].

Registres du Conseil de Genève à l'époque de Calvin, vol. 6 (1541), éd. S. Coram-Mekkey et al., 2 vols, Genève 2016.

Registres du Consistoire de Genève au temps de Calvin, vol. 1 (1542-1544), éd. T. A. Lambert – I. M. Watt, Genève 1996.

Les Sources du Droit du Canton de Genève, éd. É. Rivoire – V. van Berchem, 4 vols, Aarau 1927-1935.

Literature (and Its Abbreviations)

E. de Boer, *The Genevan School of the Prophets: The* congrégations *of the Company of Pastors and their Influence in 16th-Century Europe*, Genève 2012 [= de Boer, *The Genevan School of the Prophets*].

W. J. Bouwsma, *John Calvin: A Sixteenth-Century Portrait*, Oxford 1988 [= Bouwsma, *John Calvin*].

M. W. Bruening, *Calvinism's First Battleground: Conflict and Reform in the Pays de Vaud, 1528-1559*, Dordrecht 2005.

The Cambridge Companion to John Calvin, ed. D. K. McKim, Cambridge 2004.

A Companion to the Reformation in Geneva, ed. J. Balserak, Leiden 2021 [= Balserak, *The Reformation in Geneva*].

É. Doumergue, *Jean Calvin. Les hommes et les choses de son temps*, 7 vols, Lausanne 1844-1937 [= Doumergue, *Jean Calvin*].

M. U. Chrisman, *Strasbourg and the Reform. A Study in the Process of Change*, New Haven (CT) 1967.

J. Gaberel, *Histoire de l'Église de Genève*, 3 vols, Genève 1858.

B. Gordon, *Calvin*, New Haven (CT) 2009 [= Gordon, *Calvin*].

—, *John Calvin's Institutes of the Christian Religion. A Biography*, Princeton 2016.

C. Grosse, *Les rituels de la Cène. Le culte eucharistique réformé à Genève (XVIe-XVIIe siècles)*, Genève 2008 [= Grosse, *Les rituels de la Cène*].

H. Heyer, *L'Église de Genève. Esquisse historique de son organisation*, Genève 1909.

H. Höpfl, *The Christian Polity of John Calvin*, Cambridge 1982.

Judging Faith, Punishing Sin: Inquisitions and Consistories in the Early Modern World, ed. C. H. Parker – G. Starr-LeBeau, Cambridge 2017.

R. M. Kingdon, *Reforming Geneva: Discipline, Faith and Anger in Calvin's Geneva*, Genève 2012.

—, *Adultery and Divorce in Calvin's Geneva*, Cambridge (MA) 1995.

—, 'Social welfare in Calvin's Geneva', *American Historical Review* 76 (1971), p. 50-69.

K. Maag, *Seminary or University? The Genevan Academy and Reformed Higher Education*, Aldershot 1995 [= Maag, *Seminary or University?*].

S. M. Manetsch, *Calvin's Company of Pastors: Pastoral Care and the Emerging Reformed Church, 1536-1609*, New York 2013 [= Manetsch, *Calvin's Company of Pastors*].

E. A. McKee, *The Pastoral Ministry and Worship in Calvin's Geneva*, Genève 2016 [= McKee, *The Pastoral Ministry*].

—, *Elders and the Plural Ministry: The Role of Exegetical History in Illuminating John Calvin's Theology*, Genève 1988.

—, *John Calvin on the Diaconate and Liturgical Almsgiving*, Genève 1984 [= McKee, *John Calvin on the Diaconate*].

E. W. Monter, *Calvin's Geneva*, New York 1967.

—, *Studies in Genevan Government, 1536-1605*, Geneva 1964 [= Monter, *Studies in Genevan Government*].

W. G. Naphy, 'From Prince-Bishopric to City-State: Nationalizing the Church and Creating a Republic in Reformation Geneva', in E. Nelson – J. Wright (eds), *Layered Landscapes: Early Modern Religious Space across Faith and Cultures*, London 2017, p. 134-149.

—, 'Baptisms, Church Riots and Social Unrest in Calvin's Geneva', *Sixteenth Century Journal* 26 (1995), p. 87-97 [= Naphy, 'Baptisms, Church Riots and Social Unrest'].

—, *Calvin and the Consolidation of the Genevan Reformation*, Manchester 1994 [= Naphy, *Calvin and the Genevan Reformation*].

—, 'The Renovation of the Ministry in Calvin's Geneva', in A. Pettegree (ed.), *The Reformation of the Parishes: The Ministry and the Reformation in Town and Country*, Manchester 1993, p. 113-152.

J. E. Olson, *Calvin and Social Welfare: Deacons and the Bourse Française*, London 1989.

K. E. Spierling, *Infant Baptism in Reformation Geneva: The Shaping of a Community, 1536-1564*, Aldershot 2005 [= Spierling, *Infant Baptism*].

M. J. Tuininga, *Calvin's Political Theology and the Public Engagement of the Church. Christ's Two Kingdoms*, Cambridge 2017.

J. R. Watt, *The Consistory and Social Discipline in Calvin's Geneva*, Rochester (NY) 2020 [= Watt, *The Consistory and Social Discipline*].

—, 'Calvinism, Childhood and Education: The Evidence from the Genevan Consistory', *Sixteenth Century Journal* 33 (2002), p. 439-456.

—, 'Women and the Consistory in Calvin's Geneva', *Sixteenth Century Journal* 24 (1993), p. 429-439.

J. Witte Jr, 'Honor thy Father and thy Mother? Child Marriage and Parental Consent in Calvin's Geneva', *The Journal of Religion* 86 (2006), p. 580-605.

CONCILIUM GENEVENSE – 1541

Monitum

Archives d'État de Genève, Cp. Past. R1, fol. 1-15.

CONCILIUM GENEVENSE
1541

CONSPECTUS SIGLORUM

P Projet d'ordonnances ecclésiastiques, Archives d'État de Genève, Pièces historiques, 1384

| ORDONNANCES ECCLÉSIASTIQUES

Au nom de Dieu tout puissant. Nous Sindicques, Petit et Grand conseil avecq nostre Peuple assemble au son de trompette et grosse cloche. Suyvant noz antiennes coustumes. Ayant considere que cest chose digne de recommendation sur toutes les aultres que la doctrine du sainct evangile de nostre Seigneur soit bien conservee en sa purite et lesglise christienne deuement entretenue que la jeunesse pour ladvenir soit fidellement instruicte lhospital ordonné en bon estat pour la sustentation des pauvres. Ce qui ne se peut faire synon quil y ayt certaine regle et maniere de vivre par laquelle chascun estat entende le debvoir de son office. A ceste cause il nous a semble advis bon que le gouvernement spirituel tel que nostre seigneur la demonstre et institue par sa parolle fust reduict en bonne forme pour avoir lieu et estre observe entre nous. Et ainsi avons ordonne et estably de suyvre et garder en nostre ville et territoire la police ecclesiastique qui sensuit, comme nous voyons quelle est prise de levangile de Jesuchrist.

Premierement il y a quatres ordres doffices que nostre
seigneur a institue pour le gouvernement de son esglise.
Asscavoir

Les pasteurs. Puis les docteurs. Apres les anciens aultrement nommez Commis par la Seigneurie. Quartement les diacres.

Pourtant si nous voulons avoir lesglise bien ordonnee et lentretenir en son entier il nous fault observer ceste forme de regime:

---

1 Ordonnances ecclésiastiques] *alia manus add. in marg.* **2/15** Au – Jesuchrist] *deest P* **3** avecq] *atramento erasus* **6** et] *atramento erasus* **7** soit fidellement] *atramento erasus* **8** qui] *scriba corr., a.c.* q se] *a.c.* ce **9** par] *coniecimus* **16** Premierement] *deest P* **18** Asscavoir] Premierement *P* **19/20** aultrement nommez Commis par la Seigneurie] *in adnot. in P* **20** par] *scriba corr., a.c.* pour **21** lesglise] esglise *P* lentretenir] *scriba corr., a.c.* lentretenant

398 CONCILIUM GENEVENSE – 1541

Du devoir des Pasteurs

Quant est des pasteurs que lescripture nomme aussi aulcunesfois
25 surveillans anciens et ministres leur office est dannuncer la parolle de dieu
pour endoctriner, admonester exorter et reprendre tant en publicq comme en
particulier administrer les sacremens et faire les corrections fraternelles avec
les anciens ou commis.

Or affin que rien ne se face confusement en lesglise nul ne se doibt ingerer
30 en cest office sans vocation en laquelle il fault considerer trois choses. Asscavoir lexamen qui est le principal. Apres a qui il appertient de instituer les
ministres. Tiercement quelle ceremonie ou facon de faire il est bon de garder a
les introduire en loffice.

De l'examen des Pasteurs

35 Lexamen contient deux parties dont la premiere est touchant la doctrine.
Asscavoir si celluy quon doibt ordonner a la bonne et saine cognoissance de
lescripture. Et puis sil est ydoine et propre pour la communiquer au Peuple en
edification.

Aussi pour eviter tous dangiers que celluy quon veult recepvoir nayt
40 quelque opinion mauvaise. Il sera bon quil proteste de recepvoir et tenir la
doctrine approuvee en lesglise. Pour cognoistre sil est propre a enseigner il
fauldra proceder par interrogations et par louyr traicter en prive la doctrine du
seigneur.

La seconde partie est de la vie. Asscavoir sil est de bonnes meurs et sest
45 toujours gouverne sans reproche. La reigle dy proceder est tres bien demonstree par sainct paul laquelle il fauldra tenir.

24/28 Quant – commis] cfr Tit. 1, 5-9; cfr I Petr. 5, 1-4   **45/46** La – tenir] cfr I Tim.
3, 1-7

24/25 pasteurs – ministres] in the 1541 edition of the *Institutes*, Calvin affirmed that
he called 'indifferemment Prestres et Evesques les ministres de l'Eglise. L'ordre est icelle
vocation'. See J. Calvin, *Institution de la religion chrétienne*, éd. O. Millet, Genève 2008,
p. 1452-1453

---

23 Du devoir des Pasteurs] *alia manus add. in marg.*; *deest P*   **24/25** aulcunesfois –
ministres] aulcunesfois evesques, anciens et ministres *P*   **28** ou commis] *in adnot. in P*
ou] et *P*   **31** Apres a qui il appertient] Apres aussi jl appartient *P*   **34** De – Pasteurs]
alia manus add. in marg.; *deest P*   **36** la] *atramento erasus*   saine] *atramento erasus*,
saincte *P*   **39** tous dangiers] tout danger *P*   recepvoir] retenir *P*

CONCILIUM GENEVENSE – 1541

Sensuyt a qui il appartient dinstituer les pasteurs

Il sera bon en cest endroict de suyvre lordre de lesglise ancienne veu que ce nest que une practique de ce qui nous est monstre par lescripture.

| *De leur election*

Cest que les ministres elisent premierement celluy quon debvra mettre en loffice layant faict a scavoir a la Seigneurie apres quon le presente au conseil. Et sil est trouve digne que le conseil le recoyve et accepte selon quil verra estre expedient luy donnant tesmoignaige pour le produire finablement au Peuple en la predication affin quil soit receu par consentement commun de la compaignie des fidelles. Sil estoit trouve indigne et demonstre tel par probations legitimes il fauldroit lors proceder a nouvelle election pour en prendre un aultre.

Quant a la maniere de lintroduire pour ce que les ceremonies du temps passe ont este tournees en beaulcoup de superstitions a cause de linfirmite du temps il suffira quil se fasse par un des ministres une declaration et remonstrance de loffice auquel on l'ordonne puis qu'on fasse prieres et oraisons affin que le Seigneur luy fasse la grace de sen acquiter.

Quant il sera esleu quil ayt a jurer entre les mains de la Seigneurie duquel serment il y aura forme escripte convenable a ce qui est requis en un ministre selon que sensuit, puis fault inserer la forme dont on use.

Or comme il fault bien examiner les ministres quant on les veut eslire, aussi fault il avoir bonne police a les entretenir en leur debvoir.

58/59 les – passe] the laying of hands on new ministers was ultimately inserted in the 1576 revision of the *Ordonnances*, although Theodore Beza continued to discourage this practice   **63/65** Quant – use] cfr 'Formule du serment prescrit aux ministres, 17 juillet 1542', in *CR*, vol. 38 (1871), col. 31-44

47 Sensuyt – pasteurs] A qui il appartient d'instituer les pasteurs *alia manus add. in marg.*   **50** De leur election] *alia manus add. in marg.*; *deest P*   **52** layant faict a scavoir a la Seigneurie] *in adnot. in P*   **53/54** selon quil verra estre expedient] *in adnot. in P*   **58/62** Quant – acquiter] Quant à la manière de lintroduyre jl seroit bon de user de limposition des mains laquelle ceremonye a este gardee des apostres et puys en leglise ancienne; moyennant que cela se face sans superstition et sans offense. Mais pource que il y a eu beaucoup de superstition au temps passe et quil sen pourroit ensuivre du scandalle on sen abstient pour linfirmite du temps *P*   **60** par] *coniecimus*   **65** selon – use] *deest P*   **66/67** Or – debvoir] ce que desyrons *alia manus add. in P*

400 CONCILIUM GENEVENSE – 1541

Etablissement dun jour de la semaine pour sassembler

Premierement sera expedient que tous les ministres pour conserver purete
70 et concorde de doctrine entre eulx conviennent ensemble un jour certain la
sepmaine pour avoir conference des escriptures et que nul ne sen exempte si na
excuse legitime. Si quelcun y estoit negligent quil en soit admoneste.

Quant a ceulx qui preschent par les villages dependantz de la Seigneurie
que noz ministres de la ville les ayent a exhorter dy venir toutes les fois quil
75 pourront. Au reste si deffaillent un moys entier quon tienne cela pour negligence trop grande. Synon quil y eust maladie ou aultre empeschement legitime.

Ce quil faut faire quand il y a des differens dans la Doctrine

Sil y sortoit quelque different de la doctrine que les ministres en tractent
80 ensemble pour discuter la matiere. Apres si mestier estoit quilz appellent les
anciens et commis par la Seigneurie pour aider a appaiser la contention. Finablement sils ne pouvoient venir a concorde amiable pour lobstination de lune
des parties que la cause soit defferee au Magistrat pour y mettre ordre.

Pour obvier a tous scandalles de vie ilz sera mestier quil y ayt forme de
85 correction sur les ministres selon quil sera expose puis apres a laquelle tous se
submettent. Qui sera aussi le moyen que le ministre soit conserve en reverence
et que la parolle de dieu ne soit par le maulvais bruyct des ministres en
deshonneur ou mespris. Car comme on corrigera celluy qui laura merite aussi
sera mestier de reprimer les calumpnies et faulx raportz quon pourroit faire
90 iniustement contre les innocens.

| Mais premierement fault noter quil y a des crimes qui sont du tout into- 3
lerables en un ministre et y a des vices quon peut aucunement supporter
moyennant quon en face admonition fraternelle.

Les premiers sont
95 Heresie
Scisme

84/85 quil – ministres] cfr Gal. 6, 1

68 Etablissement – sassembler] *alia manus add. in marg.*; *deest P* **72** Si] *atramento
erasus* **74** que – exhorter] quon les exhorte *P* **78** Ce – Doctrine] *alia manus add.
in marg.*; *deest P* **81** et commis par la Seigneurie] *in adnot. in P* **83** y] *scriba corr.,
a.c.* yl **84** ilz] *sic* **84/85** forme de correction] laquelle appartiendra a la seigneurie
alia manus add. in P **85** sur – apres] *deest P* **88** on] *scriba corr., a.c.* ont
89 reprimer] reprouver *P* faulx] *atramento erasus*; *scriba corr., a.c.* fal **94** Les
premiers sont] Vices qui sont intolérables en un pasteur *alia manus add. in marg.*

CONCILIUM GENEVENSE – 1541

Rebellion contre lordre ecclesiastique
Blaspheme manifeste et digne de peine Civile
Simonie et toute corruption de presentz
100 Brigues pour occuper le lieu dun aultre
Delaisser son esglise sans conge licite et iuste vocation
Faulcete
Periure
Paillardise
105 Larrecins
Yvrognerie
Basterie digne d'estre punie par les loix
Usure
Jeux deffendus par les loix et scandaleux
110 Dances et telles dissolutions
Crime emportant infamie Civile
Crime qui meriteroit en un aultre separation de lesglise.
Les seconds
Facon estrange de traicter lescripture laquelle tourne en scandalle
115 Curiosite de chercher questions vaines
Advancer quelque doctrine ou facon de faire non receue en lesglise
Negligence a estudier et principallement a lire les sainctes escriptures
Negligence a reprendre les vices prochaine a flaterie
Negligence a faire toutes choses requises a loffice
120 Scurrilite
Menterie
Detraction
Parolles dissolues
Parolles iniurieuses
125 Temerite
Maulvaise cautelle
| Avarice et trop grande chichete   4
Cholere deshordonnee
Noises et tenseries
130 Dissolution indecente a un ministre tant en habilemens comme en gestes
et aultre façon de faire.

---

101 licite] legitime *P*   **112** separation] *scriba corr., a.c.* sp   **113** Les seconds] Vices
qu'on peut supporter pourveu qu'on les avertisse *alia manus add. in marg.*
114 traicter] *a.c.* traicte   **115** de] a *P*   **117** principallement a] *deest P*

402 CONCILIUM GENEVENSE – 1541

Quant est des crimes quon ne doibt nullement pourter si ce sont crimes civilz cest a dire quon doibve punir par les loix si quelquun des ministres y tombe. Que la Seigneurie y mette la main et que oultre la peine ordinaire dont
135 elle a coustume de chastier les aultres elle le punisse en le deposant de son office.

Quant est des aultres crimes dont la premiere inquisition appertient au consistoire ecclesiasticque que les commis ou anciens avec les ministres veillent dessus. Et si quelquun en est convaincu quils en facent le raport au
140 conseil avec leur advis et jugement ainsi que le dernier jugement de la correction soit tousiours reserve a la Seigneurie.

Quant est des vices moindres quon doibt corriger par admonition simple quon y procede selon lordre de necessite, tellement que le dernier soit de venir au jugement ecclesiasticque.

145   *Etablissement du jour des censures de trois en trois mois*

Pour maintenir ceste Discipline en son estat que de trois mois en trois moys les ministres ayent specialement regard sil y a rien a redire entre eulx pour ilz remedier comme de raison.

Du nombre lieu et temps des predications.

150   Le dimanche quil y ayt sermon au point du jour a sainct pierre et sainct gervais et a lheure accoustumee audit sainct pierre a la magdeleine et sainct gervais.

A mydy quil y ayt cathechisme cest a dire instruction de petitz enfantz en toutes les trois esglises. Asscavoir sainct pierre, la magdeleine et sainct gervais.
155   A trois heures aussi bien en toutes les trois parroisses.

Pour envoyer les enfans au cathechisme et pour recepvoir les sacrements que en tant quil se pourra faire on observe les limites des parroisses. Cest que

---

132/136 si – office] sil sen dresse quelque accusation en murmure, que lassemblee des ministres et anciens en enquerrent, affin de y proceder par raison et selon quon en trouvera quilz en jugent, et puys rapportent le jugement au magistrat affin que si mestier est le delinquent soit depose *P*   **137/141** Quant – Seigneurie] *deest P* **137** est] *supplevimus*   **139** quils] *alia manus add.* ils   **145** Etablissement – mois] *alia manus add. in marg.*; *deest P*   **146** Discipline] *atramento erasus*   **147** ayent] *a.c.* ayant   specialement regard] *scriba corr., a.c.* specialement si regard   **148** ilz] *sic* **149** Du – predications] Du nombre lieu et tems des predications *alia manus add. in marg.*   **150** pierre] *scriba add. sup. l.*   **151** a la magdeleine] *deest P*   **155** A – parroisses] A troys heures en sainct pierre et sainct gervais le second sermon *P*

CONCILIUM GENEVENSE – 1541

sainct gervais contienne ce quil avoit du temps passe la magdeleine pareillement sainct pierre ce quil appertenoit anciennement a sainct germain saincte
160 croix nostre dame la neufve sainct legier.

| Es jours ouvriers oultre les deux predications que se font que trois fois la 5
sepmaine on presche a sainct pierre. Asscavoir le lundy mecredi et vendredy. Et
que ces sermons soyent sonnez lung apres laultre a telle heure quilz puissent
estre finitz devant quon commence allieurs. Si se faict quelque priere extraor-
165 dinaire pour la necessite du temps on gardera lordre du dymenche.

Etablissement de cinq pasteurs et de trois coadiuteurs

Pour soubstenir ces charges et aultres quilz sont du ministere il sera
besoing davoir cinq ministres et trois coadjuteurs qui seront aussi ministres
pour ayder et subvenir selon que la necessite le requerra.

170 SENSUIT LE SECOND ORDRE QUE NOUS AVONS NOMME LES DOCTEURS.

Loffice propre des docteurs est denseigner les fidelles en saine doctrine
affin que la purete de levangile ne soit corrompue ou par ignorance ou par
maulvaises opinions. Toutteffois selon que les choses sont aujourduy disposees
nous comprenons en ce tiltre les aydes et instrumens pour conserver la doc-
175 trine de dieu et faire que lesglise ne soit desolee par faulte de pasteurs et
ministres. Ainsi pour user dun mot plus intelligible nous lappellerons lordre
des escolles. Le degre plus prochain au ministere et plus adjoingt au gouvernement de lesglise est la lecture de theologie dont il sera bon quil y en ayt au vieil
et nouveau testament.

161/165 Es – dymenche] Es jours ouvriers oultre les deux predications qui se font, que
troys fois la sepmaine on presche a sainct pierre, assavoir le lundy, mardy et vendredy
une heure, devant quon commence aux aultres lieux. Et que les semons soyent sonnes
en faict lun appres laultre et quant au jour de la priere lon doybje venyr au sermon au
temple sainct Pierre le jour quil sera sonne a la grosse cloche *P*   **161** oultre] *atramento
erasus*   **162** mecredi] *scriba corr., a.c.* mardy   **162/165** Et – dymenche] *in adnot. in P*
164 allieurs] *sic*   se] *a.c.* ce   **166** Etablissement – coadiuteurs] *alia manus add. in
marg.; deest P*   **167** quilz] qui *P*   **170** Sensuit – docteurs] L'office des docteurs *alia
manus add. in marg.*   le] du *P*   les] de *P*   **171** des docteurs] de docteur *P*
174 instrumens] jnstructions *P*   **175/176** et ministres] *in adnot. in P*
176 lappellerons] appellerons *P*   **177** adjoingt] conioinct *P*   **178** ayt] *a.c.* ayat

404 CONCILIUM GENEVENSE – 1541

180 *Establissement dun college*

Mais pour ce quon ne peut profiter en telles lecons que premierement on ne soit instruict aux langues et sciences humaines. Et aussi est besoing de susciter de la semence pour le temps advenir affin de ne laisser lesglise deserte a noz enfantz il fauldra dresser college pour les instruire affin de les preparer tant au
185 ministere que au gouvernement civil.

Pour le premier fauldra assigner lieu propre tant pour faire lecons que pour tenir enfans et aultres qui vouldront profiter, avoir homme docte et expert pour disposer tant de la maison comme des lectures et qui puisse aussi lire, le prendre et souldoyer a celle condition quil ayt soubz sa charge lecteurs
190 tant aux langues comme en dyalectique sil se peut faire. Item des bachelliers pour apprendre les petitz enfans ce que nous voulons et ordonnons estre faict.

Que tous ceulx qui seront la soyent subiectz a la discipline ecclesiastique comme les ministres.

Quil ny ayt aultre escolle par la ville pour les petitz enfans mais que les
195 filles ayent leur escolle a part comme il a este faict par cy devant.

Que nul ne soit receu sil nest approuve par les ministres layant premierement faict scavoir a la Seigneurie et allors de rechef quil soit presente au conseil avec leur tesmoinage de peur des inconveniens. Touteffois lexamen doibvra estre faict present deux des seigneurs du petit conseil.

200 | Sensuit le troisiesme ordre qui est des anciens qui se diront 6
Estre commis ou deputez par la Seigneurie au consistoire.

Leur office est de prendre garde sus la vie dun chascun dadmonester amiablement ceulx qui verront faillir et mener vie desordonnee. Et la ou il en seroit mestier faire rapport a 1a compaignie qui sera deputee pour faire les correc-
205 tions fraternelles et lors les faire communement avecq les aultres.

182/183 Et – advenir] cfr Matth. 18, 19 ; cfr Luc. 8, 11-15

180 Establissement dun college] *alia manus add. in marg.*; *deest P*　　**184** pour les instruire] pour jnstruyre les enfans *P*　　les instruire affin] *scriba corr., a.c.* les instruire les enfans affin　**185** au] *deest P*　**189** celle] ycelle *P*　　sa] *scriba corr., a.c.* luy la　**190** se] *a.c.* ce　　**191** ce que nous voulons et ordonnons estre faict] et de ce esperons pourvoybre en briefz a layde du seygneur *P*　**195** ayent] *scriba corr., a.c.* ayant　**196/198** layant – conseil] *in adnot. in P*　　**198/199** Touteffois – conseil] *in adnot. in P*　**199** doibvra] *atramento erasus*　　**200/201** Sensuit – consistoire] Des Anciens *alia manus add. in marg.*　　**200/201** qui² – consistoire] *in adnot. in P*　　**203** et] ou *P*　**205** lors] *deest P*　communement] *deest P*

CONCILIUM GENEVENSE – 1541

Comme ceste eglise est disposee y sera bon den eslire deux du conseil estroict quatre du conseil des soyxante et six du conseil des deux centz gens de bonne vie et honneste sans reproche et hors de toute suspicion sur tout craignans dieu et ayantz bonne prudence spirituelle. Et les fauldra tellement eslire
210 quil y en ayt en chacun quartier de la ville affin d'avoir loeil par tout. Ce que voulons estre faict.

De la maniere de les elire

Pareillement nous avons determine que la maniere de les eslire soit telle cest que le conseil estroict advise de nommer les plus propres quon pourra
215 trouver et les plus suffisans. Et pour ce faire appeller les ministres pour en communiquer avec eulx puis quilz presentent ceulx quilz auront advise au conseil des deux centz lequel les approuvera. Si les trouvent dignes, apres estre approuvez, quilz facent serment particulier dont la forme sera dressee comme pour les ministres. Et au bout de l'an apres avoir esleu le conseil quilz se presentent a la
220 Seigneurie affin quon regarde silz debvront estre continuez ou changez. Combien qui ne seroit expedient de les changer souvent sans cause quant ilz se acquitteront de leur debvoir fidellement.

| Le quatriesme ordre du gouvernement ecclesiasticque
asscavoir des dyacres

7

225 Il en y a eu tousiours deux especes en leglise ancienne. Les uns ont este deputez a recevoir dispenser et conserver les biens des pouvres tant aulmosnes quotidiennes que possessions rentes et pensions. Les aultres pour songner et

---

225/229 Il – present] cfr Act. 6, 1-3; cfr Rom. 12, 8; 16, 1-2; cfr I Tim. 5, 9-10

225/229 Il – present] see Calvin's exegesis of Rom. 12, 8 and Rom. 16, 1-2 in I. Calvinus, *Commentarius in Epistolam Pauli ad Romanos*, ed. T. L. Parker – D. C. Parker (*Ioannis Calvini Opera Omnia* II/13), Genève 1999, p. 262, 310

---

206 y sera] jl seroit *P*   **210** quartier] *correximus ex P, a.c.* cartier   **210/211** Ce que voulons estre faict] *in adnot. in P*   **212** De la maniere de les elire] *alia manus add. in marg.; deest P*   **213/214** Pareillement – cest] La maniere de les eslire semble estre bonne tellement que *P*   **217** Si les trouvent] Sil les trouve *P*   apres estre approuvez] *deest P*   **218/219** la forme sera dressee comme pour les ministres] la forme se pourra facilement dresser *P*   **219/220** a la Seigneurie affin quon regarde] a messieurs, affin quilz regardent *P*   **220** quon – changez] quilz regardent silz les debveront continuer ou changer *P*   **223/224** Le – dyacres] Des Diacres *alia manus add. in marg.*   **224** des] les *P*   **225** Il en y a eu] *sic*

penser les malades et administrer la pitance des povres laquelle coustume nous tenons encore de present. Et affin deviter confusion car nous avons procureurs et hospitalliers que lun des quatre procureurs dudict hospital soit recepveur de tout le bien dicelluy et quil ait gaiges competans affin de exercer mieulx son office.

Procureurs de l'hopital

Que le nombre des quatres procureurs demeure comme il a este dont lun aura charge de la recepte comme il a este dict, tant affin que les provisions soient faictes myeulx en temps que affin que ceulx qui vouldront faire quelque charite soient plus certains que le bien ne sera employe aultrement que a leur intention. Et si le revenu ne suffisoit ou bien quil y survint necessite extraordinaire la Seigneurie advisera de adiuster selon lindigence quon y verra.

Que lelection tant des procureurs que des hospitalliers se face comme des anciens et commis au consistoire, et en les eslisant quon suyve la Regle que baille sainct paul des dyacres I Timoth. 3. Tite I.

Touchant loffice et auctorite des procureurs nous confermons les articles que par nous leur ont ja este ordonnez. Moyennant que en choses urgentes et ou il y auroit danger de differer principallement quand il ny a point grande difficulte et quil nest pas question de grandz despens quilz ne soient pas contrainctz de s'assembler tousjours mais que un ou deux puissent ordonner en absence des aultres ce qui sera de raison.

De lhopital

Il sera mestier de veiller diligemment que lospital commun soit bien entretenu et que ce soit tant pour les malades que vieilles gens qui ne peuvent

---

242 I Timoth. 3. Tite I] cfr I Tim. 3, 8-13; cfr Tit. 1, 5-9

229/232 Et – office] *in adnot. in P* **233** Procureurs de lhopital] *alia manus add. in marg.*; *deest P* **234/235** Que – dict] Le nombre des procureurs deputes pour lhospital jcelluy nous semble bon mais nous desirons quil y ait aussi recepte apart *P* **236** que¹] *supplevimus* **238** le revenu] le revenu que messeygneurs assigneront *P* **240** se face] *scriba corr., a.c.* se fasse **241** et commis au consistoire] *in adnot. in P* **242** I Timoth. 3. Tite I] *deest P* **243** et auctorite] *deest P* nous confermons] nous trouvons bons *P* **243/244** les – ordonnez] *in adnot. in P* **248** de] *supplevimus ex P* **249** De lhopital] *alia manus add. in marg.*; *deest P* **250** veiller] beiller *P* **251** qui ne] *atramento erasus*

CONCILIUM GENEVENSE – 1541   407

travailler. Item femmes vefves enfans orphelins et aultres pouvres. Et touteffois
quon les tienne en un cors de logis a part et separe des aultres.

255 | Item que la solicitude des pouvres qui sont dispersez par la ville revienne   8
la selon que les procureurs en ordonneront.

Item que oultre lhospital des passans lequel il est besoing de conserver
quil y ait quelque hospitalite a part pour ceulx quon verra estre dignes de
charite speciale. Et pour ce faire quil y ait une chambre deputee pour recepvoir
ceulx qui seront adressez des procureurs et quelle soit reservee en cest usaige.

260 Que sur tout cela soit en recommendation que les familles des hospitalliers soient honnestement reiglees et selon dieu veu quilz ont a gouverner maison desdiee a dieu.

Que les Ministres et les commis ou anciens avec lun des seigneurs
sindicques aient de leur part soing denquerir sil y avoit quelque faulte ou indi-
265 gence de rien affin de prier et admonester la Seigneurie de y mettre ordre. Et
que pour ce faire tous les trois mois quelcuns de leur compaignie avec les
procureurs facent visitation a lhospital pour cognoistre si tout est bien reigle.

Il fauldra aussi que tant pour les pouvres de lhospital que pour ceulx de la
ville quilz nont pas de quoy sayder quil y ait un medecin et un chirurgien
270 propre aux gaiges de la ville qui neantmoings practiquassent en la ville mais ce
pendent fussent tenuz davoir soing de lhospital et visiter les aultres pouvres.

Quant est de lhospital pour la peste quil ait tout son cas separe a part et
principallement sil advient que la ville fust visitee de ceste verge de dieu.

Au surplus pour empescher la mendicite laquelle est contraire a bonne
275 police. Il fauldra que la Seigneurie commette quelcungs de ses officiers. Et
ainsi avons ordonne a lissue des eglises pour oster de la place ceulx qui voul-
droient resister. Et si cestoient affronteurs ou quilz se rebeccassent les mener a
lung de messieurs les sindicques. Pareillement que au reste du temps les dise-
niers y prinsent garde que la deffense de ne point mendier fust bien observee.

---

252 Item] *deest P*   **253** quon les tienne] quon tienne les mallades *P*   les] *scriba add.*
sup. l.   **256** que oultre] *coniecimus ex P*   **258** chambre] chambre speciale *P*   **261/**
262 maison desdiee] maisons desdiees *P*   **263/264** et – sindicques] *in adnot. in P*
265 rien] *lectio dubia, fortasse* vie   la Seigneurie] messieurs *P*   **266** quelcuns]
quelques *P*   **268** Il fauldra] Il seroit bon *P*   **269** quil y ait] *in adnot. in P*   **270** aux
gaiges de la ville] *in adnot. in P*   **272** ait] eust *P*   **273** advient] advenoit *P*   **275/**
276 Il – ordonne] jl seroit bon et ainsy havons ordonne que jl ay lun de nous officiers
P   **277** resister] belistrer *P*   **279** y] *supplevimus ex P*

408 CONCILIUM GENEVENSE – 1541

280 | Des Sacremens 9

Du baptesme

Que le baptesme ne se face qua lheure de la predication et quil soit administre seulement par les ministres ou coadiuteurs. Et quon enregistre les noms
des enfans avec les noms de leurs parens que sil se trouvoit quelque bastard la
285 iustice en soit advertie.

Quon ne recoyve estrangiers pour comperes que gens fidelles et de nostre
communion veu que les aultres ne sont capables de faire promesse a leglise
dinstruire les enfans comme il appartient.

De la Cene

290 Puis que la cene a este instituee de nostre Seigneur pour nous estre en
usaige plus frequent et aussi quil a ainsi este observe en leglise ancienne iusque
a ce que le dyable a tout renverse erigeant la messe au lieu dicelle. Cest un
deffault quon doibt corriger que de la celebrer tant peu souvent. Touteffois
pour a present avons advise et ordonne que elle soit administree quatre fois
295 lannee. Asscavoir a noel Pasques Penthecoste et le premier dymenche de
septembre en automne.

Que les ministres distribuent le pain en bon ordre et avec reverence et que
nul aultre donne le calice synon les commis ou dyacres avec les ministres et
pour ceste cause quil ny ait point multitude de vaisseaulx.

300 Que les tables soient pres de la chaire affin que le mistere se puisse myeulx
et plus commodement exposer pres des tables.

290/291 Puis – ancienne] cfr Act. 2, 46

---

281 Du baptesme] between the first and the second paragraph of the section on
baptism, *P* adds another paragraph which is erased in the original document and does
not feature in the official text of the *Ordonnances*. The paragraph says 'Que les pierres
ou baptistaire soit aupres de la chaire, affin quil y ait meilleure audience a reciter le
mystere et lusaige du baptesme'

---

281 Du baptesme] Du Bapteme *alia manus add. in marg.*; *deest P*   **282** se] *a.c.* ce
289 De la Cene] De la Cene *alia manus add. in marg. ex adnot. in P*   **292** a²]
atramento erasus   erigeant] *conieci ex P*   **293/296** Touteffois – automne] Parquoy
sera bon que tousiours unesfois le mois elle soit administree en la ville, tellement que
tous les troys moys elle revienne en chascune paroysse, Oultre que trois foys lan on la
face par tout assavoir a pasques, penthecoste et noel, en telle sorte neantmoins que ce
moys la elle ne soit repetee en la paroysse laquelle lors seroit en son jour *P*   **301** et plus
commodement] *deest P*

CONCILIUM GENEVENSE – 1541

Quelle ne soit celebree quen leglise jusque a meilleure opportunite.

| Que le dymenche devant quon celebre on en face la denuntiation affin 10
que nul enfant ny vienne devant que avoir faict la profession de sa foy selon
305 quil sera expose au cathechisme. Et aussi quon exhorte tous estrangiers et nou-
veaulx venus de se venir premier presenter a leglise affin destre instruictz silz
en avoient mestier et ainsi que nul nen approche a sa condemnation.

Du mariage

Que apres la denunce des bans accoustumes on face les exspousailles
310 quant les parties le requerront tant le dymenche que les jours ouvriers moyennant que ce soit au commencement du presche seullement il sera bon que le
jour quon aura celebre la cene on sen abstienne pour l'honneur du sacrement.

Introduction Des chants Ecclessiastiques

Il sera bon dintroduyre les chantz ecclesiasticques pour myeulx inciter le
315 peuple a prier et louer dieu.

Pour le commencement on apprendra les petis enfans puis avec le temps
toute leglise pourra suyvre.

Touchant les differentz en causes matrimonialles pource que ce nest pas
matiere spirituelle mais meslee avec la politicque cela demeurera a la Seigneu-
320 rie. Ce neantmoings avons advise de laisser au consistoire la charge douyr les
parties affn den rapporter leur advis au conseil pour assoir jugement. Bonnes
ordonnances soient dressees lesquelles on suyve doresnavant.

De la sepulture

Quon ensepvelisse honnestement les mortz au lieu ordonne. De la suytte
325 et compagnie nous laissons a la discretion dun chascun.

---

302 quen] que *P*   **303** on] quon *P*   **304** enfant ny] *a.c.* enfant y ny   la] *deest P*
306 presenter] representer *P*   instruictz] *a.c.* nistruictz   **307** ainsi] *Ioannes Calvinus*
corr. in P, a.c. aussi   **308** Du mariage] Du Mariage *alia manus add. in marg. ex adnot.*
in P   **310** moyennant] en *scriba add. sup. l.*   **313** Introduction Des chants
Ecclessiastiques] *alia manus add. in marg.*; *deest P*   **318** differentz] differences *P*
319/322 cela – doresnavant] *in adnot. in P*   **323** De la sepulture] *alia manus add. in*
marg. ex adnot. in P

410 CONCILIUM GENEVENSE – 1541

| Nous avons oultreplus advise et ordonne que les pourteurs ayent serment 11
a la Seigneurie dempescher toutes superstitions contraires a la parolle de dieu
de nen point pourter a heure indehue et faire raport si quelcun estoit mort
subitement affin dobvier a tous inconveniens quil en pourroit advenir.

330 Item apres leur mort de ne les pourter plustost de douze heures et non
plus tard que vingt et quatre.

DE LA VISITATION DES MALADES

Pource que plusieurs sont negligentz de se consoler en dieu par sa parolle
quand ilz se trouveront en necessite de maladie. Et ainsi plusieurs meurent
335 sans quelque admonition ou doctrine laquelle est a lhomme plus salutaire lors
que jamais. Pour ceste cause avons advise et ordonne que nul ne demeure trois
jours entiers gisans au lict quil ne le face scavoir au ministre. Et que chascun
advise d'appeller les ministres quand ilz les vouldront avoir a heure oportune
affin de ne les distraire de leur office auquel ilz servent en commun a leglise. Et
340 pour oster toutes excuses avons resolu que cela soit. Et sur tout quil soit faict
commendement que les parens amys et gardes nattendent pas que l'homme
doibve rendre lesperit en laquelle extremite les consolations ne servent de
gueres a la plus part.

DE LA VISITATION DES PRISONNIERS

345 En oultre avons ordonne certain jour la sepmaine auquel soit faicte
quelque collation aux prisonniers pour les admonester et exhorter. Et quil y ait
deux des Seigneurs du conseil deputez pour y assister affin quil ne se commette
nulle fraude. Et sil y en avoit quelquun aux seps lequel lon ne veulle pas tirer

---

332 De la visitation des malades] cfr Matth. 25, 35-36   **344** De la visitation des prisonniers] cfr Matth. 25, 35-36

---

326 Nous avons oultreplus advise et ordonne] il sera bon *P*   **327** a la Seigneurie] a nous *P*   **329** inconveniens] *atramento erasus*   pourroit] pourroient *P*   **332** De la visitation des malades] De la visite des malades *alia manus add. in marg. ex adnot. in P*   **334** trouveront] trouvent *P*   **335** lors] *Ioannes Calvinus add. in P*   **336** Pour ceste cause avons advise et ordonne] jl sera bon que messeigneurs ordonnent et facent publier *P*   **337** chascun] *in circulo in P*   **339/340** Et – soit] *deest P*   **344** De la visitation des prisonniers] De la visite des prisonniers *alia manus add. in marg.*   **345** En – ordonne] Jl sera bon que messeigneurs ordonnent *P*   auquel] *correximus, a.c.* auquel auquel   **346** et exhorter] et exhorter si bon leur semble *P*   **346/347** Et – assister] deputer quelquun de leur compaignie *P*   **348** sil y en avoit] silz en ont *P*   aux] en *P*

CONCILIUM GENEVENSE – 1541

hors quand bon semblera au Conseil il pourroit donner entree a quelque
350 ministre pour les consoler en presence comment dessus. Car quand on attend
quon les doibve mener a la mort, ilz sont souvent preoccupez si fort d'horreur
quilz ne peuvent rien recepvoir ne entendre. Et le jour de ce faire a este depute
le sambedy apres disgne.

| LORDRE QUON DEBVRA TENIR ENVERS LES PETIS ENFANS

355 Que tous citoyens et habitans ayent a mener ou envoyer leurs enfans le
dymenche a mydi au cathechisme dont il a este parle.

Quil y ait un certain formulaire compose. Sur lequel on les instruise. Et
que avec la doctrine quon leur donnera quon les interrogue de ce quil aura este
dict pour veoir si lauront bien entendu et retenu.

360 Quand un enfant sera suffisamment instruict pour se passer du cathechisme quil recite sollempnellement la somme de ce qui y sera contenu et ainsi
quil face comme une profession de sa crestiente en presence de leglise.

Devant quavoir faict cela que nul enfant ne soit admis a recepvoir la
Cene. Et quon advertisse les parens de ne les amener devant le temps. Car cest
365 chose fort pereilleuse tant pour les enfans que pour les peres de les ingerer sans
bonne et suffisante instruction pour laquelle cognoistre il est besoing de user
de cest ordre.

Affin quil ny ait faulte quil soit ordonne que les enfans quilz vont a
lescolle sassemblent la devant les douze heures et que les maistres les menent
370 par bon ordre en chascune paroisse.

Les aultres que leurs peres les envoyent ou facent conduire. Et affin quil y
ait moings de confusion quon observe autant que faire se pourra la distinction
des paroisses en cest endroit comme il a este dict cy dessus des sacremens.

357/359 Quil – retenu] after Calvin realised that his 1537 catechism was too difficult
for children, he completely rewrote it and rearranged its contents in questions and
answers and simplified the theological language. The first edition of this new catechism
was printed in 1542

349 quand – pourroit] quant bon leur semblera pourront *P*   **354** Lordre quon
debvra tenir envers les petis enfans] L'Ordre qu'on doit tenir envers les petis enfans *alia
manus add. in marg.*   **361** ainsi] aussi *P*   **370** bon] *correximus ex P, a.c.* bonne
372 se] *a.c.* ce   **373** il] *scriba corr., a.c.* y

412   CONCILIUM GENEVENSE – 1541

Que ceulx qui contreviendront soient appellez devant la compagnie des
375 anciens ou commis. Et sil ne vouloient obtemperer a bon conseil quil en soit
faict le rapport a la Seigneurie.

| Pour adviser lesquelz feront leur debvoir ou non que les commis susdits 13
aient loeil dessus pour sen donner garde.

De lordre quon doibt tenir envers les grands pour observer
380 ### bonne pollice en leglise

Letablissement dun iour pour le Consistoire

Que les commis susdictz dont il a este parle sassemblent une fois la
sepmaine avec les ministres. Asscavoir le jeudy pour veoir sil ny a nul desordre
en leglise et traicter ensemble des remedes quand il en sera besoing.
385 Pource quil nauroit nulle auctorite ne jurisdiction pour contraindre avons
advise leur donner un de noz officiers pour apeller ceulx auquelz ilz vouldront
faire quelque admonition.

Si quelcun par mespris refuse de comparoistre leur office sera en advertir
le conseil affin de donner remede.

390 Sensuyvent les personnes que les anciens ou commis doibvent
admonester et comme on doibvra proceder

Sil y a quelcun qui dogmatise contre la doctrine receue quil soit appelle
pour conferer avec luy. Sil se renge quon le renvoye sans scandale ne diffame.
Sil est opiniastre quon ladmoneste par quelque fois jusques a ce quon verra
395 quil sera mestier de plus grande severite. Et lors quon luy interdise la communion de la cene et quon le denonce au Magistrat.

Si quelcun est negligent de convenir a leglise tellement quon appercoyve
un mespris notable de la communion des fidelles ou si quelquun se monstre

---

374 qui] *scriba corr., a.c.* que   **375** ou commis] *in adnot. in P*   sil] *sic*   **375/376** quil
en soit faict le rapport a la Seigneurie] quon en face le rapport a messieurs *P*
377 commis susdits] anciens *P*   **381** Letablissement dun iour pour le Consistoire]
alia manus add. in marg.; deest P   **382** commis susdictz] anciens *P*   **383** jeudy] jeudy
matin *P*   **385/386** avons advise] quil plaise a messieurs *P*   **386** un de noz] ung de
leurs *P*   auquelz] *sic*; ausquelz *P*   **388** refuse] *supplevimus ex P*   **389** le conseil]
messieurs *P*   **390/391** Sensuyvent – proceder] Qui sont ceux qui doivent estre
admonestez et comment on y doit proceder *alia manus add. in marg.; in adnot. in P*
390 ou commis] *in adnot. in P*   **392** qui] *scriba corr., a.c.* quil   **394** verra] *a.c.* vevra

CONCILIUM GENEVENSE – 1541

estre contempteur de lordre ecclesiasticque quon ladmoneste et sil se rend
400 obeissant quon le renvoye amyablement. Sil persevere de mal en pis apres
lavoir trois fois admoneste quon le separe de leglise et quon le denonce a la
Seigneurie.

| Quand est de la vie dun chascun pour corriger les faultes qui y seroient il 14
fauldra proceder selon lordre que nostre Seigneur a commande.

405 Cest que des vices secretz quon les repregne secretement et que nul ne
ameine son prochain devant leglise pour lacuser de quelque faulte. Laquelle ne
sera point notoire ne scandaleuse synon apres lavoir trouve rebelle.

Au reste que ceulx quilz se seront mocquez des admonitions particulieres
de leur prochain soient admonetez de rechiefz par leglise. Et sils ne voulloient
410 nullement venir a raison ne recognoistre leur faulte quand ilz en seront
convaincuz quon leur denunce quilz en aient a sabstenir de la Cene jusques a
ce quilz reviennent a meilleure disposition.

Quant est des vices notoires et publicques que leglise ne peut pas dissimu-
ler. Si ce sont faultes qui meritent seullement admonition. Loffice des anciens
415 commis sera appeller ceulx qui en seront entachez leur faire remonstrances
amyables affin quilz aient a sen corriger si on y voit amendement ne les plus
molester. Silz perseverent a mal faire quon les admoneste de rechiefz. Et si a la
longue on ne profitoit rien leur denuncer comme a contempteurs de dieu quilz
aient a sabstenir de la cene jusques a ce quon voye en eulx changement de vie.

420 Quant est des crimes qui ne meritent pas seullement remonstrances de
parolles. Mais corrections avec chastiment. Si quelcun y est tombe selon l'exi-
gence du cas il luy fauldra denuncer quil sabstienne quelque temps de la cene
pour se humilier devant dieu et myeulx cognoistre sa faulte.

Si quelcun par contumace ou rebellion se voulloit ingerer contre la
425 deffence loffice du ministre sera de le renvoyer veu qui ne luy est licite de le
recepvoir a la communion.

Et neantmoings que tout cela soit tellement modere qui ny ait nulle
rigueur dont personne soit greve et mesmes que les corrections ne soient sinon
medicines pour reduire les pecheurs a nostre Seigneur.

430 Et que tout cela se face en telle sorte que les ministres naient nulle jurisdiction civile et ne usent sinon du glaive spirituel de la parolle de dieu comme

---

400/401 apres lavoir trois fois admoneste] cfr Matth. 18, 15-17   **405/407** Cest –
rebelle] cfr Matth. 18, 15-17   **431/432** comme sainct paul leur ordonne] cfr Eph. 6, 17

399 sil] *scriba corr., a.c.* pil   **401/402** a la Seigneurie] *in adnot. in P*   **403** qui] *scriba
corr., a.c.* quil   **408** quilz] *sic*   **411** en] *deest P*   **412** a] en *P*   **415** commis] *in adnot.
in P*   faire] feront *P*   **416** y voit] *atramento erasus*   **422** quil] *a.c.* quilz
423 cognoistre] recognoistre *P*   **430/438** Et – cas] *deest P*

sainct paul leur ordonne et que par ce le consistoire ne soit en rien derogue a lauctorite de la Seigneurie ne a la justice ordinaire. Mais que la puissance Civile demeure en son entier. Et mesmes ou il sera besoing de faire quelque
435 punition ou contraindre les parties que les ministres avec le consistoire aiant ouy les parties et faict les remonstrances et admonitions telles que bon sera ayent a raporter au conseil le tout lequel sur leur relation advisera den ordonner et faire jugement selon lexigence du cas.

Que ceste pollice soit non seullement pour la ville. Mais aussi pour les
440 villages dependantz de la Seigneurie.

---

432 le] *supplevimus*   **436** ouy] *scriba corr., a.c.* ouyr   sera] *scriba corr., a.c.* sar

CONCILIA HUNGARICA ET TRANSSYLVANICA

1545-1567-1570

edidit
Zoltán CSEPREGI

THE SYNODS OF ERDŐD, DEBRECEN, AND CSENGER
1545-1567-1570

THE SYNOD OF ERDŐD (1545)

On 20 September 1545, several pastors from the upper region of the river Tisza gathered in Erdőd and agreed upon a confession of faith consisting of twelve articles. The participants were all Hungarians, without exception, and the names of the 29 co-signers still remain. Many can be found in the records of the University of Wittenberg. ([1]) In the first eleven articles, the pastors dealt in detail with several doctrinal tenets. As a conclusion of the Synod's proceedings, they summarised the remainder of their doctrinal tenets in the twelfth and last article as follows: '[i]n all other matters we agree with the creed submitted in Augsburg in 1530'. Their choice of wording leaves no doubt that they had the so-called *Variata* – which was the commonly-used version of the *Confessio Augustana* in those years – under their eyes.

Later on, both the Lutheran Church and the Reformed Church of Hungary, as well as the Church of the Transylvanian Saxons, adopted the *Confessio Erdödina* as their confession of faith. As a result, two clearly distinguishable textual traditions of this confession emerged. However, their contents were theologically identical. The superintendents of the Transylvanian Saxons copied the *Erdödina* into their protocols. ([2]) Péter Bod (1712-1769) published this text in his *Historia* (siglum *B*) in an overall accurate fashion. The other textual tradition of the *Erdödina* is connected to the Hungarian Reformed

---

([1]) *Historia Ecclesiae Reformatae in Hungaria*, p. 93; Bod, *Historia Hungarorum Ecclesiastica*, vol. 1, p. 322.

([2]) *Codex Pancratius*; *Manuscriptum Adamianum*; G. Pöldner, *Privilegia et acta synodalia von anno 1545 bis 1713*; G. J. Haner, *Isagoge in Historiam Transylvanicam trium recentissimorum saeculorum Ecclesiasticam* (manuscripts, now in Sibiu, Archivele Statului); L. Kolb, *Acta synodorum tam generalium, tam specialium ab ineunte aetate reformationis in Transylvania sive ab anno 1545 usque ad annum 1726 ab ecclesiasticis institutarum congesta* (manuscript, Brasov, Biserica negra, Tf 74); A. Scharsius, *Compendium actorum synodalium inde a reformationis tempore a pastoribus Saxonicis Augustanae Confessionis non variatae addictis in Transilvania consignatum* (Biblioteca Universităţii Lucian Blaga Sibiu, manuscript 908).

418 CONCILIA HUNGARICA ET TRANSSYLVANICA – 1545-1567-1570

Church. In 1624 István Dési, pastor in Broos, copied the confession into the records of his congregation. This is where Mihály Ajtai (1704-1776) found it. Later on, József Benkő (1740-1814) copied Ajtai's manuscript, (3) and the text was eventually edited and published by Ferenc Tóth (1768-1844) (siglum *T*). The latter version of the *Erdödina* contains more mistakes than Bod's manuscript: however, the former helps complete without difficulty the missing parts from the latter. The text of the *Erdödina* we used as basis for this edition is the first modern critical edition of the document. (4)

THE SYNOD OF DEBRECEN (1567): THE *CONFESSIO BREVIS* AND THE *ARTICULI MAIORES*

The Synod of the Transylvanian Church held in Torda on 13 February 1567 endorsed the Unitarian doctrines of Ferenc Dávid (*c.* 1520-1579), bishop of Cluj. In response to this event the bishop of Debrecen, Péter Melius (*c.* 1536-1572), summoned fourteen deaneries from his own district east of the river Tisza as well as other three from northern Hungary to meet at Debrecen. A Synod was held there on 24-26 February 1567. (5) Melius submitted two of his treatises to the assembly: the *Confessio brevis*, a lengthy creed in Hungarian, (6) and the so-called *Articuli maiores*, a collection of dogmatic-polemical canons. His writings were mainly directed against anti-trinitarians, but also included a discussion of liturgy, predestination, and the Eucharist refuting the tenets of Rome and Wittenberg. The Synod also solemnly approved the *Second Helvetic Confession* as confirmed by the signatures of the deans who attended the meeting. (7) This Synod played a significant role in the creation of the Hungarian Reformed Church, with regard to dogmas, liturgy, and canon law.

---

(3) M. Ajtai, *Collectiones historiae ecclesiasticae, praecipue historiam Hungariae illustrantes*, Országos Széchényi Könyvtár, Budapest, Quart. Hung. 1043, vol. 2; J. Benkő, *Synodi Erdödienses geminatae, prior generalis anno MDXLV, altera partialis anno MDLV a protestantibus verbi divini ministris in Erdöd oppido Hungariae celebratae*, Biblioteca Centrală a Universităţii Victor Babeş.

(4) *RefBK*, vol. 1/2 (2006), p. 439-448, no. 33.

(5) A draft of preparatory propositions can be found in *Historia Ecclesiae Reformatae in Hungaria*, p. 164-170.

(6) *BaM*, p. 160-222.

(7) i.e. the deans of Várad, Érmellék, Máramaros, Makó, Debrecen, Szatmár, Bereg, Szilágy, Nyír, Böszörmény, Nagybánya, Ugocsa, Túr, Károly, Zemplén, Újvár, Borsod. See *RMNy*, p. 1109 (Debrecen 1616).

CONCILIA HUNGARICA ET TRANSSYLVANICA – 1545-1567-1570   419

The *Confessio brevis* was published in the summer of 1567 in Debrecen. This edition included a preface dated 28 June and addressed to John Sigismund Zápolya (1540-1571), Prince of Transylvania, encouraging him to get rid of heretics following the examples of Michael Servetus and Valentino Gentile. The excerpts from this document offered below, as well as the retrospective numbering of paragraphs, are taken from the 2009 critical edition. (8) The *Hungarian Confession* and the *Articuli maiores* were also published in Debrecen between August and September 1567. The paragraphs of the latter document have so far been inconsistently numbered, so we offered our own numeration. Due to the abundance of ambiguous Biblical references in this text, we included only the verbatim quotes in the Biblical apparatus. Our selection of excerpts from the *Articuli* represents the first critical edition of this document.

THE SYNOD OF CSENGER (1570): THE *CONFESSIO VERA*

The spread of Anti-trinitarianism prompted a stiff reaction from Calvinists. Péter Melius summoned a Synod to meet at Csenger, in eastern Hungary. In preparation for it, Melius compiled a list of 52 articles of faith, titled *Propositiones verae et consentientes Scripturis Sacris*. (9) The Synod of Csenger, held on 26 July 1570, approved Melius' *Confessio vera*. In line with the main purpose of this work, the opening five articles defended the doctrine of the Holy Trinity, and Melius' defence was further supported by an exegetical study. (10) Articles 6 to 19 were a condensation of Reformed theology and refuted Roman Catholicism, Lutheranism, and Anabaptism. The last item found on the frontispiece as well as in the table of contents – titled *De tollendi foedis haereticis et antichristis* – is missing from the text of the confession. However, Melius discussed this point in a later work, the *Principia quaedam in theologia et philosophia immota* as well as in a recommendation addressed to Transylvanian chancellor Mihály Csáky (1505-1572), dated 15 August 1570. (11) The *Con-*

---

(8) *RefBK*, vol. 2/2 (2009), p. 347-401, no. 62.
(9) *RMNy* 281. In the *Confessio vera*, theses 43 to 52 are numbered 10 to 19.
(10) *RefBK*, vol. 3/1 (2012), p. 32-36.
(11) 'Iudico Servetum et Serveti filios a Diabolo excitatos et Satanae traditos esse et captivos duci ab ipso Deo huius saeculi, II Cor. 4. Eph. 3. 4. Rom. 1. 3. Sed ut ab initio excitatae haereses ab ipso Deo sopitae et extinctae sunt, ubi electi probati sunt et dormientes post semen sparsum excitati sunt, aurum a stipulis separatum est, ita et Servetianas haereses brevi extinctum iri spero, imo et persuasi, sicut certa sunt indicia', in *Principia quaedam in theologia et philosophia immota*, Debrecini MDLXX (*RMNy* 278).

420 CONCILIA HUNGARICA ET TRANSSYLVANICA – 1545-1567-1570

fessio vera of Csenger is the culmination of a long-standing Calvinist polemics against anti-trinitarians in the region east of the river Tisza, which included the formulation of local creeds. When the critical dangers represented by Anabaptism ceased to exist, these texts were replaced by confessions of faith enjoying international prestige, such as the *Second Helvetic Confession* and the *Heidelberg Catechism*.

There is only one surviving copy of the first edition of the *Confessio vera* approved in Debrecen, published in 1570 shortly after the Synod. The text offered below and the retrospective numbering of paragraphs follow the 2012 critical edition, which also offers further detail on later editions and translations of the *Confessio*. ([12])

BIBLIOGRAPHY

Sources (and Their Abbreviations)

M. Ajtai, *Tóth Ferencz gyüjteménye a magyar reformáta egyház történetére vonatkozó iratoknak*, 4 vols [= Ajtai, *Collectiones*].

J. C. W. Augusti, *Corpus librorum symbolicorum, qui in ecclesia reformatorum auctoritatem publicam obtinuerunt*, Elberfeldi 1827.

P. Bod, *Historia Hungarorum Ecclesiastica, inde ab exordio Novi Testamenti ad nostra usque tempora ex monumentis partim editis, partim vero ineditis, fide dignis* – ed. L. W. E. Rauwenhoff, 3 vols, Lugduni Batavorum 1888 [= Bod, *Historia Hungarorum Ecclesiastica*].

Corpus et Syntagma Confessionum Fidei, quae in diversis Regnis et Nationibus ecclesiarum nomine fuerunt authentice editae, in celeberrimis conventibus exhibitae publica auctoritate comprobatae, 2 vols, Genevae 1612; [2]1654.

F. A. Lampe – P. Debreceni Ember, *Historia Ecclesiae Reformatae in Hungaria*, Traj. ad Rhen. 1728 [= *Historia Ecclesiae Reformatae in Hungaria*].

H. A. Niemeyer, *Collectio confessionum in ecclesiis reformatis publicatarum*, 2 vols, Lipsiae 1840.

Országos Széchényi Könyvtár, Budapest Quart. Hung. 1043.

Ostmitteleuropas Bekenntnisschriften der evangelischen Kirchen A. und H.B. des Reformationszeitalters Band III/1: *1564-1576*, hrsg. P. F. Barton –

---

(12) *RefBK*, vol. 3/1 (2012), p. 21-45, no. 66.

L. Makkai (*Studien und Texte zur Kirchengeschichte und Geschichte* V, 3/1), Budapest 1987 [= *BaM*].

Régi magyarországi nyomtatványok, szerk. G. Borsa et al., 4 vols, Budapest 1971-2012 [= *RMNy*].

LITERATURE (AND ITS ABBREVIATIONS)

Antitrinitarianism in the Second Half of the Sixteenth Century, ed. R. Dán – A. Pirnát (*Studia Humanitatis* 5), Budapest – Leiden 1982.

M. Balázs, *Early Transylvanian Antitrinitarianism (1566-1571): From Servet to Palaeologus*, Baden-Baden 1996.

J-.A. Bernhard, 'Von Adligen, Studenten und Buchdruckern in Ungarn: ein Beitrag zur «Wende» vom lutherischen zum reformierten Bekenntnis im protestantischen Ungarn des 16. Jahrhunderts', *Zwingliana* 33 (2006), p. 155-168.

E. Bryner, 'Die Ausstrahlungen Bullingers auf die Reformation in Ungarn und Polen', *Zwingliana* 31 (2004), p. 179-197.

M. Bucsay, *Der Protestantismus in Ungarn 1521-1978. Ungarns Reformationskirchen in Geschichte und Gegenwart*, 2 vols, Vienna – Cologne – Graz 1977-1979.

—, 'Die Lehre vom Heiligen Abendmahl in der ungarischen Reformation helvetischer Richtung', *Deutsche Theologie* 6 (1939), p. 261-281.

Calvin und Reformiertentum in Ungarn und Siebenbürgen. Helvetisches Bekenntnis, Ethnie und Politik vom 16. Jahrhundert bis 1918, hrsg. M. Fata – A. Schindling, Münster 2010.

S. Drees, *Prädestination und Bekenntnis. Die Rezeption der Prädestinationslehre Johannes Calvins in den europäischen reformierten Bekenntnisschriften bis 1619*, Kamen 2011.

Heinrich Bullinger 1504-1575. Gesammelte Aufsätze zum 400. Todestag, hrsg. U. Gäbler – E. Erkenrath (*Zürcher Beiträge für Reformationsgeschichte* 7/8), 2 vols, Zürich 1975.

I. Juhász, 'Glaubensbekenntnis und Kirchengeschichte. Die *Confessio Helvetica Posterior* in der Geschichte der Siebenbürgisch-reformierten Kirche', in U. Gäbler – E. Zsindely (hrsg.), *Bullinger-Tagung 1975: Vorträge, gehalten aus Anlass von Heinrich Bullingers 400. Todestag*, Zürich 1977, p. 99-112.

—, 'Von Luther zu Bullinger. Der theologische Weg der Reformation in den protestantischen Kirchen in Rumänien', *Zeitschrift für Kirchengeschichte* 81 (1970), p. 308-333.

L. Makkai, 'Des Péter Melius Abendmahlslehre in seiner Kolosserbriefauslegung im Vergleich mit den Kolosserbriefkommentaren Calvins und Melanchthons', in W. H. Neuser (hrsg.), *Calvinus servus Christi. Die Referate des Congrès international des recherches calviniennes / International Congress on Calvin Research / Internationalen Kongresses für Calvinforschung, vom 25. bis 28. August 1986 in Debrecen*, Budapest 1988, p. 233-236.

—, 'Melius, the Hungarian Reformer', in D. Kosáry et al. (éds.), *Études historiques hongroises 1985, publiées à l'occasion du XVIe Congrès international des sciences historiques par le comité national des historiens hongrois*, 3 vols, Budapest 1985, vol. 1, p. 1-19.

L. M. Medyesy, 'The Evolving of the Sixteenth-Century Transylvanian Reformed Church and its Impact on the Hungarians', *Communio Viatorum* 36 (1994), p. 121-134.

B. Nagy, 'Bullingers Bedeutung für das östliche Europa. Ein Forschungsbericht', in E. Kähler (hrsg.), *Reformation 1517-1967. Wittenberger Vorträge*, Berlin 1968, p. 84-119.

—, 'Geschichte und Bedeutung des Zweiten Helvetischen Bekenntnisses in den osteuropäischen Ländern', in J. Staedtke (hrsg.), *Glauben und Bekennen. Vierhundert Jahre Confessio Helvetica Posterior. Beiträge zu ihrer Geschichte und Theologie*, Zürich 1966, p. 109-202.

—, 'Quellenforschung zur ungarischen Reformationsliteratur unter besonderer Berücksichtigung der Beziehungen zu Bullinger', *Zwingliana* 12 (1965), p. 191-206.

B. Németh, 'Die Existenz der Reformierten Kirchen in Ungarn im 16. Jahrhundert zwischen Autonomie und Vernetzung', *Jahrbuch für Geschichte des Protestantismus in Österreich* 121 (2005), p. 169-185.

—, «...*Gott schläft nicht, er blinzelt uns zu...*»: *evangelisch-reformierte Lebensgestaltung zwischen Kontinuität und Wandel – Ungarn im 16. Jahrhundert als Beispiel*, Frankfurt am Main 2003.

W. H. Neuser, 'Melanchthons Abendmahlslehre und ihre Auswirkungen im unteren Donauraum', *Zeitschrift für Kirchengeschichte* 84 (1973), p. 49-59.

I. Schlégl, 'Die Beziehungen Heinrich Bullingers zu Ungarn', *Zwingliana* 12/5 (1966), p. 330-370.

E. Tempfli, 'Melanchthon und die Synode von Erdőd, 20. September 1545', in G. Frank – M. Treu (hrsg.), *Melanchthon und Europa*, 2 vols (*Melanchton-Schriften der Stadt Bretten* 6,1/2), Stuttgart 2001-2002, vol. 1 (2001), p. 203-221.

W. Tóth, 'Trinitarianism versus Antitrinitarianism in the Hungarian Reformation', *Church History* 13 (1944), p. 255-268.

A. S. Unghváry, *The Hungarian Protestant Reformation in the Sixteenth Century under the Ottoman Impact: Essays and Profiles* (*Texts and Studies in Religion* 48), Lewiston – Queenston 1989.

G. Vladár, 'Die Calvinrezeption in Ungarn', in Evangelisch-theologische Fakultät der Universität Wien (hrsg.), *Johannes Calvin zum 500. Geburtstag: Festgottesdienst, Festakt & Wissenschaftliches Symposion* (*Gutachten und Studien* 7), Wien 2009, p. 56-73.

MONITUM

Confessio Erdödina   *RefBK*, vol. 1/2 (2006), p. 439-448.

Confessio brevis, Debrecen   *RefBK*, vol. 2/2 (2009), p. 347-401.

Articuli maiores, Debrecen   *RMNy* 228.

Confessio vera, Csenger   *RefBK*, vol. 3/1 (2012), p. 21-45.

CONCILIA ERDÖDINUM, DEBRECENIENSE,
ET CSENGERIENSE
1545 – 1567 – 1570

CONSPECTUS SIGLORUM

CONFESSIO ERDÖDINA, 1545 – MANUSCRIPTA

A   M. Ajtai, *Collectiones historiae ecclesiasticae, praecipue historiam Hungariae illustrantes*. Országos Széchényi Könyvtár, Budapest, Quart. Hung. 1043, vol. 2, fol. 10r-13v (Copia ab autographo descripta)

D   St. Dési, *Articuli christianae confessionis Erdödini a pastoribus ecclesiarum Hung. conscripti 20. Septembris anno 1545*. Ibid. (vide supra), vol. 4, fol. 36r-38r (Copia ab autographo descripta)

CONFESSIO ERDÖDINA, 1545 – EDITIONES

B   P. Bod, *Historia Hungarorum Ecclesiastica, inde ab exordio Novi Testamenti ad nostra usque tempora ex monumentis partim editis, partim vero ineditis, fide dignis*, ed. L. W. E. Rauwenhoff, vol. 1, Leiden 1888, p. 322-325

L   F. A. Lampe – P. Debreceni Ember, *Historia Ecclesiae Reformatae in Hungaria*, Utrecht 1728

T   F. Tóth, *A' helvétziai vallástételt követő túl a' tiszai superintendentziában élt református püspökök élete, e' jelen való időkig lehozva*, Győr 1812, p. 247-262

CONFESSIO BREVIS, DEBRECEN, 1567 – EDITIONES

BaM   P. F. Barton – L. Makkai (hrsg.), *Ostmitteleuropas Bekenntnisschriften der evangelischen Kirchen A. und H.B. des Reformationszeitalters Band III/1: 1564-1576* (*Studien und Texte zur Kirchengeschichte und Geschichte* V, 3/1), Budapest 1987, p. 133-159

E   (Editio princeps:) *Brevis confessio pastorum ad synodum Debrecii* [sic] *celebratam 24, 25 et 26 Februa. anno D. 1567 convocatorum*, Debrecini. Excudebat Michael Töröc, An. MDLXVII. [40] fol. – 4° (*RMNy* 228)

RefBK   A. Mühling – P. Opitz (hrsg.), *Reformierte Bekenntnisschriften*, vol. 2/2, Neukirchen 2009, p. 347-401

ARTICULI MAIORES, DEBRECEN, 1567 – EDITIONES

C   *De disciplina ecclesiastica sev gvbernationis ecclesiasticae legitima forma in Vngarica natione cis Tibiscum, ex verbo Dei petita et conformi cum veterum recentiorumque in ecclesia doctorum constitutionibus, ad vitam et mores ministrorum regendos atque ad decentem ordinatamque in ecclesia functionem ac ad tuendam pietatem et honestatem composita, consilio et opera Georgij Gönci pastoris ecclesiae Debreciensis etc. Anno Christi MDLXXVII*, Debrecini 1591. [43] fol. – 4° (*RMNy* 657). – ²1613, ³1633, ⁴1646

E   (Editio princeps) *Articuli ex verbo Dei et lege natvrae compositi, ad conseruandam politiam ecclesiasticam et formandam vitam Christianam in omnibus ordinibus necessariam*, Debrecini MDLXVII. [34] fol. – 4° (*RMNy* 226)

CONFESSIO VERA, CSENGER, 1570 – EDITIONES

BaM   vide supra, p. 262-270

BuM   *XVI. századi Magyar Református Hitvallások*, ed. M. Bucsay – L. Makkai, Debrecen 1972, p. 25-75

CONSPECTUS SIGLORUM

E (Editio princeps) *Confessio vera ex verbo Dei sumpta et in synodo Czengerina uno consensu exhibita et declarata*, Debrecini MDLXX. [20] fol. – 4° (*RMNy* 278)

I

ARTICULI CHRISTIANAE CONFESSIONIS ERDÖDINI A PASTORIBUS ECCLESIARUM HUNG. CONSCRIPTI 20. SEPTEMBRIS ANNO 1545

Deus optimus maximus voluit congressus hominum fieri, ut in eorum
coetu ipse cum Filio suo unigenito et Spiritu Sancto celebretur. Ideo cum nos
quoque Dei beneficio convenerimus, cupimus, quantum in nobis est, coram
mundo gloriam eius promovere.

I. Deus trinus in unitate. – Imprimis itaque confitemur unum Deum in
trinitate et trinum in unitate iuxta sententiam orthodoxorum patrum. At
damnamus omnes aliter sentientes, et praesertim eos, qui dicunt, nos ex uno
Deo fingere tres Deos. Ac tales quidem cupimus prohibere, ut gloria Sanctae
Trinitatis maneat.

II. Iesus Deus, homo, unus mediator. – Item confitemur dominum Iesum
verum Deum et verum hominem esse, verum sacerdotem et unicum mediatorem nostrum inter Deum Patrem et nos homines peccatores, eumque naturae
esse duplicis. Damnamus itaque eos, qui sanctos carne exutos constituunt
mediatores et gloriam mediatoris Christi transferunt in sanctos.

III. Iustificatio gratuita. – Iustificationem, hoc est remissionem peccatorum coniunctam cum donatione Spiritus Sancti et acceptionem ad vitam
aeternam confitemur gratis contingere hominibus fide apprehendentibus
misericordiam Dei propter meritum Christi. Damnamus vero homines iusti-

---

8/9 Deus – patrum] cfr *Symbolum Athanasianum*, par. 3, in BSELK, p. 28   **9/ 12** At – maneat] cfr *Confessio Augustana Invariata*, Article 1, in BSELK, p. 50-52   **16/ 17** Damnamus – sanctos] *Confessio Augustana Invariata*, Article 21, and *Apologia*, Article 21, in BSELK, p. 81 and 316-325 respectively

---

1/3 Articuli – 1545] *om. tit.* B   **4** eorum] omni *A D T*   **8** Deus – unitate] De
trinitate sancta *A D T*   itaque] igitur *A D T*   **10** aliter] aliud *A D T*   **11** Ac tales
quidem] Et tales *A D T*   Sanctae] sacrosanctae *A D T*   **12** Trinitatis] *add.* defendatur
ac *A D T*   **13** Iesus – mediator] De Filio Dei, unico mediatore *A D T*   **14** et verum]
et *A D T*   verum³] aeternum *A D T*   et²] ac *A D T*   **17** Christi] nostri *A D T*
18 Iustificatio gratuita] De iustificatione hominis peccatoris coram Deo *A D T*   hoc
est] et *A D T*   **19** acceptionem] acceptationem *A D T*

430 CONCILIUM ERDÖDINUM – 1545

tiarios, qui operibus, ieiuniis, peregrinationibus, fraternitatibus religiosorum tribuunt iustificationem.

IV. Fides iustificat. – Fidem intelligimus esse donum Dei, et cum dicimus 25 fide iustificari hominem, intelligimus fidem non tantum historiae notitiam, verum et fiduciam, qua apprehendimus misericordiam Dei et acquiescimus in Filio Dei. Damnamus eos, qui fidem dicunt humanis viribus acquiri et eam intelligunt esse tantum historiae notitiam.

V. Bona opera necessaria. – Etsi autem bonis operibus non tribuimus 30 iustificationem, quae solius fidei est, tamen ea dicimus esse necessaria et requiri a renatis; arbor enim bona fructus bonos facit. Requiruntur enim bona opera propter tres causas. Primo, propter mandatum et gloriam Dei. Secundo, propter aedificationem proximi. Tertio, ut fidem nostram bonis operibus testemur, exerceamus et vocationem nostram recte faciamus. Damnamus eos, 35 qui bonis operibus tribuunt iustificationem, et hypocritas, qui nec vitam emendare nec fidem bonis operibus declarare volunt, qui tantum titulo tenus professores Christi se profitentur.

VI. Baptismus, coena Domini tollunt peccata. – In administratione sacramentorum baptismi et coenae dominicae sequimur institutionem Christi et 40 primitivae ecclesiae et confitemur per baptismum tolli omnia peccata et gratiam Dei offerri et in coena Domini sub pane et vino vere exhiberi corpus et sanguinem Christi. Volumus autem, ut Christi institutio in utroque sacramento nativo sermone, ea qua licet reverentia, in omnibus ecclesiis uno ritu eademque forma peragatur et administretur. Damnamus, qui extenuant origi- 45 nale peccatum, et eos, qui asserunt infantes non esse baptizandos. Damnamus item violatores institutionis Christi et profanatores coenae dominicae, et qui alteram speciem laicis subtrahunt et legitimum usum coenae dominicae in

---

25 historiae notitiam] cfr *Confessio Augustana Variata*, Article 4, in *CR*, vol. 26 (1858), p. 353; also in *RefBK*, vol. 1/2 (2006), p. 157   **34/37** Damnamus – profitentur] cfr *Confessio Augustana Variata*, Article 20, in *CR*, vol. 26 (1858), p. 364-365; also in *RefBK*, vol. 1/2 (2006), p. 169   **41/42** in – Christi[1]] *Confessio Augustana Variata*, Article 10, in *CR*, vol. 26 (1858), p. 357; also in *RefBK*, vol. 1/2 (2006), p. 161

---

22 religiosorum] religionum *A D*; reliquorum *T*   **24** Fides iustificat] Quid et qualis sit fides iustificans *A D T*   et] at *A D T*   **25** historiae notitiam] notitiam historicam *A D T*   **29** Bona opera necessaria] Bona opera quo et quare facienda, tribus de caussis *A D T*   **30** esse] *om. A D T*   **31** enim[1]] autem *A D T*   **37** Christi se] se christianitatis *A D T*   **38** Baptismus coena Domini tollunt peccata] Sacra duo: baptismus et coena Domini eorumque administratio et effecta *A D T*   sacramentorum] sacrorum, scilicet *A D T*   **41** gratiam] gloriam *B*   **42** utroque] vero *A D T*   **43** qua licet reverentia] quae decet, reverentia *A D*; quae decet, recurentia *T*   **44** Damnamus] *add.* eos *A D T*   **46** item] *add.* omnes *A D*; *add.* eos *T*   institutionis] iustificationis *D*   **46/47** et[2] – dominicae] *om. B*

CONCILIUM ERDÖDINUM – 1545

horrendas nundinationes et abominationes missarum verterunt. Item damnamus omnes blasphemos, qui hanc institutionem Christi, quae est in nostris
50 ecclesiis, vocant missam diabolicam. Ideo Petrus hanc blasphemiam tolli et
tales blasphemos coerceri iubet.

VII. Sanctos carne exutos colimus honore imitationis, hoc est fiduciam
cordis non ponimus in illis nec eorum auxilium imploramus; imitamur autem
eorum fidem ac bona opera vocationis et charitatis. Laudamus Deum in
55 sanctis et agimus gratias ei, quod ostenderit exempla misericordiae et fidei.
Laudamus enim ipsos sanctos, quod donis Dei pie usi sint ad aedificationem
ecclesiae et bonis operibus praeluxerint. Damnamus eos, qui fiduciam Christo
debitam transferunt in sanctos et eos invocant.

VIII. Fatemur quatuor gradus christianae libertatis. Primo, quod simus
60 liberi propter Christum ab ira Dei, a damnatione legis, peccati et aeterna morte. Secundo, in mundi periculis nos donari Spiritu Sancto et sustentari in
omnibus aerumnis, ne victi afflictionis magnitudine deficiamus ab evangelio.
Tertio, quod attinet ad iustificationem, ab omnibus legis operibus nos esse
liberatos; quod vero attinet ad obedientiam, a moralibus non esse liberatos.
65 Quarto, ab omnibus mundi traditionibus, ritibus et constitutionibus episcoporum, quae ut laqueos conscientiarum requirunt, ac si esset necessarius
cultus, nos esse liberos. Caeterum boni ordinis causa eorum ritus in pietate
christiana observari posse, qui immediate requiruntur ut cultus necessarius.
Hos in christiana libertate censemus esse servandos.

70 IX. Asserimus triplicem confessionem, divinam, fraternam et auricularem. Caeterum divinam et fraternam dicimus esse iuris divini, auricularem
non item. Etsi autem non requirimus in auriculari confessione enumerationem

---

50/51 Ideo – iubet] cfr II Petr. 2, 12

48 verterunt] vertunt *A D T*   **50** Petrus] coetus *A D T*   **52** VII] *add. tit.* De sanctis
mortuis, qui honorandi sunt imitatione bonorum operum, officio vocationis et
charitatis, non invocationis *A D T*   hoc est] at *A T*; et *D*   **54** ac] et *A D T*
charitatis] *add.* Deinde *A D T*   **55** exempla] viam *A D T*   **56** enim] ergo *A D T*
sint] sunt *A D T*   **59** VIII] *add. tit.* Gradus christianae libertatis *A D T*   simus]
sumus *A D T*   **60** propter] per *A D T*   peccati] poena *A*   **61** in²] ab *A D T*
62 afflictionis magnitudine] magnitudine afflictionum *A D*; magnitudine adflictorum
T   **64** vero] praeterea *A D T*   **65** mundi] humanis *A D T*   **66** ut laqueos] in
laqueis *A D T*   requirunt – necessarius] requiruntur, tanquam necessarii *A D T*
67 eorum] ii *A D T*   **68** christiana observari posse] servari possunt *A D T*   qui] *add.*
nempe *A D T*   **68/69** necessarius. Hos] necessarii, quos *A D T*   **70** IX] *add. tit.* De
triplici confessione et quare auricularis sit in ecclesia retinenda? Tribus de caussis: 1. ob
doctrinam 2. consolationem 3. absolutionem *A D T*   et] *om. A D T*

432 CONCILIUM ERDŐDINUM – 1545

peccatorum, partim propter impossibilitatem, partim propter laqueum conscientiarum, tamen in ecclesia retinendam esse propter triplicem censemus
75 utilitatem: doctrinam, consolationem et absolutionem, nec secus aliquem ad
communionem admittimus.

X. Adversarii nostri nos calumniantur, nos esse sine capite, principe et
ordine. Verum nos fatemur, Christum esse caput vere ecclesiae, cuius nos
membra esse credimus. Principes item et politicos magistratus honoramus et
80 eorum officium amamus verbo Dei et obedientia in rebus, quae non laedunt
gloriam Dei. Nec sine ordine sumus. Est enim certus ordo pastorum, ministrorum et auditorum iuxta illud: *Alios dedit apostolos, pastores et doctores, ne
circumferantur quovis vento doctrinae.* Et si autem in hymnis et cantionibus
ecclesiasticis non ubique eundem ordinem observamus, tamen in doctrina,
85 absolutione et sacramentorum administratione unum ordinem eundemque
ritum observamus. Nec in feriis in hac provincia celebrandis multum discrepa-
mus, ideo sine causa ab adversariis damnamur et calumniamur.

XI. Adversarii nostri calumniantur nos ab ordinaria successione episcoporum abscedere. Nos id non sine mandato Dei fecimus. Quoties enim lux
90 evangelii in successione ordinaria extinguitur, necesse est aliam doctrinam
quaeri, sicut dicitur: si *quis aliud evangelium docet, anathema sit.* Igitur testamur Deum nos libenter audire velle episcopos et illis obedientiam praestare, si
modo non discederent ab evangelio. Sed cum et puram doctrinam depravave-
rint et legitimam sacramentorum administrationem profanaverint, *oportet nos*
95 *magis Deo, quam hominibus obedire.* Itaque damnamus eos, qui ecclesiam
alligant ad ordinariam successionem episcoporum, quasi ipsi iure divino ante-
cellant caeteris ministris evangelii et quasi ecclesia sit humana politia. Item

---

82/83 cfr Eph. 4, 11 et 14   **91** Gal. 1, 9   **94/95** Act. 5, 28

---

73 propter[2] – conscientiarum] cfr *Confessio Augustana Variata*, Article 24, in *CR*,
vol. 26 (1858), p. 383; also in *RefBK*, vol. 1/2 (2006), p. 186

---

73 peccatorum, partim] peccatorum *A D T*   **74** tamen] *add.* consensus *A D T*
censemus] *om. A D T*   **75** utilitatem] *add.* propter *A D T*   et] *om. A D T*   **77** X]
add. tit. De capite ecclesiae, quod est Christus, et ordinaria episcoporum successio *A D
T*   nostri nos] nostri *A D T*   **78** Verum nos] Verum *A D T*   cuius] omnes *A D T*
79 esse] *om. A D T*   item] nostros *A D T*   **80** officium] officia *A D T*   **81** gloriam
Dei] Deum atque eius gloriam *A D T*   enim certus] enim decens *A T*; recens *D*
82 illud] *add.* Pauli *A D T*   **84** in] *om. A D T*   **87** causa] caussis *T*   et
calumniamur] *om. A D T*   **88** XI] *add. tit.* Quare ab ordinaria successione
episcoporum decessimus? Ex mandato Dei *A D T*   **89** Nos] *om. A D T*   fecimus]
facimus *A D T*   **90/91** doctrinam quaeri] quaerere *A D T*   **91** Igitur] Ideo *A D T*
94 sacramentorum] sacrorum doctrinam et *A D T*   **95** damnamus] *add.* omnes *A D
T*

CONCILIUM ERDÖDINUM – 1545

damnamus et eos, qui dicunt nullam esse ordinationem, nullum ministerium, nullam rempublicam apud eos, qui non habent episcopos ordinaria successione regentes, cum ecclesia non sit ordinata ad certum locum, aut certam personarum successionem, sicuti Christus clare inquit, cum dicit: *ecce hic est Christus aut illic, nolite credere.* Item: *Regnum Dei non venit cum observatione,* sed ecclesia Dei tantum ad verbum Dei est alligata.

XII. In reliquis articulis consentimus cum ecclesia vera, sicut patet in confessione fidei Augustae exhibita invictissimo Caesari Carolo quinto semper Augusto.

101/102 Matth. 24, 23   **102** Luc. 17, 20

---

104 In – vera] cfr *Confessio Augustana Invariata,* in *BSLK,* p. 83c-d; *Confessio Augustana Variata,* in *CR,* vol. 26 (1858), p. 373-374; also in *RefBK,* vol. 1/2 (2006), p. 177

---

102 Item] *false add.* Paulus *A D T*   **104** XII] *add. tit.* Consensus in articulis Augustanae Confessionis *A D T*   reliquis] *add.* fidei *L*   **105** Augustae] Augustana *A*; Augustanae *D T*   **105/106** exhibita – Augusto] imperatori Carolo V. semper Augusto exhibita anno 1530. 13-0 Iunii *A*; invictissimo imperatori Carolo V. semper Augusto 30. anno exhibitae. 13. Iunii 1624 Saxopoli Stephanus Dési pastor primarius, vulgo plebanus *D*; invictissimo imperatori Carolo V. semper Augusto exhibita anno 30. exhibitae *T*; Carolo V. exhibita *L*

II

BREVIS CONFESSIO PASTORUM AD SYNODUM DEBRECINI CELEBRATAM 24. 25. ET 26. FEBRUARII ANNO D. 1567. CONVOCATORUM

[...] *Verbum Domini manet in aeternum,* Esai. 32. *Consilium impiorum*
5 *peribit* et cometae haereticorum absummuntur, Psal. 134. Apoc. 8. 9. [...]

I.

Haereses omnes a Diabolo per sua organa ex vana gloria, contentione et
schismatibus ac invidia, superbia et pugna verborum (teste apostolo) ortas,
Gala. 5. 6. Psal. 2. II Cor. 12., detestamur et reiicimus. Nempe Sabellianam et
10 Servetianam contra veram Trinitatem, Arrianam, Samosateni, Fotini, Ebionis,
Eunomii contra aeternam Christi divinitatem subsistentem, coessentialem et
coequalem Patri, item Stancari, Pelagii, liberi arbitrii assertorum et patrono-
rum ac defensorum idolorum, ararum, azymi missatici et aliarum sordium
papisticarum, vestium scilicet Baaliticarum, calicis et reliquorum instrumen-
15 torum missae abominabilis et detestandae in regno Antichristi inventorum,
aut perperam ex Levitici sacerdotii imitatione ad idolum missae applicatorum,
sicut sceleste et impie Ieroboam rex Israel typum templi Salomonis, ararum,
vestium, sacrificiorum, oblationum et aliorum rituum et instrumentorum
pertinentium ad ministerium Aaronicum in Samariam per abusum transtulit
20 et convertit in foedam et turpem idolatriam, quam Achab, Iezabel, et caeteri
impii reges auxerunt, ita nunc Romanenses caupones foedam et turpem collu-
viem missae abominandae partim ex prava imitatione Levitici sacerdotii, quod
erat umbra sacerdotii Christi (Christo ergo exhibito tanquam corpore, illud ut
umbra et exemplar verorum propter inutilitatem et infirmitatem recessit cum
25 suis instrumentis, aris, vestibus, purificationibus teste apostolo, Ebre. 5. 6. 7. 8.
9. 10. 11., Christo, Matth. 11, *lex et prophetae usque ad Ioannem,* Col. 1. 2. Canes

---

4 Is. 40, 8; I Petr. 1, 25   **4/5** Ps. 1, 6; 112, 10   **26** Matth. 11, 13

---

6 1] cfr *Confessio catholica* (1562), Article 113, in *RefBK*, vol. 2/2 (2009), p. 80   **26/
27** Canes – Aesopici] cfr Phaedrus, *Fabulae Aesopiae* 1, 4

1/3 Brevis – convocatorum] *in titulo interno* Summa confessionis et conclusionum
synodi Debrecinum ad 24. Februarii convocatae, ubi ordine Sabellii et Serveti, Arii,
Fotini, Manichaeorum haereses et falsa dogmata Stancari, psychomacaristarum,
sordium Antichristi defensorum ex purissimo Dei verbo refutata et damnata sunt *E*
2 Februarii] *a.c.* Februa.   **5** Psal. 134] *sic*   **6** 1] *add. tit.* De haeresibus *RefBK*

440		CONCILIUM DEBRECENIENSE – 1567

sunt ergo Aesopici, qui corpore et veritate ipso Christo et Novo Testamento, nova et coelesti doctrina et sacramentorum ritibus a Christo institutis reiectis aut faedatis umbram sacerdotii Christi, Leviticum sacerdotium captant),
30 partim vero ex gentilismo et paganismo idolum missae proditores animarum Romanenses pontifices consarcinarunt, tanquam peram mendicam ex centonibus et variis assumentis consutam. Horum sordes hypocritae, semipapistae, defensores hostiae vel azymi missatici, ararum et idolorum amplexantur. Simul ergo cum papistis et hos detestamur, imo ex sententia Christi horum peccata
35 maiora sunt. Sunt enim servi scientes, quia sciunt idola, aras, vestes sacrificales et omnia signa et organa idolatriae et missae totaliter damnari in secundo praecepto et ubique in Veteri et Novo Testamento, tamen contra conscientiam retinent. [...]

[3]

40		Damnamus hic et Stancari dogma. Et dicimus Iesum Christum Deum et hominem esse salvatorem, mediatorem secundum utranque naturam propter has rationes ex verbo Dei sumptas. Primo: propter precii redemptionis naturam: quod imprimis hoc requirebat, ut fieret temperamentum inter misericordiam et iustitiam Dei, vel ut propheta dicit: Psal. 85. *Chesed vel Emet*
45 *niphgassa*, hoc est, *misericordia et veritas sibi occurrerent et obviarent, Zedek vesalom nassaku*, id est, *iustitia et pax sese amplecterentur et oscularentur*, hoc est, *gloria Deo in excelsis tribueretur et in terris pax esset hominibus ex bona Dei voluntate nata*. Inter misericordiam enim et iustitiam legalem Dei nostri respectu erat contrarietas, hoc est, ex aeterna praescientia, praedefinitione
50 secundum misericordiam suam nos Deus salvare et vivificare, conformes Deo reddere debebat, sicut ab aeterno in sese secundum beneplacitum voluntatis suae hoc proposuerat. Sed heus contrarius eventus: per Adae inobedientiam et transgressionem *peccatum intravit in mundum et per peccatum mors*. Homines igitur peccatores Deus (sicut Adae praedixerat: *si comederis, moriendo certissi-*
55 *me moreris*) occidere, morte aeterna destruere oportuit. Ne ergo decretum aeternum misericordiae de salvandis electis mutaretur, neque legale foedus cum Adam violaretur, quia *verbum Dei stat in aeternum*, ut Iehova immutabi-

---

36/37 damnari – praecepto] cfr Ex. 20, 4; Deut. 5, 8   **44/46** Ps. 85, 11   **47/48** Luc. 2, 14   **53** Rom. 5, 12   **54/55** Gen. 2, 17   **57** Is. 40, 8; I Petr. 1, 25

39 3] cfr *Confessio catholica* (1562), Articles 132-134; *Confessio Helvetica Posterior* (1566), par. 5, in *RefBK*, vol. 2/2 (2009), p. 93-95 and 280-281 respectively

39 3] *add. tit.* De mediatore *RefBK*

CONCILIUM DEBRECENIENSE – 1567

lis, ita verbum Dei immutabile, I Sam 15. Ebr. 1. 6. Psal 87. 102. 103. Matth 24.,
oportuit itaque utrunque decretum impleri. Decretum iustitiae legale de aeterna punitione dupliciter implebatur.

Primo: ut peccatum contra aeternam iustitiam, contra Deum factum
aeterna iustitia per mortem crucemque carnis destrueretur, ut Ro. 5. 6. 8. II
Cor. 5. Esa. 53. dicitur, *Christus factus est peccatum, ut nos fieremus iustitia in
Christo. De peccato condemnavit peccatum in carne, ut iustitia legis impleretur in
nobis.*

Secundo: cum peccato Diabolum, maledictionem legis, iram Dei, mortem et aeternam condemnationem per vitam aeternam, per benedictionem,
veritatem destruerentur, ut Ro. 4. 5. 7. 8. Gal 3. 4. Ebr. 1. 2. 7. 8. 9. 10. *Christus
factus maledictum pro nobis, ut nos fieremus benedicti.* Subiectus est Christus
legis maledicto, ut nos liberaremur a iure peccati et mortis. Iustitia autem et
vita, sanctificatio, redemptio aeterna, infinita est Christus principaliter secundum deitatem suam. Sicut Esa. 9. 40. 43. 54. Et ubique Deo Iehovae tribuitur
peccati, Diaboli, inferni destructio, Osae. 1. 13. Zach. 9. 13. *Ego sum, ego sum
Iehova, qui deleo peccata tua propter me. Peccatorum tuorum non recordabor.
Servire me fecisti in peccatis tuis, haec dicit Iehova,* Esa. 43. Hinc apostolus,
Rom. 3. 4. 5. Ebr. 1., dicit per eum fieri purgationem delictorum nostrorum,
per eum aboleri peccata, mortem, Diabolum, per eum nos Deo reconciliari in
sanguine crucis eius, qui est Filius Dei in carnem missus, per quem secula facta
sunt.

Tertio: qui fuit ante omnia, substitit in forma Dei, aequalis Deo Patri, in
quo habitat plenitudo deitatis corporaliter, qui est imago, character substantiae Dei, potentia et sapientia Dei. Sed Christus secundum deitatem suam est
aequalis Patri, Iehova subsistens, Dei unigenitus, a Patre missus in carnem,
proprius Patris Filius, Ioan. 1. 5. 10. I Ioa. 3. 4. 5. Rom. 8. Secundum deitatem
suam substitit et creavit omnia et est imago Dei. Ergo deitatis virtute peccata
remittit, destruit. Et carnis mors, passio tantum fuit deitatis organum, ut dicitur: *Deus per sanguinem suum reconciliavit,* acquisivit ecclesiam. Filius Deus
per Spiritum aeternum offerens suam carnem invenit nobis redemptionem
aeternam, Ebr. 9. 10. vide Ebre. 7. Sacrificium, mors Christi aeterna redemptio,
sacerdotium aeternum propter aeternam deitatem, propter Spiritum aeternum
immortalemque deitatem suam.

63/64 Christus – Christo] II Cor. 5, 21   **64/65** De – nobis] Rom. 8, 3-4   **68/
69** Gal. 3, 13-14   **73/75** Is. 43, 24-25   **76** dicit – nostrorum] cfr Hebr. 1, 2-3   **77/
78** per² – eius] cfr Col. 1, 20   **81/82** qui – Dei¹] cfr Phil. 2, 6; Col. 2, 9; Hebr. 1, 3
87 Deus¹ – reconciliavit] Col. 1, 20   **87/89** Filius – aeternam] cfr Hebr. 7, 25-28

58 Psal 87] *sic*

438 CONCILIUM DEBRECENIENSE – 1567

Misericordiae vero satisfactum est tripliciter.

Primo: quia imago Dei amissa per Adam per imaginem Dei infinitam, consubstantialem Patri aequalem reparata est, id est, *Christus factus est nobis* 95 *iustitia, vita, veritas, sanctificatio,* hoc est, amissas virtutes reparavit, I Cor. 1. Col. 1. 2. Eph. 1. 3. 4. II Cor. 3. I Corin. 15. Reformamur ad eandum imaginem a Spiritu Dei de die in diem. *Induite novum hominem, qui secundum Deum creatus est.* Reparata autem iustitia nostra per resurrectionem Christi, resurrectio autem deitatis virtus est, Rom. 4. 5. 8. II Cor. 13. Io. 1. 2. Mortuus ex carnis 100 infirmitate vivit virtute deitatis suae. Ego pono animam et moriar et ego propria virtute resurgam. Christus secundum deitatem suam est imago Dei substantialis, Ebr. 1. Col. 1. 2. Ioan. 1. Christus ergo deitatis suae virtute imaginem Dei, virtutes amissas restaurat. *Mortuus est propter peccata nostra et resurrexit propter iustificationem nostri,* Roma 4. II Timoth. 1. 2. *Christus mortem* 105 *abolevit, vitam reparavit. Dominus est spiritus, ubi spiritus domini, ibi libertas,* id est, Christus secundum deitatem suam est essentia spiritualis, est Iehova, Deus, habuit Spiritum Sanctum et spiritualem efficaciam, per quem nos ad amissam imaginem transformat, II Corin. 3. Ecce Christi deitas, ecce Christus secundum deitatem salvator.

110 Secundo: satisfactum est misericordiae Dei resuscitatione animarum electarum ex peccato, delicto, iniquitate, et earum vivificatio, Ioa. 5. 6. 10. Eph. 2. Col. 2. Ro. 6. 8. Cum Christo mortui estis delictis et resurrexistis cum eo. *Veniet hora in qua mortui audient vocem Filii Dei et vivent,* debuit et corpora ex pulvere resuscitare. Io. 5. 6. *Quorum animas ego vivificavi per panem vivum,* 115 *carnis meae esu, ego eos resuscitabo in novissimo die.* I Cor. 15. Sed resuscitatio deitatis virtus est, non carnis.

Tertio: satisfieri oportuit misericordiae, omnium restauratione, reconciliatione, ut caelum novum, terra nova crearentur, et a vanitate corruptionis creatura liberaretur, Rom. 8. Coloss. 1. 2. Ephe. 1. Esa. 65. Sed prima et nova 120 creatio solius deitatis opus est, Esa. 45. Psal. 102. Ebr. 1. Christus ergo causaliter divinitate est mediator. Secundo: Christum mediatorem dicimus secundum utranque naturam, quia dicit Spiritus Sanctus, Esa. 7. 9. 35. 54. Osae. 1. 3. Soph. 3. Ioel 3. Zach. 2. 3. salvatorem esse Iehovam, Deum, Filium Dei. *Salvabo eos ego Iehova Pater, in Iehova Deoque ipsorum iustitia nostra.* Vocatur Iehova, 125 homo et semen mulieris, Deus verus et homo, I Tim. 2. 3. Ignari sunt ergo

---

94/95 I Cor. 1, 30 **96/97** Reformamur – diem] cfr II Cor. 3, 18; 4, 16 **97/98** Eph. 4, 24 **103/104** Rom. 4, 25 **104/105** Christus – reparavit] II Tim. 1, 10 **105** Dominus – libertas] II Cor. 3, 17 **110/111** satisfactum – vivificatio] cfr Rom. 6, 8; Eph. 2, 5; Col. 2, 20 **113** Ioh. 5, 25 **114/115** Ioh. 6, 54 **123/124** Os. 1, 7

104 II] *supplevi, om. E*

CONCILIUM DEBRECENIENSE – 1567

antilytri caeci et stulti Stancariani dogmatis imitatores, qui negant Christum secundum utramque naturam esse mediatorem.

[4]

Damnamus hic et Manichaeorum dogma, hoc est, eos, qui Deum auto-
130 rem peccati ulla ratione faciunt.

Primo: quia scriptum est, Psal. 5. *Deus non est volens peccata*, hoc est, velle facere peccatum non potest. *Ea autem sola facit Deus, quae vult*, Psalmo 114. 135. Sed non vult peccatum, ergo nec facit. Et sicut est Deus summa iustitia, lux, vita, ita contrarium suae naturae facere non potest.

135 Secundo: quia dicitur Deum peccatum odisse, non posse ad iniquitatem respicere, nescire calumniam aut facere peccatum.

Tertio: quia prohibet peccata et punit, quaecunque autem punit et prohibet, eorum autor esse non potest.

Quarto: dicit Scriptura non posse Deum punire homines et mundi iudi-
140 cem esse, si peccata vellet, faceret, Gen. 18. Rom. 2. 3. *Si peccatum meum in gloriam Dei est, quare ergo ego tanquam peccator punior?*

[5]

Reiicimus et curiosas fundamento Scripturae carentes speculationes eorum, qui dicunt Adamum necessario ex Dei decreto ex illa beata integritate
145 excidisse.

Primo: quia prohibuit Adamum, ne laberetur. Si autem decrevisset, etiam voluisset, quia *omnis voluntas et omne decretum meum fiet*, Esa. 46. 55. 57. Sed non voluit Deus Adae peccatum et lapsum, Psal. 5. Gene. 2. 3., ergo neque decrevit. Illa enim decernit et facit tantum Deus, quae vult, Psal. 114. 135.

---

126 antilytri] cfr I Tim. 2, 6   **131** Ps. 5, 5   **132** Ps. 135, 6   **140/141** Rom. 3, 7; cfr Gen. 18, 25   **147** Is. 46, 10   **147/148** Sed – lapsum] cfr Ps. 5, 5-6

128 4] cfr *Confessio catholica* (1562), Article 12; *Confessio Helvetica Posterior* (1566), par. 8, in *RefBK*, vol. 2/2 (2009), p. 16 and 284-286 respectively   **142** 5] cfr *Confessio catholica* (1562), Article 10; *Confessio Helvetica Posterior* (1566), par. 8, in *RefBK*, vol. 2/2 (2009), p. 14-15 and 284-286 respectively

128 4] *add. in marg. tit.* De causa peccati E   **132** Psalmo 114] *sic*   **142** 5] *add. tit.* Deus non voluit Adae lapsum *RefBK*   **149** Psal. 114] *sic*

440 CONCILIUM DEBRECENIENSE – 1567

150 *Quaecunque voluit, fecit,* Eph. 1. *Qui agit omnia secundum beneplacitum voluntatis suae.*

Secundo: excusat se Deus et Adae lapsum inobedientiae Adae tribuit: *quis dixit, ut nudus esses? Non ego feci hoc, sed tu eo, quod edisti de arbore, de qua dixeram, ne ederes*: Gen. 3. Rom. 5. 6. *Per inobedientiam et transgressionem* 155 *hominis peccatum et mors intravit. Vivo ego Deus, nolo mortem peccatoris,* id est, non sum causa peccati et mortis hominis, Ezech 3. 18. 33. *Perditio tua ex te, in me autem salus. Peccata tua fecerunt tibi haec.*

Tertio: quia Eva et Adam sua sponte, nemine cogente lapsi sunt. Si sponte, nullo cogente lapsus est et excidit, ergo non necessario excidit. Nam sponte, 160 libere, nullo cogente labi, excidi et necessario excidi contrariantur, Psal. 49. *Homo cum in honore esset, non intellexit,* Sap. 7. 15. 17. 19. *Deus reliquit hominem in manu consilii aut in libertate sua. Apposui tibi ignem et aquam.*

Quarto: quia ad imaginem Dei in libertate fuit creatus, igitur ex necessitate labi non potuit, quia poterat labi et non labi: iam post peccatum necessi- 165 tate privationis labitur, sed cum habuit habitum, potestatem non peccandi, sponte lapsus est, Col. 3. Ephe. 3. 4.

Quinto: quia Esai. 48. Thre. 3. Deum peccata praevidere, praesciisse Adae lapsum, sed non necessitasse, neque decrevisse. *Vidi te, quod peccares contra me, dura cervix, frons aenea tibi, et ideo transgressorem ab utero vocavi te. Nunc facta* 170 *sunt et non ex tunc:* id est, non ego feci te labi mea praevisione, sed tu per tuam inobedientiam. Permisit ergo labi hominem, sed non necessitavit, Esai. 50. *Dimisi in peccatis matrem tuam.* Psal. 83. Dimisit gentes in peccatis suis. Acto. 14. *Permisit abire gentes in viis suis.*

Peccata autem seu mala, quae dicitur Deus facere, ut ego indurabo, deci- 175 piam, tradam in sensum reprobum, est antimisthia, id est, poena prioris peccati Dei respectu, sed culpa Diaboli et hominum peccantium respectu. Sicut dum quis per foetorem, sulphur et stercus aliquem suffumigando punit, non efficit foetorem in stercore, sulphure, sed in eis est, ita Deus dum per Diabolum, per organa irae peccata peccatis punit, non efficit in eis peccata, sed 180 naturaliter post corruptionem Diabolo et hominibus haec mala insunt, Ephe. 4. Rom. 1. *Excaecati propter ignorantiam, quae est in illis.* Exod. 7. 8. Vide Pharaonis historiam. Haec ex verbo Dei sumpta sunt. Reliquas argutias consequentiarum reiicimus, simplici enim veritate contenti sumus, maxime ut

---

150 Ps. 135, 6   **150/151** Eph. 1, 11   **153/154** Gen. 3, 1; cfr Rom. 5, 12 et 18;. 6, 16
154/155 Per – intravit] Rom. 5, 12   **155** Vivo – peccatoris] Ez. 33, 11; 18, 32   **156/**
157 Perditio – salus] Os. 13, 9   **157** Peccata – haec] Ier. 30, 15   **161** Ps. 48, 21   **161/**
162 Eccli. 15, 14 et 17   **168/170** Is. 48, 3-4 et 48, 7-8; cfr Thren. 3, 42   **172** Is. 50, 1;
cfr Ps. 83, 14-18   **173** Act. 14, 16   **175** antimisthia] cfr Rom. 1, 27; II Cor. 6, 13
181 Eph. 4, 18; cfr Rom. 1, 21

CONCILIUM DEBRECENIENSE – 1567

absurda vitemus, ne peccatis Deum involvamus, ne Deo iustum iudicium et
185 autoritatem puniendi peccatum eripiamus, quae omnia Deo eripiuntur, si
peccatis delectatur aut facit, vel vult approbatione et effectione. Velle enim
dimittendo peccata iam confessi sumus.

De vera autem et essentialis Dei unitate et forma, de reali et coessentiali et
coequali Triade deque Christi et Spiritus Sancti aeterna et adoranda divinitate
190 talem ex verbo Dei confessionem edimus.

[6] De Deo

Credimus et confitemur in unum Deum, qui est Iehova Elohim, hoc est,
tres dantes testimonium, Pater, Filius et Spiritus Sanctus. Et sicut unitatem
realem et essentialem, hoc est, unam deitatem, formam Dei confitemur in
195 Trinitate, in Patre, Filio et Spiritu. Ita veram homousion, coessentialem,
coequalem Trinitatem, distinctam substantialiter hypostatica personarum
Patris, Filii, Spiritus Sancti procedentis proprietate, officio et manifestatione
distincta, alia ac diversa. Nam Pater in voce, Filius in viri forma, Spiritus Sanctus in specie columbae se manifestavit.
200 Unum Deum credimus, quia Scriptura Iehovam et Deum unum ubique
nobis proponit, Exod. 20. Deut. 4. 5. 6. *Audi Israel, Iehova Elohiim est Iehova
unus,* Esa. 43. 44. 45. 48. *Videte, quia tantum ego sum Iehova Deus, praeter me,
extra me, absque me, ante me, post me non est Deus alius.* Trinitatem credimus
ideo, quia Scriptura hunc unum Iehovam vocat Elohiim, id est, tres subsisten-
205 tes, tres dantes testimonium, tres, qui in angelorum et virorum forma in uno
Iehova sese patefecit, deinde, quia uni Deo Elohiim pluralitatem tribuit Scriptura. *Faciamus hominem. Ecce Adam sicut unus ex nobis.*

Secundo: quia realiter propriis nominibus, hypostasi seu substantia
propria Iehova gignens, mittens a Iehova Filio misso, genito distinguitur. Alius
210 paracletus dicitur Spiritus Sanctus a Filio. Et impossibile est proprietates naturaliter, realiter, personaliter distinctas confundi. Impossibile est Patrem esse
Filium missum, incarnatum, et contra impossibile est Filium esse Patrem
gignentem, mittentem se. Distinguuntur officio diverso, aliud Patris officium,

---

193 I Ioh. 5, 7   **201/202** Deut. 6, 4   **202/203** Is. 45, 21   **207** Faciamus hominem]
Gen. 1, 26   Ecce – nobis] Gen. 3, 22   **210** paracletus] cfr Ioh. 14, 16

---

191 6] cfr *Confessio catholica* (1562), Article 1; *Confessio Helvetica Posterior* (1566),
par. 3, in *RefBK*, vol. 2/2 (2009), p. 11 and 277-278 respectively

---

208 Secundo] *correxi*, Tertio *E*

442 CONCILIUM DEBRECENIENSE – 1567

aliud Filii in sua persona, sed in una deitatis natura unum est officium totius
215 Trinitatis.

Tertio: visibili, sensibili, tractabili manifestatione, diversa forma, specie et
materia Pater in voce, Spiritus in columba, Filius in viri forma. Contra naturam faciunt, qui haec confundunt.

Quarto: quia Symbolum Apostolicum et baptismus realem Trinitatem
220 nobis proponit. Destruant ergo Symbolum et baptismum, qui negant Trinitatem. Credimus ergo in Patrem, Filium et Spiritum Sanctum et Christum aeternum Dei Filium ab aeterno genitum ex hypostasi Patris tanquam characterem
et splendorem a gloria Patris. Et ut Pater non prius Deus, quam Pater, ita Filius
Patris imago, character, sapientia, virtus, potentia, brachium, sermo non prius
225 Iehova, quam Filius. In Deo enim nulla est mutatio, Malac. 3. Iacob. 1. I Sam.
15. Esai. 40. 41. 55. 57. Psal. 89. 102. Ebr. 1. *Tu idem ille es et non mutaberis. Iesus
Christus heri et hodie idem.* Ergo non coepit esse Filius Deus Iehova, sed ab
aeterno fuit, Mich. 5. Psal. 110. *Egressus eius ab aeterno, ante uterum, ante auro-
ram, ros nativitatis tuae,* hoc est, ab initio ante creationem mundi natus,
230 primogenitus ante omnes creaturas, Col. 1. 2. Ego sapientia ab aeterno, ante
secula concepta, ordinata sum et cum eo adfui in creatione. *Sermo erat Deus, et
Deus iste Sermo ab initio, ab aeterno erat apud Deum*: Ioa. 1. I Ioan. 1.

Deinde Christus est splendor Patris, sapientia. Ergo non potuit Pater esse
sine Filio, ut sol sine radio suo. Nam Pater Deus est per suam sapientiam,
235 virtutem. *Aeterna in Deo et apud Deum vita est Sermo. Haec vita ab aeterno
erat apud Deum*: I Ioa. 1. Tertio: *extra me et ante me, post me alius Deus non
fuit.* Ergo extra Filium Pater non est Deus, nec Filius sine Patre. Et ut Patre
Filius non prior, ita non est posterior. Dicit enim, post me non erit: id est, me
Patre Deo non erit Deus posterior, sicut prior non fuit.

240 [7]

Dicimus et confitemur ergo Christum verum Deum Iehovam, magnum,
solum et unum, praeter quem non est alius, subsistentem in forma Dei et
vitam habentem in se ipso. Et triplici ratione unum et coequalem Patri. Primo;

222/223 characterem – Patris] cfr Hebr. 1, 3   **226** Tu – mutaberis] Ps. 102, 28; cfr
Mal. 3, 6; Hebr. 1, 12   **226/227** Iesus – idem] Hebr. 13, 8   **228/229** Ps. 110, 3; Mich.
5, 2   **231/232** Ioh. 1, 1-3; cfr I Ioh. 1, 1-2   **235/236** I Ioh. 1, 2   **236/237** Is. 45, 21

240 7] cfr *Confessio catholica* (1562), Articles 5-6; *Confessio Helvetica Posterior* (1566),
par. 11, in *RefBK*, vol. 2/2 (2009), p. 13 and 291-297 respectively

240 7] *add. tit.* De Iesu Christo *RefBK*

CONCILIUM DEBRECENIENSE – 1567

in naturae identitate, quia *sicut Pater habet vitam in se, ita et Filio dedit in se*
vitam habere. Sed Pater habuit vitam et substitit in se ab aeterno, non in Filio
nec in Spiritu Sancto. Ergo et Logos Filius secundum deitatem suam in se
substitit, ut Pater, non in Patris hypostasi, ut Servetici canes nugantur. Sicut
Pater subsistit, sic et Filius: Pater realiter, substantialiter, praesenter, non praedestinatione, sic ergo et Filius. Nam omnia Patris sunt Filii, sed Patris est esse
ab aeterno Iehovam subsistentem. Hoc idem ergo est et Filii, scilicet esse ab
aeterno Iehovam subsistentem, Ioan. 10. 16. 17. Secundo: in operationis, electionis, creationis, salvationis, vivificationis identitate. Quaecunque Pater facit,
haec eadem similiter et Filius facit. Tertio: sicut adoratur Pater, ita adoratur
Filius.

Triplici ratione item a Patre Filium et Spiritum distingui docemus.

Primo: proprietate hypostatica, Filius generatione aut filiatione, Spiritus
processione substantiali.

Secundo: officio dispensationis. Nam solus Filius Logos fit caro, id est,
Deus in carne manifestatus, carnem assummit, solus mediator, pontifex. Solus
Spiritus arrabo haereditatis in electis.

Tertio: apparitione. Solus enim Pater in voce clamat de caelo, solus Spiritus Sanctus in specie columbae, solus Filius baptizatur in forma servi in Iorda-
ne.

[8]

Eisdem rationibus Spiritum Sanctum Iehovam verum Deum subsistentem in Dei forma, habentem in seipso vitam confitemur et docemus. Hunc
eundem Spiritum homousion, Patri Filio coessentialem et coequalem propter
eadem deitatis privilegia, quibus Pater et Filius sunt Deus, nam Esai. 6. 11. 48.
61. Psal. 104. dicitur Iehova, Deus creator, conservator, item I Corin. 3. 6. 12.
II Cor. 6. Verus et unus Dominus autor et distributor donorum, Deus cuius
templum sunt electi. Ita Act. 5. 28. Verus Deus et Iehova esse dicitur, procedit
substantialiter a Patre, ergo ut sit Deus de Deo, oportet. Nam ex substantia
Patris substantia procedit. Credimus in Spiritum Sanctum, adoratur Spiritus
Sanctus tanquam Deus solus et verus. In quem enim credimus, hunc et adoramus. Nam fides est fundamentum adorationis.

244/245 Ioh. 5, 26   **260** arrabo] cfr II Cor. 1, 22; Eph. 1, 14   **270/271** Verus –
electi] cfr I Cor. 3, 16; 6, 19; 12, 11; II Cor. 6, 16

---

264 8] cfr *Confessio catholica* (1562), Article 7, in *RefBK*, vol. 2/2 (2009), p. 13

---

264 8] *add. tit.* De Spiritu Sancto *RefBK*

444 CONCILIUM DEBRECENIENSE – 1567

Subsistentiam autem aut hypostasin Scriptura tribuit Spiritui Sancto propter has rationes:

Primo: quia est Iah, Iehova exercituum, Esa. 6. Quicumque est Iehova, est subsistens, essentiator, in seipso vitam et hypostasin habet, sic enim Exod. 3. Iehovae vox exponitur et in Apocalypsi sic: *qui est ens, qui fuit subsistens, qui erit et deinceps venturus*. Vocatur et Deus verus. Quia est Deus adorandus, est Spiritus, id est, substantia spiritualis, Ioa. 4. II Corin. 3. *Ubi est Spiritus Domini, ibi libertas*. Si est et subsistit, ergo est substantia.

Secundo: quia creat, creator est, sustentat creata, alit, vivificat, Gen. 1. Spiritus Domini alebat massam creatam. Psal 104. *Emitte Spiritum et creabuntur*. Sap. 1. Esa. 40. 41. *Quis adiuvit Spiritum Iehovae in creando?*

Tertio: apparuit Spiritus in viri et angeli forma Abrahae, Lotho. Gen. 18. 19. Sicut Christus, ita Spiritus Sanctus patres praecessit in igne et nube. Apparuit in corporali specie columbae, Lucae 3. Mat. 3. Ioan. 1. Creare, dare aliis essentiam, vitam, motum non posset, si Iehova essentians in se non subsisteret, ut Esa. 40. 41. 43. 45. 47. Quicquid non est, non subsistit, esse et substantiam aliis dare non potest. Et nisi substantia spiritualis esset, haberet existentiam propriam, in specie corporali apparere non posset. Sola substantia potest apparere in substantia, accidentia, qualitates ut non subsistunt, ita substantias facere, in aliis substantiis extra suum esse, apparere non possunt.

Quarto: electos vivificat, regenerat, salvat, ducit, omnia opera bona efficit in electis, Ioa. 4. 5. 6. 15. 16. Rom. 5. 8. Tit. 3. Eph. 5. 6. I Cor. 12. Obsignat electos et est pignus in electis. Sed sola spiritualis, aeterna subsistens substantia potest vivificare, obsignare. Ergo Spiritus est substantia Iehovalis.

Quinto: alius paracletus a Christo dicitur, qui mundum arguit et bona Christi dispensat. Sed Christus erat substantialis paracletus, ergo talis est et Spiritus Sanctus, paracletus in seipso realiter subsistens, ut Christus.

Sexto: a Christo in statu corporali, in vento et igne corporali datur, mittitur. Nisi esset substantia realis, mitti, dari in corporali substantia non posset. Spiritus Sanctus aquae, igni, vento confertur, ergo vere est essentia spiritualis.

Septimo: credimus in Spiritum Sanctum, adoramus Spiritum, baptizamur in nomine Spiritus Sancti. Sed in eum tantum credere electi possunt, qui est Iehova subsistens, creator, salvator. Qui est creatura, accidens, qualitas, in eum credere non possunt. Et in solius Dei subsistentis Iehovalis nomine baptizari

---

278 Iehova exercituum] cfr Is. 6, 3   280 Iehovae vox exponitur] cfr Ex. 3, 14   280/
281 Apoc. 1, 8   281/282 Quia – Spiritus'] cfr Ioh. 4, 24   282/283 II Cor. 3, 17
285 Spiritus – creatam] cfr Gen. 1, 2   Ps. 104, 30   286 Is. 40, 13   288/
289 Apparuit – columbae] cfr Matth. 3, 17; Luc. 3, 21-22; Ioh. 1, 32   297/
298 Obsignat – electis] cfr II Cor. 1, 22; 5, 5; Eph. 1, 13-14   301 paracletus] cfr Ioh.
14, 16   309/310 Et – possunt'] cfr Matth. 28, 19; Marc. 16, 15-16

CONCILIUM DEBRECENIENSE – 1567

310 possunt, in nomen qualitatis, creaturae non possunt baptizari, Matth. 28. Mar. 16. I Cor. 1. 3. Solam Dei substantiam spiritualem adorare debemus, non qualitatem Dei creatam.

Octavo: nihil est in Deo accidens, sed omnia sum, nec ex Deo ab aeterno procedere qualitas creata potest. Quicquid est in Deo, increatum est et 315 substantia: Spiritus Sanctus est in Deo. Processit a Patre, Ioan. 15. Fuit ante creationem et in creatione. Ergo Spiritus Sanctus est substantia spiritualis subsistens.

Nono: quia sicut patres, ita in synodo Vasarhelina anno 1566. die 19. mense Maii convocata, existentia aut substantia tribuitur Spiritui Sancto. Et in 320 Catechesi Logo et Spiritui Sancto aequalem Deo subsistentiam tribuunt Claudiopolitani fratres. Contrarium igitur Deo et sibi sentiunt, si existentiam Spiritus Sancti negaverint.

[9]

Essentiae vero nomine utimur pro una Dei forma seu deitate essentiali et 325 dicimus cum Paulo: idem esse Patrem, Filium et Spiritum Sanctum in una Dei forma esse hyparchontas, id est, subsistentes, in seipso vitam habentes, ac si dicas: in una essentiali deitate, maiestate et gloria. Nihil enim in Deo est accidentarium, sed Ero, Sum, Iah, Iehova, existentia sunt. Nomine personae utimur pro hypostasi, prosopo. Sicut Patri hypostasin seu substantiam 330 propriam in seipso subsistentem, distinctam vitam habentem Paulus Ebre. 1. tribuit. Christo vero Paulus II Corin. 2. prosopon, id est, personam propriam in seipsa vitam habentem, distinctam incommunicabili proprietate tribuit. Trinitatis nomine utimur pro Elohiim, id est, trinitarius. Elohiim enim plurale

---

313 sum] cfr Ex. 3, 14   315 Processit – Patre] Ioh. 15, 26   329/331 Sicut – tribuit] cfr Hebr. 1, 4   331/332 Christo – tribuit] cfr II Cor. 2, 10

318/322 Nono – negaverint] cfr *Catechismus ecclesiarum Dei in natione Hungarica per Transilvaniam, quae relicto papistico Deo quaterno, verbum Dei de sacrosancta Triade, uno vero Deo Patre, et Filio eius, Domino Iesu Christo ac amborum Spiritu amplexe sunt simplicitateque pia ac puritate illud credunt ac profitentur. – Sententia concors pastorum et ministrorum ecclesiae Dei nationis Hungaricae in Transilvania de propositionibus doctoris Georgij Blandratae et Francisci Davidis etc. in disputatione Albensi coram regia maiestate, anno Domini MDLXVI die April. XXV. propositus, et limitatione fratrum, qui ex Hungaria praedictae disputationi interfuerunt, in frequenti synodo Vásárhelyensi eodem anno, die vero XIX. Maij pronunciata et publicata,* Claudiopoli 1566 (*RMNy* 215) 323 9] cfr *Confessio catholica* (1562), Articles 2-3, in *RefBK*, vol. 2/2 (2009), p. 11-12

323 9] *add. tit.* De usu nominum: essentia, persona, Trinitas *RefBK*

446 CONCILIUM DEBRECENIENSE – 1567

ab Eloha, ab El et Hova, participio ex Hava, id est, sum, fui, compositum. El
335 Patrem, Ho Filium, Va Spiritum Sanctum recte vertere poteris, Deus Trinitarius, id est, tres subsistentes et vitam habentes in seipso in una Dei forma. Nam
Deut. 6. haec duo: Iehova unus et Elohiim per conversionem dicuntur sic:
Iehova unus est Elohiim, id est, trias nostra. Et contra Elohenu, Deus trium
subsistentium, in seipso vitam habentium est Iehova unus, id est, unitas deita-
340 tis est Trinitas. Et Trinitas est una deitas, ut Ioan. 5. 8. 10. I Ioan. 5. *Hi tres sunt*
unum, id est, Trinitas est una Dei forma et unum, id est, unitas deitatis, una
Dei forma est Trinitas. Impie ergo faciunt, qui ex unitate et Trinitate quaterni-
tatem cudunt, nam extra Trinitatem nulla deitas nec extra Trinitatem ulla
deitas, Esai. 43. 44. 45. Sed tota unitas deitatis et Trinitas est in Patre, Filio et
345 Spiritu Sancto, extra hos tres nec est unitas nec Trinitas.

Filium secundum utrunque respectum, et quatenus Filius, et quatenus
Iehova de Iehova, Deus de Deo non a se, sed a Patre est, qui est principium
Trinitatis generationis et ordinis respectu, non tempore. Nam extra Patrem et
Filium nulla deitas, praeter unum principium, unam deitatem, praeter unam
350 Trinitatem non est alia. Unde ergo Filio sua divinitas extra Patrem? extra
deitatem et Trinitatem cuius principium est in Patre?

Cum Symbolo ergo Niceno, Athanasii et cum Scriptura Sacra dicimus
Christum et ut Filium et ut Deum a Patre esse.

Dicit enim: Pater dedit Filio vitam habere, id est, deitatem subsistentem.
355 *Ego non veni a meipso, non a me sum, sed ab ipso sum ens.* Ioan. 5. 6. *Nihil potest*
Filius a se facere sine Patre, ergo ut agere a se, ita esse a se non potest. Actio
enim coequalis cum Patre ex substantiae identitate et coessentialitate orta est,
Ioa. 5. 8. 10. 16. *Ego et Pater unum sumus*. Ergo, quae Pater facit, haec eadem
similiter et Filius facit. Per plenitudinem Dei et Spiritum Sanctum omnia
360 facit, agit Filius per se in seipso. Ut enim habet vitam in seipso et per se subsistit, ita agit per se, sed non a se, Ioa. 5. 6. 7. 8. Col. 1. 2.

Simul adoramus Patrem, Filium et Spiritum, quatenus sunt unum, sed eo
ordine, quem Pater proposuit: scilicet, ut Pater *in Spiritu et veritate*, in Filio et
propter Filium ex Spiritus Sancti institutione, intercessione, formatione adore-
365 tur. Nemo enim venit ad Filium, nec novit Filium sine Spiritu Sancto, neque
quis credere, adorare Patrem in Filio per fidem potest sine Spiritu, ut Ioa. 5. 6.
14. 15. 16. Rom. 5. 8. Eph. 1. 4. dicitur.

Haec est nostra confessio de Trinitate, quam copiosius deinceps
edemus. [...]

---

338 Deut. 6, 2-3   **340/341** I Ioh. 5, 8   **354** Pater – habere] cfr Ioh. 5, 26   **355** Ioh.
7, 28   **355/356** Ioh. 5, 19; 5, 30   **358** Ioh. 10, 30   **363** Ioh. 4, 24

CONCILIUM DEBRECENIENSE – 1567

447

370   [18] CONTRA HOLOPRAEDESTINARIOS

Scriptura sacra et holopraedestinarios, hoc est, qui universum mundum electum esse et ex universali promissione universalem praedestinationem esse somniant, his rationibus refutat et docet praedestinationem esse paucorum et particularem, certumque numerum et catalogum esse electorum usque ad
375 capillos, nam *et capilli capitis numerati sunt.*

Primo: literaliter sic scriptum est, Matt. 20: *Multi sunt vocati, sed pauci electi.* Id est, omnes quidem per verbum externum vocantur, sed soli ad vitam electi obediunt, et pauci sunt illi, qui ad vitam electi sunt. Mat. 7. *Pauci sunt, qui intrant ad vitam per arctam viam,* Luc. 13. *Quam pauci salvantur.*

380   Secundo: ab effectu ad causam, non omnes obediunt evangelio, non omnium est fides, sed paucorum. Sed soli credentes sunt electi, ergo ut fides paucorum, ita et praedestinatio paucorum est. Quod autem fides, vocatio, conversio, iustificatio, salvatio sint effectus praedestinationis, et quomodo ex ea fluant, ordine sic probamus, Act. 13. *Crediderunt soli illi, qui erant praeordinati*
385 *ad vitam,* Rom. 8. 9. *Quos praesciit et praedefiniit, hos et vocavit, hos iustificavit, hos et glorificavit,* Ephe. 1. *Benedixit nos Deus in Christo, sicut elegerat nos in Christo ante fundamenta mundi.* Titum 1. 2. I Pet. 1. *Gratia et pax vobis electis secundum praecognitionem Dei in fidei obedientiam et sanctificationem Spiritus Sancti.* Sic et promissio Dei restringitur. Iustitia Dei in omnes et super omnes
390 credentes, Rom. 3. 4., sed credentes sunt pauci, Ioan. 3. 5. 7. 8. 10. *Haec est voluntas Dei, ut omnis, qui credit. Nemo venit ad me, nisi Pater traxerit.* Sed Pater solos electos trahit, convertit intus Spiritu suo et verbo. Ioa. 8. 10. 16. 17. *Isti tui erant, mihi dedisti eos et ex his nemo periit. Ego nominatim novi oves meas.* Ergo habent electi catalogum, II Timoth. 2. *Novit Dominus, qui sint sui,*
395 Apoca. 3. 4. 14. 20. 21. *Nemo poterat discere canticum novum, nisi signati, quorum nomina scripta erant in libro vitae.*

Tertia ergo ratio particularis electionis haec est, quia liber vitae, catalogus certus tribuitur Deo, in quo electos, nomina electorum, membra, partes, fugas, lacrymas, ossa, capillorum numerum describat. Exod. 32. *Dele me de libro vitae.*
400 Psal. 56. 130. *Fugas et membra mea numerasti.* Matth. 10. 12. Lucae 10. 12. 21.

---

375 Matth. 10, 30; Luc. 12, 7   **376/377** Matth. 20, 16   **378/379** Matth. 7, 14
379 Luc. 13, 23   **384/385** Act. 13, 48   **385/386** Rom. 8, 30   **386/387** Eph. 1, 3-4
387/389 I Petr. 1, 2   **389/390** Iustitia – credentes[1]] cfr Rom. 3, 22; 4, 23-24   **390/**
391 Ioh. 6, 40 et 44   **393** Isti – periit] Ioh. 17, 12   **393/394** Ego – meas] Ioh. 10, 14
et 27   **394** II Tim. 2, 19   **395/396** Apoc. 14, 3; 21, 27   **399** Ex. 32, 32   **400** Ps. 56, 9

370 18] cfr *Confessio catholica* (1562), Articles 34-36; *Confessio Helvetica Posterior* (1566), par. 10, in *RefBK*, vol. 2/2 (2009), p. 25-28 and 289-291 respectively

448   CONCILIUM DEBRECENIENSE – 1567

Capilli capitis numerati sunt. Si capilli, multo magis personae, Phil. 4. *Nomina vestra scripta sunt in coelis.* Mat. 13.

 Quarto: Scriptura reliquias tantum secundum electionem salvari probat, Rom. 9. Esai. 10, *Si fuerint sicut arena maris, tantum reliquiae salvantur.* Sed
405 soli electi salvantur, Roma. 8. Ephe. 1. Ergo pauci sunt electi, et reliquiarum est electio, Esa. 37., a gratia pro reliquiis. Hier. 23. 39. *Reliquias gregis, et populi mei congregabo,* vide Osae. 1. 3. Mich 2. 4. 5. Reliquiae Iacob salvabuntur, Soph. 1. 2. 3. Zach. 8. Vide de reliquiis salvandis, Roma. 9. 11. *Reliquiae secundum electionem gratiae salvae factae sunt.* Non est ergo universalis electio.

410 Quinto: vasa misericordiae salvanda a vasis irae perdendis Scriptura distinguit: *Iacob dilexi, Esau odio habui,* Mal. 1. Roma. 9. Alios ad vitam, alios ad interitum praeparavit, II Timo. 2. *Duplicia vasa in magna domo.* I Cor. 1. 2. II Cor. 2. 3. 4. Christus, evangelium stultitia, impotentia, *odor mortis iis, qui pereunt, sed odor vitae salvandis.* Stulte errant et illi, qui Esau reprobum cum
415 Saule et Salamone idolatra salvatos fuisse nugantur, cum Scriptura contrarium asserat, Ebrae. 10. 11. 12, de Esau, Gene. 26. *Nequis sit fornicator et prophanus, ut Esau, qui locum poenitentiae non reperit.* I Thessa. 3. III Regum. 10. 11. vide Salamonis impietatem, Saulis vero I Samuelis 15. 16. 36.

 Neque sequitur ex hac doctrina Deum prosopolepsin aut personarum
420 respectorem esse. Primo: quia reddit aequalia aequalibus et idem merentibus. Quia *omnes peccaverunt,* omnes tam electos, quam vasa irae aeterna morte punit. Electos in Christo, quem peccatum et maledictum fecit pro eis, vasa irae in se, Roma. 3. 4. 5. 6.

 Deinde dare dona indebita non merentibus secundum voluntatis suae
425 beneplacitum non est prosopolepsia, Matt. 21. *Nonne ex denario convenisti mecum? Tolle tuum et vade, nonne licet de meo facere, quod volo?* Ita Roma 4. 9. 11. disputat apostolus. *Quid habes, quod non accepisti?* Non laboranti merces non imputantur secundum debitum, sed secundum gratiam. Si nulli daret, quod non debet, argui non posset, si vero paucis donat, quod non debet, quis
430 Deum culpare potest? Figulus est, nos lutum, libere format vasa ex sordido luto peccati, talia, qualia vult, Rom. 9.

---

401 Matth. 10, 30; Luc. 12, 7 **401/402** Matth. 13, 11-12; Phil. 4, 3 **404** Is. 10, 22; Rom. 9, 27 **405/406** Ergo – electio] cfr Rom. 8, 29-30; Eph. 1, 4 **406** a – reliquiis] cfr Is. 37, 32 **406/407** Ier. 23, 3 **407** Reliquiae Iacob salvabuntur] cfr Mich. 5, 7-8 **408/409** Rom. 11, 5 **411** Mal. 1, 2-3; Rom. 9, 13 **412** II Tim. 2, 20 **413/ 414** II Cor. 2, 15-16 **416/417** Hebr. 12, 16-17 **419** prosopolepsin] cfr Act. 10, 34 **421** Rom. 3, 23; 5, 12 **425** prosopolepsia] cfr Rom. 2, 11; Eph. 6, 9; Col. 3, 25 **425/ 426** Matth. 20, 13-15 **427** I Cor. 4, 7 **430/431** Figulus – vult] cfr Rom. 9, 21

417 III] *supplevi, om. E*

CONCILIUM DEBRECENIENSE – 1567

Causas electionis, sicut et iustificationis, salvationis, has Scriptura recitat: in Patre eudokian vel beneplacitum, gratiam Dei, Ephe. 1. Roma. 8. 9. 11., in Christo causam meritoriam, propter quam eligat, salvet, ex vasis irae, filiis irae, peccatoribus dilectos filios, iustos faciat. Nam Christus tradidit semetipsum antilytron, precium redemtionis. *Ille peccatum factus est, ut nos iusti fieremus, ille maledictum, ut nos benedicti fieremus.* In Spiritu Sancto causa dispensatoria, nam sicut in Christo elegit, ita per Spiritum Sanctum exequitur electionis suae effectum, hoc est, per Spiritum Sanctum applicat nobis per verbum et fidem electionis fructus et reliqua beneficia, Rom. 8. I Corin 2. 12. I Pet. 1.

Electi in Spiritus Sancti sanctificationem, hoc est, ut Spiritus Sanctus purificaret. Verbum et fides sunt organa, effectus sunt conversio, regeneratio, iustificatio, novitas vitae, fides et bona opera. Nam soli electi tantum salvantur, convertuntur, Ioan. 5. 6. 17. Acto. 13. Rom. 8. 9. 11.

Sexto: Christus sua beneficia, sacrificium, orationem solis apostolis, solis credituris applicat, Ioan. 6. 10. 16. 17. *Ego pro his oro tantum, pro his me sacrifico, non pro mundo. Gratia et misericordia super eos, et custodis pactum, servas promissionem tuam his, qui credunt, te diligunt, mandata tua custodiunt.* Esai. 54. 59. Hier. 31. Eze. 11. 36. Psal. 89. 103. 117. Rom. 1. 3. 4. 8. 9. 10. 11. 15. Ebrae. 11. Recitat longo catalogo solos credentes salvari, sed fidem pauci habent, ergo pauci et electi. Qui verbum Dei non audiunt, in peccatis regnantibus vivunt. Ebriosi, rapaces, fures, avari, idolatrae vasa irae sunt, non electi. Nam electionem necessario sequuntur conversio, iustificatio, bona opera, Rom. 8. 9. 11. Ephe. 1. 2. Apoc. 14.

[19] CONTRA AUTOEXUSIASTAS

Spiritus Sanctus et autoexusiastas, id est, qui ex se et a se hominibus potestatem, vires volendi, intelligendi, hominibus bona coelestia tribuunt, arguit et damnat.

Primo: quia scriptum est, *omnes peccaverunt et carent, spoliati sunt gloria Dei,* id est, peccando amiserunt imaginem Dei et spoliati libero arbitrio, potentia sciendi, volendi et faciendi bonum, Rom. 3 23. 5. I Cor. 15.

---

433 eudokian] cfr Eph. 1, 9 **436** Ille – fieremus] II Cor. 5, 21 **437** ille – fieremus] Gal. 3, 13-14 **439/440** applicat – beneficia] cfr I Petr. 1, 2 **446/447** Ego – mundo] Ioh. 17, 9 **447/448** Gratia – custodiunt] Neh. 1, 5; cfr III Reg. 8, 23; II Par. 6, 14 **452** Ebriosi – idolatrae] cfr I Cor. 5, 11 **459/460** Rom. 3, 23

455 19] cfr *Confessio catholica* (1562), Articles 30-31, in *RefBK*, vol. 2/2 (2009), p. 23-24

461 23] *supplevi*

450   CONCILIUM DEBRECENIENSE – 1567

2. Secundo: quia homines in delictis mortui sunt, sicut anima, dum deserit corpus, cadaver est, nihil sensit, non movetur, ita ab anima hominum anima et spiritus, quo hominum anima vivebat, intelligebat, volebat, faciebat bona, ipsa scilicet imago Dei, discessit, facti sunt ligno, lapidi, terrae, iumento similes. Ut impossibile est in mortuo manere aliquem sensu, in lapide scientiam, motum esse, in iumento intelligentiam, ita impossibile est homines mortuos in delictis et spoliatos Dei imagine posse aliquid boni scire, cogitare, velle, facere, Deo obedire, cum sint lapis. *Auferam cor lapideum, dabo carneum*, Ezech. 11. 36. *Iumentum factus sum apud te. Homo iumento comparatus est*. Psal. 49. 73.

3. Quia homo est peccatum, tenebrae, Satanae mancipium, subiectus legis maledicto, inimicus Dei, et sensus et motus, voluntas hominis inimicitia est contra Deum. Legi ergo Dei non subiicitur, nec potest, Roma. 6. 7. 8. Impossibile est lucem cum tenebris, peccatum cum iustitia, Diabolum cum Christo consentire. Homo est Satan, peccatum, hostis Dei, obedire ergo Deo et consentire Deo non potest, II Corin. 6.

4. Quia sicut Aetiops, pardus mutare pellem non potest, ita homines peccatores benefacere non possunt, Hie. 13.

5. Quia totum figmentum cogitationum cordis humani tantum ad malum est pronum, id est, tantum malum cogitare, velle et facere potest, ad bonum autem nullum habet motum, non potest Deo obedire.

6. Quia sunt sepulcrum patens, nullus est, qui intelligat, qui velit, qui faciat bonum. Omnes declinaverunt, omnes sunt mendaces. Nihil igitur boni homines non renati velle et facere possunt, Rom. 3. 5. 7.

7. Quia homines vocantur peccatum, lutum faetidum. Opera et iustitiae omnes hominum telae aranearum, ova viperarum, pannus menstruatae, stercora sunt, Esa. 59. 64. Phil. 3. Semper lex arguit et damnat opera hominum. Sed lex sola peccata damnat, ergo omnium opera sine fide peccatum est, et nemo potest placere Deo sine fide. *Animalis homo non intelligit ea, quae sunt spiritualia*, I Cor. 2. Nullum ergo est liberum arbitrium in mortuis.

8. Soli gratiae Dei, Christi merito, Spiritui Sancto tribuit caussas conversionis, poenitentiae, intelligendi, volendi et faciendi bonum. *Omnia opera nostra tu operatus es. Quid habes, quod non accepisti? Deus est, qui caepit bonum*

---

469 Ez. 11, 18-20; 36, 26   **470** Iumentum – te] Ps. 73, 22   Homo – est] Ps. 49, 21 **473/475** Impossibile – consentire] cfr II Cor. 6, 14-16   **477/478** sicut – possunt] cfr Ier. 13, 23   **479/480** totum – pronum] cfr Gen. 8, 21   **482/483** sunt – bonum] cfr Ps. 5, 10; Rom. 3, 13   **483** Omnes – mendaces] cfr Rom. 3, 12-13   **485/487** Opera – sunt] cfr Is. 59, 5-6; 64, 5; Phil. 3, 19   **489** I Cor. 2, 14   **492/493** Omnia – es] Is. 26, 12   **493** Quid – accepisti] I Cor. 4, 7   **493/494** Deus – perficiet] Phil. 1, 6

462 Secundo] *sic*

CONCILIUM DEBRECENIENSE – 1567

in vobis, ipse et perficiet. Ipse Deus efficit, ut velitis et faciatis, Phil. 1. 2. *Qui voca-*
495 *vit vos, idem faciet,* I Thess. 5. Hier. 31. Ezech. 11. 36. Ebr. 8. *Ego convertam, ego*
faciam, ut in praeceptis meis ambulent, mihi obediant.

9. Conversio, regeneratio, fides et iustificatio vocantur nova creatio, resuscitatio, sed creatio et mortuorum resuscitatio sunt solius deitatis opera, Esai.
41. 43. 45. Ioan. 3. 5. 6. 10. Rom. 8. Coloss. 2. Homines ergo converti, iustifica-
500 ri, scire, velle bonum, consentire Deo, cooperari Deo, subiici legi impossibile,
quia nulla luci cum tenebris conventio. Sunt inimici Dei, sunt peccatum,
Satan, cum Deo igitur agere, operari non possunt. Sed ubi electi, conversi
iustificati sunt gratia Dei in Christo, ope Spiritus Sancti induunt imaginem
Dei, facti sunt nova creatura, sunt iusti, resuscitati, Deo cooperantur, volunt,
505 possunt bonum cum Christo.

Stulte somniant igitur Pelagiani, assertores liberi arbitrii, ideo tribuendas
esse vires hominibus, quia lex requirit, praecipit, promittit vitam, adhortatur:
quia lex secundum primam conditionem loquitur, sicuti creati eramus. Quod
datum erat et amisimus, requirit, sed non tribuit vires. Nam impium et fatuum
510 est ex impossibli mandato ad factorem dissimilem, qui est pecus, terra, cadaver,
infans, colligere possibilitatem faciendi. Tu cadaver, lapis, lignum, vive, dabo
praemia, ergo lapis mortuus vivit. Mille aureos ab eo petere, qui terentium non
habet, impossibile est. Sed lex, dum impossibilia mandat, Deum excusat,
homines inexcusabiles facit, Exo. 20.

515 Nec sequitur inutiles esse orationes, adhortationes, nam Christus est finis
et impletio legis. Electi Christi virtute per fidem legem stabiliunt, obediunt
Deo, Ioa. 15. 17. I Ioan. 4. 5. Quod in nobis deficit, in Christo completur. Lex
impossibilia iubendo vires et merita nostra contemnere mandat, et gratiam
Dei, Christi meritum implorare iubet, Roma. 3. 6. 7. 8. Gala. 3. 4. Ezech. 16.
520 *Dixi in sanguine, vive, vive, cum non possis, ego assumsi te.* Hier. 31. Ezech. 11.
36. *Faedus novum faciam tecum, et ego leges meas in mentem inscribam et in*
corda dabo.

[20] CONTRA PSYCHOMACARISTAS

Vesaniam et stultum errorem psychomacaristarum, id est, eorum qui
525 animas sanctorum, mox ut a corpore solutae sunt, in perfectissimam beatitudinem ingredi somniant, his rationibus Spiritus Sanctus arguit.

---

494 Ipse – faciatis] Phil. 2, 13 **494/495** I Thess. 5, 24 **495/496** Ez. 11, 20; 36, 27;
cfr Ier. 31, 33; Hebr. 8, 10 **501** nulla – conventio] cfr II Cor. 6, 15 **520** Ez. 16, 6
521/522 Ier. 31, 33

CONCILIUM DEBRECENIENSE – 1567

1. Quia Symbolum et universa Scriptura sic docet: *Unde venturus est iudicare vivos.* Quando filius hominis veniet, tunc erit apolytrosis vestra, id est, tunc perfecte et absolute perficietur redemtio et liberatio vestra ab omnibus
530 malis, spiritualibus, corporalibus, a peccato, Diabolo, morte, inferis et tunc veniet Dei regnum, id est, tunc introibitis in regnum Dei, tunc facie ad faciem perfecta Dei cognitione seu vita aeterna fruemini. *Venite benedicti Patris, accipite regnum.* Rom. 8. Tunc liberabitur creatura a corruptione. Luc. 21. Matt. 24.

535 2. Quia scriptum est: *credo resurrectionem mortuorum et post hanc vitam aeternam.* Non ergo ante resurrectionem animae vita aeterna perfecte fruentur, nisi ex parte, I Cor. 13. 15. II Cor. 5.

3. Quia Christi anima ante resurrectionem sui corporis fuit in Paradiso in sinu Abrahae, sed non fuit in regno Dei, et post resurrectionem intravit in
540 regnum Dei, Luc. 24. Oportuit Christum primum pari, resurgere et sic intrare in gloriam Dei, in regnum Dei. Ergo et nostrae animae ante resurrectionem sunt in Paradiso, id est, in parte vitae aeternae, sed non in consummatione.

4. Ebrae 3. 4. 11. Vita aeterna sancto sanctorum confertur, ut per atria, per partes ingrediebantur in sancta sanctorum, primo in atrium exterius, post in
545 atrium interius, hinc in templum vel sanctum, ex sancto in sanctum sanctorum, ita primitias vitae aeternae in Paradiso, in sinu Abrahae animae sanctae percipiunt. Post resurrectionem ingredientur absque fide, sine medio fidei in vitam aeternam.

Ibidem cap. 11. *hi omnes sancti fide iustificati non acceperunt promissionem*
550 vel beatitudinem aeternam totaliter, nec in ea introducti *Deo melius de nobis providente, ne sine nobis ingrederentur* in illam aeternam beatitudinem.

5. Quia Scriptura docet nos spe salvari, id est, per spem expectare vitam aeternam, per fidem nos ambulare, non per intuitum bonorum, hoc est, mediate nos frui bonis, non immediate, II Cor. 5., et quidem ex parte, imper-
555 fecte, I Cor. 13., nos fide custodiri in salutem aeternam, sed fides, spes destruentur in vita aeterna. Animae electorum sperant et credunt, ergo nondum sunt in beatitudine aeterna, ubi ex parte imperfectio, fides, spes cessabunt

---

528 apolytrosis] cfr Luc. 21, 28 **532/533** Matth. 25, 34 **533** Tunc – corruptione] cfr Matth. 24, 30-31; Luc. 21, 28 **536/537** Non – parte] cfr II Cor. 5, 1-4 **538/ 540** Christi – Dei] cfr Luc. 24, 26 et 46 **549/551** Hebr. 11, 39-40 **553** perᵗ – bonorum] cfr II Cor. 5, 7 **554** ex parte imperfecte] cfr I Cor. 13, 10 **557** fides – cessabunt] cfr I Cor. 13, 13

527/528 Unde – vivos] *Symbolum Nicaeno-Constantinopolitanum,* in *COGD* I, p. 57 **535/536** credo – aeternam] *Symbolum Nicaeno-Constantinopolitanum,* in *COGD* I, p. 57

CONCILIUM DEBRECENIENSE – 1567

et Deus erit *omnia in omnibus*, Titum 1. 2. Ephe. 4., *expectantes beatam spem*, id est, per expectatam beatitudinem et adventum magni Dei, Iesu Christi, Tit. 2. Stulte errant ergo psychomacaristae.

6. Vita aeterna et beatitudo est immediata Dei cognitio et fruitio conspectu Dei, facie ad faciem videre, intueri. Sicut Luc. 21. redemptionem, Paulus, Roma. 8., salutem definit, et I Ioan. 3. *Tunc videbimus eum facie ad faciem, sicuti est*, I Cor. 13. 15. Fit autem hoc corpore et anima, cum totus homo reformatus erit ad imaginem Dei, II Corin. 3. 5. I Corin. 15. Sed nunc ex parte, per fidem ambulamus. Sumus cum Christo et hic in terra per fidem et ex parte, sumus cum Christo et in Paradiso. Quia Christus hic et in Paradiso et ubique praesens est. Sicut stultum est sic colligere: Christus inquit, ubi ego sum, ibi sunt servi mecum. Cum Christo resurrexistis et simul sedistis in dextera Dei. Christus est in perfecta beatitudine in coelo, ergo et nos corpore et anima ibidem sumus. Ita stultum est colligere: cupio dissolvi et esse cum Christo. Christus est perfecte in beatitudine, ergo et animae. Cum Christus aliter sit in regno, aliter animae, ille totaliter, istae animae ex parte, I Corin. 13. Utinam sophistae, vini potores, unicum Christi testimonium, Ioan. 14., didicissent: *Vado, parabo vobis locum et iterum veniam et tunc recipiam et vos ad me ipsum.* [...]

[29] DE RESURRECTIONE OMNIUM

Etsi animarum resurrectio seu electio, vocatio, iustificatio et glorificatio electorum tantum est, Rom. 8. 9. Ioan. 5. 6., sicut praedestinatione dictum est, tamen carnis resurrectio communis et omnium est, piorum et vasorum irae, virorum et mulierum, idque ideo:

Primo: quia scriptum est: *Evigilabunt omnes, qui in pulvere dormiunt. Credo carnis resurrectionem.* Daniel 12. Mulieres dormiunt et mortuae sunt, igitur et resurgent, Matth. 22. 24. Ioan. 5. 11. 12.

Secundo: I Corin. 15. Ioan. 5. 6. I Thess. 4. 5. Matth. 22. Christus et apostolus multis argumentis resurrectionem mortuorum probant. Omnes, qui mortui sunt, resurgent, Apoc. 19. 20. 21.

---

558 I Cor. 15, 28   Tit. 2, 13; cfr Eph. 4, 4   **562/563** Sicut – definit] cfr Luc. 21, 27; Rom. 8, 23   **563/564** I Ioh. 3, 2; cfr I Cor. 13, 12   **564/565** totus – Dei] cfr I Cor. 15, 49; II Cor. 3, 18   **573** ex parte] cfr I Cor. 13, 12   **575/576** Vado – ipsum] Ioh. 14, 3   **582** Dan. 12, 2

577 29] cfr *Confessio catholica* (1562), Article 203, in *RefBK*, vol. 2/2 (2009), p. 143-145
583 Credo carnis resurrectionem] cfr *Symbolum Apostolicum*

454 CONCILIUM DEBRECENIENSE – 1567

Tertio: *regina Austri resurget in iudicio et condemnabit hanc nationem.* Ergo mulieres resurgent.

590 Quarto: Christus multas puellas vivificavit in terra propter testimonium futurae resurrectionis, Matth. 8. 9. Luc. 8.

Quinto: mulieres electae iustificantur, resurgent, resuscitabuntur, I Cori. 6. 7. I Timoth. 1. 2.

[30] De anima mulierum

595 Docemus mulieres habere corpus et animam propriam, nec in viros conversuras, idque ideo:

Primo: quia factae sunt ex viro similes, ex corpore et anima Adae. Fiunt mulieres ex parentibus corpus et animam habentibus, Gen. 1. 2.

2. Maria virgo, Anna, Elizabet, Debora et sanctae mulieres ita canunt:

600 *Magnificat anima mea dominum et exultavit spiritus meus in Deo*, Luc. 1. 2.

Tertio: Christus archisynagogae filiam suscitans ex mortuis dicit Lucas spiritum puellae rediisse, Luc. 8. Mat. 9. Impie ergo mentiuntur mulieres non habere animas.

Quarto: in die resurrectionis dicit virum relinqui, uxorem assumi, et licet

605 resurgant mulieres quoque, *tamen non nubunt nec nubuntur*, Matt. 22. 24.

Quinto: meretrices antecedent iustitiarios in vita aeterna et regno Dei, ergo vere resurgent nec in viros convertentur, Matt. 21.

Sexto: virgines fatuae exclusae sunt, prudentes ingressae sunt cum sponso Christo in vitam aeternam, ergo resurgent, Matth. 25.

610 Finis nostrae confessionis.

---

588 Matth. 12, 42   **590** Christus – terra] cfr Matth. 9, 25; Luc. 8, 55   **600** Luc. 1, 46-47   **601/602** Christus – rediisse] cfr Luc. 8, 55; Matth. 9, 18-19   **605** Matth. 22, 30   **606** meretrices – Dei] cfr Matth. 21, 32   **608/609** virgines – Christo] cfr Matth. 25, 1-13

III

ARTICULI EX VERBO DEI ET LEGE NATURAE COMPOSITI AD CONSERVANDAM POLITIAM COELESTEM ET IURISDICTIONEM ECCLESIASTICAM IN UNGARICA NATIONE

[1]

Ut multorum querelae et accusationes indignae vitentur, qui nos ideo cyclopes et barbaros exleges vocant, quod locus sit inter nos anarchiae cyclopicae et disciplinae solutissimae, effreni licentia et ataxia inordinata arrogantia foedatae, dum superbi quid libet licere putant.

Contra horum ergo querelas hoc concludimus.

Sicut Deus sine certa lege, ordine, dispositione et voluntate sui arbitrii liberi nihil facit, sed omnia praedefinito consilio, praescientia et praeordinatione facit, regit et gubernat, ita ecclesia et omnis politia hominum carere legitimo, debito et iusto ordine non potest. Igitur ad naturae coelestis et politicae conservationem dicimus ordinem esse necessarium. Imo spiritum et regulam totius vitae et politiae dicimus esse iustum, legitimum et omnibus politiis congruentem ordinem. Peiores ergo et deteriores esse bestiis et vermibus dicimus, qui ataxia, inordinatione et anarchia cyclopica dominandi cupidine sanctas politias et ecclesias turbant. Cum scriptum sit: *Omnia ordine et honeste cum decoro fiant inter vos.* Deus non est autor inordinatae confusionis, sed pacis, concordiae et charitatis, Ephe. 1. 2. 4. Col. 1. 2. Ideo ecclesia corpori humano et aedificiis bene dispositis confertur, ut sicut capiti membra rite cohaerent et aedificia per suas compages, structuras compacta et commissa copulantur et uniuntur, ita capiti suo, Christo ecclesia per verbum et fidem ope Spiritus Sancti et architectorum, pastorum cohaerere debet. Ubi autem nemo nemi-

---

19/20 I Cor. 14, 40

1/4 Articuli – natione] *in titulo externo* Articuli ex verbo Dei et lege naturae compositi, ad conservandam politiam ecclesiasticam et formandam vitam christianam in omnibus ordinibus necessariam *E* **5** 1] *add. in marg. tit.* Omnia in ecclesia ordine et decenter fieri oportet *C*

nem audit, sed omnia prava licentia turbantur, locus est Diabolo, qui autor est confusionis et discordiae. Ephe. 4. 5. II Cor. 12. 13.

[2]

Nihil in ecclesia ex kenodoxia, id est, vana gloria, contentione, invidia fiat, sed omnia ex Spiritu mansuetudinis et charitatis. Unus quisque se aliis excellentiorem in humilitate putet et alios sibi non superbe, sed humiliter praeferat. I Cor. 5. 6. 12. 14. Phil. 2. 5. 10. Iacob. 1. 4. Gal. 2. 4. 5. 6.

[3]

Quia omne, quod non fit ex verbo Dei, peccatum est, et omnis traditio, *quam Pater non plantavit, eradicabitur,* et scriptum est, Matth. 16. *Non addes verbo meo quiquam, ne arguaris mendax,* et apostolus kenin apatin, vanam deceptionem, Col. 1. 2. Phil. 1. 2. 3. Gala. 2. 3. 4. 5., Samuel vero tohu bohu, rem inanem et vacuam traditionem humanam vocat, I Samuel 12. 15., dicimus ergo omnem piam et sanctam ordinationem ecclesiae ex verbo Dei petendam esse et fundatam veritate divina.

[4]

Quaecunque per Diabolum, Antichristum et per haereticos in ecclesiam invecta sunt, ut doctrinae falsae et institutiones, cum sint peccatum et tenebrae, pro reiectamentis, pro nugis et mendaciis habenda sunt. Igitur in doctrinae veritate, in ritibus ecclesiasticis semper verbum Dei sequendum est, Christus et apostoli eius in doctrina et ritibus imitentur. Impie ergo errant, qui relicta veritate, luce et exemplo Christi et apostolorum eius Antichristum, papam in suis sordibus sequuntur, ut idolorum, ararum, vestium, papalium et aliarum sordium ab Antichristo excogitatarum patroni et defensores, azymi

---

29 kenodoxia] cfr Gal. 5, 26; Phil. 2, 3   **34** omne – est] cfr Rom. 14, 23   **35** Matth. 15, 13   **35/36** Prou. 30, 6   **36** kenin apatin] cfr Col. 2, 8   **37** tohu bohu] cfr I Reg. 12, 21

---

33 3] cfr *Confessio Helvetica Posterior* (1566), par. 24, in *RefBK*, vol. 2/2 (2009), p. 336-338   **41** 4] cfr *Confessio brevis* (1567), par. 2, in *RefBK*, vol. 2/2 (2009), p. 364-367

---

41 4] *add. in marg. tit.* Doctrinae puritas conservanda et ritus verbo Dei consentientes observandi sunt in ecclesia: Haeresis vero et doctrina Antichristi fugienda *C*

CONCILIUM DEBRECENIENSE – 1567

50 missatici factitant, quibus scelus et sacrilegium est Christum et apostolos et patres, imo christianam libertatem in usu fermentati et panis communis sequi.

Sanctum autem et tutum et rectum esse somniant, si Antichristum et papam sequantur. Veritate enim Dei offendi, scandalizari pios nugantur, mendacio autem et iniquitate, hominum inventis non, sed immunes a scandalo 55 manere homines vociferantur, Matth. 19. 23. Cum Scriptura foedae scortationi et adulterio comparet Antichristi, papae sordes, idola, aras, instituta et missaticam ostiam retinere, Esai. 57. Ezech. 16.

[5]

Nemo in articulis fidei et in aliis religionis christianae fundamentis, 60 ritibus ac sacramentis privatim et propria autoritate cum multorum scandalo et offendiculis mutationem aut innovationem facere praesumat. Sed si quid innovandum aut mutandum vel corrigendum erit in consueta doctrina et ritibus, legitime cum totius ecclesiae consensu fiat. Prius coactis ecclesiae synodis ex verbo Dei et patribus fiant pie collationes et disputationes. Quicunque 65 autem ex vana gloria, superbia et logomachia moliri aliquid inordinate non cessaverint, ecclesiae iurisdictione et magistratuum authoritate puniendos iudicamus.

Scriptum est enim: *Qui vos non audit, me non audit. Si ecclesiam non audit, sit ethnicus et publicanus.* Matt. 10. et 23. Luc. 10. I Tim. 4. 5. Haereti70 cum hominem post unam et alteram admonitionem devita et fuge, et Scriptura haereticos turbatores concordiae lapidandos esse iussit, Deut. 13. 17. 28. III Reg. 13. Levi. 24. II Para. 10. 34. Ezech. 13. 14. 18. Sicut Helias iussit sacerdotes Baal occidi, qui noluerunt veritati obedire, vide Psal. 101. Hier. 14. 15. Dani. 3. Exo. 22. Chore, Datan, Abiron inobedientes et schismatici a terra absorpti, alii 75 igne consumti sunt.

---

65 logomachia] cfr I Tim. 6, 4; II Tim. 2, 14   **68** Qui – audit²] Luc. 10, 16   **68/**
69 Si – publicanus] Matth. 18, 17   **72/73** Helias – occidi] cfr III Reg. 18, 40   **74/**
75 Chore – sunt] cfr Num. 16, 32

58 5] cfr *Confessio Helvetica Posterior* (1566), par. 27, in *RefBK*, vol. 2/2 (2009), p. 341-342

58 5] *add. in marg. tit.* Conformitas rituum et Sacramentorum observanda, mutatio vero seu innovatio scandalosa serio vitanda *C*   **61** praesumat] *correxi*, praesummat *C E*

[6]

Impietati patrocinantur principes et pastores, qui falsa et mendacia prophetantes non prohibent, sed vineam Domini apris destruere permittunt, Psal. 79. Ezech. 14. 15.

80 Sedechias periit cum Acab, Ieroboam et aliis impiis regibus, qui idolatriae et impiorum doctorum patroni fuerunt, III Reg. 17. IV Reg. 10. 17. 23. 25. Et nunc igitur si Serveticas et Sabellianas haereses contra sanctam et adorandam Triadem, contra Christi et Spiritus Sancti divinitatem non puniverint principes, illos Dominus cum Sedechia puniet, Levi. 20. Num. 35.

85

[7]

Quia Deus unus est, unus Christus, *una fides, unum baptisma*, unum Dei verbum, una charitas, unum salutis fundamentum, ideo necesse est pastores primum in fundamento salutis et doctrinae, in articulis fidei in symbolo conprehensis et in sacramentorum simplici veritate et administrationis ritu et 90 forma in verbo expressa convenire. Idem sapere, sentire, ut dicitur: *Idem sentiatis omnes. Scrutamini Scripturas*. Roma. 12. 14. 15. Phil. 2. Ioa. 7. 8. 13. 14. 15. 17. I Cor. 11. 12. Exo. 30. 41. Deut. 12. 17. Nemo sapiat praeterquam, quod scriptum est. *Exemplum dedi vobis, ut sicut ego feci, et vos ita faciatis. Ego a Domino sic accepi. Estote imitatores mei, sicut ego Christi*. Unum erat doctrinae 95 in veteri testamento genus et fundamentum, uniformis ubique et administrandi ritus. Nihil quiquam mutare licebat. Convenire ergo in fundamento et ritu ceremoniarum in verbo Dei expresso oportet, ne fiant schismata et dissensiones, quae damnat apostolus, I Cor. 3. 10. 11. 12. Gal. 5. 6. Sicut coena in publico loco, ita baptismus in publico loco post contionem fiat.

---

78 vineam – permittunt] cfr Ps. 79, 14   **86** Eph. 4, 5   **90/91** Idem sentiatis omnes] Phil. 2, 2   **91** Scrutamini Scripturas] Ioh. 5, 39   **92/93** Nemo – est] cfr I Cor. 4, 6 **93** Exemplum – faciatis] Ioh. 13, 15   **93/94** Ego – accepi] I Cor. 11, 23   **94** Estote – Christi] I Cor. 11, 1

76 6] cfr *Confessio brevis* (1567) in *RefBK*, vol. 2/2 (2009), p. 360-361   **85** 7] cfr *Confessio catholica* (1562), Articles 79-89 and 174, in *RefBK*, vol. 2/2 (2009), p. 52-62 and 126-129 respectively; *Hungarian Creed* (1567), in *BaM*, p. 207-211

85 7] *add. in marg. tit.* Consensus in fundamento et in praecipuis fidei articulis et ritibus ecclesiasticis necessarius *C*

CONCILIUM DEBRECENIENSE – 1567   459

Forma baptizandi ex verbo Dei haec colligitur. Cum Christus, Ioannes et apostolus baptismum explicarent, primum de duplici baptismo, de spirituali, de igne, de spiritu, id est, de efficacia mortis, quae est ceu ignis vorans stipulas, peccata, mortem, Matt. 3. 11. I Cor. 1. 3., et de efficacia resurrectionis, qui est Spiritus vivificans, ex peccatis resuscitans, reformans, regenerans, Luc. 3. Io. 1. 3., secundo de externo baptismo locuti sunt, qui est signum prioris et spiritualis, Luc. 3. Io. 1. 3. Tit. 3. Ephe. 5. Primo igitur de duplici baptismo tractetur, secundo de significatione sive de fine baptismi externi, qui triplex est. Primo significat reconciliationem nostram, Patri nos reconciliatos testatur. Secundo causam reconciliationis in Christo praedicat. Pueri reclinatio Christi descensum, mortem, passionem, sepulturam, peccatorum nostrorum abolitionem, lotio infantis peccatorum omnium ablutionem, elevatio pueri significat Christi resurrectione nostras animas ex peccato resuscitatas et corpora nostra per eundem Christum resuscitabuntur, Ioan. 5. 6. I Cor. 15. Infantis involutio tertio aut induitio significat nostram regenerationem, iustificationem, Christum et iustitiam Christi, imaginem Christi electos induisse, Gal. 3. Rom. 6. 8. I Cor. 15. II Cor. 3. Sic et symbolum explicabitur: haec fuit forma baptizandi, I Cor. 15. Ebrae. 6. Gala. 3. Coloss. 2. 3.

Tertio, quae sit stipulatio in baptismo. Trinitas sic obligavit se nobis iuramento et promissione, quod nos, quos in Christo dilexit, elegit, adoptavit, iustificavit, non deserat, sed ab omni malo liberet, in utero suo portabit, Ezech. 16. Ose. 2. Esai. 54. Filius quoque Christus obligavit se suae sponsae similiter iuramento, quod eam diligat, alat, curet, non deserat, sed ex omnibus sordibus abluat, ne habeat rugam aut maculam, Ephe. 5. Titum 3. Spiritus Sanctus obligavit se electis sic, quod tanquam arrabo haereditatis ad diem usque redemptionis nos regeneret, ducat, doceat, illuminet, dirigat, omnia bona opera in nobis efficiat, fide, spe confirmet, Ephe. 1. 4. II Cor. 1. 5.

Obligatio autem et stipulatio electorum est:

Primo, quod Deum tantum unum invocent, adorent. Secundo, quod unicum sponsum et salvatorem Christum agnoscant. Omnes salutis causas in solidum Deo tribuant, sibi confusionem, Deo gloriam, quia nihil habent, quod non acceperint. Tertio, quod abnegata impietate et mundanis concupiscentiis iuste, sobrie, religiose vivant. Acta carnis et concupiscentiae fomites

---

124 arrabo haereditatis] cfr II Cor. 1, 22; Eph. 1, 14   **130/131** nihil – acceperint] cfr I Cor. 3, 29

---

100 Forma – colligitur] *add. in marg. tit.* Forma baptismi *C*   **101** primum de duplici baptismo] *add. in marg. tit.* Duplex est baptismus *C*   **107** secundo – externi] *add. in marg. tit.* Finis baptismi externi *C*   **110** abolitionem] obolitionem *E*

460 CONCILIUM DEBRECENIENSE – 1567

Spiritus Sancti virtute, induti armis Christi extinguant, Roma. 6. 8. 13. Col. 1.
2. 3. Ephe. 4. 5. 6. Gala. 5. 6. Et quod sordes Antichristi, papae fugiant.

135 Alias stultas speculationes et abrenunciationes reiicimus. Sicut contioni
multi interesse possunt, ita pie facient, si huic sacrae contioni plurimi adsint,
et testes tinctionis esse possunt. Compatres pro amicis et testibus approbamus,
non more papistico.

Et coena sic explicetur cum Christo et Paulo:

140 Primo de duplici coena pastor disputet: de spirituali, qui est gratia Dei,
panis vivus, Spiritus S. vivificans, fides et verbum, Ioa. 6. Secundo de sacramento externo seu signo tractetur sic: primo, quid sit coena Domini externa;
secundo, quid significet quis usus: scilicet ut sit memoria beneficii Christi,
redemptionis nostrae et satisfactionis Christi; secundo, ut doceat de confirma-
145 tione testamenti novi per Christi sanguinem; tertio, ut significet unionem
nostram cum Christo, I Cor. 11. Tertio tractetur, quomodo sumenda sit coena:
scilicet cum probatione et fide digne, I Cor. 11.

Postquam autem hanc contionem in baptismo et coena perficit pastor,
oret et tingat, immergat in aquam infantem, lavet recitando haec verba: En
150 tegedet moslac, förösztlec Atyanac, Fiunac et S. Léleknec nevében. Finito baptismo benedicat baptizatis, ut in fide, charitate, bonis operibus permaneant. Et
si fieri potest, totaliter tingatur et immergatur infans, sicut Baptista et apostoli
baptizabant, Ioa. 1. Luc. 3. Acto. 8. Et sic in Ebraeo et Graeco vis verbi baptizo
explicabitur. Sic autem coenam orans, post orationem panem accipiendo in
155 manus, Christi et apostoli exemplo recitet formam verborum et sic panem et
poculum postea distribuat idem pastor et inter distributionem potest pias
quaestiones proponere, erudire populum. Finita distributione oret et sic
coetum dimittat. Haec vera est forma sacramenta administrandi.

Papisticam consuetudinem prorsus damnamus. Sicut stultam illam abre-
160 nunciandi stipulationem, quae ut erat mendacium, ita et impossibilis. Stultum
simul est spondere pro alio, quem, qualis sit futurus, ignorat. Hic spondet pro
probitate et iurat, ille fit ipsum scelus. Sicut igitur legis impletio viribus hominum impossibilis, ita abrenunciatio, hoc est, velle peccato, mundo, Diabolo
resistere suis viribus, sine gratiae Dei praesidio, impium est. Reiicimus et illos,
165 qui negant nullam esse abrenuntiationem, imo electio, conversio, regeneratio
et iustificatio necessario tanquam causa effectum post se abrenunciationem

---

139 Et – Paulo] *add. in marg. tit.* Caenae dominicae forma et eius legitima
administratio *C* **144** secundo] *sic* **146** sumenda] *correxi,* summenda *C E* **149**/
150 En – nevében] *Hungarice, translata:* 'ego lavo, baptizo te in nomine Patris, Filii et
Spiritus Sancti' **150** et S. Léleknec] es szent Leleknec *C*

CONCILIUM DEBRECENIENSE – 1567

trahit teste apostolo, Ro. 3. 5. 6. Tit. 2. 3. Nam ubi iustificati sumus, impietatem, peccata abnegare oportet.

[8]

Sicut Scripturae sacrae, hoc est, canonica prophetarum et apostolorum scripta solum proponenda sunt in ecclesia, non autem apocrypha, ut Ecclesiastici, Sapientiae, Tobiae libri, II Pet. 3. Ita interpraetatio Scripturae ne sit privata, sicut cuique placet aut videtur, sed Scriptura Scripturam interpraetetur, antecedentia et consequentia in textu conferantur. Patres orthodoxi, salubres et sani commentarii adhibeantur. Nam agnoscimus patrum orthodoxorum et sanorum commentariorum scripta praeclara esse dona Dei, ut dicitur I Cor. 12. Ephe. 4., *dedit dona hominibus, euangelistas, doctores*, id est, interpraetes. Ita et I Cor. 14. Matt. 21. apostolus loquitur. Et Christus iubet attente legendos esse prophetas. Apostolus vero: *attende lectioni*, id est, discas et doceas et adhorteris, habens fidem et bonam conscientiam, I Cor. 2. 3. 4. Repudiamus ergo sciolos et barbaros, qui patrum scripta et pios commentarios reiiciunt et inordinate ambulant enthusiastarum more, ex vana capitis speculatione rudem populum pascunt.

[9]

Norma interpraetationis in genere haec sit, ut recte secetur verbum Dei: testamentum vetus a novo, lex ab euangelio, veteres ritus et ceremoniae a novi testamenti ritibus distinguantur, II Cor. 2. 3. Ro. 3. 5. 8. 9. 10. Causae salutis ab organis et effectibus distinguantur. Et quae Scriptura separatim proponit, ita doceantur, ne fiat confusio, tempora distingue et conciliabis Scripturas.

---

177 I Cor. 12, 28   **179** I Tim. 4, 13

169 8] cfr *Confessio catholica* (1562), Articles 141 and 165-166, in *RefBK*, vol. 2/2 (2009), p. 100-101 and 119-121 respectively

169 8] *add. in marg. tit.* In ecclesia solum verbum Dei purum est proponendum, et sani commentarii consulendi *C*   **172** interpraetatio] *sic*   **173** interpraetetur] *sic*   **177** interpraetes] *sic*   **185** Norma interpraetationis] *sic*

462 CONCILIUM DEBRECENIENSE – 1567

190 [10]

Sacra Biblia sic proponantur, ut prophetarum et apostolorum scripta doceantur et tota doctrina ordine proponatur, ne tantum in postillis comprehensa euangelia dominicalia et epistolae continuentur, sed inter perfectos, hoc est, in fide et religione confirmatos prophetarum et apostolorum scripta
195 proponantur. Nec concionatores textu ex Bibliis proposito neglecto extra septa currant et incongrua doceant, sed textus ordine iuxta seriem commatum, punctorum et versuum tractetur et explicetur, et ubi textum exposuit, summam concionis proponat. Deinde ordine textum explicet et ex textu utilia documenta populo tradat. Et ultra spatium horae unius concio ne protrahatur,
200 ne taedium pariat.

[11]

Nemo sapiat supra quam, quod oportet sapere, sed omnes ad sobrietatem sapiant, Ro. 12. 15. I Cor. 3. 11. I Tim. 1. 3. Hoc est, illa doceantur tantum, quae sunt in Scripturis comprehensa. Stultae et inanes quaestiones devitentur. Nec
205 quaerantur illa, quae in Scripturae veritate non continentur, ut curiosi homines facere solent.

[12]

Sicut maledictus est, qui relicta coelesti doctrina prophetarum et apostolorum Antichristi, papae et haereticorum impia dogmata sequitur, ita qui
210 exemplo Christi, lucis mundi, veritatis, capitis et sponsi ecclesiae et apostolorum reiecto in actionibus sacris et ritibus imitandis Antichristi, papae et haereticorum exempla, instituta et traditiones (quae sunt tohu bohu, stercus, tenebrae, fornicatio) sequuntur, maledicti sunt, Esa. 4. 28. 57. Et sic foeda pollutione tanquam scorta lectum mariti sui Christi adulterum recipiendo polluunt et
215 dilatando cubile et stratum sui mariti suscipiunt adulterum, ac prioris mariti recordantur et oleum, vinum, lanam adulterorum amant, Amos. 4. 5. 6. Eze. 16. Ut panis missatici, idolorum et ararum patroni, Matth. 13. 15. Et Christus

---

202/203 Nemo – sapiant] cfr Rom. 12, 3   212 tohu bohu] cfr I Reg. 12, 21

190 10] cfr *Confessio catholica* (1562), Article 174, in *RefBK*, vol. 2/2 (2009), p. 126-129

190 10] *add. in marg. tit.* Conciones publice quomodo instituendae sint *C*   201 11] *add. in marg. tit.* Curiosae et stultae quaestiones fugiendae *C*

CONCILIUM DEBRECENIENSE – 1567

arguit Iudaeos, quod propter traditiones suas deseruerunt praecepta Dei, Mar.
2. 10.

[13]

Christum cum Belial, lucem cum tenebris, iustitiam cum iniquitate in
unum iugum copulant et malum dicunt bonum et contra bonum malum, qui
coelestia et divina, doctrinam sacram, actiones Christi cum Antichristi foedis
sordibus, inventis claudicando in utranque partem coniungunt et utrunque
Dei sacra instituta et Diaboli sordes retinent, cum nihil malorum retineri
possint. Nec forma nec abusus in hominum inventis servari debent, quaecunque in primo et secundo praecepto damnantur. *Non sint tibi dii alii*, Exo. 20.
Deut. 4. 5. I Ioa. 5. II Cor. 10. *Non facies sculptile, non adorabis nec coles ea.*
Fugite idola! Quae communicatio luci cum tenebris? Nihil est in peccato, sordibus, quod totaliter non sit peccatum, tenebrae. Quaecunque sunt Antichristi
tenebrae, sordes, contra verbum Dei excogitata, totaliter et universaliter sunt
mala, ut dicitur: *Totum figmentum cordis hominum tantum ad malum.* Quid
ergo restat, quod non sit peccatum? Matt. 15. 23. Col. 2. Esai. 28. 29. Si tenebrae, si iniquitas, si stercus, vanitas vanitatum, omnis Diaboli plantatio, quid
ergo in ea relinquas boni? Quae lux in tenebris?

[14]

Quaecunque in papismo et regno Antichristi et divinis doctrinis polluta
et foedata fuerunt abusu turpi, illa omnia a puris et sanctis de sordibus eximi,
abstergi et purgari possunt deletis sordibus et pollutionibus papisticis, Rom.
14. 15. I Cor. 6. 8. 10. *Puris enim omnia pura sunt*, et nihil est per se immundum, ut coena Domini, baptismus et doctrina sacra, ciborum et dierum
delectus a piis corrigi et emendari possunt, I Timo. 4. Tit. 1.

221/222 Christum – copulant] cfr II Cor. 6, 15   **227** Ex. 20, 3   **228** Ex. 20, 4-5
229 Fugite idola] I Ioh. 5, 21   Quae – tenebris] II Cor. 6, 14   **232** Gen. 6, 5
240 Tit. 1, 15

225 sacra instituta] *om. C E*

464 CONCILIUM DEBRECENIENSE – 1567

[15]

Vestes missaticas cum hostia missatica et aris reiicimus. Sed vestium natu-
245 ralium et politicarum, naturae servientium libertatis christianae arbitrio relinquimus materiam et formam, ita ut usus earum necessitati naturae aptus sit
cum decoro et mediocri sobrietate contentus. Absit tantum luxus, fastus, pompa et superstitio idolatrica, ut scurrarum et Kamuriim in veteri testamento
habitus damnantur, Ose. 2. 4. Ezech. 14. 16. II Reg. 10. 11. 17. 25. Kamuriim
250 erant Baalitici sacerdotes, qui vestium superstitione fallebant rudiores. Nam
nihil de materia, forma vestium Scriptura tradit. Sed omnia filiorum libertate
et potestate disponenda committit, Psal. 34. I Corin. 10. 14. Rom. 14. 15.
I Tim. 4. Col. 2. *Domini enim est terra et plenitudo eius. Nemo iudicet et
condemnet vos in cibo, potu* nec in vestium varietate. Nam etiam in veteri tes-
255 tamento tantum vestes Aaronicae, sacerdotales erant suis formis et regulis
terminatae. Vulgares vero, politicae et quotidianae sacerdotum vestes accomo-
dabantur necessitati naturae et decoro temperabantur, ut ergo superstitiosae
vestes damnantur, ita fastuosae, parasiticae et scurris aut militari ordini con-
gruentes in ministris ecclesiae.

260 [16]

Sicut verbum Dei non est alligatum, ita stultum est ministerium verbi uni
loco astringere. Et quaecunque per se Dei sunt, sed per accidens Antichristi
per tyrannidem facta fuerunt, illa vindicari ex sordibus papisticis possunt
abiecto abusu, IV Reg. 3. 10. 11. 13. Mat. 21. Act. 4. 5. Nam sordibus de templo
265 Salomonis eiectis templum manebat. Christus et apostoli in synagogis et templis Iudaeorum docebant, Matt. 21. Act. 4. 5. I Cor. 11. 13. 14. 15. 16. Et solus
finis aut abusus damnatur in templis missaticis, materia vero et forma
nusquam (ut in idolis hostia missatica) damnantur, illorum enim tantum
forma damnatur, quaecunque adorata sunt, Deut. 4. 5. 6. 7. Sed templa non
270 sunt adorata per se, sed per accidens, propter missam, aram, idola. His remotis

---

249 Kamuriim] cfr Soph. 1, 4   **253** Domini – eius] Ps. 23, 1   **253/254** Nemo –
potu] Col. 2, 16

243 15] cfr *Confessio catholica* (1562), Articles 90-91, 96, and 128, in *RefBK*, vol. 2/2
(2009), p. 62-63, 67-69, and 91-92 respectively; *Hungarian Creed* (1567), in *BaM*,
p. 197-201   **260** 16] cfr *Confessio catholica* (1562), Article 127, in *RefBK*, vol. 2/2
(2009), p. 91; *Hungarian Creed* (1567), in *BaM*, p. 201-202

243 15] *add. in marg. tit.* Reliquiae missaticae abiiciendae *C*   **265** synagogis] *correxi,*
sinagogis *C E*   **266** I] *supplevi, om. C E*   16] *false add.* 17. *E*

CONCILIUM DEBRECENIENSE – 1567

loca pura sunt, scriptum est enim, Psal. 95. 97. 105. 107. *Non facies ullam simili-
tudinem et non adorabis eam*, Exod. 20.

[17]

Cantus usum, tanquam doctrinae, adhortationis et cultus divini partem,
cum Scriptura sacra recipimus, I Cor. 14. *Docentes admonentes vos per psalmos,
hymnos et cantiones*, Ephe. 5. Col. 3. Sed ut lingua intellecta canatur. Insaniunt
enim et destruunt teste apostolo, qui in coetu docent, canunt sine mente,
intellectu coram idiotis et barbaris, lingua ignota reboant. Pie symbolum et
orationes aut angeli cantus, antiphonae decantari possunt. Organa vero musi-
ca, saltatrici missae Antichristi accomodata cum idolis eiicimus, quia nullus
eorum usus in ecclesia, imo signa idolatriae sunt et occasiones.

[18]

Neminem sine ordinatione, probatione in doctrina et moribus citra ecclesiae iudicium admittimus, quia scriptum est, I Tim. 3. Tit. 1. 3. *Hi probentur
prius, et sic ministrent. Ipsi currebant, et ego non mittebam. Seligite mihi Paulum et Barnabam*, Rom. 8. 9. 10. Acto. 11. 13. Nemo ergo sine vocatione currat,
sed sint omnes electi in officium, vocati, ordinati et examinati. Nunquam enim
prophetae et apostoli sine legitima vocatione docuerunt, Ebr. 5. 7. 8. I Cor. 11.
13. Nemo sibi honorem docendi usurpet, nisi vocetur, ut Aaron.

271/272 Ex. 20, 4-5   **275/276** Eph. 5, 19; Col. 3, 16   **284/285** Hi – ministrent]
I Tim. 3, 10   **285** Ipsi – mittebam] Ier. 23, 21   **285/286** Seligite – Barnabam] Act.
13, 2

273 17] cfr *Confessio catholica* (1562), Articles 92 and 138; *Confessio Helvetica Posterior*
(1566), par. 23, in *RefBK*, vol. 2/2 (2009), p. 63-64, 97-98, and 335-336 respectively;
Hungarian Creed (1567), in *BaM*, p. 199-200   **282** 18] cfr *Confessio catholica* (1562),
Article 181; *Confessio Helvetica Posterior* (1566), par. 18, in *RefBK*, vol. 2/2 (2009),
p. 131-132 and 316-323 respectively

273 17] *add. in marg. tit.* Hymni, Psalmi et cantiones in ecclesia ad aedificationem
vernacula lingua cum intellectu decantari debet *C*   **282** 18] *add. in marg. tit.* Nemo
admitti debet ad ministerium ecclesiasticum absque iudicio et ordinatione ecclesiae *C*

466 CONCILIUM DEBRECENIENSE – 1567

290

[19]

Sicut uni et certo loco ordinationem non alligamus papistico more, ita indoctis et rudibus probationem et examen facere ex Scripturae fundamentis nescientibus non permittimus, I Tim. 3. 4. 5. II Tim. 1. 2. 3. Act. 1. 13. Nam apostolus Timotheum seniorum suffragio electum esse docet. Et Matthias in 295 senatu apostolorum, Paulus et Barnabas in ecclesia et synodo electi sunt. Fiant ergo ordinationes aut in synodis aut in praesbyterorum collegio a doctis et probatis ecclesiae praelatis et superintendente. [...]

[44]

Sicut totum ministerium docendi, loquendi in ecclesia mulieribus inter-300 dictum est, ita sacramentorum administratio, baptismi et coenae illis interdic-ta est ex verbo Dei. Impie ergo faciunt, qui sub praetextu falsae necessitatis obstetricibus baptizandi munus infantes in articulo mortis concedunt, cum verbum Dei contrarium doceat: *mulieri docere non permitto, ne loquantur, sed taceant in ecclesiis,* I Tim. 2. 3. 4. I Corin. 14.

305

[45]

Omnium aetatum homines, infantes, maiores nondum baptizatos, omnes creaturas, hoc est, omnes homines omnium aetatum Scriptura docere et bapti-zare iubet, Matt. 18. Igitur et nos oblatos ecclesiae, recipientes doctrinam et religionem, qui non sunt canes et porci, docere et baptizare iubemus, Marc. 16.
310 Qui autem reiiciunt verbum Dei et religionis christianae fundamentum, nec audire sermonem Dei volunt, his sacramentum baptismi et coenae non administramus, ut sunt Cygari multi et similes apostatae. *Nolite sanctum dare canibus.* Hos etiam copulari a ministris prohibemus.

294/295 Et – sunt] cfr Act. 1, 26; 13, 2-3; 15, 25 **303/304** I Tim. 2, 12; cfr I Cor. 14, 34 **307/308** omnes – iubet] cfr Matth. 28, 19-20 **309** canes et porci] cfr Matth. 7, 6 **312/313** Matth. 7, 6

---

290 19] *add. in marg. tit.* Examen et ordinatio ministrorum publice in Synodis fieri debet *C* **296** praesbyterorum] *sic* **305** 45] *add. in marg. tit.* Omnium aetatum et gentium homines oblati ecclesiae Dei recipiendi et baptizandi sunt *C* **308** Matt. 18] *sic* **312** ut – apostatae] *add. in marg. tit.* Cygari et similes apostata [*sic*] carentes fundamento verae religionis non sunt admittandi ad baptismum et caenam Domini *C*

CONCILIUM DEBRECENIENSE – 1567

[46]

Quia *omnia tempus habent*, ideo boni ordinis et pacis causa publico ministerio, scilicet docendi et administrandi sacramenta, tempus et locum aptum deligimus, ut decenter fiant omnia, Eccle. 4. Rom. 12. 13. 14. 14. Act. 1. 2. 3. Et apostoli certis horis ad templum Salomonis ascendebant. Qui inter convivia et nuptias sacramenta administrant, postquam referti sunt epulis, eos ecclesia detestatur, tanquam eutaxias, boni ordinis violatores. Et in veteri testamento sacrificandi ritui tempus designatum erat.

[47]

Sicut fures, adulteros, maledicos, periuros, ita ebriosos post unam et alteram admonitionem excommunicatione puniendos cum Scriptura pronunciamus, Rom. 13. I Corin. 6. II Cor. 6. Ephe. 5. 6. Ebrietas enim cognatum malum est fornicationi et propter malum ebrietatis captivitatem hostilem et mortem minatur Dominus, Esa. 5. Mich. 6. 7. Hab. 1. 3. Amos. 5. 6. 7. Imo qui ludunt ebriosorum sordibus et rident super eorum malitia, eos quoque damnat Dominus, et qui alios vino ingurgitant violenter, aut sub fuco et praetextu amicitiae, eos quoque damnat Scriptura, Hab. 1. 2.

Principes et iudices ebriosos non punientes, sed in aula sua eos retinentes Dominus iudicabit.

[48]

Pastores iustum et aequum iudicamus, ut citati a laicis in ius primum coram iudice proprio, hoc est, coram senatu seniorum iudicentur. Deinde et appellationi ad regem et sedes iudiciarias non contradicant. Nam oportet omnes subiici suis magistratibus clericos et laicos, Rom. 13. I Pet. 2. 4. 5. Neque libertate filiorum offendiculo simus aliis, ne habeant occasionem maledicendi nos adversarii Iesu Christi.

---

315 Eccl. 3, 1   **329** qui – violenter] cfr Hab. 2, 5 et 15-16

314 46] cfr *Confessio catholica* (1562), Article 127, in *RefBK*, vol. 2/2 (2009), p. 91
322 47] cfr *Confessio catholica* (1562), Article 177, in *RefBK*, vol. 2/2 (2009), p. 130

314 46] *add. in marg. tit.* Omnes ministerii partes convenienti tempore et loco peragi debent *C*   **322** 47] *add. in marg. tit.* Qui excommunicatione puniendi *C*

468 CONCILIUM DEBRECENIENSE – 1567

340 [49]

Non oves pastorem, sed pastor regit oves. Ideo et concionatores ex verbo Dei regant ecclesias suas, neque assentatorum et hypocritarum ventosis criminationibus circunferantur, aut fascinate ad nutum adulatorum doceant, sed contra portas inferorum veritatem dicant et doceant invito Diabolo et impiis
345 hominibus, Ioan. 10. Ezech. 33. 34.

[50]

Tempestive et intempestive pastores veri ex verbo Dei peccata et scelera omnium ordinum, regum, principum, nobilium, subditorum arguant et increpent, sicut tuba exaltent voces suas et non parcant, Esai. 58. Ezech. 3. 18. 33.
350 Hier. 18. II Tim. 3. 4. Qui vero peccatis parcunt, iudicamus canes mutos esse. Tempestive cum publice docent in coetu ecclesiae, intempestive, id est, privatim, etiam extra coetum et suggestum.

[51]

Ecclesias, pagos, villas et civitates duplici honore suos pastores non prae-
355 venientes, sed quae operarios iusta mercede et cibo defraudant, in peccatis regnantibus vivunt, eos deserendos et pastore privandos et Satanae tradendos, qui non obediunt veritati, pro publicanis habendos Scriptura iubet, Matt. 10. 18. Rom. 6. 13. II Thess. 3.

[52]

360 Sicut excommunicatio et depositio ab ecclesia et synodis fieri debet post cognitionem et delictorum requisitionem per testes, Matt. 18. II Tim. 5., ita assumtio aut reconciliatio ab ecclesia fieri debet. Sicut apostolus in exemplo incoesti eiecti et recepti docet, II Cor. 2.

---

349 sicut – parcant] cfr Is. 58, 1   **350** canes mutos] cfr Is. 56, 10

340 49] *add. in marg. tit.* Officium pastorum ecclesiae *C*   **353** 51] *add. in marg. tit.* Quales coetus sint pastoribus et verbo Dei privandi *C*   **355** quae] *om. C E*   **359** 52] *add. in marg. tit.* Excommunicatio, depositio et assumtio in ecclesia fieri debet *C*

CONCILIUM DEBRECENIENSE – 1567

[53]

365 Catechesin, hoc est, Symboli et Orationis Dominicae et Decalogi compendiosam et brevem explicationem in ecclesiis retineri volumus, ut sit introductio ad perfectiora, Ebr. 5. 6. Gala. 5. 6. Et tempore apostolorum erant catechizantes, qui religionis fundamenta iuxta Symbolum Apostolorum proponebant.

370 [54]

Sicut nulla luci cum tenebris participatio, fideli cum infideli, I Corin. 10. 11. II Cor. 6., ita sacris ritibus et sepulturae impiorum et hypocritarum minis- tros adesse nolumus, quia scriptum est: *Sine, ut mortui sepelliant suos mortuos.* Et quicunque corpus, fundamentum doctrinae, verbum Dei contemnunt et 375 non audiunt, illis nec in sacramentorum administratione nec copulandi ritu ministrari permittimus, ut dicitur: *Nolite sanctum dare canibus. Si non recepe- rint vos, exite*, Matt. 7. 10.

[55]

Peccata, quae Scriptura morte plectenda iudicat, ut homicidium, fornica- 380 tionem, periurium, idolatrium, adulterium, incoestum, scortationem aut foedam pollutionem cum masculis et iumentis, ut Levit. 18. 19. 20. Et universa- le praeceptum est de fornicationibus Levit. 18. 19. Quicunque ex his omnibus malis et abominationibus quacunque ratione fornicatus fuerit, sive sit ille in matrimonio, sive extra matrimonium, liberae personae, tamen succidantur 385 animae illorum et moriantur ambo, adulter et adultera, fornicator liber extra coniugium et fornicatrix. Nam adulteros et fornicatores Deus iudicabit et con- demnabit, I Cor. 5. 7. Ephe. 5. Gal. 5. 6. Ebrae. 12. 13.

---

371 nulla – participatio] cfr II Cor. 6, 14-15   **373** Luc. 9, 60   **376** Nolite – canibus] Matth. 7, 6   **376/377** Si – exite] Matth. 10, 14

364 53] cfr *Confessio Helvetica Posterior* (1566), par. 25, in *RefBK*, vol. 2/2 (2009), p. 338-339

364 53] *add. in marg. tit.* Catechesis in ecclesiis docenda *C*   **370** 54] *add. in marg. tit.* Ministri ecclesiae contemptoribus verbi Dei suam operam locare non debent *C* **378** 55] *add. in marg. tit.* Quae et qualia peccata sint morte digna *C*

470 CONCILIUM DEBRECENIENSE – 1567

Nam ut coniugatis prohibetur adulterium, ita et inconiugatis, et ut coniugati mortem merentur, ita et inconiugati. Sic enim scriptum: Si quis duxerit
390 puellam uxorem, et non fuerit virgo, morte moriatur et lapidibus obruatur,
Deu. 22. Si quis oppresserit virginem desponsatam in civitate vel pago, ambo
moriantur, puella, quia non clamavit, vir, quia uxorem proximi humiliavit.
Item Levi. 20. 21. *Filia sacerdotis si fornicata fuerit, exuratur. Tolletis malum de
medio vestro*, Deut. 22. Placatur autem ira Dei, cum malefici tolluntur de vita
395 et adulteri et fornicatores occiduntur. Sicut Moses patres per filios et contra
occidi iussit propter utrunque malum, propter vituli adorationem, et quia
postquam edit et bibit, surrexit ludere, etiam carnaliter fornicati sunt. Et cum
populus cum Madianitis fornicaretur, accensa erat ira Dei in populum, sed
Phinees scortatorem cum meretrice transfigens placavit iram Dei, Num. 25.
400 I Cor. 10. Impie faciunt igitur magistratus, iudices et officiales, qui adulteros et
adulteras, fornicatores, scorta publica muleta pecuniaria aut flagellatione levi
puniunt, non autem morte, sicut Dominus iudicat et praecipit. Senes, qui
Susannam opprimere volebant, Daniel occidere iubet. Et pii reges, Daniel,
Iosaphat et patres Abraham, Isaac, Iacob capitali poena puniebant fornicatores
405 et adulteros. Sicut Iudas, cum videt Thamar factam esse gravidam, morti adiu-
dicat, Gene. 18. *Producite Thamar et comburatur*. Propter fornicationem et
ebrietatem, idolatriam diluvio periit mundus. Sodoma, Gomorrha propter
foedam scortationem submersae sunt, Gene. 6. 7. 8. 18. 19. Iudic. 20. Propter
stupratam Levitae uxorem Beniamitae trucidantur. Damnat propheta et eos,
410 qui vino multant et puniunt reos, ut vulgus rusticorum factitat, Amos 2. *Vir et
pater ibant ad puellam ad fornicandum et super vestimentis oppignoratis accum-
bebant et vinum eorum bibebant, qui puniebantur, sed vae illis, quia prophanant
sanctum nomen meum*. Tales igitur ex verbo Dei detestamur.

389/390 Si – obruatur] cfr Deut. 22, 20-21   **391/392** Si – humiliavit] cfr Deut.
22, 23-27 **393** Filia – exuratur] Leu. 21, 8 **393/394** Tolletis – vestro] Deut. 22, 21 et
24 **395/397** Sicut – sunt] cfr Ex. 32, 6 et 27 **397/399** Et – Dei] cfr Num. 25, 7-8
402/403 Senes – iubet] Dan. 13, 59 et 62 **406** Gen. 38, 24 **408/409** Propter –
trucidantur] cfr Iud. 20, 48 **410/413** Am. 2, 7-8

---

398 Madianitis] *sic* **406** Gene. 18] *sic* **410** 2] *add. f. C E*

CONCILIUM DEBRECENIENSE – 1567

[56]

415 Reges et principes, magistratus, officiales et iudices Spiritus S. sanctos et inculpatos esse iubet et iuste dominari, II Samuel. 23. Psal. 101. Quomodo enim alios punient, si rei sunt malorum ipsi, propter quae alios occident? Negat apostolus cum Abraham, Gene. 18. Rom. 3., Deum iudicem mundi et ultorem esse posse, si respiceret ad peccata et in peccatis delectaretur vel
420 peccata ad gloriam suam fieri iudicaret. Principes Biblia sacra prae manibus habeant et praeferant iudicium Dei in Mose et Prophetis descriptum omnium imperatorum decretis. Deus enim est veritas, iustitia, lux. Sancte et vere igitur de omnibus iudicat. Et si autem in legibus forensibus species quaedam Iudaeos respiciunt solos, tamen genus earum specierum omnes gentes. Sicut Decalogus
425 ad omnes gentes pertinet, ita genus legum divinarum ad omnem populum et nationes. Lux igitur et norma sit lex et iudicium Dei in omnibus populorum legibus et iudiciis, Psalm. 51. Rom. 3. *Sit Deus verax, omnis homo mendax.* Decreta mentiri possunt contra Deum scripta, Deus autem non.

Impie igitur faciunt, qui propter longam et foedam consuetudinem leges
430 et iudicia reiiciunt, praesertim propter decreta. Moris est nobis adulteria taurina mulcta, flagellis punire. Ita nobis usu venit a longo tempore, decreta sic habent, etiamsi lex Dei contrarium dicat. Tales nugae audiant, Matt. 23. Vae qui reiicitis praecepta et traditiones Dei propter traditiones vestras falsas. Vide II Samuel. 23. Psal. 81. 82. 101., quam sanctitatem Dominus a magistratibus
435 requirat, quicunque igitur peccata et delicta non puniunt, dicimus eos currere cum furibus, cum adulteris portionem ponere, Psal. 50. 53. Hos socios furum, id est, omnium malorum Scriptura vocat, Esai. 1. et Mich. 6. 7. Esai. 25. 26. 31. Damnat Spiritus S. iudices, qui adulantur principibus et impiis eorum postulatis, mandatis contra Deum obediunt. Princeps postulat, iudex reddit, id est,
440 iudices, officiales iniusta mandata exequuntur. Uram, mongya, Istenre mondom, minden marhaiát el vészem. Spoliant, occidunt, mulctant, depraedantur iniuste innocentes propter principum tyrannidem. Consentiunt maleficis, qui peccata maleficorum non puniunt, Rom. 1. 2. 3. Sentientes autem et consen-

---

418/419 Negat – delectaretur] cfr Rom. 3, 6   **427** Rom. 3, 4   **435/436** eos – ponere] cfr Ps. 50, 18   **436/437** Hos – vocat] cfr Is. 1, 23

414 56] cfr *Confessio catholica* (1562), Articles 114-115; *Confessio brevis* (1567), in *RefBK*, vol. 2/2 (2009), p. 80-81 and 358-359 respectively

414 56] *add. in marg. tit.* Principes et magistratus, officiales et iudices quales esse oporteat, quibus legibus et decretis utantur, et peccata pro meritis puniant *C*   **440/441** Uram – vészem] *Hungarice, translata:* 'Domine, inquit, pro Deo omnia bona eius diripio'

CONCILIUM DEBRECENIENSE – 1567

tientes simul condemnabuntur. Universale mandatum est ad principes: Male-
445 ficos ne patiaris vivere, Exod. 21. 22. Deut. 22. Princeps ideo gerit gladium, ut
puniat malos, Rom. 13. David ita loquitur: Cito, mane maleficos tollam de
aula mea, de civitate Dei, adulator, impius, idolatra, maledicus, depraedator,
ebriosi mihi non ministrabunt, Psal. 101. Sed hos eiiciam.

Sed heus: Nunc principum aula hac colluvie malorum reserta est, paucos
450 invenias, qui haec mala detestentur, iuste, sobrie vivant.

Ideo autem ebrietas fugienda est principibus et omnibus, quia parit
asotiam, id est, luxum, fornicationem, homicidium, corda piorum aggravat et
excludit a regno Dei, I Cor. 6. 7. Nolite vino inebriari, quia in ipsa ingurgita-
tione luxus, intemperantia, fornicatio est, Osae. 4. Ephe. 4. 5. *Vinum et forni-*
455 *catio cor auferunt.* Nabuchodonozor, Darius, Artaxerxes, Balthasar puniti sunt
propter ebrietatem eo, quod se et alios vino ingurgitarent, Gen. 19. Hab. 1. 2.
Dan. 5. 6. Loth vino inebriatus foedam cum filiabus pollutionem fecit. Ex his
pronunctiamus, quicunque ex principibus ebriosos et maleficos non puniunt,
contra mandatum Dei peccare graviter.

460   [57]

Scriptura suis limitibus circumscripsit et limitavit, Exo. 21. 22. Deu. 19. 21.
22. Levi. 24., quibus gratia regis dari possit, sic: Si quis volens occiderit hominem, morte moriatur, qui non volens, nec insidiatus est, ille ne moriatur.
Solius Dei est remittere peccata, dare veniam, deinde pastorum munus est in
465 nomine Dei solvere, ligare, remittere et non condemnare, Matt. 18. 28. Ioan.
20. Perperam principes haec ad se trahunt. Non esset Deus iustus, si peccata
non puniret, quomodo igitur principes peccata inulta dimittere possunt, cum
praecipiatur illis: Tollite maleficos et ne patiaris vivere, Exo. 22. 23. Levi. 20.
Num. 35. Mortem minatur Dominus populo et principi, qui negligunt reorum
470 punitionem: *Vae, inquit Dominus, qui iustificat et absolvit impium, reum mor-*
tis, adulterum, homicidam propter munus, Esa. 1. 5. Pro. 17. Mich. 4. 5. 6. 7.
David cum non posset reos mortis occidere, filio suo Salomoni testamento

---

444/445 Maleficos – vivere] cfr Ex. 22, 17   **445/446** Princeps – malos] cfr Rom.
13, 4   **446/448** Cito – eiiciam] cfr Ps. 101, 7-8   **452** asotiam] cfr Eph. 5, 18; Tit. 1, 6;
I Petr. 4, 4   **454/455** Os. 4, 11   **457** Loth – fecit] cfr Gen. 19, 32-36   **468** Tollite –
vivere] cfr Ex. 22, 17   **470/471** Is. 5, 23; cfr Ex. 23, 6-8; Prou. 17, 15   **472/**
473 David – capitalia] cfr III Reg. 2, 6 et 9

451 Ideo] *add. in marg. tit.* Ebrietas principibus et omnibus cur serio sit cavenda C
458 pronunctiamus] *sic*   **460** 57] *add. in marg. tit.* Qui et quales malefici sunt venia
et gratia digni, qui vero non? C

CONCILIUM DEBRECENIENSE – 1567

legat, ut rei mortis occidantur propter peccata capitalia, III Reg. 1. 2. 3. Maior est ergo Dei autoritas, quam hominum consuetudo. De his infra copiosius.

[58]

Sicut loca conventus sanctorum pura et ab omnibus sordibus aliena esse debent, ne transeuntium sint cloaca aut porcorum harae, ita et a foetidis sepulturarum contaminationibus aliena esse oportet, propter has rationes:

1. Scandalum est vitandum, neque infirmi abusu nostrae libertatis offendendi sunt, quia vae per quem venit scandalum, I Corin. 8. 10. Mat. 18. Sed in terra prophana et papisticis sordibus incantata cum papistis sepellire est occasio scandali teste apostolo, I Cor. 8. 10. Nam sicut idolothyta tanquam daemoniis sacrata edebant impii cum conscientia idoli, ita papistae cum conscientia idoli et prophanae contaminationis utuntur coemiteriis, aliquam sanctitatem et religionem propter incantationem papisticam terrae illi tribuentes. Si igitur ibidem et eodem loco sepelliant et christiani, scandalo erunt infirmis. Nam iudicantur ab infirmis et papistis cum conscientia papistica eo sensu et fine et pios in eo loco sepellire, quo papistae. Iubet ergo apostolus ab idolio, de sacris impiorum egredi, ne offendantur infirmi ignorantes propter conscientiae nostrae libertatem.

2. Christus, patriarchae extra civitatem, extra locum conventus habuerunt sepulturae suae loca, Gen. 23. Abraham ab Ephron pecunia emit speluncam duplicem pro sepulchro.

Christus extra civitatem sepultus est, Ebre. 13. Mat. 27. Et omnes pii reges extra synagogas sepulti sunt. Nunquam in eodem loco sepulti sunt, ubi sacrificarunt aut docuerunt. Impie faciunt igitur, qui in terra a papistis foedata cum multorum scandalo suos mortuos sepelliunt.

---

480 vae – scandalum] cfr Matth. 18, 7   **488** idolio] cfr I Cor. 8, 10

494/497 Christus – sepelliunt] cfr *Confessio catholica* (1562), Article 175; *Confessio Helvetica Posterior* (1566), par. 26, in *RefBK*, vol. 2/2 (2009), p. 129 and 339-340 respectively; *Hungarian Creed* (1567), in *BaM*, p. 213-214

475 58] *add. in marg. tit.* Loca publica conventus piorum qualis [*sic*] esse debent *C*
494 Christus] *add. in marg. tit.* Coemiteria piorum ubi et qualia esse debent *C*

474 CONCILIUM DEBRECENIENSE – 1567

[59]

Displicet Spiritui Sancto et nobis Christum cum Belial, iusticiam cum
500 iniquitate in unum iugum velle coniungere.

In eodem templo et loco docere, sacramenta administrare, ubi daemoniis
sacrificant, missarum idolomania et reliquiae abominationes perficiuntur, sit
fornicatio foeda. Idque propter has rationes:

Nam ut ecclesia malignantium, ita et loca eorum ab initio, a Cain usque
505 ad apostolorum tempora distincta fuerunt. Soli Deo in templo Salomonis
offerebatur. Impiis vero, Ieroboam, Iezabel et Achab in Samaria locus prophanationis erat.

2. Beatus vir, qui non abiit in caetum impiorum et non audivit voces
incantantium et luporum, Psal. 1. Sed in eodem templo esse, docere, ut Budae,
510 Pestini et alibi audiuntur abominationes et foedae prophanationes Dei sine
contradictione, impossibile est, templum Dei et domum Dei posse locum eundem et etiam locum esse Belial. Christus eiecit mercatores ementes et venden-
tes, Matt. 21.

3. Quia scriptum est: Non est bonum in tabernaculis impiorum manere,
515 Esai. 52. II Cor. 9. *Exite de medio eorum, immundum ne tangatis*, a tabernaculis
et coetu Core, Datan, Abiron, hominum impiorum separemini, Psal. 84.

4. Quia nullum testimonium, nec idoneum exemplum reperiri potest
sanctos cum impiis in eodem templo, domo et synagoga obtulisse et perpetuo
in uno loco mansisse. Oves enim Christi voces mercenariorum fugiunt et non
520 audiunt, Ioan. 10.

5. Quia Scriptura iubet destrui idola, lucos excindi, aras diruere, ubi sacrificant. Iubet tolli missae idolomaniam. Quomodo igitur christiani in lupanari
Antichristi, papae manebunt? Separentur ergo a tabernaculis impiorum et
propria loca ad conveniendum habeant.

525 [60]

Sicut a tempore Cain et Abel semper vera et visibilis ecclesia seu coetus
electorum, cui admixti fuerunt semper hypocritae, perinde ac tritico zizania,

---

499/500 Christum – coniungere] cfr II Cor. 6, 15   **508/509** Beatus – luporum] cfr
Ps. 1, 1   **515** Is. 52, 11; II Cor. 6, 17   **519/520** Oves – audiunt] cfr Ioh. 10, 4-5

498 59] cfr *Confessio catholica* (1562), Article 127, in *RefBK*, vol. 2/2 (2009), p. 91;
Hungarian Creed (1567), in *BaM*, p. 201-202

502 idolomania] *correxi*, idolomonia *E*   **515** II Cor. 9] *sic*

CONCILIUM DEBRECENIENSE – 1567

coetui bonorum piscium pisces mali, qui vento Dei ventillabuntur et igni Dei,
ut separati a tritico fuerint, comburrentur, Mat. 3. 7. 8. 13. A falsa et impiorum
530 vel malignantium coetu, ut templum Salomonis a templo Samariae Ieroboam
idolatricorum, qui coetus reiecta vera Dei cognitione excaecatus per Satanam
et Antichristum, per impiaque dogmata excaecati sunt mente sua, reiecta veritate credunt mendacio, reiicientes praecepta et mandata, caeremonias et instituta Dei Bibliisque sacris Antichristi, Papae traditiones, doctrinas, instituta,
535 missas abominandas sequuntur, quae sunt stercora, stipulae, vanae deceptio-
nes, quae eradicabuntur et destruentur, ut Spiritus S. inquit. Ita ergo et nunc hi
duo coetus ut professione, doctrina, fide, institutis, tessaris distinguuntur, ut
conventuum et congregationum publicarum locis distinguantur oportet. Ut
enim impossibile est Christum et Beliial convenire et unum esse posse, ita
540 impossibile veram Dei ecclesiam (quae est corpus et sponsa Christi) posse
unam esse. Ut lupi cum ovibus, peccatum cum iustitia, lux cum tenebris, vita
aeterna et gehenna, mors unum non sunt, ita ecclesia sancta, catholica et ecclesia malignantium una esse non potest. Ut autem hypocritae paulatim et sensim
deficiunt de coetu sanctorum, ita de coetu malignantium quotidie apponen-
545 tur, qui salvi fiant. Nam ut vasa irae salvari impossibile est, ita electos perire
impossibile, quotidie ergo de medio impiorum electi colliguntur, Roma 3. 8. 9.
10. 11. Ephe. 1. 2. 3. 4. 5. Tit. 1. 2. 3. I Tim. 1. 2. 3. II Tim. 1. 2. Act. 1. 2. 3. 4. 5. 6.
7. 10. 11. 13. 16. Esai. 8. 9. 10. 54. Et ergo differunt haec duo: *Christus dilexit
ecclesiam et se tradidit pro ea.* Item: *Odivi ecclesiam malignantium.* Psal. 26. 37.
550 64. Igitur coetus piorum una est ecclesia catholica, quae in donis caelestibus,
in causis salutis, in spirituali unione est invisibilis, sed in fructu, professione,
operibus et personis homninum respectu visibilis. Impiorum vero coetus est
altera ecclesia, in quam prohibet Spiritus S., ne beati viri et electi veniant, Psal.
1. 15. 64.

555   [61]

Haereticos veritate Scripturae convictos, perfidos, generales ecclesiae consensus turbantes et in veritate doctrinae non persistentes, sed Deo et toti

---

528/529 qui – comburrentur] cfr Matth. 3, 12; 13, 30; 13, 40-42   **548/549** Eph. 5, 25
549 Ps. 26, 5

555 61] cfr *Confessio catholica* (1562), Article 113; *Confessio brevis* (1567), par. 1, and
par. 10, in *RefBK*, vol. 2/2 (2009), p. 80, 361-364, and 376-377 respectively

539 Beliial] *sic*   **555** 61] *add. in marg. tit.* Haeretici verbo Dei convicti si pergant
contumaces esse, cavendi sunt *C*

476 CONCILIUM DEBRECENIENSE – 1567

Scripturae sacrae repugnantes, patrum orthodoxorum et modernorum ecclesiae doctorum confessiones, scripta, iudicia reiicientes et damnantes et suas
560 opiniones haereticas stabilientes, quae singulis diebus et horis variantur,
tanquam solido fundamento carentes, velut arundines, stipulas, post multas
iam admonitiones devitamus, quia praeter logomachian, antitheses pseudonymu gnoseos nihil habent. Et in convitia et blasphemiam erumpunt, ut
Sabellius, Ebion, Arrius, Servetus et Servetici, I Tim. 1. 3. 4. 6. II Tim. 1. 2.
565 3. [...]

[63]

Ex verbo Dei contra furores novi Anabaptistae, Serveti statuimus infantes
cum maioribus baptizandos esse propter has rationes.
1. Res sacramenti, foedus ipsum, iustitia, vita, ingressus in ecclesia, regene-
570 ratio pertinet etiam ad infantes electorum ex pacto Dei. Ergo et signum illis
dandum est, Gen. 17. 22. Esai. 59. *Ero Deus tuus et seminis tui. Non auferam*
Spiritum meum et verba a te et semine tuo.
2. Christus iubet sibi afferri Zeirim et Nearim, id est, brephi kae poedia
Mar. 9. 10. et Luca interpraetibus cap. 18. Hoc est, infantes et puellulos, et
575 arguit apostolos prohibentes. Hos Christus in ulnas recipit, benedicit et dicit
in se credere, Matth. 18. Mar. 9. 10. Nisi autem fuissent pusilli et infantes ab
uberibus pendentes, in ulnas non recepisset. Ergo tingendi sunt infantes.
Impieque nugantur Servetici canes infantes non credere, non audire, non
discere, non regenerari, non sanctificari, quia a Deo Patre in Christi merito
580 ope Spiritus S. in arcana schola audiunt, discunt, credunt, placent Deo, ideo
credunt, quia sine fide nemo placet, Ebr. 11. Rom. 10. 14. Matt. 18. 19.
3. Circuncisi sunt infantes et mandato Dei, Gene. 17. Sed circuncisioni
successit baptismus, ut apostolus confert, Rom. 2. 4. 6. Col. 2. 3. Et plane eiusdem rei sunt sigilla et notae, regenerationis scilicet et ingressus in ecclesiam,
585 Col. 2. 3. Deut. 10. Ergo et infantes tingendi sunt. De similibus enim idem est
iudicium.

562/563 antitheses pseudonymu gnoseos] cfr I Tim. 6, 20   **571** Gen. 17, 7   **571/**
572 Is. 59, 21   **573** brephi kae poedia] Luc. 18, 15

566 63] cfr *Hungarian Creed* (1567), in *BaM*, p. 217-222

563 in convitia] *sic*   **566** 63] *add. in marg. tit.* Infantes cum adultis baptizandi sunt *C*
569 ingressus in ecclesia] *sic*   **574** interpraetibus] *sic*

CONCILIUM DEBRECENIENSE – 1567

4. Quarto, universale praeceptum: Ite in mundum, docete et baptizate omnes, qui crediderit, salvus erit. Maiores a ministris immediate foris docentur et discunt. Infantes vero mediate docentur foris per eos, qui illos ecclesiae offerunt, intus a Spiritu S. docentur et virtute Spiritus S. credunt. Credunt autem, ut Matt. 18. 19. Mar. 10. 9. Luc. 18.

5. Apostolus Paulus totam domum Stephanae baptizavit. Ad Ioannem tota Iudaea exibat, inter quos fuerunt et infantes, sicut historiae docent, I Cor. 1. Mat. 1. Luc. 3. Io. 1. 2. Omnes ergo venientes ad baptismum cum catholici et Apostolici Symboli confessione, id est, quicunque testantur se religionem, fidem, doctrinam recipere, approbare ea, quae in Symbolo Apostolico continentur. Sicut pro symbolo et tessera, nota et signo fuit symbolum ab initio in ecclesia, ut ex cap. Ebre. 5. 6. Gal. 6. colligi potest. Caetera argumenta et testimonia vide in libello Ungarico de Triade scripto anno 1567. in Augusto edito, ubi argutiae et argumenta Serveti refutantur.

[64]

Docemus ex verbo Dei blasphemos, haereticos vera doctrina legitime convictos et damnatos reos esse mortis, ab ecclesia eiiciendos, a magistratibus autem iure gladii occidendos. Ut Sabelliani, Servetici, Arriani, Fotiniani, qui distinctionem hypostaseon proprietate, persona, manifestatione et dispensatione realem ac veram Trinitatem negant et soli Patri unitatem deitatis, personae, substantiae tribuentes in Patre somniant logon et Spiritum S. esse hypostaticas virtutes. Sicut in homine anima est substantia et anima habet partes substantiales, sed tamen unus est homo, extra unum hominem anima et substantiales partes nihil sunt. Ita extra Patris substantiam et hypostasin negant Sabelliani Filium et Spiritum S. subsistere, proprietatem in se subsistentem et incommunicabilem habere, cum omne proprium incommunicabile sit et propriam hypostasin constituat. Pater Filius esse persona, nomine et proprietate non potest et contra. Et manifeste scriptum est: Sicut Pater in se habet vitam, ita dedit et Filio in se habere vitam seu subsistentiam. Ergo Pater in se et Filius in se subsistit. Scriptura item Patrem et Filium vocat duos, Patrem vero, Filium et Spiritum S. tres testes. Quaecunque autem numero, proprietate, hypostasi differunt et distinguuntur, una natura quidem sunt, sed

---

587/588 Ite – erit] cfr Matth. 28, 19-20 et Marc. 16, 16   **592** Apostolus – baptizavit] cfr I Cor. 1, 16   **592/593** Ad – exibat] Matth. 3, 5   **614/615** Sicut – subsistentiam] cfr Ioh. 5, 26   **617** tres testes] cfr I Ioh. 5, 7

594 Mat. 1] *sic*   **601** 64] *add. in marg. tit.* Blasphemi et haeretici verbo Dei convicti ab ecclesia eiiciendi et a magistratibus occidendi sunt *C*

CONCILIUM DEBRECENIENSE – 1567

una hypostasis numero et proprietate esse non possunt, ut Petrus, Iacobus,
620 Ioannes distinguuntur proprietatibus, una persona ergo non sunt. Tertio,
manifestationibus in utroque testamento, Patri, Filio et Spiritui S. distincte et
seorsim hypostases tribuuntur, ut tres virorum formae, vox sonans, columba et
viri forma in baptismo.

Docemus ex ore Dei haereticos, id est, qui contra Dei veram unitatem,
625 essentiam et Trinitatem, contra Filii et Spiritus S. divinitatem et contra Dei
voluntatem in Bibliis et symbolis patefactam, contra fidei articulos, contra
coelestem doctrinam patrum orthodoxorum et catholicae ecclesiae testimonia
et confessiones consonas Scripturae veritati impiam doctrinam repugnantem
veritati, scindentem ecclesiae unitatem et gignentem scandala et impios erro-
630 res et peccata, pugnas verborum amplectuntur et temere blasphemando, non
obediendo et non acquiescendo sacris sermonibus docent tantum ex suberba
inflatione, invidia, dissensione, scissione, odio, ut Ephe. 5. 6. Gal. 5. 6. Phil. 2.
I Tim. 2. 3. 4. Tit. 2. II Pet. 2. 3. Iud. 1. Apo. 1. 2.

Secundum originem suam per omnes circunstantias haeresis impia et doc-
635 trina haereticorum cangraenae comparata describitur.

Prima ratio haec est: Iubet Spiritus S. peccata mortalia contra primam et
secundam tabulam saeva morte plectenda. Si quis dederit idolo Moloch de
semine, si quis adoraverit idola contemnendo Deum, si quis blasphemaverit
nomen Dei, sabbata mea non custodierit. Si surrexerit falsus propheta, sine
640 miseratione interficiatur et moriatur, Lev. 19. 20. Num 35. Deu. 13.

Secundo: Reges pii et prophetae pii, ut Helias iussit occidi sacerdotes
Baal per subditos, Iosaphat, Iehu, Iosias haereticos et falsos prophetas ex iussu
et mandato Dei occiderunt, III Reg. 18. 19. 22. IV Reg. 4. 6. 10. 23. 25. Ita Hier.
5. 14. et Esai. 5. 56. 58. Ezechielis 13. 14. horrendam mortem haereticis Deus
645 minatur.

Tertio: Apostoli, cum magistratus non occiderent haereticos, divino
fulmine occiderunt, ut Petrus Ananiam, Paulus Alexandrum, Hymaeneum
anathematizavit.

Quarto: Iubet Dominus blasphemum lapidare, Levi. 24. Omnes haeretici
650 sunt blasphemi. Sunt igitur occidendi. Et apostolus post unam et alteram
admonitionem haereticum fugere iubet, Tit. 3. II Timo. 3. 4. Quod autem

---

634/635 Secundum – describitur] cfr II Tim. 2, 17   **637/638** Si – semine] cfr Leu.
20, 2   **639** sabbata – custodierit] cfr Leu. 19, 30   **639/640** Si – moriatur] cfr Deut.
13, 2 et 6   **641/642** Helias – subditos] cfr III Reg. 18, 40   **647/648** Petrus –
anathematizavit] cfr Act. 5, 3-5 et I Tim. 1, 20   **650/651** apostolus – iubet] cfr Tit.
3, 10

---

647 Hymaeneum] *sic*

CONCILIUM DEBRECENIENSE – 1567

obiiciunt quidam: Zizania non esse colligenda, loquitur de hypocritis, de paleis, piscibus malis in sagena bonis admixtis, hoc est, quorum peccata tecta sunt, non manifeste blasphemi, haeretici, homicidae, adulteri, sed latent inter
655 triticum, hos negat extirpandos. Nam hypocritae, impii plures sunt, quam electi. Si isti omnes occidendi essent, totus mundus delendus esset. Zizania ergo, quae adhuc in herbis sunt, non sunt extirpanda, sed cum maturescunt, peccata impiorum haereticorum notoria sunt, iubet Dominus occidi, tolli de medio, ne vivant, Exo. 22. 23. Deut. 17. 18. Levit. 19. 20. Num. 35. [...]

660   [74]

Etsi autem ecclesia vera alligata est verbo Dei, hoc est, scriptis prophetarum et apostolorum, et aedificata est in Christo super petram iuxta illud: *Ad legem et testimonium meum. Scrutamini Scripturas, quia illae sunt, quae de me testantur*, Ioa. 5. *Aedificati super fundamentum prophetarum et apostolorum*,
665 Ephe. 2. Tamen scripta patrum ab Ignatio usque ad Bernardum, qui Graece et Latine scripserunt, quatenus horum scripta Symbolo Apostolico et Scripturis sacris consentiunt et sunt fideles Bibliorum commentarii et expositiones, cum scriptis et confessionibus commentariisque doctorum virorum, qui post revelationem per Lutherum factam scripserunt in ecclesia Christi, quatenus et
670 horum commentarii et confessiones Symbolo Apostolico et Bibliis sacris consentiunt, recipimus et approbamus. Nam agnoscimus piam et catholicam interpretationem Scripturarum donum Dei esse, I Cor. 12., et interpretes, doctores, evangelistas, commentatores sanos et rectos coelitus ecclesiae donari et mitti, Ephe. 4. I Cor. 12. Psal. 68. Stulte, stolide et temere igitur faciunt super-
675 bi et rudes sciolique Servetiani, qui sua stercora, stultas opiniones et iudicia caeca, putidas confessiones et expositiones barbaras dissonasque a veritate Scripturae patrum ortohodoxorum, doctorum fidelium, academiarum piarum, Helveticae, Genevensis et Saxonicae ecclesiae pastorum et doctorum iudiciis, scriptis et confessionibus praeferunt. Imo etiam manifeste Scripturae testimo-
680 nia repugnantia opinioni et haeresi Serveticae detorquent et obscurant. Sym-

---

662/663 Ad – meum] Is. 8, 20   **663/664** Scrutamini – testantur] Ioh. 5, 39
664 Eph. 2, 20

661/682 Etsi – reiiciunt] cfr *Confessio catholica* (1562), Articles 141 and 165-166; *Confessio Helvetica Posterior* (1566), par. 2, in *RefBK*, vol. 2/2 (2009), p. 100-101, 119-121, and 275-276 respectively

660 74] add. in marg. tit. Scripta patrum orthodoxorum et recentium doctorum virorum sana commentaria cum gratiarum actione amplectimur et recipimus *C*

480 CONCILIUM DEBRECENIENSE – 1567

bolum autem Apostolicum, Nicaenum, Athanasii, Damasceni, quae veritati Scripturae consonant, reiiciunt.

Inter reliquas vero confessiones recepimus et subscripsimus Helveticae confessioni anno D. 1566 editae, cui et ecclesiae Genevensis ministri subscrip-
685 serunt. Et quicunque confessionem nostram in synodis confirmatam et hanc confessionem Helveticam Tiguri editam aut articulos hos ex verbo Dei temere reiecerit, solverit et contrarium docuerit, iurisdictione ecclesiastica puniendum statuimus. Finis. 22. Augusti an. D. 1567.

683/688 Inter – 1567] *Confessio Helvetica Posterior* (1566); *Confessio brevis* (1567), in *RefBK*, vol. 2/2 (2009), p. 243-401

683 Inter] *add. in marg. tit.* Ungaricae ecclesiae Helveticarum ecclesiarum confessioni subscripserunt *C*   **688** 1567] *add.* Articuli denuo editi et in generali synodo Varadini approbati et publicati anno 1591. 6. Iunii. *C*

IV

CONFESSIO PASTORUM ECCLESIAE IESU CHRISTI EXHIBITA IN CZENGER DE UNO ET SOLO DEO, QUI EST PATER, FILIUS ET SPIRITUS SANCTUS, CONFIRMATA EXPLICATIONE PHRASIUM HEBRAEARUM ET REGULIS CERTIS EX VERBO DEI DESUMPTIS

[1] DE UNO ET SOLO DEO

Vere et sincere confitemur secundum Scripturas sacras Deum verum esse unum et solum, authorem et conservatorem omnium, qui sic se patefecit, ut sit Pater, Filius et Spiritus Sanctus.

[2] DE TRINITATE UNIUS IEHOVAE

Hunc unum et solum Deum, tres in coelo testes Patrem, Filium et Spiritum Sanctum esse credimus, qui licet tres sint subsistentibus suis proprietatibus et officiis dispensatoriis, tamen *hi tres unum quoque sunt*, ut apostolus testis est, I Ioan 5.

---

13 I Ioh. 5, 7

6 1] cfr *Confessio catholica* (1562), Article 1; *Confessio Helvetica Posterior* (1566), par. 3; *Confessio brevis* (1567), par. 6, in *RefBK*, vol. 2/2 (2009), p. 11, 277-278, and 371-373 respectively; *Hungarian Creed* (1567), in *BaM*, p. 167   **10** 2] cfr *Confessio catholica* (1562), Articles 2-3; *Confessio brevis* (1567), par. 9, in *RefBK*, vol. 2/2 (2009), p. 11-12 and 375-376 respectively; *Hungarian Creed* (1567), in *BaM*, p. 167-172, 182-183, and 186-188

1/5 Confessio – desumptis] *in titulo externo* Confessio vera ex verbo Dei sumpta et in Synodo Czengerina uno consensu exhibita et declarata *E*   **9** Sanctus] *add. in marg.* Esai. 40. 44. 45. Deut. 5. 6. I Cor. 8. Mar. 12. *E*

482   CONCILIUM CSENGERIENSE – 1570

[3] DE PATRE AETERNO

Patrem vocamus ex verbo Dei Deum et Iehovam in se vitam habentem, a nullo existentem et omni origine carentem, qui ex sua hypostasi tanquam characterem et splendorem suae gloriae Filium unigenitum ab aeterno sine omni principio et mutatione genuit, per quem omnia ab aeterno praesciit et disposuit et in principio creavit et conservat, et electos iustificando salvat, impios autem condemnat.

[4] DE FILIO DEI

Christum iuxta carnem Davidis filium, per omnia fratribus similem excepto peccato credimus. Hunc eundem Christum secundum Logon credimus et confitemur Filium Dei unigenitum a Patre, Deum et Iehovam aequalem Patri et ab initio ante omnia opera ex ore altissimi tanquam splendorem gloriae et characterem substantiae eius genitum esse, per quem omnia facta sunt ante creationem, in creatione et post creationem. Qui dicitur angelus foederis et sermo Dei carnem in fine seculorum assumens, Rom. 1. 8. 9. Heb. 1. 2. 3. Gal. 3. 4.

Qui cum subsistens esset in forma Dei, Patri aequaliter, se humiliavit ac formam servi assumsit, sic totum antilytron seu aequivalens praecium virtute et potentia spiritus aeterni in carne assumta persolvit. Quia in ipso somaticos seu vere placuerit Patri totam plenitudinem deitatis inhabitare, ut sic omnia per eum restaurari possint, Eph. 1. Colos. 1. 2. II Cor. 5.

Huic Christo licet iuxta carnem temporalis tribuatur origo et nativitas, tanquam vero homini fratribus per omnia simili, excepto peccato, tamen, quatenus est unigenitus a Patre, subsistens in forma Dei, ita in se vitam habens, ut

---

19/21 per – condemnat] cfr Ps. 2, 7; Prou. 8, 23; Ioh. 1, 3 et 5, 26; Eph. 1, 4; Hebr. 1, 3
24 excepto peccato] cfr Hebr. 4, 15   **26/27** tanquam – eius] cfr Hebr. 1, 3   **28/**
29 angelus foederis] cfr I Tim. 3, 16   **31/32** Qui – assumsit] cfr Phil. 2, 6-7
32 antilytron] cfr I Tim. 2, 6   **33/34** in² – inhabitare] cfr Col. 2, 9   **37** excepto
peccato] cfr Hebr. 4, 15   **38** subsistens in forma Dei] cfr Phil. 2, 6   **38/39** ita – Pater]
cfr Ioh. 5, 26

15 3] cfr *Confessio catholica* (1562), Article 4, in *RefBK*, vol. 2/2 (2009), p. 12-13
22 4] cfr *Confessio catholica* (1562), Articles 5-6; *Confessio Helvetica Posterior* (1566),
par. 11; *Confessio brevis* (1567), par. 7, in *RefBK*, vol. 2/2 (2009), p. 13, 291-297, and 373
respectively; *Hungarian Creed* (1567), in *BaM*, p. 172-176 afnd 183-186

30 Gal. 3. 4.] *add. in marg.* Psalmo 2. I Timot. 3. Roma 3. 4. 8. Ebreo. 3. 8. 9. *E*
32 praecium] *sic*

CONCILIUM CSENGERIENSE – 1570

Pater, caret omni origine et temporali mutatione. Quia est Iehova a Iehova
40 egressus et missus a diebus aeternis, sola mystica et ineffabili generatione
unigenitus a Patre.

[5] De Spiritu Sancto

Spiritum quoque sanctum credimus et confitemur a Patre procedentem et
a Filio emissum in corda credentium, esse Adonai Iehovam, ut in Ezechiele se
45 Spiritus Sanctus appellat, capite 2. 3. 8. 10. Cui omnia elogia uni soli Deo
propria tribuuntur, perinde, ut Patri ac Filio, scilicet, primo Iehova Adonai,
Deus vocatur, Psalm. 95. Ebr. 3.

Secundo, vocatur Deus Iehova scrutans corda et renes seu Deus omnipotens.
50 Tertio, creator, conservator, regenerator, sanctificator.

Quarto, autor et distributor omnium donorum Dei, I Cor. 12. Gal. 5. 6.
Eph. 5. 6. Fructus Spiritus Sancti sunt fides, spes, charitas.

Quinto, quia futura praedixit in prophetis, elegit et emisit apostolos sua
authoritate, Acto. 13.
55 Hi tres Pater, Sermo et Spiritus, quia unum sunt in Iehovali et in aeterna
deitate, volunte, consilio et operibus, ut Ioan. 3. 5. 6. 10. 14. 15. 16. dicitur,
sunt unum et in adoratione, sicut enim Deus Pater sine Filio suo et Spiritu
Sancto eligere, creare, sanctificare non potest, ita Pater sine Filio et Spiritu
Sancto Deus Iehova adorandus esse non potest.

60 ### [6] De coena Domini

Coenam Domini vocamus sacramentum a Christo ex pane et vino institutum in memoriam mortis suae. Sicut autem papisticam transubstantiatio-

---

48 vocatur – renes] cfr Ps. 7, 10 et Apoc. 2, 2   **51** autor – Dei] cfr I Cor. 12, 11; Gal.
5, 22-23; Eph. 5, 9

42 5] cfr *Confessio catholica* (1562), Article 7; *Confessio brevis* (1567), par. 8, in *RefBK*,
vol. 2/2 (2009), p. 13 and 373-375 respectively; *Hungarian Creed* (1567), in *BaM*,
p. 176-182   **60** 6] cfr *Confessio catholica* (1562), Article 84; *Confessio Helvetica
Posterior* (1566), par. 21; *Confessio brevis* (1567), par. 21, in *RefBK*, vol. 2/2 (2009),
p. 55-57, 329-334, and 392-394 respectively; *Hungarian Creed* (1567), in *BaM*, p. 207-211

41 Patre] *add. in marg.* Matthei 1. 3. Luce 1. 2. 3. Roma. 1. 8. 9. Ebreo. 3. 8. 9. Ioann. 1. 3.
8. 10. Philip. 2. Michae 5. Zach. 2. 3. 10. Proverb. 8. Psalmo 2. *E*   **50** Tertio –
sanctificator] *add. in marg.* Esaiae. 6. I Cor. 1. 2. 3. *E*   **51/52** Quarto – charitas] *add.
in marg.* Rom. 3. 4. 8. Gal. 3. 4. *E*   **53/54** Quinto – 13.] *add. in marg.* Iob. 26. 27. 33. *E*

nem ex verbo Dei negamus, ita pernegamus sarcophagiam corporalem et cruentam, hoc est, ore corporali naturale Christi corpus ex virgine natum sumi in coena, et panem substantialiter et realiter sine ulla transubstantiatione corpus Christi esse, aut in panem corpus Christi contra fidei et naturae regulam includi et in pane ore carnali ab omnibus in coena sumi; cum Symbolum et Scriptura doceant corpus Christi ascendisse in coelum. Deinde impossibile et contra naturam est contentum suo continente, locatum suo loco maius esse, ut plantae et arbores, animalia ipsa terra continente vel orbe maiora esse, panem coenae posse totum corpus Christi capere et poculum totum Christi sanguinem continere aut includere.

Deinde, quin et post verborum Christi pronuntiationem Christus apostolis panem dedit et non corpus suum, quod pro nobis postridie obtulit. Et Paulus dicit: *Si quis panem hunc indigne comederit, reus erit corporis Christi. Panis, quem frangimus, nonne est communicatio corporis Christi?* I Cor. 10. 11.

Tertio: Quia vocatur panis memoria mortis et corporis Christi. Memoria autem vocatur ex Dei institutione signum foederis. Quicquid enim recordari facit, recte memoraculum seu signum vocatur, ut Gen. 9. 17. dicitur. I Cor. 11. Luc. 22.

Quarta ratio: Impossibile est diversas species, disparatam et aliam speciem et formam esse posse naturaliter et realiter in sua forma substantiali sine transubstantiatione et mutatione disparatarum specierum de sua forma et substantia prima aut subiecto in aliam naturam. Ut virga Mosis non fuit serpens sine transubstantiatione. Aqua non fuit sanguis in Aegypto nec aqua vinum fuit in nuptiis sine mutatione, ita nec panis coenae realiter et substantialiter ac corporaliter corpus Christi esse potest neque ore corporali sumi potest, nisi in carnem Christi transmutetur amissa forma et substantia panis.

Quemadmodum damnamus papisticum delyrium, dum sic nugantur: primo panem transubstantiari et offerri in missa, deinde sola accidentia panis manere, sed sub illa forma visibili panis corpus Christi latitari, cum impossibile sit accidentia manere sine suis subiectis, et formas substantiales, quae dant esse rei, id est, ob quas res suis nominibus appellantur, sine primis substantiis subsistere posse, ut in coena, cum panis sit forma corporalis et tamen substantia prima, aut subiectum corporis Christi naturalis lateat sub forma panis. Ita et eorum insaniam damnamus, qui asserunt sarcophagiam, id est, ore corporali sumi corpus Christi naturale, sanguinolentum sine ulla mutatione et transsub-

---

75/76 I Cor. 10, 16; 11, 27   **77/78** Memoria – vocatur] cfr Gen. 9, 12-13 et 17; 17, 11
85/86 nec – mutatione] cfr Ioh. 2, 9

---

72 includere] *add. in marg.* Matt. 26. 27. Mar. 1. 4. 16. *E*   **85** Aegypto] *add. in marg.* Exo. 3. 4. 7. 8. *E*

CONCILIUM CSENGERIENSE – 1570

stantiatione. Nam ut impossibile est accidentia manere et sumi sine subiecto, ut papistae nugantur videri quidem accidentia panis, sed corpus Christi in
100 missa sumi, ita isti creophagi aut sarcophagi delyrant, dum somniant panem quidem videri et panem non mutari in corpus, tamen pane manducato corpus Christi realiter et substantialiter ore corporali sumi, id quod contra fidei et naturae regulam est, scilicet disparatas species in aliis specierum formis esse posse substantialiter et sumi sine mutatione. Sicut aqua vinum esse in nuptiis
105 nec pro vino sumi potuit sine versione aquae in vinum, Ioan. 2. Sola ergo appellatione transubstantiatores papistae a sarcophagis corporariis differunt, sed re ipsa in re sacramentaria per omnia conveniunt.

[7] De sacramentariis

Reiicimus et eorum delyrium, qui coenam Domini vacuum signum vel
110 Christi absentis tantum memoriam his signis recoli docent. Nam sicut Christus est *Amen, testis fidelis, verax, veritas et vita,* ita coena Domini est praesentis et infiniti aeternique Filii Dei unigeniti a Patre memoria, qui se et sua bona, carnem suam et sanguinem suum, id est, panem vivum et potum coelestem Spiritus Sancti ope per verbum promissionis gratiae offert et exhibet electis
115 fide vera evangelium Christi apprehendentibus, ut Ioan. 6. 14. 15.

[8] De presentia in coena

Christum credimus ubique electis suis praesentem, ut Filium Dei Iehovam unigenitum a Patre, quatenus *hi tres sunt unum,* id est, unus Deus. Sed hic Filius Dei, ut Deus, sermo est mystice et spiritualiter quoque, dum enter prae-
120 senter Iehovali sua deitate et cum donis in unigenito et primogenito somatice et vere † habitantis adest perinde, ut Pater, sicut vitis in palmitibus, caput in

---

104/105 Sicut – vinum] cfr Ioh. 2, 9   **111** Apoc. 3, 14   **121** sicut vitis in palmitibus] cfr Ioh. 15, 1-8

109/110 Reiicimus – docent] cfr *Confessio brevis* (1567), par. 23, in *RefBK,* vol. 2/2 (2009), p. 395; *Hungarian Creed* (1567), in *BaM,* p. 212   **111/113** ita – suum] cfr *Abendmahlsbekenntnis zu Neumarkt* (1563), Article 5, in *RefBK,* vol. 2/1 (2009), p. 113   **116** 8] cfr *Confessio catholica* (1562), Article 86; *Confessio brevis* (1567), par. 22, in *RefBK,* vol. 2/2 (2009), p. 58-59 and 394 respectively; *Hungarian Creed* (1567), in *BaM,* p. 211-212

111 vita] *add. in marg.* Apocal. 1. 3. Matt. 18. 25. I Corin. 8. 10. *E*   **116** presentia] *sic*   **121** habitantis] *coniecit* habitantibus *BuM,* habitet *BaM*

membris adest, Ioann. 15. I Cor. 10. 12. Eph. 4. 5. 6. Ut autem est homo fratribus per omnia similis, adest in ecclesia sua mystice et spiritualiter. Primo: adest per unionem cum Logo, quatenus unitus est Logo ubique praesenti.

125 Secundo: adest in sua promissione per verbum et fidem communicando se electis, ut vitis in palmitibus distantibus et dissitis a vite, caput in membris dissitis a capite adest per venas, ita vitis et caput homo Christus quoque nostrum adest per promissiones gratiae, dum panem vivum et potum coelestem nobis communicat, Ioan. 6. 8. 10. 14. 15. Tertio: adest institutione sua

130 sacramentali aut Spiritus Sancti effusione in electos. Quarto: officio dispensatorio aut intercessione pro electis, Ioan. 15. 16. Ebr. 1. 7. 9. 10. Non est autem praesens carnaliter, sicut in utero matris, in Iudaea, in sepulchro fuit praesens localiter, quia ascendit in coelum corporaliter, *surrexit, non est hic*, et oportet in coelo esse usque ad diem iudicii, Acto. 3.

135 [9] De veris sacramentis

Scriptura sacra haec quatuor in omnibus signis novi foederis proponit. Primo: foedus seu pactum ipsum, quod est Dei gratia, reconciliatio cum hominibus propter Christum, dona propter Christum per Spiritum Sanctum electis fide exhibita et applicata. Secundo: materia rei ex qua sacramentum institui-

140 tur, ut iris cum Noah, praeputium carnis cum Abraham, iumenta et panis in sacrificiis, in baptismo aqua, in coena panis et vinum. Tertio: causa formalis, diversis enim formis signa erecta sunt cum Noah, Abraham et populo Iudaico, et in Novo Testamento, baptismo diversae sunt formae sacramenti. Quarta causa finalis, quae rescipit Deum et homines, hinc dicta sunt signa foederis,

145 memoria pacti aut novi testamenti inter Deum et homines: respectu causae finalis dicta sunt res sacramentariae signa aut memoria in signum foederis et reconciliationis instituta, ut iridis erectio et circuncisio vocatur Beriit, id est, foedus, deinde Otth Beriith, id est, signum foederis, Gen. 9. 17. Ita in coena panis et vinum respectu causae finalis sunt memoria mortis Christi, id est,

150 signa commonefacientia de morte Christi, Matt. 26. Lucae 22. I Cor. 10. 11. Panis et vinum sunt per se et sua natura sine ulla mutatione papistica aut creophagica, ut papistae somniant, corpus et novum testamentum aut communi-

---

133 Marc. 16, 6   **147/148** ut – foederis] cfr Gen. 9, 12; 17, 11

135 9] cfr *Confessio catholica* (1562), Articles 74-78; *Confessio Helvetica Posterior* (1566), par. 21, in *RefBK*, vol. 2/2 (2009), p. 50-52 and 323-327 respectively

122 Eph. 4 5 6] *add. in marg.* Ioann. 3. 5. 6. Colosen. 1. 2. *E*   **129** Ioan. 6 8 10 14 15] *add. in marg.* I Cor. 8. 10. Eph. 1. 4. 5. 6. *E*   **134** Acto. 3] *add. in marg.* Mar. 14. 16. *E*

CONCILIUM CSENGERIENSE – 1570

catio corporis, sunt mystica et sacra Christi institutione et appellatione sine transformatione corporaria, sicut supra dictum est, signa enim non substantiam signatorum, sed tantum accipiunt nomina, ut Ge. 9. 17. I Cor. 10. Lucae 22. Iris et circuncisio nunc foedus, nunc signum et in coena elementum nunc panis nunc corpus Christi appellatur, I Cor. 10. 11. Sed non mutatur panis in corpus Christi, sed accipit nomen corporis et vinum sanguinis, non essentiam aut naturam carnis et sanguinis Christi, ut papistae somniant.

[10] DE AETERNITATE. PROPOSITIO XLIII.

Aeternum quoque varie sumitur, primo: Dei respectu, quoties Deo Patri, Filio, Spiritui Sancto tribuitur, significat principio et fine mutationeque carentem perpetuitatem: *Tu Iehova habitans aeternitates: Tu Iehova Deus es in aeternum.*

Secundo: sumitur pro Christi descriptione filiali et infinita natura, virtute et efficatia vel nativitate, ut Pro. 8. Sap. 7. 9. Ecc. 24. *Ab aeterno ante omnia genuit me.* Mich. 5. *Egressus eius ab aeterno a diebus aeternis.* Esa. 9. Christus est Filius Dei, Deus fortis, pater aeternitatis. Hoc est, autor aeterni foederis, testamenti, salutis, iustitiae et vitae aeternae causa. Ebr. 1. 9. 13. Angelus est foederis. Testamentum in Christo confirmatum. Testamentum aeternum in sanguine Christi confirmatum est. Effectum aeternum, salutem, vitam, testamentum seu foedus aeternum tribuit Filio Dei dato, unigenito a Patre infinito, aeterno. Qualis effectus, talis causa: Sed effectus Christi, redemtio, salus, testamentum sunt aeternum, ergo et Filius est Pater aeternitatis, id est, Deus aeternus infinitus, ut Pater, Esa. 9. Tertio: sumitur pro continuo tempore, hoc est, pro spacio, quo mundus creatus est, pro diebus, in quibus mundus factus est. Hinc dicitur: *Elegit nos ante tempora aeterna,* id est, ante septem dies creationis, ante creationem ab aeterno elegit, Eph. 1. 2. 3. 5. II Timoth. 1. 2. 3. Quarto: sumitur pro infinita piorum salute et cruciatu impiorum. Quae, ut se, in electis et vasis irae habent initium, tamen iam fine carent salus et condemnatio.

156/157 Iris – appellatur] cfr Gen. 9, 12-13 et 17; 17, 11   **157/158** in corpus Christi] cfr I Cor. 10, 16; 11, 24-25   **163** Is. 9, 6-7; 57, 15   **166/167** Prou. 8, 23   **167** Mich. 5, 2 **168** Deus fortis] cfr Is. 9, 5   **168/169** autor – est] cfr Hebr. 9, 15; 13, 20   **174** Pater aeternitatis] cfr Is. 9, 5   **177** Eph. 1, 4

160 10] cfr *Confessio catholica* (1562), Article 230, in *RefBK*, vol. 2/2 (2009), p. 163-164

160 Propositio] *a.c.* Pro.   **163** aeternum] *add. in marg.* Esa. 57. cap. Esaie 9. *E* **166** efficatia] *sic*   **176** spacio] *sic*   **180** condemnatio] *add. in marg.* Genesis 13. Ioannis 18. Leviti. 12. *E*

488 CONCILIUM CSENGERIENSE – 1570

[11] De baptismo infantium. Propositio XLIIII.

Infantes omnes ecclesiae oblatos, qui canes et porci non sunt, in nomine Patris, Filii et Spiritus Sancti baptismo baptizandos esse docemus, sicut promissio et signatum vel foedus et ad infantes electos pertinet et sacramen-
185 tum circumcisionis infantibus quoque institutum fuit.

[12] XLV. Propositio

Scriptura nomen baptismi varie usurpat. Primo: pro afflictione et cruce electorum, ut Math. 20. *Potestis baptizari, quo ego baptizor?* id est, potestis ferre illam crucem infinitam aut poenas infinitas? Secundo: sumitur baptis-
190 mus pro regeneratione et causa regenerationis, pro Spiritu et igne aut gratiae Dei plenitunide. *Ille baptizabit vos igne et spiritu. Nisi quis natus fuerit ex aqua et spiritu, non poterit ingredi in vitam*, Matth. 3. Mar. 1. Ioa. 1. 3. Tertio: sumi-tur baptismus pro signo regenerationis et lavacri interioris, quod a Christo institutum est, *in nomine Patris, Filii et Spiritus Sancti*, Matth. 28. Quarto:
195 sumitur pro Christi baptismo vel pro nomine Christi, pro poenitentia et con-versione, ut Mat. 3. *Poenitentiam agite et baptizetur unusquisque vestrum in nomine Iesu Christi in remissionem peccatorum*, id est, agite poenitentiam, ut propter Christum accipiatis remissionem peccatorum et donum spiritus. Quinto: pro religione et confessione christiana et unione insertioneque fidei,
200 doctrinae et confessione Christi, ut Acto. 10. *Numquid aquam prohibere potest aliquis, ne baptizentur hi, qui Spiritum Sanctum acceperunt, et iussit eos bapti-zari Petrus in nomine domini Iesu Christi.* Hic baptismus aquae primo, secun-do baptismus spiritus et ignis, tertio baptismus nominis Christi explicatur. *Baptizati sunt in nomine Iesu.* Hoc est, primo in nomine Patris, Filii et Spiritus
205 Sancti aqua sunt baptizati, postea susceperunt nomen Christi, facti sunt chris-tiani, fidem, doctrinam et religionem Christi susceperunt et appraehenderunt, Gal. 3. I Cor. 3. *Quicunque in Christo baptizati estis, Christum induistis.* Sexto

---

182 canes et porci non sunt] cfr Matth. 7, 6   **188** Matth. 20, 22   **191** Ille – spiritu] Marc. 1, 8; cfr Matth. 3, 11-17   **191/192** Nisi – vitam] Ioh. 3, 5   **194** Matth. 28, 19 **196/197** Act. 2, 38   **200/202** Act. 10, 47-48   **204** Act. 19, 5   **207** Gal. 3, 27

---

181 11] cfr *Articuli maiores* (1567), Article 63; *Hungarian Creed* (1567), in *BaM*, p. 217-222   **186** 12] cfr *Confessio catholica* (1562), Articles 79-82; *Confessio Helvetica Posterior* (1566), par. 20, in *RefBK*, vol. 2/2 (2009), p. 52-55 and 327-329 respectively; *Articuli maiores* (1567), Article 7

---

185 fuit] *add. in marg.* Romano. 5. 6. I Cor. 15. Colossen. 2. *E*   **186** Propositio] *a.c.* Pro.   **192** Mar. 1.] 1. *add. E*   **206** appraehenderunt] *sic*

CONCILIUM CSENGERIENSE – 1570

pro lotione et communi lavacro sumitur, Iudit 12. *Baptizabat se Iudit in fonte.*
Mar. 7. *Iudaei non comedunt, nisi baptizentur prius.*

[13] DE LEGE. PROPOSITIO XLVI.

Lex ad peccata arguenda et evangelium propter annunciandam remissionem peccatorum praedicandum est. Neque enim poenitentia praedicari potest, neque peccata argui possunt sine lege. In suis ergo finibus lex et evangelium praedicanda sunt.

[14] DE RITIBUS ECCLESIASTICIS. PROPOSITIO XLVII.

Omnes honestos et pios ritus verbo Dei consentientes et servientes gloriae Dei et aedificationi ecclesiae, cantilenas scilicet ex sacris literis compositas, cum intellectu, spiritu et mente canimus, et reiicimus insanos, qui his contradicunt, aut lingua non intellecta in coetu discantizant, aut reboant ad coelum usque, ut sacerdotes Baal, I Cor. 14. Eph. 5.

[15] DE VESTITU PASTORUM. PROPOSITIO XLVIII.

Quia in sacris literis in Veteri et Novo Testamento nulla limitatione, figura aut mensura ministrorum ecclesiae vestes in usu communi circumscribuntur et limitantur, stultum et impium est haeredes et dominos omnium creaturarum a domino Deo factos facere servos in vestitu, cibo et potu superstitioso. In his ergo omnibus mediocritas pia et sancta serviens honestati, decoro et necessitati secundum circumstantias servanda est. Vitanda sunt extrema omnia, luxus, superbia, scandala, sordicies et avaritia non serviens et non parcens naturae, I Cor. 6. 14. 15.

---

208 Iudith 12, 7 **209** Marc. 7, 3 **219/220** reboant – Baal] cfr III Reg. 18, 26-29

210 13] cfr *Confessio catholica* (1562), Articles 24-28; *Confessio Helvetica Posterior* (1566), par. 12, in *RefBK*, vol. 2/2 (2009), p. 21-22 and 297-298 **215** 14] cfr *Confessio Helvetica Posterior* (1566), par. 27, in *RefBK*, vol. 2/2 (2009), p. 341-342; *Articuli maiores* (1567), Article 5 **221** 15] cfr *Confessio catholica* (1562), Articles 91 and 128; *Confessio brevis* (1567), par. 28, in *RefBK*, vol. 2/2 (2009), p. 62-63, 91-92, and 399-401 respectively; *Hungarian Creed* (1567), in *BaM*, p. 200-201

210 Propositio] *a.c.* Pro. **215** ecclesiasticis] *sic* Propositio] *a.c.* Pro.
221 Propositio] *a.c.* Pro.

CONCILIUM CSENGERIENSE – 1570

230 ## [16] De templis. Propositio XLIX.

Templa et loca conventus electorum remotis idolis et papisticis sordibus idolorum, ararum et boatuum recipimus, etiam si prius eis Baalim abusi sunt. Nulla enim creatura in terris est, qua impii abusi non sunt. Sed abusus non tollit substantiam bonae rei. Hoc est, non sunt ideo creaturae Dei per se bonae
235 reiiciendae, quia iis impii abusi sunt.

[17] De cibo et mercede pastorum. Propositio L.

Scriptura sacra et natura docet *dignos esse operarios cibo et mercede sua.* Impie ergo nugantur clamitantes mercedem non esse veris in Christo ministris dandam. Sicut novi haeretici fabulantur sub monachorum praetextu, qui licet
240 non paciscantur cum ovibus, sed tamen iis pellem et carnem excoriando detrahunt, ut Ioan. 10. 11. Hiere. 23. Spiritus Dei falsis prophetis loquitur, Ezech. 14. Esa. 58.

[18] De causa peccati. Propositio LI.

Sicut impossibile est contrarie inter se pugnantia et destruentia se mutuo
245 causam efficientem formalemque esse posse sibi contrariorum, ut lux non est causa tenebrarum neque caliditas frigiditatis, ita impossibile est Deum, qui est lux, iusticia, veritas, sapientia, bonitas, vita, causam esse tenebrarum, peccati et mendacii, ignorantiae, coecitatis, malitiae et mortis. Sed horum omnium causa Satanas et homines sunt. Quaecunque enim Deus prohibet, et propter quae
250 damnat, facere ex se et per se non potest, Deut. 32.

---

237 Luc. 10, 7; I Tim. 5, 18

---

230 16] cfr *Confessio catholica* (1562), Article 127, in *RefBK*, vol. 2/2 (2009), p. 91; *Hungarian Creed* (1567), in *BaM*, p. 201-202; *Articuli maiores* (1567), Article 16 **236** 17] cfr *Confessio Helvetica Posterior* (1566), par. 28, in *RefBK*, vol. 2/2 (2009), p. 342; *Articuli maiores* (1567), Article 34 **243** 18] cfr *Confessio catholica* (1562), Article 12; *Confessio Helvetica Posterior* (1566), par. 8; *Confessio brevis* (1567), par. 4-5, in *RefBK*, vol. 2/2 (2009), p. 16, 284-286, and 369-371 respectively; *Hungarian Creed* (1567), in *BaM*, p. 193-195

230 Propositio] *a.c.* Pro.   **236** Propositio] *a.c.* Pro.   **241** Hiere. 23.] 3. *add. E* **243** Propositio] *a.c.* Pro.   **247** iusticia] *sic*   **248** mortis] *add. in marg.* Psalmo 5. 46. 61. 66. 80. 84. 114. 135. *E*

CONCILIUM CSENGERIENSE – 1570

[19] De aprosopolipsia in Deo. Propositio LII.

Sicut qui operantibus aequaliter simul mercedem aequalem iuste reddit, et qui non merentibus donat ex gratia, libero arbitrio, quae vult, non est respector personarum, ita Deus mortem et condemnationem tanquam peccati stipendium dum omnibus merentibus aequalem reddit, ex debito secundum iustitiam et legem suam, iuste fecit. Et contra dum non merentibus donat propter Filium ex plenitudine gratiae suae et libera voluntate iustitiam et vitam, non est prosopoliptis, id est, non est respector personarum, ut dicitur: *Quod tuum est, et meritus es, tolle et vade: Annon licet mihi facere de meo, quod volo? Annon oculus tuus est nequam? non meus oculus, quia ego bonus sum,* Matt. 20.

[20] De mediatore

Christum Filium Dei et hominis totum secundum utramque naturam verum Melchisedecum pontificem, regem mediatorem et salvatorem, redemptorem confitemur propter has causas.

1. Propter iustitiae et misericordiae temperamentum: ut iustitiae infinitae et legi damnanti propter peccatum satisfaceret in carne moriendo, virtute et efficatia Spiritus aeterni. Deinde ut et misericordiae divinae vivificanti electos per eiusdem sermonis et Filii Dei unigeniti omnipotentiam satisfieret iuxta electionem aeternam in Christo ab aeterno factam, Eph. 1.

2. Propter antilytron aut aequivalens praecium, hoc est, ut perfecte mediator praecium salutis pro electis solvere possit, hoc scilicet, propter peccatum hominum mori in carne possit. Deinde peccatum, mortem, Diabolum, infernum, legis maledictionem destruere possit, imaginem autem Dei amissam, vitam, iustitiam, sapientiam Dei reparare possit et vivificare, omnia res-

---

251 aprosopolipsia] cfr I Petr. 1, 17   **258** prosopoliptis] cfr Ioh. 1, 16; Act. 10, 34
259/260 Matth. 20, 14-15   **269/270** iuxta – factam] cfr Eph. 1, 4

251 19] cfr *Confessio catholica* (1562), Articles 34-36; *Confessio Helvetica Posterior* (1566), par. 10; *Confessio brevis* (1567), par. 18, in *RefBK*, vol. 2/2 (2009), p. 25-28, 289-291, and 387-389 respectively; *Hungarian Creed* (1567), in *BaM*, p. 202-205
262 20] *Confessio catholica* (1562), Articles 132-134; *Confessio Helvetica Posterior* (1566), par. 5; *Confessio brevis* (1567), par. 3, in *RefBK*, vol. 2/2 (2009), p. 93-95, 280-281, and 367-369 respectively; *Hungarian Creed* (1567), in *BaM*, p. 189-193

251 Propositio] *a.c.* Pro.   **268** efficatia] *sic*   divinae] *correxi*, divine *E*
271 praecium] *sic* **272** praecium] *sic*

492 CONCILIUM CSENGERIENSE – 1570

taurare possit deitatis suae virtute et potentia, Rom. 3. 4. 8. II Cor. 3. 5. Col. 1.
2. Eph. 1. 3.

3. Quia literaliter mediator vocatur Filius Dei unigenitus immortalis, id
est, verus Deus, vita aeterna, id est, immortalis Iehova Deus aeternus, magnus
laudandus in secula, Deus magnus, sua potentia et virtute salvans, I Cor. 1. 3.
Col. 1. Eb 1. 7. 9. Zach. 1. 3. 10. 13. 14. Oseae 1. 2. 3. 12. Idem mediator Dei et
hominum vocatur homo Iesus Christus. Sunt ergo gloriae Dei et veritatis,
iustitiae deitatis destructores, sunt pacis inter homines hostes, qui Christum
mediatorem, id est, Filium Dei unigenitum a Patre et hominem verum negant,
Luc. 1. 2. Impossibile enim est gloriam Dei in coelis perfici, legem et evangelium impleri et salutem, pacem electorum perfici sine Filio Dei, vero Deo et
homine, et sine vero homine, Romano. 1. 3. Colos. 1. 2. Ephesio. 1. 3.

Finis

Per Petrum Melium Horhinum.

CONCILIUM VENETIANUM-FERRARIENSE

1550

edidit
Davide DAINESE

THE COUNCIL OF VENICE-FERRARA
1550

In recent scholarship, the state of the art on the subject of the so-called Anabaptist Council of Venice of 1550 ([1]) has been linked to a particularly striking event. While a still young Carlo Ginzburg was working at the behest of Delio Cantimori on the critical edition of Pietro Manelfi's depositions, aided by Aldo Stella's research on Anabaptism in Veneto, the latter finalised a significant revision to what he himself had gleaned from the studies available on the issue. ([2]) In essence, Stella's 'Nuove ricerche storiche', published in 1969, undermined the reliability of the primary source on the Council of Venice, leaving us with an authoritative, excellent critical edition ([3]) of a testi-

---

([1]) Or *collegium*. For terms and possible definitions, see Addante, *Eretici e libertini*, p. 95-116.

([2]) Cfr. Stella, *Dall'anabattismo al socinianesimo*, p. 76-83; Ginzburg, *Costituti*; Stella, *Anabattismo e antitrinitarismo*, p. 64-72. The first reviewers, Anne Jacobson Schutte and Henry A. DeWind, immediately grasped the problem: 'There is one major difficulty, however. Aldo Stella has recently proved that on many subjects where Manelfi's statements can be checked against those of his contemporaries interrogated by the Inquisition, Manelfi can be shown to be unreliable: among other things, he was a latecomer to the radical movement who was not (as he claimed) present at the "Anabaptist synod"'. See A. Jacobson Schutte, '[Review of] Carlo Ginzburg, ed. *I costituti di don Pietro Manelfi* (Biblioteca del Corpus Reformatorum Italicorum). Florence: G. C. Sansoni Editore, and Chicago: The Newberry Library, 1970. 5 pl. 102 p. L.3,000', *Renaissance Quarterly* 25 (1972), p. 364-366, here p. 365.

([3]) Carlo Ginzburg's edition, despite due corrections to the names of places and people – following, for the most part, later research that allowed for greater clarity on certain details – remains without equal from a philological profile. Among the more relevant corrections we can mention the exchange (which however depends on Manelfi's account in this case) between Badia Calavena (Ginzburg, *Costituti*, p. 32 and p. 41) and Badia Polesine, an important centre for the spread of Anabaptism in Polesine (cfr. Malavasi, 'Sulla diffusione delle teorie ereticali', p. 17-24) as well as the reading of Terra delle Fosse (Ginzburg, *Costituti*, p. 21) for Torre della Fossa (Venezia, Archivio di Stato, Savi all'eresia (Santo Ufficio), busta 158, reg. III, f. 31ʳ; cfr. Stella, *Anabattismo e antitrinitarismo*, p. 54), currently Torre Fossa, a hamlet near Ferrara in the direction of Consandolo (where the summer residence of Renée de France was located). In terms of interpretation, Ginzburg's central thesis related to Manelfi's attempt to convert Julius III is disputed: Prosperi, *Libro Grande*, p. 64 and p. 208 embraces Ginzburg's thesis, while Firpo, in *Alumbrados*, p. 100 and *La presa di potere*, p. 183 opposes it.

mony to the so-called Anabaptist Council of 1550 which, however, proves to be indirect and ultimately unreliable as far as both the actual events and the decisions of the Council itself were and are concerned.

Let us examine the facts. On 17 October 1551, Pietro Manelfi, a self-proclaimed priest from the diocese of Senigallia, appeared before the Bolognese inquisitor, Leandro Alberti. Manelfi therein stated that, after holding both 'Lutheran' and 'Anabaptist' convictions, the Holy Spirit had inspired him to 'redire ad gremium Sanctae Romanae Ecclesiae'. (4) The term 'Anabaptism' from Manelfi's account is the same label found in historiography since the end of the nineteenth century: (5) a fluid fashion of Anabaptism that had spread throughout northern and central Italy with increasingly anti-trinitarian connotations following the predominance of a current that eventually gained a majority (6) – a pre-eminence, so to speak, that was the very result of the Council of Venice itself. Manelfi went on summarising some of its traits:

> Non essere lecito secondo l'evangelio battezare gli fanciulli se prima non credeno.
> Gli magistrati non potere essere cristiani.
> Gli sacramenti non conferire gratia alchuna, ma essere segni esteriori.
> Non tenere nella chiesa altro che scrittura sacra.
> Non tenere oppenione alchuna de' dottori.

(4) Ginzburg, *Costituti*, p. 31.

(5) Both in Karl Benrath and Emilio Comba's works.

(6) Cfr. Ginzburg, *Costituti* p. 63, '[i]tem Ticiano cominciò a predicarmi la dottrina anabattista et il rebattizzarmi, dicendo ch'io non ero battizzato perché non havevo fede quando fui battizzato, et delle *altre openioni antique* [emphasis added] de anabattisti, come è che li christiani non possono esercitare magistrati et signorie, dominii et regni, prima per l'authoritate di Christo "Reges gentium dominantur, vos autem non sic", poi ancora per la legge che dice "Non occides", et perché lo apostolo dice che la spada è data a' Gentili "ad vindictam malefactorum" et non a' christiani, imperò niuno christiano può essere re, duca, principe, né esercitare magistrato alcuno, et questo è uno de primi principii de anabattisti, et altre openioni; non era però ancora fra tali anabattisti concluso contra la divinità di Christo et *altri articoli novi* [emphasis added] determinati et conclusi nel concilio che fu fatto in Venetia. Item N. consente e tiene tutte le openioni de anabattisti, et tiene in casa la scrittura volgare et non li ha altri libri, perché noi anabattisti non potemo tenere altri libri che la scrittura sacra, la qual scrittura nova et vecchia tutta accettiamo, escetto il primo et secondo capitolo dello evengelio di san Mattheo et il primo et secondo et parte del terzo capitolo di san Luca'. And especially p. 67, '[r]icordomi ancora che nel detto concilio fu concluso che quelli che non accettavano questa *dottrina nova* [emphasis added] conclusa nel concilio che fussero esclusi dalla nostra giesa d'anabattisti' (similarly at p. 36: 'quelli che la [= conciliar doctrine] ricevevano erano della nostra chiesa, quelli che non la ricevevano gli separavamo dagli altri').

CONCILIUM VENETIANUM-FERRARIENSE – 1550

Tenere la Chiesa Romana essere diabolica et antecristiana.

Quelli che sono stati battezati non essere christiani, ma essere bisogno rebattizarli. (7)

Manelfi informed the inquisitor of the decisions taken at the Council of Venice through ten schematic points:

1. Christ is human, not divine. He was conceived through the carnal union of Joseph and Mary, and yet he is endowed with all divine virtue.

2. According to several Scriptural passages, Mary had other children after Christ.

3. God did not create the angelic host. When Scriptures speak of angels, this has to be interpreted as an allusion to ministers, i.e. men sent by God for the purposes that Scriptures mention;

4. The devil is human prudence, and the serpent that according to Moses seduced Eve should be interpreted as such. As in Scriptures we will not find any creatures of God who are his enemies, with the sole exception of prudence, as it is shown in The Epistle to the Romans.

5. On Judgment Day, the wicked will not be resurrected, but only the elect, of whom Christ has been head.

6. Our sepulchre is the only hell;

7. Upon death, the elect will rest with the Lord and their souls will lie in peace until Judgment Day, whereafter they will rise. The souls of the wicked will perish with their bodies, as happens with animals.

8. God strengthens the human seed to produce both the spirit and the flesh.

9. The elect are redeemed through God's eternal mercy and charity; visible works – i.e. Christ's death, blood, and merit – are not necessary.

10. Christ died to bear witness to God's justice, i.e. all the goodness and mercy of him and his promises. (8)

Manelfi enclosed a detailed list of names of 'Anabaptists' and 'Lutherans' who were active in central and northern Italy, accompanied by their respective professions. (9) Alberti, who was evidently satisfied by this list, later sent Manelfi to Rome, where, between 12 and 14 November 1551, the latter could

(7) Ginzburg, *Costituti*, p. 33-34.

(8) Ginzburg, *Costituti*, p. 34-35.

(9) The 'geography of Alberti' was examined a few years ago in a convention held in Bologna: see *L'Italia dell'Inquisitore. Storia e geografia dell'Italia del Cinquecento nella Descrittione di Leandro Alberti. Atti del Convegno Internazionale di Studi (Bologna, 27-29 maggio 2004)*, a cura di M. Donattini, Bologna 2007.

498 CONCILIUM VENETIANUM-FERRARIENSE – 1550

display his knowledge before Girolamo Muzzarelli, Master of the Sacred Palace, and the cardinal inquisitors.

The picture that Manelfi outlined is plainly one of an anti-trinitarian reform movement of Anabaptist origins from beyond the Alps, directly exported by 'his' enigmatic Titian. (¹⁰) That being said, the historiographical critical awareness of later generations of scholars – from Cantimori (¹¹) to DeWind, (¹²) and then from Rotondò, (¹³) Williams, (¹⁴) and finally back to Cantimori (¹⁵) – helped Aldo Stella assess the problems of Manelfi's confessions, which Bainton had already questioned. (¹⁶) Stella noticed how a yet un-re-baptised Manelfi, while in Florence, (¹⁷) 'si entusiasmava esageratamente come un neofita, ed anzi travalicava con disinvoltura' the anti-trinitarian proposals, (¹⁸) providing a glimpse into the historiographic consciousness of a typically Italian situation ('spiritualism' or 'rationalism', so to speak, or a later form of 'radicalism') that was no longer seamlessly attributable to Anabaptism, and which would not replace Anabaptism – as appears in Manelfi's accounts

(10) Before Ginzburg – but also in the Italian translation of Black, *Italian Inquisition*, p. 402 – Titian was generally confused with Lorenzo Tizzano/Tissano. Cfr. Santus, 'Tizzano, Lorenzo' and 'Tiziano, predicatore'.

(11) His studies from 1936 to 1939, from Cantimori, 'Anabattismo' to Cantimori, *Eretici italiani*, make emerge Camillo Renato and Girolamo Busale along with the synergic bipolar notion of the cultured elite of varied origin and the popular component that casts doubt on Cantimori's idea that Italian Anabaptism could be the outcome of the movement from mainstream European Anabaptism. See L. Felici, 'Delio Cantimori storico della Riforma radicale nel periodo fra le due guerre', in C. Lastraioli (éd.), *Réforme et Contre-Réforme à l'époque de la naissance et de l'affirmation du totalitarisme (1900-1940). Actes du colloque international de Tours organisé par Maria Rosa Chiapparo et Chiara Lastraioli, 30 septembre – 2 octobre 2004*, Turnhout 2008, p. 11-44.

(12) H. A. DeWind, '«Anabaptism» and Italy', *Church History* 21 (1952), p. 20-38 seeks to dismantle the idea of an 'Italian Anabaptism'.

(13) His criticism of DeWind's thesis is in A. Rotondò, 'I movimenti ereticali nell'Europa del Cinquecento', *Rivista storica italiana* 88 (1966), p. 103-139.

(14) On the attempt to define 'Anabaptism', 'rationalism', and 'spiritualism', see G. H. Williams, *The Radical Reformation*, Philadelphia (PA) 1962.

(15) Cfr. Cantimori, 'Gli anabattisti'.

(16) Cfr. *Bernardino Ochino. Esule e riformatore senese del Cinquecento, 1487-1563. Versione dal manoscritto inglese di Elio Gianturco*, a cura di R. H. Bainton, Firenze 1940, p. 48 and Stella, *Anabattismo e antitrinitarismo*.

(17) Stella describes him as such, accrediting the testimony to Marcantonio Del Bon (Stella, *Anabattismo e antitrinitarismo*, p. 66-67).

(18) Stella, *Anabattismo e antitrinitarismo*, p. 67.

CONCILIUM VENETIANUM-FERRARIENSE – 1550   499

instead. ([19]) Stella's most significant finding, however, concerns the irrefutable demonstration of the unreliability of Manelfi's depositions.

As for the so-called Council of Venice, Stella gave solid evidence that Manelfi had not actually participated in the meeting. Given that Manelfi was baptised later, he neither financed nor contributed to its preparation and could not have been a trustworthy herald of its outcomes. On the whole, Manelfi exaggerated its importance: the Council lasted for four days – rather than the symbolic forty – and was attended by fewer than fifteen participants, against the 'cinquanta o sessanta' – of whom 'vinti o trenta' Grisons – Manelfi spoke of. Other inconsistencies emerge, such as its date – October or November 1550, certainly not September as Manelfi reported – and the lodgings of the participants: Manelfi spoke of 'diversi palazzi a camere locande', whereas more reliable testimony refers solely to the 'casa di madona Elena', near what is now the Ponte dei Fuseri.

These inconsistencies also impacted and impact on the credibility of the information provided by Manelfi about the decisions taken at the Council. The veracity of Manelfi's ten articles outlived its purpose, as did the 'scrittura romana' which Ginzburg included in his critical edition of Manelfi's depositions as the sixth document. ([20]) Instead, evidence suggests that this Council was, in fact, a meeting during which the participants shared their respective convictions mostly on the conception of Christ. A tendential agreement emerged concerning the notion of Christ's natural birth (i.e. from coitus) but without questioning the belief in his divinity. Furthermore, these discussions did not come to an end in Venice, but continued at a later date in Ferrara,

---

(19) As research progressively demonstrated from the end of the Second World War up to the 1960s, for instance in A. Castellini, *Figure della Riforma pretridentina*, Brescia 1948, but also indirectly in H. Jedin, *Katholische Reformation oder Gegenreformation? Ein Versuch zur Klärung der Begriffe nebst einer Jubiläumsbetrachtung über das Trienter Konzil*, Luzern 1946; cfr. P. Prodi, 'Il binomio jediniano «riforma cattolica e controriforma» e la storiografia italiana', *Annali dell'Istituto storico Italo-Germanico di Trento* 6 (1980), p. 85-98. See also Paschini, *Venezia e l'Inquisizione*; M. E. Pommier, 'L'itinéraire religieux d'un moine vagabond italien au XVIᵉ siècle', *Mélanges d'archéologie et d'histoire* 6 (1954), p. 293-322; B. Nicolini, *Ideali e passioni nell'Italia religiosa del Cinquecento*, Bologna 1962; C. Ginzburg, 'Due note sul profetismo cinquecentesco', *Rivista Storica Italiana* 78 (1966), p. 184-207.

(20) As far as the 'scriptura romana' is concerned, cfr. Ginzburg, *Costituti*, p. 83-84. It is a notice drafting the main features of Italian Anabaptism, which was hand-delivered by Muzzarelli (on Muzzarelli see also Ginzburg, *Costituti*, p. 13; Paschini, *Venezia e l'Inquisizione*, p. 87; Martin, *Hidden Enemies*, p. 99) to the Venetian authorities. The document was likely written by Girolamo Muzio and prepared using Manelfi's depositions.

500 CONCILIUM VENETIANUM-FERRARIENSE – 1550

where participants examined the Scriptural texts related to Christ's birth (Luc. 1, 34-35 and Matth. 1, 24-25). However, this second meeting in Ferrara did not coincide with any unanimous consensus, not even by Titian, who – as Marcantonio Del Bon stated – 'contrastava grandemente'. (21)

Other decisions of the Venetian Council that emerge from the source-texts involve the disavowal of weapons (indeed, they were prohibited) and substantial iconoclasm (arms manufacturers, besides painters and sculptors of holy images, were formally excluded from Anabaptist congregations). According to Stella, a final discussion seems to have taken place in Venice or Ferrara. It concerned the relationship with the *saeculum*, i.e. the complete alterity between Christianity on the one side and the civil magistrates and authority on the other: (22) as we have seen, this remains one of the cornerstones of that particular guise of Anabaptism to which Manelfi claimed to have converted to, and the latter did not omit this information in his deposition as it was the only element which proved effective (i.e. the arrest of those mentioned by the secular arm). Nevertheless, in his assessment of Benedetto Del Borgo's preaching, (23) Stella demonstrated that the Anabaptists' positions were characterised by a good deal of compliance, especially after the Venetian meeting. (24)

The most recent studies, including those undertaken after the opening of the archives of the Congregation for the Doctrine of the Faith in 1998, have not substantially changed this narrative. (25) Indeed, this state-of-the-art

(21) According to Manelfi, the community of Cittadella was the most recalcitrant; see also Zille, *Cittadella*. Addante seems more uncertain about the date of the 'Ferrara session' of the Council (see Addante, *Eretici e libertini*, p. 108).

(22) Although only partially confirmed by surviving sources at our disposal – for instance by Iseppo Sartor's deposition – this nonetheless was an important doctrinal feature.

(23) Though only partially confirmed by the sources at our disposal, i.e., by the deposition of Iseppo Sartor, it is nevertheless an important doctrinal feature.

(24) As far as Venice is concerned, see Stella, *Anabattismo e antitrinitarismo*, p. 71.

(25) In particular, both Dall'Olio, *Eretici e Inquisitori* and Firpo, *La presa di potere*, p. 179-195 shed light on the relationships between Muzzarelli's Rome and Ghislieri and Alberti's Bologna. On the functioning of the Venetian tribunal, see Martin, *Hidden Enemies*; Black, *Italian Inquisition*, p. 31-37; Del Col, *Inquisizione*, p. 342-394; Mayer, *Roman Inquisition*, p. 64-151; Seitz, 'Interconnected Inquisitors', all providing the most up-to-date and complete picture. See also P. C. Ioly Zorattini, *Processi del S. Uffizio di Venezia contro ebrei e giudaizzanti*, 14 vols, Firenze 1980-1999 and F. Barbierato, *Politici e ateisti: percorsi della miscredenza a Venezia fra Sei e Settecento*, Milano 2006 along with the dated but still useful Paschini, *Venezia e l'inquisizione*. For more detailed information see Grendler, 'Tre savii'; Seidel Menchi, 'Protestantesimo a Venezia'; Del Col, *Aquileia*, p. cxxx-cxxxvii. Among works published before 1998, see Tedeschi, *Il giudice* and Prosperi, *Tribunali*; on post-1998 works, see C. Arnold, 'The Archive of the

account has been entirely subsumed both by Simonetta Adorni Braccesi and by Simone Ragagli and Stefania Malavasi. (26) On the whole, Manelfi's inconsistencies do not seem to indicate that the entire deposition was an invention of his: it does reveal certain inaccuracies – and sometimes serious negligence – but it also suggests that this information was second-hand or indirect, and, at most, it calls for this information to be reassessed. Through the comparison of Manelfi's accounts with the material discovered by Stella, Luca Addante has meticulously reconstructed the introduction and influence of Juan de Valdés' ideas in the Neapolitan group in the Anabaptist circle of Veneto. (27) More specifically, the *condicio sine qua non* of Manelfi's credibility was the date of his (second) baptism: was it before or after the meeting in Venice? Among the numerous inconsistencies in his confessions, one in particular is specifically connected to this detail. In the Bolognese deposition of 17 October 1551, he claimed to have been catechised in Ferrara by 'messer Giuseppe da Vicenza', (28) and then to have been re-baptised 'da Titiano'. (29) However, the following month, in Rome, he mentioned only Titian as both his catechist and baptiser: 'Ticiano cominciò a predicarmi la dottrina anabattista et il rebattizzarmi'. (30) So when did Manelfi's baptism take place? He stated it took place in Ferrara – clearly before the so-called Council – and did so without going into much detail: (31) on the other hand, the more authoritative Marcantonio Del Bon clearly asserted that Manelfi's baptism had taken place after the Council – 'lui non era entrato in detta setta se non molti mesi doppo' – as he met him as late as in June 1551, when he knew Manelfi would come 'da Fiorenza e Ferrara'. (32) Giuseppe Sartori recalled he was in Florence, yet to be

Roman Congregation for the Doctrine of the Faith (ACDF): An Initial Overview of Its Holdings and Scholarship', in S. Wendehorst (ed.), *The Roman Inquisition, the Index and the Jews: Contexts Sources and Perspectives*, Leiden – Boston (MA) 2004, p. 155-168 and M. Valente, 'Nuove ricerche e interpretazioni sul Sant'Uffizio a più di dieci anni dall'apertura dell'archivio', *Rivista di storia della Chiesa in Italia* 66 (2012), p. 569-592.

(26) Cfr. Adorni Braccesi, 'Manelfi'; Ragagli, 'Manelfi'; Malavasi, 'Anabattismo'.

(27) Addante, *Eretici e libertini*, p. 106-128.

(28) Also known as Giuseppe (Iseppo) Cingano (also Sartor when referred to by his trade). Cfr. Venezia, Archivio di Stato, Savi all'eresia (Santo Ufficio), busta 24, fasc. processuale n. 2 and *infra*.

(29) Cfr. Ginzburg, *Costituti*, p. 34.

(30) Ginzburg, *Costituti*, p. 63.

(31) Ginzburg, *Costituti*, p. 34 and p. 63-64.

(32) See Venezia, Archivio di Stato, Savi all'eresia (Santo Ufficio), busta 158, reg. III, f. 37^r and cfr. Stella, *Anabattismo e antitrinitarismo*, p. 65. See also Venezia, Archivio di Stato, Savi all'eresia (Santo Ufficio), busta 158, reg. III, f. 34^v and cfr. Stella, *Anabattismo e antitrinitarismo*, p. 68.

re-baptised, together with 'don Antonio' Pagano, 'capellan de la duchessa di Ferara qual era scampato ... per paura de esser preso per heretico': (33) thus, it could not have occurred before the arrest of Giorgio Siculo in September 1550, (34) as only afterwards did Ferrara become unsafe.

The Paduan tailor Bernardino Prandi and his wife provided further details. Manelfi's baptism must have taken place after December 1550/January 1551, as at that time he was their guest and was not yet baptised. (35) After the arrest of Siculo, according to Heinrich Bullinger's letter to Pier Paolo Vergerio, Renée de France came out in public: this could imply that Ferrara – or more precisely Consandolo, her summer residence – had once again become a safe haven. Eleonora Belligni admits to this point, suggesting that it is possible that she became emboldened in this specific period. (36) If Ferrara in 1551 once again became a reference point for Titian's group, which gravitated between Padua and Ferrara and was very close to Renée de France, it must have been when the Polesine region had ceased to be safe 'per la grandissima commodità de li fiumar e canali che sono assaissimi et aperti senza alcun ostacolo' (37) – indeed, one of Titian's children was hiding in Rovigo. This must necessarily date to after the arrest of the influential Benedetto Del Borgo in Rovigo in February 1551, or after his execution the following month. (38) If this hypothe-

---

(33) See Venezia, Archivio di Stato, Savi all'eresia (Santo Ufficio), busta 158, reg. IV, f. 56ʳ and cfr. Stella, *Anabattismo e antitrinitarismo*, p. 49.

(34) E. Belligni, *Renata di Francia (1510-1575). Un'eresia di corte*, Torino 2012, p. 247-248, who also recalls how Renata kept excellent relations with Titian (p. 311). Cfr. Stella, *Anabattismo e antitrinitarismo*, p. 49.

(35) See Venezia, Archivio di Stato, Savi all'eresia (Santo Ufficio), busta 158, reg. II, f. 59ʳ-60ᵛ and cfr. Stella, *Anabattismo e antitrinitarismo*, p. 67.

(36) Belligni, *Renata di Francia*, p. 248.

(37) As Morosini, *podestà* of Rovigo, had lodged complaints in 1534 to the Consiglio dei Dieci: see Venezia, Archivio di Stato, Capi del Consiglio dei Dieci, Lettere di rettori Rovigo, busta 121, c. 60 and cfr. Stella, *Anabattismo e antitrinitarismo*, p. 75. Moreover, if 'Badia e Lendinara rappresentano per Venezia l'aspetto più "tedioso" riguardo il problema della criminalità', then Rovigo found itself in 'una situazione per nulla migliore' (Malavasi, *Criminalità e giustizia*, p. 14).

(38) Benedetto should not be underestimated: in terms of authority and competence, he carried more weight than Titian himself – once again deviating from Manelfi's accounts. Cfr. Stella, *Anabattismo e antitrinitarismo*, p. 43 and Addante, *Eretici e libertini*, p. 181. The Paduan community was also affected, as it rapidly fell apart (Stella, *Anabattismo e antitrinitarismo*, p. 79-80). Moreover, this event was exceptional as 'inquisitorial trials in Venice and the Veneto only rarely ended with a death sentence'. See C. Cristellon – S. Seidel Menchi, 'Religious Life', in E. Dursteler (ed.), *A Companion to Venetian History, 1400-1797* (*Brill's Companions to European History* 4), Leiden 2013, p. 379-419, here p. 411, note 82.

CONCILIUM VENETIANUM-FERRARIENSE – 1550

sis was correct, Manelfi's inaccuracy would boil down to backdating his association with Titian's movement.

What seems clear is that Manelfi sought to make his depositions more
credible by exaggerating his own importance in the eyes of the inquisitors: if
so, it is worth questioning the naïveté of such an intention, as his recount
would obviously deviate from the confessions of those first arrested. Therefore,
Ugo Gastaldi's hypothesis that Manelfi acted 'in pieno accordo con il Sant'Uffizio', seeking to strengthen the credibility of his statements – which exceeded
the highest expectations of his listeners, although formulated by a relatively
marginal member of the Anabaptist community – seems corroborated. ([39]).
By trusting Manelfi's statements, Rome could thus provide evidence 'per tutta
Italia' of 'una moltitudine d'anabattisti' – as shown in the curial document
delivered to the *Serenissima* – 'i quali hanno congiurato contra li magistrati,
contra le fede et contra Christo', ([40]) conditioning and seeking to redirect the
policy of tolerance hitherto adopted by Venice.

NOTES ON THE EDITION

The critical edition offered below is the result of the transcription of
excerpts from documents related to the so-called Council of Venice of 1550,
held in the State Archives of Venice, fondo Savi all'eresia (Santo Ufficio),
busta 158, libri II-IV. These three volumes contain records of heresy trials from
1551 to 1552: they were not considered in Carlo Ginzburg's critical edition of
Manelfi's account and were the ones which led Aldo Stella to dispute the
veracity of Manelfi's declarations. Some depositions were made by participants in the meeting of Venice and constitute first-hand information about
the event. There are also indirect testimonies. The depositions of the Synod's
participants – accounted for in index 303 of the archive collection Savi all'eresia (Santo Ufficio), compiled in 1876 by Giuseppe Giorno and Luigi Pasini,
which Ginzburg did consider – mostly date back to arrests and trials that
significantly precede or follow Manelfi's confessions (in essence, they are cases
of *relapsi*) and are not particularly useful for the reconstruction of the events
of autumn 1550. ([41])

---

(39) Cfr. Gastaldi, *Storia dell'Anabattismo*, vol. 2, p. 557. As Adriano Prosperi notes, it
was no coincidence that Manelfi enjoyed a stipend of five gold ducats a month from
1552 onwards (Prosperi, *Libro Grande*, p. 434).

(40) Ginzburg, *Costituti*, p. 83.

(41) In any case, however, they refer to material from previous trials as sources for the
writing of the texts of conviction or of abjuration.

As the aim of this series is to publish only synodal decrees (*decreta*), in the texts we edited the reader will find information concerning the decisions taken during the so-called Council of Venice as well as the decisions of the meeting of Ferrara, which immediately followed the former – indeed, the two events are closely linked to one another. However, since an edition of the actual details of the Council (such as venue, number and role of participants, conclusion) is still lacking, we decided to publish them as a synopsis at the end of this introduction.

Anyhow, for both the decisions and other information published as an appendix, in the main body of the text we have limited ourselves to reporting the confessions held in the participants' depositions: on the other hand, the second apparatus has been used as indirect testimony – according to the guidelines of the *Conciliorum Oecumenicorum Generaliumque Decreta* series – with the exception of Manelfi's testimony (see below). (42) Due to an inability to proceed beyond the collation of testimonies that are equally authoritative from a philological point of view, it was impossible to draft a single text: as a result, the two testimonies are juxtaposed, as some of the figures from different interrogations provide certain details on specific aspects of the conciliar event and others further clarify them (and information will be provided in full regardless of the consistency of the information found in different depositions). In an effort to ensure fluidity and legibility, we have omitted the court clerks' annotations (e.g. 'domandato', 'rispose', 'dicens') unless their omission compromised the intelligibility of the testimony. Information provided is subdivided by authors, whose names are given as they are found in the manuscript.

The main goal of this critical edition is to show how Manelfi's statements differ from those his fellow believers gave the following year. In the third apparatus, Manelfi's depositions can be read in Ginzburg's edition as variants of the body of the text. In those occurrences in which information is repeated in depositions of several participants in the so-called Synod, deviations from Manelfi's accounts will be provided in the apparatus only in their first appearance.

(42) Since the appendix has no Monitum, manuscript lines will also be included in this section's second apparatus.

The following abbreviations are used in the apparatuses of the critical edition: *Man¹*, *Man⁴*, *A*, *B*, *C* (see 'bibliography' as well as 'conspectus siglorum').

APPENDIX

Manelfi	⟨Giovanni Maria Beato altre volte Manfredino cittadino di Rovigo:⟩[2]	⟨Marc'Antonio da Prata de Asolo:⟩[1]
Preparation Andai a Vicenza con gli detti compagni, ove in una congregatione venemmo a quel passo del *Deuteronomio* ove Dio dice: «Prophetam suscitabo de fratribus tuis, et ponam verba mea in ore ipsius etc. tamquam me ipsum audite», et fussemo in differentia fra noi se Cristo fosse Dio o huomo. Et per risolvere questo dubio concludessemo che si chiamasse tutti gli ministri delle congregationi de lochi a Venetia a concilio, et perciò furno eletti doi che andassero per tutto fin in Basilea a chiamare doi per chiesa over loco, che venessero a detto concilio[4].		In Padova era venuta certa differentia: che alcuni tenevano che l'evangelio non fusse tutta scrittura delli evangelisti, ma che li fusse sta gionto et alchuni lo tenevano ad unguem[3].

(1) Marcantonio Del Bon, cfr Venezia, Archivio di Stato, Savi all'eresia (Santo Ufficio), busta 9, fasc. 7 and Venezia, Archivio di Stato, Savi all'eresia (Santo Ufficio), busta 34, fasc. Prata Marc'Antonio.

(2) cfr Venezia, Archivio di Stato, Savi all'eresia (Santo Ufficio), busta 6, fasc. 5; Rovigo, Archivio diocesano di Adria-Rovigo, Cause criminali, busta 1, fasc. 33; cfr Malavasi, Diavolo e acquasanta, p. 42-52 and 62-66.

(3) In – unguem] *B*, f. 31ᵛ l. 8-11.

(4) Andai – concilio] *Man¹*, p. 34 l. 68-77.

CONCILIUM VENETIANUM-FERRARIENSE – 1550

⟨Pasqualin quondam Francesco de Pasqualini de Asolo pelizaro:⟩	⟨Iseppo fiol de Zuan Maria di Sartori da Asolo:⟩	⟨Zuan Ludovico Bronzier dalla Badia:[5]⟩	⟨Perin calegharo da Asolo fiol de Zuanantoni favro:⟩	
Messer Augustin maestro da scuola[6] mi disse che Benetto[7] era cascato in una gran heresia che Christo non era nato de verginità de Maria ma chel era fiol de Joseph et ne disse che non dovessemo parlar con lui. Doppo venessemo a Padoa donde Marc' Antonio parlò con lui de questa cosa della vergenità et deliberarno de venir in Venetia et parlarsene – etiam de altre cose[10].	Non so ⟨a instantia de chi fu fatto tal redutto⟩ salvo che per esser stato scomunicato messer Benetto dalla giesia de Cittadella perché l'haveva detto che Jesù Christo era nasciuto de matrimonio de Joseph et de[α] Maria cioè[β] nasciuto de copula et per esser intravenuta tal dissension el fu fatto tal redutto[9].	Credo che Benedetto predetto ne invitasse a vener qui in Venetia et così venessemo[8].		Preparation

(α) de] *add. et del.* madon *C*
(β) cioè] *add. et del.* del suo *C*

(5) cfr Malavasi, *Diavolo e acquasanta*, p. 54-56.
(6) Agostino Tealdo, cfr Zille, *Cittadella*.
(7) Benedetto Del Borgo, cfr Venezia, Archivio di Stato, Savi all'eresia (Santo Ufficio), busta 9, fasc. 5 and Malavasi, *Diavolo e acquasanta*, p. 43-45.
(8) Credo – venessemo] *A*, f. 98ʳ l. 24-26.
(9) Non – redutto] *C*, f. 36ʳ l. 11-16.
(10) Messer – cose] *C*, f. 2ʳ l. 28 - f. 2ᵛ l. 3.

Manelfi	Giovanni Maria Beato	Marc'Antonio da Prata

Logistics

Et così dell'anno 1550 del mese di settembre si ritrovorno sessanta fra ministri et vescovi de anabattisti in Venetia a concilio[11], ove per quaranta giorni digiunando, orando et studiando le scritture sacre determinassemo così questi articoli[13].
Erano sino al numero de cinquanta o sessanta in circa. Quanto all'habitation nostra alloggiassimo in diversi palazzi a camere locande, dove tre dove quattro, et se io havesse una lista che tengo in Padoa vi saprei dire di chi erano li alloggiamenti[17].

Avanti Nadal prossimo passato fece un anno che io mi trovavo in questa terra con el sopraditto messer Hieronimo[12] che litigavemo al consiglio di Venetia et a quel tempo el venne in questa terra el sopraditto Benetto con tutti quelli che ho nominato di Asolo[14], et con altri che mi par che erano al numero di otto et una volta mi fecero andar in una casa verso Rialto, non so donde ma intesi a dir che la era la casa inservente, donde in una camera tra noi, che erimo da circa diese, fu ragionato di tutte

Per la qual cosa fu avisati Benedetto de Borgo et Ticiano et anchor fu mandato uno messo fino in Pisa per chiamar Nicola a a questa difficultà dove che se reducessemo in questa città in casa di madona Elena, che sta al ponte di Fusari, et eramo circa dodece over quatordece[15]. Fu ordinato di farlo in Venetia per manco tumulto et manco suspetto[16]. Credo che fosse di novembre o ottobre del 1550 et stessimo da tre o quattro giorni insieme[18].
El numero delli congregati

(11) see the indirect testimony at *A*, f. 77^rv (Mathio dalla Madalena): *'era sta fatto un concilio in Venetia dove erano intravenuti dui per città'. Dicens interrogatus: '(Jacometto stringaro) non me disse di che né di quante città ma el me disse che di Vicenza el vi era andato lui con un altro compagno ma non mi disse chi fosse, et che in questo concilio fu parlato di questo et che tutti lo sentivano che fossi così come ho detto di sopra'. Domandato: 'chi intendeste voi che fossero quelli che intravenero al detto concilio'? Rispose: 'el mi disse chel vi era quel messer Marcantonio da Asolo e messer Paolo non so come si chiama il suo cognome e quel Titian el quale io conosco per vista e gli ho parlato due volte e quel messer Nicola del qual non so il sovranome e credo chel sia o da Treviso o da Asolo e un messer Benetto non so il suo sovranome credo chel sia da Asolo over da Rovigo e mi disse chel vi era stato anche l'Abbate da Padova'. Dicens interrogatus 'el non me disse chi era questo Abbate, ma el mi disse solamente l'Abbate da Padova come ho detto et lo laudava grandemente che l'era un grand'uomo et dotto'. Domandato: 'ne disselo in che luogo qui in Venetia fosse fatto il detto concilio' rispose liberamente: 'el non mi disse né in che luogo né in che contrà né anche mi cercai di saver più oltre'. Dicens interrogatus 'el non mi nominò altri che quelli che ho detto di sopra che andavano intorno'.*

(12) Gerolamo Venezze, cfr Malavasi, *Diavolo e acquasanta*, p. 45-46.

(13) Et – articoli] *Man¹*, p. 34 l. 77-80.

(14) cfr *A*, f. 73^r: *Marc'Antonio da Asolo non so el suo cognome et uno Pasqualin Pelizaro pur da Asolo et uno Iseppo et uno Perin Calegher et uno Paulo Beltramin: questi tutti dicevano esser da Asolo.*

(15) Per – quatordece] *B*, f. 31^v l. 12-17.

(16) Fu – suspetto] *B*, f. 32^v l. 8-10.

(17) erano – alloggiamenti] *Man⁴*, p. 65 l. 672-675.

(18) Credo – insieme] *B*, f. 32^v l. 12-14.

CONCILIUM VENETIANUM-FERRARIENSE – 1550

Pasqualin	Iseppo Sartori	Zuan Ludovico	Perin calegharo	
Et così venessemo in Venetia et lozassemo al ponte de Fusi in casa de una dona che teneva camere donde fusse da tredese[19].	⟨Qui in Venetia⟩ veni a uno redutto et fussemo non so quanti insieme apresso S. Luca[γ] a pi dui ponti – non so di chi sia la casa, non credo che sapria andare – da tredese vel quator-	⟨Tal congregatione⟩ la fessemo al ponte de' Fusari in casa de una dona che aloza fores- tieri, par fussemo da otto in diese et credo che di ottobre fa uno anno over novem- bre[20]. Credo che		Logistics

(γ) Luca] *add. et del.* apr *C*

(19) Et – tredese] *C*, f. 2ᵛ l. 3-5.
(20) Tal – novembre] *A*, f. 98ʳ,l. 17-20.

CONCILIUM VENETIANUM-FERRARIENSE – 1550

Manelfi	Giovanni Maria Beato	Marc'Antonio da Prata
	le sopraditte cose[21].	qui in Venetia in quel tempo che ho nominato furono circha dodece over quatordece così anchora lo confermo – et potrebbe esser un più un mancho, ché più specialmente non mi ricordo – et non stessemo più di giorni quatro over cinque, come de questo vostre signorie cristianissime ne potria haver fede dalla patrona dove alloggiassemo, che fu una madona Elena de Cipro, sta in questa città al ponte de Fusari – potrebbe esser che doppo finito tal parlamento alchuno de noi restasse anchora in questa città per quatro over sei giorni[22].
Participants	Li convenne d'Italia Ticiano sudetto, Nicola da Terviso, l'abbate Hieronimo Buzano neapolitano et uno maestro Antonino suo compagno, et Benedetto d'Asolo di Terviso il quale fu iustitiato in Rovigo per tal causa, Iulio da Vincenza[δ] morto in Vicenza di sua morte, et un altro veronese morto, et un altro da Citadella morto, et Ioanne, Celio Secondo sfratato quale ha composto *Pasquin in estasi* qual		Et in questo sudetto eramo Benetto de Borgo, Ticiano, Paulo Beltramin[23], Iseppo Sartor[24], Zuanni Bronzier dalla Badia, Zuan Maria Beato da Rhovigo, Hieronimo da Venetia[25] et Francesco Sega[26] da Rovigo, Jacometto Stringaro[27] da Vicenza[ε], Julio Sartor da Treviso, Bastian cognato de Benetto, sta a Treviso non mi ricordo la casada et né

(δ) Vincenza] *sic*
(ε) da Vicenza] *add. in marg.*

(21) Avanti – cose] *A*, f. 73v l. 12-22. Cfr *A*, f. 77r.
(22) El – giorni] *B*, f. 36v l. 2-12.
(23) cfr Venezia, Archivio di Stato, Savi all'eresia (Santo Ufficio), busta 9, fasc. 7.
(24) Other than Iseppo (Giuseppe) Cingano, cfr *infra*.
(25) Gerolamo Venezze, *vide supra*.
(26) Francesco Della Sega, cfr Venezia, Archivio di Stato, Savi all'eresia (Santo Ufficio), busta 19, fasc. 1 and 2 and Malavasi, *Diavolo e acquasanta*, p. 45-46.
(27) cfr Venezia, Archivio di Stato, Savi all'eresia (Santo Ufficio), busta 9, fasc. 7.

CONCILIUM VENETIANUM-FERRARIENSE – 1550

Pasqualin	Iseppo Sartori	Zuan Ludovico	Perin calegharo
	dese vel circa[28]. ⟨(Domandato: « Stesse troppo in questa terra? » Respose:)⟩ Salvo el vero, tre giorni[31].	stessemo circha tre o quatro giorni in questa terra[29]. Alogiassemo tutti in la medema casa[30].	

| Benetto, Marc'Antonio, Iseppo, Paulo Beltramin, uno cognato de Benetto che sta a Treviso et credo chel sia nodaro et ha | Messer Benetto De Borgo, messer Marc' Antonio da Prata, uno Tician che altramente non so che el sia ma l'è da Ceneda | ⟨Intraveno a tal congregatione⟩: el detto Benetto, Paulo Beltramin et Marcantonio de Asolo, Jacometto stringaro, | | Participants |

(28) Qui – circa] *C*, f. 35ᵛ l. 25-30.
(29) Credo – terra] *A*, f. 98ᵛ l. 6-7.
(30) Alogiassemo – casa] *A*, f. 98ᵛ l. 9-10.
(31) Domandato – giorni] *C*, f. 36ᵛ l. 17-18.

CONCILIUM VENETIANUM-FERRARIENSE – 1550

| Manelfi | Giovanni Maria Beato | Marc'Antonio da Prata |

venne da Basilea, il Nero venne da Chiavena, Francesco bassanese che venne da Chiavena, et altri da san Gallo da quelle parti de Grisoni, et altri[33].

Fu Ticiano pratico per quelle parte et il suo compagno Ioseph d'Asolo[35].

Et tutti ch'eravamo ivi congregati eravamo episcopi di detta giesa, l'officio de quali è predicare la parola et constituire ministri nelle giese andando sempre attorno, et si chiamano vescovi apostoli, fra quali uno era io, Nicola da Terviso, Ticiano et Ioseph, li quali da poi detto concilio andorno attorno, et hora ci va ancora Marc'Antonio d'Asolo, messer Paolo da Terviso, messer Ioseph da Vicenza, Hieronimo Speranza da Vicenza, maestro Bartholomeo da Padova pianellaro, maestro Iacometto da Terviso sarto, et altri che hora non mi ricordo il nome[40].

Per tutto quel paese[41] sono molti et molti anabattisti, et el so perché in Venetia al concilio fatto, secondo che ho deto nella mia confessione, ne venero da vinti o trenta da quelle parti[42].

de altri non mi ricordo[32]. Fu mandato un Hieronimo Speranza a Pisa per chiamar Nicola de Alessandria alla sopradetta congregatione fatta in Venetia[34]. Non mi ricordo che intravenesse alchun forestiero[36]. ⟨Pietro della Marcha⟩ non era entrato in detta setta se non molti mesi doppo fatto la sudetta congregation in questa terra[37] – per quello che io ho inteso da altri et da lui stesso[38]: lui stava a Fiorenza et non era venuto in queste bande se non al tempo che noi, cioè lui et mi, andassemo in Capo d'Istria, che fu nel principio del mese de zugno prossimo passato, 1551, et la congregatione fu fatta del 1550[39].

---

(32) Et – ricordo] *B*, f. 32ᵛ l. 1-8.
(33) Li – altri] *Man⁴*, p. 65 l. 664-671.
(34) Fu – Venetia] *B*, f. 36ʳ l. 1-2.
(35) Fu – d'Asolo] *Man⁴*, p. 66 l. 682-683.
(36) Non – forestiero] *B*, f. 36ᵛ l. 16-17.
(37) Pietro – terra] *B*, f. 36ᵛ l. 23-25.
(38) per – stesso] *B*, f. 36ᵛ l. 27-28.
(39) lui – 1550] *B*, f. 36ᵛ l. 28 - 37ʳ l. 3.
(40) Et – nome] *Man⁴*, p. 66-67 l. 713-721.
(41) I.e. *In Voltelina, Basilea, et passo più oltra verso San Gallo* (*Man⁴*, p. 67 l. 728).
(42) Per – parti] *Man⁴*, p. 67 l. 729-731.

CONCILIUM VENETIANUM-FERRARIENSE – 1550

Pasqualin	Iseppo Sartori	Zuan Ludovico	Perin calegharo
nome Bastian, Jacomo Stringaro da Vicenza, Tician, Francesco da Rhovigo, messer Zuani dalla Badia et altri non mi ricordo[44].	per quello che lui ha detto, Pasqualin, messer Zuan Maria Beato da Rovigo, messer Hieronimo da Venetia da Rhovigo[ʸ], messer Francesco da Rovigo, non so el suo cognome, messer Zuani dalla Badia, messer Paulo Beltramin, Iulio da Treviso che non lo cognosceva ne pria l'haveva visto, io, et delli altri che non li ho cognosciuti altramente né avanti ne doppo li ho più veduti[46].	Tiziano, Francesco Fra Hosto[43], Hieronimo da Venezia et Zuan Maria Beato da Rhovigo, uno da Treviso, el nome del qual non mi sovien, et io et credo che non vi era altri[45].	

(ζ) Rhovigo] *sic*

(43) Francesco Della Sega, *vide supra.*
(44) Benetto – ricordo] *C*, f. 2ᵛ l. 18-23.
(45) Intraveno – altri] *A*, f. 98ʳ l. 27 - 98ᵛ l. 2.
(46) Messer – veduti] *C*, f. 36ʳ l. 1-10.

Manelfi	Giovanni Maria Beato	Marc'Antonio da Prata
Expenses Io fui eletto con un altro a cercare danari per fare le spese al concilio[47]. Toccò a me pagare li patroni per detti alloggiamenti, li quali però non sapevano queste nostre congregationi eccetto che una patrona un giorno me disse: « Che vuol dire tante gente che vengano ? ». Et io li dissi che bastava di essere pagata[51]. Nel stato di Venetia furno spesi ventisette scudi perché degiunavamo ogni giorno et magnavamo sobriamente. Questi denari si raccolsero dalli anabattisti di Vicenza, Padoa, Terviso et Citadella, et io raccolsi detti denari in queste giese et ero spenditore; per il viaggio ciascun spendeva secondo li haveva subministrato la sua giesa[52].	Me fu detto che messer Paulo Beltramin fece le spese del fitto de casa, et el ditto Benetto altre volte et anche Ticiano racomandava li poveri et tra noi gettavemo l'elemosena in una baretta et poi tra loro li dispensevano secondo che gli pareva[50].	Stessimo tutti insieme et raro si andava fuora di casa eccetto color che spendevano[48]: Messer Paulo Beltramin, messer Gioan Bronzero di quelli da Rovigo et io[49].
Closure Questi articoli furono conclusi in quel concilio et tutte le chiese accettorno questa dottrina, eccetto quella di Cittadella. Io fui eletto uno de' ministri per andare predicando la detta dottrina per tutti gli sopradetti lochi, per gli quali andai con Marc'Antonio d'Asola predicandola, et quelli che la ricevano erano della nostra chiesa, quelli che non la ricevano gli separavamo dagli altri; et così perseverassemo per tutto agosto prossimo passato[54]. Finiti quaranta giorni raccoglies-		⟨Finita che fu la sopradetta congregatione⟩ io andai a Padova dove stete circa dui giorni et doppo a Vicenza per refferir a quelli de lì quanto era stato parlato et sì come ho detto de sopra[53]. Io refferivi a quelli de Vicenza che era sta parlato de Christo, che fusse puro homo, et per la maggior parte ciaschuno così teneva quanto alla confession della fede de quelli che recevano el segno del batismo

(47) Io – concilio] *Man¹*, p. 34 l. 76-77.
(48) Stessimo – spendevano] *B*, f. 32ᵛ l. 16-19.
(49) Messer – io] *B*, f. 32ᵛ l. 20-21.
(50) Me – pareva] *A*, f. 73ᵛ l. 24-27.
(51) Toccò – pagata] *Man⁴*, p. 65 l. 675-679.
(52) Nel – giesa] *Man⁴*, p. 66 l. 686-690.
(53) Finita – sopra] *B*, f. 37ʳ l. 5-8.
(54) Questi – passato] *Man¹*, p. 35-36 l. 109-115.

CONCILIUM VENETIANUM-FERRARIENSE – 1550

Pasqualin	Iseppo Sartori	Zuan Ludovico	Perin calegharo	
		Circa la spesa spendevano quelli che si sentivano haver danari che fu Paulo Beltramin, et io quelli da Rhovigo[55].		Expenses
			Quando io ultimamente ero in Ferrara, el vene Benetto Dal Borgo et Tician et trovorno messer Nicola et mi in Ferrara. Et ghe disseno	Closure

(55) Circa – Rhovigo] *A*, f. 98ᵛ l. 4-6.

516 CONCILIUM VENETIANUM-FERRARIENSE – 1550

Manelfi	Giovanni Maria Beato	Marc'Antonio da Prata

Manelfi

simo tutta la dottrina[56].
Et tutti ch'eravamo ivi congregati eravamo episcopi di detta giesa, l'officio de quali è predicare la parola et constituire ministri nelle giese andando sempre attorno, et si chiamano vescovi apostoli, fra quali uno ero io, Nicola da Terviso, Ticiano et Ioseph, li quali da poi detto concilio andorno attorno, et hora ci va ancora Marc'Antonio d'Asolo, messer Paolo da Terviso, messer Ioseph da Vicenza, Hieronimo Speranza da Vicenza, maestro Bartholomeo da Padova pianellaro, maestro Iacometto da Terviso sarto, et altri che hora non mi ricorda il nome, li quali sempre vanno attorno visitando le giese, disseminando questa dottrina, facendo novi ministri et simil cose pertinente all'augumento di questa dottrina[58].

Marc'Antonio da Prata

era che cognoscessero uno solo Idio et Christo Segnor nostro capo de fedeli vero Messia promesso da Idio et che si separassero dalla ydolatria et constitutione di legge, santo tribunal dicendoli che non vi era altro maestro che Christo[57].

(56) Finiti – dottrina] *Man⁴*, p. 66 l. 709-710.

(57) Io – Christo] *B*, f. 37ʳ l. 12-21.

(58) Et – dottrina] *Man⁴*, p. 66-67 l. 713-723. Cfr *B*, f. 58ᵛ l. 1-8 (Julio fiol de Zuano da S. Corona da Vicenza o Calegaro): *Domandato: 'Tra di voi è mai stato fatta congregation o uno reducto generale et in questo locho?' Respose: 'Mi non lo so [...]. Ma ben ho inteso da li nostri de Vicenza che in questa terra fu fato una congregation generale, cioè del alquanti de la nostra giesa de diverse città, né so altramente per che conto salvo che intesi dir che delliberorno che dui andasseno da una banda et dui da l'altra per le terre, a parlar et predicar, et veder de tirar dele persone alla nostra giesa.*

Pasqualin	Iseppo Sartori	Zuan Ludovico	Perin calegharo
			de questa congrega-tion fatta in Venetia et ghe lesseno una lettera, ma non vol-seno che mi la inten-desse et subito letta la getorno su il fuogo[59].

(59) Quando – fuogo] *C*, f. 14ᵛ l. 25-30.

BIBLIOGRAPHY

Sources (and Their Abbreviations)

Manuscripts

Rovigo, Archivio diocesano di Adria-Rovigo, Cause criminali, busta 1, fasc. 12.

Rovigo, Archivio diocesano di Adria-Rovigo, Cause criminali, busta 1, fasc. 33.

Venezia, Archivio di Stato, Savi all'eresia (Santo Ufficio), busta 6, fasc. 5.

Venezia, Archivio di Stato, Savi all'eresia (Santo Ufficio), busta 9, fasc. 5.

Venezia, Archivio di Stato, Savi all'eresia (Santo Ufficio), busta 9, fasc. 7.

Venezia, Archivio di Stato, Savi all'eresia (Santo Ufficio), busta 19, fasc. 1.

Venezia, Archivio di Stato, Savi all'eresia (Santo Ufficio), busta 19, fasc. 2.

Venezia, Archivio di Stato, Savi all'eresia (Santo Ufficio), busta 34, fasc. Prata Marc'Antonio.

Venezia, Archivio di Stato, Savi all'eresia (Santo Ufficio), busta 158, libro secondo [= *A*].

Venezia, Archivio di Stato, Savi all'eresia (Santo Ufficio), busta 158, libro terzo [= *B*].

Venezia, Archivio di Stato, Savi all'eresia (Santo Ufficio), busta 158, libro quarto [= *C*].

Printed Source

I costituti di don Pietro Manelfi, a cura di C. Ginzburg, Firenze – Chicago (IL) 1970 [= Ginzburg, *Costituti*], p. 31-38 [= *Man¹*] and 64-70 [= *Man⁴*]

Literature (and Its Abbreviations)

L. Addante, *Eretici e libertini nel Cinquecento italiano*, Roma – Bari 2010 [= Addante, *Eretici e libertini*].

S. Adorni Braccesi, 'Manelfi, Pietro', in *Dizionario Biografico degli Italiani* 68 (2007), p. 594-596 [= Adorni Braccesi, 'Manelfi'].

K. Benrath, *Geschichte der Reformation in Venedig*, Halle 1887.

—, 'Wiedertäufer im Venetianischen um die Mitte des 16. Jahrhunderts', *Theologische Studien und Kritiken* 58 (1885), p. 9-67.

C. F. Black, *The Italian Inquisition*, New Haven (CT) – London 2009 [= Black, *Italian Inquisition*].

D. Caccamo, *Eretici Italiani in Moravia, Polonia, Transilvania (1558-1611). Studi e documenti*, Firenze – Chicago (IL) 1970.

S. Caponetto, *La riforma protestante nell'Italia del Cinquecento*, Torino ²1997.

D. Cantimori, 'Gli anabattisti', in A. M. Moschetti – M. Schiavone (a cura di), *Grande antologia filosofica*, 35 vols, Milano 1954-1985, vol. 8 (1964), p. 1405-1488 [= Cantimori, 'Gli anabattisti'].

—, *Eretici italiani nel Cinquecento*, Firenze 1939 [= Cantimori, *Eretici italiani*].

—, 'Anabattismo e neoplatonismo nel XVI secolo in Italia', *Rendiconti della classe di scienze morali, storiche e filologiche della Regia Accademia nazionale dei Lincei* ser. 6, vol. 12/5-6 (1936), p. 36-41 [= Cantimori, 'Anabattismo'].

F. C. Church, *I riformatori italiani*, 2 vols, Firenze 1935.

E. Comba, 'Un sinodo anabattista a Venezia, anno 1550', *La rivista cristiana* 13 (1885), p. 21-24 and p. 83-87.

I costituti di don Pietro Manelfi, a cura di C. Ginzburg, Firenze – Chicago (IL) 1970, p. 9-27 [= Ginzburg, *Costituti*].

G. Dall'Olio, *Eretici e Inquisitori nella Bologna del Cinquecento*, Bologna 1999 [= Dall'Olio, *Eretici e Inquisitori*].

A. Del Col, *L'inquisizione nel patriarcato e diocesi di Aquileia 1557-1559*, Trieste 1998 [= Del Col, *Aquileia*].

—, *L'Inquisizione in Italia dal XII al XXI secolo*, Milano 2006 [= Del Col, *Inquisizione*].

—, 'Organizzazione, composizione e giurisdizione dei tribunali dell'Inquisizione romana nella repubblica di Venezia (1500-1550)', *Critica storica* 2 (1988), p. 245-294.

M. Firpo, *Tra «Alumbrados» e «Spirituali». Studi su Juan de Valdes e il valdesianesimo nella crisi religiosa del Cinquecento italiano*, Firenze 1990 [= Firpo, *Alumbrados*].

—, *La presa di potere dell'Inquisizione romana 1550-1553*, Roma – Bari 2014 [= Firpo, *La presa di potere*].

U. Gastaldi, *Storia dell'anabattismo*, 2 vols, Torino 1981 [= Gastaldi, *Storia dell'anabattismo*).

P. Grendler, 'The *Tre savii sopra eresia* 1547-1605: A Prosopographical Study', *Studi veneziani* n.s. 3 (1979), p. 283-340 [= Grendler, 'Tre savii'].

P. C. Ioly Zorattini, 'The Trials of the Holy Office of Adria (Rovigo) against Jews and Judaizers', in *Proceedings of the World Congress of Jewish Studies*, 5 vols, Ithaca (NY) 1985, vol. 2.1: *The History of the Jewish People (From the Second Temple Period Until the Middle Ages)*, p. 167-174.

S. Malavasi, 'Anabattismo', in A. Prosperi (dir.), *Dizionario Storico dell'Inquisizione*, 4 vols, Pisa 2010, vol. 1, p. 57-59 [= Malavasi, 'Anabattismo'].

—, *Criminalità e giustizia nel Polesine tra Cinque e Seicento*, Rovigo 1997 [= Malavasi, *Criminalità e giustizia*].

—, 'Ancora per la storia dell'eresia a Rovigo nel Cinquecento', in *Non uno itinere. Studi storici offerti dagli allievi a Federico Seneca*, Venezia 1993, p. 55-71.

—, 'Sulla diffusione delle teorie ereticali nel Veneto durante il '500: anabattisti rodigini e polesani', *Archivio Veneto* 96 (1972) p. 5-24 [= Malavasi, 'Sulla diffusione delle teorie ereticali'].

J. Martin, 'Spiritual Journeys and the Fashioning of Religious Identity in Renaissance Venice', *Renaissance Studies* 10 (1996), p. 358-370.

—, *Venice's Hidden Enemies. Italian Heretics in a Renaissance City*, Berkeley (CA) – Los Angeles (CA) – London 1993 [= Martin, *Hidden Enemies*].

T. F. Mayer, *The Roman Inquisition: A Papal Bureaucracy and Its Laws in the Age of Galileo*, Philadelphia (PA) 2013 [= Mayer, *Roman Inquisition*].

A. Olivieri, *Riforma ed eresia a Vicenza nel Cinquecento*, Roma 1992.

P. Paschini, *Venezia e l'Inquisizione romana da Giulio III a Pio IV*, Padova 1959 [= Paschini, *Venezia e l'Inquisizione*].

A. Prosperi, *L'eresia del Libro Grande. Storia di Giorgio Siculo e della sua setta*, Milano 2000 [= Prosperi, *Libro Grande*].

—, *Tribunali della coscienza. Inquisitori, confessori e missionari*, Torino 1996 [= Prosperi, *Tribunali*].

S. Ragagli, 'Manelfi, Pietro', in A. Prosperi (dir.), *Dizionario Storico dell'Inquisizione*, 4 vols, Pisa 2010, vol. 2, p. 972-973 [= Ragagli, 'Manelfi'].

C. Santus, 'Tiziano, predicatore anabattista', in A. Prosperi (dir.), *Dizionario Storico dell'Inquisizione*, 4 vols, Pisa 2010, vol. 3, p. 1575-1576 [= Santus, 'Tiziano, predicatore'].

—, 'Tizzano, Lorenzo', in A. Prosperi (dir.), *Dizionario Storico dell'Inquisizione*, 4 vols, Pisa 2010, vol. 3, p. 1576-1577 [= Santus, 'Tizzano, Lorenzo'].

S. Seidel Menchi, 'Protestantesimo a Venezia', in G. Gullino (a cura di), *La chiesa di Venezia tra riforma protestante e riforma cattolica*, Venezia 1990, p. 131-181 [= Seidel Menchi, 'Protestantesimo a Venezia'].

J. Seitz, 'Interconnected Inquisitors. Circulation and Networks Among Outer Peripheral Tribunals', in K. Aron-Beller – C. F. Black (eds), *The Roman Inquisition. Centre versus Peripheries*, Leiden – Boston (MA) 2018, p. 139-160 [= Seitz, 'Interconnected Inquisitors'].

A. Stella, *Dall'anabattismo veneto al «Sozialevangelismus» dei fratelli Hutteriti e all'Illuminismo religioso sociniano*, Roma 1996.

—, *Anabattismo e antitrinitarismo in Italia nel XVI secolo. Nuove ricerche storiche*, Padova 1969 [= Stella, *Anabattismo e antitrinitarismo*].

—, *Dall'anabattismo al socinianesimo nel Cinquecento veneto. Ricerche storiche*, Padova 1967 [= Stella, *Dall'anabattismo al socinianesimo*].

J. Tedeschi, *Il giudice e l'eretico. Studi sull'Inquisizione romana*, Milano 1997 [= Tedeschi, *Il giudice*].

E. Zille, *Gli eretici a Cittadella nel Cinquecento*, Padova 1971 [= Zille, *Cittadella*].

Monitum

1-101:

1-3 ⟨Giovanni – ricordi] *A*, f. 73ᵛ l. 21-24

4-5 quella – terribile] *A*, f. 72ᵛ l. 30 - 73ʳ l. 1

5-6 che – David] *A*, f. 72ʳ l. 5-7

7-14 ⟨Zuan – *Idio*] *A*, f. 98ᵛ l. 11-21

15-19 La – *secula*] *A*, f. 98ᵛ l. 22 - f. 99ʳ l. 2

20-21 ⟨Quella – altramente] *A*, f. 99ʳ l. 4-6

22 Messer – giese⟩] *A*, f. 99ʳ l. 6-7

23-25 De – evangelisti] *A*, f. 99ʳ l. 16-19

26-30 Ragionassemo – figlioli] *B*, f. 45ᵛ l. 1-6

31-40 ⟨Marc'Antonio – matrimonio] *B*, f. 31ᵛ l. 17 - f. 32ʳ l. 1

41-48 Fu – Abbadia] *B*, f. 33ʳ l. 3-15

49-51 In – offensibili] *B*, f. 40ʳ l. 7-11

52-58 ⟨Pasqualin – Ferara] *C*, f. 2ᵛ l. 5-13

59-63 ⟨Iseppo – sopra] *C*, f. 36ʳ l. 18-23

64-68 El – non] *C*, f. 36ʳ l. 25 - f. 36ᵛ l. 1

69-70 El – apostoli] *C*, f. 36ᵛ l. 2-4

71-74 ⟨Della – Dio] *C*, f. 36ᵛ l. 5-10

75-76 El – ricordo] *C*, f. 36ᵛ l. 15-16

77-84 ⟨Marc'Antonio – evangelio] *B*, f. 33ʳ l. 20 - f. 33ᵛ l. 6

85-86 Io – tutto] *B*, f. 33ᵛ l. 9-12

87-91 ⟨Pasqualin – non] *C*, f. 2ᵛ l. 13-17

92-101 ⟨Perin – dato] *C*, f. 15ʳ l. 5-13

CONCILIUM VENETIANUM-FERRARIENSE
1550

CONSPECTUS SIGLORUM

Codices

A   Venezia, Archivio di Stato, Savi all'eresia (Santo Ufficio), busta 158, libro secondo

B   Venezia, Archivio di Stato, Savi all'eresia (Santo Ufficio), busta 158, libro terzo

C   Venezia, Archivio di Stato, Savi all'eresia (Santo Ufficio), busta 158, libro quarto

Editiones

Man[1]   Ginzburg, *Costituti*, p. 31-38

Man[4]   Ginzburg, *Costituti*, p. 64-70

⟨Giovanni Maria Beato altre volte Manfredino cittadino di Rovigo:⟩
Fu ragionato de tutte le sopradette cose, legendo S. Paulo et altri libri, ma non
fu deliberato cosa alchuna che mi ricordi:

2/3 non – ricordi] Manelfi (see app. 3) is referring to what he had stated at p. 33
(*Man¹*): Non essere lecito secondo l'evangelio battezare gli fanciulli se prima non
credeno. Gli magistrati non potere essere cristiani. Gli sacramenti non conferire gratia
alchuna, ma essere segni esteriori. Non tenere nella chiesa altro che scrittura sacra. Non
tenere oppenione alchuna de' dottori. Tenere la Chiesa Romana essere diabolica et
antecristiana. Quelli che sono stati battezati non essere christiani, ma essere bisogno
rebattizarli   **3** cosa alchuna] cfr *A*, f. 38ʳ l. 3-10 (Iseppo Cingano): ho sentito dire da
più persone de la nostra oppinion come di sopra che tal articulo*ᵖ·ᶜ·* fu risolto in Padoa
(Vicenza *Man¹*) et ancho in Venetia: che Jesu Christo fusse generato de seme humano
cioè de Joseph. Domandato chi forno quelli che ne disse de tal rissolutione, rispose:
Marc'Antonio de Asolo et ancho Tician el qual non fu mai de quella oppenion perché
el voleva star sul evangelio et de altre. Cfr *A*, f. 76ᵛ-77ʳ (Mathio dalla Madalena):
Domandato: sapete voi o havete mai inteso da altri chel sia stato fatto nessuna
congregatione overo concilio per discutere et diterminare questo articulo della
concettione overo altri articuli di questa dottrina in alcuna città di questo dominio?
Rispose: Signor sì che io l'ho inteso! Admonito chel debba dir che cosa l'ha inteso et da
chi, rispose: io ho inteso può essere un mese in circa dopoi [*in marg. add.*] che*ᵖ·ᶜ·* io
recevessi il segno, che, andando un dì per Campo Marzo rasonando col piccolo

2 legendo – libri] orando et studiando le scritture sacre *Man¹*, noi non studiavamo
altro che il testamento vecchio et novo volgare, non permettendo il latino nella giesa
Man⁴   2/3 non – ricordi] 1. Cristo non essere Dio ma huomo concetto del seme di
Ioseph et di Maria, ma ripieno di tutte le virtù di Dio. 2. Maria havere havuto altri
figliuoli et figliuole dopo Cristo, provando per più lochi della scrittura Cristo havere
havuto fratelli et sorelle. 3. Non essere natura angelica creata da Dio, et dove la scrittura
parla di angeli, essere ministri, cioè huomini mandati da Dio a quell'effetto che
dimostra la scrittura. 4. Non essere altro diavolo che la prudentia humana, et così quel
serpente quale dice Moisé haver sedutto Eva, non essere altro che la prudentia humana,
perché non ritroviamo nelle scritture niuna cosa creata da Dio esserle nemica se non la
prudentia humana, come dice Paolo Alli Romani. 5. Gli impii nel dì del giuditio non
risuscitare, ma solo gli eletti, de' quali è stato capo Cristo. 6. Non ci essere altro inferno
che 'l sepolcro. 7. Gli eletti quando moreno dormire nel Signore, et non andare
altrimente le anime loro a fruire cosa alchuna fin al dì del giuditio, quando saranno
risuscitate; l'anime dell'impii perire insieme col corpo, come fanno tutti li altri
animali. 8. Il seme humano havere da Dio forza di produrre la carne e lo spirito. 9. Gli
eletti essere giustificati per la eterna misericordia et charità di Dio senza nessuna opera
visibile, intendendo senza la morte, il sangue et gli meriti di Cristo. 10. Cristo essere
morto alla demostratione della giustitia di Dio, et giustitia intendevamo il cumulo di
tutta la bontà et misericordia di Dio et delle sue promissioni *Man¹*, raccogliesimo tutte
le openioni che ho confessate nella mia confessione, tenendo ancora tutte l'openioni
antique de anabattisti, et particolarmente quella de magistrati detta di sopra *Man⁴*

526 CONCILIUM VENETIANUM-FERRARIENSE – 1550

quella ⟨dottrina⟩ del incarnation de Jesu Christo la qual mi pareva grande et
5 troppo terribile, che Christo era nato del seme di santo Iseppo et de Maria
secondo le promesse, che Christo doveva nascer della stirpe di David.

⟨Zuan Ludovico Bronzier dalla Badia:⟩
Li ragionamenti nostri forno cercha alle cose della fede, ragionassemo quello
che chadauno credeva et restassemo tutti in uno medemo creder, come è che
10 tutti credevemo in uno solo Idio, credevemo uno solo Jesu Christo nostro
mediator suo figliolo et nostro redentor nato, morto et resuscitato secondo le
promesse fatte da Idio, una sola giesia, et restassemo in questo: che Jesu Christo sia nato huomo del seme di Josephe de matrimonio, come dice Pietro in li
Atti delli apostoli *homo probato da Idio.*
15 La ⟨Nostra dona credevemo⟩ fusse legitima moglier de Joseph et che de con-
ceptione matrimonial sia nato Christo che era quel concepto apresso el Padre
ab eterno promesso, nel qual lui haveva statuito de restaurar ogni cosa in cielo
et in terra, al qual el dete la plenitudine del Spirito et gli dete ogni potestà in
cielo et in terra, di sorte che come dice Paulo *sit Deus benedictus in secula.*
20 ⟨Quella conception⟩ la intendo de conception matrimonial et che in el parto
et doppo el parto ⟨Maria⟩ la non fosse vergine altramente.
Messer sì, ⟨quella oppinione fu acceptata da tutte le predette giese⟩.

13/14 Pietro – Idio] cfr Act. 1, 23 (fors.) **19** Rom. 9, 5

Jacometto stringaro, intrassemo su questo della concettione*p.c.* et contendevamo
insieme sopra questo et dicendo io non è possibile questa cosa sia, lui mi disse che era
sta fatto un concilio in Venetia

4/6 quella – David] io ragionai da poi l'oratione proponendo il dubio della
incarnatione del signor Giesu Christo, dicendo che quivi eravamo ragunati per non
andare alla ciecca di questo nostro maestro Christo, ma per rissolversi se era solo
huomo generato di seme o pur Dio concetto di Spirito santo. Et nel successo di tempo
se rissolse quanto ho confessato *Man⁴* **14** Idio] *add. et del.* et in consegratione *A*

CONCILIUM VENETIANUM-FERRARIENSE – 1550

De questa materia poteva esser che non fusse ancho ragionato, ma tenemo che Jesu Christo habbia havuto etiam altri fratelli nasciuti de Maria come notava-
25 no gli evangelisti.
Ragionassemo dela nostra fede et restassemo in uno medemo creder particu-larmente in questo: che Jesu Christo fosse nato homo del seme de Gioseph et Maria de legittimo matrimonio, concepto de conception naturale; che Maria nel parto et dopo il parto non fusse altremente virgine per haver havuto etiam
30 altri figlioli.

⟨Marc'Antonio da Prata de Asolo:⟩
Largamente parlassemo in quella materia et fu concluso che li fusse sta agionto et tal difficultà era nasciuta per certi napoletani che erano intrati in la congre-gatione – che erano Bruno et Zuani Dalla Cava – et la difficultà era che Chris-
35 to fusse o non fusse sta cognosicuto avanti el batismo et che le prophetie che erano nel evangelio avanti ditto batismo parlasseno in altro proposito et che Jesu Christo fusse nato de copula carnal come li altri homeni cioè de matrimo-nio de Joseph et de Maria. Et sopra de questo anchora che fusse stato parlato longamente si romase quasi irressoluti. Ben la maggior parte de noi tenevamo
40 chel fusse nato de matrimonio.
Fu ordinato doi che predicasseno la parola di Dio, quali fu Benetto de Borgo et Titiano, et a questi furno aggiunto compagni, cioè che andasseno con loro, che furono Francesco da Rovigo che andasse con Benetto et io insieme con Iseppo Sartore andassemo con Titiano, tamen io non andetti mai con lui
45 dapoi la partita che facessimo di questa città perché io fui mandato a Vicenza a quelli che erano de lì per riferirli quanto era sta' trattato. Credo che Titiano andette alla volta di Treviso et doveva andar a Saravalle et a Asolo, et Benetto andette verso Rovigo et alla Abbadia.

---

24 fratelli] cfr Marc. 6, 3; Matth. 13, 55

24 fratelli] cfr *C*, f. 47^{rv} (Gasparo Menzato da Castel Francho): Mi ve dirò la verità: el fu fatto uno concilio in questa terra per alchuni de nostri et mi a quel tempo ero infermo alla morte et el vene uno abbate napoletano con Jacometto stringher da Vicenza et uno Bernardin Sartor da Padoa et mi disse che haveva determinato in el ditto consilio che la Nostra dona haveva havuto altri fioli oltra Christo et mi non ghe dete mai fede a questo perché per el evangelio vedeva a uno altro modo in Esaia [cfr Is. 7, 14] che dice: *ecce virgo concipiet* [...] perché mi me trovavo in miseria et el ditto Abbate me sovigneva dissimulai$^{p.c.}$ et mostravo de crederlo$^{p.c.}$ ancho mi ma non l'ho mai credesto, come me possa giustificar per quel Bernarndin et ancho per altri et da quel tempo comenzai a starmi fuora et loro mi hano scomunicato

41/48 Fu – Abbadia] concludessimo che si pubblicasse a tutte le giesie, et così ognuno fu licentiato con la dottrina determinata *Man⁴* **48** et alla] *add. in marg. B*

528 CONCILIUM VENETIANUM-FERRARIENSE – 1550

In vero fu parlato et concluso che in quella che decevamo esser giesia de Dio
50 non potesse esser che facesseno imagine o scultara che portasseno veneration,
né anchor quelli che facesseno armi offensbili.

⟨Pasqualin quondam Francesco de Pasqualini de Asolo, pelizaro:⟩
Fu ordinato tra noi che non si admetisse in la nostra giesa persona alchuna che
fosse depentor et facesse imani, né alchuno spader et che fa armi, né alchuno
55 che fa dadi et carte, et fu anche parlato de Christo et dela vergenità de sua
madre et fu ditto che più non se ne dovesse parlar. Et qui stessemo salvo el vero
tre giorni ben et vero che doppo messer Benetto de Borgo et Francesco da
Rhovigo gle ni parlò et venero a trovarmi a Ferara.

⟨Iseppo fiol de Zuan Maria di Sartori da Asolo:⟩
60 El fu concluso che Jesu Christo era generato del seme de David secondo la
carne et dechiarato fiol de Dio in potestà et virtù. Benché ghe era etiam quelli
che credevano non so a che modo perché io li sentiva contrariar sopra de questo et io mi aderì a quanto fu concluso come de sopra.
El fu trattato cerca le arte et fu concluso che in la giesia nostra che hora non è
65 più mia – anci, la tengo per una setta perché la niega, se pol dir, tutta la scrittura – non se dovesse far imageni alle quali si richiedesse el culto de Dio, et non
mi ricordo sel fu ditto cerca delle spade et carte et dadi là – el si permeteva per
la prima necessità: o si o non.
El fu parlà anche della potestà pontificia et fu detto che S. Piero haveva una
70 preheminentia più delli altri apostoli.
⟨Della potestà temporal⟩ mi par, se ben mi ricordo, che fu concluso che uno
che ministrasse giusticia non potesse esser in la giesia et in tutte le cose portas-
semo obedientia alli giudici temporali salvo che in quelle cose che a noi pareva
che non fusseno de deretto et contrarie al honor de Dio.
75 El fu trattate assai cose ma per el tempo longo et per esser stato via non me le
ricordo.

⟨Marc'Antonio da Prata de Asolo:⟩
Ci trovassimo una volta insieme in Ferrara dove era Nicola de Allessandria,
Benetto Borgo, Titiano, Francesco da Rovigo, un Battista Tabachin de terra
80 de' Grisoni, Iseppo Sartor et potrebbe esser altri che non me ricordo, dove fu
ragionato anchora in simil materia; et anchor che tutti restorno quieti della

---

79 Battista Tabachin] cfr Del Col, *L'inquisizione*, p. 361-362

55 sua] *p.c.* C   **56** fu – parlar] ricordomi ancora che nel detto concilio fu concluso
che quelli che non accettavano questa dottrina nova conclusa nel concilio che fussero
esclusi dalla nostra giesa d'anabattisti *Man⁴*   **74** deretto] *add. et del.* al bon C

CONCILIUM VENETIANUM-FERRARIENSE – 1550

humanità di Christo et dell'evangelio, pur anchora alcuni erano che non
assentivano che Christo fosse puro huomo et che non fosse stato aggiunto
all'evangelio.

85 Io so che gliera Titiano che contrastava grandemente, ma delli altri non so
perché lui allegava che destruggendo una parte se veniria a destruggere il tutto.

⟨Pasqualin quondam Francesco de Pasqualini de Asolo, pelizaro:⟩
⟨Benetto De Borgo et Francesco Da Rhovigo venero a trovarmi a Ferara⟩ non
a posta ma per trovar Nicola de Alessandria che era lì et ne rasonorno de tal
90 cosa – ⟨de Christo et dela vergenità de sua madre⟩ – anchora che mi non ghe
credesse fermamente ma steva in dubio dal sì al non.

⟨Perin calegharo da Asolo fiol de Zuanantoni favro:⟩
El vene el detto Benetto in Ferrara et comenzò a lezer a Pasqualin, a Iseppo et
a mi, et credo che el ghe era anche presente Julio Calegaro da Vicenza, quelli
95 tre capitoli de san Mathio et dui, salvo el vero, de san Luca donde trattano che
Christo era nato de virginità et così legendo el ne disse: 'Questi capitoli va per
terra perché ne caciano carote et non è vero che Christo sia nato de verginità,
ma l'he nato de homo et de donna come nui altri, perché così li propheti dico-
no'. El che aldendo io mi tolsi via et lui restò a parlar con Pasqualin et Iseppo
100 et per questo io mi tolsi via et getai in fuogo uno testo novo che lì mi havevano
dato.

---

95 tre – Luca] cfr Matth. 1-2; Luc. 1-2

85/86 Io – tutto] *vide supra*

CONCILIA LUTETIANUM ET RUPELLENSE

1559-1571

edidit
Irene DINGEL

THE SYNODS OF PARIS AND LA ROCHELLE AND
THE *GALLICAN CONFESSION*
1559-1571

The *Confession de foi* – widely known as the *Gallican Confession* – was drafted together with an ecclesiastical ordinance – the *Discipline ecclésiastique* – during the so-called first national Synod of the French Reformed churches, held in Paris in 1559. It marked the first phase of the consolidation of French Protestantism. This phase involved doctrinal and confessional issues, as well as Church organisation. Yet these developments were not accompanied by any sort of recognition on an ecclesiastical-political level nor by any form of tolerance by the French monarchy. At that point, it became even more evident what differentiated French Protestantism from the Roman Catholic Church in theological terms, along with the aspiration toward a form of structural autonomy.

The Communities Adhering to Reform in France

The appearance of evangelical circles in France dates back to the 1530s. One of the hubs of French evangelicalism was Meaux, a town located east of Paris, where sympathisers of Bishop Guillaume Briçonnet (*c.* 1470-1534) had gathered. Briçonnet was strongly interested in reform with a background in humanistic scholarship. He had been a pupil of the well-known humanist Jacques Lefèvre d'Étaples (1450/1455-1535), also known by the name of Jacob Faber Stapulensis. These circles adopted reformist texts from outside France. Martin Luther's ideas spread throughout the nation, thanks to translations and citations of his writings in French publications, such as transcriptions of the *Leipziger Disputation*, the dispute between Luther and Johannes Eck that took place in Leipzig between June and July 1519. ([1]) In 1520, Luther's writings also began to appear in Lyon. The influence of the Reformation slowly began to mix with ideas developing in France, based on local, Biblical humanism as well as reformist leanings. Supporters of this current of thought would, in fact, be called *luthériens*, although without differentiating the several currents of thought. For a time, everything linked with the Reformation was labelled as

(1) Dingel, 'Luther und Europa', p. 213 and following.

'Lutheran', even when certain theological ideas were barely connected with Luther's. However, even after the Sorbonne condemned Luther's statements on the basis of 100 propositions – on 15 April 1521, before the Edict of Worms was promulgated on 8 May of the same year – thus lending support to the Parisian *parlement*'s battle against 'Lutheran heresy', the printing of evangelical material in France did not cease.

The *Affaire des placards* (1534) represented a significant watershed. The case originated with the circulation of manifestos challenging the Roman Catholic rite of the Mass. One of these was even found before the door of the royal chambers of Francis I. This triggered a wave of relentless persecution that would only intensify during the reign of Henry II, Francis I's son. The evangelical communities in France were well consolidated at the time and were not eradicated, although they were forced to go into hiding. A network of organised communities – no longer calling themselves Lutherans, but Calvinists – existed as early as 1550 as the ideas of Calvin had already circulated and exercised significant influence. Many of those facing persecution found refuge in Geneva, where numerous pastors active in French communities had received their training. The high nobility also began to support the Reformation. (²) These stances, along with the nobility's opposition to the pre-absolutist tendencies of the last Valois sovereigns, led to a greater consolidation and visibility for evangelical groups and ideas within France.

The circulation of Reformed doctrine and the support of politically-influential circles were only the outer face of French Protestantism. A closer look at the daily life of these congregations reveals the issue of a clandestine existence that remained unresolved and was destined to worsen. Basic precepts of doctrine and confession were not shared by all to the same degree: for instance, sacraments were not regulated, and this made legal issues emerge concerning in particular baptism and marriage (marriage was no longer held to be a sacrament); congregations were not organised systematically or in a homogenous fashion, and there was a dearth of human resources capable of filling all the specific ecclesiastical roles needed. This particular backdrop endowed the first national Synod, held in Paris in 1559, with particular significance. The Synod provided the Reformed congregations of France with a frame of reference both on a theological and statutory-ecclesiastical level. Moreover, French Protestantism officially came out of hiding. The *Gallican Confession* was accompanied in subsequent editions by a dedicatory epistle

---

(²) For example Louis of Condé and his son Henry from the Bourbon dynasty, and Gaspard I of Coligny, Lord of Châtillon.

CONCILIA LUTETIANUM ET RUPELLENSE – 1559-1571

addressed to the King of France, Francis II, (3) in the vain hope of dissuading him from persecution through a clear explanation of Reformed doctrine. (4) The loyalty of French Calvinists to the political regime remained intact. Calvin himself came out against radicalisation in the movement; yet in this period Calvinists did not receive any legal recognition.

THE FIRST NATIONAL SYNOD OF PARIS (1559)

The representatives of eleven French churches met secretly from 25 to 29 May 1559 in a home in the Saint-Germain-des-Prés neighbourhood, the site of present-day rue Visconti. The delegates came from Saint-Lô, Dieppe, Angers, Orléans, Tours, Poitiers, Saintes, Marennes, Châtellerault, and Saint-Jean-d'Angély. Their chosen moderator – in reality their *de facto* president – was François Morel, a provincial noble from Collonges and senior pastor of the Reformed Church of Paris. The *Discipline ecclésiastique* in 40 articles was drafted, along with the *Confession de foi* in just as many articles. While the *Discipline* was repeatedly discussed, annotated, and continuously updated (5) according to current needs in other synods, the *Gallican Confession* remained fundamentally unaltered. (6) The *Gallican Confession* formulated during the Synod was based on a text elaborated in Geneva. Its complete title is: *Confession de foy, faicte d'un commun accord par les Eglises qui sont dispersees en France, et sabstienent des idolatries Papales. Avec une preface contenant responce et defence contre les calumnies dont on les charge.* (7) The text was drawn up by request of Morel. It originates from Calvin, who for his part had incorporated a confession already formulated in Paris in 1557, probably by Antoine de la Roche-Chandieu. (8) When the delegates arrived in Paris with the text from Geneva, the Synod had already begun, and the *Discipline ecclésiastique* had already been written. At that point, the text from Geneva became the basis for

---

(3) For a comparative study of the *Confession de foi* and the *Confessio Augustana* see Dingel, 'Bekenntnis und Geschichte', p. 68-71.

(4) The *Confession de foi* containing the dedicatory epistle was offered to Francis II in 1560. Another version was offered by Theodore Beza to Charles IX in 1561, during the Colloquy of Poissy. See also Dingel, 'Die *Confession de foi*', p. 175 and following (erroneously marked G.S).

(5) Aymon, *Tous les synodes* refers to 14 chapters or sections, containing 222 articles.

(6) Hannelore Jahr is heavily critical of the earlier interpretation offered by Jacques Pannier. See Jahr, *Studien*, especially p. 21-23.

(7) The text is published in *CR*, vol. 37 (1870), p. 739-752. See also Peter Barth – Wilhelm Niesel (ed.), *Calvin, Opera selecta*, vol. 2, München 1952, p. 297-324.

(8) See Jahr, *Studien*, p. 19-23.

536 CONCILIA LUTETIANUM ET RUPELLENSE – 1559-1571

the *Gallican Confession* drafted by the Synod. The 35 articles of the former became 40 in the latter, which was entitled *Confession de foy, faicte d'un commun accord par les François, qui desirent vivre selon la pureté de l'Euangile de nostre Seigneur Iesu-Christ*.

STRUCTURE AND CONTENT OF THE *GALLICAN CONFESSION*

The structure and content of the *Gallican Confession* share the same characteristics and dogmatic approach of other Reformed confessions. Furthermore, they develop in parallel with the synthesis of Calvin's *Catechism* and *Institutes of Christian Religion*. Articles 1 to 8 focus on the divine decree, a concept linked to the explicit definition of the sole, fundamental authority of the Christian faith, i.e. Holy Scripture. Articles 9 through 12 expand on anthropology and deal with both sin and predestination. The doctrine of the eternal grace of God is dealt with after the explanations of the fall into sin and the inevitable presence of sin in the human condition. This clearly reveals the infralapsarian character of the *Gallican Confession*'s doctrine of predestination. However, the reference to the eternal and immutable decree of God confers a supralapsarian value on it. But the decision to place the doctrine of predestination within the structure of the *Confession* between divine decree and Christology leads this doctrine toward a context of Reformed soteriology: God in his eternal judgment chooses man, drawing him away from the corruption of which he is guilty, guiding him to salvation through Jesus Christ.

Articles 13 to 20 concern Jesus Christ as the Son of God, his divine and human natures, and how the entirety of his person achieves the salvation of humanity. Articles 21 to 24 are pneumatological. Issues of vocation, conversion and sanctification of Christian life through the action of the Holy Spirit are dealt with herein. However, good works carried out by Christians under the guidance of the Spirit have no justificatory efficacy. True believers must not detract from Jesus Christ, the sole intermediary between man and God. Articles 25 to 33 deal with ecclesiology and underline the need for good order within the Church, expanding on the ministries and offices of the Church. Articles 34 to 38 concern the sacraments of baptism and the Lord's Supper; they underline the symbolic significance of the spiritual delight of the Lord's Supper as well as the real transmission of the gift of salvation. Refraining from any spiritualist stances, the *Gallican Confession* explicitly affirms that the duty of authorities instituted by God consists in guaranteeing the correct worship of God and the pacification of society (according to the teachings of the Ten Commandments). Obedience to civil authorities, acting as God's

representatives, must not be questioned, even when those authorities do not profess the Reformed faith.

Although the *Gallican Confession* does not explicitly reject any particular doctrine, it is clear which churches, groups, or currents are called upon to affirm Reformed identity in terms of theological and/or confessional tenets. The emphasis reserved for the concept of justification centred on Christ, along with the fact that works and rites do not have any salvational efficacy, clearly demonstrate the *Confession*'s alienation from Roman Catholicism. The manner in which the divine decree is defined, along with the Christological position based on the idea of the two distinct natures of Christ, are clear stances against Anti-trinitarianism. At the same time, it becomes apparent that Lutheran Christology, with its emphasis on the communication of divine attributes from the divine to the human nature of Christ (*communicatio idiomatum, genus maiestaticum*), is also rejected in order to exclude the danger of interpenetration of the two natures of Christ. The *Confession de foi* also distances itself from spiritualist currents, positions that accept other forms of revelation alongside the Holy Scriptures, and libertine behaviour. All this is incorporated within the positive formulation of the creed. Thus, the *Gallican Confession* reaffirms the continuity of doctrine in early-Christian formulation of doctrine emerging from the ecumenical councils of the first five centuries.

Although the *Gallican Confession* was written on the occasion of the first national Synod of 1559, from 1559 to 1571 (i.e. until the seventh national Synod of La Rochelle), two different drafts circulated: the 'Genevan' version entitled *Confession de foy, faicte d'un commun accord par les Eglises qui sont dispersees en France, et sabstienent des idolatries Papales*, and the 'Parisian' version, edited on this basis and entitled *Confession de foy, faicte d'un commun accord par les François, qui desirent vivre selon la pureté de l'Euangile de nostre Seigneur Iesus-Christ*. The co-existence of these two versions came to an end after the national Synod held in La Rochelle, when the latter version with 40 articles became the only authoritative confession, ([9]) though with elucidations related to the Lord's Supper in Article 36. ([10]) Three manuscript copies were drawn up in parchment and were signed by all the attendees of the Synod to be kept in La Rochelle, Béarn, and Geneva. ([11]) This amended version of the *Gallican Confession* continues to be considered the fundamental text of the Reformed

---

([9]) Aymon, *Tous les synodes*, vol. 1, p. 98.

([10]) In this article, the term 'unit[é]' was changed into 'union'. An agreement was also reached on the explanation of the meaning of 'substance' (see the edition below).

([11]) Aymon, *Tous les synodes*, vol. 1, p. 100. Only the Geneva manuscript is extant. See Pannier, *Les origines*, p. 134.

538   CONCILIA LUTETIANUM ET RUPELLENSE – 1559-1571

Church of France and of French-speaking communities that have settled in other countries.

The historiography referring to this text is not unequivocal. Indeed, the document is labelled alternatively as *Confession de foi*, *Confession de La Rochelle*, or the *Huguenot Confession*. It is largely referred to as *Confessio Gallicana* or *Gallican Confession*. This definition likely spread in the nineteenth century, despite the fact that the *Confession de foi* has no particular 'Gallican' features to it. Given that the adjective refers to Gallicanism – the French model of Church statute grounded in the Middle Ages and the early modern period – it would be more appropriate to speak of the *Confessio Gallica*, in line with the known versions of the *Confessio Helvetica*, *Confessio Belgica*, *Confessio Scotica*, and *Confessio Hungarica*. Occasionally, however, this variant is also found.

THE SYNOD OF LA ROCHELLE (1571)

The seventh national Synod of the French Reformed churches, held in 1571 in La Rochelle, took place in the midst of the French wars of religion, begun in 1562 in the aftermath of the massacre of Vassy. When the Synod gathered, the third religious war had just ended with the promulgation of the Edict of Saint-Germain (8 August 1570). The edict was a success for the *politiques* and ensured Huguenots – as they were called following the conspiracy of Amboise in 1560 – broad tolerance. In addition to a general amnesty, it allowed for the public practice of religion to be newly granted to high nobility. Furthermore, Reformed worship could be freely held in the outer quarters of two cities within each governorship. Last but not least, from that moment on Protestants were ensured access to universities, schools, and hospitals. For the first time, four strongholds (*places de sûreté*) were accorded to Protestants for two years: La Rochelle, Montauban, Cognac, and La Charité. ([12])

During the period of military confrontation in France, theological negotiations began in the Holy Roman Empire under the leadership of the theologian Jacob Andreae to reconcile disputing groups among the adherents to the *Augsburg Confession*. Promoters of these negotiations included Duke Christoph of Württemberg, Landgrave William of Hesse and Duke Julius of Brunswick-Wolfenbüttel. During these negotiations, the understanding of the Lord's Supper and the underlying Christology were among the most hotly-contested issues. This may help explain why the national Synod held on 2 April 1571 in La Rochelle dealt, among other issues, with the article related to

---

(12) See Lecler, *Geschichte der Religionsfreiheit*, vol. 2, p. 113 and following.

the Lord's Supper contained in the *Confession de foi*. Jean Aymon's edition of the proceedings of the French Reformed national synods reports that the delegates argued that the unity of the community with Jesus Christ should not be defined as 'unit[é]', but rather as 'union'. Furthermore, following the opening of the debate on the meaning of the term 'substance' with reference to the substantial presence of Christ in the Lord's Supper, an authoritative resolution was put in place. In maintaining this concept that was so laden with significance, and at the same time a very controversial subject in confessional terms, the Synod's intention, however, was to keep distance and distinction from the Lutheran understanding of the real presence. ([13])

Along with the articles concerning Church discipline, Article 29 – which entrusted the guidance of the Church to pastors, elders, and deacons – was also discussed. This discussion came about due to an instance in Bordeaux, where a medical doctor actively opposed the *Discipline ecclésiastique*. In the face of what he perceived as the clergy's tyrannical behaviour, the doctor requested that the town council exercise control over the Church. The Synod came out strongly against this quasi-Erastian position but made no modifications to the text of the *Confession de foi*. ([14]) The rest of the debate focused on the *Discipline*, which was re-elaborated and modified. ([15])

The Synod of La Rochelle also saw the participation of high-ranking personalities who were influential in both the political and the theological spheres. Theodore Beza, Calvin's successor as leader of the Venerable Company of Pastors of Geneva, assumed the role of the Synod's moderator. The Synod met in the presence of the Queen of Navarre, Jeanne d'Albret, and her son Henry (later King Henry IV of Bourbon). The Prince of Condé, Count Ludwig of Nassau-Dillenburg (William of Orange's brother), ([16]) and Admiral Gaspard de Coligny also attended the Synod. The participation of such individuals resulted in the Synod being labelled the Synod 'of princes'. ([17]) Their involvement, as well as their signatures at the bottom of the three parchment copies of the *Confession de foi*, conferred recognition upon it as a confessional standard beyond the boundaries of particular congregations and the borders of France.

---

(13) Aymon, *Tous les synodes*, vol. 1, p. 99-100 (Article VII).

(14) Aymon, *Tous les synodes*, vol. 1, p. 99 (Article V).

(15) Aymon, *Tous les synodes*, vol. 1, p. 100-109 and 111.

(16) Ludwig of Nassau-Dillenburg (1538-1574) entered into war alongside the Huguenots and invaded the Netherlands with them in 1572.

(17) 'Synode de princes', as in Léonard, *Histoire*, vol. 2, p. 120.

540   CONCILIA LUTETIANUM ET RUPELLENSE – 1559-1571

Notes on the Edition

The manuscript of the *Confession de foi* we used for our critical edition is held in the Archives d'État de Genève, Pièces Historiques, 1905. Parchment manuscript, 1 leaf/folio, *c.* 52 × 65 cm. On the front side, it features the 40 articles of the *Confession* in three columns. Under the articles, there is a note of the approval of the text by the Synod of La Rochelle. There are also several signatures of noblemen, theologians, and delegates of the Reformed churches of France who attended the Synod. On the back side, 'Confession de Foy des Eglises de France, Signee par diuers Princes et Seigneurs, Comme aussi Par les deputes de diuers provinces'.

Our critical edition is consistently case-insensitive, except at the start of sentences and proper names. The use of *u* and *v* as well as *i* and *j* has been adapted to current usage in French. The punctuation has been normalised. Ligatures and tildes have been tacitly resolved.

BIBLIOGRAPHY

Sources (and Their Abbreviations)

J. Aymon, *Tous les synodes nationaux des églises reformées de France* [...], 2 vols, La Haye 1710 [= Aymon, *Tous les synodes*].

'Bekenntnis des Glaubens (*Confession de foi*)', übers. J. F. Gerhard Goeters, in R. Mau (hrsg.), *Evangelische Bekenntnisse. Bekenntnisschriften der Reformation und neuere Theologische Erklärungen*, 2 vols, Bielefeld 1997, Bd. 2, p. 179-194.

Die Bekenntnisschriften der reformierten Kirche. In authentischen Texten mit geschichtlicher Einleitung und Register, hrsg. E. F. K. Müller, Zürich ²1987, p. 221-232.

Bekenntnisschriften und Kirchenordnungen der nach Gottes Wort reformierten Kirche, hrsg. W. Niesel, Zollikon – Zürich ³1938, p. 65-75.

E. Campi, 'Confessio Gallicana, 1559/1571, mit dem Bekenntnis der Waldenser, 1560', in *RefBK*, vol. 2/1 (2009), p. 1-29.

'Confession de foi, faite d'un commun accord par les églises qui sont dispersées en France et s'abstienent des idolatries papales', in *CR*, vol. 37 (1870), p. 739-752.

'Die Genfer Vorlage', übers. C. Link, in E. Busch et al., *Calvin-Studienausgabe*, 8 vols, Neukirchen-Vluyn 1994-2011, vol. 4, 2002, p. 29-77.

'Hugenottisches Bekenntnis von 1559', übers. W. Boudriot, in P. Jacobs (hrsg.), *Reformierte Bekenntnisschriften und Kirchenordnungen in deutscher Übersetzung*, Neukirchen o. J. 1949, p. 109-121.

Reformierte Bekenntnisschriften. Eine Auswahl von den Anfängen bis zur Gegenwart, hrsg. G. Plasger – M. Freudenberg, Göttingen 2005, p. 107-123.

[M. Servetus], *Christianismi Restitutio*, s.l. M.D.LIII.

—, *Dialogorum de Trinitate Libri Duo. De Iustitia Regni Christi, Capitula Quatuor. Per Michaelem Serveto, alia Reues, ab Aragonia Hispanum*, s.l. M.S.XXXII.

—, *De Trinitatis Erroribus Libri Septem. Per Michaelem Serueto, alias Reues ab Aragonia Hispanum*, s.l. M.D.XXXI.

Literature (and Its Abbreviations)

J. R. Armogathe, 'Quelques réflexions sur la Confession de foi de La Rochelle', *Bulletin de la Société de l'histoire du protestantisme français* 117 (1971), p. 201-213.

P. Benedict, 'Settlements: France', in T. A. Brady – H. A. Oberman – J. D. Tracy (eds), *Handbook of European History 1400-1600: Late Middle Ages, Renaissance and Reformation*, 2 vols, Leiden – New York – Cologne 1994-1995, vol. 1, p. 417-454.

G. Braghi, 'Between Paris and Geneva: Some Remarks on the Approval of the Gallican Confession (May 1559)', *Journal of Early Modern Christianity* 5/2 (2018), p. 197-219.

—, '"Imprimée de différentes manières": The Gallican Confession and Its First Printed Editions (1559?-1561)', *Zwingliana* 46 (2019), p. 45-72.

J. Cadier, 'La Confession de foi de la Rochelle. Son histoire, son importance', *Revue réformée* 32 (1971), p. 43-54.

D. Crouzet, *La Genèse de la Réforme française 1520-1562 (Regards sur l'histoire – Histoire moderne* 109), Paris 1996.

D. Deddens, 'De eerste synode der Franse Gereformeerde Kerken te Parijs, 1559', *Lucerna* 1/2 (1958-1960), p. 99-120.

I. Dingel, 'Luther und Europa', in A. Beutel (hrsg.), *Luther Handbuch*, Tübingen [2]2010, p. 206-217 [= Dingel, 'Luther und Europa'].

—, 'Bekenntnis und Geschichte. Funktion und Entwicklung des reformatorischen Bekenntnisses im 16. Jahrhundert', in J. Loehr (hrsg.), *Dona Melanchthoniana. Festgabe für Heinz Scheible zum 70. Geburtstag,* Stuttgart – Bad Cannstatt [2]2005, p. 68-71 [= Dingel, 'Bekenntnis und Geschichte'].

—, 'Die *Confession de foi* von 1559 – Bekenntnis des hart bedrängten französischen Protestantismus', in E. Mittler et al. (hrsg.), *Bibliotheca Palatina. Katalog zur Ausstellung vom 8. Juli bis 2. November 1986 Heiliggeistkirche Heidelberg,* 2 vols, Heidelberg 1986, vol. 1, p. 175 ff. [= Dingel, 'Die Confession de foi'].

R. H. Esnault, 'La Confession de La Rochelle au XIXe siècle', *Études théologiques et religieuses* 34 (1959), p. 155-212.

P. de Félice, 'Le Synode National de 1559', *Bulletin de la Société de l'histoire du protestantisme français* 105 (1959), p. 1-8.

M. Greengrass, *The French Reformation,* Oxford 1987.

Handbuch der Dogmen- und Theologiegeschichte, hrsg. C. Andresen, 3 vols, Göttingen [2]1999.

F. M. Higman, *La diffusion de la Réforme en France, 1520-1565 (Publications de la Faculté de Théologie de l'Université de Genève* 17), Genève 1992.

P. Imbart de la Tour, *Les origines de la Réforme,* 4 vols, Paris – Melun 1914-[2]1948.

P. Jacobs, 'Das Hugenottische Bekenntnis. Ein vierhundertjähriges Zeugnis der Hochblüte reformierter Bekenntnisbildung', *Evangelische Theologie* 19 (1959), p. 203-219.

—, *Theologie reformierter Bekenntnisschriften in Grundzügen,* Neukirchen 1959.

H. Jahr, *Studien zur Überlieferungsgeschichte der Confession de foi von 1559 (Beiträge zur Geschichte und Lehre der Reformierten Kirche* 16), Neukirchen 1964 [= Jahr, *Studien*].

J. Lecler, *Geschichte der Religionsfreiheit im Zeitalter der Reformation,* 2 vols, Stuttgart 1965 [= Lecler, *Geschichte der Religionsfreiheit*].

E. G. Léonard, *Histoire générale du Protestantisme,* 3 vols, Paris [2]1988. [= Léonard, *Histoire*].

—, 'Légende et histoire du synode de 1559', *Etudes évangéliques* 19 (1959), p. 12-27.

R. Mehl, *Explication de la confession de foi da la Rochelle,* Paris 1959.

CONCILIA LUTETIANUM ET RUPELLENSE – 1559-1571   543

R. Nürnberger, *Die Politisierung des französischen Protestantismus. Calvin und die Anfänge des protestantischen Radikalismus*, Tübingen 1948.

J. Pannier, *Les origines de la confession de foi et la discipline des églises réformées de France* (*Études d'histoire et de philosophie religieuses* 32), Paris 1936 [= Pannier, *Les origines*].

G. von Polenz, *Geschichte des französischen Calvinismus bis zum Gnadenedikt von Nîmes im Jahre 1629*, 4 vols, Gotha 1857-1869.

J. Poujol, 'De la confession de Foi de 1559 à la Conjuration d'Amboise', *Bulletin de la Société de l'histoire du protestantisme français* 119 (1973), p. 158-177.

M. Reulos, 'Le synode national de La Rochelle (1571) et la constitution d'un "parti" protestant', in *Actes du Colloque 'L'Amiral de Coligny et son temps' (Paris, 24-28 octobre 1972)*, Paris 1974, p. 707-716.

—, 'L'organisation des églises réformées françaises et le Synode de 1559', *Bulletin de la Société de l'histoire du protestantisme français* 105 (1959), p. 9-24.

J. Rohls, *Theologie reformierter Bekenntnisschriften*, Göttingen 1987.

R. Stauffer, 'Brève histoire de la Confession de La Rochelle', *Bulletin de la Société de l'histoire du protestantisme français* 117 (1971), p. 355-366.

R. Stephan, *Gestalten und Kräfte des französischen Protestantismus*, München 1967.

O. E. Strasser-Bertrand – O. J. de Jong, *Geschichte des Protestantismus in Frankreich und den Niederlanden* (*Die Kirche in ihrer Geschichte* 3/M2), Göttingen 1975.

N. M. Sutherland, *The Huguenot Struggle for Recognition*, New Haven – London 1980.

M. Venard, 'Frankreich und die Niederlande', in N. Brox et al. (hrsg.), *Die Geschichte des Christentums*, 14 vols, Freiburg – Basel – Wien 1991-2004 (Sonderausg. 2010), vol. 8 (1995), p. 447-523.

MONITUM

Archives d'État de Genève, Pièces Historiques, 1905.

CONCILIA LUTETIANUM ET RUPELLENSE
1559-1571

LA CONFESSION DE FOY DES EGLISES REFORMEES
DU ROYAUME DE FRANCE

Article premier.

Nous croyons et confessons qu'il y a un seul Dieu, qui est une seule et
5 simple essence, spirituelle, eternelle, invisible, immuable, infinie, incomprehensible, ineffable, qui peut toutes choses, qui est toute sage, toute bonne,
toute juste et toute misericordieuse.

II.

Ce Dieu se manifeste tel aux hommes: Premierement par ses oeuvres tant
10 par la création que par la conservation et conduite d'icelles. Secondement et
clairement par sa parolle, laquelle au commencement revellee par oracles, a
este puis apres redigee par escrit es livres que nous appellons escripture saincte.

III.

Toute ceste escripture saincte est comprinse es livres canoniques du viel et
15 nouveau testament, desquelz le nombre s'ensuit: Les cinq livres de Moyse,
scavoir est, Genese, Exode, Levitique, Nombres, Deuteronome; item Josue,
Juges, Ruth, le premier et second livres de Samuel, premier et second livres des
Rois, premier et second livres des Chroniques, autrement dits Paralipomenon,
le premier livre d'Esdras; item Nehemmie, le livre d'Ester, Job, Pseaumes de
20 David, Proverbes ou Sentences de Salomon, le livre de l'Ecclesiaste, dit le Pres-
cheur, Cantique de Salomon; item les livres d'Esaïe, Jeremie, les lamentations
de Jeremie, Ezechiel, Daniel, Osee, Joel, Amos, Abdias, Jonas, Michee,
Nahum, Abacuc, Sophonie, Aggee, Zacharie, Malachie. Item le saint evangile
selon Saint Matthieu, selon Saint Marc, selon Saint Luc et selon Saint Jehan;
25 item le second livre Saint Luc, autrement dit les Actes des Apostres; item les
epistres Saint Paul, aux Romains une, aux Chorinthiens deux, aux Galates une,

---

14 comprinse] *intellege* comprise   **23** saint] *a.c.* s   **24** Saint[1]] *a.c.* St   Saint[2]] *a.c.* St
Saint[3]] *a.c.* St   Saint[4]] *a.c.* St   **25** Saint] *a.c.* St   **26** Saint] *a.c.* St

548 CONCILIA LUTETIANUM ET RUPELLENSE – 1559-1571

aux Ephesiens une, aux Philippiens une, aux Colossiens une, aux Thessaloniciens deux, a Thimothee deux, a Tite une, a Philemon une; item l'epistre aux Hebrieux, l'epistre Saint Jaques, la premiere et seconde epistre Saint Pierre, la premiere, deuxieme et troisieme epistres Saint Jehan, l'epistre Saint Jude; item l'Apocalypse ou Revelation sainct Jean.

IV.

Nous cognoissons ces livres estre canoniques et reigle trescertaine de nostre foy; non tant par le commun accord et consentement de l'eglise, que par le tesmoignage et interieure persuasion du Sainct Esprit, qui les nous faict discerner d'avec les autres livres ecclesiastiques. Sur lesquelz (encores qu'ilz soyent utiles) on ne peut fonder aucun article de foy.

V.

Nous croyons que la parole de Dieu qui est contenue en ces livres est procedee de Dieu, duquel elle seule prend son authorite et non des hommes. Et d'autant qu'elle est reigle de toute vérité, contenant tout ce qui est necessaire pour le service de Dieu et nostre salut, il n'est loysible aux hommes, ne mesmes aux anges d'y adjouster, diminuer ou changer. Dont il s'ensuit que ne l'antiquite, ne les coustumes, ne la multitude, ne la sagesse humaine, ne les jugemens, ne les arrestz, ne les edicts, ne les decrets, ne les conciles, ne les visions, ne les miracles, ne doivent estre opposez a icelle escripture saincte, ains au contraire, toutes choses doivent estre examinees, reiglees, et reformees selon icelle. Et suyvant cela nous avoüons les trois symboles, ascavoir des Apostres, de Nice et d'Athanase, pource qu'ilz sont conformes a la parole de Dieu.

41/43 Et – changer] cfr Gal. 1, 8; I Tim. 6, 3 seq.; Matth. 5, 18 seq.

36 les autres livres ecclesiastiques] i.e. the apocryphal or deuterocanonical books   **36/37** encores – utiles] Luther described the apocrypha as 'Bu[e]cher: so der heiligen Schrifft nicht gleich gehalten, vnd doch nu[e]tzlich vnd gut zu lesen sind' (*WA DB*, vol. 12 (1961), 2 seq.)   **37** on – foy] cfr Augustinus, *De civitate Dei: Libri XI-XXII* 18, 38, ed. D. Dombart – A. Kalb (*CC SL* 48), Turnhout 1955, p. 633-634, 22-36 (= *PL* 41, col. 598)   **48/49** Et – Dieu] Roman Catholicism, Lutheranism, and Calvinism all agree that these three creeds are canonical

29 Saint[1]] *a.c.* St   Saint[2]] *a.c.* St   **30** Saint[1]] *a.c.* St   Saint[2]] *a.c.* St   **45** conciles] *a.c.* consiles   **46** ains] *intellege* mais; plutôt

VI.

Ceste escripture saincte nous enseigne qu'en ceste seule et simple essence divine, que nous avons confessee, il y a trois personnes: le Pere, le Fils, et le Saint Esprit. Le Pere, premiere cause, principe et origine de toutes choses; le Fils sa parole et sapience eternelle; le Sainct Esprit sa vertu, puissance et efficasse. Le Fils eternellement engendre du Père; le Sainct Esprit procedant eternellement de tous deux. Les trois personnes non confuses, mais distinctes, et toutesfois non divisees, mais d'une mesme essence, eternite, puissance et egualite. Et en cela avoüons ce qui a este determine par les conciles anciens, et detestons toutes sectes et heresies, qui ont este rejettees par les saints docteurs, comme Sainct Hylaire, Sainct Athanase, Sainct Ambroise, Sainct Cirile.

51/52 ceste – confessee] cfr Article I   **58** Et – anciens] a generic reference to the councils of Nicaea (325), Constantinople (381), Ephesus (431), and Chalcedon (451) **60** Sainct Hylaire] Hilary of Poitiers (c. 315-367) polemicised with the Arians on Trinitarian doctrine. See for example Hilarius Pictaviensis, *Contra arianos vel Auxentium Mediolanensis liber unus* (*PL* 10), Paris 1845, col. 609-618; *De trinitate*, ed. P. Smulders (*CC SL* 62-62A), Turnhout 1979-1980 (= *PL* 10, col. 25-472)   Sainct Athanase] Athanasius (c. 295-373), bishop of Alexandria, is also placed here in the context of the polemics against Arian teachings. See for example Athanasius, *De incarnatione Verbi*, éd. C. Kannengiesser (*SC* 199), Paris 2016 (= *PG* 25, col. 96-197); *Orationes quattuor contra Arianos*, éd. K. Metzler – K. Savvidis (*SC* 598-599), Paris 2019 (= *PG* 26, col. 12-525); *Apologia contra Arianos*, in Athanasius, *Werke*, II/1, hrsg. H.-G. Opitz, Berlin – Leipzig 1935, p. 87-168 (= *PG* 25, col. 248-409); *Historia Arianorum ad monachos,* in Athanasius, *Werke*, II/1, hrsg. H.-G. Opitz, p. 183-230 (= *PG* 25, col. 696-796); *De decretis Nicaenae synodi*, in Athanasius, *Werke*, II/1, hrsg. H.-G. Opitz, p. 1-4 (= *PG* 25, col. 416-476); *De synodis Arimini et Seleuciae celebratis* , in Athanasius, *Werke*, II/1, hrsg. H.-G. Opitz, p. 231-278 (= *PG* 26, col. 681-793); *De sententia Dionysii*, in Athanasius, *Werke*, II/1, hrsg. H.-G. Opitz, p. 46-67 (= *PG* 25, col. 480-521); *Expositio fidei*, ed. H. Nordberg, *Athanasiana* I, Helsinki 1962, p. 49-56 (= *PG* 25, col. 200-208); *Sermo maior de fide*, ed. H. Nordberg, *Athanasiana* I, Helsinki 1962, p. 57-71 (= *PG* 26, col. 1264-1293)   Sainct Ambroise] Ambrose of Milan (c. 333-397). See Ambrosius, *De fide [ad Gratianum Augustum]*, hrsg. O. Faller (*CSEL* 78; *Sancti Ambrosii Opera*, 8), Wien 1962 (= *PL* 16, 1880, col. 549-726); *De spiritu sancto libri tres*, hrsg. O. Faller (*CSEL* 79; *Sancti Ambrosii Opera*, 9), Wien 1964, p. 15-222 (= *PL* 16, col. 731-850); *De paenitentia*, hrsg. O. Faller (*CSEL* 73; *Sancti Ambrosii Opera*, 7), Wien 1955, p. 119-206 (= *PL* 16, col. 485-546)   Sainct Cirile] Cyril of Alexandria (c. 375-444) was involved in various Christological disputes including the doctrine of the Trinity

53 Saint] *a.c.* St   **54** sapience] *intellege* sagesse

VII.

Nous croyons que Dieu en trois personnes cooperantes par sa vertu, sagesse et bonte incomprehensible a cree toutes choses, non seulement le ciel, la terre, et tout ce qui y est contenu, mais aussi les espritz invisibles, desquelz
65 les uns sont descheuz et tresbuchez en perdition, les autres ont persiste en obeissance. Que les premiers, s'estans corrumpus en malice, sont ennemis de tout bien, par consequent de toute l'eglise. Les secondz, ayans este preservez par la grace de Dieu, sont ministres pour glorifier le nom de Dieu et servir au salut de ses esleux.

70
VIII.

Nous croyons que non seulement il a cree toutes choses, mais qu'il les gouverne et conduit, disposant et ordonnant selon sa volonte de tout ce qui advient au monde, non pas qu'il soit autheur du mal, ou que la coulpe luy en puisse estre imputee, veu que sa volonte est la reigle souveraine et infallible de
75 toute droicture et equite. Mais il a des moyens admirables de se servir tellement des diables et des meschans, qu'il scait convertir en bien le mal qu'ils font, et duquel ilz sont coulpables. Et ainsi en confessant, que rien ne se faict sans la providence de Dieu, nous adorons en humilite les secrets, qui nous sont cachez, sans nous enquerir par dessus nostre mesure, mais plustost appliquons
80 a nostre usage, ce qui nous est monstre en l'escripture saincte, pour estre en repos et seurete. D'autant que Dieu, qui a toutes choses subjectes a soy, veille sur nous d'un soing paternel, tellement qu'il ne tombera point un cheveu de nostre teste sans son vouloir, et cependant tient les diables et tous noz ennemis bridez, en sorte qu'ilz ne nous peuvent faire aucune nuisance sans son conge.

85
IX.

Nous croyons que l'homme, ayant este cree pur et entier et conforme à l'image de Dieu, qui est par sa propre faute descheu de sa grace qu'il avoit receuë, et ainsi s'est aliene de Dieu, qui est la fontaine de justice, et de tous biens, en sorte que sa nature est du tout corrompue, et estant aveugle en son
90 esprit et depravé en son coeur, a perdu toute integrité, sans en avoir rien de

---

66/68 Que – ministres] cfr Hebr. 1, 14   **81/83** D'autant – vouloir] cfr Matth. 10, 29 ff; Act. 27, 34

73 coulpe] *ex latino sermone* culpa

CONCILIA LUTETIANUM ET RUPELLENSE – 1559-1571   551

residu. Et combien qu'il ait encores quelque discretion du bien et du mal, non-obstant nous disons que ce qu'il a de clairte, se convertit en tenebres, quand il est question de cercher Dieu, tellement qu'il n'en peut nullement approcher par son intelligence et raison. Et combien qu'il ait volonte, par laquelle il est 95 incité a faire ceci ou cela, toutesfois elle est du tout captive soubz peche, en sorte qu'il n'a nulle liberte a bien que celle que Dieu luy donne.

X.

Nous croyons que toute la lignee d'Adam est infectee de telle contagion, qui est le peche originel et un vice hereditaire, et non pas seulement une imita-100 tion, comme les Pelagiens ont voulu dire, lesquelz nous detestons en leurs erreurs. Et n'estimons pas, qu'il soit besoing de s'enquerir comme le peche vient d'un homme a l'autre, veu que c'est bien assez que ce que Dieu luy avoit donne, n'estoit pas pour luy seul, mais pour toute sa lignee. Et ainsi qu'en la personne d'iceluy, nous avons este denuez de tous biens et sommes tresbuchez 105 en toute povrette et malediction.

XI.

Nous croyons aussi que ce vice est vrayement peche, qui suffit a condam-ner tout le genre humain, jusques aux petis enfans des le ventre de la mere, et que pour tel il est repute devant Dieu, mesmes qu'apres le baptesme c'est 110 tousiours peche, quand a la coulpe, combien que la condamnation en soit abo-lie aux enfans de Dieu, ne la leur imputant point, par sa bonté gratuite. Outre cela que c'est une perversite, produisant tousjours fruicts de malice et rebel-lion, telz que les plus saincts, encores qu'ilz y resistent, ne laissent point d'estre entachez d'infirmitez et de fautes pendant qu'ilz habitent en ce monde.

---

100 les Pelagiens] the monk Pelagius, who had been active in Rome since about 400, maintained – unlike Augustine – that man has free will and is capable of good as well as of evil. Pelagians rejected the idea of original sin, as they understood Adam's case as merely a bad example whose imitation brought sin into the world. This led to the so-called Pelagian dispute of 411/431

105 povrette] *intellege* pauvreté   **112** c'est] *a.c.* s'est

XII.

Nous croyons que de ceste corruption et condamnation generale, en laquelle tous hommes sont plongez, Dieu retire ceux lesquelz en son conseil eternel et immuable il a esleux par sa seule bonte et misericorde en nostre seigneur Jesus Christ, sans consideration de leurs oeuvres, laissant les autres en icelle mesme corruption et condamnation pour demonstrer en eux sa justice, comme es premiers il faict luire les richesses de da misericorde. Car les uns ne sont point meilleurs que les autres, jusques à ce que Dieu les discerne selon son conseil immuable, qu'il a determine en Jesus Christ devant la creation du monde. Et nul aussi ne se pourroit introduire a un tel bien de sa propre vertu, veu que de nature nous ne pouvons avoir un seul bon mouvement, ni affection, ne pensee, jusques a ce que Dieu nous ait prevenu et nous y ait disposez.

XIII.

Nous croyons qu'en iceluy Jesus Christ tout ce qui estoit requis a nostre salut nous a este offert, et communique. Lequel nous estant donne a salut, nous a este quant et quant faict sapience, justice, sanctification et redemption, en sorte qu'en declinant de luy, on renonce a la misericorde du Père, ou il nous convient avoir nostre refuge unique.

XIV.

Nous croyons que Jesus Christ, estant la sagesse de Dieu et son fils eternel, a vestu nostre chair, afin d'estre Dieu et homme en une personne, voire homme semblable a nous, passible en corps et en ame, sinon entant qu'il a este pur de toute macule. Et quant a son humanite, qu'il a este vraye semence d'Abraham et de David, combien qu'il ait este conceu par la vertu secrette du Saint Esprit. Enquoy nous detestons toutes les heresies qui ont anciennement

---

134 Jesus – sagesse] cfr I Cor. 1, 24   **135** a – chair] cfr Ioh. 1, 14   **135/137** afin – macule] cfr I Petr. 1, 19   **137/138** vraye – David] cfr Matth. 1, 1-17 et 20; Luc. 1, 27 et 2, 4; Ioh. 7, 42; Gal. 3, 16; Hebr. 2, 16

139/140 Enquoy – eglises] this rejection focused primarily on those early-Church heresies calling into question the Church's doctrine of the Trinity and Christology, such as Arianism, Nestorianism, and Eutychianism. The arguments of these heresies were revived in the sixteenth century by some radical Protestants. This included both

---

139 Saint] *a.c.* St

140 trouble les eglises ; et notamment aussi les imaginations diaboliques de Servet, lequel attribue au seigneur Jesus une divinite fantastique, d'autant qu'il le dit estre idee et patron de toutes choses, et le nomme fils personnel ou figuratif de Dieu et finalement luy forge un corps de trois elemens increez, et par ainsi mesle et destruit toutes les deux natures.

145   XV.

Nous croyons qu'en une mesme personne, assavoir Jesus Christ, les deux natures sont vrayement et inseparablement conjoinctes et unies, demeurant neantmoins chascune en sa distincte propriete, tellement que comme en ceste conjonction la nature divine retenant sa proprieté est demeuree incree, infinie, 150 et remplissant toutes choses, aussi la nature humaine est demeuree finie, ayant sa forme, mesure et propriete. Et mesme combien que Jesus Christ en ressuscitant ait donne immortalité a son corps, toutesfois il ne luy a oste la verite de sa nature. Et ainsi nous le considerons tellement en sa divinité, que nous ne le despouillons point de son humanité.

155   XVI.

Nous croyons que Dieu envoyant sont filz a voulu monstrer son amour et bonte innestimable envers nous, en le livrant a la mort et le ressuscitant pour accomplir toute justice, et pour nous aquerir la vie celeste.

                                      XVII.

160   Nous croyons que par le sacrifice unique, que le seigneur Jesus a offert en la croix, nous sommes reconciliez a Dieu pour estre tenus et reputez justes

---

Anti-trinitarianism as well as different understandings of communion based on Christological arguments in the debate over the presence of Christ in the Eucharist. Cfr *Handbuch der Dogmen- und Theologiegeschichte*, Vol. 1: *The development of teaching in the context of catholicity*, hrsg. C. Andresen, Göttingen 1982, 2. erg. U. überarb. Ed. 1999, p. 99-283   **140** Servet] Michael Servetus (1509/1511-1553) was a Spanish medical doctor and theologian. His rejection of the doctrine of the Trinity sparked a bitter controversy with John Calvin. Servetus died at the stake in Geneva   **141/144** lequel – natures] see M. Servetus, *De Trinitatis erroribus libri septem. Per Michaelem Serveto, alias Reves ab Aragonia Hispanum*, s.l. 1531, as well as the *Dialogorum de Trinitate libri duo. De iustitia regni Christi, capitula quatuor. Per Michaelem Serveto, alias Reves, ab Aragonia Hispanum*, s.l. 1532. See also *Christianismi restitutio*, s.l. 1553

554 CONCILIA LUTETIANUM ET RUPELLENSE – 1559-1571

devant luy, pource que nous ne luy pouvons estre agreables, ne estre participans de son adoption, sinon d'autant qu'il nous pardonne noz fautes et les
ensevelit. Aussi nous protestons que Jesus Christ est nostre lavement entier et
165 parfaict, qu'en sa mort nous avons entiere satisfaction pour nous aquiter de
nos forfaicts et iniquitez, dont nous sommes coulpables, et ne pouvons estre
delivrez que par ce remede.

XVIII.

Nous croyons que toute nostre justice est fondee en la remission de nos
170 pechez, comme aussi c'est nostre seule felicité, comme dit David. Parquoy
nous rejettons tous autres moyens de nous pouvoir justifier devant Dieu. Et
sans presumer de nulles vertus ne merites, nous nous tenons simplement à
l'obeissance de Jesus Christ, laquelle nous est allouee, tant pour couvrir toutes
nos fautes, que pour nous faire trouver grace et faveur devant Dieu. Et de faict
175 nous croyons qu'en declinant de ce fondement tant peu que ce soit, nous ne
pourrions trouver ailleurs aucun repos, mais serions tousjours agitez d'inquietude, d'autant que jamais nous ne sommes paisiblement avec Dieu, jusques a
ce que nous soyons bien resoluz d'estre aimez en Jesus Christ, veu que nous
sommes dignes d'estre hais en nous-mesmes.

180 ## XIX.

Nous croyons que c'est par ce moyen que nous avons liberte et privilege
d'invoquer Dieu, avec pleine fiance qu'il se monstrera nostre pere. Car nous
n'aurions pas aucun accez au Père, si nous n'estions adressez par ce Mediateur,
et pour estre exaucez en son nom, il convient tenir nostre vie de luy, comme de
185 nostre chef.

XX.

Nous croyons que nous sommes faictz participans de ceste justice par la
seule foy, comme il est dit, qu'il a souffert pour nous aquerir salut, a celle fin
que quiconque croira en luy ne perisse point. Et que cela se faict, d'autant que

---

169/170 Nous – David] cfr Ps. 32, 1-2   **181/182** Nous – pere] cfr Rom. 8, 15; Gal.
4, 6 **183** si – Mediateur] cfr I Tim. 2, 5; Hebr. 8, 6; 9, 15; 12, 24 **184/185** et – chef]
cfr Eph. 1, 22 et 4, 15; Col. 1, 15-20 **187/189** nous – point] cfr Ioh. 3, 16-18 et 3, 36

163 qu'il] *a.c.* qu'ilz

CONCILIA LUTETIANUM ET RUPELLENSE – 1559-1571

190 les promesses de vie qui nous sont donnees en luy sont appropriees a nostre usage, et en sentons l'effect quand nous les acceptons, ne doubtans point qu'estans asseurez de la bouche de Dieu, nous ne serons point frustrez. Ainsi la justice que nous obtenons par foy, despend des promesses gratuites, par lesquelles Dieu nous declare et testifie qu'il nous aime.

195 ## XXI.

Nous croyons que nous sommes illuminez en la foy par la grace secrette du Saint Esprit, tellement que c'est un don gratuit et particulier que Dieu despart a ceux que bon luy semble, en sorte que les fideles n'ont dequoy s'en glorifier, estans obligez au double de ce qu'ilz ont este preferez aux autres, 200 mesme que la foy n'est pas seulement baillee pour un coup aux esleux pour les introduire au bon chemin, ains pour les y faire continuer aussi jusques au bout. Car comme c'est a Dieu de faire le commencement, aussi c'est a luy de parachever.

XXII.

205 Nous croyons que par ceste foy nous sommes regenerez en nouveaute de vie, estans naturellement asserviz a peche. Or nous recevons par foy la grace de vivre sainctement et en la crainte de Dieu en recevant la promesse qui nous est donnee par l'evangile, ascavoir que Dieu nous donnera son Sainct Esprit. Ainsi la foy non seulement ne refroidit l'affection de bien et sainctement vivre, mais 210 l'engendre et l'exite en nous produisant necessairement les bonnes oeuvres. Au reste combien que Dieu pour accomplir nostre salut nous regenere, nous reformant a bien faire, toutesfois nous confessons que les bonnes oeuvres, que nous faisons par la conduite de son Esprit, ne viennent point en conte pour nous justifier ou meriter que Dieu nous tienne pour ses enfans, pource que nous

---

196/199 Nous – glorifier] cfr I Cor. 1, 29 seq.; II Cor. 10, 17 seq.; Eph. 2, 8 seq. **199** estans – double] cfr Apoc. 18, 6   **202/203** Car – parachever] cfr Phil. 2, 13 **205/206** par – vie] cfr Rom. 6, 4 **206** estans – peche] cfr Rom. 6, 6 et 6, 16-20

199 estans – double] behind the idea of the double compensation is a legal thinking, which can be found in the Old Testament (e.g. Ex. 22, 3-8) but also in Roman law. Cfr *Corpus Iuris Civilis, Digesta*, in *Institutiones, Digesta*, hrsg. Th. Mommsen – P. Krüger (*Corpus Iuris Civilis* 1), Berlin 1928, 2, 8, 3; 3, 2, 13, 7; 5, 3, 55; 9, 2, 2, 1; 11, 3, 14, 5

197 Saint] *a.c.* St

556 CONCILIA LUTETIANUM ET RUPELLENSE – 1559-1571

215 serions tousjours flottans en doubte et inquietude, si nos consciences ne s'appuyoyent sur la satisfaction, par laquelle Jesus Christ nous a aquittez.

XXIII.

Nous croyons que toutes les figures de la loy ont prins fin a la venue de Jesus Christ. Mais combien que les ceremonies ne soyent plus en usage, neant-220 moins la substance et verite nous en est demeuree en la personne de celuy, auquel gist tout l'accomplissement. Au surplus il nous faut aider de la loy et des prophetes, tant pour reigler nostre vie que pour estre confermez aux promesses de l'evangile.

XXIV.

225 Nous croyons, puis que Jesus Christ nous est donne pour seul advocat, et qu'il nous commande de nous retirer privement en son nom vers son pere, et mesme qu'il ne nous est pas licite de prier sinon ensuyvant la forme que Dieu nous a dictee par sa parole, que tout ce que les hommes ont imagine de l'intercession des sainctz trespassez, n'est qu'abus et fallace de Satan, pour faire 230 desvoyer les hommes de bien prier. Nous rejettons aussi tous autres moyens, que les hommes presument avoir pour se racheter envers Dieu, comme derrogeans au sacrifice de la mort et passion de Jesus Christ. Finalement nous tenons le purgatoire pour une illusion procedee d'icelle mesme boutique, de laquelle sont aussi procedez le voeuz monastiques, pelerinages, defenses du 235 mariage et de l'usage des viandes, l'observation ceremonieuse des jours, la confession auriculaire, les indulgences, et toutes autres telles choses, par lesquelles on pense meriter grace et salut. Lesquelles choses nous rejettons non seulement pour la faulse opinion du merite, qui y est attachee, mais aussi par ce que ce sont inventions humaines, qui imposent joug aux consciences.

240 ## XXV.

Or, pource que nous ne jouissons de Jesus Christ que par l'evangile, nous croyons que l'ordre de l'eglise, qui a este establie en son authorite, doit estre sacre et inviolable. Et pourtant que l'eglise ne peut consister sinon qu'il y ait

---

218 les figures de la loy] cfr Hebr. 8, 5 et 10, 1   **225** seul advocat] cfr I Ioh. 2, 1   **227/**
228 mesme – parole] cfr Matth. 6, 5-13

229 fallace] *intellege* mensonge; perfidie   **241** jouissons] *a.c.* jouissans

CONCILIA LUTETIANUM ET RUPELLENSE – 1559-1571

des pasteurs qui ayent la charge d'enseigner, lesquelz on doit honnorer et
escouter en reverence, quand ilz sont deuement appelez, et exercent fidelement
leur office. Non pas que Dieu soit attache a telles aides ou moyens inferieurs,
mais pource qu'il luy plaist nous entretenir soubz telle charge et bride. Enquoy
nous detestons tous fantastiques qui voudroyent bien, entant qu'en eux est,
aneantir le ministere et predication de la parole de Dieu et ses sacremens.

XXVI.

Nous croyons donc que nul ne se doit retirer a part, et se contenter de sa
personne, mais tous ensemble doivent garder er entretenir l'unite de l'eglise, se
soubmettans a l'instruction commune et au joug de Jesus Christ, et ce en
quelque lieu que Dieu aura estably un vray ordre d'eglise, encores que les
magistratz et leurs edictz y soyent contraires, et que tous ceux qui ne s'y
rengent ou s'en separent contrarient a l'ordonnance de Dieu.

XXVII.

Toutesfois nous croyons qu'il convient discerner soigneusement et avec
prudence quelle est la vraye eglize, pource que par trop on abuse de ce tiltre.
Nous disons donc, suyvant la parole de Dieu, que c'est la compagnie des
fideles qui s'accordent a suyvre icelle parolle et la pure religion qui en despend,
et qui profitent en icelle tout le temps de leur vie, croissans et confermans en la
crainte de Dieu, selon qu'ils ont besoing de s'advancer et marcher tousjours
plus outre. Mesmes quoy qu'ilz s'efforcent, qu'il leur convient avoir incessam-
ment recours a la remission de leurs pechez. Neantmoins nous ne nions point,
que parmi les fideles il n'y ait des hypocrites et reprouvez, desquelz la malice
ne peut effacer le tiltre de l'eglise.

XXVIII.

Soubs ceste croyance nous protestons que ou la parole de Dieu n'est
receue, et qu'on ne faict nulle profession de s'assubjectir à icelle, ou il n'y a nul
usage des sacremens, a parler proprement, on ne peut juger qu'il y ait aucune
eglise. Pourtant nous condamnons les assemblees de la papaute, veu que la

---

252/253 se – Christ] vide Matth. 11, 29-30

247/249 Enquoy – sacremens] this article condemns spiritualist currents within the
Reformation objecting to the establishment of ecclesiastical structures per se

pure verite de Dieu en est bannie, esquelles les sacremens sont corrompus, abastardiz, falsifiez ou aneantiz du tout, et esquelles toutes superstitions et
275 idolatries ont la vogue. Nous tenons donques que tous ceux qui s'y meslent en telz actes et y communiquent, se separent et retranchent du corps de Jesus Christ. Toutesfois pource qu'il reste encore quelque petite trace d'eglise en la papaute, et mesme que la substance du baptesme y est demeuree, joinct que l'efficace et vertu du baptesme ne despend de celuy qui l'administre, nous
280 confessons ceux qui y sont baptisez n'avoir besoing d'un second baptesme. Cependent a cause des corruptions qui y sont, on n'y peut presenter les enfans sans se polluer.

XXIX.

Quant est de la vraye eglise, nous croyons qu'elle doit estre gouvernee
285 selon la police, que nostre seigneur Jesus Christ a establie. C'est qu'il y ait des pasteurs, des surveillans et diacres, afin que la purete de doctrine ait son cours, que les vices soyent corrigez et reprimez, et que les povres, et tous autres affligez soyent secourus en leurs necessitez, et que les assemblees se facent au nom de Dieu, esquelles grands et petis soyent edifiez.

290 ## XXX.

Nous croyons tous vrais pasteurs, en quelque lieu qu'ilz soyent, avoir mesme authorite et esgale puissance soubs un seul chef, seul souverain et seul universel evesque Jesus Christ. Et pour ceste cause, que nulle eglise ne doit pretendre aucune domination ou seigneurie sur l'autre.

295 ## XXXI.

Nous croyons que nul ne se doit ingerer de son authorite propre pour gouverner l'eglise. Mais que cela se doit faire par election, entant qu'il est possible et que Dieu le permet. Laquelle exeption nous y adjoustons notament pource qu'il a fallu quelquefois, et mesme de nostre temps, auquel l'estat de
300 l'eglise estoit interrompu, que Dieu ait suscité gens d'une façon extraordinaire pour dresser l'eglise de nouveau, qui estoit en ruine et desolation. Mais quoy qu'il en soit, nous croyons qu'il se faut tousjours conformer a ceste reigle, que

---

279 ne] *add. in marg.*

CONCILIA LUTETIANUM ET RUPELLENSE – 1559-1571

tous pasteurs, surveillans, et diacres ayent tesmoignage d'estre appellez a leur
office.

XXXII.

Nous croyons aussi qu'il est bon que ceux, qui sont esleux pour estre
superintendans, advisent entreux quel moyen ilz devront tenir pour le regime
de tout le corps, et toutesfois qu'ilz ne declinent nullement de ce qui nous en a
este ordonne par nostre seigneur Jesus Christ. Ce qui n'empesche point qu'il
n'y ait quelques ordonnances particulieres en chascun lieu, selon que la com-
modité le requerra.

XXXIII.

Cependant nous excluons toutes inventions humaines et toutes loix,
qu'on voudroit introduire sous ombre du service de Dieu, par lesquelles on
voudroit lier les consciences, mais seulement recevons ce qui faict et est propre
pour nourrir concorde, et tenir chascun despuis le premier jusques au dernier
en obeissance. Enquoy nous avons a suyvre ce que nostre seigneur a declare
quant a l'excommunication, laquelle nous approuvons, et confessons estre
necessaire avec toutes ses appartenances.

XXXIV.

Nous croyons que les sacremens sont adjoustez a la parole pour plus
ample confirmation, afin de nous estre gages et marreaux de la grace de Dieu,
et par ce moyen ayder et soulaiger nostre foy, a cause de l'infirmité et rudesse
qui est en nous, et qu'ilz sont tellement signes exterieurs, que Dieu besoigne
par iceux en la vertu de son Esprit, afin de ne nous y rien signifier en vain. Toutesfois nous tenons que toute leur substance et verité est en Jesus Christ; et si
on les en separe ce n'est plus rien qu'ombrage et fumee.

317/319 Enquoy – appartenances] cfr Matth. 18, 15-17 ; I Cor. 5, 4 ff ; I Tim. 1, 20

313 Cependant – humaines] cfr above, Article XXIV. Reformers considered these as
human inventions, not derived from Scripture. This included rites, ceremonies, and
religious beliefs, such as purgatory and most of the sacraments of the Roman Catholic
tradition   **322** marreaux] i.e. *méreaux*, coins used as identification marks – here used
in the sense of a guarantee – in sixteenth-century France. They functioned as tokens for
admission to the Lord's Supper

XXXV.

Nous en confessons seulement deux communs a toute l'eglise, desquelz le
premier, qui est le baptesme, nous est donne pour tesmoignage de nostre
adoption. Pource que la nous sommes entez au corps de Christ, afin d'estre
lavez et nettoyez par son sang et puis renouvelez en saincte vie par son Esprit.
Nous tenons aussi combien que nous ne soyons baptisez qu'une fois, que le
profit qui nous est la signifie s'estand a la vie et a la mort, afin que nous ayons
une signature permanente, que Jesus Christ nous sera tousjours justice et sanctification. Or combien que ce soit un sacrement de foy et de penitence, neantmoins pource que Dieu reçoit en son eglise les petis enfans avec leurs peres,
nous disons que par l'authorite de Jesus Christ les petis enfans engendrez des
fideles doivent estre baptisez.

XXXVI.

Nous confessons que la cène (qui est le second sacrement) nous est
tesmoignage de l'unité que nous avons avec Jesus Christ, d'autant qu'il n'est
pas seulement une fois mort et ressuscite pour nous, mais aussi nous repaist et
nourrist vrayement de sa chair et de son sang, a ce que nous soyons un avec luy,
et que sa vie nous soit commune. Or combien qu'il soit au ciel jusques a ce
qu'il vienne pour juger tout le monde, toutesfois nous croyons que par la vertu
secrette et incomprehensible de son Esprit il nous nourrist et vivifie de la
substance de son corps et de son sang. Nous tenons bien que cela se faict spiri-

---

331 Pource – Christ] cfr Rom. 11, 23 seq.

348 substance] at the seventh national Synod of La Rochelle, it was noted that it was
necessary to explain the 'participation à la Substance de Jesus-Ghrist [*sic*] en la Cene'.
The proceedings, in Aymon, *Tous les synodes*, vol. 1, p. 100, state: '[...] mais après une
assés longue conference, il a été resolu que le Synode aprouvant nôtre Confession,
rejette l'opinion de ceux qui ne veulent pas recevoir le mot de Substance contenu audit
Article: par lequel mot ledit Synode n'entend aucune conjonction, ni mélange, ni
changement, ni transmutation de quoi que ce soit d'une façon charnelle et grossiére qui
aît du raport à la matiere des corps; mais une conjonction vraie, très-étroite, et d'une
façon spirituelle, par laquelle Jesus-Christ lui-même est tellement fait nôtre, et nous
siens, qu'il n'y a aucune conjonction de corps, ni naturelle, ni artficiele, qui soit si
étroite; laquelle néanmoins n'aboutit point à faire que sa Substance, ou sa Personne
jointe avec nos personnes, en compose quelque troisième; mais seulement à faire que sa
vertu, et ce qui est en lui de salutaire pour les hommes, nous soit, par ce moien, plus
étroitement donné et communiqué. C'est pourquoi nous ne sommes pas du sentiment

---

342 unité] *post synodum Rupellanam (1571)* union

CONCILIA LUTETIANUM ET RUPELLENSE – 1559-1571 561

tuellement, non pas pour mettre au lieu de l'effect et de la verité imagination
350 ne pensee, mais d'autant que ce mystere surmonte en sa hautesse la mesure de
nostre sens et tout ordre de nature, bref, pource qu'il est celeste, ne peut estre
apprehende que par foy.

XXXVII.

Nous croyons ainsi qu'il a este dit, que tant en la cene, qu'au baptesme,
355 Dieu nous donne reallement et par effect ce qu'il y figure. Et pourtant nous
conjoingnons avec les signes la vraye possession et jouyssance de ce qui nous
est la presente. Et par ainsi tous ceux, qui apportent à la table sacree de Christ
une pure foy, comme un vaisseau, reçoyvent vrayement ce que les signes y testi-
fient: c'est que le corps et le sang de Jesus Christ ne servent pas moins de man-
360 ger et boire a l'ame que le pain et le vin font au corps.

XXXVIII.

Ainsi nous tenons que l'eau, estant un element caduque, ne laisse pas de
nous testifier en la verite le lavement interieur de nostre ame au sang de Jesus
Christ par l'efficace de son Esprit, et que le pain et le vin nous estans donnez
365 en la cene, nous servent vrayement de nourriture spirituelle, d'autant qu'ils
nous monstrent comme a l'oeil la chair de Jesus Christ nous estre nostre
viande, et son sang nostre breuvage. Et rejettons les fantastiques et sacramen-

---

de ceux qui disent que nous participons seulement à ses merites, et aux dons qu'il nous
communique par son Esprit, sans que lui-même soit fait nôtre: mais au contraire nous
adorons ce grand Mystere surnaturel et incomprehensible de l'operation réelle et très-
efficace de Jesus-Christ en nous, comme l'Apôtre St. Paul le témoigne dans son Epître
aux Ephesiens. Nous croions donc pour cet effet que nous sommes faits participans du
Corps de Jesus-Christ livré pour nous, et de son sang repandu pour nous, et que nous
sommes chair de sa chair, et os de ses os, en le recevant et tous ses dons avec lui, par Foi
engendrée en nous par l'eficace et la vertu incompréhensible du Saint Esprit: Et nous
entendons ainsi ces passages de l'Evangile: Celui qui mange la chair et qui boit le sang
de Jesus a la Vie éternelle, Jesus Christ est le sep et nous sommes les sarmens, et qu'il
nous faut demeurer en lui, afin de porter du fruit, que nous sommes membres de son
corps: et que tout ainsi que nous tirons nôtre mort du premier Adam, en tant que nous
participons à sa Nature, ainsi faut-il que nous participions vraiement au second Adam,
afin d'en tirer nôtre vie. C'est pourquoi tous les Pasteurs et généralement tous les fidéles
seront exhortés de ne donner aucun lieu aux opinions contraires à ce que dessus, qui est
très-expressément fondé sur la Parole de Dieu'   **354** Nous – dit] see above, Article
XXXIV **367** sacramentaires] contemporaries referred to all those who deviated from
their own communion doctrine as 'sacramentarians'

562 CONCILIA LUTETIANUM ET RUPELLENSE – 1559-1571

taires, qui ne veulent point recevoir telz signes et marques, veu que Jesus Christ prononce: Ceci est mon corps, et ce calice est mon sang.

370 ## XXXIX.

Nous croyons que Dieu veut que le monde soit gouverne par loix et polices, afin qu'il y ait quelques brides pour reprimer les appetis desordonnez du monde. Et ainsi qu'il a estably les royaumes, republiques et toutes autres sortes de principauté, soyent hereditaires ou autrement, et tout ce qui appar-
375 tient à l'estat de justice, et en veut estre recogneu autheur; a ceste cause a mis le glaive en la main des magistrats, pour reprimer les pechez commis, non seule-ment contre la seconde table des commandemens de Dieu, mais aussi contre la premiere. Il faut donques a cause de luy, que non seulement on endure, que les superieurs dominent, mais aussi qu'on les honnore et prise en toute reverence,
380 les tenans pour ses lieutenants et officiers, lesquelz il a commis pour exercer une charge legitime et saincte.

XL.

Nous tenons donques qu'il faut obeir a leurs loix et statuts, payer tributs, imposts et autres devoirs, et porter le joug de subjection d'une bonne et
385 franche volonte, encores qu'ilz fussent infideles, moyennant que l'empire

---

369 Ceci – sang] vide Matth. 26, 26-28; Marc. 14, 22-24; Luc. 22, 19 seq.; I Cor. 11, 23-25   **373/375** Et – autheur] cfr Rom. 13, 1   **375/376** aⁱ – magistrats] cfr Rom. 13, 4   **376** pour – commis] cfr Rom. 13, 3-4   **380** les – officiers] cfr Rom. 13, 4-5 **383/384** Nous – devoirs] cfr Rom. 13, 5-7

368 telz signes et marques] the *Confession de foi* condemns spiritualistic and Anabaptist-minded groups who saw the hearing of the Word of God and the receiving of the sacraments as purely external accomplishments and emphasized purely spiritual participation, considering it sufficient. This was often accompanied by the rejection of ecclesiastical offices and of an orderly Church service. The *Confession de foi*, on the other hand, refers to the institution of the sacrament of the Lord's Supper and thus also to external acts by Christ himself   **377** la seconde table des commandemens de Dieu] i.e. commandments 5 to 10 according to the Reformed list, counting the prohibition of images as a separate commandment. These commandments preserve the functioning of social coexistence in a political community   **377/378** la premiere] i.e. commandments 1 to 4, concerning the relationship of man to God. Civil authorities are therefore responsible for ensuring their subjects the right worship of God

CONCILIA LUTETIANUM ET RUPELLENSE – 1559-1571   563

souverain de Dieu demeure en son entier. Par ainsi nous detestons ceux qui voudroyent rejetter les superioritez, mettre communautez et confusion de biens, et renverser l'ordre de justice.

Ceste confession arrestee au premier synode national tenu a Paris le
390 dixneufviesme may mil cinq cens cinquante neuf, regnant sous Henry deuxiesme, et despuis publie a Charles neufiesme, par la grace de Dieu Roy de France a Poissy l'an mil cinq cents soixante et un. Aprez avoir esté leüt au synode national assemble a La Rochelle, il a este declare par ladicte synode representant toutes les eglises de ce royaume, que toutes lesdictes eglises fran-
395 çoyses approuvent et ratifient la sus scripte confession en tous ses chefz et articles comme estant entierement fondee sur la pure et expresse parole de Dieu, et en tesmoignage de ce consentement ladicte confession de foy a este signee par les ministres et anciens, deputez des provinces de ce royaume au nom des dictes eglises. Et furent presentz audicte synode tenu a La Rochelle,
400 Janne, par la grace de Dieu Royne de Navarre; hautz et puissants princes: Henry, Prince de Navarre; Henry de Bourbon, Prince de Conde; tresillustre Prince Loys, Conte de Nassau; Messire Gaspard, Conte Colligny, amiral de France; et plusieurs seigneurs gentilhommes et autres personnes. Faict a La Rochelle, le douziesme avril l'an de grace mil cinq cents Soixante et onze.

386/388 Par – justice] the *Confession de foi* rejects all those groups – mostly spiritualists and Anabaptist-minded, in the francophone world also called 'libertins' – refusing to submit to secular powers, which were understood by Rom. 13 as God-given **389/404** Ceste – onze] this final section is followed by the signatures of the individuals listed here. Among other signatures, we can find the ones of Theodore Beza and Nicolas des Gallars

---

395 sus scripte] *a.c.* sus cscripte   **397** a] *addidi*

CONSPECTUS MATERIAE

Conciliorum Oecumenicorum
Generaliumque Decreta, VI/1/1

GENERAL INTRODUCTION
(A. Melloni) .... V-XIV

EDITOR'S NOTE
(G. Braghi) XV

LIST OF ABBREVIATIONS .... XVII-XVIII

EDITIONS 1-563

CONCILIUM HOMBERGENSE – 1526
(ed. J. Schilling) 1-57

CONCILIUM IULIOMAGENSE – 1527
(ed. C. Scheidegger) 59-87

DISPUTATIO ET DECEM THESES BERNENSES – 1528
(ed. P. Hildebrand) 89-103

CONCILIUM AUGUSTANUM – 1530
(ed. K. I. Stjerna) 105-213

CONCILIUM BERNENSE – 1532
(ed. P. Hildebrand) 215-277

CONCILIUM CAMPI FORANEI (iuxta Hengroniam)
– 1532 (ed. G. Braghi) 279-311

SYNODUS TIGURINA – 1532
(ed. E. Campi) 313-345

CONCILIUM ARGENTORATENSE – 1533/1534
(ed. G. Braghi & G. Murdock) 347-379

CONCILIUM GENEVENSE – 1541
(ed. G. Braghi & G. Murdock) 381-414

CONCILIA HUNGARICA ET TRANSSYLVANICA
– 1545, 1567, 1570 (ed. Z. Csepregi) 415-492

CONCILIUM VENETIANUM-FERRARIENSE – 1550
(ed. D. Dainese) 493-529

CONCILIA LUTETIANUM ET RUPELLENSE – 1559/1571
(ed. I. Dingel) 531-563